SUCCESSFUL SMALL BUSINESS MANAGEMENT

Successful Small Business Management

CURTIS E. TATE, JR.
The University of Georgia

LEON C. MEGGINSON
Louisiana State University

CHARLES R. SCOTT, JR.
The University of Alabama

LYLE R. TRUEBLOOD
The University of Tulsa

1975

BUSINESS PUBLICATIONS, INC.   Dallas, Texas 75231
Irwin-Dorsey International London, England WC2H 9NJ
Irwin-Dorsey Limited Georgetown, Ontario L7G 4B3

First Printing, May 1975

ISBN 0-256-01693-3
Library of Congress Catalog Card No. 74–27543
Printed in the United States of America

This book is dedicated with affectionate respect to

ANDREW R. TOWL

*Director of Case Development and Director of the
Intercollegiate Case Clearing House
Harvard University
Graduate School of Business Administration*

in grateful appreciation for his efforts in stimulating
international case development, and for his inspiring
the organization, growth, and development of the
Southern Case Research Association.

Preface

Today's students are interested in being active participants in the game of living rather than being merely neutral, passive observers. "Doing their own thing," and searching for a sense of meaning, identity, creativity, and achievement, are important to them.

One of the best ways of accomplishing all these things is to become the owner of a small business. Yet, the management of all types of economic activity is becoming increasingly more complex and difficult because of the problems and pressures involved. This is especially true of small businesses, as shown by the fact that about 930 out of every 1,000 new businesses started in the United States will eventually fail. The failure rate is a shocking 93 percent!

Because of this reality, the purpose of this book is to improve your opportunity for successfully "doing your own thing." This does not mean that you will be successful after you have read and studied the material, but it should help improve your chances of succeeding. Operating a small business is a very practical job—it involves desire, theoretical knowledge, practical experience, hard work, and even some element of luck.

This book is designed to provide you with a combination of theoretical and practical knowledge. The text material presents the ideas, concepts, and philosophies of each subject area, while the cases give you the opportunity to apply that knowledge to actual situations.

Our objectives in developing this book have been to:

1. Show students, prospective owners and managers of small business, and others interested in the subject some of the advantages and disadvantages of those businesses.
2. Indicate to them how to become involved in a small business.
3. Demonstrate how to avoid some of the mistakes in conceiving, initiating, organizing, and operating a small business that have been economically fatal to others.
4. Enable them to achieve the optimum benefit from the limited economic and human resources they are able to muster for their business.
5. Assist them to succeed in managing and operating their own business.

We have tried to present a truly *readable* approach to the subject of management of small business and entrepreneurship. The presentation of the ideas is made more alive by presenting current examples of actual business applications. Cases have been gathered and written by members of the Southern Case Research Association and other teachers and most have been presented at case workshops around the country. Selection of the materials was made on the basis of their fundamental contribution to learning and their ability to stimulate interest and involvement. Many cases place the reader in the position of being an owner-manager of a small business who is faced with a decision-making situation.

In order to aid your learning process, we have divided the book into eight parts and 26 chapters. Some of the unique characteristics of small businesses and the persons who own and operate them are discussed in Part I.

Once you decide that you want to own and manage a small business, you must choose the kind of business to engage in and select the specific firm you will enter. These challenges are explored in Part II.

A most significant question you must answer is: How can I manage and operate my business successfully? Vital management functions and activities should be performed economically and effectively in order for your business to be successful. The general management functions consist of planning, organizing, directing, and controlling the firms' operations. These management functions, which are discussed briefly in Part III, provide an overview of the rest of the material.

Marketing, production, personnel management, and financing are the most important business activities you will need to perform effectively if you want to succeed. These are discussed in relative detail in Parts IV, V, VI, and VII. The practical aspects of these activities are emphasized.

Finally, the entire subject of managing a small business is brought into perspective in Part VIII.

We believe that *Successful Small Business Management* will fill the needs of students interested in small businesses. Hopefully, those using the text will identify with the individuals included in the cases and will learn to be better managers.

To John Ryan, Corporate Finance Department, Robinson-Humphrey Company; Woodrow Stewart, Attorney, Telford, Stewart, and Stephens; John Sewell and John Lattimer, Small Business Administration; and Will Hattendorf, Economic Development Administration, our thanks for their advice and assistance in keeping this book reality-oriented.

Thanks are due for the contributions made through the years by the many researchers, entrepreneurs and managers, and professional people and members of the Southern Case Research Association.

Also, a special thank you to Addie M. Scott and Wyn Trueblood for their unfailing support.

We would be remiss if we failed to acknowledge the assistance of those who provided secretarial assistance in the preparation of the manuscript and the Teacher's Manual, and who patiently proofed the material. To Janice Glab, Jo Anne Martin, and Martha Ann Wilson, thank you.

April 1975

Curtis E. Tate, Jr.
Leon C. Megginson
Charles R. Scott, Jr.
Lyle R. Trueblood

List of Case Contributors

Robert L. Anderson
N. A. Beadles
Frederic A. Brett
Harvey J. Brightman
Robert Crayne
Dennis M. Crites
Warren DeBord
Donald DeSalvia
Wayne E. Etter
Christopher French
Robert Gatewood
Joe L. Hamilton
John Hand
M. M. Hargrove
Dorothy N. Harlow
Paul Hudleston
Fred Ingerson
Omer C. Jenkins
J. C. Johnson
Rudolph L. Kagerer
David R. Kenerson
Peter R. Kensicki
Henry Key
Jay T. Knippen
Hall H. Logan
Joseph Barry Mason
Morris L. Mayer
Leon C. Megginson

Kenneth W. Olm
B. D. Perkins
George E. Passey
Sydney C. Reagan
Robert A., Rentz, Jr.
James F. Russell
Donald W. Scatton
Charles R. Scott, Jr.
David R. Seymour
Arthur D. Sharplin
A. Michael Sibley
Calvin W. Stevens
Alonzo J. Strickland, III.
Jeffrey C. Susbauer
Curtis E. Tate, Jr.
John Clair Thomson
Arthur A. Thompson
Howard A. Thompson
Henry Towery
L. R. Trueblood
Thomas F. Urban
Milton F. Usry
Kenneth R. Van Voorhis
William Vroman
Louis C. Wagner
Louis P. White
Stephen L. Woehrle
Allan Young

Thomas W. Zimmerman

Contents

**Part II
What Is Your Business?**   51

4. Selecting the Type of Business You Would Like to Enter   53

How You Can Investigate the Alternatives. How You Can Classify the Types of Business. How You Can Choose the Business to Enter. Whether You Should "Be Independent" or Acquire a Franchise: *Importance of Franchising. Considerations in Franchising. Some Pertinent Questions to Ask. Some Conclusions Concerning Franchising.* Service Stations.

5. Studying the Economic Environment for Your Business   64

Studying the Economic Environment for the Industry. Studying the Market for Your Business. Deciding Whether to Start a New Business or Buy an Existing One: *Entering an Established Business. Starting a New Business of Your Own.*

6. Planning the Legal, Financial, and Administrative Structure of Your Firm   74

Determining Legal Form: *Proprietorship. Partnership. Corporation. Holding Company. Trust.* Financial Structure: *Proprietorship. Partnership. Corporation.* Administrative Structure.

7. How to Establish Your New Business   84

Developing a Timetable. Establishing Your Business Objectives. Setting Up the Organizational Structure. Determining Personnel Requirements. Determining Your Physical Plant Needs. *Location. Buy or Lease.* Planning Your Approach to the Market: *Building an Image. Channels of Distribution. Pricing Policies.* Preparing Your Budgets: *Types of Budgets. Anticipating Difficulties.* Locating Sources of Funds: *Your Own Funds. Other Individuals. Trade Credit. Commercial Banks. Investment Banks. Major Non-Financial Corporations. Insurance Companies. Small Business Administration. Small Business Investment Corporation. Industrial Development Corporations. Economic Development Administration (EDA). State Employment Agencies. Agricultural Loans.* Implementing Your Plans: *Capital Procurement. Corporate Charter and Permits. Contracting and Purchasing Facilities and Supplies. Personnel Selection and Training. Beginning Operations.*

8. How to Enter an Existing Business   100

To Purchase, or Not to Purchase? *Determining Reasons for the Availability of the Business. Analysis of Accounting Information. Analysis of*

Pricing Formula. Appraisal of Operations, Plant, and Equipment. Preparing an Economic Feasibility Study. Implementing Your Plans: *Financing the Business. Considering Changes in Method of Operations. Developing a Formal Plan. Taking Over the Business.*

Part III
Managing Your Small Business   145

9. Planning for Your Business   147

Need for Planning. The Planning Function and Types of Plans. Management by Objectives. Barriers to Planning. How to Plan. Levels of Planning.

10. Organizing Your Business   155

The Need for Organizing Your Firm. Planning for Growth. Organizational Principles and Practices. Forms of Organization, by Types of Authority. Ways of Organizing Your Firm. Organizational Problems.

11. Directing and Controlling the Activities of Your Firm   162

Directing: *Exercising Leadership. Communicating. Motivating.* Controlling: *Process of Control. Self-Discipline. Externally Imposed Discipline. Indirect Control.* What Kind of Manager Would You Be? Sources of Outside Assistance: *The Private Management Consultant. The Small Business Administration.*

Part IV
Marketing and Your Business   195

12. Marketing: Concepts, Policies, and What-to-Do Strategies   197

The Marketing Concept: *Meeting Customers' Needs. Market Segmentation. Competitive Edge.* Strategic Marketing Policies: *Morality and Pub-*

lic Service. Products. Markets. Profits. Personal Selling. Customer Relations. Promotion. Credit Policies. Use of Credit Cards. Approaches to Marketing Strategy—What-to-Do: *Expanding Sales into New Markets. Increasing Penetration of Present Market. Make No Marketing Innovations.*

13. Marketing Operations: Market Research, Sales Forecasting, Advertising, and Sales Promotion   210

Market Research and Sales Forecasting: *Areas of Market Research. Sources of Marketing Information. Sales Forecasting. Overcoming Market Research Difficulties.* Advertising and Sales Promotion: *Advertising. Sales Promotion.*

14. Marketing Operations: Personal Selling, Channels of Distribution and Logistics, Pricing, and the Marketing Mix   222

Personal Selling: *Using Sales Agents. Using Your Own Sales Representatives.* Channels of Distribution and Logistics. Pricing. The Marketing Mix. Appendix: Guide for Improving a Sales Representative's Performance.

Part V
Producing Your Product or Service   269

15. Your Service: Changing Inputs to Outputs   271

Systems for Converting Inputs to Finished Products: *Productive Elements. Productive Elements Applied to Different Industries.* Deciding Whether to Make or Buy. Planning Your Physical Facilities: *Step 1: Determine Your Services. Step 2: Break the Product or Service into Parts, Operations, and Activities. Step 3: Determine the Times to Perform the Operations. Step 4: Estimate the Number of Machines and Workers Needed. Step 5: Decide the Best Arrangement for the Sequence of Operations. Step 6: Determine the General Layout. Step 7: Plan the Detailed Layout for Efficiency and Effectiveness.* Implementing Your Plans.

16. Your Process Plan and Control System   286

Work Design: *State the Problem. State the Function of the Work. Collect Information. List Alternatives. Analyze and Select Alternatives. For-*

mulate, Review, and Test the Selected Changes. Install and Follow Up
the Changes. Work Measurement: *Time for Work Performance. Adding
Time for Personal Needs.* Planning: The Forecast. Planning: Converting
a Sales Plan to a Production Plan. Scheduling: Setting the Time for Work
to Be Done in the Near Future. Installing an Information System to
Direct the Activities. Controlling Production: Quantity and Quality.

17. Purchasing and Controlling Your Materials   302

Materials (or Goods) Planning and Control. Inventory. Quantities per
Order. Ordering Procedure. Sources of Supply. Receiving Materials.

**Part VI
Manning Your Business**   343

18. Selecting Your People   345

Planning Your Personnel Requirements. Where to Find New Employees.
How to Recruit New People. How to Select People for Given Jobs: *Application Blank. Interviewing. Employment Tests. Checking References.
Physical Examination. Decision to Hire.* How to Introduce New People
to Their Jobs.

19. Developing and Maintaining Your People   358

Training and Developing Your People: *Need for Training. Methods of
Training. Outside Assistance You Can Use in Training. Some Guidelines
for Developing People.* Setting Wages and Salaries: *Rewarding Nonmanagerial Employees. Rewarding Management Personnel. Appraising
Your Employees' Performance.* Appendix: Guidelines for Effective Employee Training.

20. Your Relationships with Your Employees   373

Handling Your Employees' Grievances. Understanding Legislation that
Affects Your Business: *Unions and Collective Bargaining. Payroll Taxes.
Workmen's Compensation. Wages and Hours. Laws Pertaining to Age.
Equal Employment Opportunities. Sex Discrimination. Environmental
Protection. Occupational Safety and Health.* Dealing with the Labor
Unions. Appendix: Twenty-Seven Things You *Can Do* When a Union
Tries to Organize Your Company. Appendix: Twenty-Two Things You
Cannot Do When They Try to Organize.

Part VII
Maintaining Financial Health   415

Financial Accounts of the Firm: *Assets. Liabilities. Owner's Equity. Revenue and Expenses. Profit.* Methods of Evaluating the Firm's Financial Condition: *Values of Each Ratio in the Past. Values of Other Like Companies.* Important Ratios and Their Meaning.

What Information Is Needed: *Service to Customers. Services Performed for You. Other Activities.* Recording the Information: *Sales. Cash Income and Outgo. Accounts Receivable. Accounts Payable. Inventory. Expenses. Financial Statements.* The Storing of Information.

Step 1: Establishing Your Profit Goal. Step 2: Determining Your Planned Volume of Sales. Step 3: Estimating Your Expenses for Planned Volume of Sales. Step 4: Determining Your Profit from Steps (2) and (3). Step 5: Comparing Your Estimated Profit with Your Profit Goal. Step 6: Listing Possible Alternatives to Improve Your Profits. Step 7: Determining How Changes in Costs Vary with Sales Volume Changes. Step 8: Determining How Profits Vary with Changes in Sales Volume. Step 9: Analyzing Alternatives from a Profit Standpoint. Step 10: Selecting Changes in Your Plans.

Characteristics of Control Systems: *Controls Should Be Timely. Controls Should Not Be Costly. Controls Should Provide the Accuracy Needed. Controls Should Be Quantifiable and Measurable. Controls Should Show Causes, When Possible. Controls Should Be Assigned to One Individual.* Causes of Poor Performance. Establishing Standards of Performance. Obtaining Information on Actual Performance. Comparing Actual Performance with Standards. The Design and Use of Budgets: *Sales Budget. Cash Budget. Credit, Collections, and Accounts Receivable. Other Budgets.*

Insurance and Its Limitations. Alternatives to Commercial Insurance. Guides to Buying Insurance: *Financial Characteristics and Flexibility of Insurer. Services Rendered by Agent.* Types of Coverage.

CASES FOR PART VII

Part VIII
Where Do You Go from Here?

Managing a Family-Owned Business. Some Difficult Problems with Managers. Preparing for Your Successor. Appendix: Inventory of Information Used to Manage and Operate a Company.

CASES FOR PART VIII

Part I

Characteristics of Small Businesses and Their Owner-Managers

The first step you should take toward owning and managing a small business is to decide whether it is the "right" thing for you to do. The material in this part should help you make that important decision.

The role of small business in our economy and the challenges it affords are put into perspective in the first chapter. Then, considerable attention is given in Chapter 2 to the characteristics, attitudes, and objectives of the small business manager. You, as one of these individuals, have been our first and prime consideration in presenting the material. In essence, you will enter business for yourself because you want to attain the objectives of financial profits and certain non-monetary benefits. In order to achieve these objectives, however, you must give up security and other benefits achieved through working for someone else, and assume the risks inherent in ownership. These thoughts are covered in Chapter 3.

1

The Challenge of Managing a Small Business

Small business now accounts for about one-half of all this country's business activities. About 95 percent of all business enterprises are classified as small. Because small businesses are so prevalent and perform such an important function in our economic system, it is desirable to study the unique challenges involved in managing one of them. Owners and managers of these enterprises usually believe in individual freedom, initiative, and the free-enterprise system. Most people consider it important to keep this part of our business society healthy.

In managing a business, there usually must be a conscious choice between the desirable alternatives and the undesirable ones. There must be a weighing of the advantages against the disadvantages of those alternatives. The resulting decision tends to be based upon the individual's evaluation of the relative merits of the available alternatives. This relationship should also be present in a person's mind when he is deciding whether to become the owner of a business or whether he should become a manager working for someone else.

This chapter is designed to help you evaluate intelligently the alternatives of becoming the owner of a small business or of going into some other activity.

DISTINCTION BETWEEN MANAGING SMALL AND BIG BUSINESS

In distinguishing between big business and small business, some of the criteria used are relative size, type of customers, financial strength, and number of employees. For example, in the Small Business Act of 1953, Congress defined a small business as one which "is independently owned and operated and which is not dominant in its field of operation."[1] The specific criteria to be used in determining size would be set by the Small Business Administration.

Distinction According to Size

There is no generally accepted definition of a "small business." The definitions vary all the way from that of the office of the Secretary of the Treasury, which includes all firms with "receipts of less than $1,000,000," to our's, which is "an organization with a name, a place of operations, an owner, and one or more workers other than the owner." According to the first definition, there were more than 14.5 million small businesses in the U.S. in 1969.[2] According to the second definition, there were around 5.7 million independent or small businesses in 1971.[3] The Small Business Administration says there were over eight million small businesses.[4] Included in that number were "invisible" businesses such as people working out of their own homes.

A different definition is used by the Federal Reserve Bank. It says a small business is one which "is independently owned and operated but is not dominant in its field."[5] The United States Employment Service estimates that the average manufacturing firm has 60 employees; the average wholesaler has nine; the average retailer has four; and the average service establishment has two. Over 70 percent of small business involves distribution.[6]

According to Dun & Bradstreet, there are about 2,250,000 businesses in this country. Well over half are worth less than $50,000. Only 5 percent are worth more than $200,000. (See Figure 1–1.)

According to the definition used in this book—an organization with a name, a place of operations, an owner, and one or more workers other than the owner—there are around 5.7 million small businesses, making up about 95 percent of all business units. According to various Small Business Administration reports, these firms account for: around 37 percent of our gross national product; 99 percent of firms and 85

[1] W. B. Barnes, *First Semi-Annual Report of Small Business Administration* (Washington, D.C.: Small Business Administration, January 31, 1954), p. 7ff.

[2] Small Business Administration, *Annual Report*, vol. 2 (Washington, D.C.: U.S. Government Printing Office, 1972), p. 28.

[3] National Foundation of Independent Business reports.

[4] Small Business Administration, *Annual Report*, vol. 1 (Washington, D.C.: U.S. Government Printing Office, 1972), p. 2.

[5] Small Business Administration, *Strengthening Small Business Management* (Washington, D.C.: U.S. Government Printing Office, 1971), p. 42.

[6] Ibid.

FIGURE 1–1
Distribution of Business Firms by Worth, 1972

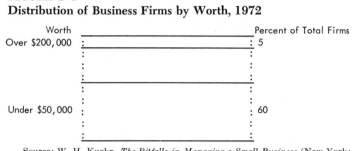

Source: W. H. Kuehn, *The Pitfalls in Managing a Small Business* (New York: Dun & Bradstreet, March 1973), p. 3.

percent of sales in construction; 96 percent of firms and 72 percent of sales in retail trade; 94 percent of firms and 70 percent of sales in wholesale trade; and 94 percent of firms and 30 percent of sales in manufacturing.

Distinction According to Intentions

An important distinction to be made is that the *intentions* of the owners and managers of small firms tend to be different from those of professional managers of large enterprises.

Intentions of Managers of Large Enterprises. The intentions of managers of large businesses are many and varied. Yet, they can probably be summarized as: the desire for job security; the desire for place, power, and prestige; and the desire for high income. Managers who desire job security are exemplified by those individuals who try to maintain an average earnings record that shows a steady—though not spectacular—increase year in and year out without taking chances that would jeopardize their position. Many managers in large firms desire the economic power that goes with such positions. These are managers who like to exercise economic power and dominance over other people and thereby control their business activities. The vast majority of American managers desire to make substantially higher incomes than the average and are willing to pay the price of increased responsibilities and the expenditure of time, effort, and energy in order to achieve this goal. Also, most of these managers enjoy their position and do not abuse it. For instance, the president of a manufacturing organization told one of us that, "Not enough attention is being paid to the satisfaction of leadership and the pleasure of being a manager. We are not enjoying the fun of being a president. We have got to do a better job of encouraging leadership in this area."

Those managers who are in the field for the extra income admit that managing a company is filled with responsibilities and worries, but they are willing to sacrifice other pleasures in order to have the benefits that go with a high income (including the large number of fringe benefits, such as expense accounts and the availability of company facilities for personal use).

Intentions of Owners of Small Businesses. While these same motives might impel someone to become the owner of a small business, it must be recognized that there is a vast difference which can be summarized by the word "independence." This distinction was made by a recent graduate of one of our larger universities, who had majored in Business Administration, when he wrote to one of us explaining why so few college graduates want to go into business for themselves.

> I believe that at least part of the answer is that the new graduates just don't know where to start and what to expect in the business world. With this lack of knowledge, they just don't have the "guts" to try it on their own. In my own case, I decided when I was in undergraduate school that I did not want to work for the other man. I always said that if I were going to make anyone rich, it was going to be myself. (Unfortunately, it has not worked out that way—yet.) Even with this burning desire to be my own boss, I was very hesitant and almost afraid to go into business for myself. However, I'm still glad I did.

This letter illustrates the objective of those who become managers of small businesses. That goal is the freedom from interference or control by "superiors." Those individuals desire autonomy in exercising their initiative and ambition, which often results in innovations and leads to great flexibility, which is one of the virtues of small business.

UNIQUE ADVANTAGES OF A SMALL BUSINESS

The small business has many advantages over its larger competitors. It is usually in closer touch with its customers, employees, and suppliers. The small business tends to have better employee relations than larger firms. It can do a more individualized job for customers and thereby can attract them on the basis of specialty product, quality, and personal services rather than on the impersonal factors of price or mass production of largely identical products.

Due to the small percentage that goes for overhead and non-revenue producing activities, there are still some activities that can be performed more efficiently by small organizations than large ones.

The small enterprise is often a source of new materials, processes, ideas, services, and products that larger firms are reluctant to provide. The big company is usually committed by its investment in tools, inventory, and personnel to producing the same product in larger quantities or for longer periods of time, and is not as flexible as a smaller firm.

Smaller companies have become a controlling factor in the American economy by keeping the bigger concerns "on their toes." With the introduction of new products, methods, services, and so forth, the small businesses help check the development of monopolies, which is sometimes the tendency in larger organizations. Therefore, small businesses encourage competition, if not in price, at least in design and efficiency.

Small local businesses usually have a more intimate knowledge of their communities, and therefore take more personal interest in them. Their owners and managers are mainstays of community projects. Another unique advantage of the small business is that *it produces people as well as goods and services.* Small companies enable their people to achieve a more well-rounded, balanced development than they could achieve in larger organizations. This development is accomplished by providing them a greater variety of learning experiences in work activities not open to individuals holding more specialized jobs in larger organizations. People have greater freedom in making decisions as well as in performing a greater variety of activities. This freedom, in turn, lends zest and interest to their work. In addition, it trains people to become better leaders and to use their talents and energies most effectively.

It has been said that the small business is a manifestation of one of the basic freedoms of American life, namely, risk taking—with its consequent rewards and punishments. The entrepreneur has *relative* freedom to enter or leave a business at will, to start small and grow big, to expand or contract, and to succeed or fail. This freedom is the basis of our economic system. Yet, the freedom to enter and leave is not absolute. Certain legal and other requirements must be met before one can start a new business. The same is true of closing a firm. The manager may have responsibilities to customers, employees, investors, and/or the community which prevent leaving at will.

This characteristic has forced the small business to be flexible. Therefore, it can switch its production readily to meet changing market conditions and can adapt itself quickly to changing demands within its field and capacity. It can even change fields. The small business is a center of initiative where experiments may be conducted, where innovations may be initiated, and where new ventures are started. Many of the new products of today originated in small business concerns. Particularly is this true in the electronic computer field where the initial developments were carried on in small companies, e.g., the Univac computer.

UNIQUE DISADVANTAGES OF A SMALL BUSINESS

Probably more has been written concerning the disadvantages of small business than any other aspect of this area of study. Usually, the discussions boil down to three things: inadequate management ability, inadequate financing (including "unfair" taxation), and a poor competitive position.

One study showed the pitfalls facing small business managers and what can be done about them. The results are shown in Figure 1–2.

FIGURE 1–2
Pitfalls Facing Small Businessmen

Pitfalls

1. Lack of experience
2. Lack of money
3. The wrong location
4. Inventory mismanagement
5. Too much capital going into fixed assets
6. Poor credit granting practices
7. Taking too much out for yourself
8. Unplanned expansion
9. Having the wrong attitudes

What Can Be Done about these Pitfalls?

1. Recognize limitations
2. Planning
3. Record keeping
4. Watch the balance sheet—not just the profits
5. Investigate
6. Suppliers and banks
7. Learning
8. Professional assistance
9. Watch your health

Source: W. H. Kuehn, *The Pitfalls in Managing a Small Business* (New York: Dun & Bradstreet, March 1973).

What are the specific disadvantages of small businesses? The problems of effective management of a small business have multiplied during recent years. During World War II, the Korean Conflict, and the Vietnam War, many independent enterprisers started in business and showed unusual profits. However, as the "seller's market" ended each time and a "buyer's market" developed, the problems confronting them began to multiply in character and intensity.

During these periods, many small business managers *relied on one-person management*. They tended to guard their positions very jealously and seldom selected effective subordinates. If they did, they failed to give them enough authority and responsibility to manage adequately. Often, the problem of "inbreeding" existed; members of the family who were not capable were brought into the firm in positions of authority.

Managers of small businesses *cannot be specialized* in one area. As they must make their own decisions and are forced to live with those choices, whether they are good, bad, or indifferent, the managers are faced with a dilemma. Because of the business's limited resources, it cannot afford to make costly mistakes; but because the organization is so small, it cannot afford to hire assistance to help prevent managers from making mistakes. Lack of sufficient time to give attention to the various managerial functions accounts for the vast majority of failures among small businesses.

A related specific limitation of small businesses is the *shortage of working capital.* This leads to the inability to keep up with their larger competitors in new facilities, equipment, tools, and methods. Many efforts have been made to overcome this difficulty by making loans available to small businesses and by trying to obtain favorable tax laws to assist them.

Another disadvantage is the *lack of coordination between production and marketing,* that is, the lack of adequately balancing and coordinating these two important functions. It is important for a small business to keep a judicious balance between (1) having too few products so that sales are lost, and (2) diversifying too fast. This means that there should be a balancing between the advantages of diversification and the advantages of product specialization.

Some other disadvantages are: a lack of proper records keeping; lack of effective selling techniques—especially market research, specialty advertising, and personal selling; too rapid and unplanned expansion; and the increasing complexity of internal management as the organization grows in size. These disadvantages, although real and of significance to the small business, cannot be adequately treated here. They are covered elsewhere throughout this book. However, some of the problems associated with growth will be discussed.

THE PROBLEM OF GROWTH

The problem of growth appears to be a built-in dilemma facing many small businesses. First, if the owners are inefficient and if their initiative or abilities are not sufficient, their organizations flounder and eventually become included among the casualties called "business failures."

Second, if the owners are mediocre, their organizations continue to be small businesses and are constantly plagued with the problems associated with smallness.

Third, if the owner-managers are efficient and capable, and their organizations succeed and grow, they run the risk of losing the very things they seek from their business firms. The very act of growing means losing some of the autonomy and control the owners seek. If nothing else, the owners now must please a larger number of people, including customers, the public, and their employees. They also have the problem of controlling other people, exercising the very thing they resented in others. All too frequently, owner-managers are not equipped to control other people well, and they begin to have interpersonal problems in their firms. If they become large enough and require outside capital for future success and growth, they may lose autonomy and control over their organizations. However, even if they lose control, they may still retain a sense of achievement for what they have been able to create within their "own" organization. They can still say, "This is something I've built."

Historically, the ownership and management of small businesses have

FIGURE 1–3
Stages in the Development of Small Business

First Stage--One person operation, where the owner does all the activities.

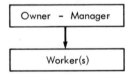

Second Stage--Separation of management and nonmanagement functions; hired subordinates to do some of the manual and/or mental activities while owner manages.

Third Stage--Separation of ownership and management functions; owner begins to relinquish the responsibilities for the day-to-day running of the business activities to a professional manager.

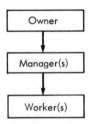

Source: Adapted from L. C. Megginson, *Providing Management Talent for Small Business* (Small Business Management Research Reports; Baton Rouge, La.: College of Business Administration, Louisiana State University, 1961), p. 7.

tended to follow the growth pattern shown in Figure 1–3. During the first stage, the owner both manages the company and performs all the work himself. As the organization grows into the second stage, the owner hires one or more employees to help perform the manual and/or mental activities. Later, as the organization begins to get larger, it enters the third stage in which the owner hires a manager to run the business. Thus, the business takes on the form, characteristics, and many of the problems of a big business.

An insurance firm began in the late 1920s with a husband and wife selling policies during the day and doing the paper work at night. As chairman of the firm, the man described the process of growth in this way:

> A company's success and growth is a chain reaction. First, there is the growth which leads to new responsibilities. This, in turn, leads to a search for executive talent to undertake the new responsibilities. If the search is successful, the effective management leads to better business, which leads to more profits. Then, the decision must be made to expand again. Thus, the cycle is repeated.
>
> However, the chain reaction can be broken at any point in the cycle. For instance, if the attempt to find another manager is unsuccessful, the growth may stop. Somewhere along the line, the founder ceases being the owner-manager of a small company with its unique problems and rewards and becomes the manager of a large company with all of its problems.

In this connection, it should be emphasized that the length of service of professional managers (as opposed to owner-managers) in small organizations *tends* to be relatively short. They move from one company to another as they progress. Often, owners must give managers an interest in the company to hold them.

THE PROBLEM OF "FAILURE"

The threat of failure is ever present for small businesses. Discontinuances result from many factors, including health, changes in family situations, and the apparent advantages of working for someone else. These are voluntary decisions to quit.

There are, however, other discontinuances which are the result of inability or failure to make the business "go." Things just don't work out as planned. These are "failures."

There are two types of failures. One ends up in court with some kind of loss to the creditors. There are relatively few of these failures. In fact, there were only 10,326 such failures in 1971 and 9,566 in 1972.[7] The underlying causes of these "formal failures" for 1972 are shown in Figure 1–4.

What are the characteristics of the firms which suffer this type of failure? Retailers and service establishments tend to fail earlier than

---

[7] *The Business Failure Record, 1972* (New York: Business Economics Department, Dun & Bradstreet, 1973), p. 3.

FIGURE 1-4
Causes of 9,566 Business Failures in 1972

Overall Causes	*Underlying Causes*

Neglect:
Due to . . . . Bad habits, poor health, marital difficulties, etc.

Fraud:
Due to . . . . Misleading name, false financial statement, premeditated overbuy, irregular disposal of assets, etc.

Lack of experience in the line:
Lack of managerial experience:
Unbalanced experience:
Incompetence:
Due to . . . . Inadequate sales, heavy operating expenses, receivables difficulties, inventory difficulties, excessive fixed assets, poor location, competitive weakness, etc.

Disaster:
Due to . . . . Fire, flood, burglary, employee fraud, strike, etc. Some of these occurrences could have been provided for through insurance.

Source: *The Business Failure Record, 1972* (New York: Business Economics Department, Dun & Bradstreet, 1973), pp. 11–12.

other type businesses, while manufacturers, construction firms, and wholesalers fail later. This is shown in Table 1–1.

The other kind of failure is more important, numerically, and probably emotionally as well. This involves situations where individuals have

TABLE 1-1
Formal Business Failures Classified by Year and Size of Liability

Year	*Under $5,000*	*$5,000 to $25,000*	*$25,000 to $100,000*	*$100,000 to $1 million*	*Over $1 million*
1970	4.0	29.7	40.9	22.8	2.6
1971	3.8	27.2	42.7	23.5	2.8
1972	4.1	26.1	43.4	23.4	3.0

Source: *The Business Failure Record, 1972* (New York: Business Economics Department, Dun & Bradstreet, 1973), p. 6.

put their savings—or income—into a business only to see losses wipe out their investment. Creditors don't suffer, for the owner has put up the funds to absorb the losses and pay off the debts. The owner is the one who packs up, closes the door, and says, "That's it! I'll never try starting a business of my own again." In summary, the Service Corps of Retired Executives (SCORE) estimates that around 400,000 small firms go out of business each year in the U.S., and 100,000 of these fail in the first year of existence.[8] The causes of failure, in descending order,

[8] "Failing Businesses," *Parade,* September 8, 1974, p. 24.

are: (1) lack of business records, (2) lack of business experience, (3) insufficient stock turnover, (4) accounts receivable, (5) inventory shrinkage, (6) poor inventory control, (7) lack of finances, (8) improper markup, and (9) lack of sales.

SUMMARY

In summary, the most valid distinction between small and big business is based on the *intentions, aims, goals,* or *objectives* of the owner-managers. Small business managers primarily crave independence and freedom from control. They enjoy the autonomy they have in the exercise of their initiative and ambition.

The unique *advantages* of small business include the following:

1. More personal contacts with customers, suppliers, and employees.
2. Better interpersonal relationships.
3. More efficiency in many respects.
4. A source of innovation, including flexibility of action.
5. A controlling factor over big business' tendency toward monopoly.
6. Greater community life.
7. Development of leaders.

The primary disadvantages are:

1. Inadequate management ability caused by a lack of training and development.
2. Insufficient financing, including "unfair" taxation.
3. A poor competitive position.
4. Lack of coordination between producing and selling.
5. Lack of proper record keeping.
6. Lack of effective marketing techniques.
7. Increasing complexity of operations.

The specific *causes of failure* for small businesses are:

1. Neglect.
2. Fraud.
3. Lack of experience, including incompetence, inadequate managerial training and experience, and unbalanced experience.
4. Disasters.

This type enterprise is often faced with a dilemma, for if the owner is inefficient or mediocre, he fails; but if he is too successful, he becomes so large that he loses the independence that he craves. You should recognize that remaining small is not a sign of failure. You can remain small, successful, satisfied, and find a niche for yourself in the business world. In other words, there is a place for the small business if the owner works at making it effective and successful.

Finally, small businesses provide the dynamism, innovation, and effectiveness that has led to our productive economic system.

QUESTIONS FOR FURTHER DISCUSSION

1. What would you say is the most valid distinction between small and big business? Explain.
2. Discuss the unique advantages of a small business.
3. Briefly discuss some of the primary disadvantages of a small business.
4. Explain the phrase, "The problem of growth appears to be a built-in dilemma for the small businessman."
5. Briefly discuss the stages in the development of a small business. Have you seen any examples of this growth pattern? Explain.
6. What are some *overall* causes of failures? Explain.
7. Distinguish between two types of failure.
8. What are the characteristics of firms which suffer "formal failures"?
9. What would you say are the intentions of managers of large businesses?
10. What is the vast difference between the intentions of managers of large businesses and small businesses?

2

What Are Your Objectives?

After presenting to you the challenges afforded by owning and operating a small business, we would like to explore the role you could play as the owner of one of these important units. In this chapter, we discuss: (1) your philosophy of life, (2) your personal objectives, (3) the objectives of small businesses, and (4) the importance of meshing together these objectives.

YOUR PHILOSOPHY OF LIFE

It is essential that you define the kind of ethical standards and value system that make up your philosophy of life. The process of sorting and choosing the type of business you enter will be influenced by these characteristics.

As indicated in Chapter 1, the chances for success in small business are not great. Of every 1,000 new firms, about 930 eventually fail, merge, or otherwise cease to exist. Thus, you should consider the alternative of choosing a managerial job in government or big business and avoiding the many and complex worries of running a small business. Another alternative is to become a staff specialist in an area of your interest, have set hours of work and enjoy leisure time for recreation and hobbies, have a set income and don't worry about having your own money tied up in a business that has a good chance of failing. In other words, you can choose a reasonably safe economic life for yourself and your family instead of the more challenging and rewarding life of an entrepreneur.

15

Thus, at the outset, you should ask yourself some questions about *your personal philosophy of life* such as these:

What are my reasons for being?
Why am I here?
What do I really want out of life?
Why should I have my own business?
What is it that excites me about owning a business?

YOUR PERSONAL OBJECTIVES

A person's occupation represents much more to him than just a set of skills and functions; it represents a way of life. It largely provides and determines the environment—both physical and psychological—in which the individual lives; it selects, and often strengthens, the traits that he most frequently uses. The occupation usually carries with it a status in the community and provides the individual's social roles and patterns for living. Since it largely determines with what sorts of persons one spends much of his life, it greatly influences value judgments and ethical standards. Occupational preference and personality traits are also usually related. Consequently, the ultimate objective in choosing your occupation should be the satisfaction of individual needs.

Theoretical Needs

Many efforts have been made to classify and explain human needs. The more popular efforts are summarized for the readers who have studied them elsewhere, or as an introduction to those who have not.

Maslow's Needs Hierarchy. Abraham Maslow, a psychologist, said that human needs could be grouped together in an increasing order, or hierarchy, from the bottom up.[1] As one need is satisfied, the next higher need comes into play. The needs, which were modified by McGregor, are:

5. Self-Fulfillment.
4. Ego.
3. Social.
2. Safety.
1. Physiological.

Herzberg's Motivators and Maintenance Factors. Frederick Herzberg, another psychologist, said there are two sets of factors present in every job situation.[2] One set of factors is necessary in order to *main-*

---

[1] Douglas McGregor, *The Human Side of Enterprise* (New York: McGraw-Hill Book Co., 1960), pp. 36–39.

[2] Frederick Herzberg et. al., *The Motivation to Work* 2d ed. (New York: John Wiley & Sons, Inc., 1959).

tain a good working relationship, but they *do not motivate the individual to produce at a higher level.* They are:

1. Supervision.
2. Company policies and administration.
3. Employee benefits.
4. Job security.
5. Working conditions.
6. Salary.
7. Relationships with others.

The other factors, if present, *motivate people to produce at a high level.* They are:

1. Achievement.
2. Recognition.
3. Responsibility.
4. Creative and challenging work.
5. Advancement.

McGregor's Theory X and Theory Y. Considering many of these and other ideas, Douglas McGregor concluded that two basic assumptions can be made about human behavior and, therefore, about the motivation of individuals to perform in the business world.

Under *Theory X,* human beings are thought to be lazy, to dislike work, to shun responsibility, and to require coercion to achieve effective productivity.[3]

Under *Theory Y,* humans are generally thought to accept work as normal, to need and desire work, and to be using only part of their intellectual and productive capabilities.[4] The entrepreneur is a classic example of Theory Y in practice, exhibiting ambition, drive, initiative, and hard work.

Motives of Small Business Owners

The above discussion of human needs will provide you the background for further study. As the owner of a small business, you have the potential for fulfilling all of these needs through managing your own firm. The manner in which your needs are fulfilled depends upon the knowledge, skills, and personality traits you bring to your business. Your personal objectives express the type of life you wish to lead.

A great deal depends on the type of person you are and your dedication to your business. Owning your own business can be very rewarding in the following ways:

---

[3] McGregor, *Human Side of Enterprise,* pp. 33–44.

[4] Ibid., pp. 45–47.

1. You can make a great deal of money, including certain expense account benefits. Be sure to bear in mind the legality and tax accountability of these!
2. You can perform a satisfying service to your community.
3. You can obtain prestige in your community.
4. You can find the challenges and new experiences many and varied.
5. You can be proud of what you have built.

There is a certain satisfaction in managing something you have built that does not come to you from directing a business that others have built. But before you decide upon this course, other questions must be answered—if you are to succeed. Ambition, desire, capital, and willingness are not enough. You still need:

1. Technical and managerial know-how.
2. Preparation.
3. Experience.
4. Ability.
5. Perseverence.
6. Willingness to work.
7. Personality.
8. Judgment.
9. Competitive spirit.
10. Health to use all of them.

Now, one last time, before you consider risking your money, time, and effort to become an entrepreneur, ask yourself the following questions:

> Am I willing to make the personal and family sacrifices?
> What is my objective—to make a lot of money or to perform a useful service?
> Do I have the patience and tenacity required of this type of activity?
> Do I have the skills and knowledge so that I can collect the resources needed; can I convert those resources so that customers will want them; and can I organize and direct the activities needed to succeed?
> How much of me do I want to put into the business?
> How much money do I need to get started and where do I get it?

There are many other questions which you should raise, but we will discuss these later.

OBJECTIVES OF A SMALL BUSINESS

Since the most valid distinction between small and big business is based on the *intentions, aims, goals,* or *objectives* of the owner-manager and the firm itself, these factors deserve considerable attention on your part at the very beginning of your interest in small business. One of the most important functions you—as the owner-manager—will perform is setting these goals and objectives. The *objectives are the ends toward which all the activities of your organization will be aimed.* Essentially, they determine the "character" of the firm and are the purposes toward which all the activities of your organization—including plans, policies, and programs—will be directed. They are the focal point of all your entrepreneurial functions.

An important distinction should be made between the objectives of the organization itself and those of its owner(s), managers, and employees. This distinction is important because the two sets of objectives are not necessarily the same. We will now look at some organizational objectives which should be considered along with the personal objectives which have just been discussed.

As for the business itself, there are at least two sets of objectives—the *overall enterprise objectives* and the *subsidiary goals* of the individual parts of the organization. There must be overall objectives, for without them there is the danger that individual goals may not be consistent with each other. The enterprise's objectives give unity of direction to the organization and provide standards by which actions of members of the firm can be measured. Each part of the firm will then set its objectives in order to contribute to the objectives of the enterprise.

Among the *overall enterprise objectives* that are important for you to consider are:

1. Service.
2. Profit.
3. Social.
4. Growth.

Service Objective

The overall objective of any business organization must be to perform a useful *service* for society by producing and distributing goods or services (or the satisfactions associated with them) to the public. A private organization is expected to receive a profit for its operations. In a capitalistic free-enterprise economy, profit is acceptable and considered to be in the public interest. Even in a profit-oriented organization, however, the primary objective is service to the public in the form of producing goods or services at a cost which will ensure a "fair" price to the consumer and "adequate" profits to the owners. Thus, the person who aspires to operate a small business must keep uppermost in mind the necessity for having service as his primary objective, but with profit as a natural consequence. If the enterprise ceases to give service, people will not accept the organization and it will go out of business. The reverse is also true, for if profits do not result, the owners will cease operating the firm.

When you make decisions concerning the type of business you desire to establish or enter, your firm's products and the type(s) of customers you will serve, you will be considering the service objective.

Profit Objective

The *profit motive* is not always understood, so a word of explanation may be needed by some readers. The production of profits is the reward for taking risks—such as investing your funds in an untried business and trying to anticipate the needs and wants of the public—and they are required if any private business is to survive. Profits are needed to create new jobs, acquire new facilities, and develop new products or services. The making of profit is fundamental to a capitalistic society and it is considered to be in the public interest. Profits are not self-generating, however, as they are residual and come into existence through satisfying the demand for a product or service. Products and services must be produced efficiently and effectively. In turn, the types of goods and services demanded are so numerous and varied that multiple objectives must be formulated if the product or service is to satisfy those demands.

In summary, profits compensate you for your acceptance of business risks and for performance of economic service. They are needed to assure continuity of your business.

Social Objectives

Your firm also has *social objectives* for people in the community other than customers—employees, suppliers, the government, and the community itself. All of these groups should be served effectively. You—as owner—therefore, have a social responsibility. You occupy a trusteeship position and should act to protect the interests of your customers, employees, suppliers, and the general public, as well as to make profit. Your personal moral code should have a sound basis if you are to act fairly and honestly in your relationships with all these groups.

Growth Objective

You should be concerned with your firm's *growth* and select a growth objective early in your career. Some of the questions you need to answer in setting this objective are:

Do I seek relative stability or merely survival?
Do I seek a rate of profit which is "satisfactory," considering my efforts and investment?
Do I seek to maximize profits?
Will I be satisfied to remain small?
Do I want to grow and challenge larger firms?

Walter Barnett* is a local contractor specializing in commercial construction. He has had many offers to expand locally, regionally, and even statewide. He has consistently chosen to remain small, bid on the jobs he wants, have few labor problems, earn a comfortable living, and "enjoy life." He appears to be succeeding in achieving these objectives.

Ray Williams, who built residential housing, had an excellent reputation for quality at a reasonable price. He received an offer to associate with a firm in an adjoining state, and he accepted. When the economy slackened 18 months later, construction declined, money became "tight," and he found himself overextended. He is now back working for another contractor.

Subsidiary Goals

The primary function of the small business manager is to direct the activities of the business toward attaining its overall objectives. Subsidiary objectives should be set for each functional unit of the organization (such as production, marketing, finance, personnel, and research) to provide guidelines in meeting the overall objectives of the business. In addition, the personal objectives of all individuals performing tasks within each functional unit must be considered and directed toward the organization's overall objectives.

This process is not as simple as it may appear, for each level of objectives may consist of several related objectives. In a practical business situation, the attainment of two or more objectives on any given level is often achieved only at the expense of other objectives on the same level or between levels. Consequently, conflict sometimes arises between objectives. This conflict must be resolved or minimized if productivity and profitability are to be achieved.

MESHING OF OBJECTIVES

A survey of 97 small, owner-managed firms in the San Antonio area revealed a correlation between profitability, customer satisfaction, man-

---

* The names in these incidents, illustrations, and in the cases at the end of the parts are disguised, although the events are real.

ager satisfaction, and psychic rewards.[5] It also showed that the chances of success are greatly increased when the objectives of the business—service at a profit—are meshed with owners' personal objectives. The results of the study indicate that it is possible for you to integrate multiple objectives into a unified whole.

Questions arise as to whether this integration of objectives can actually be accomplished and to what extent it can be achieved in small business establishments. An integration of objectives can be accomplished if the emphasis is directed toward *optimizing objectives* and *minimizing company and personal conflicts.* Communication plays an important part in the process. The close interpersonal relationships between owners of small businesses and their subordinates, customers, and others speed up communications and make integration easier.

Speaking from a social viewpoint, the small organization offers a sense of belonging that is missing in larger groups. There is a feeling of *esprit de corps* that cannot be duplicated in a large company. According to the sales manager of a small distribution company:

> A small business is both an economic and a social system. There is a sense of belonging that is hard to find in a big company. Also, in a small company, the job carries with it a position which gives the person a sense of prestige that he would lose if he went to a larger company.

SUMMARY

In this chapter, we have discussed four ideas:

1. Your philosophy of life.
2. The objectives of small businesses.
3. Some personal objectives of business owners and managers.
4. The importance of meshing business and personal objectives.

In order to set objectives effectively, you must consciously or unconsciously adopt a philosophy of life that will govern you in the choice of the firm's long-range objectives and intermediate goals, and guide you in your personal conduct. This philosophy is a way of thinking as to what the purpose of your company should be and how this purpose can best be achieved. If you develop such a basic philosophy of management, your major decisions will be easier to make and the problems that arise in the day-to-day conduct of your business will be much easier to solve.

Some of the questions you should seek to answer in developing your

---

[5] Hal B. Pickle and Brian S. Rungeling, "Empirical Investigation of Entrepreneurial Goals and Customer Satisfaction," *The Journal of Business*, vol. 46, no. 2 (April 1973), pp. 268–73.

philosophy were posed. Some of the ways a working philosophy will assist you are to:

1. Help you win effective support and followers.
2. Provide guidelines for you and provide a foundation for your managerial thinking.
3. Supply a framework within which you can improve your thinking.

In choosing objectives for your small business, there are at least four important ones. These are *service, profit, social,* and *growth*. The two overriding objectives are *service* and *profit*. Profit is your reward for accepting business risks and performing an economic service. *It is necessary if you are to continue doing those two things.*

A primary objective of your firm should be the *service objective.* A privately-owned business is an economic institution which has the purpose of producing and distributing goods or services or, more basically, the satisfactions associated with them. If your firm fails to fulfill the service objective, it will go out of business.

Next, you must decide upon your own objectives which motivate you to become a small business manager. The most important ones are *achievement, challenge, stimulation* of new experiences, *growth* and *advancement,* a seeking for *identity, recognition,* and *esteem* of others.

Business objectives must be integrated with your personal objectives for the most successful operation of a small business.

In summary, the personal rewards to proprietors of small businesses are many and varied. However, they can be summarized by saying that the owners can see clearly the cause-effect relationships between their enterprise, ability, and energy, and the material rewards they receive as a result of exercising those talents in running a small firm. They determine their own rewards and do not have to wait for someone above them to approve (or disapprove) an increase in their rewards. Thus, they are responsible for their own achievement, advancement, the feeling of pride that comes from creating and building something to pass on to one's family, and the inherent satisfaction of being part of a dynamic, growing entity.

QUESTIONS FOR FURTHER DISCUSSION

1. What are three major advantages of using a conscious, well-formed philosophy of management?
2. What are some of the more important objectives that seem to motivate small businessmen?
3. Explain the interrelationship between the *service* and *profit* objectives.
4. Why is the setting of objectives one of the most important functions of the owner-manager?

5. Is it necessary to distinguish between the objectives of the organization and those of its members? Why?

6. What is the purpose of *enterprise objectives?* Briefly discuss those objectives.

7. What is the relationship between enterprise objectives and subsidiary goals?

8. Explain the statement: "A person's occupation represents much more to him than just a set of skills and functions; it means a way of life."

9. Is the small businessman an example of theory X or theory Y? Why?

10. Is an integration of objectives possible? When and how?

3

You as Owner of a Small Business

In Chapter 1, we tried to show you some of the characteristics, advantages, and disadvantages of small business enterprises. You were asked to look at your philosophy of life and to study your personal and business objectives in Chapter 2. Now, we would like to present to you:

1. Some unique characteristics of successful small business managers.
2. Some personal requirements for success in a small business.
3. An introspective personal analysis you can make to see if you have the characteristics needed for success in a small firm.

These points are quite important, for as one studies the behavior of people who choose careers in small business, one is made acutely aware that all too often failure resulted from one or more of the following weaknesses:

1. Too much was left to chance.
2. The crucial obstacles went unnoticed through ignorance.
3. The amounts of time and physical effort demanded of the small business manager were not recognized and planned for.
4. The amount of capital required for a particular business was not determined, or—as is more often true—was grossly underestimated, and therefore not provided for.
5. Too many decisions were made by "hunch" or through intuition, without adequate background and experience upon which to base vital judgments.

CHARACTERISTICS OF SUCCESSFUL SMALL BUSINESS MANAGERS

The skills, abilities, and personal characteristics of owner-managers exert a more powerful influence on the fortunes of small companies than they do on larger firms. Whether you have these characteristics or not should then weigh heavily in determining whether or not you enter a small firm. Also, the kinds of methods and procedures you adopt in a small firm should be designed not only to offset any personal deficiencies you may have but also to build upon your strengths.

What, then, are the characteristics of successful owners of small enterprises? There are at least seven unique characteristics of such individuals, namely:

1. A great sense of independence.
2. A strong sense of enterprise.
3. Dominated as much by personal and family considerations as by professional choices.
4. Enters small business more by chance than design.
5. Jealously guards his time.
6. Limited formal education.
7. Expects quick and concrete results.

No individual will have all these characteristics to be sure, but they are the ones we have found to be present most frequently in owner-managers of the smaller firms.

A Great Sense of Independence

Successful small business managers have *a highly developed sense of independence* and they have *a strong desire to be independent of outside control*, whether this control is financial, governmental, or any other type of restraint on their initiative. They are the unreconstructed rebels of the business world who enjoy the feeling of freedom which comes from being "captain" of their own fate.

Robert Smith worked his way through college sweeping floors in a lighting fixture store. Later, he set up a wholesale division for his boss. He believed that success depended upon "never working for a company that you can't own," and building a firm of moderate size that "you can control completely." Seven years ago, at age 23, he borrowed $75,000, purchased some metalworking equipment, and set up shop producing and selling modern lighting fixtures. Now, he sells several million dollars worth of lamps each year.

A Sense of Enterprise

The managers of small businesses have a strong sense of enterprise which gives them a desire to use their ideas, abilities, ambitions, aspirations, and initiatives to the greatest degree possible. They are able to conceive new ideas, plan them, see them carried out, and profit from the results of those plans. This is not always true in a larger organization where different specialists do different phases of the work.

> George Martin was born in Europe under Nazi domination. His goal, from the time he came to the U.S. at age 16, was to become a millionaire. During college and while in the Army, he dabbled in buying and selling securities. This activity provided him with the savings to start a service putting together tax-sheltered investments for wealthy people. At 31 years of age, he attributes his millions to "hard work, intuitive skills, persistence—and luck."

Another aspect of enterprise which is almost always present in small businessmen is their drive for achievement and their willingness to work long, hard hours to reach their goal.

> Dick Crowe, from a middle-class New York neighborhood, worked his way through college doing odd jobs. After graduation, he became a real estate agent and later bought a weight-watchers' franchise. According to his own appraisal, he is totally committed to the firm, works long hours, and doesn't "know how to enjoy myself. I can't relax for my mind is always working, thinking, calculating."

Personal and Family Considerations

Small business managers are probably dominated as much by personal and family considerations as by the profit-making motive. Quite frequently, our students tell us they are returning home to start a business because that is what their family expects them to do. Even more frequent is the comment that they are going back to run the family business rather than go somewhere else and work for another company. In both cases, the person is doing it from a sense of obligation to his family rather than from the desire for profit.

Other examples are:

> A young man resigned a regular commission in the U.S. Army, where he was quite satisfied to make a career, in order to return to the wholesale distributorship and replace his father whose health was failing.

Another young man gave up a promising career as a professional personnel administrator in order to replace his father in their automobile agency. His father had died and his mother either had to sell out or get the son to run the firm.

A third man resigned from college in his senior year to run the family-owned picture-framing business when his father died.

Enters Small Business More by Chance Than Design

Many people have gravitated by chance into a position of ownership or management of the small firm rather than having prepared for it by design. This is especially true when the person has grown up in the business, has lived with it from day to day, and then one day finds himself in the position of having to take over the business. These are the owners or managers who quite frequently ask for assistance in the form of management training and development. This type of individual differs sharply from one who comes to college with the ambition to become a professional manager and gears his whole program toward that end.

Joe Ditta graduated from college in music and sought a career in the music profession. He had worked in the family restaurant while attending school. Soon after he became a professional singer, his father died and he returned home to manage the restaurant for the family.

Guards His Time

Time is very valuable, because of the many hours that must be dedicated to a small business. The position of a small business manager is to be differentiated from that of the manager of a large corporation who is expected to give a certain percentage of his time to "public relations" and have someone else perform his duties while he is away. The small business manager must still perform all the duties even if he engages in outside activities. He is very jealous of his time and appears irritable if someone infringes upon that time.

Dudley Moore has an insurance agency. While he is active in his church's activities, he takes certain steps to preserve his time. He accepts only those positions where his expertise is really needed and he feels he can make a contribution. Also, he is usually the last one to arrive at a committee meeting—only after the "chit-chat" is over—and leaves as soon as the business activities are over.

Limited Formal Education

Small business managers are apt to have only limited formal education. Yet, they tend to supplement this learning with informal learning through reading, "picking the brains" of more learned friends, and through extension and correspondence courses.

Expects Quick Results

Entrepreneurs expect quick and concrete results from an investment, whether it is an investment of time or capital. They seek a quick turnover of a relatively small amount invested in the firm rather than engaging in the long-range planning which is common in large businesses.

In general, small business managers can be characterized as unreconstructed rebels, who are free and wish to remain free from the artificial conformity required in the larger organizations. They are rugged individuals who are willing to take risks and who have the determination and perseverence to capitalize upon those risks.

EFFECTS OF EXTERNAL ENVIRONMENT

While we accept these characteristics of successful small business managers, there is another theory developed from several small-sample studies at Harvard and MIT.[1] The researchers examined entrepreneurs who were involved in substantial ventures. They found that while very successful entrepreneurs may ultimately stand apart, at the beginning (when they make the decision to become entrepreneurs), they are in most respects very much like other ambitious, striving individuals. It was also found that the entrepreneurial interests for those who became small business managers were more a function of external differences than internal ones. Their decisions were more the result of practical readiness and cost income constraints than of individual psychology or personality.

PERSONAL REQUIREMENTS FOR SUCCESS IN SMALL BUSINESS

Although it is impossible to determine or state *all* the requirements for success in small business, at least we know that the following are important:

1. A sensitivity to internal and external changes affecting the business.
2. The ability to react quickly to those changes.
3. Accurate and useful operating and marketing information.

[1] Be sure to read Patrick R. Liles, "Who Are the Entrepreneurs?" *MSU Business Topics*, vol. 22 no. 1 (Winter 1974), pp. 5–14.

4. The effective, but humane, use of human resources.
5. Obtaining sufficient investment capital, at a reasonable price.
6. The effective handling of government laws, rules, and regulations.

Understanding the Uniqueness of Small Firms

As the owner-manager of a small business, you should have a thorough understanding of the peculiarities of the size of your business. You should not seek to duplicate or copy the management techniques of larger firms. Rather, you should develop your own techniques to meet the needs of your business.

Adaptability to Change

An important characteristic of small business enterprises is their vulnerability to technological and environmental changes. Because they are small, such changes have a greater impact upon their operations and profitability. Yet, small businesses can have an advantage over larger firms in this respect, for they can react faster to change because they have fewer people making decisions. It is extremely important that you *be sensitive to the changes taking place both inside and outside your firm and that you be ready to act or react quickly to these changes.*

Accurate Operating and Marketing Information

Gathering *accurate and useful information concerning the operations of your business and its market* is extremely important. You must keep informed—on a regular and frequent basis—of the financial position and market position of the business. You must know how to analyze this information and develop plans to maintain or improve your position. This task may be done faster and more economically by using one of the computer service firms which provide such information at a nominal cost. Your customers are another source of information relative to the product, service, or operation of your business. Small business enterprises usually have a close association with their customers, who are not only one of the best sources of information, but perhaps the cheapest source.

Using Human Resources

The *effective, but humane, use of your human resources* is extremely important to a small business enterprise, because its owner-managers have a close and more personal association with their employees. These workers can be an economical source of information and ideas and their productivity greatly increased if you allow them to share ideas with you—and if you are *willing to recognize and reward their contribution.* Human resources are extremely important to a small business because the loss of a key employee, coupled with the difficulty in finding a replacement, can seriously jeopardize its operations. This aspect of small business management will be discussed in detail in Chapters 18–21.

Obtaining Investment Capital

One of the most difficult problems facing small business managers is *obtaining sufficient investment capital—at a reasonable price.* This requires that you plow back more of the profits into your business. You must be willing and able to delay your immediate desire for dividends in favor of the best long-run interest of the business. You must develop a strong credit rating and pay your debts promptly. Often, in an effort to keep large customers, a small business will postpone collecting from large customers who are accustomed to doing business with larger firms who enjoy a more favorable credit position and, as a result, are slower at paying their debts. This practice has the immediate effect of tying up cash vital to the operations of a small business. Continued neglect in collecting accounts receivable from customers has frequently led to the loss of the customer and the loss of the business.

Handling Government Regulations

You need to be able to *handle "red tape" effectively,* for the day when small business firms enjoyed an exemption from governmental legislation and regulation has passed. It is now even argued that small businesses are taxed disproportionately higher than larger businesses. Recent civil rights, occupational safety and health, and environmental legislation no longer exempts small business establishments, but frequently adds tremendously to their costs of operation. (These subjects will be discussed later.) Faced with the high costs of complying with these laws and regulations, the inability to pass the cost on to the consumers, and the large penalties for noncompliance, a growing number of small business firms are left with no alternative except liquidation.[2] Yet, there are various assistance programs available to you, and about which you must become aware.

AN INTROSPECTIVE PERSONAL ANALYSIS

Now that you have seen some of the characteristics of successful small business managers, as well as the personal requirements needed

---

[2] For example, see Dale D. McConkey, "Will Ecology Kill Small Business?," *Business Horizons,* vol. 15, no. 2 (April 1972), pp. 61–69.

for success in a small firm, you should be particularly interested in whether you possess a sufficient number of those characteristics and requirements to be successful. The following personal evaluation should help you decide this important question.

What Is Your Philosophy of Life?

As shown in Chapter 2, your management philosophy will provide a basis for decision making in your company. In order to manage your firm effectively, you need an ethical value system and some basic principles that you believe in and which you can use as guidelines. Among the more important questions related to this ethical value system are the following:

1. What are your true motives?
2. What real objectives do you seek?
3. What psychological and social relations do you consider to be needed for success?
4. What general economic atmosphere do you prefer to operate in?

To begin with, let us state clearly that everyone has a philosophy, whether it is conscious or unconscious, whether it is well-defined or ill-defined. Therefore, if you have and use a conscious and well-formed philosophy of management, many major advantages will be yours. Such a philosophy should:

1. *Help you win effective support and followers.* People will know what you stand for and what overall action you are most likely to take. They will know why you act as you do and will therefore have more confidence in your actions.
2. *Provide guidelines for you and provide a foundation for your managerial thinking and decision making.* Your management philosophy should be especially useful because conditions are changing so rapidly that you will face new management challenges to which there are no tailor-made solutions.
3. *Supply a framework within which you can improve your thinking abilities.* Your thinking process will be directed and stimulated so that you achieve more effective and satisfactory developments.

There are many types of people with an infinite variety of philosophies. However, we will discuss only the following philosophies:

1. Rugged individualism versus group-centered.
2. Activities-oriented versus results-oriented.

Characteristics associated with these philosophies vary, but in general the *rugged individualist* is highly self-reliant and is a decision-maker.

Most of the strong-willed, powerful industrialists in the 1890s and early 1900s—such as Henry Ford—were guided by this philosophy. On the other hand, many present-day managers believe that the group should be considered in all managerial decisions and actions. These *group-centered* individuals rely upon planning and decision-making groups, use committees extensively, and consider the many mutual interests of management and other employees.

The *activities-oriented* manager stresses what must be done, tends to be a "one-person show," prescribes the organization structure, determines the tasks of subordinates, delegates decision-making authority, determines the best methods to perform the work, and exercises tight control over employee performance. The *results-oriented* manager prefers to use the full resources of his people, emphasizes goal-setting, assists in achieving goals, wants himself and his subordinates to develop self-commitment and self-direction for results, has his subordinates play a large part in determining the methods of work, and exercises control by results.

Your philosophy, in turn, depends upon your personal values, or of what you consider to be *right* or *wrong, good* or *bad, desirable* or *not desirable.* Based upon your philosophy and value system, your business objectives and policies are formulated.

There are two categories into which the philosophy should be divided:

1. An impersonal professional approach.
2. A personal, moral-ethical approach.

We have found in counseling and consulting with prospective business owners that on occasion it is essential to approach the issues in this fashion. For example, an individual may come in to discuss the prospects of opening a bar or tavern. *Impersonally and professionally*, it is pointed out that certain licenses and permits must be obtained. The services of a local attorney familiar with these matters needs to be acquired, because certain additional hidden payments may be needed. The approximate capital investment involved for building, fixtures, inventory, and the type of location desirable for this establishment is defined. The consultant may point out certain specific locations that are available and explain why these locations are desirable and other locations undesirable. Also, the amount of net income that may be anticipated will be stated. From a *personal, moral-ethical point of view*, it might be pointed out that there are social implications of being involved with this type of business, such as the local tendency to brand people involved in those businesses with a stigma that becomes a lifetime mark. In addition, it might be pointed out that there are certain local ethical sensitivities which might be offended by such businesses. Therefore, it might be best in the long run, from a personal viewpoint, to avoid those activities that would be in direct conflict with these ethical standards, even though the economic benefits might be substantial.

What Are Your Mental Abilities?

If you still want to become an entrepreneur, then you should make a penetrating analysis of your personal attributes in order to determine the type of business that may satisfy your personal objectives and needs. You might ask yourself questions about *your mental abilities,* such as these:

1. Are you able to conceptualize your choice of a business; i.e., can you visualize it in its entirety, physically and functionally?
2. Are you able to observe things in perspective?
3. Can you generate ideas in a "free wheeling" fashion?
4. Can you generate ideas relating to new methods and new products?
5. Are you technically oriented?
6. Can you interpret and translate activities into a technical framework?
7. Are you sensitive to the human factor?
8. Are you sensitive to the feelings, wants, and needs of others?

What Are Your Attitudes?

If you are still thinking of entering a small business, you should make a self-analysis of your *personal attitudes* in specific areas. Some of these areas are your:

1. Aspiration level.
2. Willingness to accept responsibility.
3. Mental and emotional stability.
4. Commitment to the idea of small business.
5. Willingness to take risks.
6. Ability to live with irregular hours.
7. Self-discipline.
8. Self-confidence.

Each of these attitudes is discussed in detail.

Are you able to define your *aspiration level?* Aspiration is the driving or motivational force behind the individual. It is what he wants to achieve in life. You may want to express this level in terms of education, marital and parental status, dollars, status in the community, doing physical or mental labor, being of service to others, or other things.

> For example, an excellent student wanted to go into the heating and air conditioning pipe-wrapping business, but did not consider the income from the business to be satisfactory. Consequently, he became a manager in a large business.

The degree to which you are willing to accept *responsibility* determines the relationship you will have with the public and the customer. So far in your life, have you willingly accepted responsibility? Are you willing to assume responsibility in the future? Are you willing to admit to the last error you made? Are you an individual whose attitude toward responsibility is to accept it even though this may mean personal sacrifice? Are you willing to be responsible for the actions of others, even if you have delegated to them the authority to act for you?

> Faye Fendley, daughter of a poor restaurant owner, dropped out of school at 14; moved to Manhattan, using $300 saved from baby-sitting; worked part-time in a real estate agency; received her own license at 21 and started her own real estate business; married at 23. She was widowed, with three children, at 29. Spurning offers to buy the bakery she and her late husband owned, she assumed the full responsibility for running and expanding the business.

Are you a *stable person,* or are you a person who is impatient and unwilling to wait for success? If success is not immediately achievable, are you willing to continue to work toward its achievement? Do you seek immediate gratification of your wants, or are you willing to postpone them in order to reinvest in the firm? When given an opportunity that offers a significant potential, but may not be readily achievable, many young people tend to grow weary and move to another activity. These people in their limited progression may, on occasion, generate a "good income" in their chasing after "fast buck" opportunities, but these opportunities may lack stability and security. The successful entrepreneur does not work this way.

> Stan Bernthal, college dropout, worked in a garment factory. In his spare time, he designed clothing for young people out of scraps of material. He and his college roommate organized a firm to provide these good-looking, inexpensive clothes. In spite of initial success, Stan limited himself to $12,000 a year salary until the firm was assured of success.

Are you *committed?* This is the trait that determines whether an individual will endure the trials, tribulations, and personal and family sacrifices necessary to move ahead toward the achievement of one's objectives. How committed are you to your idea for the business you have dreamed of? Unless this commitment is firmly implanted, it is suggested that you forego the idea and seek that vocation to which you can be committed.

Do you enjoy *taking risks?* Are you willing to take the chance of "losing your shirt" to gain other benefits? Or, do you "play it close to your vest" and seek the "sure thing" in life? It does make a difference!

Can you live with an *irregular schedule?* Are you willing to forego regular hours and be worried during your time off? Are you willing to give up your weekends if something goes wrong or it becomes necessary to prepare a proposal for that new contract? Or, would you prefer regular hours, holidays, and vacations?

Are you *self-disciplined?* Are you able to exercise discipline over yourself and your affairs? The old cliche applied to early business owners, "Don't take too much out the front door," still applies. It is important that sufficient resources remain in the business to provide working capital and to provide for growth and contingencies.

> A local home building contractor had a very profitable business. Coming from a low economic background, he began to purchase luxuries he had always wanted for himself and his family. Soon, there were insufficient funds to meet bills, payrolls, taxes, and other business expenses. The end result was bankruptcy.

Are you *self-confident?* Do you have confidence in yourself and can you make decisions alone?

If the answers to these questions are "yes," or if you feel that you can make them "yes" at some time in the near future, you may have the qualities that would make your small business venture a satisfying and rewarding activity.

You are now at the point of deciding whether to go into your own business or not. As you approach the point of making a decision, you are in a position comparable to a person driving an automobile who is approaching a "stop light." Just as the light control mechanism is outside the influence of the driver, there are factors beyond your control that should influence your decision about entering a business of your own. These external factors—social, economic, cultural, and natural elements—are beyond your control. In the same manner as the driver approaching a traffic light must be responsive to the control mechanism in observing the status of the light, so must you be responsive to the environmental factors pertinent to the success or failure of your business.

SUMMARY

We have tried in this chapter to impress you with three things, namely:

1. Some unique characteristics of the successful small businessman.
2. Some personal requirements for a successful small business.
3. A personal analysis you can make to see if you have the necessary characteristics for success in managing a small business firm.

The key requirements needed for you to succeed in a small business are:

1. Sensitivity to internal and external changes which affect the business.
2. The ability to react quickly to those changes.
3. Accurate and useful operating and marketing information.
4. Effective, but humane, use of your human resources.
5. Obtaining sufficient investment capital, at a reasonable price.
6. Effective handling of government laws, rules, and regulations.

The personal characteristics usually found in successful small business managers are:

1. A great sense of independence.
2. A strong sense of enterprise.
3. Dominated as much by personal and family consideration.
4. Enters small business more by chance than design.
5. Jealously guards his time.
6. Limited formal education.
7. Expects quick and concrete results.

Finally, a personal analysis program was suggested whereby you may be able to determine whether you have the attitudes required for success in this area.

Before reaching a final decision on what career you want to follow, you should decide what you want out of life. If your personal objectives and the company objectives are not in harmony, you will not derive the personal satisfaction you seek from your business.

QUESTIONS FOR FURTHER DISCUSSION

1. All too often, certain crucial factors are overlooked when one chooses a career in small business. What are some of these factors?
2. What are some key personal requirements needed for one to succeed in small business? Briefly explain their importance.
3. What is meant by the cliche, "Don't take too much out the front door"?
4. Conduct your own personal analysis by honestly trying to answer the questions raised in the last section of this chapter.
5. What characteristics have been found to be present most frequently in owner-managers of smaller firms? Briefly discuss each of these characteristics.
6. How would you summarize the characteristics of small business managers?
7. If one were to ask himself, "What is my philosophy of life?," or "What are my mental abilities?," what specific types of questions should he ask himself?

8. Contrast the philosophy of rugged individualism with the group-centered philosophy. Do the same for the activities-oriented philosophy with the results-oriented philosophy.

9. When one is conducting a personal analysis program, he should make a self-analysis of his *personal attitudes* in specific areas. Briefly discuss each of these areas.

WHERE TO LOOK FOR FURTHER INFORMATION

"Are You One of Them?" *MBA*, vol. 7, no. 6 (June–July 1973), p. 5.

Buchan, P. Bruce. "Corporate Risk Policies," *Journal: Management Advisor*, vol. 10, no. 5 (September–October 1973), pp. 45–51.

"Now It's Young People Making Millions," *U.S. News & World Report*, vol. 74, no. 8 (February 25, 1974), pp. 47–50.

Roscow, James P. "Can Entrepreneurship Be Taught?" *MBA*, vol. 7, no. 6 (June–July 1973), pp. 12, 16, 50, and 51.

"Some Hints on Small Business Company Success," *The Iron Age*, vol. 199, no. 22 (June 1, 1967), p. 25.

Cases for Part I*

I–1. Shaffer's Drive Inns[1]

About 20 years ago the Shaffer family (mother, father, and son) decided to open a drive-in in a Midwestern city of about 200,000 people. They figured that the general area was lacking a drive-in that would offer a variety of quality services such as malts, sandwiches, curb service, and modern inside eating facilities as well, so they built a facility that incorporated all the above features and named it Shaffer's Drive Inns.

The son, Albert Shaffer, put a lot of energy into managing the store and worked harder than most people realized. In fact, he was soon able to buy his mother and father out and gain exclusive control of the store for himself.

It was 15 years before Mr. Shaffer decided to build another store; four years later, he built a third one. He always issued stock for each store that he built, but controlled at least 51 percent of the stock in each one.

Mr. Shaffer was respected and admired by his employees and had a "great man" image among them. He was an authoritarian-type leader,

---

* The cases in this book are *actual situations* involving *real people* in *real organizations,* although the names have been disguised. The cases are not designed to present illustrations of either correct or incorrect handling of administrative problems.

[1] This case was prepared by Joe L. Hamilton, formerly at Louisiana State University, but now with Container Corporation.

but his employees accepted his judgment as law because, in the opinion of his employees, he was right 99 percent of the time. Mr. Shaffer, when discussing anything that might arise with his employees, would never "tear into" the people, but would argue the point with them and listen to what they had to say and would then point out where they were either right or wrong. Once he had his mind made up though, it usually stayed made up.

The organizational structure used by Shaffer's Drive Inns was complicated. There were two managers and an assistant for each store, and assistants were to be trained to become future managers. In addition to these managers in each store, there were other people including kitchen help, curb boys, and so forth. Not only did this organizational structure have some serious flaws in it, but it led to some personality conflicts, as will be discussed later.

Shaffer's Drive Inns proved to be very popular. A lot of research went into the proper location for each of them and each was located where it could make its appeal either to college students or to heavy automobile traffic. The Drive Inns became well known for their quality service. These were specific objectives of Mr. Shaffer, and were in tune with his business philosophy.

Shaffer's Drive Inns proved to be so popular that a decision was reached to build three more Drive Inns in a nearby city. These three stores opened during a one month period. It was at this point that Mr. Shaffer realized his business was getting away from him. The people he chose for managers were well trained to go into the stores, but they had very little contact with the main office and consequently were forced to make most of their own decisions. In addition, the two managers in each store were constantly bickering with each other. The tendency to pass the buck was a serious temptation. The employees were quick to realize they could play one manager against the other to achieve desired goals.

Mr. Shaffer believed in personal contact to get his views across. But, as the stores were now becoming geographically separated, he was having a difficult time spending the proper amount of time at each store. He decided he needed an assistant to be his right hand man and carry on when and where he could not. He wanted someone from inside the organization who knew all the ropes. Mr. Shaffer chose Marc Mason, known as a "self-made man," to be his unofficial assistant. Although Mr. Mason was entirely capable of handling the job, his selection caused serious complaints and criticisms from three of the store managers.

These three men had been with the organization for a combined time of over 30 years, and each one assumed himself to have certain authority he didn't actually possess. They were described as "completely set in their ways and resisted any and every planned change." When Mr. Mason became Mr. Shaffer's unofficial assistant, they resisted every move he made in every conceivable way.

Mr. Denney had a high school education. He was known "to argue just for the sake of arguing." He was not known as a "go-getter" and was content to work in the slowest store of the chain. He seemed to have an inferiority complex in that he thought he wasn't as good as everyone else. In the opinion of some of his associates, he was not even capable of managing his own money. His strongest feature was his length of service, for he had been with the organization so long that he assumed he had high status. Mr. Denney shared the managership of one store with Mr. Riley.

Mr. Riley was a quiet-spoken man; he seldom raised his voice to anyone. He was "of average intelligence, but was not able to communicate properly with his employees." As a result, he wasn't able to get as much out of his employees as he should have.

Mr. Nettles once shared the management of a store with Mr. Mason. He was an ex-marine, and was considerably older than Mr. Mason. Mr. Nettles was known "to be pretty sharp and to know quite a bit about the business." Mr. Nettles could never bring himself to believe that he had been bypassed by Mr. Mason, and was frequently vocal about his feeling of dissatisfaction.

"Mr. Mason," it was said, "was treated very unfairly in the early days of his career. He was not brought into decisions or taken into the confidence of the man he worked with. However, he was a diligent worker and put in many hours of hard work. He was the type of man who really made a place for himself, and his hours of long, hard work were recognized by Mr. Shaffer."

Despite the growing communications problems, Mr. Shaffer went ahead with plans for another Drive Inn (the eighth one) in still another town. Now the lines of communication were really split. Mr. Shaffer, even with the assistance of Mr. Mason, was not able to devote as much time as he should to each of the stores. This left the store managers to their own discretion in many of their decisions. They started making more and more of their own decisions and started relying less and less on Mr. Shaffer and Mr. Mason. This was much to the displeasure of Mr. Shaffer it might be said. The eighth store caused Mr. Shaffer to seek outside help.

QUESTIONS FOR DISCUSSION

1. What does this case show about the problems involved in organizing a small business?
2. What were some of the organizational problems facing the owner?

3. What does it show about the problems resulting from growth of a small firm?
4. What were the objectives of the owner of the business?
5. What does the case show about interpersonal problems in small business?

I–2. *Bob Jones*

A former employer described Bob Jones as, "an employee who is personable, very willing to receive supervision and correction, but continually fails to comply with suggestions for improvement and has little regard for established rules, procedures, and policies. It is readily apparent to everyone that the employee's personal attitude, friendliness, and cooperation with other employees is beyond reproach. He seldom has a personality clash or disagreement with other employees in the office."

Bob Jones had been with a state organization for four years. His job required him constantly to come in contact with the public, and a great deal of good (or bad) publicity could result from his actions on the job. The employee was "quite capable as evidenced by his entrance examination, references, and past work experience." However, at frequent intervals Bob had to be told to improve his work habits. During these discussions, he indicated an interest in correcting the various deficiencies as they were pointed out to him by his manager. Each time he was in complete accord with the recommendations made to him and pledged to do a better job. The "payoff" never came, however. A follow-up revealed little or no adherence to established procedures and new suggestions. Bob would fall right back into his old habits.

The principal areas of weaknesses the manager found were "an almost complete disregard for details in every phase of his work. Although Bob was capable, and did the over-all job fairly satisfactorily, he was completely negligent in preparation of the details associated with each job." As time went on, it was noticed that Bob was spending an excessive amount of his office time engaged in personal activities. It was found that he used office time primarily for social purposes rather than for business. When questioned about this, Bob would always promise to improve, but as with the details of his work, he would soon forget his good intentions. It was also noticed that he requested an excessive amount of annual and sick leave, often for one hour or less.

This situation fluctuated over a period of time, would get better and then worse. However, it never reached a point requiring drastic action until Bob bought half interest in a restaurant. The purchase of this business aggravated two already bad practices. First, the amount of time required in the office to manage his private business increased. Second, and equally as bad from the office manager's point of view, he did not get his normal rest because he tried to work at his business between six and eight hours a day after his normal workday at the state office.

His efficiency continued to decline until the office manager decided something should be done.

After reciting these details, the manager turned to the professor and said, "What would you do if you were me?"

The manager finally told Bob that his private business was interfering with his official duties. He was further told that if he continued to have outside business activities, he must write to the head of the agency at the state capital, describe his business involvement, and obtain the administrator's opinion as to the advisability of continuing in the business.

When the agency head denied Bob the right to operate his private business, he resigned from the organization to devote himself full time to his restaurant business.

QUESTIONS FOR DISCUSSION

1. Do you think Bob's personal objectives are compatible with those of a small business? Explain.
2. To what extent are Bob's personal characteristics compatible with those needed to operate a small business successfully?
3. What must Bob do to operate the business successfully? Explain.
4. What future do you predict for Bob in his new venture? Explain.

I–3. The Son-in-Law

Fred Clayton, a college graduate with a degree in geology, was inducted as a commissioned officer in the Navy in 1952. While in the service, he married the daughter of Art Carroll, a prosperous manufacturers' agent in the electronics industry.

When Fred's military service was terminated in 1955, he accepted a sales position in his father-in-law's organization, the Carroll Sales Company. Mr. Carroll had high hopes that Fred would take an interest in the business and eventually relieve him of some of the managerial responsibilities. Fred was trained for a short while in the home office and was assigned a territory in which to make sales calls and to promote the products offered by his company. A new car and a liberal expense account were provided. He presented a pleasing personal appearance to the customers. However, it was soon evident to Mr. Carroll that Fred did not possess the necessary characteristics to become a good salesman.

For a number of years, Fred continued to receive a share of the available business in his area with little sales effort. This condition was primarily due to the tremendous demand for electronic equipment which far exceeded the supply at that time.

Mr. Carroll was concerned with the fact that Fred was not spending sufficient time in his territory. Frequently, he would leave town on Tuesday and return on Thursday of the same week after attempting to cover an area which, to be properly serviced, would normally take from Monday through Friday. Fred's expenses were extremely high for the time he spent in the field. On occasion, Mr. Carroll would discuss Fred's progress with him. As a future officer in the company, Mr. Carroll requested that his son-in-law set the example for the other sales personnel by putting in more time in his territory and by cutting down on his weekly expenses. After these talks, Fred would improve, but within a short time he would return to his original routine.

The company continued to prosper and to expand due to good sales effort from most of the sales force and because of the continued demand for their products. By 1968 the company covered a sales area consisting of nine states. At that time, the son-in-law was appointed district sales manager of a two-state territory and was responsible for the supervision of a warehouse and five salesmen. Fred did not work closely with any of his salesmen, but he took time to scrutinize every expense account and often returned them with items marked "not approved." The salesmen felt he was very petty about this and were frequently infuriated by his actions. He also controlled all of their correspondence and information flowing to and from the territory. The other sales districts within the company had more liberal expense accounts and salesmen could make decisions on their own. The district under the supervision of Fred Clayton never led the company in sales, although it contained the greatest potential of all the districts.

Mr. Carroll was quite disappointed in the lack of sales progress in Fred's division. He was also very concerned over the results of a 1971 survey which indicated that Fred's district had an unusually high turnover of sales personnel.

In 1972, Mr. Carroll took his son-in-law out of sales. He still hoped that there might be some position in the firm where the young man would be a real asset. With this thought in mind, he placed Fred in charge of operations to supervise and regulate the operation of the warehouses. Fred was to control inventories. He continued to have problems with personnel, causing so much unrest among employees that a number of key men talked of leaving.

A year later, Mr. Carroll realized the situation was critical. "In what way is Fred unhappy?" he asked himself. "Is he completely unmotivated to succeed because he thinks he doesn't have to? Doesn't he feel at least a moral obligation to try to get along with his associates? How have I failed to give his best abilities an opportunity? How far must I go in trying to fit him into the situation?"

QUESTIONS FOR DISCUSSION

1. Comment upon Fred's capabilities for managing a small business.
2. What could Mr. Carroll do to help Fred become a better manager?
3. What qualities should a "good" manager possess in a company such as this? Does Fred possess them?
4. Who was responsible for developing Fred into a capable executive? Has each of these succeeded or failed? Explain.
5. How do you explain the unusually high turnover of sales personnel in Fred's district?
6. How would you answer each of Mr. Carroll's questions?

I-4. The National Insurance Company

At the time of this case, the National Insurance Company was a medium-sized, profitable concern located in one of the largest cities in Louisiana and incorporated under Louisiana laws. The company was largely owned and controlled by four families. In addition to the home office, there were 12 district offices located throughout the state. There were approximately 25 employees in the home office, in addition to six officers, and about 225 field personnel operating in and out of the district offices.

Recently, a meeting of the officers of the company was called by the chairman of the board of directors. The president, executive vice president, vice president, secretary, treasurer, and Pete Cassity—an outside consultant—were asked to attend.

As soon as the pleasantries of the day were exchanged, the chairman called the meeting to order and said, "Gentlemen, we have an important series of decisions to make. The time has come for us to decide whether to expand our operations outside of the state of Louisiana. If we decide to expand, we then have a question concerning what additional state or states to go into. Further, what specific areas within the states to go into and the extensiveness of our operations. Finally, what effect will these decisions have upon our management personnel?

"Before making these decisions, I would like to bring Mr. Cassity up to date on the history of our company so that he will better understand the thinking that must go into making these choices.

"During the mid-20s, my brother, Fred, and I had been working for a national insurance company for about ten years. We began being dissatisfied with our situation and decided we would like to go into business for ourselves, for we had the desire to become independent and to be free of the shackles of working for someone else. If we were going to make anyone rich with our efforts, we decided that it might as well be us as anyone else. Also, we had the desire to make more money than we were making serving as salesmen for the other company.

"These facts, coupled with the desire to 'be on our own,' led us to make the break and organize an insurance group of our own. We asked H. P. Harris, a friend, to join us and we organized National as a mutual company, with $5,000 capital and with a one-room office in one of the downtown office buildings.

"We were the only employees of the company for several years. Consequently, we had to do all the field work, as well as the clerical work.

"I will never forget the excitement when Fred wrote the first application for the company. However, this enthusiasm was dampened a little when we had to sit down and type the policy ourselves. We were writing only one type of policy at that time, that is, a health and accident policy. The only major difficulty we encountered was the harassment by the major companies whose salesmen were telling our policyholders that we didn't have any money, that we wouldn't be in business for six months, that we were a 'fly-by-night' operation, that we could not legally write a policy outside the city limits, and doing everything but insulting our character and integrity. (Sometimes, I think they even did that.)

"Under the mutual arrangement, we were carrying on a business of selling industrial life insurance, where the stipulated premium and advance assessments were regularly payable and collectible every week. We were organized as a non-stock corporation that was based upon members holding certificates in accordance with the mutual assessment plan. There were only 15 members when we started operating.

"Our business was progressing nicely in 1927 when we had the worse flood in the city's history. Unfortunately, in addition to doing serious damage to the city and surrounding areas, it also adversely affected our business so that our sales of policies and collection of premiums were considerably slowed down.

"By 1928, the company looked like it was going to be successful and the mutual idea was becoming less desirable, so we decided to incorporate as a stock company. We surrendered our old charter and reinsured the mutual business in the stock company.

"When we incorporated as a private stock company in 1928, there were 15 shareholders and the capitalization was $10,000, composed of 100 shares of non-assessable stock with a par value of $100. There were five members of the board and three officers.

"Things were going nicely until the stock market crashed in October, 1929. Then the depression really started and things began to get tough for us and our new company. As with all other business organizations of that time, we had a hard time collecting money. As a matter of fact, we sometimes almost did not collect enough money to pay our claims to the policyholders, which would probably have made the larger companies happy. Also, the depression caused some of our policyholders to turn their insurance into an investment rather than a form of protection.

"Things had become so rough by 1931 that Fred accepted a position with a national company in Jackson, Mississippi. At that time, I was made president of the company and began the unpleasant task of trying to consolidate and save the business that we had. These were strictly 'times that tried men's souls.'

"To try to make ends meet, Mr. Harris and I each remitted $10 a week to the company, even if it had to come out of our personal money. Mr. King (one of the stockholders who was also selling for us) was on a different basis. After paying all of his claims and his salary, he was to remit to the company the remainder of his premium collections. By these two means, the company showed a profit of around $900 at the end of 1931.

"From there on, things got worse. At the end of 1932, we didn't have *any* money. Mr. Harris and I had to put up money which we raised by mortgaging our houses before we could file the annual report with the state Insurance Commissioner. In the latter part of 1932, Fred came back and was put on the same contract basis as Mr. Harris and I were on. By doing this, we had $30 a week definitely coming in; Mr. King was giving us a pretty good profit from his debit. That is the way we finally pulled things out and saved the company.

"In retrospect, I have to laugh at our brashness and perseverance. In the early part of 1932, we were definitely broke and would have sold the company if we could have found a buyer for it. We tried to sell the stock in the company, but people would only laugh at us and not buy.

"By 1935, we hired two agents who had been with a national company for a long time. They were very good agents and soon built two good debits for us. One of these men is still with us, while the other one has retired.

"I have been asked what factors have contributed most to the success of our company. It seems that the following factors pulled us through. First, there was the desire we had to be on our own, to be independent of outside control. Second, there was our determination to succeed—in other words, pure stickability and the desire to show our detractors that we could succeed. Third, there was our ambition to create a successful company to leave for our heirs. Fourth, there was our hard work, as exemplified by our getting out and beating the bushes for 16 to 18 hours a day because we could not afford the luxury of paid employees in those days. Fifth, there was plain 'good management,' or the ability to operate the company successfully. Sixth, there was our desire to make money."

QUESTIONS FOR DISCUSSION

1. What does this case show about the characteristics of a small business?
2. What does it show about the characteristics of small business managers?
3. Although these events happened over 40 years ago, do you see any similarities between then and today?
4. What lessons have you learned from this case?

I–5. *Tanner's Grocery Store*[1]

Star City is a southern town of 50,000 people located in a primarily rural area. There are several small industrial plants and a great deal of farming, but the identifying characteristic of the city is the major state university located within it. This, coupled with a relatively large

---

[1] Written by Rudolph L. Kagerer and James F. Russell, University of Georgia.

number of impoverished blacks enabled the city to obtain federal funds in the form of a Model Cities Program to aid the city in providing assistance in the areas of housing, recreation, education, and employment to the blacks.

One of the efforts initiated under the program was directed at preparing a group of blacks in the fundamentals of small business operation. Faculty members of the university were employed to provide instruction in management, marketing, and accounting to a group who were theoretically selected on the basis of overall ability, motivation, and potential to succeed. The major emphasis in the training was placed on providing the fundamental skills needed in making business decisions. In addition, the effort included assistance in researching business opportunities, preparation of materials for loan applications, and consultative assistance once the business has been acquired, if an ongoing one, or started, if a new one. These services were provided by graduate students in business under the guidance of the director, who was primarily an administrator.

William Tanner was one of the blacks selected for the training. A native of Star City, he was 25 years old, married, and the father of one child. He had completed two years of college and served in the U.S. Army as a medical technician. Soft spoken and intelligent, Tanner showed great enthusiasm for the opportunity the program represented, but did not continue his enthusiasm, attending only 21 of over 100 class sessions in a period of a year. He had worked for two years as an inventory clerk and timekeeper for a manufacturing firm, and for one year as an employment interviewer for the state employment service. He had held several smaller jobs as a teenager, but none of them were long lasting or responsible in nature. His record in the jobs he had held appeared to be good, such that he was offered a promotion when he considered leaving his last job to undertake his own business. Tanner was a faithful church attender, a junior deacon and choir member, and had shown some organizational ability in that he had taken part in the formation of a local chapter of a national black fraternity in college and had served as the first president of the chapter. He did have some financial resources, in the form of $1,000 in savings, but obviously not enough to launch a small business of any substantial size. In short, Tanner appeared to have the educational qualifications and interpersonal skills for operating a small business. Little can be inferred concerning his motivation, except that he stated that he wanted to "make it," so that young blacks could view him as a model, and see that they, too, might have a chance. He believed that the blacks would support him because he, too, was black, and so did not concern himself with many of the more onerous aspects of business training such as financial management and accounting.

An opportunity presented itself to Tanner in Greenwaite's Grocery Store. John Greenwaite and his partner, James Slater, both white, had been operating the store for the past three years. They had started out in a smaller store three blocks away and had moved to their present location when the need arose for more floor space to allow for expansion. Both stores were in the same primarily black neighborhood. The partners operated the store daily from 7:00 A.M. until 11:00 P.M., carried a limited inventory of name brand products and a cut-to-order meat department specializing in less expensive cuts of pork and beef. They managed to draw "reasonable profits" from the business by sharing the work load, minimizing extra labor costs, and by maintaining a 25 to 30 percent markup on their shelf products, justified by the convenience aspect of the hours of operation and made possible by the judicious granting of credit. By virtue of their long stay in the neighborhood, they had eliminated many of the bad credit risks and granted credit only to those who were known by them to be prompt payers. In addition, they were known to grant small high interest loans to good customers to meet emergencies, although the repayment terms are not known. When Tanner came around and began asking whether they wished to sell the business, the partners felt pleased at the possibility of turning a profit on the sale.

QUESTIONS FOR DISCUSSION

1. What were Mr. Tanner's objectives in wanting to go into business for himself?
2. What personal characteristics did he have for becoming a small businessman?
3. What does the case illustrate about the university's role in small business development?
4. What does it show about the government's role?

Part II

What Is Your Business?

In Part I, we looked at some of the challenges of entering a small business, some personal and business objectives of small business managers, and some characteristics which lead to success in owning or managing that type of business.

We assume you have now decided you want to become a small business manager. We hope you have decided to take that challenging and difficult—but rewarding—route instead of the easier—but more routine—career as a professional manager in a large business, government, or another organization. If so, the material in this part should be of great use to you.

Its chapters provide some insights into the types of business you might enter, such as manufacturing, service, research and development, and consulting. Some thoughts on evaluating the business environment in which you will operate are also presented. As a prospective owner of a small business, you have these two broad alternatives available: (1) to establish a new business, or (2) to enter an ongoing business. Detailed procedures for each of these alternatives are presented.

Specifically, you will need to do the following things: Decide what's for you ⟶ Explore a business idea ⟶ Determine economic feasibility of the idea ⟶ Develop detailed plans ⟶ Determine legal form of organization ⟶ Estimate financial needs ⟶ Arrange financing ⟶ Select business site ⟶ Obtain or build facilities ⟶ Purchase equipment ⟶ Install equipment ⟶ Acquire inventory ⟶ Select employees ⟶ Give them preliminary training ⟶ Initiate operations ⟶ Attract potential customers ⟶ Make sales ⟶ Obtain revenue ⟶ Pay bills ⟶ Make profit.

FIGURE II–1
Concept of Entering Business

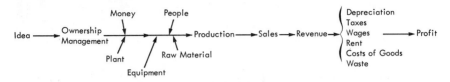

Figure II–1 is a graphic presentation of these and other activities involved in starting up a firm. It moves you from your idea for a business
through the various activities to the final objective, profit. This illustration is intended to assist you in visualizing the nature of your firm
and what is needed for it to become a reality.

4

Selecting the Type of Business You Would Like to Enter

It is now time for you to give careful consideration to the type of business that satisfies your personal goals and objectives. This important decision will probably determine whether you will be successful and satisfied during your business career.

The process of picking and choosing the type of business you enter will be influenced by your personal value system, education, training, financial ability, and family situation. Since owning a small business is a very personal matter, you should consider as broad a range of options as is feasible. In conducting this survey and in analyzing possible business opportunities, you should not become so involved that you lose sight of your overall objective—whatever it might be. Your mission is to find that business which helps you achieve your objectives while satisfying your other personal needs.

The material in this chapter covers:

1. How you can investigate the available alternatives.
2. How you can classify the types of business.
3. How you can choose the business to enter.
4. Whether you should "begin from scratch" or acquire a franchise.

HOW YOU CAN INVESTIGATE THE ALTERNATIVES

It seems to us that the best point of departure for you is to review the introspective personal analysis you made of yourself in Chapter 3.

The purpose of this reevaluation is to eliminate those options which are not compatible with your personal likes and dislikes. You would probably be miserable if you chose an activity which you found to be inconsistent with your abilities and personality.

The main thrust of that analysis should be to identify what physical, mental, emotional, and spiritual abilities you have—including:

1. Your intellectual abilities.
2. Your education, training, and experience which determine the expertise you have for certain types of business.
3. Your philosophies and ethical value system, which will keep you from being satisfied in many kinds of business.
4. Your attitudes and feelings, which will limit your success to only a small variety of activities.
5. Other considerations, such as the likes and dislikes of your spouse, whether to be near your parents, and what would it take to make you a satisfied—and therefore a successful—person.

This analysis is the first culling procedure and should drastically reduce the number and variety of choices available to you.

If you would feel more comfortable by taking attitude, interest, and aptitude tests to assist you in making your decision, such tests are available through your university, college, junior college, or vocational-technical school. In addition, you may find a professional psychologist to assist you.

The next rejection process is to eliminate the businesses which will not provide you with the challenges, opportunities, and rewards—financial and otherwise—which you are seeking. Be rather ruthless in asking, "What's in it for me?", as well as inquiring, "What can I do to be of help to others?" Ask yourself questions similar to the following about each business you consider:

1. How much capital is required to enter and compete successfully in this business?
2. How long will it take me to recoup my investment?
3. How long will it take me to reach an acceptable level of income?
4. How will I live until that time?
5. What is the degree of risk involved? Am I willing to take that risk?
6. Can I hack it on my own? Or, will I need the help of my family? Others?
7. How much work is involved in getting the business going? In running it? Am I willing to put out that much effort?
8. Do I want to acquire a franchise from an established company, or do I want to "start from scratch" and "go it on my own"?

9. What are the potentials of this type business? What are my chances of achieving that potential?
10. Are sufficient data available for me to reach meaningful decisions? If so, what are the sources of information?

You might want to prepare yourself a check list in order to be more methodical and objective in this evaluation. Figure 4–1 shows a list used

FIGURE 4–1
Business Selection Survey Checklist

Capital Required	Degree of Risk Involved	Amount of Work Involved	Independent Ownership or Franchise	Potential of the Business	Source of Data

by a consultant who helps people decide what business to enter. This list may be modified to meet your unique needs.

Where can you find the information needed to make this type of analysis? The first place to look is in the technical section of your nearest library—or the Government Documents section. The librarians in either of these sections can assist you in finding industry data. You will probably want to study carefully the *U.S. Census* data on *Population, Business, Housing* and possibly even *Agriculture*. The Small Business Administration in Washington or a regional office can be of great help to you. Also, contact:

1. The research division of your local chamber of commerce.
2. The trade association for the industries you are interested in.
3. Local business leaders.
4. Bankers and other financial experts.
5. Even "write your Congressman."

HOW YOU CAN CLASSIFY THE TYPES OF BUSINESS

While there are several ways of classifying the types of business available, we chose to group them as: (1) retailing; (2) service; (3) wholesaling; (4) research and development; (5) consulting; and (6) manufacturing.

A more detailed grouping, showing the options in each group, is shown in Figure 4–2.

FIGURE 4–2
Some Business Options, Classified into Related Groups

I. *Retailing*
   1. Food
      a. Grocery
      b. Fast-prepared
      c. Convenience
      d. Restaurant
      e. Lounges
      f. Specialty shops
   2. Appliance
   3. Hardware and building material
   4. Specialty
   5. Clothing
II. *Service*
   1. Service station
   2. Auto repair
   3. Appliance repair
   4. House and commercial repair and renovation
   5. Janitorial
   6. Plumber
   7. Electrician
   8. Floor covering
   9. F.O.B. (fixed base operation-aircraft)
  10. Travel agencies
III. *Wholesaling*
   1. Jobbers
   2. Brokers
   3. Distributors
   4. Manufacturing agents
IV. *Research and Development*
   1. Materials
   2. Products
   3. Software information systems
   4. Specialized machinery
   5. Manufacturing systems

V. *Consulting*
   1. Management
   2. Management information systems
   3. Financial
   4. Investment
   5. Marketing
   6. Risk management
   7. Land use and development
   8. Engineering
   9. Economic
  10. Government
  11. Various additional highly specialized areas
VI. *Manufacturing*
   1. Metals
      a. Sheet metal
      b. Machine shop
         (1) General
         (2) Special equipment
      c. Foundry
      d. Mini-steel mill
   2. Plastics
      a. Extrusion
      b. Applicators
      c. Formulators
   3. Food
      a. Processors
         (1) Meat
         (2) Vegetables
         (3) Bakery
         (4) Specialty items

HOW YOU CAN CHOOSE THE BUSINESS TO ENTER

The point has now been reached where you need to have an exercise in "brainstorming." Get a group of your friends together and ask them what kinds of products or services they need. Then, ask them if those needs are being met adequately. If not, what would be necessary for their needs to be satisfied? Try to get them to identify not only existing types of business, but also as many new kinds of business as possible. You should then consider the kinds of products and services not now available, but which are needed and could—if available—find a market.

You might also assemble a diversified group of local small businessmen to "brainstorm" with you on business opportunities. Another possible source of participants for this exercise might be members of the local

ACE (Active Corp of Executives) or SCORE (Service Corp of Executives) chapters.

An example of a business which originated from ideas of local business managers was a sheet metal shop that was established to supply the sheet metal requirement of a machine shop.

When you are obtaining advice from outsiders, always remember that it is your resources that are at stake when the commitment is made. Thus, the ultimate decision must be yours.

After this exercise in free-wheel thinking, the next step is to actually select that business which seems best for you. Your earlier checklist would now come in handy in making your choice.

In fact, you may want to make more than one choice and leave yourself some options. Remember to consider your personal attributes in order to best utilize your capabilities. In the selection process, the business should fit one's reason for being and one's life objectives. Yet, an effort should be made to maintain an attitude of objectivity and let your mind govern—not your emotions.

Once the choice has been made, it is necessary to conduct an economic feasibility study to determine, as best you can, its economic possibilities. Chapter 5 contains guidelines for such a study. As one former student put it, "The time spent in doing these various exercises pays off in the end. It actually helps achieve your purpose in less time by guiding you to do those things you need to do." He has evidenced this by starting three businesses in distinctly different but related fields and achieving success in sales and profits in the first year of operation of each of them.

WHETHER YOU SHOULD "BE INDEPENDENT" OR ACQUIRE A FRANCHISE

Now you have another choice to make—whether to have an independent operation or to buy a franchise from one of the hundreds of franchise companies.

Importance of Franchising

Franchising has been one of the most rapidly expanding areas of business activity in recent years. The large percentage of new businesses that fall in this category explains its prominent treatment in this part of the book. A discussion concerning aspects of franchising considered to be most important to the prospective new owner is presented below.

While service stations are considered a form of franchising, government documents separate service station franchises from other types. We also make this distinction in our discussion.

TABLE 4–1
Franchising: Size Distribution by Number of Establishments—1971*

Size Groups	Franchising Companies (Number)	Establishments		Sales	
		Number	Percent	Millions of Dollars	Percent
Total	791	175,549	100	$24,010	100
1,001 and greater	39	111,352	63	13,620	57
501 to 1,000.	23	15,373	9	3,220	13
151 to 500.	93	26,377	15	3,850	16
51 to 150	158	14,126	8	2,190	9
11 to 50	268	7,268	4	1,010	4
0 to 10	210	1,053	1	120	1

* Size group distribution not available for automobile and truck dealers, gasoline service stations and soft drink bottlers.
From *U.S. Industrial Outlook,* Dept. of Commerce.

Table 4–1 shows that there were 791 franchising companies in 1971. The average company had between 11 and 50 franchises. Yet, 39 companies had over 1,000 franchises, and they accounted for 63 percent of the establishments and 57 percent of the sales.

Franchise activities are growing, as shown by Table 4–2. Sales in-

TABLE 4–2
Franchising: Trends and Projections, 1971–73 (in millions of dollars, except as noted)

	1971	1972*	Percent Increase 1971–72	1973*	Percent Increase 1972–73
Sales					
Total	$128,880	$141,450	10	$156,060	10
Franchisor	18,650	20,220	8	22,140	5
Franchisee	110,230	121,230	10	133,920	11
Establishments					
Total	431,169	443,815	3	466,049	5
Franchisor	74,721	77,408	4	80,662	4
Franchisee	356,448	366,407	3	383,387	5

* Based on estimates by respondents to recent survey by Bureau of Domestic Commerce.
From *U.S. Industrial Outlook,* Department of Commerce, p. 407.

creased 10 percent each year from 1971 to 1973. The number of establishments grew three percent from 1971 to 1972, and five percent from 1972 to 1973. So, it is an expanding field. In fact, it has been estimated that at least 60 percent of all business will be some sort of franchise by 1979.[1] It

---

[1] Charles Swayne and William Tucker, *The Effective Entrepreneur* (Morristown, N.J.: General Learning Press, 1973), p. 150.

is also estimated that franchising accounts for about $177 billion in annual sales.[2]

Considerations in Franchising

Each name-brand franchise should be investigated on its own merits. Experience has proven that the array of franchise activities runs from "an excellent opportunity" to "a very poor risk" for the franchisee. You should be cautious in dealing with franchisors, particular vending machine franchisors, who promise you a guaranteed return on your investment. Often, contracts with these elusive or vanishing organizations have proven worthless. The *Franchise* magazine, as well as certain trade association publications, may serve as a useful source of information.

In deciding whether to franchise or not, you should consider these services offered by the better franchising organizations:

1. Selection of location site.
2. Purchase of site, and construction of a standardized structure identified as a part of the trademark of the franchise.
3. Provision for additional financing when minimum equity requirement is met by the potential franchisee. This financing would cover land, building, equipment, inventory, and working capital.
4. Standardized accounting and cost control systems. These records are audited periodically by the franchisor staff. In many instances, standard monthly operating statements are required. The franchisor develops a set of standard performance figures based on composite figures of reporting franchisees and returns a comparative analysis to the franchisee as a managerial aid.
5. A set of customer service standards. These are established by the franchisor and professional staff who make regular inspection visits to assure the compliance by the franchisee.
6. National or regional advertising programs, establishing and maintaining a uniform image.

Some Pertinent Questions to Ask

Many franchise situations are loaded with pitfalls. Some of these dangers were pointed out in a Small Business Administration press release[3] of a study done for the U.S. Senate Select Committee on Small Business. Such franchises have left hundreds of disgruntled, disappointed, disillusioned people strewn in the aftermath of their onslaught.

---

[2] "Companies," *Business Week*, August 31, 1974, p. 75.

[3] See Urban B. Ozanne and Shelby D. Hunt, *The Economic Effects of Franchising* (Washington, D.C.: Small Business Administration, 1971), especially pages 1–2.

Unfortunately, many have naively placed their life savings in ventures that were doomed to failure from the start. There has been a broad array of these activities from gum-vending machines, candy machines, and stamp machines to fast food (fried chicken, specialty food items, soft custard, and hamburgers), motels, coin-operated laundries, ice cream parlors, and so forth.

> A man put up $2,000, on a guaranteed investment, for gum and candy machines. The franchisors promised to find good locations for the machines. However, these failed to materialize as all desirable locations were already being used. As a result, the man lost his $2,000 because the machines did not produce the projected guaranteed revenue. In the meantime, the franchisor evaporated and the guarantee on the investment was of no value.

> A well-known radio-T.V. entertainment personality became involved with a fried chicken franchise operation. After a lot of fanfare and national publicity, a public offering of stock occurred. The fine print on the front page of the prospectus revealed more "padding" of assets than real value. From the outset, the franchisor did a poor job in assisting the franchisees. Consequently, the franchisees went down along with the company's stockholders.

> A flurry of activity in mobile home sales and home park franchises led many people to invest in the stock of the companies and buy their franchises. Many "fast-buck" operators rode to the pinacle of paper success, but most investors lost substantial sums when the house of paper came crashing down.

> Camping park franchises appeared vacant or sparsely populated during the recent "energy crisis."

In viewing a franchise possibility, you should probably question the objectives of the franchisor. Here is a simple list of questions you might want to investigate before "putting your money on the barrel head."

1. What is in it for me?
    a. Return on investment
    b. Salary I can reasonably expect
2. Is the franchisor just unloading a "white elephant" on me?

> An example was a franchisor who tried to sell home swimming pools by requiring the franchisee to purchase a display model at a price comparable to a standard retail price.

3. What services does the franchisor provide the franchisee? Are the services priced at a discount or priced above the benefits they offer?

4. What is the attitude of the existing franchisees? Are they seeking to "unload," or are they happy with the results they are achieving?

5. What is the attitude of your banker, CPA, Better Business Bureau, chamber of commerce, and the community toward the franchisor and existing franchisees?

Some Conclusions Concerning Franchising

Even in the best franchise situations, the franchisor tends to hold an advantage. Usually, this relates to operating standards, supply and material purchasing agreements, and agreements relating to the repurchase of the franchise. However, franchise operations may offer you an opportunity to derive a satisfactory income on your investment and efforts.

A large number of court cases relating to franchise activities are now being adjudicated. Among the issues involved are territorial rights held by the franchisor and by the franchisee, and the right of the franchisor to require the franchisee to purchase supplies and inventory from the franchisor. Decisions seem to indicate that the franchisee may acquire some advantages and lose some from these legal actions.

Some outstanding examples of franchises are Holiday Inns, Mac-Donalds, Dairy Queen, Hardees, Tastee-Freez, Ramada Inns, and Downtowner Motels.

SERVICE STATIONS

One should not confuse service station operations with other forms of franchise relationships. The local distributor and petroleum company screen applicants for individual locations. The type of location and the type and size of inventory determine the amount of investment the individual makes.

During "normal" times, a station operating 12 hours with two to three pump islands should average 40 thousand to 50 thousand gallons of gasoline per month, supported by a good volume of TBA (tires, batteries, and accessories). Fast, high-quality, friendly, dependable service is the requisite for building a successful business in this highly competitive field. Stations operating 24 hours per day located on interstate highways should have a diversity of drink and snack vending machines. These provide a significant monthly income when adequately serviced.

The mortality rate is very high in the service station industry due to these factors:

1. Changes in traffic patterns produced by such activities as neighborhood transitions, opening of a new shopping center, and the construction of streets, expressways, and interstate highways.

2. Poor service and dirty facilities.
3. Using open-account credit rather than requiring cash or company credit cards.
4. Stocking excessive inventory, including items that have little demand but tie up working capital and reduce cash flow.
5. Poor quality of employees.
6. Pilferage by customers and employees.
7. Poor merchandising, which does not assure adequate volume of TBA.
8. In times of shortages, the lack of products to assure an adequate volume of sales to generate a satisfactory level of revenue and profit.

Many major petroleum companies provide training schools for incoming dealers. In some instances, one might question the quality or effectiveness of these programs. In addition, a number of companies provide "in-house" advisory services to their dealers.

The "energy crisis" has created an atmosphere of uncertainty around the service station industry. The stronger "dealer operated" stations have been under pressure to survive. The shortage or absence of the main product, gasoline, has had a major impact on the volume of the stations' TBAs and other products. In some areas, the major companies have been accused of terminating dealer contracts and converting to company-operated stations.

The future of independent service station operations seems to be clouded by much uncertainty. Until the petroleum industry achieves stability as to direction, volume of product, methods of retailing, and pricing, you should be cautious before venturing into this type of business.

SUMMARY

In this chapter, you have been provided with some ideas on how to select the type of business you would like to enter.

You should begin by investigating the alternatives *available* to you, based upon your abilities and personality. A checklist was provided to guide you in making this analysis.

A classification of businesses for a more logical evaluation was provided.

"Brainstorming" was suggested as a method to assist you in choosing your business.

Another important question is whether you wish to remain independent or to become part of a franchise. Arguments for and against were provided.

Finally, it was suggested that you be wary of operating a service station until the energy situation is clarified and the major oil companies clarify their policies.

QUESTIONS FOR FURTHER DISCUSSION

1. Explain how you can investigate the alternatives for starting a business.
2. What are some types of business available to you?
3. How can an exercise in "brainstorming" help you to choose your business?
4. What considerations are important in deciding whether to buy a franchise?
5. What are the pertinent questions which should be asked in franchising?
6. Would you open a service station at this time? Explain your answer.

5

Studying the Economic Environment for Your Business

By now, you should have decided whether you want to enter a small business and what type of business would interest you most. Now you are ready to study the economic environment for your potential business, and decide whether to start a new business or buy out an existing enterprise.

The economic environment plays a vital role in the success or failure of small firms. All too frequently, it is obvious from later events that little effort had been made to determine whether the economic environment was friendly or hostile. Our intent here is to outline a procedure for you to use in studying the economic environment. It is necessary to have a guide to help you determine if your idea for a business is economically feasible, and to aid you in deciding whether to build or buy a firm.

The method of making these decisions may be carried out rationally and objectively or with little thought. The purpose of Figure 5–1 is to dramatize the manner in which entrepreneurs have been observed approaching the decision-making process—and, hopefully, to help you do it more effectively. You may either use the analytical and rational approach of a computer, or you may play the odds and rely on chance, as in playing a slot machine. The game of business requires the best objective, rational, and reasoned effort from you, if you are to succeed.

FIGURE 5–1
Which Method to Use in Making Your Decisions

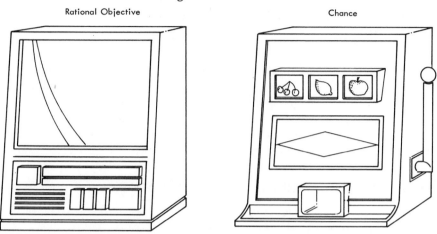

The material covered in this chapter includes:

1. Studying the economic environment for the industry.
2. Studying the market for your business.
3. Deciding whether to start a new business or buy an existing enterprise.

STUDYING THE ECONOMIC ENVIRONMENT FOR THE INDUSTRY

You should begin your study by analyzing the characteristics of the economic environment related to the particular kind of business in which you are interested. An overview of the economic status of the industry—of which your potential business will be a part—may be provided by obtaining answers to these questions:

1. How many firms are there in this type of industry?
2. Do they vary in size, or do they seem to be uniform in size and general characteristics?
3. What is the geographic distribution of the firms in the industry? Are they concentrated in one area, or are they widely distributed? (Rising transportation costs have increased the importance of this factor.)
4. What is the relationship between small firms of this type and larger firms and other industries? There may be adverse features associated with this relationship. As an example, carpet plants solely dependent on the auto industry for customers are subject to the whims of auto sales for their business.

5. Does the firm serve only the domestic market? Or, are there opportunities to serve foreign markets as well?
6. What are federal, state, and local government agencies' attitudes toward this type of business?
7. What is society's attitude toward this type of business?

After deciding the overall economic environment in the industry, you need to study the business climate for your business in the area in which you would like to operate. One approach that is frequently used in analyzing an area is to evaluate the objective and subjective factors which influence the region's business climate. Additional data which pertain to your particular type of business may also be obtained.

STUDYING THE MARKET FOR YOUR BUSINESS

You should next determine what is happening in the market place, and the possible future your business will have in that market. The size, nature, and other characteristics of the market, as well as your firm's future possibilities, may be derived from answers to questions such as these:

1. What is the relationship of population to the proposed business?
    a. Identify the age and age distribution among the population. Is a specific age group of greater importance to this business than others?
    b. Identify the population by sex, race, education, fertility rate, occupations, and other characteristics that affect the demand for goods and services.
    c. Define the size of the population and trends in size, age, sex, racial, educational, and occupational distributions. A declining population, or a declining population segment, in a specific geographic area may indicate an unsuccessful future for some businesses. The declining birth rate is affecting many industries oriented toward the baby, teenager, and youth markets.
2. What is the size and distribution of income within the population?
3. Is the sales volume for this kind of business growing, stable, or declining?
4. What is the number and size of competitors?
5. What is the success rate of competing businesses?
6. What are the technical aspects? (state of the art)
7. What are the sources of supply?
8. What are the capital requirements?
9. What is the rate of return on investment?

This information should help you estimate the size of your market. Additional data may be obtained from trade associations, chambers of commerce, and various federal, state, and local government agencies. Examples of specific sources are the U.S. Department of Commerce (through its Office of Business Economics) and the Bureau of Census. The divisions of research of colleges and universities also may be of assistance to you.

Statistical information gathered and tabulated by the Bureau of the Census may be particularly useful in evaluating the following variables which determine the size and composition of your market:

1. Population characteristics.
2. Employment patterns.
3. Personal income.
4. Business sales and income.

Now, you should be able to arrive at a "ball park" figure for your total sales volume and your share of the market. In arriving at this kind of estimate, you should select reasonable and conservative figures. For example, you—as the planner of a new business—should first define the geographic boundaries of the market area and then, from your knowledge of the potential customers in the various communities located in this area, make an estimate of products that might be purchased. It is better to plan for a lower level of sales in order to budget more effectively the business' operation.

In studying the market area, you should ascertain the number of similar businesses that have been liquidated or merged with a competitor. The latter is usually a sign of economic weakness.

You should determine the kind of technology being applied by other firms in your industry. For example: Are other machine shops using hand equipment? Or, are they using the latest equipment, including numerically-controlled devices? The state of technology is significant in determining operating costs.

The adequacy of the size and cost of inventory is determined by the number and location of suppliers.

If you call on your own resources and those of other people who are specialists in your business area, you may be able to develop a detailed plan for your business. This plan would include land, building, equipment, inventory, working capital, and personnel. You should then be able to determine the capital requirements for each of these productive factors, as well as the total of your capital requirements. Some additional capital should be provided for contingencies.

Information concerning your capital requirements may be obtained from potential competitors. You may even find that owners of existing businesses will cooperate with you by supplying various types of useful information, so long as you approach them in a manner to merit confidence. Some owners cling to the old adage of "I've got a secret." However, our experience indicates these people are in the minority. Other sources of information may include suppliers, wholesalers, and manufacturers.

A consultant was searching for comprehensive information relating to the opening of a retail fabric shop. He called a major textile manufacturer who indicated that this information was readily available from "McCall Patterns" and "Simplicity Patterns." Each of the pattern makers maintained comprehensive market research programs, and made such information readily available.

By using the capital requirements and developing an estimate of your expected profits after taxes, you should be able to estimate the rate of return you can hope to receive on your investment and on each dollar of sales. You will probably want to set a "return on investment" objective which, when added to your estimated value of your own services, should compare favorably with the profit potential for your type of business. There is no generally acceptable guideline as to how much this rate of return should be.

By using the rate of return figure you decide upon, and given the knowledge of the market in which you plan to operate, you can compute what sales will be needed to give you a satisfactory return.

For example, suppose you invest $25,000 in a small business and your objective is to receive a 12 percent return on your investment. You also think you could earn $12,000 a year working for someone else. You should then expect to receive an annual income from the business of at least $15,000, which is the equivalent of $12,000 salary plus $3,000 return on investment.

You further estimate your market to consist of 5,000 companies spending an average of $1,000 per year for the items you will sell. This represents a total market potential of $5 million. You know that the typical profit-to-sales ratio for that industry is about 6 percent. By dividing your hoped-for earnings of $15,000 by the profit margin of 6 percent, you find that you must have sales of $250,000 in order to achieve your profit objective. This means you would need at least a 5 percent share of the market for your products.

In addition to the data sources previously listed, the Small Business Administration has developed a variety of information resources that may be obtained by contacting the nearest Small Business Administration office, one of the U.S. Printing Office retail outlets, or the Superintendent of Documents, Washington, D.C.

After completing all these mental exercises, you should know if the rate of return for the business you have chosen is acceptable, based on current economic information. Since you want to achieve the highest possible rate of return, you should make fresh comparisons with alternative investment opportunities. You should decide whether this business is the opportunity sought. If it is, then the decision is "Go"!

DECIDING WHETHER TO START A NEW BUSINESS OR BUY AN EXISTING ONE

You have now decided that you are the entrepreneurial type and that you want to own a business. You have also determined what type of business you want to enter and have found it to be economically feasible. The next step is to choose the specific business which affords you the opportunity you seek. In surveying the situation, you may want to look at the alternatives of either entering an established business or conceiving, planning, organizing, and operating a new business of your own. In this respect, you are like the traveler on the road in Figure 5–2, who must make a decision. You will want to select the alternative

FIGURE 5–2
Which Fork to Take

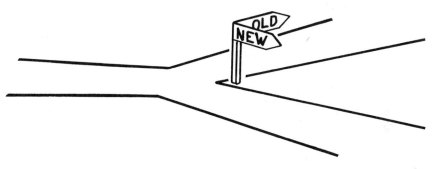

which seems to afford you the best opportunity of accomplishing your goals. However, just as the traveler, you may find yourself in the dilemma of not knowing which direction to take. After viewing the options, you must make a decision—hopefully, a decision that will carry you to success.

The following material should help you make this decision most effectively. Specifically, it presents the reasons for and against entering an existing firm and starting a new one "from scratch."

Entering an Established Business

Before you are able to make the type analysis you desire, you must first locate that business, or those businesses, that are available for purchase. In your search, you will find that some firms are not available at any price; others will become available, but at a high price (as is often quoted in the cliche, "I'll sell anything I have for a price"); and there will be those firms whose owners are actively seeking a buyer.

Some Considerations in Acquiring an On-Going Firm.   One important factor is always the *price* asked for the firm. Sometimes a successful on-going business may be acquired at a bargain price. For some reason, it can be bought at a fraction of the dollar cost, or its replacement value.

> For example, a small stone company was owned by a few stock-holders who wanted to sell out in a hurry for personal reasons. The company had more assets, including accounts receivable and cash on hand in the bank, than the purchase price the owners were ask-ing. Some outsiders purchased all the outstanding shares. They were able to take the cash on hand and that received from the receivables to reimburse themselves for all the shares they had bought.

You should be ready to grab similar opportunities.

A retailer may be willing to sell his business for the current price of his inventory. However, you should be cautious. You should not pur-chase his accounts receivable and you should be certain that his payables and other liabilities are established. Be sure to have your own CPA audit the records and verify the inventory and its values. Some examples are:

> A grocer who wanted to sell her store, reduced her retail prices in order to attract a large number of customers. It mattered little to her that many items were reduced to cost or less. A "sucker," who saw the large number of customers, took the bait and bought the store. About three weeks after assuming ownership and manage-ment, he had to replenish his stock. After raising prices, his business dropped off and he was very unhappy over his situation.

Another element of consideration is *your managerial ability.* There are those who have a talent for acquiring businesses that are in economic difficulty or are not achieving the optimum results possible. These per-sons are able to come into a business and initiate changes that turn the business around. Once the business prospers, the new owner looks for another buyer to purchase the successful business from him. The seller then seeks another similar opportunity.

Reasons for Acquiring an Established Business.   While it is difficult to discuss this subject intelligently without knowing the specific details of each situation, at least there are some generalizations which can be made. Some advantages of acquiring an established business are:

1. The facilities—building, equipment, inventory, and personnel—are in a functioning status.
2. A product or service is already being produced and distributed.
3. A market has been established and exists.
4. Revenue and profits are being generated.
5. The location may be very desirable.
6. Financial relationships have been established with banks and trade creditors.

An experienced small businessman recently sold one of his businesses. He searched for an existing business in which he might become involved. His interests were managerial challenge, economic growth, and profit. After viewing several possibilities, he acquired a small company that manufactured a top quality airport service vehicle. The company needed additional capital and more effective management. The new owner was able to bring these two ingredients.

Reasons against Acquiring an Established Business. Buying an on-going business may also have these disadvantages:

1. The physical facilities (building and equipment) may be old and obsolete.
2. The personnel may be stagnant and have a poor production record.
3. Union-management relations may be poor.
4. The inventory may contain an excessive amount of "dead stock."
5. Too high a percentage of the assets may be in poor-quality accounts receivable.
6. The location may be bad.
7. The financial condition, and relations with financial institutions, may be deteriorating.
8. There may be some poor customers who are draining the assets of the firm.

A firm in the extractive industry had failed. The owners were seeking new financial assistance in order to reactivate its operation. While a favorable market environment existed, the inferior quality of the firm's raw material made it unacceptable in the marketplace. Had the principals sought a new site with a better quality material, the business could probably have been reactivated. Substantial quantities of acceptable material were available near the existing property, but the owners did not choose to use it.

Starting a New Business of Your Own

In considering the possibilities of establishing a new enterprise, you should recognize that you have more freedom of choice in defining the nature of the business than if you purchase an existing firm. Remember that there are both pluses and minuses in choosing this alternative. You should view a particular business in terms of whether it will enable you to achieve your personal objectives. Also, how do the advantages and disadvantages of this option compare with those of entering the on-going business? Is there—on this basis—a reasonable opportunity for success?

As previously stated, some people have as their goal in life the initiation of new businesses. They find pleasure in establishing new ventures, getting them operating at a profit, and then finding a buyer for them. Then they start the process over again.

Other people enjoy the challenge and sense of accomplishment which come from creating something new. They feel that they have been useful, and will probably keep the business and run it themselves. Yet, they may later start and operate other firms.

Reasons for Establishing a New Business.   Some of the reasons for starting a new business of your own may include the opportunities to:

1. Define the nature of your business.
2. Create the type physical facilities you prefer.
3. Take advantage of the latest technology in selecting equipment, materials, and tools.
4. Utilize the most recent processes and procedures.
5. Obtain fresh inventory.
6. Have a free hand in selecting, training, developing, and motivating personnel.
7. Design your own management information system.
8. Select your competitive environment—within limits.

> A young entrepreneur wanted to enter the food, beverage, and lodging business. He could purchase one or more of a number of existing facilities. Each had a community image. His other option was to restore a historic building, which had earlier served as a hotel, into a superior-quality facility.

Reasons Against Establishing a New Business.   Some of the disadvantages of starting a new business "from scratch" are:

1. Problems of selecting the right business.
2. Unproven performance records in sales, reliability, service, and profits.
3. Problems associated with assembling the composite resources—including location, building, equipment, material, and people.
4. Necessity of selecting and training a new work force.
5. Lack of an established product line.

6. Production problems associated with the start up of a new business.
7. The lack of an established market and channels of distribution.
8. Problems in establishing basic accounting system and controls.
9. Difficulty in working out the "bugs" that develop in the initial operation.

A new restaurant, catering to a high-class clientele, was established in a questionable neighborhood and not very accessible. In spite of advertising and the support of influential people, the business failed. Yet, a small business specialist had counseled the potential investors against making an investment in the venture because of the many negative factors.

SUMMARY

The purpose of this discussion of the environment of small business was to enable you, by following the outlined analysis procedure, to reach a conclusion with which you can be comfortable. You should do this analysis yourself because it will enhance your probability of success.

Also, in deciding whether to buy an existing business or start a new enterprise, no one can really advise you what to do. Instead, you must "do your own thing." Thus, you must match the available alternatives with your abilities and inclinations.

QUESTIONS FOR FURTHER DISCUSSION

1. What are the major factors which should be considered in studying the economic environment for a given industry?
2. What are the major factors which should be considered in studying the business climate for the market area?
3. What are the major factors which should be considered in studying the composition of the market for your product?
4. How can capital requirements be investigated?
5. How can the return on investment be estimated?
6. Discuss the importance of price and managerial ability in acquiring an on-going firm.
7. What are the reasons for acquiring an established business?
8. What are the reasons against acquiring an established business?
9. What are the reasons for establishing a new business?
10. What are the reasons against establishing a new business?

6

Planning the Legal, Financial, and Administrative Structure of Your Firm

Now that you have studied the economic feasibility of your firm and have decided whether to buy an existing firm or start a new one, you are about ready to begin the organizing process. However, you have at least two more important decisions to make. First, you must determine what legal form you wish your enterprise to have. Second, you must decide your financial structure.

The material in this chapter should help you make these important choices. First, though, a word of caution is in order. While we will provide you with a summary of the most important basics in these areas, complete coverage is not feasible. Instead, we recommend that you seek the professional assistance of a lawyer specializing in business and corporate law, a reputable CPA, and a local banker familiar with local business conditions.

DETERMINING LEGAL FORM

In many small businesses, too little attention is paid to selecting objectively the legal form that best serves the owner's interests. There seems to be an appalling lack of knowledge relating to the advantages and disadvantages of using the various forms of legal organization. Our intent is to provide you with a better understanding of the legal form a business may have. The most popular of these legal forms are the: (1) proprietorship; (2) partnership; (3) corporation; (4) holding company; and (5) trust.[1]

Proprietorship

A proprietorship is an enterprise owned by a single individual. It is the easiest and simplest form of business to organize. Many people prefer this type of organization because of its simplicity and their inherent preference for individual control. It does provide for relative freedom of action and control, as well as being simple to enter and leave. In these respects, you may find it an attractive form to use.

You should consider at least two negative factors, though. First, as you and your business are one and the same, they cannot legally be distinguished and separated. Consequently, the legal life of the business terminates with your death. Some legal action must be taken to reactivate and reinstate it. Second, you have unlimited liability for the debts of the firm. If there are not sufficient assets to pay for all the obligations of the firm, you must use your personal assets to pay for them. Conversely, if you have unpaid personal debts, the creditors can use the assets of your business to satisfy their demands.

Partnership

A partnership is the joining together of two or more individuals to form an organization. Partnerships are quite popular because of these *advantages:*

1. Pooling of the resources of more than one individual.
2. Specific specialized skills possessed by the individual partners.
3. Division of labor and management responsibility.

Partnerships are more effective than proprietorships in raising financial resources and in obtaining better management.

Yet, there are *disadvantages* inherent in the partnership arrangement, including:

1. Death of any of the partners terminates the life of the partnership. This may be offset by an agreement which states that the remaining partner(s) will purchase the interest of the deceased partner from his estate. Frequently, the partnership itself carries insurance to cover this contingency.

---

[1] If you wish further information on this subject without seeing a lawyer, refer to Harold F. Lusk et al. *Business Law: Principles and Cases,* 3d. U.C.C. ed. (Homewood, Ill.: Richard D. Irwin, Inc., 1974).

2. Members of a general partnership, or the general partners in a limited partnership, have unlimited liability for the debts of the firm.
3. Partners are responsible for the acts of each and every other partner.
4. A partner cannot obtain bonding protection against the acts of the other partner(s).
5. An impasse may develop when the partners become incompatible.

Because of this last disadvantage, you should include in your partnership agreement a "buy-sell" arrangement to provide for the perpetuation of the business. This clause can be activated in the event of one or more of the following:

1. An impasse develops between the partners in reaching an agreement on an important issue.
2. One or more of the partners develops other interests and wishes to leave the partnership.
3. A partner dies.
4. A conflict of interests develops.

Types of Partnerships. Partnerships may be general or limited. In a *general partnership,* each partner is held liable for the acts of the other partners. A *limited partnership* can be created only by compliance with a state's statutory requirements. Such a partnership is composed of one or more *general partners* and one or more *limited partners.* Management of the firm is performed by the general partners, who have unlimited personal liability for the partnership's debts. The personal liability of the limited partners is limited to the amount of capital contributed by them.

The exemption from personal liability of limited partners is conditional upon their not participating in any way in the management of the firm. However, the limited partners are permitted to be employees of the firm. Unfortunately, legal decisions do not make it very clear as to how far the limited partners can go in giving advice or reviewing management decision making without losing their exemption from personal liability. There is no requirement that a limited partnership so designate itself in its name or otherwise in its dealings. Yet, the surnames of the limited partners may not be used in the firm name.

Tests of a Partnership. It is sometimes difficult to tell if an enterprise is a proprietorship, partnership, or corporation. There is no simple test for the existence of a partnership, but the major requirements are: the intent of the owners, co-ownership of the business, and carrying on the business for a profit. Also, no formalities are required to create a partnership. You may form one and not realize it.

As a general rule, the sharing of profits, together with having a voice in the management of a business, are sufficient evidence to imply the existence of a partnership.

Rights of the Partners.   If there is no agreement to the contrary, each partner has an equal voice in the management of the business. Also, a majority of the partners has the legal right to make decisions pertaining to the daily operations of the business. However, all partners must consent to the making of fundamental changes in the structure itself. Each partner's share of the profits is presumed to be his or her only compensation and, in the absence of any other agreement, the profits and losses are distributed equally.

Corporation

A corporation is sometimes defined as a legal entity, or an artificial being, whose life exists at the pleasure of the courts of law. The formation of a corporation is more formal and complex than is required for the other legal forms. The number of persons required as stockholders varies with individual state laws. Usually, the number varies from three to five, and frequently two of these may be "dummies" who serve as incorporators in name only and remain inactive as far as the activities of the firm are concerned. The procedure for formation is usually legally defined and requires the services of an attorney. Incorporation fees frequently cost from $300 to $1,000.

Advantages and Disadvantages.   The primary *advantages* the corporate form offers you as a small investor are:

1. It is a legal entity separate and distinct from you as an individual.
2. It offers permanence. If you or another one of the owners dies, the shares can be transferred to others without the legal life of the firm being affected.
3. Your liability for the firm's debts is limited to the amount you invest in its stock. Your private resources cannot be touched.
4. You can have representative management.
5. Large amounts of capital can be raised relatively easily. Some authorities would question the validity of this statement.

Some offsetting *disadvantages* which might keep you from using this form of structure are:

1. Taxes and fees are high.
2. The procedures, reports, and statements required become cumbersome and burdensome.
3. Your powers are limited to those stated in the charter.
4. You may have difficulty doing business in another state.
5. The other stockholders may not be interested in the firm.
6. It tends to be a more impersonal form of business.

Because of the limited liability feature, the corporate form is considered superior to all other forms of organization.

Other Considerations. If other individuals are involved in your venture, and you decide to incorporate, a pre-incorporation agreement should be drawn up and signed by the incorporators. This agreement should provide protection against any member, or members, of the group taking off on their own with the proprietary basis for establishing the organization. It at least provides you the restitution of damages that may have been incurred.

In order to protect you and the other parties involved, a buy-sell arrangement for the major stockholders should be included in the articles of incorporation. Also, if the success of the venture is dependent on your, or certain other individuals' participation in the firm, "key man insurance" should be carried on you and those persons. This type of insurance will protect the resources of the firm in the event of such a loss and provide protection during the period of adjustment that follows. (See Chapter 25.)

Adequate bond and insurance coverage against losses which result from the acts of employees and others should be maintained. Also, liability and Workman's Compensation insurance coverage should be maintained.

Holding Company

As your firm grows larger, or as you wish to expand your activities while conserving your own resources, you might consider it desirable to establish a parent corporation to serve as a holding company for your corporation. Under certain conditions, you may gain tax advantages from this arrangement. Furthermore, the assets of the parent company may be protected by limiting the liability.

Trust

For estate and other reasons identified under the tax laws, the trust arrangement established a method of providing the owner of a business with certain tax advantages. A popular one in recent years has been the "real estate investment trust" which gives higher tax-bracket individuals certain income tax advantages.

A trust differs from a corporation in that it is established for a specific period of time—or until certain designated events have occurred. It is administered by a trustee, or a board of trustees. The trust receives specific assets from the person, or persons, establishing it. The trust covenant defines the purpose of the trust, names the beneficiary or beneficiaries, and establishes a formula for the distribution of income and trust assets.

FINANCIAL STRUCTURE

The nature of the legal structure you choose for your firm will have a direct relationship with the nature of the financial structure. However, it should be emphasized that the methods of financing a business are varied, although certain patterns do seem to occur more frequently than others. Innovations that work are common place. In the material that follows, we attempt to discuss the more popular financial practices and structures.

Proprietorship

Frequently, we think of the proprietorship as being financed from the personal funds of the proprietor. However, there are many instances where only a small portion of the funds required are financed from his own resources. He may obtain a bank loan, a loan from an individual, a loan from or guaranteed by a government agency, or a loan from a business. The amount of money which can be obtained in addition to those of the proprietor will be determined by the amount of personal funds he possesses and the amount and quality of personal assets that may be pledged for a loan. The amount and percentage of money for a loan available above those of the proprietor, will be determined by:

1. The "track record" of the individual proprietor; that is, his prior record of performance.
2. The nature of the business venture itself, including the amount of fixed assets, size of inventory, the rate of inventory turnover, market potential, profit potential, and so forth.

The usual proportion of debt ranges from 25 to 60 percent of the owner's equity.

Partnership

In starting a partnership, one of the factors to be considered in selecting your partners is whether the individuals possess adequate financial resources to contribute. The capital contribution made by each partner goes into the "paid-in capital" account.

Occasionally, one or more of the partners may make the partnership a loan after the business has started operating. In such instances, the loan will be evidenced by a note. The loan may be secured by fixed assets of the partnership or unsecured, that is, issued against the general credit of the partnership.

In some instances, additional funds may be obtained from outside sources such as banks, individuals, government agencies, and other businesses. Usually, this type of financing will be in the form of short- or intermediate-term loans.

Corporation

In establishing a new business, the amount of equity capital required of the initial stockholders will usually range from 40 to 100 percent. The amount is dependent upon such factors as the nature of the venture, abilities and past performance of the management group, kind of assets involved, and market potential.

Equities. During the period immediately following World War II, more than one class of equity (*common stock*) was frequently used. For example, Class A stock would be made voting, but would be subordinated to Class B stock as far as dividends were concerned. Class B stock would be non-voting.

Debt. A favorite debt device has been the *convertible debenture,* which provides investors with not only the security of a debt instrument, but also an opportunity to shift from debt to equity when the firm's stock appreciates.

Recently, many institutional lenders, because of tight money, demand for funds, and a changing market environment, obtained *stock purchase warrants* of up to 50 percent of the total equity. These warrants give the investors the right to purchase a certain number of shares of the firm's common stock at a stated price. The volume of debt, whether it was debentures or mortgage bonds, was usually about 25 to 50 percent of the total capital structure.

Other Considerations. Under certain conditions, it may be advantageous for the incorporating investors to invest a portion of their funds in equity securities and the remainder in debt because of tax advantages and a more favorable priority position in case the firm liquidates.

Sometimes, *subordinated instruments,* such as *second mortgages, junior notes,* or *bonds,* are used.

Preferred stock, which pays a stated percent of dividend before the common stockholders receive any returns, may be desirable even though it tends to restrict the flexibility of the capital structure.

Warrants, as mentioned above, may be used or required by certain investors as part of the financial package. Examples of investors demanding these are: S.B.I.C.s (Small Business Investment Companies), and insurance companies.

Industrial revenue bonds provide a cheaper means of acquiring funds when your business will be located in an industrial park, community, or region where the use of such an instrument is available.

The use of debt in financing enables you to obtain *leverage* upon your equity investment, i.e., by using debt you are able to expand your income relative to your equity.

You should be careful that the indenture provisions of debt instruments are not restrictive and do not limit your actions too much. You want to have the opportunity to work through any periodic adversity without being "washed out" by covenants in the indenture that fail to provide adequate "running room."

Section 1244 Stock. Your corporation may be made more attractive to investors if you comply with the statutory concept of a "small business corporation," as defined in Section 1244 of the "Small Business Tax Revision Act of 1958." For this to happen, (1) the total amount of stock offered under the plan, plus other contributions to capital and paid-in surplus, may not exceed $500,000 and (2) the total amount of the stock which may be offered, plus the equity capital of the corporation, must be less than $1,000,000.

Section 1244 stock is common stock (voting or non-voting) in a domestic corporation. *Losses* on the sale, exchange, or worthlessness of this stock *are treated as ordinary losses rather than capital losses sustained by an individual.* The total amount that may be treated as an ordinary loss must be less than $25,000 or, if a husband and wife are filing a joint return, $50,000. This provision could give you a considerable tax advantage.

The stock must be issued to the taxpayer in exchange for a transfer by him of money or other property. Stock issued in exchange for stock or securities of another corporation, or for services rendered, does not qualify. Also, only the individual to whom the stock is issued qualifies for the benefits of Section 1244.

Finally, taxpayers who are owner-operators of a closely held corporation should make certain that they qualify a maximum amount of their stock under this special provision. When planning their business, most potential owners are so optimistic that they simply cannot see the need for anticipating tax differences which become important only if their new ventures fail. Historical data do not support this conclusion, however, for many more small businesses fail than succeed. If for some reason your business should fail, the opportunity to obtain a tax refund based on a $50,000 ordinary net operating loss deduction is substantially more valuable to you than the potential use of a $50,000 net capital loss carry-forward. This provision should also be of special interest to you in seeking venture capital for your new corporation. High marginal tax bracket investors are attracted by the possibility of investing in a new firm if they know that the government will share their risk of loss on a 70–30 basis, but will only share in the potential profits on a 25–75 basis. Also, except for knowledge of the provision and a little timely action, the cost associated with this tax-saving opportunity is essentially zero.[2]

If outside sources of funds are desired, in addition to equity, there may be convertible preferred stock with warrants and bonds. The nature of the structure under these circumstances is determined by the tenor of the money market.

> At the end of 1973, the slow response of the money market indicated that it might be necessary for the original owners of a company to share ownership interest based on a dollar for dollar basis. In other words, the securities accepted by the outside investors might have been convertible preferred with warrants and bonds. However, a "sweetener" was necessary for the consummation of the deal. The "sweetener" was in the form of partial ownership of the firm.

ADMINISTRATIVE STRUCTURE

You must also set up an administrative structure to run the business. This process will be discussed in greater detail in Chapter 10, but the subject is presented here as part of the overview of your entering a new business.

You should set up a series of authority and responsibility relationships expressed in a formal organization chart. Even if you have a one-man business, a chart can be useful as a reminder of how your time might be most effectively utilized.

You may select a traditional formal organization structure that may be described as a triangular pyramid. (See Figure 6–1.) This relationship provides for a tighter and narrower span of control. It requires more centralization of authority and more detailed supervision.

On the other hand, you may select the flatter, broader span of control. (See Figure 6–2.) If so, you will provide your subordinates with less centralized authority and less detailed supervision.

A chart should not only be a useful tool for the present, but also an aid in planning for the future development of your organization and in projecting personnel requirements.

A list of job titles and job specifications should accompany the chart. Job specifications consist of the duties, responsibilities, and working conditions of the work assignment and the qualifications necessary to fulfill the jobs acceptably.

---

[2] If you desire further information on this important subject, see your tax attorney or refer to Ray M. Sommerfeld, *Federal Taxes and Management Decisions* (Homewood, Ill.: Richard D. Irwin, Inc., 1974).

FIGURE 6–1   **FIGURE 6–2**

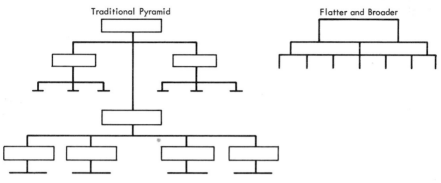

SUMMARY

We have tried to show you how to set up your legal, financial, and administrative structure. The usual progression is to determine what legal form you desire (or must have) for your business, decide the sources of your funds and your capital structure, and choose your administrative organization.

We hope you have learned enough from this presentation to permit you to know when to call in an outside expert and to know what questions to ask him when you do.

QUESTIONS FOR FURTHER DISCUSSION

1. What are the negative and positive factors of the proprietorship, partnership, and corporation when it comes to selecting the legal form of business?
2. Briefly discuss the financial structure of the three legal forms of business, the proprietorship, partnership, and corporation.
3. Describe the holding company and trust.
4. Make contact with a small business and report on its legal, financial, and administrative structures.

7

How to Establish Your New Business

After having made the choice to enter a new business, and after having determined that your idea is economically feasible, you are now prepared to make the business a reality. The material in this chapter presents a plan of action for achieving the reality. It is intended to take you step by step into operating a business.

Specifically, the steps to be taken include the following:

1. Developing a timetable.
2. Establishing your business objectives.
3. Setting up your organizational structure.
4. Determining your personnel requirements.
5. Determining your physical plant needs.
6. Planning your approach to the market.
7. Preparing your budget.
8. Locating sources of funds.
9. Implementing your plans.

Figure 7–1 is intended to present a schematic of the business process. In general, you inject financial, physical, and human resources into your company. It, in turn, distributes goods and services to other companies, to wholesalers, to retailers, or to the final consumers.

DEVELOPING A TIMETABLE

You should establish a timetable for developing the business in an ordered, coordinated fashion. Data should be developed relating to per-

FIGURE 7-1
The Business Process

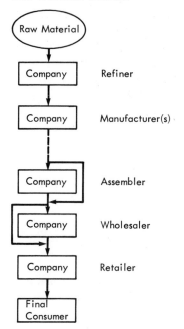

forming each step in starting the business. Next, a time frame for accomplishing each of the steps should be determined. Many of these steps can be, and often are, performed simultaneously. You, as the owner, have the responsibility of meeting the time schedule.

ESTABLISHING YOUR BUSINESS OBJECTIVES

In order for your enterprise to have purpose and direction, you should establish the objectives you hope to achieve for yourself and your firm. These should be compatible with the objectives discussed in Chapter 2. An example of some possible categories of objectives are:

	After 1 Year	After 5 Years	After 10 Years
I. Size			
Physical			
Financial.			
II. Type of products			
Number			
Kind of product lines.			
III. Number of employees			
IV. Sales			
V. Profits			

SETTING UP THE ORGANIZATIONAL STRUCTURE

As previously stated, you must develop a unified organizational structure, taking into consideration the legal, financial, and administrative aspects of your business. Keeping in mind the basic premise that "My business is very personal," it is important that you select those forms that are in *your best interest*. Also, you should organize for the "long run" and not just for the "short run." The outline which follows is intended to aid you in considering the options available to you at each junction and, hopefully, to assist you in making the best choice.

1. Legal Alternatives
   You must choose the form which seems most appropriate to you based upon your needs, objectives, qualifications, and philosophies.
   a. Proprietorship.
   b. Partnership.
   c. Corporation.
   d. Holding Company.
2. Capital Structure
   The extent to which equity and debt are used will be determined by the interrelationships and the interactions between:
   a. Amount of personal funds you wish to commit to the business.
   b. Amount of personal funds other principals wish to commit.
   c. Amount of leverage desired.
   d. Availability of equity and borrowed capital and at what costs—interest and concessions.
   e. Degree of risk you wish to assume.
3. Administrative Structure
   You now must develop a formal organizational plan based upon these factors:
   a. The *raison d'être* (reason for being) of the business.
   b. Your primary personal and business objectives.
   c. The plans, programs, policies, and practices that will enable you to achieve your objectives.
   d. The authority and responsibility relationships that will permit you to accomplish your mission.

An element often overlooked by the small business manager is the importance of having access to a board of directors (or advisers, if not a corporation) to evaluate the firm's operation and to make recommendations relating to future activities. You *must* be willing to be responsive to its guidance. You should expect to pay these people a minimum of $100 per meeting, plus expenses, and as the firm prospers, an increased amount. The board should be composed of at least three people from outside the business and an equal number from within.

In selecting outside members, you should look toward a balance of expertise and experience, such as: (1) a business manager with a record of success in business, preferably in a related but different field; (2) another business manager with a different background, but equally successful; and (3) if available, a professorial type, with a general management background that encompasses the operations of small businesses.

DETERMINING PERSONNEL REQUIREMENTS

The next organizational step is to determine the duties and responsibilities (job descriptions and specifications) needed to perform the activities of your business. Then, the process of estimating your personnel requirements can be undertaken. (See Chapter 10.)

One problem area seems to be more prevalent in smaller firms than in larger organizations. Frequently the business is closely related to the family unit, and this relationship may contribute to morale problems if outsiders are brought in. The small business owner-manager should be aware of these potential problems and take deliberate steps to prevent them. (See Chapter 26.)

DETERMINING YOUR PHYSICAL PLANT NEEDS

There are two important decisions you must now make, namely, (1) what location to choose, and (2) whether to buy (build) or lease your physical facilities.

Location

You should seek that location which satisfies your requirements and provides you optimum benefits. For example, if you are going into the retail business and are considering a specific piece of vacant property, it is desirable to determine the reason behind the vacancy. Often, a particular location seems to be a "born loser," experiencing a whole series of failures. Also, you are concerned about the means of transportation (foot, car, or public transportation), traffic patterns, and traffic volume.

Factors that should be considered in choosing a location are: access to your work force, availability of utilities, the type of business, relationship to your market, and availability of transportation.

Access to Work Force. The availability of people with the personal attributes and skills your business requires is essential for success. You should consider the possibility of blending part-time with full-time personnel in order to provide more flexibility and a more economic operation. Another consideration is the distance and type residential areas from which you will draw people. If you can locate where people can walk to work and possibly even go home for lunch, you may have an advantage in pay negotiation, worker loyalty and interest, as well as better job attendance.

Availability of Utilities.   Access to needed utilities, such as electric power, gas, water, sewage, and steam, is also very important. Two other factors to consider are flexibility in operation and economics (not only the initial installation of costs, but also operating costs).

Type of Business.   The type of business you are going to operate, such as retail, service, or manufacturing, will also influence your locational decisions. This factor is important as it relates to access to customers, suppliers, work force, utilities, transportation, and compliance with zoning regulations. The *mission* of the business serves as a basic consideration in seeking the "right" location.

Availability of Vendors.   Is there a sufficient number of vendors to supply the needs of your business? In the selection of vendors, you should determine the types of supportive service each seller can provide. The kinds of support that may be derived are: (1) assistance in designing a product or products; (2) aid in the selection of machinery and plant; (3) technical assistance in solving problems; and (4) assistance with pricing and formulating trade credit practices.

Relationship to the Market.   What is the relationship of the location to your market? Is it a central location? Is there an adequate number of customers in the market area to sustain your business? You must identify and focus on the competitive advantages you can offer that will enable you to obtain your target share of the market. Evaluate any "tie ins" that will enable you to expand your business, such as equipment sales, service, gas, and/or supplies.

Access to Transportation.   Can the most economical form of transportation for both your in-bound and out-bound shipments be made? Are there railroad spurs to the location? Truck lines? Buses?

Buy or Lease

The question of whether to buy or lease your physical plant is important. The supply of capital may be the determining factor. Also, the rate and amount of return you can receive on capital invested in other ways will be another consideration. The nature of space requirements and the availability of a structure will also be significant. You should not overlook the role of depreciation and its effect on cash flow. Also, do your building requirements indicate the need for specialized or general purpose structure? You should be cautious in committing yourself to a special purpose structure because of the long-range ramifications of disposing of it if you decide to move or go out of business.

PLANNING YOUR APPROACH TO THE MARKET

Three marketing factors you need to consider before opening your business to the public are: (1) building an image; (2) what channels of distribution to use; and (3) pricing. While these factors are discussed in greater detail in Chapters 12, 13, and 14, those facts you should know before starting your business are provided here.

Building an Image

A number of factors should be considered in building an image for your firm. What segment of the market offers the best potential opportunity? What advertising media will best reach this market?

A radio station operated on both AM and FM frequencies. After a substantial time period, its sales manager evaluated the results of their efforts to sell alvertising, and discovered that its advertising customers obtained 45 percent or more of their business volume from the black community. However, the members of this community made up a meager portion of the station's FM listening audience. The FM had never attracted the desired volume of advertising revenue. A shift to black disc-jockeys and a program format attuned to this community produced a substantial increase in advertising revenues.

Too much money may be spent on the exterior of the building, the decor, billboards, or an ineffective advertising program. Funds spent in these areas often result in a reduction in the quality of service and merchandise. It would be better to reverse the pattern by giving excellent service and good quality merchandise, for these are remembered longest and provide the desired customer appeal and following.

A hotel coffee shop was located in a small town on a major tourist route. The building of an interstate highway on the periphery of the town has not caused a loss of customers. People say, "I have been coming here for 25 years and I enjoy the service and food." Others say, "I have driven an extra 150 miles to get here."

While this business has continued to survive and even be successful, one is aware of numerous other instances where quality and service deteriorated and the business ultimately failed.

Channels of Distribution

The nature of the business and the economic characteristics of the industry will partially determine your channels of distribution. There are various classes of business and each has a number of options for marketing its products. Some alternatives you have are:

I. Industrial Products.
    A. Direct sales to customers.
    B. Manufacturers agents.
    C. Distributors (wholesalers–warehouses).
II. Consumer Products.
    A. Direct sales.
        1. Door–to–door.
        2. Independent retail outlets.
    B. Wholesalers.
    C. Chain retail outlets.
    D. Establishing your own retail outlets.
        1. Direct ownership.
        2. Franchise.
III. Service.
    Examples of services are: TV, radio, appliance, and automobile repairing; day-care nursery, catering; real estate, insurance; care of aged; and consumer finance. The usual channel is direct to the ultimate consumer.

Pricing Policies

Whatever the business, pricing is important. However, the focus usually should not be on *price,* but on *service.* In pricing your good or service, you should consider *all* the *cost factors,* and then add an additional percentage to provide you with your planned profit. (See Chapter 23.)

Certain rules-of-thumb are available for use in determining the price in most businesses. For example, in the restaurant industry total food costs generally have not exceeded 33 percent of the sales price. More recently, a price based on food costing from 33 to 44 percent is believed to be more realistic. In the upper range, the owner may elect to go with word-of-mouth advertising rather than spending money with various advertising media.

A restaurant owner in a college town was not sensitive to the relationship between food cost and price. He was in financial difficulty and sought the aid of the Small Business Administration. A SCORE volunteer was assigned as a consultant. His first question was, "What's the most popular item on your menu?" The restaurant owner replied, "Our $2.25 steak." The consultant asked for a scale and a raw steak. He showed the businessman that the raw steak cost $1.85. Obviously, the reason for the steak's popularity was the mark up of less than 22 percent. It was also the reason why the business was in financial difficulties.

PREPARING YOUR BUDGETS

It is now time to pull together all the revenue and cost items for which you have planned. This process is called budgeting and will be discussed in Chapter 24.

The budget should be considered as an instrument of both planning and control. It helps you plan how you will allocate your firm's scarce resources. The main objective is to maximize your revenue, minimize your cost, and increase your profit. Profit should be included in the total budget. Specific profit figures depend upon many factors, including the type industry you enter, your location, and your efficiency.

Concerning "management information," you need to ask yourself these two questions:

1. What decisions do I need to make?
2. What information do I need in order to make those decisions?

Your answers to these questions should serve as guidelines in preparing your budgets. Some of the items you should consider are: expenses, including the cost of the money you will use (remember that money has a cost, whether it is owned or borrowed), depreciation, obsolescence, utilities, maintenance, supplies, personnel, fringe benefits, insurance, material handling, waste, transportation, cost, and start-up cost; revenues, including sales of your product or service, sale of property, and interest on money invested; and the resulting profit—or loss.

Types of Budgets

The most important budgets for a small firm such as yours are:

1. An operating budget.
2. A capital budget.
3. A cash flow budget.

Operating Budget. In preparing the operating budget, you try to anticipate the costs of obtaining and selling your products and the income received from selling them. This budget will serve as a basis for comparing budgeted activities with actual performance and as a basis for determining the cause of variances from your plans.

Capital Budget. The capital budget reflects your plans for obtaining, replacing, and expanding your physical facilities. It assists you in beginning operations and being able to have the needed buildings, tools, equipment, and other facilities.

Cash Flow Budget. The cash flow budget is a statement of what *cash* will be needed to pay what expenses at what time, as well as indicating from where the cash will come to pay them. The lack of *ready cash* resources is the primary cause of firms getting into an illiquid position and causing a forced liquidation. By using the cash flow budget, such a dilemma may be avoided.

Anticipating Difficulties

At the danger of being called "alarmists," we should point out that you should realistically look at the possibility of failure and begin to prepare for it. In preparing the budget for your new business, you must understand and accept the equity risk and investment required. You should look at the costs involved in acquiring assets, using them, and then having to liquidate the business if it fails. Figure 7–2 should help you understand your risks.

FIGURE 7–2
The Value of Assets in a Going Concern and in Case of Liquidation

Items	Going Concern Value	Liquidation Value
Start-up costs	0	0
Cash drain until breakeven level of operation is attained	0	0
Basic working capital investment for a mature level of business (includes cash position adequate to take care of _ weeks of payroll and operating expenses)	Good value	Cash 100% Accounts receivable depends on quality of debtors or depends on inventory market (less handling cost)
Equity in plant, product, and equipment	Some value	Some value
Goodwill and other intangible assets	No value	No value

LOCATING SOURCES OF FUNDS

After you have budgeted the amount of funds needed for capital expenditures and to begin operations, you must locate the sources from which you can obtain those funds.

Your ability to raise funds is one of the significant determinants of the size and type of business you can enter. You should recognize that methods of financing change and that there is no one best method. While some methods have advantages over others, the attitude and desires of the investors or lenders will determine the sources of financing available to you at a given point in time.

The following discussion should help you find the needed money to begin operations. (See Chapter 6 and the related materials in Parts V and VII.)

Your Own Funds

Some people have the philosophy of using only their personal funds and that borrowing is to be avoided in any business venture. Other people believe that they should use as few of their personal funds as possible, and instead they should obtain as much leverage as possible by using the funds of others.

Assuming that you either must, or wish to, use funds of others, there are several sources of outside funds.

Other Individuals

You may find other private individuals with excess funds who are interested in investing in a venture opportunity. You may find such a person among your friends, or through your attorney, CPA, banker, or securities dealer. These people often have a specific preference for the type of business in which they are willing to invest. In general, they prefer a business with which they are familiar.

Commercial and industrial financial institutions may provide you with funds. The proportion of funds such institutions make available may range from 25 to 60 percent of the value of the total assets. Usually, the cost of such financing is higher than other alternatives, but such funds may be the most accessible. These institutions may help you through:

1. Loans on your fixed assets.
2. Lease-purchase arrangements.
3. Accounts receivable financing.
4. Factoring arrangements on accounts receivable.

Trade Credit

Trade credit should not be overlooked. This source of credit refers to the purchase of inventory, equipment, and supplies which are made on an open account in accordance with customary terms for this type of business.

Commercial Banks

In the past, commercial banks have been a good source of credit for business managers having funds of their own and with proven successful experience. More recently, because of the higher rate of return, banks have shifted a greater portion of their funds into consumer financing. The large demand for funds in recent years has pushed interest rates and terms of bank loans to higher levels and less favorable terms.

You should also consider the following services offered by commercial banks, which include:

1. General account (demand deposit).
2. Payroll accounting.
3. Income tax service.
4. Various computerized services.
5. Lock box collections to expedite payments and cash flow.
6. More individualized services.

Investment Banks

Investment banks serve to bring together those who need funds and various sources of funds. Many of them are sound and have developed a reputation for integrity and providing their clients with good service.

Preferably, you should select a banker who specializes in regional business, for they are frequently more familiar with the geographic area, the economics of the region, and are accustomed to servicing specialized needs. These bankers also maintain established relationships with insurance companies, large individual investors, and investment managers of pension trusts.

The availability of an investment banker and his service are determined by:

1. Your present financial requirements.
2. Your market potential.
3. Your projected status for two years in advance.

Unless you can reasonably anticipate that your firm will be classified as a regional or national firm within two years, you cannot expect to have access to an investment banker.

Major Non-Financial Corporations

Major producing corporations, through their financial subsidiaries, often play a significant role in financing certain types of activities which are closely related to some phase of their operations. Some examples are:

General Electric, Westinghouse, and others have been active in helping finance mobile homes and apartments. The mobile home manufacturers will install the appliances of a specific supplier, who then helps finance the producer. In addition, the appliance-financing subsidiary often finances the sale of the home to the ultimate consumer.

The "Big Three" auto firms operate through their financial subsidiaries to aid their dealers in financing dealerships, provide a floor plan arrangement for financing the dealers' new car inventories, and finance the sale of cars (including used cars) to customers.

Insurance Companies

Insurance companies may be a source of funds for your firm. You can go directly to the company, or contact its agent, an investment banker, or a mortgage banker.

While insurance companies have traditionally done debt financing, more recently they have demanded that equity purchase warrants be included as a part of the total package.

Small Business Administration

One of the primary purposes of the SBA is to provide financial assistance. The main difference between the SBA and a private lending agency is in the terms of the loan. Where banks may be limited by regulation or law on the terms of their loans, the SBA tends to permit longer periods of repayment and make other concessions to small firms. Yet, as far as credit risks are concerned, the SBA has requisites very similar to banks. The borrower should be a good credit risk.

The SBA has been limited in its financial activities by the constraints imposed by Congress in allocating funds for loan purposes. The type loans it can provide to you, and the manner of their utilization, are discussed in the following paragraphs.

Direct Loans. These loans usually fit into three categories: (1) *Ethnic loans*—significant interest has been shown in this type loan, especially loans ranging up to $25,000; (2) *Catastrophic* or *disaster loans*—these loans are made in an area where some form of disaster has struck. The terms are usually three percent interest and an amortization period of 20 years; and (3) *Small loans*—made to business firms needing between $1,500 and $3,000. Direct loans have been restricted because of the limited supply of such funds.

Participating Loans. With participating loans, the SBA takes a portion of the total loan on a direct cash participation basis, and the bank or other lender provides the remainder. In this type of loan, the SBA assumes a subordinated position to the other lender in the event of liquidation. Due to the limitation of funds, only a small number of these loans are made.

Guaranteed Loans. Guaranteed loans have been the most popular in recent years. The SBA guarantees the lender 90 percent of the loan up to a total of $350,000. The borrower may contact the SBA directly or through a bank whose policy is to make SBA guaranteed loans. The practice of using the bank as an intermediary seems to produce more satisfactory results.

Lease Guaranty Program. The lease guaranty program was initially established to enable small businesses to locate in major shopping centers where a credit rating of AAA is required. Current regulations require:

1. Paying three months' rent at the outset to be placed in escrow.
2. The amount of lease that may be guaranteed is limited to $2.5 million, i.e., the total rent for the life of the lease.
3. A 2.8 percent single insurance premium is required for guaranteeing the total rent of the lease.

Small Business Investment Corporation

SBICs are chartered by the SBA and make qualified SBA loans. For each dollar they put into a loan, the SBA matches it.

Loans are usually made for a period of 5 to 10 years. The SBICs may stipulate that they be given a certain portion of stock purchase warrants or stock options, or they may make a combination of a loan and a stock purchase. The latter combination has been preferred.

Industrial Development Corporations

Industrial development corporations have greater freedom in the types of loans they are able to make. They make "501" or "502" loans.

501 Loans. 501 loans are granted from state chartered industrial development corporations whose initial capital is provided by member commercial banks which are members of the Federal Reserve System. These corporations make term loans, working capital loans, mortgage loans, and contract performance loans, and can borrow up to one half of the loan amount from the SBA.

502 Loans. 502 financing is arranged by an individual community establishing an industrial development corporation. The amount of equity and number of stockholders required are determined by the community's population. The SBA has a ceiling of $350,000 per individual borrower, and the repayment period may extend for 25 years.

Economic Development Administration (EDA)

The EDA makes direct loans to industries located in communities classified as economically depressed areas or in communities that are declared as regional economic growth centers.

The loans made by the EDA may be used for acquiring plant and equipment. The agency may loan up to 65 percent of the total cost of the assets for which the loans are made, but the agency prefers to remain in the 50 percent range. A rule of thumb used as a guide in determining the amount of a loan is from an average of $5,200 to a maximum of $10,000 per employee for each new job the project will create. The rate of interest is reviewed quarterly. The life of the loan may reach 25 years, but the average maturity is 18 years.

State Employment Agencies

Grants may be available through your local state employment agency for obtaining employees because of the changing nature of their work assignments, or for training employees for a new business where the needed skills are lacking.

Agricultural Loans

A number of sources of funds for agricultural loans are federally funded. The Cooperative Extension Service, or one of its local agents, may be checked for information concerning availability and procedures. Some sources of funds are:

1. Federal Land Bank Association;
2. Production Credit Corporation; and
3. Farm Home Administration.

IMPLEMENTING YOUR PLANS

Now you are ready to take the plunge! It is time to obtain your funds, get a charter, purchase your facilities and supplies, hire and train your people, and start operating.

Capital Procurement

Using your capital structure plan and the sources of funds you have developed, obtain the funds, put them in your checking account, and start writing checks.

Corporate Charter and Permits

You should obtain the services of an attorney in acquiring your charter, if you are incorporating. He can help you obtain any occupational licenses and permits.

Contracting and Purchasing Facilities and Supplies

After the funds, charter, and permits are obtained, you should refer back to your timetable and start negotiating contracts and purchasing equipment, products, and supplies needed to run your business.

Personnel Selection and Training

As the time approaches for the beginning of operations, you should refer to your organization chart, job titles, and job specifications in order to determine your personnel requirements. Methods of selecting and procuring personnel will be influenced by local conditions. The presence of a Community College, Liberal Arts College, University, or Vocational-Technical School will influence your decision to use all full-time employees or to use some full-time and some part-time employees. You can receive assistance in obtaining prospective employees from institutional placement offices, state employment agencies, and private employment agencies. It may be necessary to use local advertising media to attract prospective employees. However, this practice usually increases the amount of time required for screening.

The nature of your business and the background of the newly-hired employees will influence the amount of time needed, and the methods to be used, in employee training.

Beginning Operations

You are now a business manager; you are operating your own firm, you have all the risks and hopefully you will receive the benefits and rewards of "being on your own." However, some unforeseen problems should be anticipated, for they will surely occur during the "crank-up" period.

SUMMARY

The material in this chapter has outlined the steps you should follow in establishing a new business of your own. You should by now have:

1. Developed and followed a realistic timetable.
2. Established your business goals and objectives.
3. Set up your organization structure, including the legal, financial, and administrative aspects.
4. Estimated, selected, and trained your people.
5. Determined your physical plant and facility needs, and contracted for, or purchased, them.

6. Planned your marketing activities, including advertising, channels of distribution, and pricing.
7. Prepared budgets.
8. Found sources of funds and obtained the money needed.
9. Secured your charter and the permits needed to begin operating *your own business.*

QUESTIONS FOR FURTHER DISCUSSION

1. Explain how you would determine the organizational structure of your business.
2. Discuss the procedure for estimating your personnel requirements.
3. What are the factors which should be considered in determining the location of your business?
4. What is meant by "building an image" for your firm?
5. Describe how you would set your pricing policy.
6. What is a budget and why is it useful for a business?
7. Explain briefly the major sources from which you might raise capital.
8. Describe the Small Business Administration and how it might help you raise funds.

8

How to Enter an Existing Business

While there is some similarity between establishing a new business and entering an on-going enterprise, there are several significant differences which are covered in this chapter. The procedures and analyses that follow are intended to provide you with an overview of how to evaluate a given firm and to aid you in determining :(1) whether or not to purchase the business; and (2) if you do buy it, what you should do in order to begin operations.

TO PURCHASE, OR NOT TO PURCHASE?

In considering your options in selecting an established business, it is likely that you will narrow them down to a single choice. At that point, you should check the business out before making your final decision. It might be compared to the steps involved in moving an aircraft from the boarding gate of the terminal to the taxiway, to the runway, and into the air. Certain items must be checked off at each step of the way, with the pilot having the right to abort the flight—up to the point where he is committed to taking the aircraft into the air. So it is with you and your purchase of an established business; up to a given time, you may cancel out, but at that point you are committed to take over the business. Figure 8–1 is intended to illustrate this comparison.

FIGURE 8–1
To Go or Not to Go

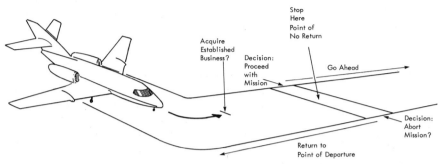

Determining Reasons for the Availability of the Business

You should determine why the firm is available for purchase, as this—in itself—is a "red flag" warning that something is wrong. You need to determine what is wrong, why, and what you should do about it.

The following discussion is designed to help you determine whether a particular business, which is available, is right for you.

Why Available. The question, "Why is this business available for purchase?" should help you establish the validity of the owner's stated purpose for selling the business. Maybe it is in accordance with the old cliche, "Anything I have is for sale—at a price. That is, the *right* price." Some reasons provide a positive opportunity, while others may be negative opportunities for you. The following analysis should help you determine the potential opportunity to be found in a firm.

Does the present owner have "too many irons in the fire"? Too many businesses are run by one individual who is unable to allocate sufficient time to successfully manage all of them.

> Bob Bleckley had dropped out of college in his senior year for financial reasons. After working several years for a building supply firm, he went to work for a partnership engaged in diversified construction of commercial buildings. He was made manager of the metal door division. The partners were so busy with their other activities that they gave him little assistance or interest. Bob was running the division.
>
> He offered to buy the division from the partners and they accepted. He now is the owner-manager of that firm and two other small activities.

Condition of the Business. You should also seek answers to the following questions.

Are the Physical Facilities Worn Out? If the plant, equipment, tools, and furniture are worn out, it is likely that the business' maintenance costs will be excessive. It is also likely that the firm can no longer effectively compete in the marketplace.

A druggist and his wife had been running their drugstore for 40 years—largely without making changes and improvements in their physical plant. After the death of his wife, the druggist, who was approaching 70, decided to sell the business. He was unable to find a buyer, for the equipment was so ontiquated and in such poor codition that it was practically useless. He finally sold his stock, including his prescription file, to another pharmacist, who moved them to another place of business.

Does the Inventory Contain Mostly "Dead Stock"? The firm's inventory may be unsalable at any price because it is no longer in demand, or has deteriorated.

The owner of a hardware store decided to sell it in 1970. The prospective buyer found 200 horse collars among the antiquated stock.

Is the Market for the Firm's Product Declining? The demand for a business' product may be declining for one or more of the following reasons:

1. Changing neighborhood—There may be a change in the residents' economic status; there may be a change from one ethnic group to another, from one age group to another, or in the life style of the inhabitants.
2. Declining population—The outward movement of the population in both urban and agrarian areas has had a devastating economic effect on some firms.
3. Technological change—The advent and installation of new technology may immediately cause the firm to become obsolete.

The owners of a company in Florida processing large cans of grapefruit juice decided to build a new, more efficient plant. As soon as it was completed, they found themselves competing with a new plant producing "fresh frozen juice" concentrates.

Is the Business Solvent? The business may be insolvent. Unfortunately, there have been instances when people have discovered all too late that the firm they purchased had less assets than liabilities.

A building contractor sold 150 homes for down payments of over $500,000. Because of *abysmally inadequate financing,* he was unable to complete the houses. The firm was sold, but the new owners had to either return the money or give title to their property to the purchasers.

An audit by a reputable accounting firm could be effective in uncovering such information. Another protective measure is the use of escrows, whereby part of the purchase price is put in safe keeping until all aspects of the sale have been completed.

Owner's Intentions. Will the present owner remain in competition? Sometimes, for reasons of location, the age of the facility or equipment, an owner can decide to dispose of his firm, open another one, and compete with the purchaser of his old firm. For protection, you should have an attorney draw up an agreement that the present owner will not re-enter a like or similar business in the community or market area for a reasonable period of time. These agreements are sometimes difficult to enforce, but most businessmen do live up to their agreement.

The owner of a pest control franchise needed to change locations for family reasons. The new location was within the franchise area, so the purchasers required him to sign an agreement that he would not re-enter the business for five years.

In the meantime, he opened a restaurant and related business and became quite successful. At the end of five years, he opened an independent pest control business in his new location.

Is the Present Owner in Good Health? If the owner is in poor health, you should determine that it is physical and not economic.

Bob Howard was interested in owning his own business. One Sunday, he was reviewing the want ads in the newspaper, when he spotted an item of interest.

> For reasons of health, owner willing to sacrifice successful, profitable sandwich shop. Priced for immediate sale.

Bob grabbed his coat and dashed over to "Easy Sandwich Shop." The place was full and business looked great. (All the owner's friends just needed a sandwich that day.) After some delay, Bob was able to engage the owner in serious negotiation. After some haggling, the principals shook hands, and Bob wrote a check from his savings for $10,000.

A month later, Bob was chagrined to learn that the business was "ready to fold" when he took the bait. The former owner's friends were gone and business was "lousy." The $10,000 received by the former owner had worked a "fast cure" for his ill-health.

Does the Present Owner Desire to Retire? The owner may have reached the age where he wishes to retire, which is a valid reason for offering a business for sale. Because of taxes, the owner may want to be paid for the business over a number of years, In addition, he may want to contract for a specified number of years to serve as a consultant or to fill some managerial role.

A word of caution is appropriate. Sometimes the continued association of a former owner may be detrimental to the welfare of the new owner. By continued association with the firm, the former owner may cause the new owner to be unsuccessful, thereby regaining ownership of the business.

At least, the presence of the old owner restricts the freedom of action of the new man and can otherwise inhibit his actions.

> Joe Jones, an experienced insurance man, became the controlling partner in an insurance firm, which also owned a savings and loan association. The previous owner, 75 years old, remained as chairman of the board of the savings and loan association and active partner in the insurance company.
>
> The next 10 years were miserable for Joe, for he was treated as a junior clerk by the minority partner. He finally sold his interest to someone else.

The following procedure should be helpful in uncovering undesirable economic conditions in a firm you are considering purchasing.

Analysis of Accounting Information

The reason for analyzing the firm's accounting data is to determine its economic health. You should do a physical inventory to determine the accuracy of the recorded information, as well as a qualitative analysis of the economic value of the assets and liabilities.

In performing your analysis, there are innumerable items you should check. The most important of these are now presented in general terms. (The specific details and examples will be discussed in Part VII.)

Cash Position. Is the firm's cash position high or low, considering the industry, location, and so forth? Due to taxes, a firm may accumulate a strong cash position. The owner may prefer to sell the firm and take advantage of the "capital gains" benefit over ordinary income. Other reasons for having a strong cash position are to take care of poor funds management, or to provide for flexibility so you can take advantage of any profitable opportunity that presents itself.

Analysis of Ratios. Many financial ratios can be used in estimating the economic health of a firm. While these are usually used in managing a going concern (as shown in Chapter 21), they can also help you make the purchase decision.

Current ratio is defined as *current assets* divided by *current liabilities,* and is a measure of short-term solvency. Current assets normally include cash, marketable securities, accounts receivable, and inventories. Current liabilities are composed of accounts payable, short-term notes payable, income taxes payable, and accrued expenses. A general rule of thumb is the current ratio should be 2 to 1.

Quick ratio is obtained by dividing *current liabilities* into *current assets minus inventories.* You can use this ratio to estimate the ability of a firm to pay off its short-term obligations without having to sell its inventories. Inventories tend to lose value faster than other assets when sold in a hurry. A rule of thumb for the quick ratio is 1 to 1.

Debt-to-equity ratio shows the firm's obligations to creditors, relative to the owner's funds. Debt includes current liabilities and bonds; owner's funds include common stock, preferred stock, capital surplus, and retained earnings.

Ratio of net income to sales is calculated by dividing *net income* by *net sales.* You may use net income before taxes or after taxes. No set guideline exists, as the ratio varies among industries, and even among companies.

Net income to investment ratio is found by dividing *net income* (before or after taxes) by *investment.* Here, again, there is no convenient rule of thumb.

Determination of Debt.   You need to check both the amount of debt and the terms of debt. The *amount of debt* is important, for it shows your financial obligations. You are primarily concerned with short-term notes (less than one year), term notes (one- to five-year maturities), and long-term debt (anything in excess of five years).

Concerning *terms of debt,* you should learn the rate of interest; the firm's ability to repay the debt in its entirety, without penalty; whether a minimum deposit balance is required by the lender; and if an acceleration clause is present in the event of default in payment of interest and principal.

Validity of Financial Statements.   You should determine the validity of the financial statement items. Each item listed on the financial statements should be verified by physically counting the listed items to determine if they agree with the amount shown. Also, you need to find out whether the items are of the stated value, or are worthless.

You should check on the age of accounts receivable. Some businesses continue to carry accounts receivable that should be charged off to "bad debts," resulting in an overstatement of the firm's profit, income tax liability, and value. A tabular summary classifying them by age: such as 30, 60, 90, 120, 180 or more days, would give some perspective of the effectiveness of the existing management's credit policies and practice. The *age of accounts payable* should also be determined.

Cash Flow Analysis. Managers often overinvest in inventory without being aware of the total annual cost of carrying it. Yet, when all elements of cost for carrying inventory are considered, the annual cost may range from 25 to 35 percent. You should prepare a cash flow analysis in order to determine the effectiveness of management in allocating its resources. In preparing it, you should remember that money has a cost in the form of real or imputed interest. If you consider this cost, you should try to use this resource most advantageously in producing a profit.

It is important that you consider the monthly cycle of cash revenue and cash pay-out. In addition, you should take into account the yearly cycle of cash in-flow and out-go.

Adequacy of Cost Data. You should determine whether cost data are adequate and accurate. One often finds that the accounting system used, even when supervised by a CPA or by one of the national accounting firms, fails to reveal the actual costs of individual activities. Thus, it is impossible to determine the price for each product or service in order to satisfy a predetermined profit criterion. Nor is it possible to explain undesirable variances.

Analysis of Pricing Formula

You should analyze the pricing formula used by the firm. Be sure that the price for individual products or services includes all elements of costs, including a provision for an adequate profit.

Appraisal of Operations, Plant, and Equipment

The objective of the following discussion is to help you study the total management operations of a firm, and not just that of the chief executive officer.

Management Effectiveness. How effective is the firm's management? In acquiring an on-going business, you may decide to keep key management personnel. Therefore, it is desirable to look for performance and behavioral characteristics that may serve as a basis for appraising how effectively each manager performs—as an individual and as a part of the managerial group.

Plant Efficiency. Some questions to ask in specific production areas are:

1. *How effective are the personnel?* You can approximate the productivity of individual employees, as well as of the total group of workers. You can look for the portion of time spent productively

compared to that which is wasted on non-productive efforts. Other questions concerning labor cost, waste and scrap, product image, company image, and competitive position are:

a.   What is the rate of labor turnover?

b.   What is the percent of absenteeism?

c.   Do employees deliberately commit acts of sabotage that reflect on the image of the product and company?

2.   *What is the amount of waste?* The amount of waste serves as an important key to profit or loss. By being particularly observant of operations, you can determine the amount of material and supplies being needlessly wasted in the operations.

A carpet mill was observed to be looping out to the edge of the jute or polypropolene backing. Yet, from one to three inches was sliced off of each linear side after the carpet was finished. It was estimated that the mill was unnecessarily using about $10,000 worth of fiber per day by not stopping the looping process approximately an inch from the edge of the backing.

Machine time that is not being utilized is an important waste. Investment in equipment is usually costly, and this cost must be offset by keeping the equipment operating as much as possible.

3.   *What is the quality of production?* The quality of products, or the quality of service produced by the employees, should be graded. The grading may be done by answering questions such as:

a.   What portion of production is completed without defects?

b.   What portion of the rejects may be reworked, and, if so, how much time is involved in this process?

c.   What portion of production results in rejects that can not be reworked?

d.   In terms of cost, how many shipments must be reshipped because some of the shipped material is not of usable quality?

4.   *What is the physical condition of the plant?* You should consider present and future demands made on the plant, as well as:

a.   Adequacy of the size and design of the plant. Is it of sufficient size and design to meet current and projected requirements?

b.   Efficiency of layout. Optimum results can be attained only by effectively laying out the plant. Important items to consider are:
     Where the equipment is spaced and laid out in a sequence of productive steps, only a nominal amount of *work-in-process inventory* is needed. The greater the number of operations that require doubling back and crossing over, the greater will be the requirements for this type of inventory.

Materials-handling cost is also important, for the more frequently work-in-process inventory has to be moved, the greater will be the cost of handling it.

The manner in which a plant is laid out has a direct relationship to labor requirements and therefore to *labor costs.*

A veneer mill and plywood plant was designed and laid out to take advantage of "cheap labor." There was a minimum of conveyors and a maximum amount of handling by the workers. The net result was excessive cost and negative profit.

Some other layout considerations are:

What is the age of the equipment?

How does the present equipment compare with the latest equipment in terms of operating costs and rate of production?

What about the state of repair of the present equipment? Is it well-kept, or does it appear that as little effort as possible is spent on maintenance?

Answers to these questions are significant in terms of their relationship to future capital requirements and efficiency of operations. Occasionally, old equipment that is well-maintained, but that has been fully depreciated, offers a cost advantage over newer, more modern equipment. It may be possible that the continued use of older equipment may produce a greater profit, but it also may not. Sometimes, it is necessary to purchase new equipment on an installment basis. However, its impact on the cash flow should be carefully analyzed.

Preparing an Economic Feasibility Study

An economic feasibility study for an on-going business is similar in nature to the economic feasibility study for a new enterprise, which was presented in Chapter 7. If you are to avoid being trapped by economic conditions that may either result in an economic disaster or stagnation, you should determine the business' feasibility. While most of this material has either been presented or will be presented in later chapters, it is summarized here. The data for the study could be gathered and analyzed under the following classifications:

1. *Population Trends of the Market.* Is the area experiencing an increase or decrease in population. Is the make up of the population stable, or is one ethnic, economic, or age group moving out and another moving in?

2. *Age Distribution of the Population.* Since there is a correlation be-

tween the demand for a firm's product or service and a particular age group, the size of that group should be identified.

3. *Income Levels and Distribution of the Population.* Sales are affected by both purchasing power and its distribution within the population. You should study the relationship between the income distribution among specific age groups and the demand for goods and services.

4. *Market Size.* From the *Journal of Marketing, Sales Management, Census Reports,* local chambers of commerce data, area planning and development commissions, local newspapers' market data and other sources, you can obtain information to help you define the size of the firm's market.

5. *Share of Market.* By estimating the size of the market, and by defining the amount of competition and its quality, you can search for areas of weakness upon which you can capitalize.

6. *Amount of Investment.* The amount of investment may be determined by seeking answers to these questions:

    What is the owner's asking price?

    Is the asking price favorable?

    What is the opinion of an appraiser specializing in this type of business?

7. *Return on Investment.* You should consider available investment opportunities to determine if the return on investment (after-tax profit divided by investment) in this particular business is adequate.

8. *Impact of Expected Changes.* Changes in the legal, physical, social, cultural, economic, and religious environments can have adverse effects on your chances of success. Some of these are:

    a. Zoning changes may have some influence if the business is retail in nature.

    Over 30 families deposited $5,000 each for new homes to be constructed. None was finished. According to town officials and engineers, the builder was incompetent and was *unable* or *unwilling to comply with the building code regulations.*

    b. Construction of traffic arteries or changes and relocations may cut businesses off from their transient traffic customers.

    Jo Anne's Dress Shop was located in a small shopping center on a highway leading out of Capital City. The street was closed for about 18 months for widening and relocation. Jo Anne's clientele, composed primarily of middle-income housewives, shifted their traffic patterns. By the time the street reopened, Jo Anne's business had declined to the point that she went bankrupt.

    c. The emphasis being placed on the environment and ecology has resulted in constraints on some businesses. You should be careful that a confrontation with the environmentalists does not occur. Changes in laws regulating pollution controls have also increased the costs of doing business.

d. Tax law changes, as well as government regulations, have an impact on the volume of paper work, as well as the time necessary to prepare the required reports.

e. Labor laws have a direct relationship to the cost of doing business. An example is the Federal Occupational Health and Safety Law (OSHA), that establishes specific safety standards. (See Chapter 20 for details).

f. Technological changes may adversely affect you. Innovations in the local newspaper equipment field, such as new and cheaper offset systems, and computers aiding in the composition of the paper, have caused many publishers to abandon their existing equipment.

IMPLEMENTING YOUR PLANS

If you have decided to buy the business, you are ready to activate "operation acquisition." Figure 8–2 indicates the sequence of steps that you will probably follow in the procedure of moving from the decision to purchase the old business to the point of taking over and running the business' operation. The rooms may be considered as the places that the important designated activities will take place. The sequence of rooms is intended to impress upon you the importance of following the appropriate sequence of activities.

Financing the Business

You are now ready to develop a plan for financing the business. As indicated earlier, financing an existing business will depend to a significant extent on the terms asked by the seller.

Considering Changes in Method of Operations

As a result of the operational analysis suggested earlier in this chapter, you should have developed some ideas concerning the proposed changes you would like to make in the business' existing method of operations.

Developing a Formal Plan

You should now prepare a formal plan of *change* to be integrated with a formal plan of *action*. You may wish to call this a Manual of Operating Procedures.

FIGURE 8–2
Points of Decisions

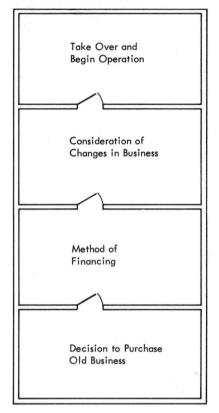

Taking Over the Business

It is now time to start operations. If you have followed the procedures outlined above, the probabilities of your succeeding in your new business will be greatly increased. Yet, you should be prepared for unforeseen contingencies and be ready to move promptly on any difficulties that may arise.

SUMMARY

Well! You are now committed to being a small business manager.

You have: (1) found a business you like; (2) determined that the reasons why the present owner wishes to sell are valid; (3) analyzed the accounting information and found it acceptable; (4) determined the accuracy of financial statements; (5) appraised the operations, plant, and equipment; (6) studied the economic feasibility, and found the firm to be needed and potentially profitable; (7) decided to buy it; (8) found, and arranged for, financing it; (9) decided on changes you would like to make in the firm's operations; (10) developed a formal plan for acquiring and running the firm; and (11) "taken over the reins" of your firm.

Now, you must manage it. How you can successfully do that is the main thrust of the next part.

QUESTIONS FOR FURTHER DISCUSSION

1. Discuss some of the reasons why a business may be available. How could you tell if they are valid?
2. What are the *current ratio* and *quick ratio?*
3. What is meant by the *validity* of financial statements? How can you determine their validity?
4. Discuss *cash flow analysis.*
5. Discuss the problem of the amount of waste in considering plant efficiency.
6. Considering plant efficiency, what factors should be considered in studying a firm's lay-out?
7. Briefly discuss what areas should be considered in an economic feasibility study.
8. If you decide to buy a business, how do you go about implementing your plans?

WHERE TO LOOK FOR FURTHER INFORMATION

Barker, Phyllis A. *Budgeting in a Small Service Firm.* Washington, D.C.: Small Business Administration, 1971. (Small Marketers Aids, No. 146)

Blicksilver, Harold. "Organizational and Financial Planning for New Business Ventures." *The Vital Majority.* Washington, D.C.: Small Business Administration, 1973, pp. 274–75.

Bunn, Verne A. *Buying and Selling a Small Business.* Washington, D.C.: Small Business Administration, 1969, pp. 3–119. (If you are serious about buying an existing business, this is *must* reading!)

Cornwell, Arthur W. *Sales Potential and Market Share.* Washington, D.C.: Small Business Administration, 1972. (Small Marketers Aids, No. 112)

Denton, Charley M. *Franchising in the Economy, 1971–1973.* Washington, D.C.: U.S. Department of Commerce, 1973, pp. 7–16.

Kudrle, Albert E. *Motels.* Washington, D.C.: Small Business Administration, 1970, pp. 4–6. (Small Business Bibliography, No. 66)

Rosenblatt, Samuel M. *Franchising in the Economy, 1972–1974.* Washington, D.C.: U.S. Department of Commerce, 1974, pp. 1–15; 41–42.

Cases for Part II

II–1. Tanner's Grocery Store (B)[1]

Mr. William Tanner decided to buy Greenwaite's Grocery Store, and the partners agreed to sell it to him. Tanner applied for a loan to the Small Business Development Corporation, a wholly owned subsidiary of a national bank which had several branches in Star City. The Corporation was formed specifically to make relatively high risk minority small business loans, provide loan capital primarily to minority group members with "good character" but no cash to facilitate house purchasing, and to grant property improvement loans on an extended term basis to what might ordinarily be termed "marginal applicants." The officers of the Corporation were also officers of the bank, and loan officers were ordinarily "officers in training." The loan officers were relatively new bank officer trainees, who served temporarily in the corporation as a part of their initial officer training.

---

[1] Written by Rudolph L. Kagerer and James F. Russell, University of Georgia. See "Tanner's Grocery Store (A)" in Part I for previous details.

113

When an applicant applies for a loan there are five major steps that are taken in the initial processing. The individual character of the applicant is evaluated by means of a careful check with credit and character references and a personal, in-depth interview. The applicant is asked to prepare a personal financial statement, and is given assistance if he is unable to do so. He is asked to make projections, both personal and business, to detail somewhat his personal and business goals so that his financial management capability and grasp of reality can be assessed. The ability of the applicant to conduct the business he has in mind, and his experience and ideas about the business are evaluated. Finally, assistance is given in an attempt to determine the real value of the business the applicant intends to initiate or assume.

If a loan is granted, a follow-up team consisting of one officer of the corporation and one management associate (ordinarily a bank officer trainee) works with the account, requiring a monthly profit and loss statement and annual balance sheet and giving financial guidance to the borrower.

During this period, there was considerable federal, state, and local pressure to place minorities into business. The Corporation, which had been in business for three years, had granted several such loans. In fact, the president of the bank, who was extremely public minded, had stated that "the greatest untapped resource of the state is in the black race." As a result, the Corporation aggressively sought such loans, and was quite anxious for Tanner to negotiate a loan for assumption of a business which seemed to be successful.

In Tanner's case, Mr. Bowden, the loan officer, reported a book value of assets in excess of $30,000, including accounts receivable, inventory, equipment, and good will. Greenwaite's unaudited profit and loss statements had shown a steady profit for the past year. Inventory was estimated by adding up shelf price for all items in the store, and subtracting 25 percent of the shelf price, since Greenwaite had marked up his items 25 to 30 percent. The equipment was priced at replacement value, even though some of the equipment had outlived its depreciation value. Tanner was granted a loan in the amount of $30,000, with which he paid $28,000 to Greenwaite. He retained $2,000, and added $1,000 from his savings to serve as liquid capital.

QUESTIONS FOR DISCUSSION

1. What does the case show about entering an existing business?
2. What does it show about the sources of credit?
3. Discuss the basis used by the Corporation to evaluate an applicant's credit worthiness.
4. Discuss the method used in evaluating the assets of the store.

II-2. University Cinemas (A)[1]

Mr. Gary Benjamin, 48, managed the University Cinema for CTW, Inc., a chain owning about 50 theaters in the Midwest. Some like University Cinema were located in small university towns; others were located in metropolitan areas. CTW had been experiencing severe cash-flow difficulties, and by early 1972 management had decided to sell some of the less profitable theaters. The managers of the theaters to be sold were offered the first opportunity to buy. Since the University Cinema had not been profitable, CTW notified Mr. Benjamin that the theater would be sold, and offered him the opportunity to buy. The asking price for University Cinema was $20,000 for the equipment and $130,000 for the building.

Mr. Benjamin was most anxious to buy the operation. He was convinced that it had the potential to be highly profitable, and that the poor results in the past were due to CTW's tendency to ignore differences in local markets and to the parent firm's poor reputation among film distributors. The distributors were reluctant to release any but the cheapest films to CTW because the firm was consistently late in remitting rental fees for the films. Mr. Benjamin was positive that he could make University Cinema profitable by correcting these problems and by making the building more attractive and comfortable.

Mr. Benjamin did not have the personal wealth to finance the purchase. He had to find one or more partners. Roman Johns expressed an interest. Mr. Johns, 28, was employed as manager of a successful men's clothing store. However, he had previous experience in theater, and Mr. Benjamin fully respected his ability. Unfortunately, he, too, was short of cash. Both Benjamin and Johns were friends of John D. Lundgren. Mr. Lundgren, 38, was a successful local businessman, and was seeking investment opportunities. His knowledge and respect for both Gary Benjamin and Roman Johns convinced him that backing the theater operation would be a sound investment. He agreed to put up $20,000 cash and assume personal liability for the $120,000 mortgage. The remaining $10,000 was contributed by Johns and Benjamin in equal shares. The deal was closed in August of the same year. The company

[1] Prepared by Peter R. Kensicki, Cincinnati Financial Corporation, and John Hand, Auburn University.

115

had some second thoughts when these eager buyers appeared in New York, but no major difficulties arose.

With CTW out of the way, the next problem was to establish the structure of ownership. The original proposal was to set up two corporations: Lafayette Corp. would hold the real estate and University Cinemas, Inc. would operate the theater. Initially, Lundgren would own two thirds of Lafayette and the other two men one sixth each; in five years Benjamin and Johns could increase their shares to 20 percent. Lundgren was to own 20 percent of University Cinemas while Benjamin and Johns held 40 percent each.

All three men had misgivings about the structure of ownership. While each was enthusiastic about the prospects of success, each had different objectives and thus preferred a different arrangement. Lundgren's sole interest was in the building. He had little interest in the theater business, and had no time to participate in the management even if he wanted to. Johns wanted to run a movie house; he did not want to be bothered with managing a piece of real estate. All he wanted was a lease so that someone else would pay the taxes and fix the roof. Benjamin also wanted to concentrate on the theater's operation, but he also wanted to own part of the building. His reasons were not clear to the others; perhaps after so many years of taking orders from a distant and unimaginative boss he needed assurance that at last it was really his. These differences were entirely friendly, but they obviously had to be settled before operations could proceed.

QUESTIONS FOR DISCUSSION

1. What are the definitions of the legal types of organizations?
2. What are the advantages and disadvantages of each type of organization?
3. What are the variations of the partnership form of organization?
4. What does each of the following really want: (*a*) Roman Johns? (*b*) Gary Benjamin? (*c*) John D. Lundgren?
5. What unique talents does each of them bring into the proposed business?
6. What are the advantages and disadvantages of the structure proposed by the management consultant?
7. Would you suggest a separate corporation to manage the building and another one to manage the theater operations? Who should own each of them?

II–3. Kiddies' Kare Korners, Inc.[1]

On April 30, 1969, Professor J. J. Brittain was wondering how to respond to new developments in a consulting assignment he had been offered. The problem had begun unfolding on April 13th when he had received a blind telephone call asking him to make a trip to Capitol City "as soon as possible" to discuss the analysis of site locations for a new type of franchise business.

The following Monday his flight was met by a driver and he was taken to the offices of the parent firm—a "fast-foods" franchising company which he learned was soon to open a new campaign. There, Joe Root, the executive vice-president, explained to Professor Brittain that the new endeavor—day-care centers for the children of working mothers—gave every appearance, on the basis of preliminary studies, of being profitable as well as a socially-useful enterprise.

He went on to diagram the financial profile of the typical franchiser whose high initial income from the sale of locations would taper off severely before the dollar level would be sustained by the percentage share of operating revenues flowing in from the franchises. For this reason, Root pointed out, he felt that it was exceedingly important that the new division identify and retain some choice locations for its own account, relying on them to provide from the early stages a source of significant amounts of revenue and, thus, sustained growth.

With this background, Professor Brittain was taken to the nearby residence which had been converted into the working headquarters for the handful of people assigned to the day-care center project. The intensive discussion which ensued quickly made it apparent that substantial thought had been put into the physical design, operating requirements, and even the fiscal character of the proposed centers. What was missing, according to the team of three handling the sales and promotional aspects, was any reliable insight into the market potential for the centers.

Because of their inexperience—one had been a Bible salesman and the other two were former IBM representatives—and their conviction

---

[1] Prepared by John Clair Thompson, University of Connecticut.

that solid information was the key for sound decisions, they had called in a firm of market researchers from Chicago. In the two weeks it had taken the firm to submit its work proposal, the trio from management had gone ahead on its own. With the deadline inching ever closer, the three found that the consultant firm presented not one new idea. At that point it had been determined that Professor Brittain should be called in.

Further exploration of the problem indicated that the usual practice in the sale of franchises—due to begin for the day-care centers on May 15—was to sell exclusive rights which covered a given area to one franchisee. Management believed in this instance that it was crucial to be able to demonstrate to bidders that a given area would support a specified number of centers. Thus, it was planned to go beyond designating an exclusive area and place maximum and minimum levels on development, perhaps even reserving for the franchiser the right to add new centers after an agreed waiting period.

Although members of management had visited existing centers in Capitol City, Atlanta, and Dallas, they had not been able to discover any pattern of analysis which explained the success or lack of it in the individually-operated locations. Providing Professor Brittain with all of the materials which had been prepared in the six months of existence of the project, the team leader drove him to the airport. It was decided that Brittain would study the data and analyses and telephone within two days to indicate whether or not he could complete work before May 15th which could be of use to the firm.

On Wednesday, Professor Brittain did call to outline the work he deemed necessary to put workable "handles" on the question of "density"—the number of day-care centers each of the major metropolitan areas of the country would accommodate. An exchange of letters detailing the specifics of the plan followed and on the 29th, a Tuesday, Brittain was commissioned to proceed with a study requiring the equivalent of 22 days of consulting which would result in usable criteria for determining the number of centers to be allocated to each area.

The next day, Wednesday, the 30th, Professor Brittain's work on other matters was interrupted by a call from Joe Root asking him to postpone beginning his analysis in order to permit the firm to reconsider its approach. Management had, after some discussion, come to the view that what it really needed to know was where the centers should be located; the question of "density" had been appraised as much less important than first believed and Root and the others were rethinking the need for study of the matter.

After completing the call, Professor Brittain pondered what he should do, if anything, in the circumstances.

QUESTIONS FOR DISCUSSION

1. What should Professor Brittain recommend to the management for inclusion in a set of measures able to reveal the marketing "density" for a given metropolitan area?
2. Drawing as necessary on the general marketing and planning analysis, what information should be utilized in locating the actual centers?
3. How do you evaluate the overall corporate planning which had been devoted to this diversification to date?

II–4. Ruth's Dashiki (A)[1]

Bill was a finance major at a large university located in a major Northeastern city. He was registered for Finance 559, an independent study course in which each student was given the assignment of studying a small business firm and recommending courses of action the firm should take. The course was a cooperative effort between a professor at the university and the Small Business Administration. The SBA identified those firms needing ass:stance, and the faculty member assigned, guided, and evaluated the student "consultant."

After being told what was expected of him in terms of a final report, Bill had been assigned to Ruth's Dashiki. From the meager information he had been given, he learned that Ruth's Dashiki was a small firm owned and operated by a black woman who specialized in designing and making Afro-American clothing.

He found Ruth's Dashiki in a small somewhat run-down business district in the south side of town. The store was located next to a rather run-down pawn shop. Small display windows on either side of the door contained several brightly patterned garments.

The business had grown out of Ruth's sewing hobby. She had always made most of her family's clothing, and relatives frequently asked her to sew something for them. She possessed an obvious talent for selecting fabrics and designing garments and, through family and friends, developed a reputation as a skilled seamstress.

---

[1] Prepared by Donald DeSalvia and Allan Young, Syracuse University.

Although friends frequently suggested she go into business, Ruth never took the suggestions seriously. After all, working full time at General Electric left her little time for sewing. Also all of her work was hand sewn since she didn't own a sewing machine.

After she accepted the offer of the deacon of her church group to pay her to make several choir and ministerial robes, she began to take the prospect of forming a business more seriously. She purchased some equipment and material, and took orders from people referred to her by friends and relatives. She operated on a part-time basis.

She felt the business could be expanded sufficiently to warrant her full-time attention, and left General Electric. At the same time, she applied for a Small Business Administration loan. After an investigation, the loan was approved, and an initial installment of $2,000 was granted in April, 1971. A major portion of this installment was used to cover the debts she had contracted in setting up and running her business to that time.

A new storefront location was found with a rental of $125.00 per month. It required extensive renovation, however, and new display cases, racks, and counters had to be installed. The relocation and delays in completing renovations cost the firm several months' output and absorbed a good share of a second $7,000 installment of the SBA loan.

A seamstress was hired at $1.85 per hour, one-half of which would be paid for fifteen weeks by the New York State Department of Labor under an On-The-Job-Training Contract. Ruth believed the contract could be extended to cover as many additional employees as needed.

Bill was impressed with the product line and the quality of craftsmanship embodied in the finished garments. The Dashiki was the primary item in the line. A Dashiki is a loose-fitting type of shirt made in a variety of styles and patterned fabrics. Although a small inventory of finished garments was available, most items still were made to order. Their retail price varied from $17.00 to $20.00, depending upon the fabric and the amount of decoration on the garment. Vests sold from $12.00 to $15.00, and floor-length women's robes varied from $30.00 to $35.00. Ruth also carried some purchased accessories and jewelry. In the past, choir and ministerial robes also had been made. There had been no orders for them in several months.

Sales at the moment were entirely dependent upon word-of-mouth advertising. The firm was located in a low income area with a high proportion of welfare families and with little consumer traffic in the area.

Bill could find no direct competitors, but wondered if a sufficient market could be developed for the product. He knew that not everyone would be interested in this type of garment. There were about 200,000 residents in the city with approximately 250,000 in the surrounding area.

The minority segment amounted to about 30,000 and the university community about 20,000. He thought the paramount problem was bringing potential customers into contact with the product.

As shown in Exhibit IV–1, the store consisted of a showroom/salesroom

EXHIBIT IV–1
Ruth's Dashiki Layout

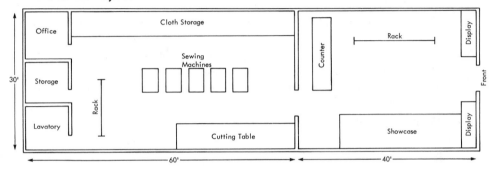

in which the items were displayed and a back room in which they were produced. Equipment used in making the garments consisted of five sewing machines, a hand iron, an ironing board, a cutting table, a clothes rack, one electric scissors, seven manikins, several pairs of scissors, and sales display and office equipment.

The production process was fairly simple. One person did all the operations needed in making a garment. These included cutting, sewing, and pressing. There was sufficient work space and equipment to greatly expand output. An item was seldom completed without frequent interruptions, making it difficult for Bill to ascertain how long it took to make each item. He estimated the average Dashiki could be made in three or three and one-half hours. Vests took four to five hours and robes took about five hours. A Dashiki required one and one-fourth yards of material as compared with three and six yards for vests and robes respectively. Ruth purchased fabrics from the Fabric Center at prices which varied from $2.00 to $3.00 per yard.

Bill also was concerned with the management of the firm. Ruth, although personable and talented, had no business background. Activities were performed haphazardly and few records were kept. Friends and relatives frequently spent hours visiting the store. During these visits, little work was accomplished. Ruth occasionally hired people for one or two days to "straighten up a bit." When asked about this practice, Ruth explained that those employed were relatives who were out of work and "hard up" and she had to help them if she could.

QUESTIONS FOR DISCUSSION

1. What do you consider to be Ruth's objectives? Are there indications that she is following these objectives? Not following them?
2. What kind of planning has she done? What should she do? (Remember that this is a very small business.)
3. What problems will she most likely face? How would you advise her to cope with them?
4. Does the store location appear to be good? What advice do you have for this?
5. Does a reasonable sales volume appear to be possible?
6. How should the product be distributed and promoted?
7. Which activities should Ruth devote herself to and which activities should she delegate?
8. What information should Ruth have to run the business?

II–5. *Ski Lodges and Second Houses*[1]

Pete had been feeling restless and uneasy about his job and his career for about six months or so. As he looks back on it, this restlessness was probably a normal period in the career of a young executive. An MBA, working for the same company for the 3½ years since graduation, Pete was advancing at the normal pace—and that was the problem. He and several friends at the company discussed their futures frequently. "The glamour of working for a large, manufacturing organization had worn off," Pete recalls. "We all had been doing the same thing for about three or four years and couldn't look forward to any significant promotion or change for another three to five years."

A few of the fellows, including Pete, began looking around for other jobs. Fortunately, the job market was good and some promising positions turned up. Pete had two offers from smaller firms which he considered to be a definite step up. Another idea, however, also fascinated him. He had been following the progress of a ski slope that was being built

---

[1] Prepared by Curtis E. Tate, Jr., and Robert Gatewood, University of Georgia, Athens, Georgia.

in the northern part of the state, where his family had long resided. It was now completed and doing a brisk business. This facility coupled with the natural recreation spots of the land (lakes, rivers, and mountains) made a highly desirable year-round family vacation area. Pete's family owned a large tract of land near the ski area and he felt sure it could be developed profitably.

After much internal debate, Pete decided to try his luck with land development, reasoning that if he couldn't get anything going successfully within three years, he would still be young enough to easily find another job in an industrial organization.

From his MBA program, Pete knew all the standard ways of obtaining financial support for business endeavors. Unfortunately, they all involved selling stocks, bonds, property, and so forth, or using them as collateral for loans. Pete had no such holdings. As a matter of fact, he had only enough to sustain himself for a few months while he got started on his ideas. His first action, therefore, was to find himself a job helping to run a lodge and restaurant in the area. He also immediately enrolled in a real estate course being offered locally. Pete reasoned that the best way to gain information about land development and its financing was to gain entrance into the group most likely to be working with such matters.

Within a few months, Pete had completed the course and had passed the state examination "with flying colors." He had also, by this time, re-established some contacts in the area and succeeded in obtaining a position with a real estate firm in his town. He then quit his job at the lodge and was able to devote full time to learning about land transaction and development. Various ideas filtered through his mind during this time, but nothing seemed to be that "right" idea.

Finally, it occurred to him that the best way to capitalize on the recreation value of the area was not to build another amusement facility, but rather to provide the housing that families need in such an area. Consequently, he studied his family's tract of land carefully. It was near enough to the ski facility to provide lodging for the skiers. That seemed like a good idea, but the tract was also large enough to serve other purposes. The best idea seemed to be to divide it up and sell off lots to individuals as sites for second homes. So Pete, with his parents' permission and cooperation, set about creating this dual purpose for the land.

Arranging for the distribution and sale of the second home sites was no problem at all; Pete did that himself. The development of the lodging facilities for skiers was quite a bit more difficult, because it required a good deal of financial support.

Pete determined that he could comfortably build 10 chalet type individual units, a trout lake that might be used for ice skating in the winter, a small swimming pool, and picnic areas on the 85 acres allotted for this facility.

Of the 10 chalets, three were to be four-bedroom; three, three-bedroom; two, two-bedroom; and two, one-bedroom. All had kitchen and dining facilities. When he questioned contractors in the area about the cost of building such a development, Pete soon learned he was into a high-cost project—about $125,000. Unfortunately, he was no better off financially than he was a few months before when he started this endeavor.

Pete then started around to the various lending institutions for funds. His first stop was a savings and loan association. This institution was very interested in some tangible demonstration of business success or something of marketable value before it would contribute to the project. Needless to say, Pete was forced to look elsewhere. "Who else," he wondered, "would be able to lend large sums?" He answered his own question by looking at his monthly paycheck stub. Why not try the federal government? It certainly had a lot of the money he and his friends earned. Pete's next visit, then, was to the Small Business Administration. They were quite interested in the idea, but Pete decided that their interest rate and repayment schedules were prohibitive.

Pete then went to more obscure agencies, i.e., the Federal Land Bank and the Production Credit Association. Both were able to lend money under a farm recreation provision in their charters and were quite interested in the project. From the former, Pete borrowed $40,000 for 30 years and from the latter $72,000 for 10 years. Both loans were on a floating interest basis tied to the prime lending rate. The combined amount of $112,000 was a little short of his needed amount, but certainly enough to get started. On further discussion with the contractor, the building cost went up even higher because Pete decided to build very high quality units both to ensure their longevity and also to make them easier to sell individually if renting did not succeed. He made up the difference by raising an additional $20,000 at 8¼ percent for 20 years from the savings and loan he originally talked with and by deciding to do most of the landscaping work himself. With this amount of capital amassed, the construction proceeded quickly and the project was completed within 10 months.

Pete figured that to meet loan payments and operating expenses, the project would have to generate $28,000 income yearly. He then did a survey of the nearby motels and hotels to aid him in setting rates for the chalets. From this survey, he decided upon $150 per week for the four-bedroom units, $125 for the three-bedroom, $115 for the two-bedrooms, and $100 for the one-bedrooms. If the units averaged 35–40 percent capacity throughout the year, this would generate $21–24,000 income. The difference Pete felt could be made up from the sale of the lots for second homes. Advertisement for the operation was handled through brochures, signs, and mass media in towns within a 125 mile radius.

Once the venture had been set up, Pete turned his attention to another matter. During the construction of his chalets, Pete became more enamoured with the second-home market. The problem was he didn't have any more land and definitely not any more money. He did, however, know of some land that would suit his purposes nicely. His solution to the dilemma was straight-forward. Simply take in partners who would purchase the land in return for 60 percent of the profit on the houses and the return of their costs. The reliable savings and loan was quite willing to finance the construction of individual houses to be sold on the open market, so the cost of construction was financed and begun. Pete thus found himself in the land development profession in a short time. Now came the long part—waiting to see if he would be successful.

QUESTIONS FOR DISCUSSION

1. In looking at Pete, what personal attributes seem evident that would cause him to leave the security of corporate employment to assume the risk and insecurity of a new venture?
2. Do the facts seem to indicate that we can label an individual as being an entrepreneurial type, i.e., possessing identifiable personal characteristics that enable the individual to assume the role of business ownership?
3. Evaluate the methods used by Pete in planning and implementing the new business. If you were carrying out an undertaking of this kind, how would you proceed?
4. Would you have attempted to obtain contractual commitments from prospective lessees or purchasers prior to launching these ventures? Explain.
5. What type of presentation would you have prepared to present to the prospective customers?
6. Do you consider Pete assumed too much risk in establishing the business? Please discuss.

II–6. *Aluminum Products Company of America*[1]

On May 12, 1970 Mr. Robert Green, a loan officer at Community State Bank, received a detailed report concerning the formation of a business

---

[1] Prepared by Wayne E. Etter, Texas A&M University.

enterprise to manufacture and distribute aluminum steps for mobile homes. The report, prepared by Mr. Joseph Belson, a graduate engineer, was submitted in support of his request for $429,000 to finance the formation and initial operation of the company. It contained information about the market for these steps, budgets, and pro-forma financial statements. Mr. Green was to analyze this information during the next week so that he could advise Mr. Belson on the prospects of financing the formation of a company to manufacture and sell these steps.

ALUMINUM PRODUCTS COMPANY OF AMERICA: A PROPOSAL FOR FORMATION OF THE COMPANY

Need for the Product

Manufacturers presently do not deliver a set of steps to the purchaser of a new mobile home, because different size steps are required for different sites. Consequently, inexpensive wooden steps for temporary use are usually provided by the dealer when a mobile home is sold.

Mobile home owners generally purchase better steps because the wooden ones soon become unattractive due to warping, splintering, cracking, etc. Improved steps are principally of three types: concrete, iron rod, and aluminum. Concrete steps are heavy and difficult to transport; they are also breakable. Iron rod steps corrode easily and require upkeep; if they are welded together they are bulky, and if they are bolted together they tend to be unstable. Aluminum steps are light in weight, but the types currently being sold are not entirely satisfactory; some models are available only in three step heights.

The most undesirable features of present steps are that they have a rigid, solid base and are not adjustable. This means that if the buyer wishes to add a porch later he must discard his present steps; or, if the mobile home is moved to a new location, the steps may be unsatisfactory for the new site.

Consequently, there exists a need for the product proposed in this report—an improved mobile home step—one that is rugged and durable, light in weight, and adjustable for different locations. These new steps were shown to several dealers, park managers, and mobile home owners. All those interviewed indicated they preferred the adjustable aluminum steps to conventional types.

Market Analysis

Four channels of distribution exist for these steps: (1) manufacturers of mobile homes; (2) mobile home dealers; (3) mobile home parks; (4) hardware stores, discount stores, and department stores. Through these channels, the immense market for these steps can be reached. Since World War II, over 3,000,000 mobile homes have been sold. During 1970, about 400,000 units were sold in the U.S.; projected sales for 1971 are 450,000 units and, by 1974, annual sales should reach 665,000 units.

If steps are sold directly to the manufacturers of mobile homes, an aggressive marketing program will be required. The goal is to penetrate 5 percent of this market in 1971, 10 percent in 1972, 20 percent in 1973, and 25 percent in 1974. The balance of the market consists of those mobile homes in existence (in 1970, about 2,387,770 units) plus those which will be produced in the future and sold without satisfactory steps.

Operating Analysis

Based on a wholesale selling price of $29.85 per set, a pro-forma income statement has been developed and is attached. It is apparent from this pro-forma income statement that the firm will be profitable in the first year and that profits will increase rapidly in the ensuing years. To increase the conservatism of this statement, the value of gross sales has been reduced by 15 percent, whereas costs have been entered at 100 percent of their estimated value. Manufacturing, selling, advertising, and administrative costs have also been estimated and are attached.

From the sales forecasts, asset needs have been projected. The needs for the first year will be substantial—about $429,000—and these will rapidly increase. Because of the relatively simple manufacturing process, fixed asset needs will be small.

Manufacturing processes are limited to cutting, notching, bending, and welding extruded aluminum. Furthermore, highly-skilled labor is not required; it will be possible to hire low-skill workers and train them in a period of not more than two to three weeks.

Pro Forma Income Statement

	1971	1972	1973	1974
Gross Sales*	$1,384,323	$2,550,921	$4,789,432	$6,657,326
Less 15%	207,648	382,638	718,415	998,599
Net Sales	$1,176,675	$2,168,283	$4,071,017	$5,658,727
Less				
Manufacturing Expenses . . .	643,885	1,184,793	2,224,347	3,192,143
Sales Expense	215,800	234,500	254,150	271,765
Advertising Expense	139,200	120,500	100,450	83,235
Administrative Expense . . .	100,000	120,000	160,000	180,000
Total Expense	($1,098,885)	($1,659,793)	($2,738,947)	($3,727,143)
Net Income before Tax	$ 77,790	$ 508,490	$1,332,070	$1,931,584
Federal Income Tax	(30,840)	(237,575)	(632,894)	(920,660)
Net Income after Tax	$ 46,950	$ 270,915	$ 699,176	$1,010,924

* Selling price is $29.85 per set.

Projected First-Year Sales

Month	Value of Net Sales* Shipped
1	$ 0
2	19,746
3	69,112
4	88,858
5	108,605
6	118,478
7	118,478
8	128,351
9	128,351
10	128,351
11	134,172
12	134,173

* Net Sales = 85% of Gross Sales.

Cost of Goods Manufactured Budget

	1971	1972	1973	1974
Cost of Materials*.	$500,860	$ 922,946	$1,732,860	$2,408,681
Cost of Packaging†	57,970	106,822	200,562	278,782
Factory Rent and Welding Materials . .	35,355	68,762	131,959	292,144
Direct Labor‡	49,700	86,263	158,966	212,536
Total	$643,885	$1,184,793	$2,224,347	$3,192,143

* $10.80 per unit.
† $1.25 per unit.
‡ Includes Supervisory personnel: 1971, $8,000; 1972, $8,800; 1973, $9,680; 1974, $10,648.

Sales Expense Budget

	1971	1972	1973	1974
12 salesmen	$115,000	$126,500	$139,150	$153,065
12 cars at $500 a month	72,000	72,000	72,000	72,000
Other expenses	28,800	36,000	43,000	46,700
Total Sales Budget	$215,800	$234,500	$254,150	$271,765

Administrative Expense Budget

	1971	1972	1973	1974
President	$ 20,000	$ 22,000	$ 24,200	$ 26,620
Accountant	12,000	13,200	14,520	15,972
Two secretaries at $5,000 each	10,000	11,000	12,100	13,300
Bookkeeper	4,000	4,400	4,840	5,324
Sales manager	12,000	13,200	14,520	15,972
Office expense.	20,000	25,000	35,000	40,000
Automobile	5,000	7,500	10,000	12,500
Rent and other	14,000	25,700	67,820	50,312
Total	$100,000	$120,000	$160,000	$180,000

Pro Forma Statement of Assets

	1971	1972	1973	1974
Cash	$ 25,000	$ 25,000	$ 25,000	$ 25,000
Accounts Receivable*	173,040	318,865	598,679	832,166
Raw Materials Inventory	76,800	76,800	76,800	76,800
Finished Goods Inventory†	144,200	225,863	498,899	693,471
Current Assets	$419,040	$646,528	$1,199,378	$1,627,437
Fixed Assets	10,000	20,000	30,000	35,000
Total Assets	$429,040	$666,528	$1,229,378	$1,662,437

* Based on an average collection period of 45 days.
† Based on an average inventory of 125% of monthly sales.

QUESTIONS FOR DISCUSSION

1. Evaluate the market potential for the product.
2. Evaluate the channels of distribution for the product.
3. Is the real need for assets as great as shown? What action would you recommend to Mr. Belson to reduce the need for funds? Prepare a cash budget to show the minimum funds required to support your plan.
4. What are your feelings regarding Mr. Belson's plan to borrow 100 percent of the required funds?
5. What other sources of capital are available to a new business?

II–7. The A-B Clearing Corporation [1]

Utility companies have used outside organizations to clear vegetation from the right-of-ways of transmission lines. These right-of-ways may include power lines of electrical systems and pipe lines transmitting natural gas or petroleum products. The clearing operation involves the periodic cutting of vegetation to a level of six to eight inches. Successful clearing operations enable the utility companies more effectively to survey and maintain optimum functioning of the system.

Contracts are let to prime contractors who may, in turn, subcontract

---

[1] Prepared by Curtis E. Tate, Jr. and William Vroman, University of Georgia.

a portion of the work to other clearing operators. The traditional channel of acquiring clearing contract grants has been through the various district offices of the utility companies. Personal relationships between the contracting officer of the utility company and the clearing operator are significant in the allocating and awarding of specific clearing contracts, which are let on an acreage basis.

Some utility companies have relied upon the use of herbicides as a method of controlling vegetation growth along the right-of-ways. However, where geographical conditions permit, the general trend has been the use of farm type tractors and bush hogs[2] as a means for clearing vegetation growth ranging up to two inches in diameter. Natural restrictions of vegetation of more than two inches in diameter and swampy or marsh-land terrain have forced the use of hand labor, resorting to axes and chain saws to clear the land.

As the size of the clearing firm increases, the firm is confronted with certain specific problems. Among these problems are the procurement and maintenance of an effective labor force. The distribution of activities over an increasing number of geographic areas creates problems of supervision and communication. The lack of adequate communication facilities may result in equipment being out of operation for half a day to a full day. Typical problems encountered in the maintenance of equipment include a ruptured tractor tire, a tractor ceasing to function because of mechanical failure, and breaking of the housing or blades of a bush hog.

Problems of dealing with an incompetent work force are always present. Attendance to work is often sporadic and undependable. On Monday morning, it is often necessary to bail a number of the work force out of jail following a weekend "drunk." There is also difficulty in communicating with workers and getting them to follow directions. The workers often fail to use a direct access route or neglect to work an acreage as directed.

A–B Clearing Corporation began as a proprietorship and later became a partnership. Initial capital was generated by an illicit moonshine operation. The clearing activities came into existence as a result of the owner's desire to shift into a legitimate business operation. The owner entered the world of legitimate business as a subcontractor for an established clearing operator.

Early in 1971, John Bost discussed with a former professor the clearing firm which he and his father owned and operated. John enumerated many of his problems and ambitions to his former professor.

---

[2] A large rotary mowing machine towed behind and powered by the farm type tractor.

John was an only son, and joined his father in the family business. His objective was that the clearing firm grow to become the dominant operation of the industry. However, there were certain obstacles in the achievement of this objective. Existing accounting practices had failed to define the cost of implementing individual contracts. Some work was still done on a subcontract basis. The fear of incurring the ill will of the prime contractor had created restraints in attempting to obtain direct contracts in certain districts. Also, the inefficiency of the available labor, the lack of more efficient equipment (which would reduce labor requirements and could operate effectively in all terrain), and weather conditions had restricted operations.

There had been an underlying insecurity concerning John's future in the event of his father's death. His only sister lived in a distant city with her husband, who was employed by a large financial institution. At the present time, she had no personal or business affiliation with the clearing company. His father had been reluctant to make available an insurance or purchase agreement which would enable John to acquire his sister's interest in her portion of the estate.

The cash flow status had also created problems. Utility companies had frequently been slow in making payments on direct contracts. In addition, the subcontract work generated a slower cash flow because the prime contractor often used these funds to satisfy his requirements for working capital. Therefore, a major problem that existed was an inadequate capital base from which to supply working capital or the replacement and expansion of capital equipment.

The professor responded to John's interest in seeking solutions to some of the problems. He made the following recommendations:

1. That the partnership be incorporated with provisions in the articles of incorporation to satisfy the needs of any future estate problems.
2. That an effective system of accounting and control be devised which would enable the determination of cost and profit on each contract.
3. That some agreement be reached between father and son on the division of managerial responsibilities.
4. That a search be launched to locate the type equipment needed to operate effectively in the field.
5. That a visit be made to larger banks in a nearby metropolitan area in search of more satisfactory banking relationships.
6. That some thought be given to future capital requirements and how these requirements might be satisfied.
7. That consideration be given to the elimination of the subcontract phase of activities and a plan be formulated to deal with the central

office of the utility companies to expedite payments on those portions of contracts completed.

8. That an attempt be made to establish a contractual relationship that would permit by-passing district offices.

After receiving these recommendations, John began attempting implementation. The firm was incorporated, and the accounting system was refined to achieve more complete management information. Much of the remainder of the calendar year found the cash flow slow and the firm continuously strapped for funds to meet payroll and other current obligations.

John's father suffered a ruptured disc, requiring hospitalization and a spinal fusion operation. This incident increased John's workload for six months at a time when he thought managerial demands had already stretched him to the limit. At times during this period, the father-son relationship became strained. The father tended to continue to think of John as a young boy rather than as a son who had achieved maturity. In the rare moments when time permitted, John continued a search for the needed types of new equipment.

In the beginning of 1972, some changes began to evolve. After much effort, the cash-flow cycle began to change. One company began paying on a 10 day basis, another on 15 days, and the remainder moved to a 30-day payment plan. In addition, a type of equipment was located that could satisfactorily function in all kinds of weather and in all types of terrain. This equipment could substantially reduce labor requirements.[3] The major consideration was that the manufacturer's terms were F.O.B. site and cash upon receipt of the equipment.

As the fiscal year ended on April 30, 1972, John was confronted with a number of important issues. He needed to induce his father to review possible advantages of shifting from the traditional methods of operation to a more innovative procedure. He needed to determine whether to purchase the new equipment, and he had to assess the possible impact of this new equipment on labor cost and contractual relationships. He also had to prepare to meet the changes that might result from the environmentalists' demands to stop using herbicides[4] as a method of control. Means had to be found to increase the capital structure necessary to satisfy the firm's growth requirements. Another need was to eliminate dealing with the district offices and to establish a relationship with the central office, which might bring negotiated contracts and/or letters of commitment.

---

[3] The approximate cost of new equipment was $40,000 per machine. The labor saving estimate was about $300 per week.

[4] Herbicides then accounted for approximately 10 percent of vegetation growth control.

Balance Sheet
Year Ending 4/30/72

Assets

Current Assets

Cash in Bank	$15,500.83		
Accounts Receivable (Trade)	23,113.78		
Accounts Receivable (Employees)	1,869.41		
Prepaid Interest	1,728.96		
Total Current Assets			$42,212.98

Long-Term Assets

Machinery and Equipment.	$33,609.62		
Less Accumulated Depreciation.	12,689.74	$20,919.88	
Trucks, Autos, and Trailers	$26,472.39		
Less Accumulated Depreciation.	5,122.95	21,349.44	
Total Long-Term Assets			42,269.32
Total Assets			$84,482.30

Liabilities

Current Liabilities

Accounts Payable.	$ 4,638.16		
Note Payable (Farmers Bank)	8,025.00		
Note Payable (Ford Motor Credit)	16,102.90		
FICA Taxes Withheld	1,309.30		
Total Current Liabilities			$30,075.36

Long-Term Liabilities

Note Payable (Stockholders)	$24,406.94		24,406.94
Total Liabilities			$54,482.30

Owner's Equity

Common Stock	$30,000.00		$30,000.00
Total Equity and Liabilities			$84,482.30

Income Statement
Year Ending 4/30/72

Gross Income		$250,588.40

Operating Expenses

Salaries and Wages	$ 97,734.33	
Repairs.	22,424.67	
Gas and Oil	15,203.46	
Insurance	6,262.37	
Utilities	480.64	
Supplies	16,460.63	
Sub-Contracts (Labor)	1,495.30	
Travel	1,204.34	
Payments.	19,409.34	
Taxes—Unemployment.	1,903.93	
Taxes—Other	109.89	
Total Operating Expenses	$182,688.90	

Administrative Expenses

Officers' Salaries	$ 29,403.50	
Telephone	1,604.80	
Office Expense	382.92	
Legal Expense.	313.53	
Total Administrative Expenses	$ 31,704.75	
Total Expenses		$214,393.65
Net Income		$ 36,194.75

QUESTIONS FOR DISCUSSION

1. After viewing the facts, do you think it wise for John to be associated with his father in a joint endeavor of this kind? Explain the basis for your answer.

2. Should you conclude that you would suggest John continue his association with his father, develop a plan of action to convince the father that changes are desirable and essential if the firm is to grow and increase its profits.

3. If you assume the role of John Bost, based on the material presented, how would you undertake to develop a master plan, including a time table of performance?

4. What strategy would you formulate to become independent of the prime contractors, i.e., to rid yourself of the role of subcontracting?

5. Do you consider the profits adequate at the present volume of revenue? Why?

II–8. Floyd Bean Bonanza Steak House (A)[1]

Bonanza International is a franchised chain of over 200 family steak restaurants with headquarters in Dallas. The concept is a limited menu of steak dinners which a family of four can eat for less than $10. Service is modified cafeteria with no tipping, and guests are invited to "come as you are."

In July, 1971, Mr. Floyd Bean signed an agreement with Bonanza International to open up the Bonanza Sirloin Pit #590, located at 1111 East Ledbetter Drive, Dallas, Texas.

MR. FLOYD BEAN

Mr. Floyd Bean is 37 years old, married, with two daughters. His health is excellent. Mr. Bean was born in Galveston, Texas, where he graduated from Central High School. He went to Southern University in Baton Rouge, Louisiana and majored in Sociology with a minor in

---

[1] Prepared by Sydney C. Reagan and Calvin W. Stephens, School of Business Administration, Southern Methodist University.

Physical Education. He graduated from Southern University in the top ten of his class after playing four years of college football.

Upon finishing college he returned to Galveston, Texas, and worked as a substitute teacher in the Galveston School System for seven months.

In 1962, he went to work for the Falstaff Brewery in Galveston, Texas, as a Field Sales Representative and Chief Tour Guide. During this time he had four men working under his supervision. His main responsibility was to book parties for the hospitality room, which was used every night. He and his men took guided groups on tours of the brewery, then to the hospitality room for a beer party.

In 1963, Floyd Bean was promoted to Branch Sales Department. He was responsible for the sales of three route men in the Galveston County area.

In 1964, Mr. Bean was promoted to a Special Division Sales Representative covering five states for Falstaff. His duties then were to assist the distributors in these five states. He called on each account in the salesmen's market with the salesmen and made recommendations to the distributor on how he could improve his sales.

In 1969 he resigned from Falstaff to take a position with Bonanza International as Director of Minority Franchising. As a part of his training, he attended the Bonanza School of Management. His duties were to find qualified minority people to go into business as owner-operators of Bonanza Steak Houses. Mr. Bean, in that capacity, temporarily took over the management of several of the Bonanza Sirloin Pits that were having problems. There he proved that he had managerial talent, and there he developed a taste for running a business of his own.

In May, 1971, Mr. Bean decided to resign his position at Bonanza International to pursue the ownership of a Bonanza franchise. He had two reasons for this move. He wanted to go into business for himself; he also felt that he would have more opportunities.

THE FRANCHISE DEVELOPMENT

Floyd Bean's ability and his desire to have a business of his own were not enough. He found that going into business takes money, and before bankers and others would lend to an entrepreneur they wanted to know that the entrepreneur or someone was going to be putting enough equity, or ownership money, into the enterprise to have something at stake—enough to make the entrepreneur work hard to make it succeed. So Floyd Bean's first problem became one of how to raise the necessary money.

Everyone who knows him well says that one quality Floyd Bean has is tenaciousness. He absolutely refuses to quit trying. And through months of negotiations and many a disappointment, even after one financing effort turned out to be all wrong, he would not give up.

"I wanted to operate my own business," Bean now says, "and I've got to admit, I got a little sore against the establishment because I thought they were playing games with me. But I told them I'm not going to quit."

Bean also found some people who could help him put his project together. Mr. Hal Gordon of the Chica Corporation of Dallas, the area distributor of Bonanza had seen an old church on Ledbetter and thought it could be rebuilt into a good Bonanza location. Mr. Gordon was able to purchase the property after seeking and obtaining a loan, and was able to offer a long-term lease to Bean. This required that a lease guarantee be built into the financing package.

The major target service area for the Bonanza Steak House is comprised of low-income, lower-middle and middle-income families. Of these families, approximately 20 percent own their homes. Total persons per occupied dwelling unit in the target service area is approximately 3.89.

The target service area is an integrated neighborhood with blacks comprising about 78 percent of the total, whites comprising 21 percent, and other ethnic groups making up the remaining one percent. (See below for additional information on the site and neighborhood.)

Site Information

1. Address: 1111 East Ledbetter, Dallas, Texas 75216

2. Location: Southwest Dallas on State Highway Loop 12, one mile east of Interstate 35.

3. Size: 87,590 square feet
   Frontage 335 feet
   Depth 300 feet

4. Building: The building to be converted to a Bonanza Steak House is an old church located on the back side of the property about 150 feet from Loop 12.

5. Access: State Highway Loop 12, known as East Ledbetter in this portion, is four lane and is the loop around Dallas. Traffic count at this location is 20,330 in a 24-hour period (1969). Traffic moves at between 40 and 50 miles per hour, with a speed limit of 45 miles per hour.

6. Major Businesses within one mile: South Park shopping center (85 acres) with all major stores
   K-Mart
   Target
   Gibson
   Jack-in-the-Box

7. Market Area: There are 3,200 homes in the immediate area, and they range in price from about $6,000 to $25,000. The residential areas just south of Loop 12 are known as Glenview with a population over 19,000 and Singing Hills with a population over 15,000. The restaurant would serve a population in a three-mile radius of over 150,000 persons.

Walter J. Sodeman, Director of Franchise Development for Bonanza, Bean's former boss, saw a lot of potential business within the black community. Sodeman cites a recent article in *Sales Management* magazine which pointed out that, while the total population of Dallas increased 25 percent from 1960 to 1970, the black population increased 63 percent; blacks went from 19 percent of the Dallas population in 1960 to 25 percent in 1970. Sodeman contends that the food service business, a service business with high profit potential and large turnover of inventory compared to other capital-intensive businesses, is a good one for black enterprisers to get into.

Also among the people who helped, was Mr. Tony F. Martinez, an Indian from Taos, New Mexico, who was the first Indian to get a Master's in Business Administration from Baylor and was senior analyst for the Dallas Alliance of Minority Enterprise (DAME). With documented experience of other restaurants, with pro-forma cash flow statements, with estimates of the cost of equipment in hand, and everything else needed to sell the project, Martinez helped Bean find the sources of funds he was looking for.

SOURCE OF FUNDS

A first $5,000 was provided by University Computing Corporation Venture Corporation, a Minority Enterprise Small Business Investment Company (MESBIC), on a five-year, 7½ percent subordinated note. Another $5,000, later increased to the needed $15,000, was similarly provided by Motor Enterprise of Detroit, a MESBIC created by General Motors to help minority enterprisers find capital. The Oak Cliff National Bank then provided $45,000 on a five-year note, with the restaurant's equipment pledged. The Small Business Administration of the federal government provided $20,000, on a five-year, 6¼ percent unsubordinated note, under the Equal Opportunity Loan Program. And finally the SBA also provided a fifteen-year lease guarantee totaling $261,000.

Thus was the package put together to cover the needed lease guarantee, organizational expenses, and working capital for Floyd Bean to get his business started.

Mr. Bean began operations on October 1, 1971.

QUESTIONS FOR DISCUSSION

1. Was Floyd Bean's decision to start a business of his own a wise decision?
2. If the answer to Question 1 is positive, did Mr. Bean select the right business to enter?
3. Was the choice of location a good one for Mr. Bean? Is this location a desirable one for this type of franchise?

4. How could Mr. Bean make his restaurant more visible to the people who pass by when driving on Ledbetter Street?
5. Evaluate the following sources of financial support for minority businesses:
    a. Banks
    b. Small Business Administration (SBA)
    c. Office of Minority Business Enterprise (OMBE)
    d. Economic Opportunity Loans (EOL)
    e. Minority Enterprise Small Business Investment Corporations (MESBIC)
    f. Insurance Companies
    g. Churches
    h. Friends and/or Mentors
6. What role should the Federal government play in the development of more viable minority businesses?
7. How can large corporations and major lending institutions help minority businesses?
8. How can universities and colleges help develop managerial and technical expertise in minority businesses?

II–9. *The Mother and Child Shop*[1]

As Mick McGregor describes it, "I've never really been the type to devote myself to just one thing for very long. Trying something new has always been fascinating for me." Maybe that's why a married man, with a first child due shortly, a full-time job, who is also working on a Ph.D., decides to fill his free moments by starting his own business.

Mick had toyed with the idea of starting a business but had never really done much about it until a friend and neighbor of his, Jack Pollach, mentioned at a Halloween party in 1967 that there was some store space available in a large shopping complex in town. Jack was developing plans for a candy store and discussed his ideas with Mick. He also mentioned that there were a few stores still to be leased.

Mick was intrigued by this idea of starting a store and encouraged by his friend's actions. He had some money set aside for investment and felt that putting this into a small business could be a profitable decision. The problem, however, was deciding what kind of store it should be. What products should be carried? The town Mick lived in

---

[1] Prepared by Professor Curtis E. Tate and Dr. Robert Gatewood, University of Georgia.

was a community of about 40,000 located about 65 miles from one large city and about 150 miles from another. Mick's reasoning was that he needed to find some store or goods that his town didn't have yet, but was ready to have. In other words, he needed something for which there was a market but for which people had to go to the larger cities to buy at the present time.

Off and on during November, Mick pondered this problem. There really wasn't a specific thing that he was interested in selling; he was just trying to maximize his chances of success by coming up with a "sure-thing" stock of merchandise. After all this effort, it was actually Mick's wife Cathy, who wasn't very interested at all in going into business at that particular time, who gave him the idea. Cathy was due to have their first child late in November. During that last week, she commented to Mick that she would certainly be happy when her pregnancy was over if for no other reason than to be able to buy clothes again.

Maternity clothes were sold only as a sideline by a few of the larger stores in town. Their selection was, at best, limited. The comment didn't register immediately with Mick, but later that evening the full impact hit him. It seemed like the very idea he had been looking for. He didn't have much time to act on the idea in the next days, however, for four days later their first child was born.

Once mother and child were home and as settled as possible, Mick began to pursue his idea vigorously. He first spent several evenings at the local library reading about manufacturers and suppliers of maternity clothing and specifically about their marketing. His main concern was deciding whether or not his town was large enough to support a maternity shop. He thought that the best way to do this was to first develop a list, from within his state and three adjacent states, of cities that were approximately the same size as his. Then he would determine how many of these had maternity clothing shops. This would give him an idea of how active the market was in similar, nearby cities and whether such a store in a city of his size was, in fact, possible. To do this Mick first went to the latest census information and listed those cities within his four-state sample that had populations between 35–45,000. To get the names of merchants in these towns, he first went to the trade journals and noted the stores in the towns on his list and the lines they carried. He also was able to find telephone books for most of the cities and determine whether any maternity clothing shops were indexed. From this he found that nearly 80 percent of the cities on his list had at least one shop like the one he was considering, and about 25 percent had two or more shops. Mick concluded that, based on these findings, his idea was at least generally sound.

He next wanted to find out some specific information about his own community in order to decide if the store was practical in his own city. He was able to find data on both the per-family income and the amount of money spent on mothers' and children's clothing each year for his area and other areas on his list. His area compared very favorably with the others on this basis. Finally, from the county planning commission, Mick obtained information on the estimated population increase over the next five and ten years and the areas of projected growth within the county. These data told him that the county would grow by 10–15 percent for the next five years and by 15–25 percent over the next ten. In addition, areas near his tentative site were projected to increase in population. From all these data, Mick was greatly encouraged. He felt that he had a sound idea that was indeed feasible based on all the marketing information he could find.

It also occurred to him during this time that a better bet might be to have a combination maternity and baby store. Women could become familiar with the store and its merchandise during their pregnancy which might influence them to come back afterward to buy clothing for their small babies. The combination seemed natural and was quickly adopted.

By mid-December of 1967, then, Mick had the idea for a combination maternity-children's store which appeared to have very little competition in town and which tentatively could be located in one of the largest and busiest shopping centers in town. That all seemed fine. The next question was, "Who's going to run this thing?" Mick wasn't confident enough in his idea to quit his job and his graduate education to go into it full-time. The logical choice, at least to him, seemed to be Cathy. Cathy, being a mother for all of two weeks, was less than wildly enthusiastic about the prospects of managing a store too. But she agreed if two conditions were met: (1) that a full-time sales clerk would be hired, and (2) that a room in the back of the store could be designed for the baby.

That problem solved, Cathy and Mick moved on to the next one— finding out something about how to run a business like this. In mid-December, while they were visiting Cathy's parents in one of the nearby large cities, they decided that the best way to find this information might be to talk with someone in the business. So they selected a maternity store that Cathy and her mother knew, and drove over to talk to the owner or manager. In retrospect Mick describes that afternoon as perhaps the most important of that time period, both informationally and psychologically. The owner and his wife were extremely helpful and encouraging, discussed many financial and managerial details, and sent Mick and Cathy on their way feeling very confident of their decision to start this business. The visit was so positive that in early January Mick and Cathy signed a three-year rental lease with the owners of the shopping complex for a 1,000 square-foot store.

Among other things that they found out from the friendly store owner was that the next buying show for the region was to be held on January 28 and 29. This was the main opportunity for comparing all the clothing lines' styles and prices for the coming spring and summer. The short time until the show was disconcerting. If they went to the show and bought merchandise, that meant they would have to open for business in a few months to sell the spring and summer clothing. If they didn't buy merchandise at this show they most likely would have to wait several months for the fall-winter show. They decided to take the risk and try to make it in time for the spring clothing.

To have a chance of meeting this deadline, Mick and Cathy decided to divide responsibilities. Cathy, because of her recent experience with maternity clothing, was in charge of selecting manufacturers' lines and styles and buying the inventory. Mick, calling on his undergraduate background of industrial engineering and his graduate training in business, took responsibility for designing and preparing the store layout and deciding on the financial and managerial aspects of the store.

Cathy suggested that the store stock high-quality, name brand merchandise. She would pick styles and particular items at the show, depending mostly on her own tastes and advice gathered from product salesmen.

Mick's immediate problem before the show was to decide how much inventory to carry initially. From his estimates of per family income and amount of money spent on mother and children's clothing, and mainly from his discussion with the store owner, Mick estimated that first year sales would be about $19,500. He also decided that he would be happy if the store broke even for the first year. So he figured total expenses should be kept to $19,500 for that year. From this figure, Mick subtracted fixed costs (personnel, rent, utilities, licenses, and estimated remodeling costs), which were about $7,500, to determine how much could be spent on inventory. This figure was $12,000. Knowing from his business courses that inventory should turn over about four times a year, it was simple to estimate an initial inventory costing about $3,000. However, after estimating the amount of merchandise he could buy for $3,000, Mick realized how little clothing that would actually be. He was concerned about the image such a sparse inventory might project. So he totaled up his projected initial expenditures to see if he could afford to start with a larger inventory. Remodeling, rent, utilities, and personnel salaries for the first two months would come to about $2500. If Mick increased his starting inventory to $4500, that would mean an initial outlay of about $7,000. This figure was within the amount of money Mick had set aside for investment, so he decided that he would take the chance and increase his inventory to $4500.

He then categorized the various items the store would be carrying into the following groups: maternity casual, maternity dresses, lingerie, and children's wear. Again going back to his previous discussion with the store owner, he decided to divide his inventory among these categories in the ratios 30 percent, 30 percent, 7 percent, and 33 percent respectively. This information on total inventory and how it should be divided among product groups was then given to Cathy who would have to work out the number of each size, etc., that should be bought. She estimated this through talks with salesmen and the store owner they had visited previously.

This task completed, Mick, from the middle of January to the middle of March, turned his attention to decorating the store. Drawing from his experience as an industrial engineer and ideas he gathered from visiting other stores, he designed the layout himself and did most of the work. Tasks such as the wiring and the counter and cabinet construction, he hired others to do but was able to specify exactly what he wished done. He was also careful not to omit the special room in the back of the store for the baby.

Everything went very smoothly at the merchandise show for the two prospective merchants. They were able to meet the salesmen they wished and purchase clothing they liked. Almost all articles were promised within six weeks.

February was spent working on the store, obtaining the necessary city and state licenses, selecting a full-time sales-woman, and becoming very nervous at the thought of actually opening the store. The person hired was an experienced sales-woman who had been recommended by a friend of Mick and Cathy.

By the beginning of March all was almost ready for an opening. The only advertising that had been done up until this time was a large paper sign across the front windows. Also, Mick belonged to several civic organizations in town and informally passed the word about the store to other members. News traveled fast in town, and quite a few people knew about the proposed opening. Mick and Cathy decided that it might be better to hold other advertising until a few weeks after the store actually opened. This would give them some time to get a feel for operating the store. So it was decided to have the grand opening in mid-April with newspaper and radio advertising to precede the opening by two weeks. The actual opening would be as soon as the store was completed and a majority of the inventory in stock. This turned out to be March 17, 1968—less than four months after Cathy's comments about the difficulty of finding maternity clothes.

QUESTIONS FOR DISCUSSION

1. How might the owners have changed their procedure in planning the business?

2. Do you think their method of researching the business was adequate? What changes would you have made?

3. Do you think adequate plans were made for determining capital requirements?

4. After some individual research on your part, would you accept their inventory allocation?

5. What weight would you give the special knowledge of the wife? the husband?

6. Do you think an adequate effort was made to determine the feasibility of the market? Give reasons for your answer.

7. What have you gained from studying this case?

8. Do you note any apparent personality characteristics that seem to indicate Mick to be the entrepreneural type?

Part **III**

Managing Your Small Business

You have now decided either to establish a new business or to enter an on-going enterprise. This business needs to be managed effectively by someone, so you must answer a most significant question, namely, "Should I be only the owner and hire someone else to manage it for me, or should I both own and manage it myself?" This decision is one of the most important you will make for your company, for wrong answers to this question account for the high rate of failures amd marginal success characteristic of many small businesses. In far too many small businesses, the man who selects the manager is not qualified to make such a judgment. Therefore, you should consider this decision carefully.

If you choose to be the manager yourself, you should be prepared to become a generalist manager and cease being a specialist in your own area of interest and competence. The generalist manager has conceptual skills which enable him to analyze the total situation, detect problems, determine causes, and bring about effective solutions.

You should not try to be the "whole show." You want to run your company, rather than let it run you. You should decide how best to guide your organization toward its predetermined objectives.

"Management is getting things done through people," said Lawrence Appley, Former President of the American Management Association. We agree with his conclusion, but there is more to managing a small business than that. As Figure III–1 shows, you must also make decisions and allocate your scarce financial, physical, and human resources so that your business will achieve its objectives. Achieving your business objectives should, in turn, help you reach your personal objectives.

145

FIGURE III–1
Definition and Functions of Management

Management is:

1. Doing through others;
2. Decision making; and
3. Allocating scarce resources; so that
4. Objectives are reached.

In order to utilize these resources effectively, you perform basic managerial functions of planning, organizing, directing, and controlling. These functions are discussed in this part; the first two in Chapters 9 and 10, and the last two in Chapter 11.

9

Planning for Your Business

Let us assume that you have chosen to manage your own business, rather than to hire a professional manager to run it for you. As the owner-manager, you must perform certain basic managerial functions effectively in order to have a profitable company. These functions are:

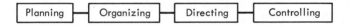

| Planning | Organizing | Directing | Controlling |

Although these managerial functions are shown separately and in sequence, that is not true in the real world of small business; you often perform them together or at the same time. However, for practical purposes, we discuss them separately and in the order shown. The planning function is covered in this chapter and the others are explained in Chapters 10 and 11.

NEED FOR PLANNING

Small business managers need to plan as thoroughly—if not more thoroughly—than managers of larger companies. The reasons are that most small firms:

1. Do not have sufficient resources to overcome their future problems.
2. Cannot afford to underwrite losses that can occur while adjusting to unexpected changes.

You should recognize that changing circumstances will probably affect your plans. A means should be provided for modifying your company's objectives to meet such changes. Activities that are profitable today may not be so in the future.

Your company is especially vulnerable to bold moves by competitors. Besides managing your company well internally, you should keep yourself informed about your competitors and be able to predict closely what they will do.

THE PLANNING FUNCTION AND TYPES OF PLANS

An explanation of the planning function and the types of plans that you as a small business manager will probably have to make are shown in Figure 9–1.

MANAGEMENT BY OBJECTIVES

To be most effective, you should probably practice Management by Objectives (MBO) in your firm. If you do, the first step you should take is to set overall objectives for the firm. These objectives should be specific and understandable; quantifiable in order that progress can be measured; and realistic, meaning that they are attainable—with difficulty.

An objective of "increasing sales" should not be set, because it is not clear what is meant. Instead, an objective should be set, say, "to increase sales by a minimum of five percent and a maximum of 15 percent over the next fiscal year at prices which will provide a gross profit of 35 percent."

Desirable objectives to be accomplished should probably involve profitability, competitive position, productivity, and employee relations, and be stated specifically, as *how much* profit, *what percent* of the market, *how much* cost of production, and *how much* labor turnover.

All of your subordinates should be asked to set objectives for themselves, their people, their material, and so forth. You should meet with each of them to agree jointly on those objectives, how they can be accomplished, and how they relate to achieving the overall company objectives. You should review everyone's objectives with them and make suggestions for how those objectives can be achieved.

Each subordinate should be provided a continual feedback of the results being attained, and these should be reviewed against the objectives. You should help each person overcome obstacles that stand in the way of reaching the objectives.

Near the end of the period, each subordinate should prepare a brief statement concerning how the performance compares to the objectives.

FIGURE 9–1
Planning Function and Types of Plans

Planning Functions	*Examples*
Planning Selection from among alternatives of future courses of action for the firm as a whole and for each department.	
Objectives Purposes, goals, results of the firm and its parts.	*Company Objectives*—Overall objective is to perform useful service for society. *Product Line*—Manufactures and distributes high-quality, custom-made, special living room and dining room furniture. *Scope of Market*—Markets its furniture in the states of Georgia, Florida, Alabama, and Louisiana. *Personal Objectives*—Statement of the type of life you wish to lead.
Strategies Major objectives or goals defining what business the company is in and the kind of company it is; plans for achieving these goals.	
Policies Overall guides to action which provide some consistency in decision making, particularly in repetitive situations.	*Personnel Policy*—Promoting from within, whereby preference for promotions is given to present employees.
Standards Values to be used as norms; these are necessary for control, because they assist in measurement.	*Specifications*—Machines and materials should be arranged in order and close together in order to produce economically and effectively.
Budgets Plans of income or outgo, or both; including money, sales items, purchased items, etc.	*Sales budgets, cash budgets, pro-forma income statements* and *balance sheets.*
Procedure Series of related tasks to be performed in a given sequence, using an established method of performing the work. A procedure includes how and when each task is to take place, and by whom it is to be performed.	*Selection Procedure*—Used in selecting employees with the proper qualifications and placing them in positions in the firm where their talents can best be used.
Method Prescribed manner for performing a given task. A method deals with a task comprising one step of a procedure, and specifies how this one step is to be performed.	*Task*—Performed by a production employee in the machining department.
Program Comprehensive plan which includes objectives, standards, budgets, policies, procedures, and methods. A given program may not necessarily include all of these components.	*Production Program*—Which designates the materials, processes to be followed, machines to be utilized, production schedules to be met, and warehouses to which shipments are made.

Each subordinate's report should be reviewed in detail and then discussed.

An agreement should be reached with each subordinate on how good performance has been. If the objectives were not achieved, an effort should be made to find out why.

An MBO program can be operated on a daily, weekly, or monthly basis. If it is working effectively, quick feedback, immediate weighing of measures of success, and good results for your company should follow.

An application of MBO on a monthly basis is shown in the Appendix for Chapter 14, Guide for Improving a Saleman's Performance.

Other applications of MBO on a *daily basis* may pertain to your production supervisor and office manager. For example:

> An order may be received by your supervisor for 1,000 widgets. This order sets a goal, and performance leads to its accomplishment.
>
> The office manager may be assigned 10 contracts to be processed. This assignment also sets a goal.

In essence, we are saying you should be concerned with survival of your company, not only five or 10 years from now, but also next week. You should act and react quickly in order to keep your firm alive—now!

Your MBO program can also be used as an effective training tool for your employees and as a critique of their efforts, on a continuing basis.

BARRIERS TO PLANNING

Why do so many small business owner-managers neglect long-range planning? Certain barriers, such as the following, tend to discourage them:

1. Fear.
2. Inexactness.
3. Changeability.
4. Lack of planning knowledge.
5. Lack of proper time and place.

Fear causes some owner-managers to believe that careful thought about their companies' future will reveal new trouble or problems. A common reaction is, "I have enough problems now without worrying about the future." The real fear they should have, however, is facing the future without an adequate plan for their businesses.

Another barrier is *inexactness*. Many small business managers believe planning is so inexact that it does not seem worth doing, for no matter how carefully they plan, things often do not work out according to the plan. This statement will always be true to an extent—planning is uncertain because the future is uncertain. However, you should realize that even though certainty is impossible, probability is sufficient to govern action. Essentially, you are better off trying to determine the best way to play the odds. The problem is to get some idea of those odds. For example, what are the odds that more customers will need your product two years or ten years hence?

Another complaint of small business managers is that *plans change* too rapidly to make planning worthwhile. The solution lies in the frequency and flexibility with which you plan. Perhaps you should not try to plan 10 years ahead, or even five years; plan for only one or two years. You should consider how you might alter plans if a change materializes. To illustrate, in planning a new plant, you could consider what to do if the demand for your product turns out to be substantially greater or less than you had expected.

Lack of planning knowledge is another serious barrier to planning. You should consider this approach:

1. Set goals and objectives.
2. Develop plans to achieve goals.
3. Assess the progress being made to achieve the objectives.

Another barrier is the *lack of proper time and place.* However, this may be an excuse to avoid a task which you prefer not to do. Also, it is easy to let planning slide when you are "busy." But you should make a conscious effort to find the time and place for planning—some peace and quiet, and some protection from continual interruptions, are needed.

Many small business managers "kill the day" doing things they enjoy, while neglecting duties they dislike but which nevertheless should be done. Effective time utilization includes careful planning of work prior to performance and uninterrupted concentration during performance. You should first do the things that should be done—not the things you like to do.

HOW TO PLAN

You should start planning by getting a complete picture of your operations. The types of information that you need to do better planning are:

1. A brief description of your company's present practices in all important areas, including products, purchasing, quality control, labor relations, and sales outlets.
2. A statement of your present organization, procedures, and reports.
3. A list of the principal external factors—such as government regulations, the state of the economy, competition, the community environment, technology, and the labor markets—which affect your company most.

4. A list of changes you expect in any of these factors in the next few years.
5. A list of the main strengths and weaknesses of your present operation (based on items 1 through 4).

You should find that writing these things down clarifies your own thinking and helps you convey your ideas to others who will participate in implementing the plans. You should be in the right frame of mind when you plan.

Planning consists of these steps:

1. Recognizing and making a tentative statement of the problem.
2. Collecting and classifying relevant facts.
3. Setting forth alternative courses of action.
4. Evaluating the pros and cons associated with these courses.
5. Selecting the course of action (the plan).

In order to ensure that your plans are complete, you should be able to answer these questions:

1. *Why* must it be done?
2. *What* action is necessary?
3. *Where* will it take place?
4. *Who* will do it?
5. *How* will it be done?
6. *How much* control (including the kind and degree) should be exercised?

The sequence of these questions is also important. The "why" of the action should be determined first, while the questions of control should come last.

LEVELS OF PLANNING

You should be able to distinguish between "executive-level," "operational," and "program" planning.

Executive level planning is broad in scope, long-range, and abstract. It entails selecting the company's objectives and policies and establishing programs and procedures for achieving them. Long-run trends in income levels, market size, product use, business location, and manufacturing and merchandising operations are involved. This type of planning is neglected by many small business managers. Too often they are engaged in fire-fighting, crisis-type management, and are so immersed in daily operations and routines that they cannot perform executive-level planning.

Operational planning is limited to separate departmental or functional activities. It tends to be narrow in scope, short-range, and concrete.

It depends to a considerable extent on prior planning decisions made at the executive level. Often, operational plans consist of budgets which are prepared one year in advance with a detailed breakdown by months.

Planning is also concerned with a specific *project* or *program*. However, you should recognize that a particular course of action in implementing a project should conform to the overall operations of your company.

Planning is especially important during your company's first year of operations. When you approach a banker, one of his first questions will concern a proposed budget.

You should delegate some planning, particularly operational and program planning, because it is required of all managers and non-managers in your company. Your employees' ideas are often helpful in providing solutions to your firm's problems. In addition, you should consult periodically with an attorney, an insurance agent, and various other specialists (such as a tax accountant).

Too often, small business managers do not analyze popular programs adopted by other companies before adopting them for their own operations. Results of programs should be thoroughly studied to be certain that they will be beneficial for your company.

Irrespective of how well plans have been formulated, some crises will arise. You should act decisively in these situations.

In planning your use of time, you should survey the time you normally spend on various activities. For a period of time, say four weeks, record every minute of time spent on every activity during the day. Then, analyze these data to determine those projects and tasks involving the greatest expenditure of time and the factors responsible for any waste of time. You should then plan your workday based upon this analysis. Perhaps you should deliberately arrange for planning by using evenings and weekends.

To help you analyze your own activities and their relative usefulness to achieving your firm's objectives, you should ask these questions:

1. Can this activity be eliminated or delegated?
2. Can this activity be combined with others?
3. Can the time required to perform the activity be reduced?
4. Can the sequence of activities be changed?

Some other methods of saving your valuable time are:

1. Organizing the work, including delegation of as many duties as feasible to your subordinates.
2. Selecting a competent secretary to sort out unimportant mail, screen incoming calls, and keep a schedule of appointments and activities.
3. Using dictating equipment.
4. Adhering to appointment and business conference times.

5. Preparing an agenda for meetings, and confining discussions to only those items on the agenda; making "follow-up" assignments to specific subordinates.

SUMMARY

In this chapter, we assumed that you would run your business yourself and perform these managerial functions:

1. Planning.
2. Organizing.
3. Directing.
4. Controlling.

Planning is selecting the future courses of action for the firm as a whole and for each department within it. The types of plans you will need are objectives, strategies, policies, standards, budgets, procedures, methods, and programs.

You should use some form of *Management by Objectives*, whereby your subordinates set their own performance goals—with your guidance.

Some barriers to effective planning are fear, inexactness, rapid change, lack of knowledge, and lack of proper time and place. However, these barriers can be partially overcome.

Planning consists of the following steps:

1. Recognizing and making a tentative statement of the problem;
2. Collecting and classifying relevant facts;
3. Setting forth alternative courses of action;
4. Evaluating the pros and cons associated with these courses; and
5. Selecting the course of action (the plan).

QUESTIONS FOR FURTHER DISCUSSION

1. Why is the following question critical? "If you own a small company, should you hire someone else to manage it for you? Or, should you manage it yourself?"
2. Describe four basic managerial functions that should be performed effectively.
3. Define and illustrate the following types of plans: (*a*) Objectives; (*b*) Policies; and (*c*) Budgets.
4. In a Management by Objectives (MBO) program, what criteria should the objectives meet?
5. List some reasons why many small business managers neglect long-range planning.
6. List the steps in planning.
7. Cite six questions that should be answered to ensure that plans are complete.

10

Organizing Your Business

The managerial functions you must perform if your business is to succeed are being discussed in this part. Planning was discussed in the previous chapter, and directing and controlling will be discussed in the following chapter. Although some aspects of organizing were covered in Chapter 6, the administrative portions are covered in detail in this chapter.

Organizing involves deciding what activities are necessary to attain your firm's objectives, grouping them into small work groups, and assigning each grouping to a manager possessing the necessary authority to carry out the activities and reach the objectives. A major problem with many small business managers is that they do not organize their activities properly. The material in this chapter should help you be more successful by helping you organize your firm better. The subjects covered are:

1. The need for organizing your firm.
2. Planning for growth.
3. Organizational principles and practices.
4. Forms of organization, by types of authority.
5. Ways of organizing your firm.
6. Some organizational problems.

THE NEED FOR ORGANIZING YOUR FIRM

If you (or a partner and you) have a small unincorporated company, there may be no "president" or other management title. Instead, the

FIGURE 10–1
Organization for a Small Manufacturing Firm

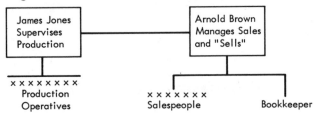

organization structure might be similar to that shown in Figure 10–1. In fact, a tight, formal organization structure should not be imposed, because it could "choke the life" out of your company.

As your firm grows beyond a certain size, you will often find that some specialized skills are required which you do not possess. You should first attempt to obtain outside, part-time assistance to aid, say, your sales manager who may lack advertising expertise or your plant manager who may lack industrial engineering training. You may also decide that you cannot manage the detailed operations any longer because the size and complexity of your operations are increasing too rapidly. You should preferably seek people in your company to designate as managers. Figure 10–2 portrays such an organization.

FIGURE 10–2
Organization Structure of a Small
Manufacturing Firm

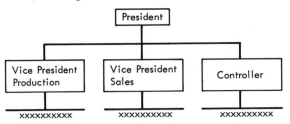

PLANNING FOR GROWTH

With respect to organizing, you should recognize that your business may undergo four stages of growth. They are:

1. The direct supervision stage.
2. The supervised supervisor's stage.
3. The indirect control stage.
4. The divisional organization stage.

In the *direct supervision* stage, you usually have less than 25 employees and you directly supervise all their work.

In the *supervised supervisor's* stage, you have a first-line supervisor who reports to you. You analyze results through the supervisor's reports.

If your company has 250–300 employees, you enter the *indirect control* stage and will need to supervise managers who, in turn, supervise first-line supervisors. Also, you will have staff people to establish policies and procedures, while you depend on reports.

If your company grows to 1,000 employees, the *divisional organization* stage is entered and you have other managers in charge of certain product lines.

ORGANIZATIONAL PRINCIPLES AND PRACTICES

An important principle of organization that you should follow is *unity of command.* Under this principle, employees should have only one superior to whom they are *directly responsible* for certain matters. When subordinates must report to two bosses concerning the same assignment, they may become frustrated if they receive conflicting instructions from the two supervisors.

In assigning work to your subordinates, you should try to arrange for *authority to be coequal with responsibility,* although this is not always possible. Sometimes—in the short run—your managers must assume responsibilities greater than their authority. However, try to give your subordinates sufficient authority to carry out their responsibilities. Otherwise, they lack the means of performing their duties. On the other hand, avoid delegating greater authority to your subordinates than they need to fulfill their responsibilities. Otherwise, they may use that authority unwisely and encroach upon the decision-making power of someone else.

The meaning of delegating and placing responsibility is "letting others take care of the details." Delegation is perhaps the hardest thing owner-managers have to learn. Some never do. Others pay lip service to the idea, but actually run everything themselves.

When you delegate, you should be assured that your subordinates are technically competent in their areas. They should either be managers or be capable of becoming managers.

The owner-manager of a small factory established three departments—a production department, a sales department, and an administrative department—and appointed a manager for each. He specified the following responsibilities:

1. The production manager was responsible for manufacturing, packing, and shipping.

2. The sales manager was responsible for advertising, customer solicitation, and customer service.
3. The administrative manager was responsible for personnel, purchasing, and accounting.
4. The production manager was designated as "assistant general manager" and delegated authority to make all operational decisions in the owner's absence.

The owner gave each manager a detailed statement of the function of his department and the extent of his authority. Actions which the managers could take on their own initiative and actions which required approval by the owner-manager were enumerated.

Each department manager was instructed to designate and train an assistant who could manage the department when the need arose.

The owner coordinated the departments. The sales manager and production manager set customer delivery dates together.

Control was exercised by holding each subordinate responsible for his actions and checking the results of those actions. The owner neither "breathed down his managers' necks," nor lost control of things. He relied upon reports and periodic staff meetings.

The owner kept his subordinates informed so that they would have the facts they needed for making their decisions. He tried to communicate effectively with them. He explained the "why" of his instructions.

His managers were given freedom to do things their way and he did not evaluate them upon whether they did a particular task exactly as he would have done it. He judged them by their results—not their methods.

If a manager deviated too much from policy, the owner brought him back into line. He avoided "second-guessing" his managers. If the subordinate did not run his department to the owner's satisfaction and if his shortcomings could not be overcome, the owner replaced the manager.[1]

Another principle you should follow is that *decisions are best made by the person "closest to the spot."*

You should watch carefully the *span of control* of each supervisor or manager. By this span we mean the number of subordinates reporting to one superior. First-line supervisors may have 10, 15, 25, 30 (or more) employees reporting to them, because of the similarity of their work. On the other hand, middle managers may have only 5, 8, or 10 supervisors for whom they are responsible, because of the diversity of their work. You should be especially careful of how many managers are reporting to you personally. If the number becomes too large, operations of your business could be severely hampered.

---

[1] Stanley Wantola, *Delegating Work and Responsibility* (Washington, D.C.: Small Business Administration, 1972), Management Aids for Small Manufacturers, No. 191.

Division of labor, or *specialization,* should be used wherever feasible, as it leads to increased expertise.

You should provide your employees with a written statement of their *duties, responsibilities, authority,* and *relationships.* Inform each of them what they can and cannot—or should not—do. Remember, though, that if you delegate authority for certain duties, you relinquish the responsibility for how those duties are performed. Yet, you cannot relinquish responsibility for their effective performance.

FORMS OF ORGANIZATION, BY TYPES OF AUTHORITY

You should be familiar with the forms of organization, according to these types of authority:

1. Functional.
2. Line.
3. Line and staff.
4. Informal.

Your business may start as a *functional organization,* whereby each supervisor is in charge of a specific function. For example, a supervisor may be assigned repair work; another, inspection; and another, production control. This form of organization is effective only in the very small business, because of span of control and duality of command limitations.

Your business may be better organized as a *line organization.* "Command" authority is used in this type of structure. Each supervisor is in charge of a specific operational unit and the employees assigned to work in it.

Further company growth may require *line and staff* authority. "Advisory" authority, specialty, and service characterize the staff. The staff assists line personnel in carrying out their activities.

An *informal organization* will always exist within the formal structure of your business. This organization consists of many interpersonal relations which arise as a result of friendships which develop on and off the job. Two examples are *informal leaders* and the *grapevine* communication system. You should determine who the informal leaders are, obtain their support for your programs, and encourage them to "sell" your programs to the rest of your employees.

WAYS OF ORGANIZING YOUR FIRM

With respect to your company's formal organization structure, you may choose to group the activities into manageable units by:

1. *Function.* Like skills are grouped together to form an organizational unit, such as *production* or *marketing.* The lowest level of the organization should probably be structured on this basis.

2. *Product.* Production or sales activities may be grouped by product, such as *men's wear, ladies' wear,* and so forth.
3. *Process.* Small companies often base their organization upon manufacturing processes, such as *welding* and *painting.*
4. *Geographic area.* If your company requires a strong, local marketing effort, organizing the sales force by areas or territories can be appropriate.
5. *Type customers.* A firm's customers may be classified as *industrial, commercial,* or other designation.
6. *Project.* To illustrate, a small public accounting firm may be organized on the basis of its clients' projects.
7. *Individual abilities of subordinates.* You may assign work to people according to their particular talents. However, a limitation is that the organization structure tends to change whenever a key employee is replaced.

ORGANIZATIONAL PROBLEMS

If they exist in your company, organizational problems are the first, or at least among the first, types of problems that should be solved.

To help you detect organizational problems—and hopefully to be able to correct them—see Figure 10–3. This figure describes the symptoms of problems, the possible underlying causes, and some possible actions to remove or correct the problems.[2]

SUMMARY

Organizing involves grouping the activities needed to achieve your objectives into small workable groups, delegating authority to carry out the responsibilities, and assigning a manager to each group.

The *organizational principles* which should guide you are practicing unity of command; maintaining a fairly equal relationship between authority and responsibility; having decisions made by the person "closest to the spot;" and having written statements of duties, responsibilities, authority, and relationships.

You may use the functional, line, or line-and-staff types of authority relationships in setting up your formal organization.

In grouping the activities together for supervisory purposes, you may group them by function, product, process, geographic area, type customers, projects, and/or individual abilities of subordinates.

---

[2] Robert G. Murdick, *et al., Business Policy: A Framework for Analysis* (Columbus, Ohio: Grid, 1972).

FIGURE 10-3
Small Business Organizational Problems

Symptoms	Possible Problems	Needed Action
1. Company seems to be drifting aimlessly or trying to go in all different directions.	The organization lacks an effective planner.	The board of directors should recognize these symptoms and formulate 1-3 year plans.
2. Conflicts occur among managers and key personnel. Confusion arises about current objectives and operations.	The manager is not working closely and personally with his people to develop unified objectives and a team approach.	Daily conferences should be held between the manager and his staff to build a working organization.
3. When the manager is not available, the organization is paralyzed.	The manager may believe no one else can make a decision without his being available.	The manager should delegate authority. A committee of the more capable employees may suggest to the manager that they be given more responsibility in decision making.
4. Supervisors make decisions which frequently are reversed by the manager.	The manager has not developed a consistent set of policies.	Some policies and procedures should be put into writing to cover the major repetitive actions and areas of decision making.
5. One activity, such as sales or production, cannot keep abreast of its work.	The manager is incompetent. Personality problems are present.	An immediate objective study is needed. If the manager cannot determine the cause of the problem, he should obtain a business consultant to study the situation and make recommendations.
6. Administrative costs have grown more rapidly than sales.	Big-company organization structure is being imposed upon the small company.	The number of managers should be reduced and the remaining managers' responsibilities broadened.

QUESTIONS FOR FURTHER DISCUSSION

1. With respect to organizing, describe four stages of growth a small company may undergo.
2. Define these organization principles: (*a*) unity of command, (*b*) co-equality of authority and responsibility, and (*c*) span of control.
3. Describe these forms of organization, according to the types of authority: (*a*) line organization, (*b*) line and staff organization, and (*c*) informal organization.
4. Describe five ways in which activities can be grouped into organizational units.

11

Directing and Controlling the Activities of Your Firm

The management functions of planning and organizing were discussed in the previous two chapters. Directing and controlling, the last two, are covered in this chapter, along with a look at what kind of a manager you might be. The topics to be discussed are:

1. Directing.
   a. Exercising leadership
   b. Communicating
   c. Motivating
2. Controlling.
   a. Process of control
   b. Self discipline
   c. Externally imposed discipline
   d. Indirect control
3. What kind of manager would you be.
4. Sources of assistance to help you manage your firm.

Much of this material is covered elsewhere in this text in considerable detail, while some of the other is not. However, it is all mentioned here as an overview of the subject.

DIRECTING

Directing is guiding and supervising the performance of duties and responsibilities by your subordinates. It consists of:

1. Exercising leadership.
2. Communicating ideas, orders, and instructions.
3. Motivating performance.

Exercising Leadership

Effective leadership involves democratic directing rather than autocratic commanding. Leadership refers to your interpersonal influence. To exercise effective leadership, you should create a good work climate which contributes materially to motivation of better work performance. You should then be skillful in communicating your orders down the chain of command, using formal and informal channels.

You should have empathy—the ability to put yourself into the shoes of other individuals and consider matters from their point of view.

Do you understand your personal leadership characteristics? It is probably more important for you to find subordinates who will respond to your style of management than it is for you to attempt to reorient your own personality, attitudes, and self-image.

Once you have chosen good subordinates, you should try to build effective supervisory relationships into your company. The following factors are significant in doing this:

1. Your attitude toward your supervisors.
2. Your choices for supervisors.
3. Training given to them.
4. Opportunities for their job satisfaction.
5. Rewards for work well done.

Your *attitude toward supervisors* is at the heart of the matter. It can make them believe that they are either errand runners, police, or leaders. If you consider them as errand runners, they will tend to follow instructions without question or suggestion. Since they have little authority, independence, or prestige, they will be resentful and avoid responsibility. If you consider them to be police, they will see that rules are obeyed and that the work is carried out. However, if you consider them to be leaders, they will probably see that company policies are followed and that the work gets done in an efficient manner.

Supervisors are expected to be your management representatives in dealing with nonmanagement employees. You should treat them as members of your management team with responsibilities for human relations, training, and liaison in addition to work performance. You should listen to their ideas and respect their opinions.

You should consult all your subordinates for their ideas. They have some good ideas, because they look at a problem from a special point of view. Also, asking them for their ideas will give them a sense of importance.

Communicating

You should recognize that most workers understand only about 20 percent of what you think and hope they understand. Communication should be two-way. You should be able to communicate your ideas to subordinates, and they should be able to communicate ideas to you. You should be an effective listener.

To be most effective in communicating ideas, orders, and instructions, you should understand these principles of effective communication:

1. Know what is to be communicated to subordinates and the most appropriate communication medium that will "reach" them.
2. Understand the subordinates' expectations and hopes.
3. Understand your own motives and objectives, and what you intend to gain from the communication.
4. Follow up to determine whether subordinates clearly understand the message.

Another part of communicating is counseling. In order to counsel effectively with subordinates, you should have this information:

1. What your subordinates are doing.
2. What unsolved work problems they have.
3. What suggestions they have for improvement.
4. How they feel about their jobs, their fellow employees, and their company.

Motivating

In motivating your employees, you should understand Maslow's hierarchy of needs and Herzberg's motivation-hygiene theory which are discussed in Chapter 2.

Motivation is rather complex and difficult to understand, at best. Understanding has been further complicated by the use of jargon by some writers and speakers. We will try a simplified approach to help you stimulate your workers, from a *practical, not a theoretical approach.*

In essence, motivation is applying an incentive, which will *promise* to satisfy the predominant need of the worker at the moment of time. However, once that need is satisfied it will no longer motivate the worker; another need must be appealed to.

A practical approach to motivating your employees might be viewed as in Figure 11–1. In general, you should know what the employees

FIGURE 11–1
Practical Approach to Motivating Your Employees

You, the Owner		Incentives You Can Use to Motivate Your Subordinates	Your Subordinates	
Your Objective	*What Is Needed to Achieve Your Objectives*	*Incentives You Can Use to Motivate Your Subordinates*	*What Needs Must Be Satisfied for Their Objectives to Be Achieved*	*Their Objective(s)*
Service and profit	Performance and productivity	Challenging work Merit increases and promotions Praise and recognition Personal publicity Responsibility	Self esteem	Self satisfaction
		Job enrichment Status systems Suggestion system Communications system Staff meetings	Social	
		Training and development Wage incentive plans Savings plans Profit sharing Seniority systems Insurance Pensions Other employee benefits	Security	
		Money, or sustenance for survival	Survival	

need in order for them to have self satisfaction; then try to find an incentive to apply in order to unlock their springs to motivation.

Motivation is difficult, for you always motivate—either positively to produce, or negatively to withhold production, as shown by the following example.

> A man went into an ice cream shop and ordered a banana split. When it came, something was obviously wrong. There was about two times as much of the goodies as there should have been.
>
> The man asked the young man who was serving him, "What's the matter?"
>
> The young man replied, with a shrug, "I'm mad at the boss."

There is a further discussion of motivation in Chapter 20.

CONTROLLING

Controlling is the measurement and correction of the performance of subordinates to assure that the company's objectives and plans are accomplished. The bridge between planning and controlling is the standard that was established in performing the planning function.

Process of Control

The process of control consists of these steps:

1. Set up planned standards of performance.
2. Measure actual performance.
3. Compare actual performance with planned performance.
4. Determine if deviations are excessive.
5. Determine appropriate corrective action and take it.

You should appraise the employees' performance by comparing it with the objectives that were set for the time specified. Your rewards or corrections should follow closely the performance review.

Self-Discipline

You should encourage self-discipline by your employees rather than using direct control. As owner-manager, your personal example will be important. Your employees should have confidence in their abilities to perform their jobs, believe that their performance is compatible with their own interests, and believe that you will provide support if they run into difficulties.

Externally Imposed Discipline

Regarding discipline, you will probably find that 95 percent of your employees conduct themselves reasonably; they rarely cause any problems. However, if you do not deal effectively with the few who violate rules and regulations, employees' disrespect will likely become widespread. In order to be effective in administering discipline, you should:

1. Know the rules.
2. Move promptly on violations.
3. Gather pertinent facts.
4. Allow employees an opportunity to explain their positions.
5. Set up tentative courses of action and evaluate them.
6. Decide what action to take.
7. Apply the disciplinary action, observing labor contract procedures.
8. Set up and maintain a record of actions taken.

You should also be able to distinguish between major and minor offenses and consider extenuating circumstances, such as the employee's length of service, prior performance record, and duration of time since the last offense. You should never be punitive or vindictive with an employee for violating a rule.

Indirect Control

In referring to the stages of growth described under the organizing function, it is evident that the very small business usually lends itself to direct control. But indirect control will be necessary at later stages of growth. Your means of indirect control are reports.

Some guidelines that you should follow with respect to reports are:

1. They should cover separate organizational units.
2. They should be designed to be updated as needed.
3. They should be factual and not designed just to make someone look good.
4. They should also be designed to indicate actions which are taken or planned to be taken.
5. They should be designed to highlight comparisons of performance between various organizational units and/or individuals within your company.

These reports should be given to all executive and supervisory personnel concerned. You should operate on the basis of the *exception principle,* which requires an immediate investigation of the causes of significant variations, whether favorable or unfavorable. You should arrange for immediate remedial action to prevent a repetition of bad results or to preserve and continue good results.

WHAT KIND OF MANAGER WOULD YOU BE?

You should recognize that the above-described managerial functions are universal in nature. They apply in all types of institutions, at all levels of management, and to all business functions. Thus, to emphasize a point related to general management attitudes and abilities considered earlier in this book and in this chapter, you should have determined by now whether or not you have the general management skills and the temperament to be in business for yourself. The material in this chapter should help you determine whether or not you have the specific know-how to be a manager in a particular industry. So often, that know-how is obtained only from experience in that industry. A rule-of-thumb of a minimum three years' experience is sometimes cited.

As your business grows, you should have the ability to make the transition from being a "doer" to being able to delegate authority to others. You will accomplish results through the leadership of others so that you can concentrate on long-range planning and financing.

Too many small business managers rely on "thinks" instead of "facts." "Thinks" consist of hunches, guesses, and intuition. You should make every effort to collect and use low-cost, readily-available, published data to verify these "thinks."

SOURCES OF OUTSIDE ASSISTANCE

You may encounter problems that you cannot solve by yourself. You should then seek outside assistance from a private management consultant, or through the Small Business Administration (SBA).

The Private Management Consultant

A management consultant can assist you in areas such as accounting, legal matters, insurance, marketing, organizational problems, and operating problems. You should expect an objective point of view, new ideas, and a knowledge of cost-saving methods which could help you improve your decision making. You may be able to save 10 to 20 percent of annual operating costs in your firm. The consultant can help you out of trouble or prevent trouble from occurring by anticipating and eliminating its causes. Fees will usually be more than $100 per day, plus expenses. You should insist that the fees to be paid, the clear definition of duties to be performed and the time stipulated for accomplishment of results be contractually specified.

You should check with past and present clients to obtain their appraisals of the consultant's competence.

The Small Business Administration

If your small firm is in trouble, you can obtain free assistance from the Small Business Administration by contacting the nearest SBA field office.

There are several ways in which this agency offers its assistance. First, it has developed several types of special materials covering a variety of topics. Some of these are free, while the others may be purchased at a nominal cost. Forms for this printed resource material may be acquired from the SBA office that services your area.

Some years ago, the agency organized the *Service Corps of Retired Executives* (SCORE) and the *Active Corps of Executives* (ACE). The latter group is composed of persons still functioning as active business executives. Consultive talent may be obtained through the local chapters of these organizations, or by contacting the nearest office of the SBA.

The SBA also operates the *406 Program* on a contract basis. It contracts with a private consulting firm to help a small business. In this program, the consulting firm does both an analysis of activities and a follow-up by becoming involved in the day-to-day operations of the enterprise.

Additional means of obtaining free assistance are contacts with instructors of Small Business Management courses and faculty advisers of accounting societies in colleges and universities. Furthermore, over 300 colleges and universities are members of the *Small Business Institute* (*SBI*), which is co-sponsored by the SBA and the American Assembly of Collegiate Schools of Business (AACSB). Contact may be made with a Program Coordinator of the SBI, and arrangements may be made for a student team to counsel and assist you in your management and operating problems.

The SBA contracts with the institution to provide consulting service on a case-referral basis, for which the agency provides a per-case expense allowance. A faculty coordinator guides students from different fields in working with an individual business needing assistance. The students go into the business, make an analysis of its operation, return to the campus, and meet with the faculty coordinator and other students involved in similar kinds of activities. In a seminar-type environment, the difficulties the firm is experiencing are identified and discussed, along with alternative courses of action. The students then return to the business and become actively involved in trying to improve its operations.

The success rate of this program seems higher than that of some of the other management assistance programs.

SUMMARY

This chapter finishes the part on how to manage your business and what functions you must perform. It has discussed the directing and controlling functions.

Directing is guiding and supervising the activities of subordinates. It involves exercising leadership; communicating ideas, orders, and instructions to subordinates; and motivating them to perform.

Controlling is measuring and correcting actions of subordinates in order to ensure that your objectives and plans are achieved. It involves the following steps:

1. Setting up planned standards of performance for you and your employees.
2. Measuring your actual performance.
3. Comparing the actual performance with your planned performance.
4. Determining if variations between actual and planned performance are excessive.

5. Taking the appropriate action to bring actual and planned performance together.

Finally, we have urged you to ask yourself again whether you want to be a small business manager. We asked what type of manager would you be, and offered some suggestions for assistance. You can obtain help from private management consultants or the SBA. The latter offers printed materials and personal assistance, including SCORE, ACE, contract consultants, and the SBI.

QUESTIONS FOR DISCUSSION

1. Define the following terms.
   a. Leadership
   b. Empathy
2. Cite three principles of effective communication.
3. List the steps in the process of control.
4. List the criteria that effective reports should meet.
5. Define the exception principle.
6. What services can management consultants provide the small company?
7. What assistance can the SBA give?

WHERE YOU CAN FIND FURTHER INFORMATION

Broom, H. N., and Longenecker, Justin G. *Small Business Management.* Cincinnati, Ohio: Southwestern, 1971. pp. 394–433.

Golde, Roger A. *Breaking the Barriers to Small Business Planning.* Washington, D.C.: Small Business Administration, 1972, p. 2. (Management Aids for Small Manufacturers, No. 179.)

Murdick, Rogert G., et al. *Business Policy: A Framework for Analysis.* Columbus, Ohio: Grid, 1972. (For information on organizing *any* type of firm.)

Sommer, Howard E. *How to Analyze Your Own Business.* Washington, D.C.: Small Business Administration, 1973. (Management Aids for Small Manufacturers, No. 46.)

Wantola, Stanley. *Delegating Work and Responsibility.* Washington, D.C.: Small Business Administration, 1972. (Management Aids for Small Manufacturers, 1972.)

Cases for Part III

III–1. Tanner's Grocery Store (C)[1]

Mr. Tanner assumed operation of the store in January, and was immediately struck by the fact that he knew very little about the grocery business, and had a great deal to learn. He delayed a decision to quit his job with the State Employment Agency, and continued to work there for three months after the opening of his store. While he was absent from the store, he left a variety of family members and trusted people in charge, none of whom knew much about the grocery business. In addition, he employed several young blacks as delivery and stock clerks, but gave them little or no training or guidance. Tanner decided that the credit business was too risky for him, and eliminated the granting of credit except to personal friends and family. He successfully collected around 60 percent of the accounts receivable, but was unable to collect the remainder as the customers avoided his store and him when the grapevine reported his action with regard to credit.

---

[1] Prepared by Rudolph L. Kagerer and James F. Russell, University of Georgia. See "Tanner's Grocery Store (A) and (B)" in Parts One and Two for previous details.

171

Visits to the store by consultants from the university based training and consultative center were fruitless since Tanner could not be found there. When he was there, the consultant, in attempting to work with him, found him at first quite confident and totally unreceptive to suggestions. Later, when Tanner realized that he was heading into trouble, he rejected assistance on the basis that it was not there when he needed it.

For the first two months of operation, Tanner's Grocery Store showed a net profit. Tanner purchased a new pick-up truck for deliveries, and a new automobile for his own use. As profits declined, Tanner's behavior changed drastically. Initially, he had worn a shirt and tie to the store, and attempted to keep himself, his employees, and his store neat and clean. After three months, he was seen in the store with a dirty sport shirt, out at the waist, and his employees and store reflected his attitude.

One of the consultants stated, in a report filed on March 19, the following problems:

1. Severe labor problems, with high turnover and loose supervision.
2. Periodic lack of adult supervision.
3. Unbusinesslike behavior, i.e., yelling across the store at employees.
4. Stock on shelves low or out.
5. General atmosphere of store strained and tense.
6. Ordering procedures spotty, and major items out of stock on Monday.
7. Employees sullen or non-responsive to customers.

When the consultant made suggestions for rectifying these problems, Tanner replied, "I can handle it," but took no action.

Another action taken by Tanner was to advertise in the university student newspaper and via handbills that students would be granted a 10 percent discount on steaks and other selected items. He made no such offer to his regular customers, who were low income public housing residents. He realized losses in his red meat department as a result of failure to attract steak-buying students, and further antagonized his customers.

QUESTIONS FOR DISCUSSION

1. Evaluate the way Mr. Tanner managed his store. What does this tell you about the need for managerial abilities for small businessmen?
2. What does the case illustrate about the performance of the management functions?
3. Explain Mr. Tanner's unwillingness to accept help from the consultants.
4. What would you have suggested to him about correcting the problems described in the March 19 report?

III–2. Metal Fabricators (A)[1]

Metal Fabricators, Inc., was a small firm engaged in the fabrication of metal products. Practically all its income came from small subcontracts from general contractors in the area. However, since its incorporation in early 1970, the two owner-managers had been attempting to develop and market a sand-blasting machine with a new type of control mechanism, which they had conceived. Only two of the sand-blasting machines or "pots," as they are called, had been sold, although most of the company's efforts had been directed at this part of the business.

The two owner-managers, Jerry Rogers and Joe Benson, had similar education and work experience, including about three years of college, with several engineering courses. They were both competent welders and both had served as construction superintendents on several medium-sized projects. Jerry's work experience had been much broader and more successful than Joe's, and he was still much in demand as a construction superintendent. He had turned down several job offers during the last year. Jerry came from a "low-income, small-town" family, while Joe was from a relatively "well-to-do" family.

Larry Ford, who owned 51 percent of the stock in the firm, was a local businessman who devoted little of his time to Metal Fabricators. But it was Larry Ford's initiative that brought Metal Fabricators into existence. Jerry and Joe were temporarily unemployed, as construction superintendents often are, when Larry asked them if they could build a special type of hopper for Ford's construction company. Jerry and Joe rented a building and welding machine and constructed the hopper. This job led to others and the firm was incorporated in March, 1970. Larry Ford, who purchased most of the stock, appointed Joe president and Jerry general manager, with the mutual consent of the two men.

Regardless of their titles, Jerry and Joe worked side by side to complete the small contracts they obtained. Within about a month there was more work than Jerry and Joe could do, and they began to hire two or three welders on a part-time basis. As the work load increased and became more dependable, three full-time welders were hired.

During its first 10 months of operation, the firm encountered difficulties similar to those normally encountered by small, new firms. Cash-flow

[1] Prepared by Arthur D. Sharplin, Louisiana State University.

problems occurred and there were times when Jerry and Joe felt obligated not to draw their salaries so that funds would be available to purchase required materials and to pay the welders. Inexperienced welders from a near-by trade school were hired at first, but these proved unsatisfactory. Organizational difficulties were also encountered. It didn't matter at first that Joe was president and Jerry was general manager, but when there were employees to be supervised, areas of responsibility and authority had to be established.

At first, Jerry and Joe discussed each new problem and usually arrived at a mutual conclusion as to what to do about it. Later on, though, Joe began to handle more and more of the "business end of the operation" and Jerry began to run the shop. As the responsibilities of the two men became more clearly defined, they began to take unilateral action—often without informing each other.

The result of all these trends was that there were often disagreements as to whether the action taken was proper. When the men were together, they often argued about one thing or another. Several of the arguments were quite heated.

One day in November when Joe was at the shop for one of his almost daily visits, the following interchange took place:

JERRY: Joe, there are several things I'd like to talk to you about. I think we should get together for an hour or so right away.

JOE: What's bothering you buddy? Looks like things are going pretty well on your end of the operation.

JERRY: I'd rather not discuss it now. Can we get together Wednesday night at about 7:00?

JOE: Yes, I suppose that'll be all right.

When the men arrived for their meeting, each had made up a list of items they wanted to discuss. They went to the small, cluttered office which was built into one corner of the fabrication shop and started to talk:

JOE: We need to work out a plan and market our pots so that we can get them moving as soon as I get this valve ready. That should be within about two weeks.

JERRY: I don't want to discuss what we are going to do. I want to discuss what we have done and what mistakes we've made and how we are going to keep from making the same ones in the future.

JOE: Okay. Well, what's on your mind?

JERRY: Well, to begin with, you're handling the business end of this operation. You've prepared monthly financial statements but you didn't seem to know that we had a shortage of cash until we had no money to pay our salaries. You should have anticipated the shortage so that we could do something about it.

JOE: You saw the financial statements, too, and you thought they were okay.

JERRY: Anyway, Joe, I wish you would try to have a little more foresight and let me know about these things before they get serious. Another thing, you've only been here about two hours a day recently. You spend the rest of the time working on our new control system. So I'd rather you not give the men any directions when you are here without my approval.

JOE: Jerry, when I see the men doing something wrong I'm going to feel free to correct them with or without your approval. Anyway, the things that I've told them have been pretty obvious.

The conversation went on in this vein for about 30 minutes with Jerry bringing up points that had been bothering him and Joe commenting on those points. After Jerry had completed his list of items the session proceeded as follows:

JOE: Now, I have several things that I'd like to mention. Particularly, you seem to be so concerned about my end of the business, I think you should pay more attention to running the shop.

JERRY: Running the shop! Why, everything is running perfectly in the shop. The men are happy and we get every job out within the estimated time. All we need is a little better financial management and a few more sales calls on your part.

JOE: Jerry, I've also been concerned because you keep pushing to make the company bigger. You want to hire more welders, and take on more of these humdrum little fabrication jobs. I'd rather we just do enough of that to get by. We are never going to be successful unless we do something really big. And, if we can develop this sand-blast machine and get just a few sales I think we might really hit pay dirt.

JERRY: I'm not trying to make a killing, Joe, and I don't have a lot of faith in long shots anyway. I'd rather just sit back and build the things that we know how to build, and just do it a little cheaper and better than the next fellow.

JOE: Well, we are not going to settle that tonight! There was one other thing I wanted to ask you to do and that is to set up a wage allocation system so that we'll know how much of the men's wages are expended on each job. Several times in the past you haven't been able to tell me whether we even made money on a job or not.

JERRY: Sometimes we haven't made money, and that's because you keep changing the amount of the bids after we've agreed upon a figure. Last week on the Enjay job I spent an hour convincing you that we ought to bid $4,500 and you said "okay." But yesterday I found out that you bid the job at $4,000. We are not going to make a cent on that contract, Joe. Sam said that he even called you and asked if you had left something out because our bid was so much lower than any of the others. But, rather than admit that you had made a mistake, you stuck with the original bid.

JOE: We disagree about that, but I'm president of this company and I have to be able to make decisions.

JERRY: We've talked for 45 minutes and I don't think we've settled a thing.

JOE: Sure we have, you are going to set up a labor schedule for each job and I hope you are going to try keep your nose a little more out of my business. I'm going to have the control system ready for the sand-blast pot week after next. Also, I'm not going to give any more orders directly to the men.

JERRY: You said, too, that you would make 35 sales calls within the next 60 days.

JOE: Yes, I said that, and I will.

JERRY: Well I still don't think we've accomplished much, but I suppose we've about talked it out. I'll see you tomorrow.

QUESTIONS FOR DISCUSSION:

1. What does the case indicate about the need for organization?
2. What does it suggest about the need for planning?
3. What does it imply about control?
4. How do you explain the shortage of finances? How could this problem be overcome?
5. What does the case show about the differing objectives of the two owner-managers? The silent partner, Mr. Larry Ford?

III–3. Eaker's Dixieland Tomato Company, Inc.[1]

Mr. L. H. Eaker, president of Dixieland Tomato Company, was facing a serious problem in his efforts to coordinate his employees and ensure a "going concern." Mr. Eaker had realized that there was a lack of coordination, control, and desire to work on the part of his work force. His efforts in these directions had failed miserably. Subsequently, Mr. Eaker did not believe that the problem lay in his management style, but rather he believed that the inherent attitudes, behavioral characteristics, and general abilities of his employees lay at the heart of the problem. He believed this so strongly that he had seriously considered closing down.

---

[1] Prepared by Thomas W. Zimmerer, Florida Atlantic University.

BACKGROUND OF THE COMPANY

Mr. Eaker began in the produce business in 1955 selling boxes of tomatoes to hotels, restaurants, and fruit stands. His operation then consisted of himself, his wife, and their station wagon. His base of operation was his home in Fort Lauderdale. After a year of operation at this level, product demand and his selling ability enabled him to add another station wagon to his small business. Both Mr. Eaker and his wife sold tomatoes from their station wagons, concentrating mainly on the Fort Lauderdale area.

In 1957, Mr. Eaker acquired a 15-year lease on a warehouse style building in downtown Fort Lauderdale. The building was equipped with a large loading dock, a walk-in cooler, and a small office with a restroom. Mr. Eaker was able to add a quarter-ton truck to his small fleet. Business expanded rapidly and Dixieland Tomato Company was soon covering most of Fort Lauderdale and the beach hotels of Hollywood and Pompano. Mr. Eaker's brother, Roy, entered the business at this time and was responsible for packing the tomatoes and preparing the orders to be delivered. Hard work and long hours produced a profit large enough to permit the addition of two more trucks.

Deliverymen were needed, and Mr. Eaker's employment practice consisted of driving through the black section of Fort Lauderdale and literally taking a man off the street. He acquired a man named Chester in this fashion. Chester was illiterate, but had a chauffeur's license and was capable of delivering in the truck. Mr. Eaker also employed a white man named Bill Rainey, who delivered only when capable—due to his long affiliation with alcohol. In 1959, Mr. Eaker added an "all-purpose" manager named Bill Vernor. His job was never clear-cut. He delivered, packed tomatoes, and attempted to oversee the total operation in Mr. Eaker's absence. None of these men ever had a job or position description.

It was at this point, with the addition of Bill Vernor, that Mr. Eaker's functions and tasks changed. Mr. Eaker turned from delivering to spending his time acquiring the tomatoes and produce to sell. He also attempted to manage the overall operations: bookkeeping, the packing of tomatoes, sales, and delivery. The years, 1962–67, were a period of tremendous growth. Total yearly sales went from approximately $50,000 in 1962, to approximately $350,000 in 1967. Accompanying this growth was a high rate of turnover of deliverymen and plant employees. Employee dissatisfaction was the rule of the day. Mr. Eaker concentrated his efforts on managing the procurement, production, and selling functions, placing little importance on the management of his employees.

This period of growth (1962–1967) saw the addition of several trucks, (bringing the total to six), a bookkeeper, a tomato grading machine, and three large walk-in coolers. There was also an expansion of the product-line to include lettuce, cucumbers, peppers, potatoes, and other vegetables, but the main sales effort remained with tomatoes. The sales territory was expanded to include Miami and Miami Beach to the south, and Deerfield and Boca Raton to the north. Mr. Eaker also began to make sales to other wholesale produce houses, and he personally acted in a produce-broker capacity to buyers in the northern states.

During this period, Dixieland Tomato Company was incorporated under the name of Eaker's Dixieland Tomato Company, Inc. It remained family-owned with the Eaker family acquiring the officers' titles. The newly acquired prosperity enabled the Eaker family to travel during the hot Florida summers (beginning of June to the end of August), leaving the operation of the business to Bill Vernor, the intended, but not titled, manager. Mr. Eaker's directions during these periods of absence were, "Do the best you can, Bill. Just hold the fort down." Mr. Eaker and Bill knew that the summer months were devastating in terms of the produce business. It was generally accepted that even maintaining status quo was impossible. On the average, a loss of approximately $5–10,000 could be expected.

This factor placed a tremendous amount of pressure, and disappointment, upon Bill. Bill was a non-aggressive, timid man. Being basically nervous and overly fearful, Bill was not capable of handling this authority and responsibility which was placed upon him every summer. Understandably, Bill was upset because he was in the position of authority and responsibility during the summer when a larger portion of "Mr. Eaker's money" was lost. Mr. Eaker was capable of handling the long hours (from 6:30 in the morning until sometimes 1:00 or 2:00 at night, six days a week). But Bill was far from being able to cope with those conditions. Bill remained at Dixieland in this capacity until January 1971, when he voluntarily left. Mr. Eaker never attempted to remove him or to change his position in the company.

DIXIELAND'S SITUATION

As previously stated, Dixieland Tomato was experiencing severe employee problems. Employee turnover was high, while morale, motivation, and job satisfaction were at an unbelievably low level. Tardiness, absence, and drinking on the job were frequent.

The work force consisted of: Mr. Eaker, acting in his usual capacity; a bookkeeper; five deliverymen; and two housemen, or plant production people. Mr. Eaker still used his "off the street" method of recruitment. There were no formal training procedures. The deliverymen, besides delivering, were also responsible for picking up tomatoes and produce at packing houses in Pompano and Delray Beach. This could mean very long hours. All deliverymen arrived around 7:30 in the morning, and most were usually finished with their deliveries by 2:00 in the afternoon. But, if tomatoes or other produce were to be picked up, this could require remaining at a packing house until 1:00 or 2:00 in the morning, the average being around 10:00 or 11:00 at night. Most of the men could expect to pick up produce at least once or twice a week.

Goals of the company and goals of the employees had never been communicated. Mr. Eaker believed that the workers were to be motivated by wages and various monetary benefits given for extra effort, such as picking up tomatoes or produce. His attitude toward his employees was "you have got to constantly push those people, or they won't do a damn thing!" He delegated very little authority and responsibility to anyone. He believed the employees were not capable of handling any authority, so he had never delegated any, especially after his experiences with Bill Vernor. Mr. Eaker's distrust of them was sensed by all of his employees. Mr. Eaker ran the show!

There was no commitment to the organization by the employees. Equal status existed among all employees, and recognition for achievement was rare. There never had been, nor were there future plans for, an employee meeting in which goals or problems would be discussed.

An interesting example of the possibility for future progress was evidenced in January. George, one of the housemen, was noted for his drinking and for his verbal expression of his dislike for the company. Mr. Eaker placed George in a position of authority and responsibility by making him responsible for maintaining the coolers and making daily inventory checks. This was probably the first time George had been given this chance to act on his own judgment with little or no supervision. The coolers were in the best shape ever, and George displayed a feeling, however slight, of commitment to his job. Mr. Eaker had not sensed this change of attitude or progress.

Steady growth had continued since 1967, and total sales for 1970 were approximately $400,000. A reasonable profit was being realized from these sales. The market potential was excellent and future increases in sales, profit, and overall growth could be attained with proper coordination of effort on the part of Dixieland Tomato.

QUESTIONS FOR DISCUSSION:

1. Is the low morale and high turnover of employees caused by the managerial style of Mr. Eaker, or, are they the natural result of managing marginal employees? Explain.
2. How would you describe Mr. Eaker's leadership style? Explain.
3. Should he care whether the employees like the working conditions or not? Explain.

4. How valuable are the employees of the firm? Explain.
5. Explain the predominant strengths and weaknesses of Mr. Eaker's managerial actions?

III–4. Panther Inn[1]

In October 1972, Midland University became a member of the Small Business Institute (SBI), an experimental program under the auspices of the Small Business Administration (SBA). The objective of the SBI was to provide management assistance to small businesses by university students. The student consultants, in turn, had an opportunity to complement their academic experience through exposure to "real world" problems.

One of the 20 cases assigned to the students at Midland University was the Panther Inn, a family restaurant and lounge located at the intersection of I–88 and State Route 127. The Inn was located in the Panther Valley with a scenic view of rolling farmland from the lounge and restaurant serving area. It was geographically located in Midland County about 40 miles from Midland University.

The project was assigned to a team of three M.B.A. students: Dave, Harold, and Jim. All three of the consulting team were a little older than the average student, having served in the military prior to continuing their education. All three had prior small business experience.

The Inn was originated by Harvey Adams, who had secured a loan of $300,000 from the SBA. The loan was 90 percent guaranteed by the SBA, with an interest rate of 8 percent on the unpaid balance. Four months later, he secured a loan of $350,000 from the SBA. The first $300,000 of this loan was to cancel the original note, while the remaining $50,000 was for additional financing. An additional $10,000 was borrowed from relatives to provide working capital. The restaurant and surrounding property had a current net worth of $700,000, but was expected to reach over $1,000,000 at completion.

Since Mr. Adams was involved in other business activities, he handed the business over to his son, Chuck, who became owner and manager. Chuck was 22 years old, married, and a high school graduate with no prior business education or experience.

---

[1] Prepared by Thomas F. Urban and Harvey J. Brightman, Miami University (Ohio).

In their initial meeting, both Mr. Adams and Chuck enthusiastically welcomed the proposed team counseling. Chuck admitted that he knew nothing about a restaurant and that he originally just wanted to be the bartender for the lounge. Since the restaurant was entering the operational phase, Dave, Harold, and Jim outlined their approach to its problems. They initially concluded that special attention should be directed toward market research, inventory control, financial and accounting operations, and overall management of the restaurant and the lounge.

In touring the facility, the team noted that there were two distinct operations. The *restaurant* was on the main floor and the *lounge* was on the lower level. Seating capacity for the restaurant included two counters with 15 seats and a table capacity of 175 customers.

At the time of the case, the party rooms were not operating at full capacity (approximately 200 persons). The lounge area was operating at 100-person capacity, but when fully completed, two bars would be operating with a capacity of 200 customers.

Chuck stated that they had 24 full-time and part-time employees. Because of the constant turnover and anticipated increases in personnel needs, Chuck had been spending a lot of time interviewing prospective employees and filling positions.

After touring the restaurant facilities, the team began to discuss the specific needs of Panther Inn. Chuck stated that he didn't know that much about business. He thought he should be making a profit because a lot of customers came in, but there didn't seem to be any money left over. He was too busy hiring people and tending bar "to look into money matters." Chuck wasn't sure where the customers were coming from, but a lot seemed like tourists. He also wanted to know how to order the supplies needed for the restaurant. Sometimes they ran out of food while at other times the employees had to eat it in order to keep it from going to waste. Chuck concluded his difficulties by stating, "I want to be a good manager, but how? I never have any time left over to take care of anything. Just tell me what to do and I'll do it."

The team told Chuck that they needed to develop a cost analysis of the restaurant and lounge as well as an analysis of the current wage structure. Since Chuck had no idea as to whether the restaurant and/or the lounge was making a profit, he relied on his accountant to provide these figures. The team indicated that they would need more data and figures to analyze the situation. Chuck said that they could get these from the accountant if he had them. He stated that the accountant was an old family friend of his father and was a "nice guy."

In addition, the team recommended a market research program in order to determine the extent of his market segmentation. Finally, Chuck wanted an analysis of his parking lot layout and facilities in order to efficiently park the customers. The first meeting closed on a friendly note as Chuck had to return to the lounge to tend bar. He promised to get all the records from the accountant and said, "You guys can do anything you want. I just don't know that much about business and you're the experts. I'm glad the SBA put you in to do the work for me."

Several weeks later, Dr. Urman was grading papers when he was interrupted by Dave, Harold, and Jim. "We're quitting Panther Inn," said Jim, "He's not going to get any more cheap labor from us. He never does anything and now he took off for Florida—a two-week vacation because he 'had to get away'."

"Yeah!" said Harold, "We drove all the way up there and he's in Florida. That's it! He never does anything we want him to."

"Hold on a second," said Dr. Urman, "We just can't drop a case because it's too tough. We have a contract with the SBA and that's one of our cases. Let's start at the beginning."

"O.K.," said Jim, "The first time we went out, we told him what we were going to do and what we needed. He never did anything. He wanted us to do everything. When we went back a few days later, he hadn't gotten the records from the accountant. In fact, the accountant hadn't even filed a tax return for the Inn. We told him to place a register at the door to have people sign in. We could get our market information from this as to where the customers come from—tourists, families, and so forth. We drew up a plan for his parking lot. He wanted us to go out and paint the lines for parking spaces for him. Us—M.B.A.'s!"

"Yeah!" said Harold, "Look at our progress reports. We tell him to do something and it's never done. The only way we get him to do anything is to do it ourselves. Look at that accounting mess! We finally drove out to his accountant's and got the books. That dumb bookkeeper! He even wears green eye shades! He still uses a single entry system. We analyzed the books and he didn't have any of the data we needed. We finally worked up a cost analysis by collecting the data ourselves. Then, we found he made a $2,300 error. He didn't post figures in the ledger and when he did post, he put the figures in the wrong places. We finally broke the figures down into separate listings for the lounge and restaurant. When we told Chuck to get rid of him, he said that he couldn't because the accountant was a friend of his father's."

"I took care of his personnel problems," said Dave, "We prepared a wage analysis. Then I wrote ads for the papers and went to the employment agencies myself. I made up an organization chart and a job description for each position. All Chuck wants to do is tend bar. He keeps saying 'Do what you guys want to do. The SBA sent you in. You're the experts.' He just thinks that everything will work out. He doesn't have any experience and wants us to take care of everything. He doesn't want to be a manager!"

"I had to take care of his marketing," said Jim, "I wrote the ads and put them in the paper. He can't rely on tourists all year. We designed the billboard for him and he never put it up. We have to do everything for him. We advertise low prices and he raises everything on his menu by $1.00 to $2.50. He didn't need to do that without asking us. Then, we advertise a family restaurant and he still won't put in a kid's menu. We wanted him to give out balloons or panthers or something and he still hasn't even looked into it. Chuck apologizes to us for not carrying through and he admits that he's lazy. All he wants to do is tend bar.

"If we can't quit this case, Dr. Urman, how can we get him to do the things we want him to? We've done more work on this than any of our other courses and we don't have anything to show for it. He just wants us to do the busy work—and now he goes to Florida."

QUESTIONS FOR DISCUSSION:

1. What does this case show about outside assistance for a small firm?
2. What should be the role of the owner-manager and the team in this type of situation?
3. What should the team do now? Dr. Urman?
4. How could Chuck be induced to do a better job of managing his firm?
5. Evaluate each of the suggestions made by the team as to feasibility, applicability, and expected effectiveness.

III–5. *Bill's Service Station*[1]

Bill's Service Station was a full-line service station owned and operated by Bill Richardson and located in a medium-sized southeastern metropolitan area. The city had a population of 75,000, of which 35 to 40 percent were black. The metropolitan area (SMSA) population was approximately 120,000. The local economy was based partly on agriculture with heavy emphasis on timber and wood pulp operations. This was supplemented by several manufacturing firms (chemicals and rubber) which employed several thousand people. The economy received an additional boost from 14,000 students attending a state university located in the

---

[1] Prepared by Joseph Barry Mason and Morris L. Mayer, University of Alabama.

town. A small four-year college, several hospitals, and state and federal government offices added a sizeable service base to the economy.

Bill started the business in 1962 and located it in a concrete block building which he converted from earlier use as a car wash operation. In front of the station were three gasoline pumps situated on an unpaved driveway which led into two open bays for automobile servicing. Inside the station was an office for customer service and accessory displays and a back room used for storage and rest room facilities. An enclosed area at the side of the office, originally the car wash tunnel, had been remodeled for use as a community meeting room.

A station wagon and a half-ton pick-up truck with road service equipment were used to provide full road service to customers. The hours of operation for the station were daily, including holidays, from 7:00 A.M. to 8:30 P.M. In addition to the owner, who was a qualified mechanic and a graduate of a vocational training school where he specialized in auto repair, there were two other full-time mechanics and six part-time employees. The full-time employees were both partially disabled veterans who worked in a motor pool while in the Korean War, and the part-time workers were high school students in need of financial support. Bill's wife provided the bookkeeping and accounting services for the station. She was an accounting graduate of a local vocational training school.

The service station offered a wide range of products and services. Tire service, both at the station and on the road, mechanical services ranging from minor tune-ups to major overhauls, and maintenance services, including oil changes and air filter replacement, were all available through the station. The accessory line was limited to high-turnover items, such as automotive chemicals. Although facilities were available, no car washes were performed. A 30-day credit service was also provided for selected customers who did not have credit cards. Bill's merchandising policies were a result of attending a dealer sales school and of having helped his father operate a service station while he was in high school.

FINANCIAL POSITION

The financial records indicated that the business was highly success-ful. The entire facility, including land, building, and all equipment associated with the business, was purchased by Bill on a 10-year mortgage of $40,000. Gross income per month ranged from $8,700 to $9,000, while expenses, including cash payment for inventory items, ranged from $7,500 to $7,600, which yielded a gross profit of $1,100 to $1,500 per month—from which the owner's salary, depreciation, and periodic expenses such as tax payments must be deducted. The first year of operation resulted in a loss of $3,000, but since then the profitability of the business had improved to such an extent that the mortgage was paid off in 1970, two years ahead of schedule.

In terms of individual product lines, the gross margin on gasoline was 5¢ per gallon, 30 percent on oil, and 40 percent on automotive chemicals. However, the service aspects of the business were the most profitable. Tire changing, for example, produced about a 90 percent margin—providing that modern equipment was used to hold down labor costs.

GEOGRAPHIC AND SOCIO-ECONOMIC MARKET CONDITIONS

The business was located in a primarily residential neighborhood of one-family homes with a few local businesses dispersed throughout the area. The station was one-half mile from the nearest main highway and was situated on the second lot from an intersection and fronted on a street of residences.

The area surrounding the station was totally a black residential area. Living conditions in the immediate vicinity ranged from "extreme poverty" to "relative affluence." Within two blocks of the station there was a relatively new subdivision of brick homes which sold in the $25,000 range. A few blocks east was a federally-funded housing project for low-income families. Many of the residents of the housing project were unemployed and on welfare, but as noted, the immediate area around the station was comprised of one-family residences in the moderate to low-income class.

BACKGROUND INFORMATION ON THE OWNER

Bill was a native of this city. In 1948, he began to be involved in community affairs in an attempt to obtain better economic, social, and political opportunities for blacks in the area. He became involved in community affairs and civil rights while he was in high school in 1948, when he participated in a move to get the black vote franchised. After high school he joined the Army, served in Korea, and returned home in 1956. At that time, he became involved in the unionization of local industries while he was employed as a mechanic in a local heavy industry. Several strikes occurred in the following period, and during a strike in 1958 he was fired from his job. His case was appealed to the National Labor Relations Board where he argued his own case and won a decision after three years of litigation. During the 1958–1962 period, he worked for the city in the municipal garage.

Since the early 1960s, Bill had been politically active and was currently serving on the city school board, the board of the Veteran's Hospital, and was Chairman of the Community Advisory Board, which functioned primarily in the area of race relations.

In 1968, he sought election as Police Commissioner of the city, but was defeated by the white incumbent. However, he continued to have political aspirations and planned to enter other municipal elections.

CONSUMER INFORMATION

Bill stated that the losses suffered by his business during the first year of operation were due to his efforts to attract customers who were middle-income professional people and white collar workers. Problems arose from offering credit to middle-income customers, including ministers and other self-employed individuals, and even with those he knew through his involvement in community affairs.

After the first year, an improvement in profitability followed Bill's efforts to concentrate on customers with lower incomes. Most of his customers were city employees and blue collar workers (laborers, etc.) with annual incomes between $4,500 and $7,000. A large number of industrial shift workers lived in the area, but relatively few of these were customers. He consciously avoided encouraging their trade because of layoffs and strike problems and the resulting pressure for credit.

Bill made a major effort to make his customers feel comfortable at the station. All customers were asked to address him simply as Bill. Employees and owner alike wore plain work clothes. Since his home was only half a block away, customers regularly visited him at home. The house was modest and unassuming in appearance. It was furnished with comfortable furniture, few pieces of which were new or expensive.

Bill drove an older model station wagon, while his wife drove a newer full size, but low priced, automobile.

BUSINESS PHILOSOPHY

Bill worked hard at establishing a reputation for honesty, speed, and dependability among his customers. If a customer called for road service, a truck was immediately dispatched. If it was not possible to reach the customer within a few minutes of the call, the customer was advised of the delay so that he might call another station. Likewise, employees were sent home if they arrived for work in such a disagreeable mood that "they might lower the quality of service rendered, or if they arrived at work under the influence of alcohol."

All advertising was done through three local radio stations. Spot announcements were used on musical radio shows catering generally to either rock or spiritual music. Initially, the advertising budget was $100 per month, and the strategy was to inform potential customers of the business. As the business became established, however, the advertising budget was reduced to $40 per month, with less money going to radio, and more money being spent in community activities, such as providing shirts for ball teams, and in similar community involvement projects.

Before extending personal credit to a person, Bill used the services of a credit bureau and also did some personal investigation. He did not extend any credit to the clergy or to self-employed people. If credit was approved, he used a rule of thumb of 35 percent of the customer's weekly salary to establish the upper limit on the amount extended. By such attention to detail, he reduced his loss on bad debts to 3.5 percent. To avoid loaning money to customers, Bill did not carry money on his person and had himself bonded so that he could explain to a customer why he could not take money out of the cash register.

The station kept maintenance records on the automobiles of regular customers and reminders were sent to the customer at specified intervals. The strategy had been highly successful.

DISCUSSION

The mortgage on the business was now paid off and money was available for capital improvements and expansion. Bill was in a quandary as to what direction the business should take in the future. His wife desired to move to a home out of the neighborhood and into one more in keeping with their new affluence. Bill was afraid this would endanger the success of his present business. He did not have sufficient capital for a major new investment elsewhere but could engage in a modest expansion program. Money was available through the white financial structure, but he had stated that "any time I tie myself to the white banks, I lose my independence in supporting causes I believe in." He was unsure as to how a change in his present method of doing business would affect his effectiveness in the community as a leader, apart from the economic viability of the business.

QUESTIONS FOR DISCUSSION:

1. Discuss the advantages and disadvantages of Mr. Richardson's intermingling of his business, personal, and political life. Can this type of problem be avoided in small businesses where the owners are in constant contact with their customers, or is this a major potential advantage over larger, less personal businesses of the same type? Can he or should he avoid involvement with the white financial structure?

2. What are the major decisions (business, personal, and professional) you see facing Mr. Richardson at this time? What would you recommend to him? Why?

3. Discuss the planning, organizing, directing, and control aspects of the case.

III–6. Ideal Sheen Cleaners (A)[1]

Mr. William E. Miller, a respected black businessman of Cleveland, Ohio, had been engaged in various aspects of the laundry and dry-cleaning business since 1939 in the area known as the Central City Market. He became self-employed because of his dissatisfaction with other employment opportunities. His goals were to overcome poverty and job uncertainty and to leave a business to his sons. He believed that hard work and empathy with his customers were prime ingredients for success. Mr. Miller learned early in his career that effective communications with the public was required, and he attributed much of his success to lessons he learned from Dale Carnegie's book, *How to Win Friends and Influence People*.

The owner continued his education over his business career by attending lectures and participating in conferences at local universities. He was an active participant in his trade associations for continuous learning about techniques, processes, and business practice. He believed that there was no shortcut to success. Rather, one must continue to learn about his business and adapt its services to an ever-changing environment.

EARLY GROWTH OF THE FIRM

The Laundry Route

Mr. Miller became a self-employed laundry route operator in 1939. He borrowed $200 from a loan shark to purchase a vehicle with which to pick up and deliver laundry to his customers. Forty percent of the retail dollar collected from customers was retained by him, and the remaining 60 percent was paid to the commercial laundry that cleaned the garments. His ability to generate business depended upon his personality and the price, speed, and quality of the laundry service.

---

[1] Prepared by Donald W. Scotton and Jeffrey C. Susbauer, The Cleveland State University.

Purchase of a Dry Cleaning and Tailor Shop

The desire to increase revenues caused the owner to purchase a dry cleaning and tailer shop in 1943. This acquisition made the firm identifiable as a business establishment. The cost of this expansion was $1,000, which was financed by private lenders at illegal rates of interest. Although this diversification was modest, the services then included: (1) dry cleaning and laundry routes, (2) over-the-counter dry cleaning and laundry services at the store, (3) pressing, and (4) limited garment repairing. Mrs. Miller operated the store while her husband conducted the route services.

Expansion in the 1950s

The business continued to grow, and a dry cleaning machine was purchased in 1952. This action eliminated the payment of 60 percent of the dry cleaning revenue to the commercial cleaning plant previously doing the work. Another reason for the purchase was recognition that customers wanted to do business with a shop that cleaned garments on the premises. A final reason for the purchase was the reduction in time for completing the service.

During the decade, further expansion took place. Modern pressing machines were purchased, and the next-door property was leased to provide needed work space. During this period commercial bank loans were negotiated on the strength of a financially strong co-signor. It was no longer necessary to deal with illegal lenders.

Expansion in the 1960s

In 1960, a third store, next to the existing property, was taken over to provide adequate storage for finished garments awaiting delivery by the two route men. The firm was incorporated as the Ideal Sheen Cleaners, Inc., in 1963. Sufficient financial progress had been made for the firm to arrange for a regular line of credit with a commercial bank. This negated the necessity of obtaining co-signors. An additional expansion was planned in 1965 at which time property was acquired to serve as a more modern dry-cleaning plant. The old plant was to be converted into a shirt laundry to widen the service offerings.

GROWTH AND CRISIS

Sales and profits continued to grow through 1969. However, it was determined early that 1970 would not be a profitable year. The dry cleaning plant expansion became operative in October, 1969, but was not run at more than 50 percent of capacity.

Several reasons for the decline were present. One was that the sales potential for the existing way of doing business in the Central City Market probably had been reached. This area was populated primarily by black families. The average family income in this area was the lowest in the city. Most of the business was done with consumers. Virtually no dry cleaning or laundry services were provided for business firms. Another reason was the rapid spread of wash-and-wear clothing. Emphasis was on easy-to-care-for and do-it-yourself garments. Still another reason was the prolonged popularity of the casual look that minimized the need for well-cared-for clothes. A final reason for the decline in profits was the unsuccessful operation for 11 months of a retail store for receiving and returning dry cleaning and laundry to customers in a downtown office building.

Mr. Miller recognized that his firm was at a critical point in its business life cycle. The alternatives were to: (1) accept a decline in growth and profits and eventually close the firm, or (2) seek new ways to revitalize the business. The latter option required drastic changes in the concept of doing business, the market to be served, the services, and the internal operations. He chose to pursue the second alternative.

STRATEGY TO OFFSET BUSINESS MATURITY AND MARKET CHANGE

It was Mr. Miller's contention that he had coped with the necessity for change throughout his business career. To avoid complacency, he pursued industry changes in the market environment through activity with his trade association, and participated with other dry cleaners across the country in market surveys about the buying behavior of customers. He believed that his firm should react to business maturity within the market served and to the changing environment by: (1) expansion of the services, (2) penetration of the existing market, (3) expansion into new markets, and (4) plant expansion. These activities are summarized below.

Expansion of Services

Five service expansions were planned to satisfy customer needs consistent with those revealed in the surveys mentioned above, information received from trade associations, and the results of a mail survey of Ideal's customers.

Cleaning by the Pound. This service was offered because there are different categories of dry cleaning. For example, a man's suit required cleaning and pressing, while a child's snowsuit needed only to be cleaned. Dry cleaners offering this service charged by the pound for a quantity of garments requiring only cleaning and not pressing.

Easy Care Service. This service was devised to reduce the finishing process, and in so doing reduce the price by 40 percent to the customer. The new process involved standard dry cleaning and then use of a steam tunnel machine rather than pressing. This process removed wrinkles from the garments. At least 30 percent of the garments could be processed completely by this method. The remainder required a minimum of "touch-up" pressing after passing through the steam tunnel.

Carpet and Upholstery Cleaning. This service was added in the spring of 1973. The equipment was purchased from the International Equipment Company of Denver. Mr. Miller attended a one-week training program at the vendor's plant to gain experience in operating and repairing the machines, use and knowledge of cleaning chemicals, and marketing techniques to aid in communicating and selling the service. He anticipated broadening his market by making the service available to household and industrial customers. Much of the cleaning could be done on the customer's premises.

Drapery Cleaning. There was an untapped demand for drapery cleaning, and plans were made to provide the service. Drapery cleaning would be available to households and to businesses. However, it was not possible to promote it until further expansion of the processing plant was completed. This expansion would provide additional space and specialized machines.

Coin-Operated Laundry. Plans were considered for the addition of a coin-operated laundry at the main plant. Customer traffic at the retail counter of the plant was supportive of this venture. Market surveys confirmed the affinity of dry cleaning and laundry services and the need for both in this Central City Market. Again, the plan could not be implemented until plant expansion and financing were arranged.

Penetration of Existing Market

Additional services were considered to develop the existing market through deeper penetration. Supportive of the effort to draw more business from the Central City Market were plans to:

Sell More to Existing Customers. This action was to be achieved by additional training to driver salesmen and retail counter clerks. Advantages, reasons, and techniques for carpet cleaning were included from information received by Mr. Miller during his training at the equipment vendor's plant. A part-time employee was hired to call customers before the route salesman came. This contact would enable customers to have sufficient time to consider which garments should be cleaned or laundered. The anticipated impact was larger sales and time savings for route salesmen.

Attract New Customers. New emphasis was to be devoted to methods for locating prospective customers and presenting the merits of the Ideal's variety of quality services. It was anticipated that the owner would assume primary responsibility for this action.

Increase the Number of Routes. It was believed that the added services would increase business in the present market and require establishment of more routes and driver salesmen. Action was to be delayed until the new services and sales training had been in operation long enough to have an effect.

Expansion into New Markets

The plans included the opening of new sales routes in the Eastern suburbs and a retail outlet in a new apartment complex being built in downtown Cleveland. Priority was given to the latter.

Park Centre was part of the effort to revitalize downtown Cleveland. It was under construction in the summer of 1973. Already, 160 of the planned 1,000 apartments were completed and occupied. Three other apartment buildings were immediately adjacent to Park Centre. One was eight years old and was the first attempt to revitalize residency in the downtown area. The other two buildings were nearing completion. These buildings would contain 877 apartments and would appeal to professional people and retired families.

Park Centre was to contain a 75-store shopping mall. Mr. Miller signed a 10-year lease in the spring of 1973 to obtain a retail outlet for Ideal Sheen Cleaners, Inc. He estimated that there were at least 4,000 housing units in downtown Cleveland. At $50 per unit he could obtain an extra $200,000 annual sales within the next four or five years. This volume was impressive when added to $240,000 sales in the Central City Market presently served.

A temporary store was opened in June 1973 in the building's laundry room lounge to offset the disadvantage of waiting until fall when the stores were to be completed. This store gave Mr. Miller an opportunity to meet new tenants as they moved in and provide a service for the 160 families that were in residence. The new store was to offer the complete line of services mentioned above and the additional amenity of a one-hour cleaning service to be performed at the retail store.

Plant Expansion

An additional plant and equipment would be required for the planned expansion described above. A building and the land next door to the existing dry-cleaning plant were available for purchase. This could house the coin-operated laundry and the added machinery needed for traditional dry cleaning; provide space for cleaning rugs and carpets, and upholstering furniture; and permit the transfer of the firm's office from the shirt laundry, which was located 20 blocks from the main plant. In addition, considerable equipment would be needed. The expansion was estimated to cost approximately $191,000, of which $27,000 would be required for leasehold improvements and equipment at retail store in Park Centre.

QUESTIONS FOR DISCUSSION

1. Does Mr. Miller possess the characteristics and philosophy commonly associated with the entrepreneur?
2. Evaluate the growth strategies used by the firm from its inception in 1939 until the crisis faced in 1969.
3. Evaluate the growth strategies proposed by the firm to offset the conditions of business maturity and market change.
4. Evaluate the sales forecast of $200,000 for the Park Centre and downtown market to be achieved within four or five years. Is it reasonable? Was the method used properly? Did he choose the correct forecasting method? What alternative methods could have been selected?
5. Was sufficient information presented to enable you to recommend or reject the planned expansion after 1970? Explain.
6. What does this case illustrate about the functions of management?

Part IV

Marketing and Your Business

Marketing, production, manning, and financing are all essential business functions. Each of them should be performed economically and effectively in order for your firm to be successful. The following three chapters pertain to the marketing function.

Marketing refers to the distribution of your firm's product or service to your customers in order to satisfy their needs and to accomplish your firm's objectives. Marketing includes the development of the product or service, pricing, distribution of the product, advertising, personal selling, promotion, and directing the sales and service people. It appears to be the most appropriate business function to be covered initially, because unless your firm has a market, or can develop a market, for the product or service, production, manning, and financing are unnecessary.

The marketing function and the philosophy that underlies its performance are presented in the following diagram:

Schematic of Marketing Function

The approach used in presenting the discussions about marketing follows this schematic. Chapter 12 covers the marketing concept, market-

ing policies, and the "what-to-do" marketing strategies. The "how-to-do-it" marketing operations are described in Chapters 13 and 14. In Chapter 13, market research and sales forecasting, merchandising, and advertising and sales promotion are described. Finally, in Chapter 14, personal selling, channels of distribution, logistics, pricing, and the market mix are covered.

12

Marketing: Concepts, Policies, and What-to-Do Strategies

In this chapter, the marketing concept, marketing policies, and "what-to-do" strategies are covered. The pertinent questions to which you need answers if you are to succeed are:

1. Is your firm adhering to the marketing concept?
2. Have broad marketing policies been established in your firm?
3. Has the marketing (what-to-do) strategy of your firm been well-defined?

THE MARKETING CONCEPT

The marketing concept is based upon the importance of the customers to a firm. If you decide to use this approach in your firm, you will need to: (1) determine what your customers' needs are, and how those needs can be satisfied; (2) select the market you will try to serve; and (3) decide what advantage you have which will give you a competitive edge over other firms.

Meeting Customers' Needs

The underlying principle of the marketing concept, as it applies to your business, is that your firm should seek to meet the needs of customers—at a profit to you. Customers' needs are your firm's primary focus, and your resources should be organized to satisfy those needs.

The marketing concept should guide the attitude of all employees in your firm. They should be devoted to stimulating and satisfying the wants and needs of customers. Too often, only the sales people in a company follow the concept, while other employees (say, delivery people, cashiers, or clerks) are rude and create customer ill will.

You should learn your customers' likes and make them feel that you are interested in them. You should give them extra service, because your customers will remember it and inform others. You should be an expert on your products and tell the truth about them even if sales are lost. You should build your trade around existing customers.

You should possess an ability to "read" customers—that is, to determine what they want and how you can best fulfill their needs and desires.

> The owner of a small ladies ready-to-wear store in a rural community had a good business going. It was discovered that most of the store's customers lived in a city 50 miles away. Some wondered why people shopped at her store when they could have patronized a store in their own city.
> Answer: She knew her customers by name, understood their needs, and bought with them in mind as individuals. "This dress should please Mrs. Adams." She then called each customer to inform her of the special purchases.[1]

You should sell your customers only as much as they can afford. An "over-sold" customer will not be a "repeat." You should encourage your sales people to build personal followings among customers. One retail salesman built his following by writing 20 letters each day to them. Each letter described new stock which would appeal to the personal preference of the customer.

You should have a customer policy whereby salesmen give the benefit of doubt to customers who return merchandise.

> When the new owner of a men's clothing store checked the records, he found that the last purchase made by one of his close friends was more than six years ago. He asked the friend why. The latter replied that the previous owner had refused to make an adjustment on a tuxedo that did not fit.
> This policy probably lost the store about $2,000 at retail because the customer would probably have bought about 15 suits plus accessories during that period of time. The new owner assured the friend that he would make future adjustments when needed. He regained a customer.[2]

[1] Irving Schwartz, *Personal Qualities Needed to Manage a Store* (Washington, D.C.: Small Business Administration, 1970), Small Marketers Aids, No. 145.

[2] Ibid.

You should rate your business once each quarter and determine what kind of image your firm has by letting yourself think about it as a customer would do. Looked at from his standpoint, ask yourself:

1. Is my firm doing all that it can to be customer-oriented?
2. Can the customer find what he wants, when he wants it, and where he wants it at a cost-effective price?
3. Do my employees and I make sure that he leaves with his needs satisfied and with a feeling toward our company that will bring him back again?

Customers want a business to be helpful! The American Institute of Banking makes this observation: "The easiest way to make money is to learn what people want and sell it to them. The fastest way to lose money is to offer something, regardless of what people want, and try to make them buy it."[3]

You should do little favors for your customers; they like your thoughtfulness more than any gift. However, people dislike receiving big favors which they cannot repay.

In the following examples, the marketing concept was not followed by the salespeople involved:[4]

The customer asked for a certain kind of fishing rod in a sporting equipment store. The salesman replied, "Sorry, we don't carry that brand," and did not offer to show the store's own brand to the customer. The store's brand had features which the competing brand did not have, and it cost no more. But the customer never knew it, unless he heard about it elsewhere.

In an appliance store, the salesman's facial expression said, "Make up your mind," as he waited for a customer to decide which washing machine she liked best. His "message" reached her because she did not buy a washer. He said, "I know she must have thought I had all day to wait on her." He did not know that she planned to buy a drier also.

If you are interested in the marketing concept, you will look for these *danger signals:*

1. Many customers walk out of your store without buying.
2. Many of them no longer visit the store.
3. They are not urged to buy additional or more expensive items.

[3] Robert G. Murdick, et al., *Business Policy: A Framework for Analysis* (Columbus, Ohio: Grid, 1972), p. 71.

[4] Kenneth Grubb, *Are Your Salespeople Missing Opportunities?* (Washington, D.C.: Small Business Administration, 1970), Small Marketers Aids, No. 95.

4. Traffic (pedestrian and vehicle) in front of your store has fallen off.
5. Customers are returning more merchandise than they should.
6. Your company's sales are down this month over the same month last year, and sales for the year-to-date are down over the same period last year.
7. Your employees are slow in greeting customers.
8. Your employees appear indifferent and make customers wait unnecessarily.
9. Your employees' personal appearance is not neat.
10. Your sales people lack knowledge of the store's merchandise.
11. The number of mistakes made by your employees is increasing.
12. The "mantle of greed" is evidenced through raising prices.
13. Your better qualified employees leave for jobs with competitors.

All of these signals are evidence that your store is not following the marketing concept.

Market Segmentation

Your firm should specify what market it is attempting to serve. A product or service which fulfills the needs and wants of a specifically-defined group of people is preferable to the product or service that is a compromise to suit widely divergent tastes. A marketing segment should be defined in terms of various characteristics such as economic status, age, education, occupation, and location. Your best opportunity is to identify a market segment which is not well-served by other firms. One authority has said:

> If we are to market successfully, we must in one way or another continually search for "holes" in the market. These holes are nothing but consumer needs and wants that exist because of inadequate or non-existent products or services.[5]

In determining your segment of the market, there are some fundamental questions you should ask yourself, such as:

1. What is my place in industry, and how can I find my competitive niche?
2. Am I known for my quality or my price?
3. If I sell industrial products, do I sell to more than one customer?
4. What image do the customers and the public have of my firm?
5. I serve only a limited number of customers. Why?

---

[5] Allan Wickman, Jr., "Marketing Ideas Make or Break a Company," *Marketing Insights* (January 19, 1970), p. 3.

A common error found in many small retailing firms is "straddling the market," or attempting to sell both high-quality and low-quality goods. As a result, the retailer is carrying a limited inventory of everything, but does not have a good selection of anything.

Competitive Edge

In order for your firm to be successful, you should seek a "competitive edge." Your business, as well as all other firms, needs some reason for being, something that is desirable from the customers' viewpoint that sets it apart from, and gives it an edge over, its competition. You should be stressing quality, reliability, integrity, and service rather than lower prices.

The competitive edge should be realistic. To determine whether it is realistic in your firm, you should answer these questions:

1. Is the competitive edge based on facts?
2. Do you know specifically what your customers are seeking?
3. Do you have an edge that is sufficiently important to entice the customer away from his present source of supply?
4. Have you used market research to make this determination?
5. Is the competitive edge compatible with your firm's capabilities and constraints?
6. Does your firm have the necessary resources—e.g., manpower to accomplish it?
7. Is the competitive edge based on conditions that are likely to change rapidly?[6]

Your firm should focus on earning profits instead of increasing the volume of sales. You should not increase sales without considering production costs, adequacy of capital, position of competition, and so forth. Expenses incurred in achieving the increased volume may exceed the revenues achieved and result in losses. You can literally "Sell yourself into bankruptcy." Sales increases should not far exceed your company's well-rounded growth in vital areas such as working capital and productive capacity.

STRATEGIC MARKETING POLICIES

You and the top managers in your firm should formulate strategic marketing policies for certain areas, including:

1. Morality and public service.
2. Products.

---

[6] Murdick, et al., *loc. cit.*

3. Markets.
4. Profits.
5. Personal selling.
6. Customer relations.
7. Promotion.
8. Credit policies.
9. Use of credit cards.

Morality and Public Service

Policies on morality and public service consist of general statements expressing your firm's desire to be honest in its dealing with the public and its customers.

To illustrate, the importance of policies prohibiting collusion with competitors became evident when executives of some turbine-generator suppliers were found guilty of market and price collusion in the 1950s.

Products

Policies on products will determine the direction in which your firm may grow in the future and may keep your company from "running off in all directions." If you are a manufacturer, you should generally restrict your products to custom, special purpose, low-volume products rather than high-volume, assembly line products where big companies are competitors and have advantages over you. If you have a small department store, you may deal in either low-quality, low-price goods or high-quality, high-price goods. If you are a retailer, you may specialize in either soft goods or durable goods.

The small firm often finds its most effective competitive weapon in the field of product strategy. It may concentrate upon a narrow product line, develop a highly specialized product or service, or provide a product-service "package" containing an unusual amount of service. Competitors' products, prices, and services should be obtained and examined to determine whether your company can build a better product.

Markets

Market policies are designed to clarify what geographic areas you wish to serve and other market characteristics appropriate for your firm. Perhaps you desire to remain only a local business. You may decide to market only consumer, industrial, or defense goods. You may decide to sell only at retail, wholesale, or to manufacturers.

Profits

Profit policies may require that sales goals be specified which will provide your firm a sufficiently large sales volume and a certain dollar profit. Or profit as a percentage of sales may be specified, which calls for low marketing costs.

Personal Selling

Personal selling policies may range from those guiding the structure of your sales organization to those covering your sales representatives' behavior. For example, you may have a policy stating that only one representative of your company may call upon an account. You may not permit "hard-selling." Other sales policies may relate to your representatives' qualifications and compensation and to constraints on your sales managers.

Customer Relations

Your company's relationship with your customers may be illustrated with this question: Should you have a policy that the customer is always right?

Promotion

The pattern of your firm's advertisements may reveal your company's promotion policies. You should follow a policy of tasteful advertising at all times. You may restrict your promotion to trade shows, or to industrial publications, or to some other advertising medium.

Credit Policies

In order to stimulate sales, you should provide credit for your customers. However, an appropriate credit policy is essential if you wish to be successful in granting credit.

Typical problems that face owners of retail and service firms when they get involved in the over-extension or unwise extenion of credit are presented below:

> Martin's Restaurant, a new business, was located in an area where many families and individuals were receiving public assistance, and its owner-manager gave credit freely. Within the first few weeks of operation, the firm had accounts receivable of $250, more than one-fourth its total capital.

Recognizing his predicament too late, the owner declared: "I have been unable to make enough money to pay my bills. I cannot pay my bills if my customers do not pay me. If some money is not received from them soon, I will have to close the restaurant."

The restaurant closed less than one year after it was established.

Mr. Neely and his wife had invested almost $6,000 of their savings in a venture. They paid $4,000 cash for equipment, and allocated the balance for working capital needs.

Sales increased during each of the 13 months they had been in business, and all bills had been paid. However, much capital was tied up in accounts receivable which could not be collected. The trouble was that Mr. Neely was soft-hearted. He stated: "I do not want to extend credit to anyone, but the problem is to tell that to my customers so their business will not be lost." The owners stopped giving credit altogether, but the firm's gross profits dropped by almost one-half. Mr. Neely was so discouraged that he sold the firm for only $2,500.[7]

Retailers lose far more from slow accounts than from bad debts. Costs related to slow accounts are the most important item in the total cost of doing credit business. Some adverse effects of slow-paying charge accounts are:

1. Increased bad-debt losses.
2. Increased bookkeeping and collection expenses.
3. Increased interest expense due to greater capital requirements.
4. Reduction of capital turnover and profit.
5. Loss of business because "slow payers" tend to transfer their patronage elsewhere.

The longer a charge account goes unpaid, the more difficult it is to collect. (See Chapter 24.)

You should establish a definite credit policy covering the following factors:

1. To grant or not to grant credit.
2. To require a down payment or not to require one.
3. How much should the typical down payment be.
4. How much time should be allowed on installment sales.

In selecting your credit customers, you can use the three C's of credit as your guideline:

Character: What is the customer's reputation in business and the community?

---

[7] *Records and Credit in Profitable Management*, (Washington D.C.: Small Business Administration), Administrative Management Course, pp. 27–28.

Capacity: What is the customer's ability to repay?

Capital: What is your customer's financial condition, or how much equity does he have invested in his company?

You should explain your credit terms to your customers clearly and unmistakably.

The customer's position should be investigated to obtain the following credit information:

1. Address and length of residence in your locality.
2. Occupation and earnings.
3. Marital status and number of dependents.
4. Ownership of property.
5. Amount of debts or payment and other credit accounts.
6. References, including bank references.

Additional questions include: Does your credit applicant change residence frequently? Change jobs often? Pay accounts slowly?

Your retail credit bureau can be contacted and asked to provide reports on prospective credit customers.

Other credit pointers are:

1. Set definite limits concerning the amount a customer can charge. Keep his credit within bounds.
2. Keep accurate, complete records.
3. Send statements at regular intervals.
4. Watch past-due accounts.
5. Take legal steps when necessary.

A well-planned collection policy is very beneficial to your firm.[8] Such a policy should include specific rules on such matters as:

1. When are accounts to be payable.
2. How soon after the due date shall the first reminder be mailed.
3. How soon after the due date shall the credit privileges be suspended on a past-due account.
4. How many steps shall be in the standard follow-up procedure, and what duration of time shall elapse between the steps.
5. What tools and methods shall be used in the follow-up.
6. When shall past-due accounts be given to a collection agency or an attorney.

Use of Credit Cards

In order to stimulate sales, you, as a retailer, should seriously consider the use of credit cards. Their objectives are to attain more rapid comple-

---

[8] Ibid., pp. 32–33.

tion of credit sales, reduce customer waiting time and inconvenience, and eliminate certain recordkeeping costs.

Bank credit cards, such as BankAmericard and Master Charge, have become important in generating sales. In 1970, there were about 24 million cardholders. Merchants report sales, sales returns and allowances, and other credits; and banks charge and credit their deposit accounts. Retailers pay a joining fee, a fee on sales made, and other fees.

You should recognize the advantages of no bad debt losses; no collection problems; and no personnel, equipment, or space requirements for servicing accounts receivable.

These policies should be examined relative to your company's strategic marketing plans. Are they consistent with your marketing strategies?

APPROACHES TO MARKETING STRATEGY—WHAT-TO-DO

In order to obtain a competitive edge, your company must innovate in product design, marketing, or manufacturing. You may find it necessary to adopt developments made by others in two of these areas while you innovate in the other. You should determine which of these three "what-to-do" marketing strategies to follow:

1. Expand sales into new classes of customers.
2. Increase penetration in market segments corresponding to existing customers.
3. Make no marketing innovations, but copy new marketing techniques and attempt to hold the present market share by product design and manufacturing innovations.

These strategies are elaborated upon below.

Expanding Sales into New Markets

To reach new markets, you may consider these possibilities:

1. Develop additional related products or models within your product line.
2. Develop completely new products unrelated to your present line.
3. Find new applications in new markets for your product.
4. Develop customized products; perhaps you desire to upgrade from low-quality to medium-quality goods.

In introducing new and improved products, you should recognize their relationships to the existing product line and established channels of distribution, cost of development and introduction, personnel and facilities, and competition and market acceptance.

The new and improved products should be consistent with the existing product line. Otherwise, major costly changes in manufacturing methods, channels of distribution, advertising, and personal selling may be necessary.

Significant capital outlays for design and development, personnel and facilities, market research, advertising and sales promotion, patents, and equipment and tooling may be involved. Profits may not be realized from one to three years on the sale of the new product, and financing should be adequate to cover this "breaking-in" period.

Competition should not be too severe. A rule-of-thumb is that new products can be introduced successfully only if a five percent share of the total market can be obtained. Your small firm may compete effectively with: (1) a non-standard product, either a higher-priced product or an economy model; (2) fast deliveries or short production runs of special items; or (3) high quality that makes your product superior to comparable products offered by competitors.

The following example pertains to the acquisition of a product or product line to certain specifications.

> The management of a defense-aerospace oriented, precision metal-stamping and machine shop desired to acquire a product or product line that met the following specifications:
>
> *Market*—The product is one for use by industrial or commercial firms of a specific industry, but not by the government or general public except incidentally.
>
> *Product*—The product sought is one on which 60 percent of the total direct manufacturing cost consists of metal stamping and/or machining processes.
>
> *Price Range*—The price range is open, but preferably should be $300 to $400.
>
> *Volume*—The volume is open, but preferably should produce $200,000 in sales in the first year with a potential sale of $1 to $2 million annually.
>
> *Finance*—Capital of $50,000 in addition to present plant capacity are available for manufacturing a new product.
>
> *Type of Acquisition*—Royalties are preferred to a patent, although purchase of a patent, joint venture, merger, or purchase of a company outright will also be considered.[9]

You should carefully consider diversification, or product line expansion. Advantages may be:

1. Increased profits.
2. Contribution to long-range growth.

---

[9] John B. Lang, *Finding a New Product for Your Company*, (Washington, D.C.: Small Business Administration, 1972), Management Aids for Small Manufacturers, No. 216.

3. Stabilization of product, employment, and payrolls.
4. Filling out a product line.
5. Lowering of administrative overhead cost per unit.

Availability of necessary facilities and skill are relevant factors. Diversification costs may exceed increased sales.

Increasing Penetration of Present Market

Perhaps you have been selling replacement parts primarily, but are attempting to expand by selling to original equipment manufacturers. Or, you may reduce the variety of products and models, which can produce substantial operating economies.

Make No Marketing Innovations

This strategy of adopting current marketing practices without trying to innovate is particularly suitable for your firm if its strength lies in its technical competence. In retailing, it is often advisable for store managers to follow this strategy.

Over the long-range, your firm may follow one strategy for several years with the intent to change after certain marketing goals have been achieved.

SUMMARY

We have tried to emphasize the importance of adopting the marketing concept, establishing broad marketing policies, and determining what marketing strategies you will use in selling your goods or services.

The *marketing concept* means you will give special consideration to the needs, desires, and wishes of your prospective employees.

Marketing policies will provide the guidelines you and your employees need in satisfying the needs of your customers.

Marketing strategies are the careful plans and methods you need in order to have a competitive advantage over other firms.

Once the what-to-do strategy (objective strategy) has been determined, your next step is to evaluate current "means" strategies. These strategies are described in the next chapter.

QUESTIONS FOR FURTHER DISCUSSION

1. Define the *marketing function*.
2. What is a proper priority of marketing questions for which the management of a small company should seek answers?

3. Define the *marketing concept* and cite three illustrations of its application.
4. Explain *market segmentation*.
5. Explain a *competitive edge*.
6. Describe briefly five strategic marketing policies.
7. Cite three adverse effects of "slow" charge accounts.
8. Briefly describe the three Cs of credit.
9. Give five types of credit information that should be obtained in the investigation of a customer.
10. Cite three advantages of using credit cards in a small company.
11. Cite three "what-to-do" marketing strategies.
12. Cite three methods of expanding sales into new markets.
13. Cite three advantages of diversification, or product line expansion.

13

Marketing Operations: Market Research, Sales Forecasting, Advertising, and Sales Promotion

In this and the next chapter, the "marketing means" strategies, or the "how-to-do-it" strategies, are covered. The "means" strategies involve the following marketing subfunctions or operations:

1. Market research and sales forecasting.
2. Advertising and sales promotion.
3. Personal selling.
4. Channels of distribution and logistics.
5. Pricing.
6. The marketing mix.

The basic question asked in these chapters is: Are your marketing operations being performed economically and effectively? The first two of these marketing operations are discussed in detail in this chapter, along with several practical examples. The last four will be covered in the next chapter.

MARKET RESEARCH AND SALES FORECASTING

Market research should provide a basis for more effective decisions by you and your marketing managers. It consists of fact-finding and forecasting and reporting the findings to you or your managers, who make the decision whether or not to take the indicated action.

Areas of Market Research

Areas of market research that you should consider are: identification of customers for your firm's products or services, and determination of their needs, evaluation of sales potential for your industry and your firm, selection of the most appropriate channel of distribution, and evaluation of advertising efficiency.

Market research studies may be directed toward the measurement of population, income level, purchasing power, and other indexes of sales potential in your trading area. The establishment of accurate sales quotas and measurement of effectiveness in selling depend upon the determination of sales potential.

To show the importance of researching the customers for a company's products, the following example is presented.

> The manager of a customer durables manufacturing firm set a goal of industry leadership and a target share of the market to be obtained within a certain period of time.
>
> *Problem:* The company did not attain the desired share of the market. The product line was styled above mass tastes. The designer was designing the product line for department store buyers (prestige stores at that). But three-fourths of the product's sales were through furniture stores. The manager realized that he had failed to research the customer adequately.
>
> *Solution:* He then arranged for market research, which indicated that many furniture store buyers were seeking products styled quite differently.[1]

Market research consists of the following steps:

1. Recognition of a problem.
2. Preliminary investigation and planning.
3. Gathering factual information.
4. Classifying and interpreting the information.
5. Reaching a conclusion.

The real nature of the difficulties facing your firm should be determined by a careful analysis of the situation. A problem creates the need for information. Your next step is a review of the facts already known, perhaps discussions with people inside or outside your firm, and reading trade publications. Once the facts are gathered, their significance, interrelationships, and implications for your firm should be determined.

---

[1] T. Stanley Gallagher, *Sound Objectives Help Build Profits* (Washington, D.C.: Small Business Administration, 1965), Management Aids for Small Manufacturers, No. 11.

Sources of Marketing Information

The sources of marketing information consist of: (1) secondary sources of published data, (2) primary sources of published data, and (3) primary sources of unpublished data.

Secondary Sources of Published Data.   Secondary sources pertain to data originally compiled and published elsewhere. Examples of these sources are:

1. Government publications, such as *Survey of Current Business* and *Statistical Abstract of the United States.*
2. Trade association reports.
3. Chambers of commerce studies.
4. University research publications.
5. Trade journals.
6. Newspapers.

The U.S. Bureau of the Census regularly collects data on the number of industrial establishments, their sales volume, and number of employees for many industry groups, broken down by county and Standard Metropolitan Statistical Areas (SMSA). An SMSA contains one city of 50,000 or more inhabitants or "twin cities" with a combined population of that size.

The data are reported for Standard Industrial Classification (SIC) Codes, which facilitate research by firms where sales can be related to their customers' type of activity. The Code breakdowns start with broad industrial categories, for example, apparel classification, such as men's, youths, and boys' furnishings, work clothing, and allied garments; and subclassifications, such as shirts, collars, night wear, underwear, and neckwear.

Many trade associations and other organizations which gather industrial data also use the SIC Code.

Metropolitan newspapers often develop important market data, such as purchasing power information, for their advertising clients. Examples are Scripps-Howard publications and the Memphis *Commercial Appeal.*

Primary Sources of Published Data.   A primary source of published data refers to the compilation and initial publication of the data. The U.S. Census Reports are illustrations.

Primary Sources of Unpublished Data.   Examples of primary sources of unpublished data are your firm's records and external data obtained from your dealers, customers, and competitors.

Sales Forecasting

You should measure your company's potential market in terms of both units and dollars. A sales forecast, both long- and short-range, should be prepared. It is the foundation of budgeting for your firm. Typically, it indicates sales during the last planning period, current sales, and future sales. (See Figure 13–1.)

Your firm's sales quotas provide targets for your firm, individual sales-

FIGURE 13–1

JONES SOAP COMPANY
Sales Forecast for Brands A, B, and C

Sales	Geographical Market Atlanta, Ga.
Last Year	
Brand A	$10,000
Brand B	56,000
Brand C	37,000
This Year	
Brand A	$12,000
Brand B	69,000
Brand C	42,000
Next Year	
Brand A	$15,000
Brand B	62,000
Brand C	45,000

The Jones Company obtained actual data from its records.
Source: Harry Lipson and John R. Darling, *Introduction to Marketing* (New York: John Wiley, 1971), pp. 184–85, 347.

men, departments, or sales territories. They should be realistic. Market sampling studies and a study of Census data may be used in deriving the quotas.

A small manufacturer of automobile dashboard accessories had a problem.

Problem: What new sales territories should be added?

Solution: The manufacturer used *Census of Population* data as an aid in making his decision. His first question was: "Where are the high concentrations of automobiles?" Then he determined which of the geographic areas being considered had concentrations of automobile supply stores and variety stores, the most appropriate kinds of retail outlets. He found this information in the *Census of Business.*

The manufacturer of paneling and room accessories had franchise arrangements with local contractors who used these materials to convert basements into finished rooms.

Problem: What new areas will be best for franchises?

Solution: From receiving *Census* statistics on housing, he determined: (1) the type of houses that predominated in a particular area; and (2) whether the houses were built on concrete slabs or with a full basement. He eliminated areas where the houses had no basements.

Another question: Could people in the particular areas afford to finish off their basements?

Answer: To answer this question, he examined *Census* data on family income, the number of children, and car ownership—particularly families that owned more than one car, which indicated they had discretionary income which might be spent for home improvement. He granted franchises in areas which had a good market potential.

Problem: An apparel manufacturer wanted to determine possible trends that might affect his business.

Solution: He used *Census* population data for keeping his company in step with its customers. These data indicated that the areas in which he was selling had a high concentration of teenagers and young adults. He then added new clothing styles appropriate for these groups.[2]

Salesmen's knowledge obtained through customer contacts should also be used in establishing sales quotas.

A small company used its salesmen in developing market plans for a new product, an item used by the steel industry.

Problem: The manager needed to estimate the new product's market potential.

Solution: A steel plant's use of the new product would be proportional to the amount of water used by it for cooling purposes. Salesmen, in their regular calls, asked about the amount of water used at each plant.

The water usage data were compared with each plant's known capacity for producing steel, pig iron, and coke. A ratio between production capacity and water usage was calculated. Statistics from the American Iron and Steel Institute were used to calculate the total amount of cooling water used by the steel industry. A list of water usage data was compiled for every steel, iron, and coke plant in the country. With this list, salesmen determined which plants had the best potential.[3]

When information is needed from a large number of companies, you should consider using *mail questionnaires.* Sometimes confidential infor-

---

[2] Solomon Dutka, *Using Census Data in Small Plant Marketing* (Washington, D.C.: Small Business Administration, 1972), Management Aids for Small Manufacturers, No. 187.

[3] Warren R. Dix, *Getting Facts for Better Sales Decisions,* (Washington, D.C.: Small Business Administration, 1966), Management Aids for Small Manufacturers, No. 12.

mation can be obtained that customers prefer not to give to salesmen. Such information as commission percentages that competitors pay their agents, market shares obtained by competitors, and market potential for your products in various geographic areas may be obtained from these mail surveys.

> A small company made a product used by meat packing plants.
> *Problem:* The manager wanted to determine the sales potential for an area consisting of 300 counties.
> *Solution:* From *County Business Patterns* (a series of booklets published by the U.S. Department of Commerce), he determined the total number of meat packing plants and their employment. He mailed questionnaires to these plants. Upon analyzing them, he learned that an average plant bought $200 worth of his product per employee per year. In multiplying the total employment in these plants by $200, he derived the potential sales.[4]

Certain kinds of questions can best be answered by *interviews with your customers and distributors.* Some of these questions could be:

1. Why are you losing business? Because of price?
2. Is something wrong with your product? Your salesmen?
3. Why don't your distributors push your line harder? Is it your discount schedule? What is the future for your product?
4. Are your customers experimenting with processes that may replace your product? Are they likely to shift to "in-house" manufacturing of your product?

Sometimes, respondents tell you what they think you want to hear. Some people don't want to hurt your feelings, and they won't tell you if they think that your company is behind the times or that your competitor's new models give better service.

You should consider the extent and intensity of your competition. One way to determine how much merchandise you and your competitors sell is using direct data.

> The manager of a furniture store obtained information on total furniture sales for counties A and B, and determined that his store accounted for 25 percent of county A's furniture sales and 10 percent of county B's. For county A, total furniture sales totaled $3 million, and his store's sales were $75,000.
> Alternatively, he could have determined the per family expenditure for furniture and multiplied it by the estimated number of families in his area. Population data could have been used (e.g., total population divided by three) in estimating the number of families.

---

[4] Ibid.

If sales data are not available for your type of goods in your market area, you should *estimate the volume of business* by relating sales of your type of merchandise to other merchandise which is sold in conjunction with yours, or by relating known national data to known local data.

A tire dealer determined that the sales of new cars three years ago had a strong effect on present retail tire sales. He also found that national sales of replacement tires in any one year had been consistently representing 10 percent of auto sales three years earlier. He could have used 10 percent of the 1971 automobile sales in his area as his market potential for 1974.

In analyzing your firm's records, *statistical analysis and projection* based on past sales may be utilized in developing sales quotas. Also, an accounting analysis of the profitability of selling to particular customers or of selling particular products may be made, and certain low-quality, high-cost customers to whom sales are unprofitable may be identified. Furthermore, analysis of your sales records on profitable credit customers may provide good information for merchandising decisions and sales promotion programs. An analysis of your company's accounts receivable aging data—current, 30–day, 60–day, 90–day, and over 90 days—is beneficial.

If your store sells many varieties of products, market share should be measured in total dollar volume rather than in product units sold. You should determine the total sales and the rate of growth for the type of goods you offer.

An area with apparel sales of $2,000,000, $2,200,000, and $2,420,000 in three successive years shows a 10 percent annual rate of growth. Other things being equal, it may be expected that these sales will amount to at least $2,662,000 in the fourth year. To *match* that growth, a store's volume should increase by 10 percent; to *increase* its market share, it would have to increase by more than 10 percent.

Overcoming Market Research Difficulties

A major disadvantage associated with market research in small businesses is the lack of "know-how" in research techniques. However, the services of outside experts—such as the market research consulting firm—may be secured. Other possibilities include help from trade associations, local chambers of commerce, banks, and field offices of the U.S. Department of Commerce and the Small Business Administration. You should consider cooperative research with other small businesses—say, evaluations of traffic flow and parking availability.

Your firm/should closely follow market changes due to shifts in the composition of your customers, their values and preferences, and their locations. "Fad" items and services tend to have a short lifecycle. You should plan to "get in and get out" within an appropriate time frame in order to maximize profits.[5]

You cannot afford all the market research you would like, so projects where the payoff is greatest should be selected. The objectives of each research project should be carefully specified. Selection of research techniques should be based upon cost considerations and the value of the decisions to be made. Market tests should be made before the introduction of new products.

ADVERTISING AND SALES PROMOTION

Advertising and sales promotion activities are important for you to consider.

Advertising

Advertising is used to inform your customers of the availability of your products or services and the uses they can make of them, and to convince customers that your products are superior to your competitor's. In order to be successful, advertising should be based upon your firm providing quality workmanship and efficient service. It should be closely related to changes in your customers' needs and desires. Rather than spend the money available on a random unplanned basis, you should establish an advertising program.

The types of advertising are *product* and *institutional*. The first type is self-explanatory, but the latter pertains to the selling of an idea regarding your company. The purpose of institutional advertising is to keep the public conscious of your company and its good reputation. The majority of small business advertising is of the product type. Determinants of the type of advertising are:

1. The nature of the business.
2. Company objectives.
3. Industry practice.
4. Media used.

Your *advertising programs* should be of a continuous nature. One-shot advertisements which are not part of a well-planned program are usually

---

[5] Successful products go through a life cycle. The stages of the cycle are: (1) the introductory period, in which there is low customer acceptance; (2) a growth period, in which gains are rapid; (3) maturity, in which sales level off; and (4) decline, in which sales fall. In general, the average life of products is decreasing due to rapid technological development and business change.

ineffective. All funds allocated for advertising should usually not be spent on a single medium. The proportion of your advertising budget allocated to each medium will be determined by the nature of your market.

> The owner of three laundromats, which were clean, well-maintained, and had a few loyal customers, could not increase the volume of sales in one of them.
>
> His prior advertising practice was to advertise in newspapers on a "one-shot" basis every four months at a high expense. He wasted money because most newspaper readers lived outside the marketing area of the problem unit.
>
> He tried a new advertising plan. He arranged for three successive mailings of handbills to potential customers in the immediate vicinity of the problem unit. The desired volume in this unit was soon reached.

On the other hand, noncontinuous advertising could be used to prepare your customers to accept a new product, to suggest to them new uses for established products or to bring to their attention special sales.

The question of *when to advertise* is very important for your business. Advertising media should reach—but not overreach—your present or desired market. Generally, you will have many media available, but you should choose those that will provide the greatest return for your advertising dollar. You should determine whether your advertising and sales promotion will be used to back up your sales representatives or used in place of them. To back up the representative, the ad should "pave the way" so that your company and product are well-known.

You should develop an *advertising budget,* a plan for the outlay of funds for advertising. Standard advertising ratios for your line of business or type of industry are effective guides. *Advertising expenditures* vary with:

1. The type of product.
2. The location, age, and prestige of your firm.
3. The extent of its market.
4. The media used.
5. The current state of the business cycle.
6. The amount of advertising by your competitors.

If advertising is a percent of projected sales, then the less your company's sales, the less the advertising when it is needed most to increase sales. On the other hand, diminishing returns may be realized from your advertising.

Your *advertising policy* may also govern the amount spent for advertising given products. You may decide to spend the major portion of the total outlay on one of your products and give only incidental advertising to others. If your firm's sales vary seasonally, you may also want to vary advertising expenditures seasonally.

Advertising should be truthful and in good taste. An advertising agency may be invaluable in designing your firm's advertising program, evaluating and recommending advertising media, attempting an evaluation of the effectiveness of different advertising appeals, performing design and art work for specific advertisements, advising on sales-promotion problems, furnishing mailing lists, and making market-sampling studies to evaluate product acceptance or area sales potentials. Suppliers and trade associations may also be beneficial in the performance of these activities.

Measuring the results of your advertising—comparing sales with advertising—is important. Assume that you are the owner of a small retail firm and you desire to determine whether your advertising is doing the job that you intend it to do. Before the advertisement is composed, you should answer this question: "What do you expect the advertising to do for your store?" You should divide your advertising into two kinds: *immediate response* and *attitude* advertising. The purpose of immediate response advertising is to entice the potential customer to buy a particular product from your store within a short period of time—today, tomorrow, the weekend, or next week. This type of advertising should be checked for results daily and at the end of one week, two weeks, and three weeks for appearance. The carry-over effects of advertising are the reason for checking after the first week.

Attitude or "image-building" advertising is the type you use to keep your store's name and merchandise before the public. You continually remind people about your regular products or services or inform them about new or special policies or services. This type of advertising is more difficult to measure, because you cannot always attribute a specific sale to it. You can measure some attitude advertising, such as a series of ads about your store's brands, at the end of one month from the ad's appearance or at the end of a campaign.

Your success in measurement depends upon how well the ads have been planned. These pointers are pertinent in planning your ads:

1. Identify your store completely and clearly.
2. Select illustrations which are similar in nature.
3. Select a printing type face and stick to it.
4. Develop easily-read copy.
5. Use coupons for direct mail advertising response.
6. Get the audience's attention in the first five seconds of a television or radio commercial.

For example, a retail monument dealer used a regular T.V. spot to advertise a $133 monument. Few customers came to purchase that item, but the advertisement proved to be a successful traffic builder for higher-priced items.

In using radio spots, saturation or blitz may prove to be successful techniques. Radio stations usually have a special package of spot rates, for example, 70 spots in seven days. Alternating between saturated coverage and prime-time spots is economical and effective.

You should consider using these tests for immediate response ads:

1. Coupons to be brought to your store.
2. Letter or phone requests referring to the ads.
3. Split runs by newspapers.
4. Sales made of the particular item.
5. Checks on store traffic.

Record-keeping is essential in testing attitude advertising, because you want to compare ads and sales for an extended time. You may make your comparisons on a weekly basis.

When ads appear concurrently in different media—newspaper, radio and television, direct mail pieces, handbills—you should try to evaluate the relative effectiveness of each.

Measuring the results of advertising is imprecise because of many complicating factors, including the time element, other forces affecting the customers' behavior, changing business conditions, and changes in competitors' advertising.

Sales Promotion

Sales promotion consists of activities which have the purpose of making your other sales efforts (e.g., advertising) more effective. Some of the more popular techniques are:

1. Creating special displays.
2. Offering premiums.
3. Running contests.
4. Distributing free samples.
5. Offering free introductory services.
6. Demonstrating products.

It may be directed toward ultimate consumers, the trade, and sales representatives.

If you become a retailer, you may consider using promotions, stamps, "two for the price of one," and premiums to obtain new customers. However, you should determine whether they are really effective or are merely reducing your profits. Your window and counter displays should be changed frequently to help bring the merchandise to your customers' attention. Some manufacturers and wholesalers advise on store layouts and personnel training programs, provide free advertising mats, provide short training courses for sales personnel, and maintain a staff of sales engineers to assist in solving customers' problems.

If you are a manufacturer, you may consider trade shows as an advertising and sales promotion medium. These shows are particularly beneficial when your buyers are widely scattered geographically and when significant innovations in equipment are being made each year.

Your sales representatves should be furnished good sales kits, up-to-date promotional materials, and catalogs. If you are selling two or more products, you should decide whether to promote them jointly or separately.

SUMMARY

In this chapter, we have tried to provide you with some "how-to-do-it" marketing strategies. Some specific information was provided to help you with your market research and sales forecasting. Several sources of data were mentioned, including published and unpublished material.

Concerning advertising and sales promotion, the subjects covered were the types of advertising, the timing of advertising programs, budgeting for this purpose, and measuring the results of advertising.

Personal selling, channels of distribution and logistics, pricing, and the marketing mix are covered in the next chapter.

QUESTIONS FOR FURTHER DISCUSSION

1. What are three areas of marketing research that small business managers should consider?
2. List the steps in market research.
3. Describe briefly sources of market information.
4. What are the benefits of sales quotas in a small company?
5. Give three kinds of information that can best be answered by interviews with a company's customers and distributors.
6. What are three values of analyzing a company's records in performing market research?
7. Describe briefly the stages of a life cycle.
8. What is the use of advertising in a small company?
9. Define institutional advertising.
10. Cite four factors that affect advertising expenditures.
11. Give four types of assistance rendered small companies by advertising agencies.
12. Define sales promotion.

14

Marketing Operations: Personal Selling, Channels of Distribution and Logistics, Pricing, and the Marketing Mix

The materal in this chapter is a continuation of the "how-to-do-it" marketing strategies started in the last chapter. The following marketing operations are covered:

1. Personal selling.
2. Channels of distribution and logistics.
3. Pricing.
4. The marketing mix.

PERSONAL SELLING

In spite of all your efforts spent in doing market research, sales forecasting, and advertising and sales promotion, someone ultimately must do some personal selling of your products or services. Therefore, you should determine whether your own sales representatives, independent representatives, agents, or brokers would do the best job for your firm.

Using Sales Agents

Some of the advantages and disadvantages of using sales agents are presented below.

Advantages of Using a Sales Agent. Some of the more valid advantages of using a sales agent to market your product are:

1. They can give you immediate entry into a territory.
2. They can make regular calls on your customers and prospects.
3. They can provide quality salesmanship into a territory.
4. Their cost is a predetermined selling expense to you, because their commissions are a percent of sales.

Disadvantages of Using a Sales Agent. Some of the main reasons why you should not use sales agents are:

1. Control over selling techniques is more limited than over your own sales representatives.
2. Selling expense on a large volume of sales may be excessive.
3. Allegiance to your company and products is not total, because the agent also serves other clients. An agent wants extra financial incentives to promote your products.
4. If you cancel the contract, the agent may take many of your customers to a new client.[1]

Using Your Own Sales Representatives

Having your own sales representatives will require the greatest investment. Yet, in the case of a highly specialized technical product, it will probably be most effective.

Effective selling should be built upon a foundation of product knowledge. The sales representative who understands the product's advantages, uses, and limitations can educate the potential customer and may be able to suggest new uses of the product.

The critical part of personal selling is the sales presentation to the prospect. A sales representative should adapt the sales approach to the customer's needs and meet every objection. Enthusiasm, friendliness, and persistence are valued traits of a successful sales representative. A "hard-sell" approach is sometimes advocated for intangible products and services, e.g., selling life insurance.

A decision should be made whether your sales representatives should be assigned to industry, government, and institutional customers, or assigned by product classification.

Your firm should have a basic sales strategy which includes these features:

1. Number of accounts per representative and average account size.
2. Compensation plan—salary, commission, salary plus commission, salary plus commission with bonus—and method of payment of expenses.

---

[1] Edwin E. Bobrow, *Is the Independent Sales Agent for You?* (Washington, D.C.: Small Business Administration, 1968.), Management Aids for Small Manufacturers, No. 200.

3. Cost of obtaining new accounts *vs.* the cost of holding old accounts. This comparison determines the amount of time a representative should spend servicing certain-sized accounts.
4. Use of overlapping or exclusive territories.
5. Sales representatives who are specialists in one of your products or lines, or who are generalists and will handle your entire line.

Specialists are easier to train and provide greater impact. One generalist representative per customer may be less confusing. Fewer high-quality, highly-paid representatives may be preferable to a larger number of less competent representatives. Owner-managers of small businesses often find that only a few customers account for a major proportion of total sales.

> The owner of a company distributing supplies to an industrial market analyzed the firm's accounts, and found that two percent of his customers accounted for one-half the total sales and more than one-half of the gross profits. More than 90 percent of the customers were small, and accounted for less than 10 percent of the sales. An analysis of representatives' call reports showed that they were spending most of their time on the small accounts and that many big accounts with good sales and profit potential were neglected.[2]

Through analysis of your sales records, you may find which products should be promoted, which products should be carried even though their profit margin is small, which products should be dropped, which territories are overstaffed or undermanned, and which customers are profitable.

You should provide for continuous or special training programs for your representatives and hold regularly-scheduled meetings with them each year. *Contests* tied into promotions, which stimulate representatives several times a year, are often desirable. The effectiveness of contests may be improved when the rewards include benefits for the representatives' spouses. A guide for improving a representative's performance is presented in the Appendix at the end of this chapter.

Your sales organization should be working closely and cooperatively with the manufacturing department. The representatives' delivery promises and production's capabilities and willingness should be matched. Good working relationships between your sales organization and market research should also exist.

You should determine whether your sales organization should place its best representatives in the most lucrative markets to compete with

---

[2] Warren R. Dix, *Getting Facts for Better Sales Decisions* (Washington, D.C.: Small Business Administration, 1966), Management Aids for Small Manufacturers, No. 12.

your top competitors, or seek untapped markets. Efficient routing of your traveling representatives and the making of appointments prior to their arrival are cost-saving practices that should be adopted.

Your representatives can maximize profits by emphasizing high-margin items. But they should look beyond the immediate sale to build customer good will and to help create satisfied future customers. *High ethical standards are vital.*

In determining whether to enter a territory, you should make a comparison of incremental costs and incremental income. You should drop a territory when its cost contribution exceeds its income contribution.

Either you or one of your top executives should support a representative when he is experiencing difficulties in obtaining a big account. Preferably, he should initially seek and request your assistance. Your representatives should be given an opportunity to be trained and promoted into management positions.

You should utilize sales reports, and stress major facts and trends rather than details. Reports show all variances between budgeted and actual sales. You should immediately investigate all excessive deviations upward or downward in order to find their causes. Long-term sales contracts with customers should have protective escalation clauses incorporated in them, particularly under inflationary conditions.

CHANNELS OF DISTRIBUTION AND LOGISTICS

A marketing channel is the pipeline through which a product flows on its way to the ultimate consumer. The choice of channels of distribution is not a simple one, but is important, as shown in these examples.

A small firm manufactured perishable salads which were sold direct to retail food stores. The salads required frequent delivery and close control to ensure freshness. The company diversified into two new lines: pickles and jelly. The manager selected the same marketing channel for these lines as for the salads. Although sales increased at the stores, expansion was necessary. As pickles and jelly had a longer shelf life, they could have been put into a separate, less expensive channel of wholesalers and chain warehouses.

A small manufacturer added an infant cereal to its product line, and selected its existing marketing channel of drug stores.
Problem: Consumers considered cereal as a food item and bought it at food stores.
Solution: The manufacturer started using food brokers as a channel.[3]

[3] Richard M. Clewett, *Checking Your Marketing Channels* (Washington, D.C.: Small Business Administration, 1963), Management Aids for Small Manufacturers, No. 9, p. 38.

Channels should be tailor-made to meet the needs of your firm. For example, in order to obtain regional or national coverage of its products, a company may find it productive to use distributors or manufacturers' agents in conjunction with its own sales force.

New products commonly require different distribution channels from those needed for products which are well-established and widely accepted.

A company started selling its new high-priced germicidal toilet soap through drugstores and prestige department stores. When consumer acceptance made the soap a staple, the company selected food stores.[4]

A company may have new markets for its products, and new marketing channels may be required.

A pneumatic drill manufacturer originally sold directly to the mining industry.

Problem: The volume of sales and profitability were inadequate.

Solution: The manufacturer selected distributors who were able to cater to the construction market.

A paint manufacturer selected hardware and paint stores, its existing channel of distribution, to distribute a new household floor wax.

Problem: The new product was reaching only a small part of the potential market.

Solution: The manufacturer switched to food stores as the channel.[5]

Multiple channels sometimes create conflicts. Distribution can be adversely affected unless these conflicts are resolved.

A manufacturer introduced a ladder attachment and selected a large mail-order house as the channel.

Problem: The company was shipping small quantities to many points which greatly increased costs.

Solution: The manufacturer sold the attachments through hardware stores.

Results: Hardware stores refused to sell the attachments, because of greater discounts provided the mail-order house and a much higher retail price.

[4] Ibid.

[5] Ibid.

In contrast, the manufacturer of do-it-yourself wood-working equipment selected a large mail-order house as the sole channel for a definite period of time. Later, the manufacturer planned to sell through its customery channels.[6]

Changes in buyers' locations may dictate a change in marketing channels. Changes in concentration of buyers may also require a change in marketing channels. Due to the rapid growth of markets in the far west and southwest, many manufacturers have stopped using agents and started selling directly to wholesalers and distributors.

Changes in your marketing channels may be revealed through examining the following indicators:

1. Shifting trends in the types of sources from which consumers or users buy.
2. Development of new needs relative to service or parts.
3. Changes in the amount of the distributors' profits.
4. Changes in policies and activities of each type of outlet according to customer types and areas, inventory, and promotion advertising.
5. Manufacturer's own organization relative to change in financial strength, higher or lower sales volume of existing products, and changes in marketing personnel or organization.
6. New objectives concerning customer groups and marketing areas.
7. Items of new products.
8. Changes in competitors' distribution plans.

You should establish a *distribution plan* which includes these factors:

1. Geographical markets and consumer types arrayed in order of importance.
2. The coverage plan: Whether distribution will be through many outlets, selected outlets, or exclusive distributors.
3. The kind and amount of marketing effort expected of each outlet.
4. The kind and amount of marketing effort you, the manufacturer, will contribute.
5. Policy statements concerning any areas of conflict.
6. Provision for feedback information.
7. Adequate incentives to motivate resellers.

Another problem a manufacturer may face is whether to ship directly from the factory or establish regional warehouses. The latter will provide more rapid service, but likely at higher inventory-carrying costs. However, transhipments between warehouses may permit lower inventories.

---

[6] Ibid.

If you are a manufacturer, your ultimate outlets should be willing to work with you on product promotion. You may arrange cooperative advertising with your dealers to share promotion costs. You should specify in advance criteria for selection of outlets and apply them.

PRICING

All items should be priced at a level to provide an adequate profit margin. The policy of pricing "to cover costs" has dangerous long-run implications. In periods of rapid inflation, particularly, costs should be constantly monitored and price changes made to provide for continued profitability.

If your firm has idle facilities, your price may be less than total cost. Provided your price covers the variable costs and makes some contribution toward the fixed costs, this practice may be desirable.

A word of caution is appropriate at this point. You should constantly check the package price structure and profits based on units sold.

A new club lessee of a food-beverage concession decided to adopt a pricing policy of selling food at cost and making profits from the sale of beverages. He overlooked the fact that a significant portion of his customers were either non-drinkers or light drinkers. Therefore, his profits were not as anticipated.

Your goal should be to find the price-volume combination that will maximize profits. When setting a price strategy, you should consider these factors:

1. The customer and channel of distribution.
2. Competitive and legal forces.
3. Annual volume and life-cycle volume.
4. Opportunities for special market promotions.
5. Product group prices.

The product, price, delivery, service, and fulfillment of psychological needs form the total package which the customer buys. A price should be consistent with the product image. Since customers often equate the quality of unknown products with price, raising prices may increase sales.

Price-cutting should be considered as a form of sales promotion. You should reduce price whenever the added volume resulting from the reduction produces sufficient sales revenue to offset the added costs. However, if an inelastic demand exists for your product, a lower price will not result in a greater number of units being sold. Your competitors' probable reactions should be considered in determining whether to reduce prices. Small firms generally should not consider themselves price leaders.

Markups, price-lining, and odd-pricing are other aspects of pricing you should consider. In calculating the selling price for a particular product, retailers, wholesalers, and manufacturers should add a *markup* to the purchase or manufacturing costs. An initial markup should cover operating—particularly selling—expenses, operating profit, and subsequent price reductions (e.g., markdowns and employee discounts). An initial markup may be expressed as a percentage of either the sales price or the product cost. A markup of $8 on a product costing $12, say, would produce a selling price of $20. The markup would be 40 percent of the sales price and 66⅔ percent of cost. Although either method is correct, consistency should be followed in the use of either base. Your business should have effective cost analysis by products in order to price the product effectively. You should recognize that modifications or markup percentages may be needed because of factors such as competitors' prices and the use of loss-leaders, or promotional, pricing.

Price-lining refers to the offering of merchandise at distinct price levels. To illustrate, women's dresses might be sold at $40, $60, and $80. Income level and buying desires of a store's customers are important factors. Advantages of price-lining are the simplification of customer choice and reduction of the store's minimum inventory.

Concerning *odd-pricing*, some small business managers believe customers will react more favorably to prices ending in odd numbers. Prices ending with "95," such as $29.95, are common for merchandise selling under $50.

By adding extra service, warranties, or paying transportation costs, your firm may sometimes effectively lower price without incurring the retaliation of lower prices by competitors with no volume gains.

THE MARKETING MIX

You should develop a marketing mix. Four basic variables in this mix are the "four Ps":

1. Product.
2. Place.
3. Promotion.
4. Price.

The right *product* for the target market should be developed. *Place* refers to the channels of distribution. *Promotion* refers to any method that communicates to the target market. The right *price* should be determined to move the right product to the right place with the right promotion for the target market.

> The manufacturer of a line of good-quality costume jewelry sold to retail jewelry stores. The owner wanted his company to grow faster. The company had been advertising in monthly trade magazines, using no sales representatives but employing order-takers, attending trade shows, and having good services, pricing, and packaging.
>
> *Owner's Study:* Company sales volumes for each area of the country were examined over a three-year period. The southeastern area sales were lagging.
>
> *New Marketing Mix:* Advertising outlays were reduced in the southeastern area. A sales representative was hired for this area.
>
> *Results:* Sales in the southeastern area began growing more rapidly than in any other area of the counry. The sales representative concentrated her efforts on retail jewelry stores that had the largest growth potentials.
>
> *Next Phase:* Different types of point-of-purchase displays and advertising mats for retailers were developed. More sales representatives were hired.
>
> *Results:* Sales doubled in two years and continued to increase substantially[7]

After developing an integrated marketing strategy, you should check it by getting affirmative answers to these questions:

1. Are all marketing activities—market research, personal selling, advertising and promotion, distribution, and pricing—directed toward selling the same product and product image?
2. Are tradeoffs made so that each activity contributes the same net marginal benefit? For example, if money is taken away from the sales organization to be used in market research, are profits likely to fall? Have priorities been established in the use of personal selling, advertising, sales promotions, packaging, and pricing within limits dictated by the volume of sales needed and funds available for the marketing program?
3. Are programs, budgets, and schedules prepared at regular intervals (yearly, quarterly, and so forth)?

SUMMARY

The material in this chapter has covered the subjects of personal selling, channels of distribution, pricing, and the marketing mix. This completes the presentation of the marketing aspects of your business.

---

[7] Harvey C. Krentzman, *Managing for Profits* (Washington, D.C.: Small Business Administration, 1968).

APPENDIX: GUIDE FOR IMPROVING A SALES REPRESENTATIVE'S PERFORMANCE[1]

One goal in measuring a representative's performance is to create improvement. The three steps in bringing about improvement are *planning, measuring,* and *correcting.*

Planning

Get the representative's agreement about goals to be attained or exceeded in the next year:

1. Total profit contribution in dollars.
2. Profit contribution in dollars for each major product line, each major market (by industry or geographical area), and each of 10–20 target accounts (for significant new and additional business).

Get the representative's agreement about expenses for the next year:

1. Total sales expense budget in dollars.
2. Budget for travel, customer entertainment, telephone, and other expenses.

Have the representative plan the number of calls to accounts and prospects during the next year.

Measuring

Review at least monthly the representative's record for: (1) year-to-date progress toward the 12–month profit contribution goals, and (2) year-to-date budget compliance.

Correcting

Meet with the representative if the record shows a variance of ten percent or more from target. Review the number of calls, plus major accomplishments and problems. In addition, you may need to help the representative in these ways:

---

[1] From Raymond O. Loen, *Measuring the Performance of Salesmen* (Washington, D.C.: Small Business Administration, 1972), Management Aids for Small Manufacturers, No. 190.

1. Give more day-to-day help and direction.
2. Accompany the representative on calls to provide coaching.
3. Conduct regular sales meetings on subjects the representatives want covered.
4. Increase sales promotion.
5. Transfer accounts to other representatives if there is insufficient effort or progress.
6. Establish tighter control over price variances allowed.
7. Increase or reduce selling prices.
8. Add new products or services.
9. Increase the financial incentive.
10. Transfer, replace, or discharge representatives.

QUESTIONS FOR FURTHER DISCUSSION

1. Cite three advantages and three disadvantages of using a sales agent in a small company.
2. Cite three valued traits of a successful sales representative.
3. What are three components of a basic sales strategy in a small company?
4. Cite three benefits obtained from analysis of a company's sales records.
5. Define a marketing channel.
6. Cite three indicators that may be examined to determine whether changes are necessary in marketing channels.
7. Cite three factors that should be considered in setting a price strategy.
8. A product costs $16 and the markup is $8. What percentage of the sales price is this markup?
9. Define price-lining.
10. Cite the four basic variables in the marketing mix.
11. Define odd-pricing.
12. Describe Management by Objectives (MBO) as applied to a sales representative.

WHERE TO LOOK FOR FURTHER INFORMATION

Cornwell, Arthur W.   *Sales Potential and Market Shares.* Washington, D.C.: Small Business Administration, 1972. (Small Marketers Aids, No. 112.)

Dutka, Solomon.   *Using Census Data in Small Plant Marketing.* Washington, D.C.: Small Business Administration, 1972. (Management Aids for Small Manufacturers, No. 187.)

Feller, Jack H.   *Keep Pointed toward Profit.* Washington. D.C.: Small Business Administration, 1972. (Management Aids for Small Manufacturers, No. 206.)

Goodpasture, Bruce.   *Danger Signals in a Small Store.* Washington, D.C.: Small Business Administration, 1970. (Small Marketers Aids, No. 141.)

Grubb, Kenneth. *Are Your Salespeople Missing Opportunities?* Washington, D.C.: Small Business Administration, 1970. (Small Marketers Aids, No. 95.)

Lang, John B. *Finding a New Product for Your Company.* Washington, D.C.: Small Business Administration, 1972. (Management Aids for Small Manufacturers, No. 216.)

Lipson, Harry, and Darling, John R. *Introduction to Marketing.* New York: John Wiley, 1971, pp. 184–85, 347.

Loen, Raymond O. *Measuring the Performance of Salesmen.* Washington, D.C.: Small Business Administration, 1972. (Management Aids for Small Manufacturers, No. 190.)

McCarthy, E. Jerome. *Basic Marketing.* 5th ed. Homewood, Ill.: Richard D. Irwin, Inc., 1975.

Murdick, Robert G., et al. *Business Policy: A Framework for Analysis.* Columbus, Ohio: Grid, 1972, pp. 61, 99–121. Credit is given to these authors for the approach used in developing this chapter, and for many of their ideas included in it.

Schabacker, Joseph C. *Strengthening Small Business Management.* Washington, D.C.: Small Business Administration, 1970.

Schwartz, Irving. *Personal Qualities Needed to Manage a Store.* Washington, D.C.: Small Business Administration, 1970. (Small Marketers Aids, No. 145.)

Small Business Administration. *Why Customers Buy (and Why They Don't).* Washington, D.C.: Small Business Administration, 1972. (Administrative Management Course.)

Sorbert, Elizabeth. *Measuring the Results of Advertising.* Washington, D.C.: Small Business Administration, 1972. (Small Marketers Aids, No. 121.)

Wikman, Allan, Jr. "Marketing Ideas Make or Break a Company," *Marketing Insights* (January 19, 1970), p. 4.

Cases for Part IV

IV-1. Roberts' Tire Service[1]

Roberts' Tire Service, owned and operated by James Roberts, was a franchise dealer for a national petroleum products company carrying a full line of national brand tires, batteries, and accessories. In addition to the normal service station business, Roberts operated a recap tire plant which sold recapped tires at retail and at wholesale to service stations and trucking companies within a fifty-mile radius of Centertown.

The station was located on one of the two main through streets connecting the business section of Centertown with its principal residential areas. Four other gasoline service stations were located within two blocks of Roberts, and all but one sold a national brand gasoline. Comparative sales data for 1961 showed Roberts as ranking second in the area with an average monthly gasoline volume of from 18,500 to 23,000 gallons.

In 1957, trading stamps began to flood the area, and Roberts decided to go along with the other service stations in the area and give stamps for all retail sales made by the station. S & H Green Stamps were chosen

---

[1] Prepared by Frederic A. Brett and George E. Passy, University of Alabama.

234

by Roberts and two of the other station operations, because of the proximity of a shopping center where the supermarket used the S & H Green Stamp plan.

Business did not increase any marked degree with the giving of trading stamps, and in March, 1959, Roberts decided to discontinue the practice as the cost of stamps was eating into his profits. Two other service stations in the area also discontinued the giving of trading stamps at about the same time and for the same reason. Sales of gasoline and oil immediately fell off and the retail business began to decline. After two months of declining sales, Roberts decided to again offer Green Stamps to his customers because "Once the super markets and other merchants start giving trading stamps, you have to go along with the practice or you just can't get the business. I wish they'd never started this mess." Business picked up almost immediately. Only one of the other service station operators who had discontinued giving trading stamps resumed the practice.

Roberts analyzed the situation and decided that if the giving of trading stamps was so important to increasing sales he would go the other merchants one better and give extra stamps to obtain a larger share of the trade. In July 1959, Roberts placed an advertisement in the local newspaper which included a coupon for 30 additional Green Stamps. These additional stamps would be given to anyone who purchased at least 10 gallons of gasoline during the week that the advertisement appeared in the paper. The coupon had to be clipped from the newspaper and given to the attendant when the gasoline was purchased.

Within two weeks after Roberts started giving the extra stamps, his sales of gasoline and oil increased by more than 10 percent. By the second month of this practice, he was attracting customers from all parts of the city and his sales climbed to an all-time high—up almost 20 percent. Sales at the other service stations in the area were not noticeably affected.

Roberts was elated over the increased sales until he noticed that his costs had gone up more than his revenue, due to the need for an additional station attendant and the cost of the extra stamps. However, service income also had increased, and since no figures were available to analyze what part of this increase in service income could be attributed to customers attracted by the extra stamp plan, the practice was continued on a trial basis.

In September 1961, Roberts decided to omit the coupon for the extra stamps from his advertisement in the newspaper. Almost immediately his sales of gasoline and oil declined with a corresponding drop in the sale of TBA[2] items and service.

---

[2] Tires, batteries, and accessories.

To help stem the declining sales, Roberts increased the size of his advertisement (beginning in December), but did not insert the coupon for the additional stamps. Instead, he ran specials on recapping tires, brake adjustments, and relinings, wheel alignment and balancing, etc., with the hope that business volume would increase to its old level.

By Februray 1962, the expected high sales volume had not been attained, and Roberts decided to reinstate the extra stamp plan. Within a relatively short period of time, gasoline sales increased as expected, but again the increased cost of labor and stamps was in excess of the additional revenue from the sale of gasoline and oil.

QUESTIONS FOR DISCUSSION:

1. Should Mr. Roberts have initially decided in 1957 to give S & H Green Stamps for all retail sales made by the station? Explain.
2. Was the reason—proximity of a shopping center whose supermarket used the S & H Green Stamp plan—sound for the choice of the same plan? Explain.
3. Do you agree with Mr. Roberts' statement: "Once the supermarkets and other merchants start giving trading stamps, you have to go along with the practice or you just can't get the business?" Explain.
4. Was the practice of giving S & H Green Stamps sound? Why, or why not?
5. Should Mr. Roberts have been striving to increase the volume of sales or profits of his business? Explain.

IV–2. *Clearview Optics*[1]

The Clearview Optics Company was a producer and seller of sunglasses. Their main competitor was the Not-Brite Eyewear Company. These two firms were dominant in the industry, although there were several smaller producers and there was competition from imports. Together, Clearview and Not-Brite accounted for 70 percent of the industry's sales.

Clearview's price range was from $2.50 to $10.00, and the product line included a clip-on model for prescription glasses. Not-Brite's price range was from $5.00 to $15.00, and it also included a clip-on model

---

[1] Prepared by Robert L. Anderson, University of South Florida.

which sold for $.50 less than Clearview's. The products of both companies had polarizing lenses; however, Not-Brite had gained a large advantage in the market by naming its line after the process of treating the lenses. The average consumer generally did not know that Clearview's products had polarizing lenses.

Clearview sold through the traditional manufacturer-wholesaler-retailer channel of distribution. The company had attempted to establish itself in every type of retail outlet where the consumer would expect to find sunglasses. In addition to the salesmen who called on the drug wholesalers, the firm employed representatives whose responsibility was to contact the retailers at regular intervals to promote Clearview Glasses, check the merchandise racks for out-of-stock condition, and to take orders which were forwarded to the appropriate drug wholesale house.

The company recently engaged an advertising agency that developed a television campaign centered on "the many moods of sunglass wearers." The main idea of the campaign was that different styles can change the mood of an individual.

The company had also attempted to use "push-money" as a promotional tool. It offered sales representatives of the drug wholesalers "push-money" to promote its sunglasses to retailers. The company representatives also traveled with the drug wholesaler's own representatives to help familiarize the retailers with the Clearview product line.

John Jones, a senior marketing major at a large southern university, had been employed by Clearview for the summer as a representative. John was 21 years old and had "a well-groomed professional appearance." He worked with Clearview for the summer in the university's co-op program, which allowed students to attend school while gaining valuable experience working for a company. John expected to graduate in one year and was considering going to work for Clearview full-time after graduation.

John's superiors were Mr. Smith, the regional manager in Atlanta, and Mr. Jones, the vice president of marketing in New York. However, for purposes of supervision and direction, John reported to Mr. Smith in Atlanta.

After a month on the job, John visited one of his marketing professors and said that he was having difficulty selling and promoting Clearview glasses to the retailers. Asked what seemed to be the problem, John stated that the retailers said that "they just don't want to handle Clearview glasses when they can sell Not-Brite." John's usual response was to explain to the retailer that Clearview recently had committed in an excess of a million dollars to a consumer advertising campaign, and further that there was no significant difference between the products of Clearview and Not-Brite, since they both had polarizing lenses.

The following are some of the retailers' comments to John:

"I have a pharmacy to run and I don't have time to talk to customers about sunglasses."

"I handle too many items to be concerned with just pushing one item."

"Why should I take time to promote your sunglasses when the customers come into my store asking for Not-Brite's?"

"Not-Brite's sell themselves; I don't have to bother with them."

"The previous salesman was too young and dressed too wildly. He didn't even know what my customers are like."

"My customers are older and they want a brand they can trust."

"My customers are older and are not concerned with the 'mod' styles you offer. They want sunglasses for eye protection."

"The Not-Brite Company will swap me good movers for non-movers at no penalty. Clearview will not do this."

John said he often made a sale of 10 to 15 dozen pairs of open stock glasses to replenish a retailer's display rack, but they were never delivered by the wholesaler. Such inaction left the retailer in an "out-of-stock" position, and that in turn created a great deal of ill-will against the Clearview Company.

Asked why the glasses were not delivered after they were sold, John said the drug wholesalers did not want to be bothered filling small, open stock orders from Clearview when they could sell whole racks of the Not-Brite brand. John went on to say that the wholesalers wanted to carry only one campany's open stock and that they preferred to carry the Not-Brite brand because it had a faster turnover.

When asked why he did not send his orders direct to the factory, John said the factory would not ship this type of order because they did not want to get involved in the wholesaling function.

John further explained to his professor that he had attempted to obtain information from his superior in Atlanta about Clearview's advertising campaign and had been rebuffed with the comment, "I don't know why we advertise as we do. That's not my job; my job is to sell the product and so is yours."

John recognized some of the problems that he was experiencing in his new job but felt that he had no place to obtain information to help him solve his problems. If he did circumvent the chain of command to point out some of the problems or try to obtain information, he could lose his job.

QUESTIONS FOR DISCUSSION

1. If Not-Brite has capitalized on the polarizing feature of their lenses, why doesn't Clearview also do it in their promotional program?

2. Should the company continue to use "push-money"? Is the practice ethical?

3. Define the concepts of "push" and "pull" theories of distribution. What are the requirements of price, place, product, and promotion if a company is to be successful using either strategies.
4. Do the promotion and distribution programs complement each other?
5. Should the company attempt to by-pass the wholesaler and sell directly to the retailer?
6. Is it possible to use a more selective method of distribution and eliminate the small retailers?
7. If you were John, would you circumvent established lines of authority to suggest changes in the marketing program to the vice president of marketing?

IV–3. Reach-A-Lamp[1]

The Raymond Johnson Manufacturing Company was formed in Oklahoma City in 1972 to produce and market the Reach-A-Lamp, a device or tool for changing fluorescent and slimline lamp tubes. Although other devices for this purpose were on the market in several areas, the Reach-A-Lamp, designed and patented by a friend of Mr. Johnson's, was described by Mr. Johnson as easier-to-operate, more versatile, and more capable than the somewhat unsatisfactory competitive changers. Disappointed with sales results after several months of distribution, Mr. Johnson, a general construction contractor, was studying actions that might be taken.

Constructed of lightweight aluminum, the Reach-A-Lamp, consisted of a long shaft with a crossed T "hand" at the upper end. At each end of the "hand" were two rubber covered "fingers" which could be controlled by the operator through manipulation of levers at the lower end of the shaft. One lever was about one foot from the lower end of the tool. When depressed by the operator's left hand, it caused a chain linkage through the shaft to close the "fingers" firmly around the lamp. Another lever at the lower end of the tool was manipulated by the operator's right hand. It turned the "fingers" to rotate the lamp and remove it from the socket. An attachment could be added which equipped the Reach-A-Lamp to remove and replace the starters found in many lamps. The "fingers" could also grip a sponge or dust-cloth

---

[1] Prepared by Dennis M. Crites, University of Oklahoma.

for cleaning the lamp and fixture surfaces. In addition, the tool was capable of removing and replacing a number of the diffusers and louvers which covered many types of fixtures. In two lengths, six-foot and eight-foot, the tool could be used on fixtures up to about 14 feet above the floor.

One maintenance man equipped with the Reach-A-Lamp could service many times more fixtures than before, and could replace the two men and ladder normally required for lamp-changing. The tool permitted changing lamps above machines and desks without an interruption of work, as might be necessary if a ladder were used. The manufacturer portrayed the tool as making lamp-changing faster, safer, less expensive, and less of an interruption. Supermarkets, department stores, offices, and factories where fluorescent or slimline lamps were used in quantity were seen as markets where the Reach-A-Lamp could be effectively used.

Before setting up for production, Mr. Johnson contacted a number of manufacturer's agents and representatives, calling mainly on electrical goods wholesalers. Agents in several key areas were contacted and agreed to distribute the tool whenever production was begun. A display of the Reach-A-Lamp was also set up at the National Lighting Exposition in New York. High interest in the tool was displayed by many of the manufacturers, distributors, contractors, and dealers in attendance at the exposition; a number of the visitors attempted to place orders. Names of the interested persons were taken in order that they could be contacted when production was started. Based on this reception and distribution prospects, Mr. Johnson concluded a royalty agreement with the inventor and arranged to begin production.

A building large enough for production operations was secured at a rental of $150 monthly. Dies and machinery required an expenditure of over $15,000; materials for production of the first lot of about 1,000 tools resulted in an additional $4,000 outlay. A work force of 10 persons was recruited, and production was begun at a rate of about 200 tools per week. Royalty payments were $1.38 per tool sold.

Manufacturers' representatives were obtained to carry the line in nine territories covering most of the area from the Atlantic Coast to the western plains region. Carrying noncompeting electrical goods lines for a number of different manufacturers, these representatives called on most of the leading electrical goods wholesalers in the territory they covered. At times, they might also make calls upon industrial buyers and purchasing agents. They received a commission of 20 percent of the selling price. Through the services of a local advertising agency, catalog price lists, instruction sheets, and advertising folders were prepared. (See Exhibit III–1). Over 20,000 mailings were made to electrical supply houses, grocery chains, and a selected list of manufacturing com-

EXHIBIT III–1
Front and Back of Advertising Folder

Back of folder

Front of folder

...for SUPER MARKETS...

DEPARTMENT STORES...

FACTORIES...

WHEREVER FLUORESCENT AND SLIMLINE
LAMPS ARE USED IN QUANTITY!

Reach·a·Lamp

Manufactured By
RAYMOND JOHNSON MFG. CO.
P. O. Box 7504 • Oklahoma City, Oklahoma

DISTRIBUTED BY . . .

WITH

Reach·a·Lamp

FLUORESCENT AND
SLIMLINE
LAMP CHANGER

the mechanical hand for

changing Hard-to-Reach

lamps and starters

IN SECONDS!

panies. New product news releases were sent to leading journals and papers serving the electrical goods trade, including *Maintenance, Southwest Electrical,* and *Contractors Electrical Equipment.* Descriptive announcements of the product appeared in several of these publications.

Retail or user prices were set at $27.50 each for the six-foot tool and at $29.50 for the eight-foot model. Wholesale discounts were established at 40 percent for lots of one to 24 and at 50 percent on larger quantities. Shipments of one to 24 were designated as F.O.B. factory while larger shipments inside the U.S.A. were shipped prepaid.

After several weeks of distribution, sales were running far below the

EXHIBIT III–1 (continued)
Inside of Advertising Folder

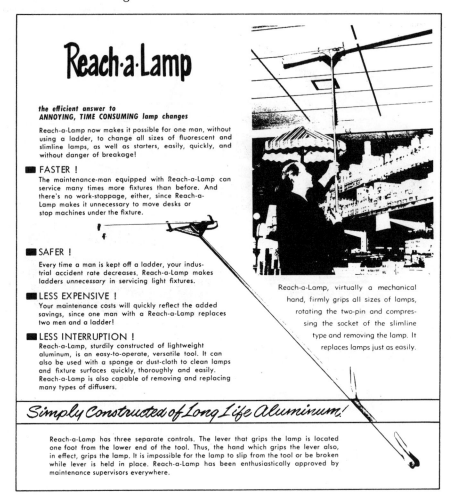

Reach·a·Lamp

**the efficient answer to
ANNOYING, TIME CONSUMING lamp changes**

Reach-a-Lamp now makes it possible for one man, without using a ladder, to change all sizes of fluorescent and slimline lamps, as well as starters, easily, quickly, and without danger of breakage!

■ FASTER !
The maintenance-man equipped with Reach-a-Lamp can service many times more fixtures than before. And there's no work-stoppage, either, since Reach-a-Lamp makes it unnecessary to move desks or stop machines under the fixture.

■ SAFER !
Every time a man is kept off a ladder, your industrial accident rate decreases. Reach-a-Lamp makes ladders *unnecessary* in servicing light fixtures.

■ LESS EXPENSIVE !
Your maintenance costs will quickly reflect the added savings, since one man with a Reach-a-Lamp replaces two men and a ladder!

■ LESS INTERRUPTION !
Reach-a-Lamp, sturdily constructed of lightweight aluminum, is an easy-to-operate, versatile tool. It can also be used with a sponge or dust-cloth to clean lamps and fixture surfaces quickly, thoroughly and easily. Reach-a-Lamp is also capable of removing and replacing many types of diffusers.

Reach-a-Lamp, virtually a mechanical hand, firmly grips all sizes of lamps, rotating the two-pin and compressing the socket of the slimline type and removing the lamp. It replaces lamps just as easily.

Simply Constructed of Long Life Aluminum!

Reach-a-Lamp has three separate controls. The lever that grips the lamp is located one foot from the lower end of the tool. Thus, the hand which grips the lever also, in effect, grips the lamp. It is impossible for the lamp to slip from the tool or be broken while lever is held in place. Reach-a-Lamp has been enthusiastically approved by maintenance supervisors everywhere.

rate of production. Representatives reported a number of difficulties. The length and shape of the device made it somewhat awkward for salesmen to carry, yet customers were reluctant to purchase without seeing the tool and observing it in operation. Some interested firms found that some of their lamps or fixture diffusers were of a type that could not be serviced by the Reach-A-Lamp. Some of the representatives failed to follow-up on the leads that were sent to them by Mr. Johnson, who was receiving several dozen mail inquiries weekly in response to the publicity and advertising released.

Mr. Johnson made a number of sales calls himself and found that demonstration of the Reach-A-Lamp almost invariably aroused interest on the part of those who saw it work. Sales were difficult to close, however, and in a number of instances, the representative was referred to someone else in the firm who had more knowledge or authority in the purchase of equipment for lighting maintenance. Some persons were enthusiastic about the need for a tool of this sort. As one electrical contractor expressed it, "This is something for which the lighting industry has had a real need for years." Other persons who might be customers saw the tool and admitted its ability and advantages, but believed that their existing method of handling lamp-changing was sufficient for their needs. For example, some supermarket operators contracted their entire lighting maintenance with electrical service contractors. Others had clerks or stock-boys change the lamps after the store was closed.

QUESTIONS FOR DISCUSSION

1. Would the favorable comments and reactions about Reach-A-Lamp indicate better sales than those attained?
2. Was there really a need for the Reach-A-Lamp on the part of the users visualized as markets by Mr. Johnson?
3. If you were a salesman selling the Reach-A-Lamp, on whom would you call?
4. How would you evaluate Mr. Johnson's choice of sales representatives?

IV–4. Graham's Pet Food[1]

The Pet Food Institute reported that dog and cat food sales in the United States, including canned, dry, semi-moist, and snacks, had grown at a rate of about 10 percent per year from 1962 to 1970. Sales had risen from $600 million to $1.16 billion. Of the $1.6 billion market, canned dog food accounted for 36 percent of the sales and canned cat food accounted for 20 percent.

Canned dog and cat food sales had increased from $354 million in 1965 to $680 million in 1970. Canned pet food sales in the Pacific Northwest, primarily Oregon and Washington, were about 1.4 million cases, with a value of $8.4 million.

---

[1] Prepared by Louis C. Wagner, University of Washington.

A National Can study predicted that by 1979 the dollar volume for all pet foods would reach $2.1 billion, an increase of 91 percent over 1970. Volume grocery products were expected to increase only 19 percent in the same period.

It was estimated that in the United States about 54 percent of the households owned a dog, cat, or both. In the western states, ownership of cats and/or dogs was higher than the national average. In addition, the 1969 Brand Rating Index showed that western families used about 40 percent more canned pet food on a per-household basis than the United States as a whole.

COMPETITION IN SEATTLE-TACOMA MARKET

The one dog food canner in the Seattle-Tacoma market produced a quality product in the medium-priced field that retailed for 22–28 cents a can in 1973. In Portland, Oregon, there were four pet food canners. In California, the San Francisco Bay area had four, and the Los Angeles area had six pet food producers. Most of these firms shipped their brands or supplied private brand products that were sold in the Seattle-Tacoma market. Some of these producers packed a canned product aimed specifically at dogs, while others attempted to appeal to both dog and cat owners.

In spite of the fact that several national brands were heavily advertised, two regional brands, "Blue Mountain" (Portland) and "Tyrells" (Seattle) led in local popularity. Table IV–1 shows the sales of canned pet food by brand in the Seattle-Tacoma market for 1973.

TABLE IV–1
Dog Food Sales by Brands: Seattle-Tacoma Market, 1973

Brand	Percent	Brand	Percent
Blue Mountain	20	Kal Kan	4
Tyrell's	17	Ken L. Ration	3
Skippy	15	Recipe	2
Vets	10	Others	2
Friskies	10	Private Label	8
Alpo	9		

In 1973, about 40,000 cases of private label dog food were sold in the Seattle-Tacoma market. Most of this dog food was produced by California canners. The only Seattle producer, Tyrells, was not interested in producing a private-label product.

There were three quality levels of canned dog food sold—economy, medium-grade, and high-meat. In addition, a few plants packed economy and medium-grade dog food in large 26-ounce cans as well as in the more popular 15-ounce size. The volume of dog food by these varieties in the Seattle-Tacoma area, as well as prices at which these varieties were sold, is shown in Table IV–2.

TABLE IV–2
**Volume of Canned Dog Food by Types: Seattle-Tacoma
Market, 1973**

Size and Type	Price per Can	Percent of Volume
15 oz. Economy	$ .15–.16	25.0
15 oz. Medium grade	.22–.28	42.0
14 oz. High meat	.31–.38	13.0
26 oz. Economy	.27	7.0
26 oz. Medium grade	.34–.37	5.0
15 oz. Private label (economy)	.14 ⎫	8.0
26 oz. Private label (economy)	.23 ⎭	

In the economy line, two California firms producing Vets and Skippy dominated the market. In the medium-price field, two regional brands, Tyrell's and Blue Mountain led the market. Although competition was increasing in 1973, Alpo secured over two thirds of the high-meat segment.

GRAHAM'S PET FOOD

A Seattle resident, Mr. Graham, who had extensive experience in the canned food industry and had worked for canning companies with a dog food line, believed that there was a good opportunity for a new high-quality dog food producer in the Seattle area. After considerable experimentation with varying dog food formulas, he developed and tested three qualities of dog food which he believed were ready to be introduced to the consumer market in the Pacific Northwest. All three grades were used by a number of kennels raising and boarding dogs in the Seattle area. He received excellent reactions from kennel owners, and had several letters endorsing his product from them. In both the economy and medium-grade fields, Mr. Graham was using 25 percent more meat products in his dog food than were his competitors. This additional meat made the product more appealing to the pet as well as to the owner.

Mr. Graham believed that locating in the Seattle area would provide him with advantages over other packers shipping into the Seattle-Tacoma market. Freight per case from Oregon producers amounted to 15 cents, and California producers paid about 40 cents to ship their products to the Seattle area. In addition, there were adequate supplies of low cost raw materials, particularly meat by-products and grain. Some Oregon and California producers obtained meat by-products in the State of Washington to fill their needs.

GRAHAM'S MARKET MIX OBJECTIVES

Mr. Graham planned to adopt the following market mix:

1. Introduce three qualities of dog and cat food in the Pacific Northwest.
   For My Love—Economy pet food
   Town N'Country Ration—Medium-grade pet food
   Town N'Country Super Ration—A 100 percent meat product
2. Introduce beef, pork, liver, and chicken flavors in the economy and medium-priced varieties.
3. Pack pet food in the economy and medium-priced varieties in the 26-ounce (large) can as well as the more popular 15-ounce size. No regional brands were packed in the larger size.
4. Obtain a portion of the local private label business which was being supplied entirely by out-of-state firms.
5. Push the economy and medium-priced pet food as suitable for cats as well as dogs.

By providing a complete product mix—three quality grades, two can sizes, and private brands—Mr. Graham hoped to obtain a 10 percent penetration of the Seattle-Tacoma and Portland market. Since the variety of his product mix would avoid having too much impact on any one segment of the market, he believed this strategy would avoid aggressive retaliatory moves by competitors already well established.

To assist in getting food stores to stock and push his line of pet food, Mr. Graham planned to offer retailers higher margins than competitors. Most manufacturers were providing retailers with margins of 18–28 percent, with 24 percent being most common. Mr. Graham planned to offer retailers margins of 36 percent for the 60-day introductory period and 28 percent later.

INTRODUCTORY OBJECTIVES

To secure sufficient volume to operate efficiently, Graham planned to introduce his line of canned pet foods in both the Seattle-Tacoma and Portland wholesale markets. He was considering allocating from $12,000 to $24,000 for the first year's promotion. Since the Seattle-Tacoma wholesale market had a population of 1,450,000 compared with a little over 1,000,000 for the Portland wholesale market, he was considering putting more of his promotional funds into the Seattle-Tacoma market.

QUESTIONS FOR DISCUSSION:

1. Does Graham have a good opportunity to enter the pet food field?
2. Evaluate his proposed product and brand mix.
3. Should he attempt to introduce his pet food in both the Seattle-Tacoma and Portland markets at the same time?
4. Develop a promotional plan for a two-month introductory period in the Seattle-Tacoma area including
   a. Level of expenditures recommended for introductory period.
   b. Types of media recommended. Justify your selection.

IV–5. Anders' Bakery[1]

In January 1947, Ronald R. Anders, the 26-year-old son of W. W. Anders, went to work in his father's business, Anders' Bakery. The bakery had been established by Ron's father in 1924. It served an area of approximately 50 miles around Midtown. According to Ron Anders, the quality of Anders' products had never been very good during the war years. Purchases were made from a large number of places and the variation in the quality of goods purchased caused noticeable variation in the final product. This variation in quality of Anders' products caused them to lose sales leadership even in the home area of Midtown.[2] The firm made a profit of $25,000 in 1946, but a loss of $21,000 was incurred in 1947.

Ron Anders first attempted to establish more rational management techniques and to change the company over from a one-man operation to a management team operation, in which no one man would be indispensable and any man could be replaced without adverse effects on the business.

Gradually, Ron's drive for improved quality and a larger share of the local market began to pay off; however, Anders' Bakery still had a substantial amount of excess capacity. In order to increase the volume of sales, Ron found, in 1950, a distributor in the Atlanta market who was willing to sell Anders' rolls and specialty products. Profits gradually

---

[1] Prepared by N. A. Beadles, University of Georgia.

[2] There were approximately seven other bakeries that served the Midtown area in direct competition with Anders' Bakery.

increased during the period 1949–1956. However, Ron Anders was still striving to maintain the $25,000 profit the corporation showed in 1946. In 1955, Ron went to the Cut-Rate Supermarket and persuaded them to sell Anders' Bakery products on a private label basis in 1956. By 1959, Anders was selling two trailer loads of bread a day through the Cut-Rate Supermarket, plus one trailer load of specialty products. Their goods were sold to the Cut-Rate Supermarket for the wholesale price less 25 percent. Ron computed that the selling costs of his own goods ran from 28 percent to 33 percent, depending upon the nature of the item, and this meant that the arrangement with the Cut-Rate Supermarket was a very profitable one for Anders' Bakery.

In late 1959, Ron Anders decided to expand into the city of Henderson in order to continue expanding the sales volume. Henderson, located about 90 miles away from Midtown, was roughly twice the size of Midtown.[3] In December, 1959, Anders obtained a warehouse in Henderson and moved his best salesman and route supervisor, George Harrison, to the area. Harrison established six new routes, offering the retail merchants in Henderson a full line of service in both bread and specialty bakery items. Due to the excellent work by Mr. Harrison, the six routes were approximately breaking even by September, 1960, and showed promise of becoming profitable in the immediate future.

Also in December, 1959, Cut-Rate Supermarket came to Ron and requested that before they renewed their contract on January 1, 1960, he produce for them a small economy loaf of bread weighing approximately 13 ounces. This loaf would sell for "two for 25¢" to "two for 29¢." No other bakery in the State of Georgia at that time produced an economy loaf, with the exception of A & P, Colonial Stores, and Winn-Dixie. Ron Anders felt that the traditional reluctance of bakeries to change the size of the loaf would be sufficient to overcome any willingness on the part of other independent bakeries in Georgia to produce an economy loaf. Anders considered that changing the size of the loaf would be looked upon as unethical by the other bakeries, and he did not wish to be the first to enter upon such a course of action. Therefore, he refused to bake an economy loaf.

After consulting with his father, Ron decided that Cut-Rate would be unable to find another independent bakery who would come out with the new economy loaf. Therefore, in late December, 1959, Ron Anders informed Cut-Rate Supermarket that he would be happy to continue the relationship as it had been in the past, but he was unwilling to produce the size loaf requested.

Anders' estimation of Cut-Rate's ability to find another bakery was wrong. Cut-Rate Supermarket's management immediately informed Mr. Anders that the contract would be terminated at the beginning of the

---

[3] Population was approximately 40,000 in 1960.

new year, and that they had already found another bakery that would bake any size loaf requested. This news came as a great shock to Mr. Anders who had told his father that at the worst, Cut-Rate would indulge in further negotiation and would eventually agree to another three-year contract similar to the one they signed in late 1956. In January, 1960, when the Cut-Rate Supermarket contract was cancelled, Anders' Bakery was faced with a loss of almost one-third of its volume of sales.

In August, 1960, Mr. Al Wilson, Anders' Atlanta distributor, came to visit Anders in Midtown. He stated that he was going to get out of the bread distributing business. He told Mr. Anders that so far as he was concerned the distributing business was nothing but a headache and that he had not been able to make any profit in the 10 years he had operated as a distributor. He stated that his relation with Anders had been a very pleasant one; and therefore, he would like to sell his Atlanta routes and equipment to Anders for $35,000, which represented the depreciated value of the equipment. Wilson said that if Anders did not buy the routes, he would sell to any other buyer he could find. Wilson stated that he had been approached by one or two other bakeries who wanted to get into the Atlanta market.

After consulting with his father, who by 1958 had virtually retired from active management in the bakery, Ron decided that the bakery could not afford to give up the Atlanta market. Ron made the decision that Anders' Bakery should take over distribution in the Atlanta market.

Once the decision was made, Ron transferred George Harrison from Henderson to take charge in Atlanta. A warehouse was rented, a secretary and clerk were hired for the Atlanta operation, and by mid-1961 Anders' Bakery was operating 14 routes in Atlanta. This meant that Anders' Bakery was operating 31 routes out of Midtown, 9 in Henderson, and 14 in the Atlanta market. These high sales were not obtained without extensive costs to the company. For example, during the week ending September 19, 1961, 43.4 percent of the bread put out for sale in Atlanta had to be picked up and returned as stale merchandise. In Henderson, 34.1 percent of the bread put out had to be picked up and returned to the company. On the other hand, only 21.1 percent of the bread put out in Midtown was picked up as stale. For the week ending September 26, the situation had not improved very much. The corresponding stale figures were 20.76 percent in Midtown, 48.5 percent in Henderson, and 58.2 percent in Atlanta.

Ron and his father both had expected penetration of the Atlanta market to be difficult, but not as difficult as the route sheets now indicated. Ron found from the sales sheets that none of the routes in either Atlanta or Henderson showed sales of $300 per week. The average for all 23 was about $175 per week.

In 1961, despite the fact that sales were higher than in 1959, the company lost $19,388.

QUESTIONS FOR DISCUSSION:

1. What changes in management practices should Ron Anders have implemented prior to the expansion of his business?
2. What should he have known about the Atlanta market before he expanded operations there?
3. What were the hazards of selling to Cut-Rate Supermarket?
4. Was Ron Anders' decision not to produce a small loaf of bread for Cut-Rate reasonable in light of his company's market position? Why?
5. What should Anders' Bakery do in light of its experience in the Atlanta market?

IV–6. Sam Frevert and Associates[1]

In March 1973, Mr. Sam Frevert, a Tulsa real estate broker, referring to the McClellan-Kerr Waterway, commented, So many industries are not even aware that we have a Waterway. We need to publicize it more.

Mr. Frevert studied civil engineering at Texas A. and M. University, but did not earn a degree. He had seven years of experience in the industrial development department of the Frisco Railroad and participated in developing over 20 industrial parks, including two in Tulsa. He also was employed for four years with a development firm that specialized in industrial properties in Dallas. He was appointed the first Director of the Tulsa Port of Catoosa, and remained in this capacity for about six years. He located several industries at the Port and observed that had he located them as a broker, he would have made several times as much money. In June 1971, he resigned and formed his own business as a real estate broker. He stated that over the years he had contemplated establishing his own brokerage firm for financial reasons.

THE FIRM'S ASSOCIATES

The Associates consisted of Mr. I. E. Chenoweth, Mr. Andy Anderson, and Mr. Charles Patchen. Mr. Chenoweth was an attorney and a rate

---

[1] Prepared by L. R. Trueblood and J. C. Johnson, University of Tulsa.

and traffic expert, whose services were procured on a contract basis. The others contributed capital to the firm.

In March 1973, Mr. Frevert and his wife were the only two involved in day-to-day operations of the firm. She was the bookkeeper and receptionist. Their office was located in their residence. Within two months, he planned to hire two other employees to sell industrial real estate.

The firm was licensed by the Port Authority as one of the 23 real estate brokers for the Tulsa Port. All leasing arrangements at the Port had been accomplished by Mr. Frevert and Col. Harley W. Ladd, who succeeded him as Director. Mr. Frevert believed that the other Port brokers were unsuccessful because they were not sufficiently aware of the transportation problems involved in order to arrange leases. His firm was the only Tulsa real estate broker which specialized in the industrial development area.

ACTIVITIES OF SAM FREVERT AND ASSOCIATES

Activities of Sam Frevert and Associates had been concentrated on the Waterway. However, Mr. Frevert planned an expansion of the firm's markets to industrial parks in the City of Tulsa.

The firm was the agent for the Seltzer Interests, of Philadelphia, which owned many Eastern industrial parks. The Seltzer Interests were establishing a transport terminal near the Tulsa Port. This terminal would have a capability that the Port did not have—individual lots facing the water to permit an overhead crane that would go directly over the water and enable a manufacturer to load his own cargoes. Also, property could be bought in the Seltzer's industrial park while it could only be leased at the Tulsa Port's industrial park. The Seltzer project was scheduled for completion by December 1973; however, no tenants had been procured by April 1973.

PROSPECTING FOR CLIENTS

Efforts were carried out to obtain marketing prospects for the Tulsa Port's industrial park, the Seltzer's park, and along the Waterway. Mr. Frevert analyzed prospective industries and selected only those in which a major part of their price (and cost) was transportation. Prospecting was accomplished through analyses of companies and industries described in Standard and Poor's and Moody's Manuals. Their products and markets were analyzed. Industries that had large volumes of dry-bulk cargoes, liquid bulk products, and heavy equipment transported were prime prospects. Several railroad carriers, with their industrial development departments, were another source of leads. Also, contacts with the Tulsa Chamber of Commerce and the Oklahoma Industrial Development Department were productive in obtaining leads.

Tulsa had a large number of steel fabricators who were prospects. Some of them manufactured heat exchangers, of great length, susceptible to barge transportation. Additional prospects were foreign steel companies. A greater volume of foreign steel than domestic steel was moved through the Tulsa Port.

Mr. Frevert stated that the first step involved in dealing with potential clients was determining their transportation needs. The second step consisted of the calculation of transportation costs in using the Waterway.

A brochure had been developed to aid the firm in publicizing its services.

RELATIONSHIPS WITH TULSA PORT FACILITIES AUTHORITY

The Tulsa Port Facilities Authority was a nonprofit trust which aided clients in financing their Port facilities. The latter could receive certain tax benefits by obtaining financing through it.

For an additional fee, Mr. Frevert would secure the necessary banking and leasing information and arrange for an attorney to draw up the contract. He represented the client in the leasing arrangements with this Authority and attempted to negotiate the most favorable leasing rentals.

Mr. Frevert often prepared pro forma statements concerning the client's physical requirements. He also contacted local builders and manufacturers of overhead cranes for cost estimates. However, he did no appraisal work.

COMMISSIONS

Exhibit VI–1 shows the suggested real estate brokers' fees at the Tulsa Port:

EXHIBIT VI–1
Suggested Real Estate Brokers' Fees at Tulsa Port of Catoosa

Duration of Lease (in years)	Percent of Lease Payment
1 through 5	10
6	9
7 and 8	8.5
9 through 17	8
18 and 19	6
20 and over	5

The prices quoted by the Tulsa Port Authority were the same whether the property was leased by the Authority's staff or by real estate brokers. The Port paid the brokers' commissions.

Commissions due from the Port Authority were payable over a two-year period. The scheduled basis of payments was: one-fourth of the commission when the lease was closed; one-fourth a year later; one-fourth six months later; and one-fourth at the end of the period.

Mr. Frevert referred to a lease covering about five acres for 24 years which he had procured. The brokerage fees were about $10,000, for which an account receivable was established for two years.

FINANCES AND ASSETS OF THE FIRM

Mr. Frevert stated that the firm had no indebtedness and nominal overhead. A private airplane and an automobile had been acquired. The plane was used when the destination was within 300–400 miles of Tulsa. Commercial flights were taken to the West and East Coasts. About one-fourth of Mr. Frevert's time was spent in traveling. Most prospects were located in New Orleans, Houston, St. Louis, or Chicago. No other fixed assets were owned.

Mr. Frevert sought downtown space for his office, because the firm's workload was increasing and additional employees were needed.

THE McCLELLAN-KERR WATERWAY

Probably the Tulsa Port had the best physical facilities of any inland port in the United States. The key to the development of the McClellan-Kerr Waterway was to convince companies (and industries) of savings associated with locating their facilities on it. The idea of water transportation or combination of water transportation with other forms of transportation had to be sold.

Economic development of the Waterway would not be exclusively at the Tulsa Port. Private industry customers building their own facilities along the Waterway would produce economic growth.

During economic recessions, barge lines prospered more than they did during boom periods. Shippers wanted to move their products more cheaply and were in less hurry.

Industrial prospects were aware of their competitors' actions. When the first company in an industry decided to ship by water, other companies would follow suit.

Since the Port was established, Tulsa had water-controlled freight. The Frisco and Santa Fe Railroads had built trackage into the Tulsa Port area. Mr. Frevert cited two problems relating to railroad rate structures: (1) the rate structures were very complicated—one could call three railroads for a rate and be given three different rates; and (2) information concerning transportation charges was not sufficiently available. All rate departments—e.g., at the Tulsa Chamber of Commerce and Oklahoma Industrial Development Department—in Oklahoma had been dissolved.

QUESTIONS FOR DISCUSSION:

1. How do you evaluate the qualifications of Mr. Frevert for managing and operating his firm?
2. How do you evaluate the industrial development potential of the Seltzer Interests's transport terminal compared with the Tulsa Port's terminal?
3. How do you evaluate Mr. Frevert's method of prospecting for clients?
4. With respect to leasing and selling sites at or near the Tulsa Port, what type of sales promotion would be effective in enticing clients (shippers) to use barge transportation rather than trucks?

IV–7. University Cinemas (B)[1]

University Cinemas, Inc., recently purchased by Gary Benjamin and Roman Johns, was a motion picture theater operating company. The building which housed the theater was owned by John Lundgren, a local businessman. At the outset, the only asset held by University Cinemas was the theater equipment valued at $20,000.

Under previous management, a theater chain known as CTW, Inc., the theater had not done well, as it had grossed only $90,000, including concession stand revenue management. Gary Benjamin and Roman Johns were certain that it could gross $160,000 and that it had failed to do so in the past only because of CTW's inadequacies, the most serious being a cash-flow problem. They habitually delayed payment to film distributors, in many cases for as long as six months. The distributors responded by refusing to supply higher quality films unless payment was received in advance. Consequently, CTW did not book the better films into their theaters. Most films shown were "X-rated" or "hard R" types available from independent producers at low cost. This, too, was self-defeating; without good shows, people did not attend the theater.

---

[1] Prepared by Peter R. Kensicki, Cincinnati Financial Corporation, and John Hand, Auburn University. See "University Cinemas (A)" in Part II for further details.

CTW's second major failing was its insistence on scheduling movies for each theater out of a central office. Benjamin was convinced that different towns do not necessarily have the same preferences. This is especially true of university towns. In an area with a large student population, students would be interested in a different type of film than would a farming community. He noted that on the rare occasions when an appropriate show was booked, it attracted good audiences.

University Cinemas was in a small isolated town where the university's 17,000 students were the primary economic force between September and May. Their preference was for "A" quality films with a strong artistic flavor and a social "message." If sex and violence were also prominent, so much the better. "Serpico," "Papillon," "Midnight Cowboy," and "A Clockwork Orange" were favorites. The students preferred late hours. Many students remained in the downtown area until well past midnight—at least until the bars closed.

There were roughly the same number of permanent townspeople as students. They formed the major market during the summer and during the month of December. The "townies" also desired "A" movies, but their preference lay in the direction of clean, wholesome family entertainment, "Sleuth," "Fiddler on the Roof," and "101 Dalmations" were popular with this group. The townspeople attended in the early evening hours and also appreciated summer afternoon shows appealing to children.

Competition for University Cinemas came from two sources. The Tigercat Theater, across the street from University Cinemas, had only 400 seats, compared with the 1,100 capacity of University Cinemas. The other source of competition was the university itself, which showed films in the main auditorium at 25–50¢ during the school year. The films offered by the university were predominantly "A" quality movies, two to 10 years old. These were limited to a single showing on Friday and Saturday nights at 7:30. Alternative uses of the auditorium prevented expansion of this service into the midweek period or multiple viewings.

The immediate goal for Benjamin and Johns was to raise the gross to $160,000 per year, the figure they considered to be the reasonable potential of the theater and its concessions. They felt obligated to raise the overall quality of the films, review the prices charged, and use the facilities more intensively.

The theater needed refurnishing. In order to obtain the funds, University Cinemas entered into an agreement with an outside firm for lease of the concession stand. In addition to paying 47½ percent of the gross receipts (less wages to stand employees), the lessee agreed to provide a one-year loan of $10,000 at 8½ percent interest. Benjamin and Johns expected the loan to be repaid out of the first year's receipts. Additional remodeling costs were partially absorbed by the landlord through an agreed reduction of the rent.

Acquisition of quality films proved to be no problem. Distributors did not hold the "sins" of CTW against the new management. Better films were available. University Cinemas quickly established that they would return the films promptly, remit film rental when due, and give honest reports of gross receipts. Not only were better films available, but the theater was able to obtain exclusive showing rights. Once a theater signs a contract to run a film, another local theater cannot obtain that film until after the first engagement. The establishment with the exclusive arrangement can choose the right time for showing the movie, secure in the knowledge that its competitor cannot "scoop" it with an earlier showing.

The rental fees for "A" quality films are usually set as a percentage of gross revenue. Box office "blockbusters" are expensive. When the Tigercat Theater obtained "The Godfather" for an eight-week run they paid the distributor 90 percent of the gross receipts from the first three weeks against a $15,000 guarantee. For the fourth week, the distributor received 70 percent; his share dropped 10 percent per week for the remainder of the engagement. An "A" quality film of less than blockbuster appeal, "Deliverance," would rent for 50 to 70 percent of gross. Older films and the classics, as well as poor grade movies, either rent for about 25 percent of gross or for a flat fee of $50 or $100. Occasionally, a double feature obtained from the same distributor is available for 30 percent of gross.

The two other problems, price structure and more intensive use of the facilities, were interrelated. Under CTW, the admission charge was $2 for all showings. The summer shows for the children were free; local merchants paid $15 per week for 100 to 200 tickets which they gave away to their customers. Average attendance figures are presented in Exhibit VII–1. Attendance depended on two factors: quality of film and day of the week. It seemed to Benjamin and Johns that the price should be lower on week nights.

EXHIBIT VII–1
Attendance and Prices Under CTW Ownership

	M–Th	Weekend	Kiddie Matinee
Quality A	200–400	300–500	500
Quality B	40–50	40–50	
Price	$2.00	$2.00	Free*

* Fifteen to 20 merchants paid $15 per week for tickets to be given to children. The merchants received about 100–200 tickets, depending on how many they could use. The program ran for 10 weeks during the summer.

In addition, since the theater was rarely more than half-filled, they thought $2 might be too high. Perhaps a lower price would increase attendance. As a result, an admission of $1.75 was set for weekends and $1.50 for weekdays, as shown in Exhibit VII–2. University Cinemas

EXHIBIT VII–2
Attendance and Prices under University Cinema's Ownership

	M–Th	*Weekend*	*Kiddie Matinee*
Quality A	300–500	700–900	
Quality B	100–150	100–150	500
Price	$1.50	$1.75	Free*

* See Note to Exhibit VII–1.

also decided to continue the summer matinees for the children. The revenue from the tickets was not large, but children did consume a lot of popcorn and soft drinks.

At this point, Benjamin and Johns were ready to attack the problem of more intensive use of the facilities. One of the first innovations was the Friday "Classic Movie Matinee," to be run while the university was in session. The films chosen were 16mm classics such as the original "Cleopatra" and Charlie Chaplin's "Modern Times." They were purchased from the distributors for a flat fee of $50 to $100. To attract nostalgia buffs, a price of $.69 was set. No formal price analysis was performed. Advertising consisted entirely of a sandwich board set up outside the theater. Attendance averaged about 60, not enough to pay the rent of the films. However, revenue from the concession stand enabled the venture to pay its direct costs. It was hoped that people who attended might see a preview they liked and attend a regular feature.

Benjamin and Johns then thought of another possibility. They booked two horror films for the Friday and Saturday nights before Halloween, with the intention of running them at midnight. The films were inexpensive "oldies." The employees would have to be overtime to work the midnight show, but otherwise costs should not rise significantly. The question was again, "What price should we charge?" If the "midnight flicks" were to become a permanent feature, Benjamin and Johns would have to decide whether to use "A" or "B" grade films. The horror shows were obviously a gimmick for Halloween. They were not intended as a permanent type for the midnight shows. They also could be sure that the Tigercat Theater would copy the "midnight flick" idea if it proved successful.

QUESTIONS FOR DISCUSSION:

1. What is the definition of demand elasticity?
2. What is the mathematical formula for demand elasticity?
3. What is the importance of demand elasticity to total revenue?
4. What are the consequences of setting too high an admission price?
5. What are the consequences of setting too low an admission price?
6. If the price is found to be too high, is it feasible to reduce the price?
7. If the price is found to be too low, is it feasible to raise the price?
8. What happened to total revenues when University Cinemas raised the quality of the films?
9. How can the theater please everyone in town?
10. What problems will arise if the competing theater copies the midnight movie idea?
11. What real advantage does University Cinemas hold over the Tigercat theater if the midnight movies prove successful?

IV–8. *Martin's Clothes, Ltd. (A)*[1]

Martin's Clothes, Ltd. was a small family owned men's clothing store featuring suits, sport clothes, and accessories. Located in Suncoast, Florida, a suburb of Tampa, Martin's had gross sales of $350,000–$383,000 annually.

Frank Martin took over the management of Martin's Clothes, Ltd. when his father died in the early part of 1957. The store operated with the objectives of providing a quality product with reliable, courteous service to its customers. A local family, the Martins were well known. Based on the objectives of the store and the local recognition of his family, Frank Martin instituted no major changes or deviations from the way the store had operated previously.

EMPLOYEES

Frank Martin handled purchasing as well as some selling. He was assisted by his son, Richard, who was primarily a sales clerk but also watched for low inventory items. Frank also had another full-time sales-

---

[1] Prepared by Jay T. Knippen and Dorothy N. Harlow, University of South Florida.

person. The busy period of the day was between 11:00 A.M. to 1:00 P.M. In such a downtown area many individuals do their shopping during their lunch hour. Based on past records, the store did about forty percent of total sales during this two-hour period. It was also during this time that Frank was primarily engaged in his selling function.

PRODUCT

Martin's Clothes, Ltd. handled only top-line men's apparel and accessories. When Frank took over the store, it carried primarily the essentials of men's apparel—suits, sport coats, slacks, shirts, ties. Frank had increased the selection carried to include shoes, socks, colognes, robes, swim-wear, and jewelry boxes. These were added at the urging of Richard, coupled with numerous customer requests made directly to Frank. Customers had also suggested that a comparable high-quality line of women's apparel and accessories be added. He had been reluctant to implement these requests. He felt that the store's image was built upon men's clothing as well as his expertise with the line; and to attempt to change or expand into women's apparel would be costly if it were to fail.

Prices were in line with the quality of the merchandise. Examples of the prices charged by Martin's were: suits $120 to $400, shirts $10 to $25, shoes $30 to $100, and ties $7.50 to $20.

Frank carried the more conservative, well-established lines and attempted to avoid items that were inclined to be fads. Richard disagreed with his father on this point. He felt that men's clothing was constantly changing and going through cycles. Due to this, Richard felt that even if particular clothing items were just a fad, the store should attempt to meet the peak demand for such merchandise. He wanted the store to carry more "mod" fashions. This would attract a segment of the market the store had previously ignored—young men 16–25 years old.

ADVERTISING

The store did essentially no advertising. Frank relied on the quality of the merchandise and the service he provided his customers to do the advertising for him. He expected this word of mouth technique to retain his present clientele as well as add new customers. Only rarely did Frank advertise in the local newspaper. His position was, "Why should I pay to advertise when my customers do it for me?"

LOCATION

Martin's Clothes, Ltd. was located in the center of the downtown area of Suncoast, Florida. Suncoast had a population of 200,000 and there was a great tourist influx from October to March. The downtown area was comprised of retail outlets, theaters, restaurants, and other business enterprises. The downtown area grew quickly in the war years, but the pace in the sixties slowed tremendously because of rapid suburban growth. Sears was the first major store to exit from the downtown area in 1963. This was followed by J. C. Penney's move to the suburban area in 1965.

The city council had discussed the necessity of revitalizing the downtown area. The revitalization program would include the destruction of some of the older vacant buildings, the construction of underground parking facilities, and the construction of a large mallway decorated with landscaping and better lighting. This project was estimated to cost over 25 million dollars. No action had resulted as yet from this proposal.

STORE HOURS

Martin's Clothes, Ltd. was open 9:30 to 5:30 Monday through Saturday, except on Friday when the store stayed open until 9:00. Frank was almost compelled to stay open Friday nights to compete with other stores who were open that night. There had been a trend to open on Sunday afternoons, and many stores followed this pattern. Frank refused, because he felt that opening Sunday was not consistent with the quality image projected by his store.

COMPETITION

Direct competition stemmed from three major sources. First, there was a large, nearby retail chain department store that sold clothing in an intermediate price range. The higher-priced merchandise in this department store was comparable to the lowest price goods carried by the Martin's store. Second, there was a small outlet which custom tailored suits and shirts. The customer selected the material he liked and he was then measured for an exact fit of the suit or shirt. The prices at this outlet were competitive with Martin's top line. Finally, there was a medium-sized local firm that handled both men's and ladies' apparel. This was an established firm with over 25 years at the same location. Its prices were somewhat lower than Martin's, but Frank believed customer preference was based more on previous shopping habits than on price.

Throughout the city there were several clothing outlets comparable to Martin's. The downtown area was in competition with other sections of the city. If the downtown area could attract more customers, then each of the stores should get some share of this increase.

SALES AND PROFITS

The sales and profits of Martin's since Frank took over the store are shown in Table VIII–1.

TABLE VIII–1
Martin's Clothes, Ltd. Sales and Profits: 1957–72

Year	Sales	Profits	Profits as Percent of Sales
1957	$350,000	$22,500	6.4
1958	363,000	25,000	6.9
1959	365,000	25,500	7.0
1960	377,000	27,000	7.3
1961	372,000	28,000	7.5
1962	374,000	26,000	7.0
1963	381,000	25,500	6.7
1964	383,000	27,000	7.1
1965	372,000	23,500	6.3
1966	370,000	21,800	5.9
1967	374,000	22,600	6.1
1968	366,000	21,000	5.8
1969	362,000	20,000	5.5
1970	367,000	21,600	5.9
1971	365,000	19,200	5.3
1972	360,000	18,500	5.2

Richard had noted that a minimum of eight percent (profits as a percentage of sales) was very common among retail outlets comparable to Martin's.

Martin's experienced a seasonal demand notorious in the retail industry even though summer clothing, in this temperate climate, was worn by some people all year. The greatest volume of sales occurred during October, November, and December. The lowest volume of sales was in the summer, particularly July and August. There also occurred smaller peak periods such as Father's Day and Easter.

FUTURE

Frank was approached by Mr. John Williams, a representative of the Sunshine Development Company. Mr. Williams informed Frank that his firm was in the process of planning a 36-store shopping mall. It would be an entirely new concept in shopping centers for this area. The mall would be completely enclosed with temperature-controlled heating and cooling. There would be parking facilities to accommodate over 2,000 cars.

The proposed mall would be located in a heavily-concentrated residential area, adjoining one of the exits of the expressway. Mr. Williams gave Frank a map of the area (see Exhibit VIII–1). The new mall would enable Frank to increase the 3,000 square feet of selling space he had to 4,600 square feet at the same rental price per square foot. Frank

EXHIBIT VIII–1

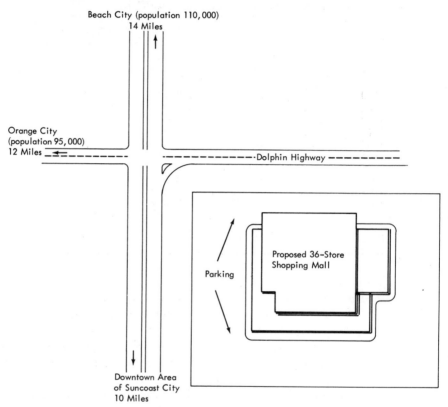

was not certain whether this new mall was a good idea. He was extremely concerned about moving his store, which had been in the same location for thirty years.

QUESTIONS FOR DISCUSSION:

1. What additional information is needed before making the relocation decision? How would you obtain this information?
2. How do you account for the profit trend?
3. Contrast and compare the problems faced by Martin's with a comparable store in your city.

4. Should Frank consider Richard's suggestion of adding fad items? If so, what items would you recommend? In what price range?

5. Do you agree with Frank's decision on advertising?

IV–9. The Stair-Chair[1]

A wheel chair which would also climb curbs and stairs has been the subject of inventors' efforts for decades. None has been really practical, and none has reached the market on a commercial scale. Excellent motorized chairs have been available for many years, and stairway-mounted elevators could be purchased to overcome a specific stairway barrier. However, the combination of a motorized chair that would permit paraplegics, quadraplegics, and others to overcome curbs, stairs, and other architectural barriers which deny those in wheelchairs much desired independence (from being assisted, chair and all, over these barriers) had not been developed.

Recently, Eugene Richison, an inventor from Kinta, Oklahoma was discussing his patented design for such a chair with Gary Keel, owner of East Side Machine Shop in Broken Arrow, Oklahoma. Mr. Keel believed that such a product would be in great demand, and suggested that he could further refine the design and perhaps market the product from his shop. Mr. Richison shared Mr. Keel's faith in the invention, but was not certain he could devote the necessary time and money to its further development. Nevertheless, a patent assignment contract was worked out between them, and within another year Mr. Keel had a prototype model, called the Stair-Chair, ready for a public showing.

The first demonstration was for the Tulsa newspapers. The resulting feature story, complete with a picture of the Stair-Chair being maneuvered up a stairway by a pretty girl, produced a high level of response. Mr. Keel's telephone rang frequently for the next couple of weeks with inquiries from individual wheelchair users and also from wheelchair manufacturers who wanted to purchase rights to manufacture the Stair-Chair, now covered by the original and subsequent patents. But, Mr. Keel did not want someone else to manufacture the product; he wanted to do it himself.

---

[1] Prepared by Howard A. Thompson, Eastern Kentucky University.

At that point in the series of events, principals from a Tulsa firm beginning to diversify its investments suggested that their organization would be interested in a joint venture wherein they would provide the financial backing for producing and marketing the Stair-Chair. The offer was accepted by Mr. Keel, and two initial steps were agreed upon. First, a design and production feasibility study was undertaken by an outside consultant. The results were "very satisfactory" with the Stair-Chair receiving high marks as to sound design and performance capability. Next, a marketing forecast was requested. These results, summarized in the Appendix, were also "highly encouraging" to Mr. Keel and to the investors.

Mr. Keel immediately began work on building nine of the now improved prototype models of the Stair-Chair. (See Exhibit IX–1 for a picture and description.) These were to be placed in strategic locations in order to gain actual experience under diverse operating conditions and also to gain approval of important centers of influence. A list of recommended locations was provided by the marketing study.

As with any complex product, ideas for further modification and improvement occur constantly. This was true of the Stair-Chair experience. For instance, the problem of transporting a heavy (185–200 pounds) motorized chair of this type was partially resolved in that it could now be reclined and folded to a height of 25 inches, permitting it to fit into the trunk of most "full-size" cars or into the rear of a station wagon. With the aid of a ramp device it could be driven into the trunk of a car, eliminating the need to lift it. Actual running time had also been extended to $4\frac{1}{2}$ hours (constant use) without a battery recharge. A plug-in battery recharge device was standard equipment on all models. Expansion of plant facilities permitted installation of a more efficient production line to replace the job-shop arrangement which was used to produce the nine prototypes. Actual layout and installation of the production line would be delayed pending results from tests of the nine Stair-Chairs, which would be completed in six months.

Mr. Keel engaged a consultant to design a marketing plan and budget for introducing the Stair-Chair following the test market. He was instructed to make the following assumptions:

1. The basic patent rights, good for 17 years, would not be successfully infringed or circumvented by any of the present wheelchair manufacturers such as Everest and Jennings. This assumption was based on a statement by a patent attorney engaged by Mr. Keel. The patented feature that was especially unique was the seat positioning device which permitted the operator to remain seated vertically while the Stair-Chair climbed or descended.
2. Sufficient development and working capital existed for producing

EXHIBIT IX-1

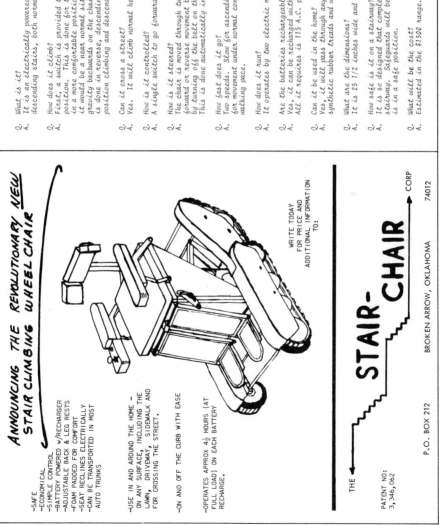

ANNOUNCING THE REVOLUTIONARY NEW
STAIR CLIMBING WHEELCHAIR

-SAFE
-ECONOMICAL
-SIMPLE CONTROL
-BATTERY POWERED w/RECHARGER
-ADJUSTABLE BACK & LEG RESTS
-FOAM PADDED FOR COMFORT
-SEAT RECLINES ELECTRICALLY
-CAN BE TRANSPORTED IN MOST
 AUTO TRUNKS

-USE IN AND AROUND THE HOME -
 ON ANY SURFACE, INCLUDING THE
 LAWN, DRIVEWAY, SIDEWALK AND
 FOR CROSSING THE STREET.

-ON AND OFF THE CURB WITH EASE.

-OPERATES APPROX 4½ HOURS (AT
 FULL LOAD) ON EACH BATTERY
 RECHARGE.

WRITE TODAY
FOR PRICE AND
ADDITIONAL INFORMATION
TO:

THE STAIR-CHAIR CORP

PATENT NO:
3,346,062

P.O. BOX 212   BROKEN ARROW, OKLAHOMA   74012

Q. What is it?
A. It is an electrically powered wheelchair that is capable of ascending and descending stairs, both normal and circular.

Q. How does it climb?
A. First, a switch is provided to lower the seat (tilt backward) to a semireclining position. This is done for two reasons, the first being to place the occupant in a more comfortable position when ascending and descending the stairway; i.e., it would be a neat normal sitting position; and secondly it shifts the center of gravity backwards on the chair base, which is necessary for climbing. Climbing is done in reverse, descending is done forward. The occupant attains the same position climbing and descending.

Q. Can it cross a street?
A. Yes. It will climb normal height curbs forward and abnormally high curbs backward.

Q. How is it controlled?
A. A single switch to go forward, backward, right and left.

Q. How is it steered?
A. The chair is moved through two identical motor driven tread-belt mechanisms. In forward or reverse movement both belts move at the same speed. Steering is done by turning off the belt on the side of the direction you wish the chair to move. This is done automatically in high or low speed by the control switch.

Q. How fast does it go?
A. Two speeds. Slow for ascending and descending stairs and a second faster speed for movement under normal conditions. The faster speed is comparable to a normal walking pace.

Q. How does it run?
A. It operates by two electric motors powered by two 12 volt batteries.

Q. Are the batteries rechargeable and if so, how?
A. Yes, it can be recharged with a built in recharger to replenish one day's running. All it requires is 115 A.C. power source.

Q. Can it be used in the home?
A. Yes, it will pass through any standard 2 foot 6 inch door. It also has nonmarking synthetic rubber treads and wheels.

Q. What are the dimensions?
A. It is 25 1/2 inches wide and 45 inches long. It weighs approximately 185 pounds.

Q. How safe is it on a stairway?
A. It is so designed that complete loss of power will immobilize the chair on a stairway. Safeguards will be built in to permit climbing only when the chair is in a safe position.

Q. What will be the cost?
A. Estimated in the $1500 range.

an initial inventory of Stair-Chairs and for a modest $25,000 promotional budget administered by a marketing manager and full-time secretary-assistant.

3. The sales goal was a total of 50,000 Stair-Chairs over the first three years of operation.

4. The cost estimate to produce the basic Stair-Chair with average accessory equipment (most orders would require some special fittings) was $650–750. Learning-curve experience was expected to reduce this cost to approximately $500 per unit after the first few thousand Stair-Chairs were produced.

5. Maintenance problems would be relatively simple and well within those which a dealer or regional service center could manage.

6. The Stair-Chair would not compete directly with regular or with other nonclimbing wheelchairs, but would be desired as a second chair.

7. The Stair-Chair would not be price sensitive within a reasonable range up to $1,500.

APPENDIX: SUMMARY OF MARKETING FEASIBILITY STUDY

SECONDARY RESEARCH OF MARKET POTENTIAL

Estimate of population needing wheelchairs in the United States is 500,000. The annual sales of all types of wheelchairs is approximately 20,000. Wheelchairs in constant use require replacement or major overhaul about twice each year. Assuming that users are well-pleased with the product, a conservative estimate of the United States market for this type of chair would seem to be 25,000 to 50,000 Stair-Chairs per year.

Statistics concerning the number of hospitals, nursing homes, retirement villages, and so forth, are not as meaningful as originally anticipated, because they are usually designed to reduce architectural barriers to the use of wheelchairs to a minimum. Therefore, the Stair-Chair would not offer significant advantages on the premises. However, many of the larger hospitals do have physical therapy departments where such a chair might be kept on hand to demonstrate its potential use to patients. Whether or not this is probable was not resolved. Even more likely would be the purchase of one or more Stair-Chairs for demonstration to potential users at rehabilitation centers. Often it is in such centers that the suggestion of a special type of prosthetic appliance is first made and the confidence in its use first acquired.

The Veterans Administration would likely be interested in evaluating the Stair-Chair toward possible inclusion on the approved list of products which could be submitted to the V.A. in New York for their testing and approval, without charge. At least one year should be allowed for this procedure before approval could be obtained. Approximately 50,000 disabled veterans required wheelchairs in 1973.

A basic wheelchair without accessories can be purchased from $100 to $300. Accessories can double this cost. Motorized wheelchairs can be purchased in a range from $750 to $1,500. Eight firms list wheelchairs in *Thomas' Register*. The largest wheelchair manufacturer, Everest & Jennings produced 90,000 wheelchairs in 1970, according to a 1971 *Barron's* report. The entire industry produced an estimated 200,000 wheelchairs in 1972.

RESULTS OF DEMONSTRATION TO AN INVITED SAMPLE OF TULSA AREA RESIDENTS

The statistics concerning airports serving scheduled airlines may become more meaningful than first anticipated. Respondents representing airlines (American, Braniff, and Continental) suggested that the Stair-Chair might be used to load nonambulatory passengers in areas not having second-level loading bridges. Nearly every airport, regardless of size, has some passenger loading areas requiring boarding stairs. Airlines prefer to use their own passenger loading equipment rather than to use airport-owned equipment. The Stair-Chair would avoid the frightening experience of unfamiliar people carrying non-ambulatory passengers up and down the boarding stairs. Assuming the prototype placed with American Airlines is well received, a conservative demand by all airlines would appear to be 500 to 1,000 Stair-Chairs per year for this use.

Respondents representing various nonprofit organizations interested in the treating or rehabilitation of wheelchair users saw the Stair-Chair as overcoming barriers not possible with a regular or motorized wheelchair. Some wanted to be convinced further regarding specific points, such as maneuverability and fitting into the trunk of car (in spite of claim on advertising material).

Wheelchair users and their relatives were especially pleased with the Stair-Chair's mobility and the added independence from other architectural barriers and uneven outdoor terrain. They were quick to point out the need for many special fittings and accessories, not all of which have been anticipated by the inventors but which are not difficult to incorporate.

MISCELLANEOUS COMMENTS FROM PARTICIPANTS IN STAIR-CHAIR DEMONSTRATION

When asked where they would purchase wheelchairs, some thought they would purchase direct from the manufacturer. Institutional users possibly would want to purchase direct in order to achieve a lower cost. However, some individuals also thought they would like to be able to purchase direct from the manufacturer. When questions of service, adjustments, parts, and so forth, were raised, some thought perhaps the chair should also be sold through a dealer, even though this would add 40 percent to the total cost. Dealers who attended felt that they could handle the chair without any conflict of interest. None of the dealers indicated a franchise agreement which would prohibit him from carrying this make of chair.

When asked how potential users would learn about a chair and decide to try one, most everyone indicated that users would have to learn through the rehabilitation center. The endorsements of the rehabilitation center and of the Veterans Administration were considered important. Certainly the V.A. endorsement would be a requirement if they were to assist veterans by purchasing the chair for them. The endorsement and recommendation from the therapist, physiatrist, orthopedist, internist, and neurosurgeon were seen as confidence builders that would be necessary prior to being willing to try a chair. Therefore, it was believed essential that such chairs be available as training devices in physical therapy areas at hospitals and rehabilitation centers. The physical therapist would be the first contact at such centers. It was thought also that perhaps even the physical therapy department might assist the person in ordering the chair direct from the manufacturer or through a dealer.

When asked how one would learn of the Stair-Chair, they thought the center of influence—the therapist, physiatrist, etc.—would learn through sales representatives, journals, conventions, and publicity. The individual would probably learn through the *Paraplegic News* or *Accent on Living*.

QUESTIONS FOR DISCUSSION

1. How comprehensive and expensive a marketing plan can be justified?
2. What target markets should be reached first?
3. What is the consumer adoption process for those target markets?
4. Should the marketing plan be national or regional?
5. What channel(s) and price margins are appropriate?
6. What promotional strategy will reach the target markets selected?

Part V

Producing Your Product or Service

Previous parts of this text have been concerned with managing and operating the business you have inherited, bought, or organized. The previous section has dealt extensively with marketing your products.

Now it is time to look at the internal process of "producing" your good or service. This is no easy or simple task, for many and diverse activities are required to carry on the "production" function.

You must be concerned with determining what products to sell; deciding whether to buy them from someone else or produce them yourself; planning, acquiring, laying out, and maintaining the physical facilities required for operations; procuring or producing the "right" quantity of the "right" products, at the "right" time, and at the "right" cost; controlling the quality and quantity of your inventory; maintaining a work force; and doing all this as economically as possible! All these activities make the production function interesting, challenging, and rewarding, but awfully frustrating also.

Specifically, this part will cover:

1. *Changing inputs to outputs, including acquiring your physical facilities.*
2. *Setting up your process plan and control system.*
3. *Purchasing and controlling your materials.*

These subjects are covered in Chapters 15, 16, and 17.

15

Your Service: Changing Inputs to Outputs

All business firms produce something, either a product or a service. Thus, all firms are engaged in some form of operations, which could be called "production." Yet, this term itself may be misleading, as will be seen.

In this chapter, we will talk about performing the service of changing inputs into outputs. The inputs are manpower, money, machines, materials, and methods. The outputs are the product(s) or service(s) for your customers. Specifically, the chapter will discuss:

1. Systems of converting inputs to finished products.
2. Deciding what part of the process to perform yourself, and what part to have others do (make or buy decisions).
3. Planning your physical facilities.
4. Implementing your plans.

SYSTEMS FOR CONVERTING INPUTS TO FINISHED PRODUCTS

The term *production* often refers to manufacturing, because production methodology was first developed and applied in manufacturing industries. Yet, in reality, *production* can be defined as *the creation of value or wealth by producing goods and services*. This definition includes other activities, as well as manufacturing. As indicated above, all companies receive inputs and convert them to outputs, as do industrial companies. Managers must have a system to do this. Figure 15–1 shows the transformation or movement of goods for a number of types of companies. Note that the conversion of the inputs to outputs repre-

FIGURE 15–1
Examples of Production Systems

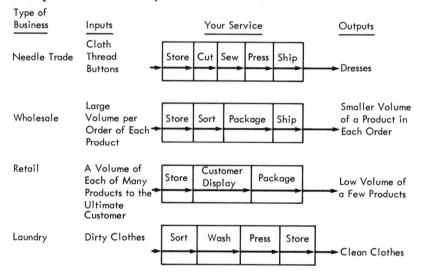

sents the major activity of the business—the reason for the company's existence—and may be a transforming of form, place, or time.

Other examples of inputs and outputs, which must have conversion processes, are shown in Figure 15–2.

Productive Elements

How can the production methodology used by industrial firms be applied to all types of small businesses? The processes of changing inputs to outputs have some characteristics which are common to all situations, and have the following common elements:

1. Systems to transform the input as to form, place, or time.
2. A sequence of steps or operations to convert the inputs into outputs.
3. Special skills and often tools, machinery, or equipment to make the transformation or conversion.
4. Some time frame in which the work is to be done.
5. Instructions to identify the work to be performed and the units being produced.

FIGURE 15–2
Examples of Inputs and Outputs

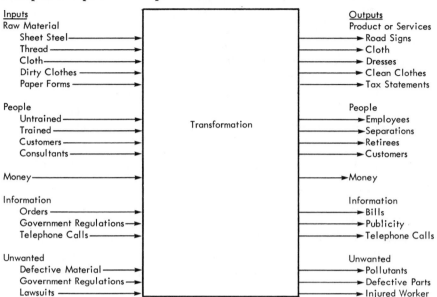

6. Standards and maximum rates of input and output.
7. Exceptions and errors which must be handled.

Productive Elements Applied to Different Industries

Not only do the inputs and outputs within a company have many common characteristics, but the transformation processes within different classifications of businesses have common characteristics. Let us look at some of these different applications to firms in different industries.

A Manufacturing Company. To *manufacture* means to *make,* or process a raw material into a finished product. "Raw material" may be the outputs from other companies, such as synthetic rubber, resistors, or plastic powder, which is changed in form and/or assembled. Usually, a series of operations is commonly performed by machines in the conversion process. Formerly, these operations were usually performed by blue-collar workers using tools and machines. Now, manual labor has largely been replaced by machines, some of which are either automatically controlled or controlled by other machines. These devices can turn out more uniform products, with greater precision, in greater volume, and with less skill required than manual production.

Manufacturing companies may produce only one standard product, while others, at the other extreme, produce a product to special order, with no product ever being repeated. The former type of process, called *continuous production,* operates automatically. The production system, once established, keeps performing the same actions. Also, the inputs and outputs can be stored with less chance of obsolescence or loss of value because of style or use changes.

Companies producing goods for customers requesting nonstandard products must produce these when the customer wants the product. These companies are called *job shops*—they produce to the customer's order, or by the job. Seasonal and other variations in demand cause production to vary up and down considerably, and tend to result in idle time and varying employment levels.

In both processes, planning and controls must be exercised. The product is usually designed by an engineer, who usually not only does the designing, but also converts it into production specifications. The operations to be performed, the machines to use, the skills of workers needed, and the material inputs needed are determined for each product or order. The time to produce is set, and instructions for workers and tools to use are designated. The information is used in performing and checking the work to assure output conformance with specifications. Thus, a procedure is set to guide and check production.

A Service Company with Manufacturing Characteristics.   Many small businesses fall into this category. Cleaning and laundering, cabinet making, short-order food processing, patient processing, printing, and machining organizations are examples. The inputs are converted to finished products through one or a series of operations. The required operations are repeated with variations for special orders. However, different emphases are placed on the design of the system of transformation than in manufacturing.

The service company usually receives smaller orders, with some variation in the input and the desired output. For example, a customer may bring into a laundry different items, such as sheets, clothing, rags, and linens. These, in turn, are made from different combinations of white, colored, natural, and synthetic cloth. Greater emphasis is put on individual handling and contact. This extra activity results in higher unit costs than for single-product, high-volume processes. Also, the related systems needed to plan, identify, and control are relatively more complex.

These companies fit the job shop classification. However, when they are designed properly, they may take on the characteristics of continuous production. In the laundry, for example, all clothing is sorted into different types of cloth. Then, each type of cloth follows a set process.

However, some units such as short-order food processors, can reduce the supporting systems needed by building into the physical facilities controls over the process. The amount of communication is reduced by limiting the variety and fixing the procedures to a small number. A hamburger stand with high volume works on an inventory replenishment basis, and hamburgers follow set variations on the same pattern.

Wholesalers. This group of companies receives large volumes of many items and distributes smaller volumes of selected items. The transformation process involves converting large packages of like items into large and small packages of a variety of items. The sequence of operations can be planned and controlled in the same manner as for the manufacturing process. The emphasis moves from transforming by machinery to storing, materials handling, and packaging.

Retailing. Again, the process within a store has subprocesses, but the organization includes movements of customers, as well as the materials. The primary emphasis is directed toward convenience to the customers and only secondarily toward material flow. The place of goods in the store and the movement of customers in relation to the goods are important contributors or detractions to the sale of goods.

Other Types of Companies. Many other small businesses not included in the prior classifications can benefit from the same type of internal analyses as those discussed. Automobile repairing, home building, and accounting firms have similar flows of material, people, or forms.

The set of processes in each organization tends to reflect its reason for existence. For example, materials and parts are converted to finished goods in a manufacturing company; patients are processed through operations in a hospital; and goods are moved to the proper place, the customer is guided to that place, and the transaction is completed at another point in a self-service store. All other processes, including paper work, are supportive and needed to assure achieving the objectives of the firm.

DECIDING WHETHER TO MAKE OR BUY

The process of changing raw material to a finished product which is delivered to the customer is a long process, usually involving many companies performing different productive functions. Figure 7–1 showed the sequence of steps raw materials go through to become a finished product you use as a consumer. One company may refine the raw materials, several may perform manufacturing processes, another may assemble the parts into the finished product, and so on. A given company may perform a large or small part of this process. The place and the size of the segment is an important decision.

Part II discussed how you would decide your place in the chain and what segment you wanted for yourself. Now, let us look at how the size of each segment is determined. Such determination depends on what you decide to buy and process, and to whom you decide to sell. The following two examples will illustrate this point.

For birdhouses made of wood, you can:

1. Buy wood and cut the parts, or buy pre-cut pieces.
2. Assemble the birdhouse, or sell the packaged pieces to be assembled by the customer.
3. Sell to a wholesaler, retailer, or the final user.

A food processor can:

1. Grow or buy its vegetables.
2. Sell its output to a wholesaler, retailer, or directly to the consumer.

For best results, you should try to specialize in the segment of the total process where you have the greatest expertise.

The *advantages of specializing* and concentrating in a small area that the company performs best are:

1. Less capital investment is needed for machinery and for people with differing capabilities.
2. Management can concentrate better on a small segment.
3. Planning, directing, and controlling are less complex.

The *advantages of a larger segment* are:

1. More control of the process.
2. Less idle machine and man time.
3. Greater potential for growth.

The decision as to what segment you will seek is usually based on the economics of the situation. It might be advantageous for you to make some of the parts you normally buy in order to use idle time of the machines and people. You might drop some of the early or late operations instead of buying more machinery when you do not have enough capacity. Remember, though, that any additions or reductions must be evaluated from a cost viewpoint, and that some of these costs may vary with changes in volume, while others do not.

Having decided on the segment of the total transformation process you wish to perform, you can now begin to plan, obtain, and install your producing unit.

The physical facilities of your company—including the building itself, machines and equipment, furniture and fixtures, and others—must be designed to aid the employees in producing the desired product or service at a low cost. The design function includes the layout and selection of machines and equipment and the determination of the features desired in the building. For purposes of discussion, the function is divided into two parts: (1) planning and (2) implementation.

PLANNING YOUR PHYSICAL FACILITIES

Good selection and arrangement of your physical facilities can pay dividends. Planning your physical facilities requires the following steps:

1. Determine the services you plan to perform (discussed in earlier chapters).
2. Break the production into *parts, operations,* and *activities.*
3. Determine the times required to perform each operation.
4. Using these time figures as a guide, estimate the number of machines and workers you need.
5. Decide the type of arrangement you feel is best for the sequence of operations.
6. Determine the general layout, using blocks for sections of the plant.
7. Plan the detailed layout which will provide the most effective use of your personnel, machines, and materials.

Step 1: Determine Your Services

This step was discussed in earlier chapters, but in general the business you are in will determine what good(s) you will need to produce or what service(s) you will perform.

Step 2: Break the Product or Service into Parts, Operations, and Activities

Assuming you are going to produce a product to sell to customers, you need to break the product down into:

1. Parts going into it.
2. Operations needed to produce it.
3. Activities surrounding its production.

Parts are the divisions of the product which, when assembled, form the output. Some outputs have only one part; others, such as radios, have many. The part or parts must be identified.

Operations are the steps or segments of work performed to accomplish the conversion of the inputs into outputs. The segments are often identified by the specialized work of a machine, as for example drilling, typing, or wrapping. The conversion process usually requires a series of operations. Figures 15–3 and 15–4 show the operations for making metal signs and collecting groceries. The circles indicate operations.

FIGURE 15–3

Operation Process Chart and Calculations for Making a Typical Metal Sign

Operations	Symbols for Sequence	Machine	Hours Required per Machine	Forecasted Volume per Hour	Number of Machines Needed
Cut Sides	①	Shear	.12/100 Cuts	500 Cuts	1
Cut Corners	②	Press	.17/100 Corners	600 Corners	2
Punch Holes	③	Press	.10/100 Holes	500 Holes	1
Wash	④	Tank	.005/Sign	300 Signs	10 Ft.*
Dry	⑤	Oven	.01/Sign	300 Signs	15 Ft.*
Phosphate Coat	⑥	Tank	.008/Sign	300 Signs	12 Ft.*
Dry	⑦	Oven	.02/Sign	300 Signs	30 Ft.*
Paint Metal	⑧	Spray Gun	.28/100 Signs	300 Signs	1
Bake	⑨	Oven	.10/Sign	300 Signs	150 Ft.*
Print Sign	⑩	Silk Screen	Varies (see table)	300 Signs	2
Bake	⑪	Oven	.10/100 Signs	300 Signs	1
Box Signs	⑫	Bench	1.00/100 Signs	300 Signs	3 Workers

* Conveyors are used to move signs into, through, and out of tanks and ovens at 10 feet per minute. Tanks and ovens are measured in feet.

FIGURE 15–4

Operation Process Chart for a Customer in a Supermarket

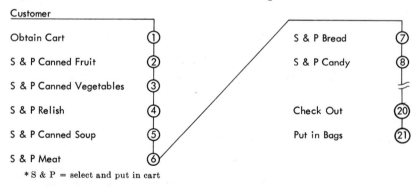

Customer			
Obtain Cart	①	S & P Bread	⑦
S & P Canned Fruit	②	S & P Candy	⑧
S & P Canned Vegetables	③		
S & P Relish	④	Check Out	⑳
S & P Canned Soup	⑤	Put in Bags	㉑
S & P Meat	⑥		

*S & P = select and put in cart

Activities, such as moving materials, are necessary for the performance of the operations. Nonactivities, including delays, are caused by imbalance of the times of the operation. Activities and nonactivities may not be identified fully until the final layout planning is performed. The number and extent of nonactivities should be minimized.

To determine the parts and operations, you start with the output and work backward to the inputs. In an assembled product, the disassembly process is called *exploding*. The process identifies the parts. Then, the operations on each part and their sequence can be identified. The sequence may be fixed or rigid, as the cutting of boards precedes their assembly as a bookshelf. Or, the sequence may not be important, as in the order of cutting the boards. In other cases, the proper sequence of operations is important to obtain a high volume of sales, as in a cafeteria or a supermarket. Flexible sequences of operations are desirable to allow for high utilization of machines and personnel.

Step 3: Determine the Times to Perform the Operations

Each operation required to produce a good or perform a service consumes the time of machines and personnel. The times can be obtained by making an estimate, or by using one of the several time measurement methods discussed in the next chapter. The total time includes the time to perform the operation plus time for unavoidable delays and personal needs. Some operations are routine and are easily measured; others are more variable and not so easily measured. The times obtained are used to determine the number of machines and the number of people needed to perform the work and the speed of conveyors.

Step 4: Estimate the Number of Machines and Workers Needed

Knowing the time that a machine takes to perform an operation on a product, and knowing your planned production, you can determine the number of machines needed. Figure 15-3 shows the number of machines required to make 300 signs per hour. Operation 3, punching holes, requires half the time of a press $[(.10 \div 100) \times 500$ holes$]$. Either one machine can be purchased for this operation, or it can be combined with operation 2, cutting corners, which requires less than half the time of a second machine.

Step 5: Decide the Best Arrangement for the Sequence of Operations

You should try to obtain the least movement of product and people. However, people and machines should not be idle and space should not be wasted. The plant can be planned according to one or a combination of two types of layout:

1. Product, or service.
2. Process, or function.

The *product layout* places the machines or serving units in such a way that the product moves along a line as it moves through its sequence of operations. Assembly lines in the automobile industry are the best-known examples of this type layout. As the automobile frame moves on a conveyor, the engine, axles, steering mechanism, and other components are added until a finished car comes off the conveyor.

This type layout has been spreading from the large manufacturing operations to nonmanufacturing and small businesses as more standardized routines have been developed and as demand volume and the capacities of machines and people have been better matched. Some examples of small businesses using this layout are the short-order line in a cafeteria, packing materials for an order in a warehouse, and one-product companies. In fact, all layouts should generally conform to this concept, as shown in Figure 15-5.

FIGURE 15–5
Product Layout

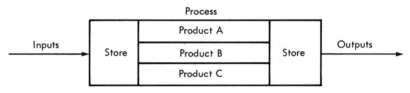

With this type layout, material or people move forward from operation to operation with little backtracking. A supermarket could set up this type of layout if it knew that a large enough number of customers wanted the same items. The customers could move down the line picking up the items as they went, and be through in a short time. If the customer selects purchases according to the order in which the goods are displayed, there is no need to backtrack. The advantages of this type of layout plan include:

1. Specialization of workers and machines.
2. Less inventory.
3. Fewer instructions and controls.
4. Faster movement.
5. Less space for aisles and storage.

The second type of layout, *process,* is based on keeping the machines and workers busy, thus keeping the idle time to a minimum. Machines performing the same type of work are grouped together, and the same is true of workers with like skills. Some examples of this type layout include presses grouped together so that each press can keep busy and typists put in a "pool" to perform typing for many offices. This type of layout increases the movement of material or people, and necessitates higher inventory. The *advantages* of the process layout include:

1. Its flexibility to take care of change and variety.
2. Its use of general-purpose machines and equipment.
3. Its more efficient use of machines and personnel.

Few layout plans are confined to either the one type or the other. Instead, they consist of combinations of the two to take advantage of the situation. Idle time created by differing production rates is more than compensated for by decreased inventory.

Layouts can be planned to move material, people, tools, or machines. Thus, in some stores the customers move through self-service lines; in others, the sales person moves about to bring the goods to the customer. Products move through some production processes; in others, people and tools move to the product. For part of the physical examination in a clinic, doctors and nurses move to the patient; for others, the patient moves from room to room.

Some of the factors to be considered in planning for movement are:

1. Size of goods and machines.
2. Safety requirements.
3. Volume of input and output.
4. Type of service.

Step 6: Determine the General Layout

The next step is to determine the general layout, using blocks for sections of the layout. A block can be a machine, a group of machines, a group of products on shelves, or a department. This step is intended to establish the general arrangement of the plant, store, or office before spending much time on details. Estimates are made of the space needed in each block using past layouts; summation of space for machines, men, aisles, and other factors; or the best judgment available. The intent is to plan the general arrangement before planning the detailed layout.

Figure 15–6 is an illustration of a block layout. The dashed lines and solid lines show the general block areas for presses, painting, shipping, and so forth.

Besides the activities directly concerned with the main services of the company, space for maintenance, planning, food, personal needs, and other services, is provided. These should be placed conveniently near the units being serviced. Estimates of the space required can be obtained from books, pamphlets, trade associations, and past experience.

If you are replanning the layout of an existing building, or are planning to move into one, the location of outside walls is predetermined. The size and shape of the land may be confining.

FIGURE 15–6
Plant Layout for Metal Sign Company

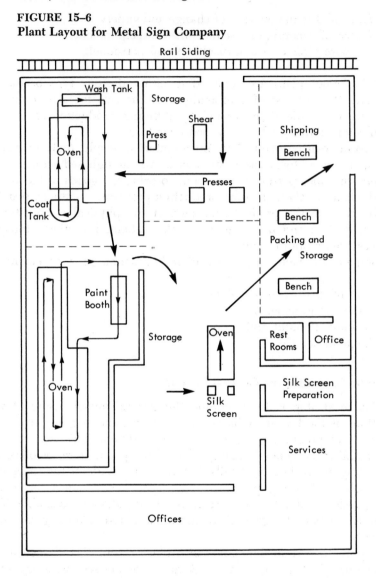

On the other hand, if you are planning a new building, you have greater flexibility. This allows you to design it so that changes can be made easily in the future. Buildings are usually designed to provide space for several years, while the number of machines planned is for only the near future—as machines can be added at a later date. In most operations, single-story, square, and columnless buildings with movable utility outlets are preferred. The building is designed from the inside out.

Entrance locations are important in the layout, particularly for service establishments. Customers enter downtown stores from the street and goods usually enter from the back. These entrances may be fixed, setting the flow of goods from back to front. Some producing plants use the same transportation units for delivering supplies and materials as for shipping the finished goods. The flow is thus U-shaped. Other—usually less important—external factors are:

1. Entrances for employees.
2. Connections to utilities.
3. Governmental restrictions.
4. Weather factors.

Included in the layout should be plans for expansion and other future conditions.

Step 7: Plan the Detailed Layout for Efficiency and Effectiveness

You must plan in detail the layout of your people, machines, and materials if you are to have efficient performance. Each machine and piece of equipment is located, and space allocated for its use. As with blocks, templets—or models—of the machines, equipment, and workers help you perform this step. These templets can be moved about to obtain your best plan. Figure 15–6 shows machine locations for the Metal Sign Company plant after using templets for placing machines.

In manufacturing, many methods are used to move materials. Conveyors, carts, by hand, trucks, and cranes are examples. For example, the materials shown in Figure 15–3 could be moved by fork-lift truck, carts, and overhead and belt conveyors. Notice that, as shown, the conveyor carries the metal plates through washing, drying, coating, and drying without stopping. The objective is to minimize materials handling and its cost without increasing other costs.

Each operation should be examined with enough care to assure easy performance of work. If the worker spends too much time standing, walking, turning, and twisting, the work will take longer and be more tiring. Large-volume items or tools should be located close at hand for quick service. An understanding of methods study is helpful in this relationship.

Some specific matters which you should include in your final layout planning are:

1. Space for movement
   Are aisles wide enough for one- or two-way traffic? Is there enough room if a queue forms? Can material be obtained easily and is space available when it is waiting?

2. Utilities

   Have adequate provisions been made for incoming wiring and gas or for disposal of water at each machine? Will any future moves be necessary?

3. Supply of equipment

   Can shelves be restocked conveniently?

4. Safety

   Has equipment using inflammable material been properly isolated and proper fire protection been provided? Are moving parts and machines guarded and the operator protected from accidents?

5. Working conditions

   Does the worker have enough working space and light? Have you provided for low noise levels, proper temperature, and no objectionable odors? Is the worker safe; can he socialize and take care of his personal needs?

6. Cleanliness and maintenance

   Is the layout designed for good housekeeping at low cost? Can machinery, equipment, and building be maintained easily?

7. Product quality

   Are provisions made to protect the product as it moves through the plant or sits in storage?

IMPLEMENTING YOUR PLANS

The first step in implementing your plans is to test them to see if they are sound. There are many ways you can do this. One method is to have employees—or other persons who can give some experienced opinions—review the plans and give you their suggestions. Another method is to simulate the process by moving templets or models of the goods or people through the process so that you can foresee their movements. You might deliberately include some mishaps to see what happens. It might be well to use the processing plans which will be discussed in Chapter 16 to see how the production plan works with your layout.

The actual implementation of your plans will depend on whether this is a brand new venture, a layout for an existing building, or a rearrangement of the present layout. Construction of a new building requires further steps in the design of the building and its surroundings. These steps include at least consideration of the following factors:

1. Type and method of construction.
2. Arrangements for parking.
3. Roads and transportation of goods.
4. Landscaping.

A new layout and the rearrangement of the layout in an existing building may require some changes, but the latter may be mainly a matter of scheduling the change-over to keep production downtime to a minimum. In all cases, the steps in implementation should be carefully planned to minimize costs.

SUMMARY

This chapter has shown you how to organize your productive system in order to transform your inputs of manpower, money, machines, methods, and materials into the outputs, goods and/or services. The systems to do this have essentially the same elements, regardless of the type industry involved.

Some illustrative industries and their use of these elements were discussed. Then, some factors for you to consider in deciding to buy your materials from outside or produce them yourself were presented. The decision should be based upon a balancing of costs.

After making these decisions, you are able to plan for, purchase, and install your physical facilities. Some principles of laying out these facilities were also presented.

QUESTIONS FOR FURTHER DISCUSSION

1. List the parts and operations needed for a set of shelves for your study room.
2. Show the transformation processes that must occur for inputs to be changed to outputs. Start with the items in Figure 15–2.
3. Analyze the layout of a kitchen. Can you make some recommendations for an improved layout?
4. Describe the differences among the layouts of several stores. List the good and bad points of each.
5. Do you think the layout of the Metal Sign Company, Figure 15–6, is a good one? Explain.
6. How would you move the material in the Metal Sign Company?
7. What advantages would the Metal Sign Company gain if it purchased cut and punched metal plates? Disadvantages?

16

Your Process Plan and Control System

So far in this book, you have determined the good(s) and/or service(s) you plan to produce or perform, how you will market them, what physical facilities you need, and how your facilities should be laid out. Now you are ready to start producing the good(s) and/or service(s). This includes designing work methods, measuring work, providing instructions, and directing and controlling the activities. (Some of these activities have been designed into the systems already described and will be referred to as the total system is described.)

The planning and control process is a communication system designed to convey to employees the what, how, where, who, and when of the work. It is also a check on what has been done to correct and adjust the work and process to assure that the customer receives good service, in terms of both time and quality. The specific topics which will be covered in this chapter are:

1. Work design.
2. Work measurement.
3. Planning—the forecast.
4. Planning—converting sales plan to a production plan.
5. Scheduling—setting the time for work to be done.
6. Information to direct activities.
7. Controlling production—quantity and quality.

WORK DESIGN

In Chapter 15, we showed how to plan the layout of a plant. However, we did not study the detailed movement of materials and the layout of the workplace. These topics now need to be studied. For example, in the metal sign plant, are the metal plates properly placed so that the operator cutting the corners has short and easy moves? How many machines can one man operate? Are there new methods of moving materials? The following steps are used in work design and improvement:

1. State the problem.
2. State the function of the work.
3. Collect information.
4. List alternatives.
5. Analyze and select alternatives.
6. Formulate, review, and test the selected changes.
7. Install and follow up the changes.

Each of these steps will be discussed briefly.

State the Problem

As usual, you should begin by stating the problem. Why study the work? Is the cost of the work too high? Is the work delaying other work? Is the quality of the service low? Is the service to the customer delayed? The reason(s) for making a study of the work should be clearly understood and stated in order to provide direction.

State the Function of the Work

Often a given production function appears obvious, as for example to sew a seam, to drill a hole, or to sell to a customer. However, you should begin by asking questions. Is this operation necessary? Is it the only alternative? A clear statement of the reason for the operation starts you toward finding the best method.

Collect Information

Collecting information breaks the work into parts and establishes appropriate relationships. The purposes are twofold—training and informing.

The reason for *training* is to develop your ability to observe work as a series of activities. For example, a machine operation might include statements such as "prepare material," "do the work," and "remove finished product." The term "prepare material" might include reaching for material, selecting material, grasping material, moving material to the machine, and positioning the material. This type of training, combined with the use of some common-sense principles, develops your ability to identify inefficiencies.

The reason for *informing* is to aid you in recording the details of the work being done for later analysis. Several types of charting procedures are shown in Figures 16–1, 16–2, and 16–3, and are discussed.

FIGURE 16–1
Flow Process Chart for Making Metal Signs

Item Description	Operation / Transportation / Inspection / Delay / Storage	Distance in Feet	Pick-Ups / Lay-Downs	Time in MIN.	Quantity	Analysis Why? What?	Where?	When?	Who?	How?	Notes
IN STORAGE AREA	O ⇨ □ D ▽										
To SHEARS BY CART	O ⇨ □ D ▽	15'	/	2	/		√			√	FORK TRUCK CONVEY
IN STACK	O ⇨ □ D ▽			10	/	√					
CUT SIDES, SHEAR	O ⇨ □ D ▽		/	2							
IN STACK	O ⇨ □ D ▽			10	3	√					CONVEYOR-ROLL TO PRESS
To PRESS, CART	O ⇨ □ D ▽	10	/	6		√		√			"
IN STACK	O ⇨ □ D ▽			3	3						
CUT CORNERS, PRESS	O ⇨ □ D ▽		/	/	/						

Figure 16–1 shows a flow process chart for the first and second operations in making a metal sign, as shown in Figure 15–3. Not only does it show the cutting of sides and corners, but it also adds transportations, delays, and storage. Observe the number of delays and transports which occur for each operation. You will want to reduce these, because they are costly. Symbols are used to simplify your understanding of the process. Data are also collected on methods of movement, distances, time, and quantity.

Figure 16–2 presents a motion study of a simple operation of assembling a bolt, washer, and nut. Note that the assembler is holding the bolt well over half the time. His hand is a very expensive vise.

Figure 16–3 shows the relationship between an operator and a machine. The operator loads and unloads the machine and the machine performs its operations automatically. Note that the idle time for the operator amounts to over half his time. Figure 16–4 can be used to analyze your decisions involved in getting up in the morning.

FIGURE 16–2
Motion Study of Assembling Bolt, Washer, and Nut

Left Hand Description	Activity	Activity	Right Hand Description
To bolt	→	→	To washer
Grasp bolt	O	O	Grasp washer
To washer	→	→	To bolt
Hold	D	O	Assemble
Hold	D	→	To nut
Hold	D	O	Grasp nut
Hold	D	→	To assembly
Hold	D	O	Assemble
Dispose	→	D	For disposal

Legend: O = Operation; → = Movement; D = Delay.
Note the large percentage of delay.

FIGURE 16–3
Man Running an Automatic Machine

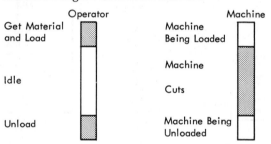

List Alternatives

Listing of alternatives is the core of any analysis and is a critical step in decision making. All work and services can be performed in many ways and products can be made from many different materials. For example, your pencil can be made of wood, metal, or plastic; it can have an eraser and clip, or not have them; and it may be cylindrical or hexagonal. A hole can be punched, drilled, burned, or cut. You should question the whole process, parts of the process, and each individual activity by recording all alternatives. The following questions are helpful.

1. Why is the activity being performed?
2. Can it be eliminated?
3. What, where, and who is performing the activity?
4. Can it be combined with another operation or operations?
5. When is the activity performed?
6. Can the work sequence be changed to reduce the volume of work?
7. How is the activity performed?
8. Can it be simplified?

FIGURE 16–4
Computer Diagram on How to Get Up in the Morning

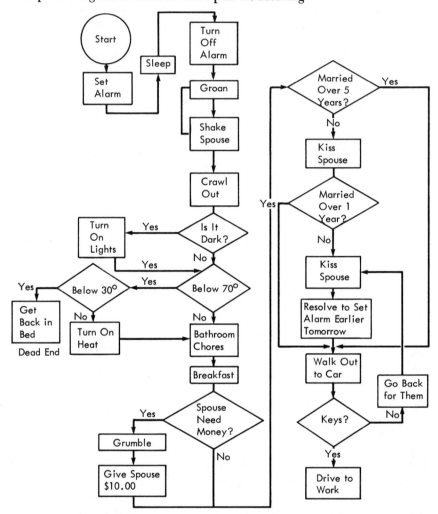

How many alternatives can you list for the bolt and washer assembly in Figure 16–2? Why assemble? Can you devise a holder to eliminate the *hold* and *dispose* activities? Can the operator in Figure 16–3 run another machine also? Or inspect? Or perform the next operation? The objective is to remove or otherwise simplify as many activities as possible without reducing the quality and quantity of output.

Analyze and Select Alternatives

This step is the evaluation of the alternatives based on practicality, cost, acceptance by workers, and the effect on output. In a good list of alternatives, a small percentage will be finally acceptable. However, the extra time invested in exploring alternatives improves your chances of finding the best design.

Formulate, Review, and Test the Selected Changes

This step converts ideas into reality, checks for any errors or missed possibilities, and makes sure the proposals will perform as expected.

Install and Follow Up the Changes

Installation includes placing the physical equipment (as for example a foot pedal), gaining acceptance by the people involved with the operation, and training workers. The objective is to improve performance to its optimum level.

WORK MEASUREMENT

One of the most difficult problems is the measurement of work. We have few precise tools for these measurements, but rely heavily on the fallible judgment of people to make the measurements. Physical work can be measured more precisely than mental work, but it still requires judgment.

This section is concerned with measuring the time for doing physical work. Once time standards are set, they can be used to:

1. Determine how many people or machines are needed for a desired output.
2. Estimate the cost of sales and other orders.
3. Determine the standard output for incentive systems.
4. Schedule production.
5. Measure performance.

The time to perform can be divided into: (1) the time to perform the work, or (2) the time for personal needs and irregular activities.

Time for Work Performance

The methods which can be used to obtain the time to perform the work are:

1. Estimates by people experienced in the work.
2. Time study, using a watch or other timing device.
3. Synthesis of the elemental times obtained from tables.

Time Standards Set by Experienced People. This is the simplest and least costly method of obtaining a time for work, but it is also the least precise. No breakdown of the work is made, and the standards often include past inefficiencies. These standards are often adequate if the person setting the standard is careful.

Time Study. This is probably the best method. Yet it has the poorest reputation, because time studies have often not been properly done or used. A time study is made by a person—usually an industrial engineer—actually observing the work being done. The observer uses a stop watch; makes many recordings of the time for each segment of the work; evaluates the worker's performance against the observer's standard of normal speed and effort; adjusts the time values; selects the *normal* time, using some averaging method; and adds a certain amount of time for personal needs and irregular activities.

Synthesis of Elemental Times. This is a pencil-and-paper method based on the accumulation of data from research studies. Tables of manual times have been developed for a wide range of activities used by workers, including reaching, moving, grasping, positioning, turning, walking, and bending. A synthetic time can be set for assembling the bolt, washer, and nut shown in Figure 16–2. Tables are also available to compute times for machining operations. By analyzing the work into the proper elements, times from the tables can be applied to obtain a *normal* time for an operation.

Adding Time for Personal Needs

Personal and irregular time allowances are added to normal time to obtain the total time in which an operation should be performed under "normal" conditions. Allowances for personal needs in time-study and synthesis methods include times for use of the rest room, poor working conditions, and fatigue. Tables are available for these times. The time for irregular activities, as for example getting material, receiving instructions, repairing minor breakdowns, and cleanup can be determined by work sampling or by estimating the frequency and length of time for each type of activity.

Work sampling is based on making a large number of observations at random times. For each observation, you record whether a worker is producing, idle, or doing irregular work. The percentage of observations in each category is the estimate of the percentage of his total time spent in that activity.

Standard time is usually expressed in *standard allowed hours* (SAH) per unit of output. Workers on incentive plans, who are paid on the number of SAH they produce, usually will earn five percent to 30 percent more SAH than their actual hours. Research indicates that the introduction of a good incentive system will increase production by about 30 percent.

PLANNING: THE FORECAST

Sales forecasting and marketing research were discussed in Chapter 13. Converting those forecasts into a sales plan is the starting point for your production plan. Before the sales plan can be fixed, your production capacity must be checked. The best sales plan from a marketing viewpoint may not be the best plan for the company as a whole. It may require too much overtime, too much idle time, or some combination of the two.

The optimum plan from a production standpoint is to maintain a constant level of production—near capacity for both machine and man—of one product, with inputs arriving as needed and outputs taken by customers as they are completed. This is an ideal to shoot for, and the concept provides the direction toward which you should move.

If the sales plan does not keep production busy, what can be done? Should the company advertise more heavily, reduce prices, or redesign its product to increase the volume? The loss in income from these actions may be more than made up for by more efficient operation of the plant. Should another product, or a variation of your product, be added to the company's service? Or would this increase the change-over costs and cause such confusion in production that it would cost more than the value received from the added sales?

Maybe the sales plan is for more output than the capacity of the production process. If so, the plan can be satisfied by expanding the capacity, by producing on overtime, or by subcontracting. Each of these can be very expensive and is capable of causing you more problems than benefits.

PLANNING: CONVERTING A SALES PLAN TO A PRODUCTION PLAN

You will be told that it is impossible to predict the sales of a small business with any reasonable degree of accuracy. This may be true, but even crude estimates are usually better than none at all. Time is required to purchase, produce, and deliver an item if it is not in stock when the customer orders it. On the other hand, the company incurs extra cost when material is held in inventory. As is mentioned in Chapter 15, inventory is used to give flexibility to a production process. While this practice results in savings, it also adds to the cost. These costs and savings should be balanced.

The largest inventories are planned for the beginning and end of the process, where the company has the minimum of control over its environment. The sales plan is affected primarily by the customer. Sales volume fluctuates up and down from one time period to another. How can the production plan and sales plan be aligned for optimal results?

Planning starts with the longer periods and proceeds backward to the day-to-day operations. Chapter 15 discussed the long-range planning needed to plan for and install physical facilities. The next step is to plan for the next shorter time period, which may be the annual plan. The sales plan, which is usually done for the year ahead, is broken down into months (or perhaps by quarters for the last six months). The production plan should be prepared for these same periods.

Some alternative *production plans* (PP) which you may consider are:

PP–1. Produce what is demanded by your customers at the time they need the goods.

PP–2. Produce at a constant level equal to the average monthly demand for the year. Inventories will increase when the volume of demand is lower than the production volume, and will decrease when demand is higher.

PP–3. Produce complementary products which balance out increases and decreases in the volume of demand for individual products. The sum of the monthly demands should result in a constant production level.

PP–4. Subcontract production which is in excess of a certain level.

PP–5. Decide not to expand production to meet demand.

PP–6. Have special sales inducements, perhaps extra advertising and lower prices, when your sales volume is expected to be low.

One of the major causes of predictable variations in demand is the yearly change of seasons. Examples of this variation include demands for sports equipment, heating and cooling facilities, and landscaping. Alternative production plans will be discussed using seasonal variations in the examples.

Figure 16–5 shows a possible monthly plot of the sales plan for your company for the year ahead. The measure of sales volume can be dollars, standard allowed hours (SAH), tons, or other units, whichever best measures production capacity, inventory level, and sales demand. Under Production Plan One (PP–1), production and sales volume lines are the same, and the inventory of finished goods can be held at a constant minimum level. As plant capacity is large—equaling 80 units—overtime work can be avoided. Production is at plant capacity during only a small part of the year, and the plant is idle up to 30 units per month during another part of the year. With the trend to increase fringe bene-

FIGURE 16–5
Sales and Production Plans with Seasonal Changes in Demand

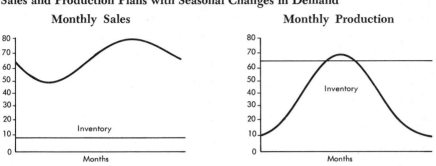

fits, annual wage systems, and severance pay, this type of production plan is becoming outdated.

Production Plan Two (PP–2) shows a constant level of production with a heavy build-up of inventory. The advantages of this plan are:

1. Decrease in capacity needed.
2. Constant level of manpower, with a minimum of hiring and layoff costs.
3. Reduction in paper work needed in running the production system.

This type of production is ideal from the production viewpoint.

The major disadvantage of PP–2 is the large inventory cost, which can bankrupt your company if it is not evaluated carefully. (See Chapter 17.) Companies ordinarily do not attempt to level production completely, but try to find some compromise between PP–1 and PP–2. An analysis can be made by finding the minimum cost plan, using the following formula:

Annual added costs = inventory costs + overtime costs
+ change in level costs.

Production Plan Three (PP–3)—producing complementary products—might be likened to producing both furnaces and air conditioners. The furnaces are produced for winter and the air conditioners for summer. If the same machines and skills can be used in producing both products, and if the volumes produced and sold can be balanced, the sales and production forces will be kept working at a constant rate the year round. This is one of the reasons many companies have a variety of products in their product lines.

Production Plan Four (PP–4)—subcontracting excess production—has several variations. You might make more of the parts yourself during slack periods, and subcontract to others during peak periods.

Production Plan Five (PP–5)—not expand production to meet sales—is often rejected without much thought, as this means a loss of sales. However, these extra sales may be so expensive to produce that they are unprofitable. Extra capacity and/or overtime may be required.

Production Plan Six (PP–6)—offer special sales inducements—is a marketing activity which was covered in Part IV.

After you have established your production plan for the year, other plans or budgets can be developed. The amount of materials, parts, and goods; the manpower required; and the financing needed can be determined.

SCHEDULING: SETTING THE TIME FOR WORK TO BE DONE IN THE NEAR FUTURE

The previous section discussed the development of the general production plan for a period of one year. This section covers day-to-day scheduling. As orders are received, they are either filled from inventory or ordered into production.

Most companies keep an inventory of standard items in order to give quick service. They stock the items for which they have forecasted sufficient demand and for which the value of fast service is greater than the added cost of carrying the inventory. These are the types of items which are produced to stock when the plant would otherwise be idle.

Orders are scheduled into production:

1. On a preplanned schedule.
2. When inventory is reduced to a certain low level.
3. When orders are received and inventory is not available.

The preplanned schedule works best for standard items, the demand for which can be forecast. Customer order scheduling is used for specialty items and for items too expensive to keep in inventory. In each case, the number of units in a production order is determined by balancing the costs involved. A large order increases inventory costs per unit; a small order increases the planning, machine set up, handling, and paper-work per unit. Producing to customer order usually sets the size of a production order, except when future orders of the same item are expected. (A further consideration of these costs is included with the discussion of purchase order sizes in Chapter 17.)

Schedules set the times to produce specified goods. A company producing the same units continuously can automatically set how many units to produce by setting the total number of man and machine hours per week. Job shops, on the other hand, must schedule each order. This scheduling can be done by one of the following methods:

1. Sending orders into the shop in sequence. The shop processes the jobs through the operations on a first-come, first-served basis.
2. Setting priorities, and processing orders accordingly. "Rush" orders have top priority.
3. Using either 1 or 2 for each operation.
4. Setting a specific time for each operation for each job.

Note the following relationships:

Method	Scheduling Cost	Idle Time	Processing Time	Inventory Level
1.	Low	High	High	High
4	High	Low	Low	Low

In doing all your scheduling, an effort should be made to keep inventory as low as practical. A long-time sequence of operations on a part which is to be assembled to a short-time sequenced part should be started early. This can be illustrated by the often used bar, or Gantt chart, shown in Figure 16–6.

FIGURE 16–6

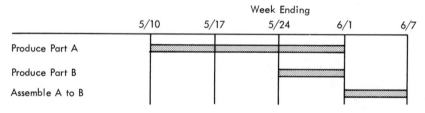

By scheduling Part A to start on May 10 and Part B to start on May 24, the two parts are expected to be completed at the time they are needed for assembly. If the delivery date for the order is June 7, the delivery may be made soon after the work is completed.

A recently developed chart is used for scheduling "networks"— sequences of operations, each of which may be dependent upon the completion of several other activities. This chart, called the *critical path method* (CPM) or *program evaluation and review technique* (PERT), is used by many companies in the construction industry. Figure 16–7 shows a chart for the installation of an underground pipe.

The circles represent the start and end of activities, and lines show activities (the length of the line has no meaning). The times at the circles give the earliest and latest times for the end of the prior operation and the beginning of the next one; the difference is called "slack." The

FIGURE 16–7
PERT Chart for Putting in a Pipeline

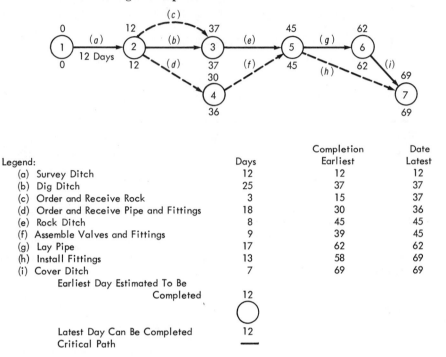

Legend:	Days	Completion Earliest	Date Latest
(a) Survey Ditch	12	12	12
(b) Dig Ditch	25	37	37
(c) Order and Receive Rock	3	15	37
(d) Order and Receive Pipe and Fittings	18	30	36
(e) Rock Ditch	8	45	45
(f) Assemble Valves and Fittings	9	39	45
(g) Lay Pipe	17	62	62
(h) Install Fittings	13	58	69
(i) Cover Ditch	7	69	69
Earliest Day Estimated To Be Completed	12		
Latest Day Can Be Completed	12		
Critical Path	—		

circles with zero slack time are on the "critical path," and the sum of the times for all the activities between those circles determines how long the whole process will take. This is the critical path. The times are usually the best estimates of knowledgeable people.

INSTALLING AN INFORMATION SYSTEM TO DIRECT THE ACTIVITIES

Orders received and plans made must be communicated to those doing the work. The information is provided by paper or oral instructions, by training workers, and/or by having a fixed flow of material. Each worker must know what and how many he is to produce, when and where he is to produce them, and what he needs in order to perform the job satisfactorily. You should design a simple, yet adequate, system to do this in your firm.

The route sheet shown in Figure 16–8 is used in a garment plant and travels with a bundle of cut cloth. This form tells the workers what to sew, the type of operation, the time for the operation, and what the next operation is. The size of bundle sets the quantity. As

FIGURE 16–8
Route Sheet Used in Garment Plant

	SKIRT	SCH.NO. LOT NO. AMT.	7732 24	SKIRT	
	.NR-24-7732 Thread bkle.on tab.tack to fnt. ****			.060-24-7732 Reverse	1:00
11:00	.448-24-7732 Hem Waist & Btm. BS			.132-24-7732 Serge Btm.	3:00
3:00	.128-24-7732 SS 2nd Side Seam ***			.196-24-7732 Serge Elastic to Waist	5:00
4:00	.164-24-7732 SS One Side Seam T&L			1.134-24-7732 Topst.fnt.pleats bste.across top **	27:00

each operator completes an operation, the proper tab is clipped to be returned to the office. More complex systems are needed for other processes.

CONTROLLING PRODUCTION: QUANTITY AND QUALITY

Even if the best of plans are made, the information is communicated, and the best work is performed, controls are still needed. If no control is exercised over the operations, the process will fail. Thus, the principle of exception should be followed.

Controlling by exceptions involves your comparing your plans with the plant's performance. In simple systems, this comparison can be made informally by personally observing the performance. Usually, though, a system of formal checks is needed.

Orders may be filed by due dates, work to be completed in each department may be recorded each day, or bar charts or graphs may be used. The record of performance is obtained through feedback, or by having forms returned with information on work performed. For example, press operators clock their time in and out on the edge of a job envelope carrying instructions; workers in a garment plant clip off pieces of the route sheet and return it pasted on their time ticket; a garage repairman enters his time on the order form.

You need not make changes when performance equals or exceeds your plans. You have an exception when performance does not reach the level desired. You need to decide what to do to improve future performance.

One example of an important control system is that used for quality control. The methods used in quality control have been developed further than those for other control systems, and are used in many other systems, including cost control. The system begins with setting the level of quality desired. The quality level is based on:

1. The value of quality to the customer.
2. The cost of the quality.

Customers want high quality, but are often willing to pay only a limited price for the product. Production costs rise rapidly as the demand for quality rises beyond a certain point. Therefore, you should ask the following questions:

1. Who are my customers, and what quality do they want?
2. What quality of product or service can I obtain, and at what costs?

Then you need to establish controls to obtain that quality. Do not try to exceed that level, for your costs will increase. But do not allow quality to go below that level; you will lose customers. Design your process to produce products or services within the desired quality range. Then, design your quality control system to check performance.

The steps needed in any system of control are:

1. Set standards for your quality range.
2. Measure your actual performance.
3. Compare 1 and 2.
4. Make corrections when needed.

Standards of quality may be set for dimension, color, strength, content, weight, service, and other characteristics. Some standards may be measured by instruments, as for example rulers or gauges for length, but color, taste, and other standards must be evaluated by skilled individuals. Measurement may be made by selected people at certain places in the process—usually upon the receipt of material, and always before it goes to the customer. You can spot-check (sample), or check each item.

Inspection reduces the chance of a poor-quality product being passed through your process and to your customer. But not all defective work is eliminated by inspection. By recording the number of defective units per 100 units, you can observe the quality performance of the process and make needed corrections. The final check might be to keep a record of the number of complaints received per 100 sales made.

SUMMARY

Planning and controlling a company's internal operations involve:

1. Analyzing individual steps of the processes to eliminate inefficiencies.
2. Setting time and quality standards.
3. Planning the work and informing the workers.
4. Checking performance.

Some of the techniques for implementing these activities have been presented in this chapter.

QUESTIONS FOR FURTHER DISCUSSION

1. Make a flow chart of registering yourself for classes.
2. List alternatives for the process charted above. Do you see any improvements that can be made?
3. How would you determine how many tables a waitress should handle?
4. Recall a secretary you have observed in the past. What percentage of time was spent typing, talking on the telephone or to people in person, etc.? How did you measure these times? Might this be a form of work sampling?
5. In some parts of the country, building construction varies seasonally. Is this a problem for company management? What decisions must management make concerning these variations?
6. How can a building contractor schedule the building of a house so as to keep idle time and inventory to a minimum?
7. Newspapers have reported a variety of complaints about the quality of service from automobile garages and other shops. If you were managing a shop, how would you control the quality of your service?

17

Purchasing and Controlling Your Materials

A major cost of most businesses is for the materials or goods purchased, processed, and sold. The activities relating to these physical inputs can make or break a business. It may pay too much, obtain the wrong materials, hold the materials too long, fail to sell the materials, or sell them at too low a price. This chapter pertains to performing these activities most effectively. The specific topics covered are the:

1. Materials (or goods) planning and control.
2. Inventory.
3. Quantities per order.
4. Ordering procedure.
5. Sources of supply.
6. Receiving materials.

MATERIALS (OR GOODS) PLANNING AND CONTROL

In the previous chapters, we discussed the flow of materials in a business and the use of inventory to take care of seasonal variations in demand. Now, we need to consider the decisions regarding materials planning and control, including:

1. Amount of material needed for the output desired.
2. Amount of inventory and its storage and recording.

3. Quantity and time of order.
4. Vendor relations.
5. Quality of materials and price per unit.
6. Methods of receiving and shipping.
7. Handling of defective materials and stock-outs.

Policies and procedures should be established so that most of these decisions become routine in nature. When exceptions occur, they should be handled by you or someone to whom you delegate the decision. These policies and procedures should minimize the total cost of materials to the company. But remember that total cost includes more than just the price of the materials themselves. It includes costs which are charged to the goods, as well as other costs which are hidden in other expenses—usually in overhead. Overhead consists of expenses which cannot be charged directly to the product or service.

Trade-offs must be made to obtain the best cost. Materials are a form of investment, and until they are sold and produce revenue, the money cannot be used for other income-producing purposes. Consequently, you want to buy in small quantities and sell them rapidly in order to obtain income. But if the quantities you have on hand are too small, you may miss income-producing opportunities and may lose customers. Also, purchasing in small quantities usually results in higher prices. Another problem concerns the controls established to keep losses from theft to a minimum. While increasing controls may reduce the cost from losses, it also increases the control cost. The problem is to find the optimum balance between the two costs.

In materials planning and control, you should recognize that most of your income will come from a small percentage of your products or services, and that some of your materials will be of high value and some of lower value. About 80 percent of the average firm's income comes from 20 percent of its products. Materials planning and control should be directed mainly toward the 20 percent. You may want to classify the goods in categories and set a procedure for each category. Thus, for the 20 percent, you may set standards and procedures for each item; for the next, say, 30 percent, you may handle items in groups; and for the last 50 percent, you consider all items as a single group. The percentages given are only guides for your consideration. You will need to analyze your product line in the light of the procedures discussed in the rest of this chapter.

Another important area is the study of products and services to determine whether all the particular inputs are needed. This is called *value analysis,* and is based on relating the purpose of each part to its cost or value. It determines the best material or design for each part or input.

INVENTORY

The inventory of materials, parts, goods, and supplies represents a high investment in all businesses. Many companies have failed because their inventories tied up too much money, or the items in inventory became obsolete, impaired, or lost. You should have an appropriate set of policies concerning the items to carry in inventory, the level of inventory, and control of the stock.

The purpose of an inventory is to disconnect one segment of a process from another, so that each segment can operate at its optimum level of performance. A process composed of several operations, with inventory between them, might be diagrammed as in Figure 17–1.

FIGURE 17–1

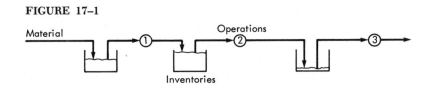

Note that the inventories are shown at different levels at different stages of the process. The level depends on the prior activities of the supplier to, and the user of, the inventory. For example, operation 1 may have been running recently and operation 2 may have been shut down. Also notice that operation 3 may not have enough material if operation 2 does not start up soon.

Inventories exist in various places in the business, and in different stages of production, as:

1. Raw materials and parts.
2. Goods in-process or between operations.
3. Finished goods at the factory, storehouse, or store.
4. Purchased goods and materials.
5. Repair parts for machines.
6. Supplies for the office, shop, or factory.
7. Patterns and tools.

Each of these types of inventory is performing basically the same function and can be studied in the same way. However, some of the inventories represent a much greater investment, cause more serious trouble if the items are not in stock, and are more costly to restock than others. The amount of attention and time spent on these should be greater than on the others.

Even a small company may have thousands of items in stock. The total investment should be kept in a proper relation to the finances of the company. This relationship will be discussed in Chapter 23 when the financial analysis of the company is considered. The detailed analysis made to determine the economical inventory level must consider the total inventory so as not to jeopardize the company's financial position. The total investment in inventory should not be so great that it deprives you of enough cash to pay your current bills.

Figure 17–2 shows how the number of units of a *purchased item* varies over a period of time. When a purchased item is received, the

FIGURE 17–2
Graph of the Changing Level of Inventory of an Item

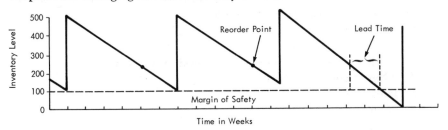

inventory increases instantly. The units are removed from inventory as they are demanded. At a certain point in time, or when the inventory reaches a given level, a purchase order is sent to the vendor for a certain quantity. The order will be received some time later. In the meantime, more units may be drawn from inventory. This cycle is repeated for each item purchased.

For items *in process* and *in finished goods,* the inventory builds up over a period of time as goods are produced, so the vertical line in Figure 17–2 would be sloping upward to the right. The inventory builds up because production is greater than demand. The following discussion pertains to purchased items, but with minor adjustments it would apply to "in process" and finished goods also.

The level of inventory at which an order should be issued is based on:

1. The quantity to be used between the time an order is issued and the items are received.
2. A quantity needed to provide a margin of safety.

The time to be allowed in (1) is determined by the sum of the times for:

1. Order to be processed in your company.
2. Order to be transported to the vendor.

3. Vendor to make and package the items.
4. Items to be transported to your company.

The total delay varies from time to time, so a margin of safety is added to obtain the quantity at the reorder point. The margin of safety, in turn, depends upon:

1. Variability of the time to obtain the items from the vendor. A higher variability requires higher margin of safety.
2. Variability of usage.
3. Cost of not having inventory—losses from stock-outs.
4. Cost of carrying inventory, estimated for each item or group of items. These inventory costs include:
    a. Space charges.
    b. Insurance and taxes.
    c. Profits lost because money is tied up in inventory.
    d. Obsolescence of items.
    e. Deterioration.
    f. Theft.

Estimates of the costs of carrying inventory range from 15 percent to over 100 percent of the average inventory for a year. Values of 20 percent to 25 percent are often used.

You can compute, or estimate, the reorder point quantity by trying various levels and reordering points and adding the cost of carrying the inventory and the cost of running out of goods multiplied by the probability of running out. The lowest total cost is the best reorder point. Note that more attention should be focused on some items than on others.

QUANTITIES PER ORDER

The quantity you include on each order affects the level of inventory and the time between orders. You may place your orders:

1. At certain intervals, such as once a week, month, or quarter, when you order an amount which brings the level of the inventory up to a predetermined standard amount.
2. When the inventory reaches a certain quantity, such as 250 units in Figure 17–2. The quantity ordered is a fixed amount called the *economic order quantity* (EOQ).

The quantity to order in (1) and (2) can be computed or estimated in the same manner, but in (1) it is used only as an expected average. The economic order quantity is determined by balancing:

1. The cost of the order, which includes
   a. The costs of processing and handling the order.
   b. The costs of the item, realizing that larger orders usually warrant price discounts.
   c. Transportation costs.
2. The inventory carrying costs.

Figure 17–3 shows the way the costs per unit vary as the quantity ordered is changed. The point of lowest cost is the EOQ. This can

FIGURE 17–3
Changes in Purchase Unit Costs

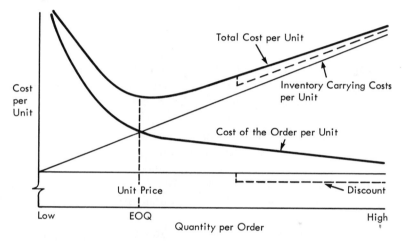

be found by using a formula or by comparing the unit costs for different order quantities. Note how a discount affects the curve and that a range in quantities has approximately the same low cost.

ORDERING PROCEDURE

Many items can be ordered on a routine basis. The procedure starts with the need as reflected by the reorder point and requires keeping a:

1. Perpetual inventory, which records when the inventory has reached the reorder point. Figure 17–4 shows a perpetual inventory card.
2. Quantity set aside which will not be used without making out a purchase order.
3. Method of calling attention to the need for the order, such as a gauge for a tank of oil.

The amount to reorder is shown on the inventory card or on some other form. The vendor and method of packaging and transporting are on a record.

FIGURE 17–4
Inventory Record Form

Date	Received		Issued		Balance on Hand
	Order No.	Units	Req. No.	Units	
7/13	3401	400			450
7/17			1075	10	440
7/22			1090	10	430

Reorder Point: 70 Bags   Reorder Quantity: 400 Bags
Item No.   Description   Unit
   315   Zinc Oxide (3Z33)   50# Bags

The major items of purchase require more analysis as their cost and quality can have a greater effect on your company. You, or someone in authority in your firm, should be involved in these purchases. A number of the considerations which require higher-level decisions are:

1. Expected changes in price. Short delays in buying for expected decreases in price or increased quantities for expected increases in price can result in savings. However, stock-outs or too heavy inventory costs should be guarded against.
2. Expected changes in demand. Seasonal products fall into this category.
3. Orders for a demand for specialty goods. The quantity ordered should match the amount demanded so that no material is left over. When the quantity of the demand is known, estimates of losses in process are added to the order. When the quantity of the demand is not known, you must depend on the forecasts plus the estimates of losses.
4. Short supply of materials.

Speculative buying should be avoided unless you are in that business. While all business decisions have a certain element of speculation, a small businessman cannot afford to gamble with money required in his business. The procedure for processing a purchase order and receiving the goods is flow-charted in Figure 17–5.

One person should have the responsibility for ordering all materials, but he should obtain the help of those people knowledgeable in the area where the goods are needed. By having a single person responsible, duplicate orders for the same material are avoided, the specialized skills needed for purchasing can be used, and responsibility for improvements in the buying process is localized.

FIGURE 17–5
Purchase Order Procedure

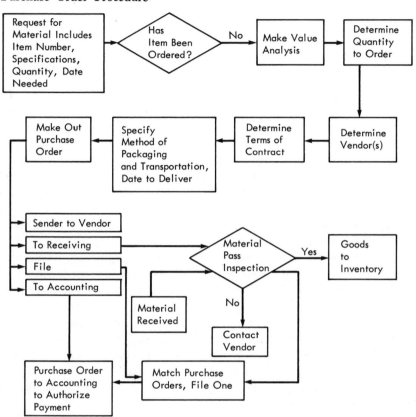

The number of forms needed for obtaining and controlling products, and the number of copies of these forms, depend on the amount of formality desired. A simple requisition form can be forwarded to the purchasing agent. He, in turn, reviews the requisitions, issues the purchase order to the vendor, follows up on orders when needed, checks the receipt of the material, takes corrective action when needed, and sees that the material is delivered to the proper place.

SOURCES OF SUPPLY

Sources from which you obtain your inputs are important because:

1. Price of purchased goods is a major cost in your outputs.
2. Reliability in delivery and quality affects your operations.
3. Vendors can be valuable sources of information.
4. Vendors can provide valuable service.

The prices from different vendors are not the same. Higher prices may be charged for:

1. Higher quality.
2. More reliable and faster delivery.
3. Better terms for returning goods.
4. More services, such as in advertising, type of packaging, and information.
5. Better, or delayed, payment plan.

You may be able to purchase an item at a lower price, but your total cost of processing the item may be higher. For example, the price plus transportation cost from a distant source may be less than from a local source, but the faster service from the local source may allow you to carry less inventory. The reduction in inventory may more than compensate for higher local price. One source may be able to supply you a wide assortment of goods you need, reducing the expense of ordering from many sources.

Your sources of supply may be from brokers, jobbers, wholesalers, manufacturers, or others. Each of these sources provides a type of service which may be valuable to you. For example, the wholesaler stocks many items so that he can give fast delivery of a wide variety of items. A manufacturer ships directly with no intermediate handler, but he is restricted in the product he can supply. However, he may have sales representatives or agents who can help the small business. Regional and national trade shows and private trade associations provide valuable information and services for keeping up-to-date on sources and their products and services.

Should you buy from one or many sources? The argument for a single source is the closer and more individual relationship which can be established. When shortages occur, you probably can obtain better service than if you have many sources. Discounts may be obtained with larger volume buying. On the other hand, multiple sources allow you to find the source with a greater variety of goods and, often, better terms. Some companies put out requests for bids, and negotiations can result in better arrangements.

Care should be exercised on the ethics of the supplier and your relationship to him. Many unethical practices exist and should be guarded against, including gifts, entertainment, misrepresentation, and reciprocity. A small company should try to maintain a good image in its dealings with vendors in order to obtain good service.

RECEIVING MATERIALS

The receipt and forwarding of materials to inventory is the last step in acquiring inputs. This step is performed to check that the material is what has been ordered, is in the proper condition, and is the proper quality. Purchasing is informed that the goods have been received, and are ready for processing.

A copy of the purchase order and other desired specifications are sent to those receiving the material. The material is checked for damage in transportation; for specified characteristics such as color, size, and the item specified; and for the proper quantity and price. Those processing the materials are delayed if they do not find the right kind and quantity of material in inventory. Proper receiving procedures can eliminate these discrepancies.

Materials can be stored in the containers in which they are received, in separate containers, or by individual item. Receiving prepares the material for storing.

SUMMARY

In this chapter, we have tried to present a helpful discussion of the importance of obtaining the proper materials, in the right quantity, of the right quality, at the right time, and for the right price.

In an era of shortages, the success of firms will depend upon their skill—and luck—in finding and acquiring adequate supplies of goods, materials, and supplies.

If you are to succeed, you will need to manage efficiently and effectively the planning and controlling of materials, including inventories, ordering points, sources of supply, and receiving and storing merchandise.

QUESTIONS FOR FURTHER DISCUSSION

1. In what ways can inventories serve to reduce costs? To increase costs?
2. How would you make an economic study to determine the quantity of a food item to buy for your family on each trip to the store? How often should purchases be made?
3. Discuss the advantages and disadvantages of having a food freezer in your home.
4. What are the advantages and the disadvantages of shopping at a single store rather than at several?
5. How would a hardware store be affected by running out of a stock item (stocking-out)?
6. Discuss the advantages and the disadvantages of buying locally versus buying from a distant seller.

WHERE TO LOOK FOR FURTHER INFORMATION

Buffa, E. S. *Modern Production Management*, 4th ed. New York: John Wiley and Sons, 1973.

Hedrick, F. D.   *Purchasing Management in the Small Company.* New York: American Management Association, Inc., 1971.

Hopeman, R. J.   *Production, Concepts Analysis Control,* 2d ed. Columbus, Ohio: Charles E. Merrill, 1971.

Improving Materials Handling in Small Business, 3d ed. Washington, D.C.: Small Business Administration, 1969. (Small Business Management, No. 4.)

Kline, J. B.   *Pointers on Scheduling Production.* Washington, D.C.: Small Business Administration, 1970. (Management Aids for Small Manufacturers, No. 207.)

Mayer, R. R.   *The Equipment Replacement Decision.* Washington, D.C.: Small Business Administration, 1970. (Management Aids for Small Manufacturers, No. 212.)

Miles, L.   *Techniques of Value Analysis and Engineering.* 2d ed. New York: McGraw-Hill Book Company, 1972.

Moore, F. G.   *Production Management.* 6th ed. Homewood, Illinois: Richard D. Irwin, Inc., 1973.

Cases for Part V

V–1. Drake Printers[1]

"Do I have any problems? I have plenty of them," said Bill Strickland, owner and president of Drake Printers. "You are interested in the production area? Let me start with the space problem. We do not have enough space on the first floor and only stairs to the second. H. J. thinks he can find an elevator to help us. Also, we cannot move our machines because special flooring was placed under each machine when we moved into this rented building 15 years ago. It would take too much money to fix the floors or to move to another building."

Mr. Strickland continued: "Let me describe our system. We did about half a million dollars of business last year. The jobs range from a few dollars for some personal calling cards to several thousand for multicolored booklets—averaging about $100 per order. Jobs are phoned in or the customer comes to the office. Either Will or I put the information for the order on a three-part order form (Exhibit I–1). The top copy we keep in the office filed by customer. Each day, I receive a list of these orders and lists of jobs to be processed in each of the press and bindery departments so that I can set the priority for processing (Exhibit I–2). These schedules are sent to the shop.

"The second copy is the stockman's copy. However, it is used for making a purchase order when I judge that we do not have an item

[1] Prepared by Charles R. Scott, Jr., University of Alabama.

313

EXHIBIT I–1
Customer Order

1 MAY 21 1974

GALLEY PROOF ; REVISED GALLEY ; PAGE PROOF ; REVISED PAGE ; VELOX

PROOF Yes ( ) No ( ) | Proof OK with Corrections | Letterpress (set change

TO | Proof OK | № 25188

DATE | Give Revised | OFFSET (X)

JOB BY DATE May 14, 1974

NAME Brewer State Junior College

ADDRESS

JOB PROMISED Friday Morning PURCHASE ORDER NO.

JOBS IN SHOP MAKE-UP MAN

Deliver (X) UPS Will Call ( ) Paid ( ) Collect ( )

QUANTITY	DESCRIPTION		PRICE
1500	Fight Inflation Flyers	Last Price	3805/1A - $74
		Art	40.40
		Cuts	
		Printing	2.46
		TOTAL 4P2 —	T.E. 42.86

Printed on Back ( ) Head to Head ( ) Tumble Head ( )

SPECIAL INSTRUCTIONS – 2 folds for mailing - Punkey In | FOLDER PAGES | SADDLE STITCHED | SIDE STITCHED

ORIGINAL DUP. TRIP. QUAD. QUINT. INVOICED

COLOR OF INK (BLACK) (RED) (BLUE) OTHER: MAY 29 1974

PADDED TAGBOARD MARBLEBOARD BOX

PUNCHING: NO. OF HOLES SLOT Invoice No. 19530

PERFORATIONS: Across Up and Down On Press Round Hole Slit

BEGIN NUMBER END NUMBER (Hand) ROUND CORNER

CARBONS: Pencil ( ) Typewriter ( ) SNAPOUT: Black ( ) Blue ( )

FINISHED SIZE 8½x11 SHEET SIZE

NO. OUT CUT FROM QUAN.

GRADE & WT. 50 lb Offset White

RETURN: ART WORK ☐ PICTURES ☐ ENGRAVINGS ☐ № 25188

TO DATE RETURNED

for the order. Most of the time the paper will be delivered in time for printing. The third copy, an envelope, is the shop processing order. We put any aids needed for processing in it and send it to the shop. The envelope moves through the shop with the material. When the envelope is returned with the delivery time stamped on it, Will or I figure the price. We use our knowledge of our operations and, sometimes,

EXHIBIT I–2
Priority List

		Dept. TYPESETTING	Page 1	Date 5/15		
Priority	Job No.	Description	In	Out		Progress
6	24655	SECA/COP. SO EAST LATIN AMER.	5/6	5/29		
3	24952	CONT. ED. U OF A/COMM AFF. SEM.	5/10	5/17	✓	
2	24955	" " " /5TH ANN. NAT. GAS	5/10	5/16	✓	
1	20519	CHAMBER OF COMM./MAPS	5/10			
25	25038	TUSC. ACADEMY/ENVELOPES	5/9	5/16	✓	
27	25030	FOR REPORT	5/9			

the Franklin catalogue which is a pricing book for the printing trade. We plan to set up systems for obtaining the time and material used on each job. At present, we do not have these.

"We figure the price for about 30 percent of the orders at the time of ordering and, on the others, give a ball park figure."

Just then, a worker came in about a rush job. When he had left, Mr. Strickland said, "Here's another question. How do you charge overtime?"

"Yes, we are having the problems with getting paper. It is not so much how much but more the type of paper. Now, we are having to keep six to eight weeks of paper inventory. Except for special orders, we order at least four cartons of paper on each order in order that transportation costs will not be too high. We have Jimmy, a business administration student, listing all our stock on this form (Exhibit I–3)—his list will include from 400 to 500 items. We hope to design

EXHIBIT I–3
Inventory List

Quantity	Size	Wt.	Kind	Color	Price (Unit)	Price (Total)
17500	17x22	16 lb	SPRINGHILL BOND	WHITE		
3700	17x28	16 lb	"	"		
8000	19x24	16 lb	"	"		
8000	17x22	20 lb	"	"		
0	17x28	20 lb	"	"		
7500	19x24	20 lb	"	"		
21000	17x22	16 lb	"	COLORS		
16,000	17x28	16 lb	"	"		

EXHIBIT I-4
Shop Layout

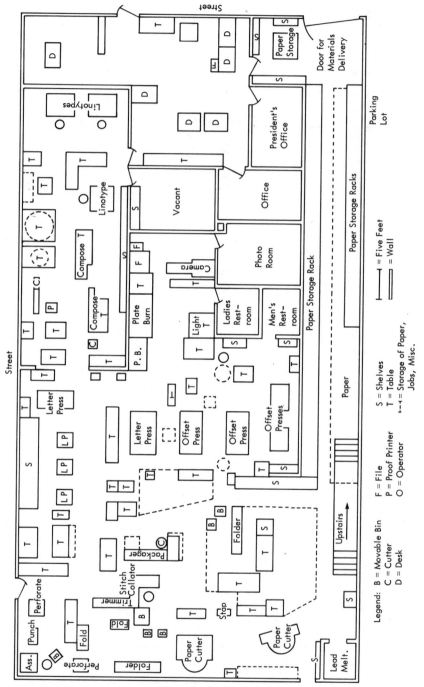

Legend: B = Movable Bin   F = File |———| = Five Feet
         C = Cutter   P = Proof Printer |----| = Wall
         D = Desk   O = Operator
                               S = Shelves
                               T = Table
                               |—◁ = Storage of Paper,
                                     Jobs, Misc.

a good inventory system to eliminate taking physical inventory each four months. We estimate our profits monthly but, now, we must estimate our inventory.

"A stockman is watching the stock level constantly to determine when to place an order for more stock. We have the paper stored in racks behind this office (See Exhibit I–4) but we have so much paper and so little room that it is now stored in the aisle. Sometimes, we have to move the paper outside the building to get it to the presses.

"We have paper, jobs in process and clutter in the plant. About once a week, I go around with an employee to point to material for him to throw away. We need more space. Oh yes, we have type set for repeat orders stored on the tables in the type-setting room. Storage of plates is becoming a problem. Also, we have about 100 file drawers upstairs full of past job orders.

"We need more productivity—more volume. Our paper cost has increased from 33 to 38 percent of our cost, and labor has risen from 33 to 43 percent. We have seven employees setting and composing type and preparing the plates, six press operators, seven in the bindery area and five in the office."

Exhibit I–4 shows the shop layout. The second floor is not shown. (It is the same size as the first floor and is an open attic except for the art office above the downstairs offices and past-order files in a hall at the top of the stairs.)

The process starts with typesetting, lines of metal letters, or offset plate making. After the proof-reading, the printing is performed on the presses. Paper is moved from storage to the paper cutter, then to the presses, and on to the bindery. The bindery has many operations—collating, drilling holes, cutting, stapling, stitching, and several methods of binding. Supervisors direct the workers concerning the jobs and their sequence. The shop has machines for most operations, but some operations are done manually. Completed jobs are returned to the front office. Material is moved by hand, by dolly, and by hand-hydraulic lift of pallets along narrow aisles.

QUESTIONS

1. Make a process chart (1) following the order forms and (2) following the paper. Show on your layout the general movement of the form and paper through the shop.

2. Does the company appear to have a good flow of material through the plant? Explain.

3. Does the company appear to have space problems? If so, list them.

4. What are the alternative methods Mr. Strickland might use to solve the space problems?

5. Which of these methods do you believe are the best? List the advantages and disadvantages of each.

6. Make specific recommendations for Question 5 which can be given to Mr. Strickland for him to install.

7. Do you believe that the one form is adequate for instructing the workers and for scheduling? Explain.

8. How can you determine the productivity of the workers? Is this necessary? Explain.

9. Do inventory problems exist? If so, what are your recommendations to Mr. Strickland?

V–2. Florida Builders Supply Company[1]

Florida Builders Supply Company was a 50 year old concern that had operated most of its life as a conventional lumber company catering to builders and contractors. Management realized in 1970 that 85 percent of the customers were home owners or do-it-yourself customers. On this basis, it decided it would try one of its new stores as a self-service operation. However, the design of the store and the layout and merchandise display had not been changed from the previous type store and the self-service efforts were not working up to the expectations of management. One of the weaknesses felt to exist was the sale of related items. It became apparent to management that a more scientific approach to design and layout would have to be undertaken if the self-service approach was to be successful.

At that time consultants, who had worked for Florida Builders Supply on other projects, were called in to help with the problem. They were charged with the responsibility of determining the best layout and design for the showroom of a new store, the design and layout of a prototype store, and the monitoring of this layout after the new store opened. If successful this layout would become the standard for all new stores. It would employ the self-service concept.

The stores were housed in a 36,000 square foot facility including an air conditioned, carpeted showroom of 4,200 feet; the remaining area

---

[1] Prepared by Warren DeBord and Henry Towery, University of South Florida.

served as a warehouse type display area. The higher-margin, more attractive merchandise was displayed in the showroom and the remainder was housed in the warehouse. The dimensions and shape of the showroom and building are shown in Exhibit II–1. The showroon had one

EXHIBIT II–1
Location of Showroom for Self-Service Stores

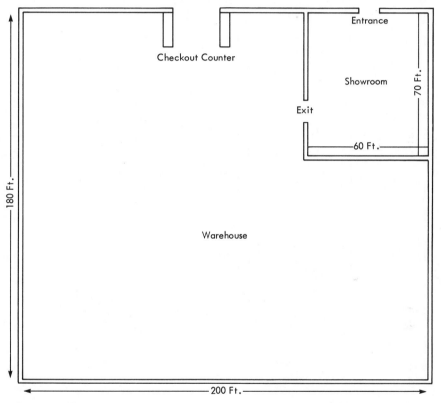

Drawn to scale.

entrance (one-way traffic) and one exit into the warehouse. This entrance and exit could be placed wherever the consultants suggested in order to maximize customer traffic control.

In an extensive research effort involving both observation and questioning of customers in other stores, several types of data were obtained. First, customer movements in several stores were observed in order to determine which areas of the showroom received the least amount of traffic. These are shown on Exhibit II–2 and II–3. The percentage figures

EXHIBIT II–2
Conventional Showroom Traffic Patterns

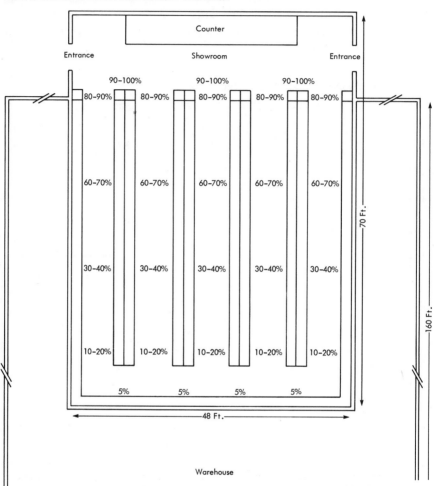

This diagram represents one type of layout used by conventional Florida Builders Supply stores. The percentage figures represent the percent of people who passed each point.

shown at various points in the two showrooms represent the percentage of customers who passed that particular point.

A second type of information, obtained by questioning customers after they had finished shopping, was a list of the items they had purchased on a pre-planned basis and a list of items purchased on impulse after entering the store. The results of the responses of approximately 1,000 Florida Builders Supply's customers are shown in Exhibits II–4 and II–5.

In addition to this information, it was determined that three displays in the showroom tended to draw customers, primarily because of the

EXHIBIT II–3
Conventional Showroom Traffic Pattern

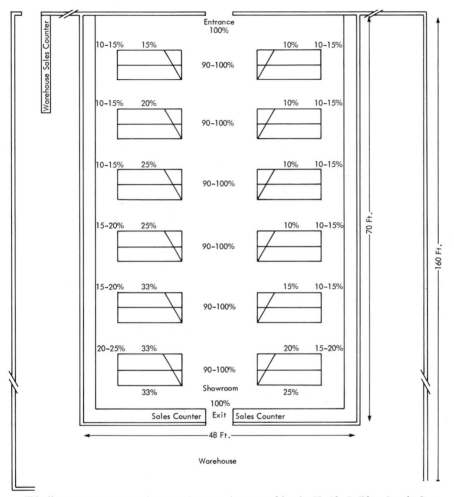

This diagram represents another type showroom layout used by the Florida Builders Supply Company. The percentage figures shown represent the percent of the people who passed each of these points.

appearance of these displays. These were the kitchen, the light fixture and the carpet displays.

The consultants were also constrained by the fact that certain types of displays, because of design, had to be placed on the walls of the showroom. The showroom had solid concrete block walls, without windows, so the entire perimeter of the showroom could be used for display purposes. Items that had to go on the outside walls are listed below with the amount of space required for each display:

1. Hand and power tools—28'
2. Garden tools—20'
3. Nails—20'
4. Mirrows and medicine cabinets—10'
5. Spindle novelty items—4'
6. Kitchen—12' × 12'
7. Bead novelty items—4'
8. Mirror tile—4'
9. Wall light display—6'
10. Spray paint—2'
11. Paint (large cans) display—36'
12. Carpet rolls—16'
13. Carpet samples—9'
14. Information booth—6' × 6'

Merchandise that was not to be displayed on the outer walls of the showroom would be displayed on free-standing gondolas throughout the store. These gondolas were 54" high and had adjustable shelving. They came in 4' sections, but could be placed end-to-end to make continuous display racks. They could also be placed back-to-back so that one aisle could afford the customer access to two gondolas of merchandise displays.

It was determined that the merchandise displayed in the showroom could be divided into two major categories: (1) home decoration items,

EXHIBIT II–4
Impulse-Purchase Items

Item	No. of Customers Purchasing*
Hand tools	84
Screws and bolts	39
Electrical items	39
Plumbing	33
Paint brushes	30
Paint	30
Cabinet hardware	27
Nails	24
Furniture legs	15
Shelving	15
Sandpaper	15
Garden hoses	15
Sprinklers	15
Wall anchors	12
House numerals	12
Light bulbs	12

* These are the customers of the approximately 1,000 interviewed who indicated they purchased these items on impulse.

EXHIBIT II–5
Planned-Purchase Items

Item	*No. of Customers Purchasing* *	*Item*	*No. of Customers Purchasing* *
Nails	188	Cabinet hardware	32
Paint	138	Garden hoses	28
Screws and bolts	134	Paneling	27
Hand tools.	126	Shelving	27
Electrical items	110	Sprinklers	25
Adhesives	64	Gardening tools	24
Caulking	64	Paint thinner.	22
Door locks.	58	Wall anchors	22
Paint brushes	56	Saw blades.	21
Pipe fittings	49	Electrical tools	20
Plumbing items	43	Light bulbs.	19
Hinges	40	Windows	14
Doors.	39	Guttering.	12
Sandpaper	36		

* These are the customers out of the approximately 1,000 interviewed who said they had planned to purchase these items before entering the store.

and (2) home repair items. The merchandise lines that were classified in each of these two categories and the amount of gondola space required to display each category are shown below. A total of 416′ of gondola space is needed to display all these items. This length indicated is for one side of the gondola.

Home Decorator Items
Shelving and table legs—32′
Decorator electric covers—8′
Fancy toilet seats—8′
Electrical items—32′
Light fixtures in boxes—16′
Extension cord sets—8′
Light bulbs—8′
Glue and adhesives (assorted)—8′
Caulking tubes (assorted)—8′
Paint brushes—12′
Paint supplies—20′
Paint (small cans)—20′
Paint accessories—20′

In addition, a 12′ × 14′ overhead light fixture display is required. Nothing can be displayed underneath this.

Home Repair Items
Hand tools—20′
Sprinklers—20′
Fancy faucets—20′
Plumbing and pipe fittings—40′
Door and window hardware—20′
Locksets—20′
Cabinet hardware—20′
General hardware items—20′

In addition, six 2′ × 2′ portable impulse racks are used to display various items from time to time.

The showroom was air-conditioned, carpeted, and had an acoustical tile ceiling. The lighting was continuous strips of fluorescent lights mounted below the ceiling surface. Every area of the showroom received the same level of illumination, except peripheral areas which had a lower level.

QUESTIONS FOR DISCUSSION

1. What factors should be considered in layout and design to control customer traffic flows?
2. How can known factors relating to preplanned and impulse purchases be utilized in planning the merchandise displays?
3. What points in the showroom will be most difficult to get customer traffic into? How can this difficulty be overcome?
4. What additional information could have been collected to help in the relayout of the showroom? Would it have been worth collecting?
5. Should gross margin for specific items be used in locating items in the showroom?
6. Make a critical analysis of the two layouts shown (Exhibits 2–2 and 2–3).
7. Based on the information presented, locate the general categories of items in the showroom, the entrance, and the exit. Explain your reasoning.
8. Show a detailed layout, including the arrangement of gondolas and location of the items of merchandise.
9. What lighting guidelines would you suggest?
10. Develop a set of generalized rules for developing a layout.
11. What influence could such things as promotions, the introduction of new product lines, theft, and the size of the showroom have on layout requirements?

V–3. La-Tex Casket, Inc.[1]

Following his father's death in 1932, Mr. Ralph Harris became the sole owner of La-Tex Casket Company. In 1947, a corporation was formed in which Mr. Harris held 51 percent of the stock. Mrs. Ann Jenkins,

---

[1] Prepared by Hall H. Logan, University of Arkansas.

a widow, held 19 percent; John McClearly, 15 percent; and Albert Mayer, 15 percent. The four comprised the board of directors.

The company was located in northwestern Louisiana. The only product of the company was caskets, though unupholstered furniture and ammunition boxes had been made in the past. In 1955, Mr. Harris died, leaving his interest in the business to his wife Marie. In 1962, Mrs. Jenkins was president; Mrs. Marie Harris served as secretary-treasurer; Mr. McCleary acted as general manger; and Mr. Mayer was production manager.

Mrs. Jenkins and Mrs. Harris were about 65 years of age, had graduated from high school, had had no business experience prior to 1955. They supervised the office work jointly, and assisted or filled in where needed. Each averaged about 30 hours a week.

Mr. McCleary, as general manager, was responsible for sales and promotion and supervised the finishing department. He had been with the company almost from its beginning, had most of his experience in the finishing department, had completed two years of high school, and was over 65 years of age. Mr. Mayer was in charge of the rest of the production. He had started as a sweeper, and was only a few years younger and less senior than Mr. McCleary.

SALES

Sales had increased each year beginning with 1956. In 1962, they approximated three quarters of a million dollars. The company sold to morticians in all 48 continental states, the Caribbean countries, and Canada.

The proportion of sales of metal caskets was increasing, reaching about 20 percent of sales in 1961. The choice of wood or metal could be influenced by the funeral home in some cases. In other cases, the family of the deceased had definite likes and dislikes. In localities where wood was a native product, wooden caskets were favored. Metal caskets were thought to be more permanent. Cremation was slowly increasing, and some crematories would not take metal caskets while others would.

Good standards of workmanship were maintained for each quality of product. Deliveries were scheduled within two weeks after receipt of order. Overtime was required on occasion to maintain this schedule. Rush orders could be shipped the same day if received before 9:00 A.M.

PRODUCTION

The standard line consisted of a relatively small number of models. However, custom manufacture made up a considerable portion of the production. From basic box construction, variation in design was accomplished in the finishing operations and materials. Mr. McCleary kept abreast of design trends. Three or four new designs were introduced each month. The number of basic box designs varied from 45 to as high as 70. Generally, caskets were made in five different widths, three depths, and four lengths. (The standard line came in 3, 1, and 3 alternatives respectively.) Usually 10 colors were available for most boxes, and 12–15 variations in hardware. Not all hardware was furnished for all box designs.

Dried lumber was purchased, and the company performed all operations on wooden caskets. Metal boxes were purchased, as the company had no facilities for metal stamping or shaping. The metal caskets were finished, both on the exterior and interior, including application of handles and special hardware. Though metal boxes were purchased, most competition could be met and undersold. Facilities, plant, and equipment were old, but well maintained. Work areas were very clean and well lighted.

Production rates had been gradually increased over the past seven years from an average of six caskets per hour to 7.5 caskets per hour. For the year ending October 31, 1961, the company produced about 12,000 caskets, for a daily average of about 48, and at an average price of about $56, F.O.B. the factory. However, no cost records were kept by part, product, or department. Mr. Mayer determined the orders to be run. Caskets were produced only to order; no caskets were carried in stock.

Seasonal production followed the death rate.

January	9.4%	May	7.4%	September	6.0%
February	9.9%	June	7.8%	October	7.8%
March	11.0%	July	7.4%	November	8.4%
April	9.4%	August	6.5%	December	9.0%

Seasonal fluctuation required about 12 additional employees for the winter peak. Unskilled employees were readily available. The two managers decided whom to hire or fire, but the annual turnover rate was considered low. Wages and salaries paid were equal to or above those paid locally.

Information on manpower requirements and pay, on production requirements, and on supervisors is shown in Exhibit III–1. The floor plans for the two floors and the flow of material are shown in Exhibits III–2 and III–3. A supervisor managed the production in each of the areas—first floor, painting, assembly, and finishing.

Parts and assemblies were moved on hand-pushed 4-wheel trucks through the plant and up and down by elevator.

Low priced boxes, about 60 percent of production, used nailed and screwed boards instead of laminated ones, usually did not have molding,

EXHIBIT III–1
Production Information

Labor Classification, Pay, and Number

Unskilled operators (U)	$1.15 to 1.35/hr.	average 19 people
Machine operators (M)	$1.35 to 1.90/hr.	average 12 people
Finishers (F)	$1.50 to 2.40/hr.	average 14 people

Production Operations, Machines, and Skills Required

Operation	Machine	Floor	Number of Employees
Rough-cut	Cut off saw	one	2(M),1(U)
Plane	Planer	one	
Laminate wood pieces	Laminator*	one	
Cut to finished dimension (1/32″ tolerance)	Saws	one	7(M)
Shape and round pieces	Molder	one	
Subassemble ends, sides, bottoms, tops	Assembly area	two	10(U)
Assemble box	Assembly area	two	8(U)
Paint (when required)	Paint offset	one	3(M)
Finish	Finishing area	two	
Apply box cover	Finishing area	two	
Fasten on hardware.	Finishing area	two	14(F)
Insert bedding.	Finishing area	two	
Finish interior of box	Finishing area	two	

Location, Age, Service and Pay of the Four Supervisors

First floor plant, 49 years of age, 20 years service	$325/month
Second floor plant, 68 years of age, 28 years service	$325/month
Paint shop, 56 years of age, 25 years service	$300/month
Finishing department, 61 years of age, 31 years service . .	$350/month

* Most expensive machine costs about $25,000.

and were covered with cloth rather than painted. Number-three grade lumber, used in the majority of boxes, was spray-painted, usually in pastel. A small percentage of fine-quality walnut, cherry, and mahogany was used in custom models. This wood was beautifully finished close to the natural color.

PURCHASING

Lumber, cloth, hardware, and bedding were the major items purchased. Local area sources had, until a few years ago, supplied most of the lumber. Local prices had then increased to the point that West Coast lumber could be landed in Louisiana at lower prices. An arrangement had been made with a local broker to warehouse his West Coast lumber on land owned by the casket company in exchange for the privilege of drawing daily needs from this pool. This virtually eliminated the raw material inventory of lumber and minimized the inventory cost.

EXHIBIT III–2
First Floor Production Layout

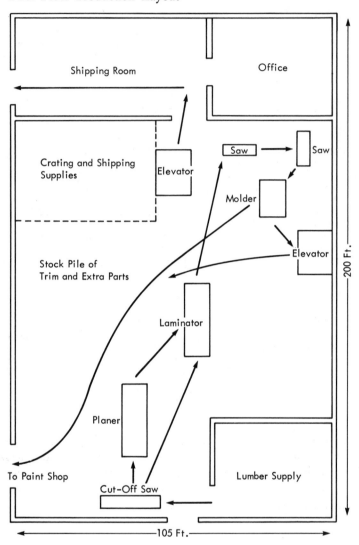

A large selection of cloths and hardware was considered necessary, even though various combinations provided a wide selection for the customer. Only on large volume items could Mr. McCleary afford to buy in quantities to obtain lower unit costs. Sales representatives brought new items of cloth and hardware to his attention. Some items were very expensive. Bedding could be anything from a simple pad to an innerspring mattress in the higher priced line.

EXHIBIT III–3
Second Floor Production Layout

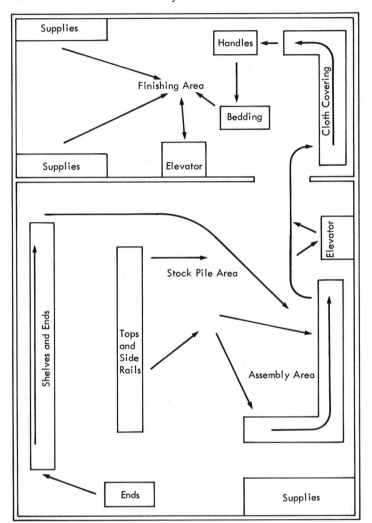

Mr. McCleary, for finishing, and Mr. Mayer, for other items, depended upon their long experience in purchasing. They had no written purchasing policies or procedures. Few records were maintained.

QUESTIONS FOR DISCUSSION

1. Can you equalize monthly production for the entire year? List the factors for a decision.

2. Estimate the costs and savings if, in Question 1, production is equalized for the machine operations. The rest of the production would fluctuate with sales.

3. Make a process chart of the process showing distances moved and methods of moving.

4. What production-flow problems do you see?

5. Do you see any advantages in mechanizing transportation in material handling operations? Any disadvantages?

6. What production and cost records, if any, are needed? Explain.

7. What changes, if any, would you make in the purchasing activities? Explain.

8. Do you feel that the inventory policy is good or poor? Explain.

V–4. Bobby Rivers
Sportswear, Inc.[1]

Bobby Rivers Sportswear had prospered from its first year of operation. First year (1953) sales of $275,000 were followed by a steady growth in sales until they were at the $1,000,000 level. Financial and operating results were considered highly confidential. Bobby Rivers Sportswear was admittedly operating profitably, and the rate of profit was generally comparable to that of other garment firms in the state. Whenever sales were in the 8300 dozen garment range annually, profits were comparable to the industry average of approximately 3.5 percent margin on sales, after taxes.

All capital stock in the company was owned by the three founders. Mr. H. H. Fancher, owner of 65 percent of the stock, assumed responsibility as president and general manager, and supervised all activities related to design, production, sales, finance and personnel. Mr. Dunning, with a 25 percent ownership, was responsible for miscellaneous activities in the plant, including shipping, receiving, and maintenance. Mr. Archer, a brother-in-law of Mr. Fancher and a son of the former owner, held 10 percent of the stock but took no part in the management of the company.

The company attempted to serve only a limited segment of the ladies ready-to-wear market. Its goal was to produce dresses and suits using

---

[1] Prepared by Kenneth W. Olm and Fred Ingerson, University of Texas.

basic, popular fabrics and designed to sell in the medium-low price range. No high-style garments were included in the line, hence the styles produced tended to have more permanancy, which in turn resulted in greater emphasis on cost and quality.

Fancher felt that much of his success was due to his ability to supply quality goods within specified time deadlines. Many manufacturers in the industry were lax in meeting contractual agreements which sometimes resulted in costly delays or gaps in the product lines of retailers.

The designing process began with the selection of a retail price for the garment. The selected retail price thus determined the wholesale price and the target cost of the garment. The designer then selected materials, style details, zippers, buttons, and other features to conform to the cost limitation previously established.

The production process started when the designer made the style and drew up the original pattern. Then a pattern girl graded the pattern up or down for different sizes and made different-size patterns. The marker girls fitted the pattern to cloth to obtain the least yardage per garment. Fancher stressed that "that's what makes your money." Fancher made out *cut sheets* which were used to order the correct number of cuts to fill the size and color requirements for a particular style. These cut sheets were given to a cutter who stacked piece goods in alternate colors (to prevent shading), stapled markers to piece goods to prevent shifting, and cut out pieces with an electric cutting knife. A stack of piece goods could be cut out for 100 to 500 dresses at once.

Goods were bundled by size and color (all 8's, all 10's, etc. of one color together), and the correct cuts of interlining were included for that number of dresses. Each bundle was numbered, and these bundles were issued to sewing operators. The supervisor had a master book in which she recorded the bundles as they were given to sewers. The employee number, bundle number, part number, amount, style number and color were recorded in the master book which also logged each bundle through each operation. Each worker maintained record cards of what work had been done, and these cards were checked with the master book. All operations had part numbers (i.e., sleeves #6, blouses #7, etc.). The master book provided a record of who did what work, and what rate they were to get per garment or per dozen garments. Operations were highly specialized in that one operator performed one operation only, such as pinking, hemming, making button holes, etc.

At an output level of approximately $1 million, employment varied from 90 to 100 employees, with 90 percent of the employees residing within a 5 mile radius of the factory and the remaining 10 percent living in rural settlements within 15 miles of the factory. Mr. Fancher estimated there were fewer than 25 persons available for employment in the immediate area who were capable of being trained.

Standard output was not determined from formal time studies. Based upon his own long experience, plus the fact that the basic operations performed changed very little from one year to the next, Mr. Fancher was confident that he could estimate standards to a satisfactory degree of accuracy. Any discrepancies would likely be noticed by the one experienced sewing-line supervisor.

Bottlenecks in the flow of work tended to occur on occasion, because of the absence of a key worker for whom there was no fully trained substitute or because of the breakdown of a critical machine Mr. Fancher felt that the company was not large enough to support a fully trained specialist mechanic, so when complicated machines like the button-holer required servicing, either the machine was rushed to Dallas (a two-hour drive) for service, or a specially trained mechanic was called from Dallas. Simple jobs could be handled by the firm's general maintenance mechanic.

Inspection was performed at four points in the production process. Bolts of material were inspected visually at the time they were laid out in layers on the cutting tables preliminary to the cutting operation. After sewing, seams were inspected when trimmed and threads were clipped. Later, the pressers were expected to check for spots, stains, or other flaws. A final inspection was performed by the packer preparing garments for shipping.

Flawed garments were seldom reworked. Instead, in conformity with industry practice, they were sold as "seconds" or "rejects" at cut-rate prices. Judging from the very few returned garments and the relatively small percentage of rejects, Mr. Fancher considered his quality control and inspection procedures quite satisfactory. Less than 1 percent of units produced were faulty.

Problems encountered in the scheduling of production could be divided into three types. Fancher alone handled all scheduling, basing his decisions upon his personal experience and "feel" for the problem.

The master production schedule was decided by Fancher twice a year for each season. Based upon an intuitive feel of the market, developed from 22 years of selling experience plus 10 years of general management, he felt that he could estimate the total demand for garments, even if he could not guess the individual colors and sizes. Because their key customer was primarily interested in a fixed quality level at a fixed, minimum price, and ordered fairly large quantities at one time, Fancher was able to set his production schedule with considerable assurance as far as basic styles were concerned. Changes had to be made, of course, as reports of sales established which styles were the better sellers and which were poorer. Detailed schedules were then altered to reflect demand for specific styles, colors, and sizes.

Frequently-changed schedules, combined with layout and cutting mistakes, sometimes resulted in fabric shortages. Difficulty was encountered in reordering specific patterns or weaves from suppliers, because most fabrics were produced on a one-run basis. To compensate for possible fabric shortages, Fancher formerly had ordered more of each type of fabric than was expected to be needed. The costs of such overpurchases became prohibitive and, although Fancher took pride in the company's reputation for meeting all promised orders, a policy was adopted to fall short on certain orders and refuse some reorders rather than to continue the extra cost of buying excess fabrics.

In setting weekly schedules for particular styles, care had to be exercised to maintain a balance because certain styles required more time on particular operations than others. For example, a shirtwaist required many more buttonholes than most other dresses. Fancher attempted to balance the scheduling of particular styles in any one day so as to keep everyone working at approximately the same pace. Rescheduling also was necessary occasionally to avoid disruptions caused by the absence of a key worker or a key machine, or because of materials delayed in transit to Maryhill.

On at least one occasion, when Fancher was on an out-of-state trip, the company was unable to accept a large reorder because of the lack of authority of the minority stockholders to make decisions concerning large purchases of fabrics. In this case, the supplier had the desired fabric in stock.

The third type of scheduling problem faced by Fancher occurred only when current sales exceeded an annual rate of 8300 dozen dresses, which was the normal capacity of the plant on a one-shift basis. Translated into dollars, an annual sales volume of $1,000,000 was the capacity of the plant. Because Fancher was not inclined to expand the facilities or add a second shift, he chose to subcontract sewing to two nearby independent contract shops. The company delivered the necessary piece goods and patterns, and received the garments in a finished condition. All subcontract work was inspected, invoiced, and shipped from Maryhill to customers.

Inspection of contract work often showed a much lower quality of workmanship than was considered acceptable at the Bobby Rivers plant. For this reason, Fancher tried to keep orders within the capacity of the Maryhill factory. The lack of suitable facilities to produce over $1 million worth of garments caused Fancher to reject feelers for a large contract business with a second dry goods chain rather than chance sacrificing the quality image of his goods.

Mr. Fancher often wondered about the future course the company was going to take. While he was not disappointed in the progress which had been made to date, the fact that his sales had stabilized at a $1 million annual volume disturbed him a little whenever he found time to reflect on the situation.

QUESTIONS FOR DISCUSSION

1. What production advantages did Bobby Rivers obtain from staying away from high-style garments? Disadvantages?
2. What do you think of Fancher's scheduling procedure? Recommend changes if you feel some should be made.
3. Evaluate Fancher's decision to subcontract. What alternatives does he have?
4. What effect would an increase in sales have on production? What might be the effect of automating part of the operations?
5. Make an analysis of the record keeping for work performed.
6. Do you feel that the lost order incident due to Mr. Fancher's being out-of-state is serious? If so, how would you recommend the company guard against its reoccurrence?
7. Evaluate the designing process. Should production people be included in the process? How?

V–5. *Hofmann Paint Company*[1]

Management of the Hofmann Paint Company reluctantly considered the advisability of an addition to its manufacturing plant, because it had become crowded as production grew. The main offices, the factory retail store, the laboratory, painting shop, warehouse, and all production operations were located in a single building with 12,800 square feet of floor space. After deciding that expansion was necessary, the management had to consider whether to add a second story or to expand on the ground level. The building foundation had been designed to hold several more stories, but the plant supervisor believed it would be excessively expensive to put in another floor that would be strong enough to hold necessary raw materials and finished stocks. If the new floor were used to store empty drums and cartons, however, the cost would be less. The supervisor further believed that it would be necessary to

---

[1] Prepared by Kenneth W. Olm and Omer C. Jenkins, University of Texas.

do something before the end of 1963 if sales continued to expand as they had in recent years.

Hofmann was established in 1947 as a privately-held paint manufacturing company to serve all of Texas and portions of surrounding states. In 1961, over 130,000 gallons of paint were produced, an increase of 30 percent over the previous year. Production was scheduled at a rate of 150,000–175,000 gallons in 1962, and net profit for the period was considered adequate to justify expansion. Manufactured products included varnishes, water-base and latex paints, and special paints for industrial use. Linseed oil and other thinners were retailed under the Hofmann label.

All manufacturing activities were carried on in a 60′ × 200′ brick building. A 20′ × 90′ balcony along one side accommodated the premix vats and a storage area for part of the pigment stock. Located underneath the balcony were a number of washbasins, a worktable, and more storage space for pigments and drum stock. A railroad spur along the rear of the building permitted materials to be unloaded directly into the storage area and the outbuilding. A 36′ × 30′ area between the main building and the outbuilding, enclosed with chain-link fence, was used for storage of vehicle drums. The plant layout of the Hofmann plant is shown in Exhibit V–1.

MIXING THE PAINT

After a batch ticket was completed, it was taken upstairs to the premix area. Sacks of dry pigment were stored on the balcony close to the premix agitator vats, and the liquid vehicle was piped to the balcony from storage tanks outside. Normally a batch of 100 gallons was made from 60 gallons of premixed paste. Each 60-gallon batch of paste was stirred by electrically-driven paddles for approximately 30–40 minutes until the pigments were in a fairly uniform suspension in the vehicle. Next, the paste flowed to grinders to complete the mixing and wetting of the material.

On the ground floor, under the balcony holding the premix vats, were the various grinders. Three different types of grinders were used according to the type of paint to be made. The grinding process took approximately two to three hours for 60 gallons of paste for high gloss paint, somewhat less for semigloss, and still less for latex paints.

FILLING

From the grinder, the thick paste mixture was poured into large steel vats (2½′ dia. × 2½′) which stood on rollers to facilitate moving (see Exhibit V–2). The remainder of the thinner was added, and the mixture

EXHIBIT V-1
Plant Layout

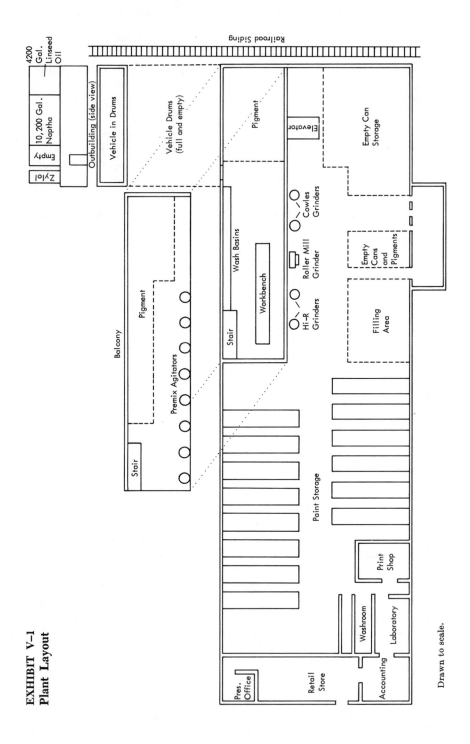

Drawn to scale.

EXHIBIT V–2
The Hi-R Grinder

was again stirred for fifteen to twenty minutes. The vat was then lifted about three feet off the floor by an electric chain hoist and carried by overhead trolley to the filling area. The shop foreman stated that an automatic filler was available, but it was used only for batches of 500 gallons or more. It seemed uneconomical to use the automatic filler on 100-gallon batches, because several hoses in the filling spout made clean-up very timeconsuming. Thorough cleaning after every batch was necessary to eliminate any residual paint, which would ruin the next batch.

All batches under 100 gallons were filled by hand. The vat was hoisted off the floor and pushed down the trolley to the filling area. A second tank, smaller in size, was placed on a small portable platform directly under the spigot of the suspended tank (see Exhibit V–3). The operator sitting on a low bench, then opened the valve of the vat to fill the smaller tank, and from this smaller tank the paint flowed through a hand-controlled valve into paint buckets. When a bucket was filled, the operator closed the spigot and slid the full can of paint along the floor to a worker sitting on a bench next to him. The second worker placed a lid on the can and sealed it with a rubber hammer. The sealed can was then slid approximately 10 feet across the floor to an area

EXHIBIT V–3
Filling and Capping

near the labeling machine where it waited until the operator was ready to run the batch through the labeler. Approximately 1,200 gallons could be filled per day using this method.

LABELING

The labeling operation normally required at least two men—one to put cans into the labeler and one to remove them and attach the wire handles. When the labeling operation was moving rapidly, it required two men to put on handles and stack the cans. After the cans were labeled and the handles attached, they were normally put on shelves in the warehouse section. Often, however, there was insufficient storage space in the warehouse area, and the cans were piled up around the labeling area.

MANUFACTURING PROCESS

The shop supervisor made a daily check of stock items and filled out a batch ticket for those which needed replenishing. Experience enabled him to know which items were selling fast and required a larger inventory and which items could be sold from inventory without replenishment. The authority and responsibility for inventory decisions were left entirely to the supervisor.

A batch ticket showed the raw material requirements to be mixed. The information on the batch tickets was taken from formulas developed by a combination of experience and trial-and-error formulation. According to the chemist, there were over 1,000 formulas in the files for different types and colors of paints which Hofmann had produced. The formulas specified the amounts of pigment and vehicle that were required per gallon of paint produced. Each time the supervisor made out a batch ticket, it was necessary to determine the quantities of materials and enter them in the appropriate columns. The theoretical yield of the batch and the filling order were also computed and put on the batch ticket.

PACKAGING

When a sales order was processed, the stock clerk would remove the cans from the shelves (or from the labeling area) and put them into cardboard cases, which were closed with staples. The supervisor said,

> I feel that we have the packaging problem in hand as well as can be expected under the circumstances. With so many small dealers we can't prepackage anything. We never know what case lots they will order, and we have some small dealers that can't afford a case lot on one item. The majority of our sales are made because we can make up a case of four colors if the dealer wants it. So we go out and take them off the shelf and make up a case of four different colors, and he doesn't have to buy four cases to get four colors.

QUALITY CONTROL

Quality control was not considered a problem at Hofmann Paint Company. Whenever a new item was being produced, it was watched carefully in every stage of production by the plant supervisor. If the item became a stock product, workers soon became familiar with it and could be left to do their work without supervision. They became so familiar with the product, the supervisor reported, that on rare occasions when a mistake was made on the batch ticket, the workers would call it to the supervisor's attention. A grind-check was made after grinding to ensure that the grinding had been right, and a yield-check for volume was made before filling. It was usually a simple matter to correct mistakes by adding the proper ingredients to balance the formula and then remix. Special items were always thoroughly checked for grind, color, weight, viscosity, and volume.

STORAGE FACILITIES

The liquid vehicle required for the various products was stored in drums and in three large steel tanks atop the outbuilding, as well as in several places in the production area, the fenced yard, and the outbuilding.

Vehicles stored in the tanks were piped directly to the premix balcony and to the grinding area. Special vehicles needed in limited quantities were purchased in drums and stored inside the outbuilding, in the storage yard, and also inside the main building near the grinding area. The drums were brought by elevator to the balcony. As the drums were emptied, they were generally taken to the storage yard, although empties were frequently stored among full drums in the main building. All finished products, sacks of pigments, and empty paint cans were stored within the main building. Sacks of pigment were stored mainly on or under the balcony near the lift, and at times overflow was stored adjacent to the filling area. The pigments used most were kept on the balcony nearest the premix vats. Finished paint was stored on shelves in the warehouse section of the building. The area above the shelves was utilized for storing nonpaint items, including wallpaper, masking tape, canvas, and other items which Hofmann did not manufacture but stocked for the retail stores.

ORDERING RAW MATERIALS

Raw materials were ordered from suppliers in Houston and Dallas. Carload orders were received by rail, but smaller orders were picked up by a company truck. This truck was needed for deliveries, and had sufficient unused time to permit its use for the nearly 400-mile round-trip distance to obtain supplies. All raw material orders could be received within 48 hours. The limited storage capacity at Hofmann generally made it difficult, if not impossible, to accommodate all the raw materials which might otherwise be ordered at one time. The plant supervisor originated all raw material requisitions, checking the stock, deciding which materials needed replenishing, considering the available storage space, and making out a requisition for purchase. The purchase requisition notified Mr. Hofmann of the quantity needed and also of the present stock on hand. Mr. Hofmann would then make out the purchase order and send it to the supplier. The available storage space would not accommodate a full stock of all raw materials if large enough quantities were ordered to receive the benefits of volume discounts and carload freight rates. Therefore, ordering was staggered to allow one material to run low while another was built up.

Exhibit V–4 gives a typical order schedule for pigments, and shows the pigments inventory as of October 9, 1962.

EXHIBIT V–4
Typical Order Schedule of Pigments and Pigment Inventory
October 9, 1962

Name of Material	Delivered Cost per Pound ($)	Usual Frequency of Order (months)	Size of Order (no. of 50# bags)	Inventory (no. of 50# bags) Oct. 9, 1962
RCHT	.09375	1	600	668
RCHT-X	.09375	1	200	148
R-900	.27500	1	200	205
R-901	.27500	1	200	200
Aluminum silate (W)	.03250	4–6	1,400	80
Aluminum silate (HO)	.03000	4–6	200	81
Atomite	.2150	4–6	600	408
Duramite	.01500	4–6	1,000	480
Asbestine (325)	.03250	4–6	1,600	316
Zinc Oxide (3Z33)	.12500	2½–3	400	43

QUESTIONS FOR DISCUSSION

1. Make a process chart and show movement of materials through the plant.
2. Using (1) and other materials, list any changes which might improve the operations.
3. Make a study of the can filling and sealing operation, and recommend desirable changes. Report these to management.
4. Evaluate the purchasing and inventory procedure. Does the inventory level for the items in Exhibit 5–4 seem reasonable? Explain.
5. Evaluate the "packaging problem."
6. Give some specific recommendations for expanding the paint production capacity. Explain your reasoning.

Part VI

Manning Your Business

According to Lawrence Appley, former president of the American Management Association, "Management is the development of people and not the direction of things . . . Management is personnel administration."

As Mr. Appley indicates, the primary duty of every manager is the proper selection, placement, development, and utilization of the talents of the firm's personnel. How well—or how poorly—he does these things is a major factor in the success or failure of the business. Of all the resources the manager has, only people have the ability to vary their own productivity. While a machine can perform only the tasks for which it was designed and within the limits of its capacity, employees have almost limitless performance capabilities, can be motivated, and can be innovative and adapt to changing circumstances.

You, as an owner-manager, should understand that the personnel function is involved in all aspects of either establishing a new business or entering an ongoing business, as well as in performing the general management and business functions described throughout this book.

Every small business manager is a "personnel manager" in the sense that work is done through people, with people, and for people. Consequently, you should be personally capable of handling employee relations until your company becomes large enough to afford a personnel manager.

This part of the text deals with the personnel function. It contains some valuable insights that can help you be effective as a personnel manager in your business. It contains information about planning your personnel requirements, selecting the sources from which you can recruit new em-

ployees, recruiting them, choosing the people you need, training and developing them into productive workers, evaluating their performance, compensating them, and dealing with various personnel relationships, including industrial relations.

The relationship between these activities is diagrammed in Figure VI–1.

FIGURE VI–1

Some of these functions may not be of value to the very small firm, but they will become important as your firm grows.

18

Selecting Your People

You can be successful in your business only if you select the right kind of people to help you, for you cannot do everything yourself. As with your other managerial activities, finding and hiring the number of people you need who have the productive qualities you need is not easy. Yet, it can be done successfully if you use the same care with, and give the same attention to, this activity as you do others.

The ideal procedure for selecting your people is to determine what jobs are to be performed, decide what qualities you are looking for in the people to be hired, search for individuals with those qualities, select the best persons available, and properly introduce them to your organization and their particular job. These subjects will be covered in this chapter under the headings:

1. Planning your manpower requirements.
2. Where to find new employees.
3. How to recruit new people.
4. How to select people for given jobs.
5. How to introduce new people to their job.

PLANNING YOUR MANPOWER REQUIREMENTS

Manpower planning is one of the most frustrating situations which the typical small business manager will encounter. Perhaps the primary reason is that the small business is not big enough to hire the exact type and number of people needed. Typically, it lacks facilities for properly recruiting, selecting, developing, and utilizing its personnel. Lack of economies of scale so far as record keeping and administration of a systematic personnel program may also exist. Another problem may be personality conflicts. One disgruntled person represents a much larger percentage of the total work force in the small firm than in the larger one. Therefore, it is important for the small business manager to try to keep from hiring the wrong employee. A related aspect of this problem is the fact that because of the usual practice of promoting from within, an incompetent worker may rise to higher levels in the organization. This point is illustrated in the case entitled "Shaffer's Drive Inns" in Part I.

When you do manpower planning, you are concerned with what type and quality of personnel your firm has and what it will need in the future. Therefore, you should:

1. Determine the jobs to be performed and the qualities needed to perform them—namely, job specifications.
2. Forecast the total number of people needed in each category by collecting and analyzing industry growth data and by studying your firm's growth data.
3. Develop manpower plans for a given period—perhaps one year—by job classification or skill.
4. Inventory the skills of all your present personnel—their education, training, and experience; their talents, abilities, skills, and trades; and their potential for growth.
5. Compare your manpower plans with your personnel inventory to identify shortages.
6. Determine the sources of supply from which you can recruit extra people as needed.

Because the quality and quantity of your work force are both important, your manpower plans should be complete and detailed, but flexible and updated at least semi-annually. The statement is frequently made that one should organize around "what is to be done" rather than "who is to do it." The use of *job specifications* will enable you as a small business manager to follow this principle of matching the person to the job to be filled.

A retailer's business was growing rapidly. While he was busy with customers, the telephone was ringing and correspondence was piling up. He believed he needed a secretary. But did he? Secretaries and stenographers are scarce and expensive. Perhaps a typist would "fill the bill." Finding a qualified typist would probably be easier, and the salary savings would be substantial. While the retailer might find it a chore to write out letters rather than dictate them, he would probably not be skilled at dictation anyway, and he could probably compose a letter more effectively by seeing how it appeared before typing.[1]

Job specifications are written statements covering the duties, authority, responsibilities, and working conditions of the job and of the *personal qualifications* required of a person to perform the job successfully. A typical job specification includes at least the following types of information:

1. The physical demands of the job and the minimum physical requirements of the individual to fill the job.
2. The working conditions—including physical conditions and psychological conditions such as relationships with others and responsibilities for other people, money, equipment, etc.
3. A summary of the duties and responsibilities of the job.
4. Educational background and knowledge, skills and techniques, and training and experience required to perform the job, as well as special training and development needed.
5. Days and hours of work.
6. Machines, tools, formulas, and other equipment used.
7. The pay classification and promotional opportunities.
8. Desirable personal characteristics.

The specifications should provide a statement of the minimum acceptable standards the person should meet in order to perform the job satisfactorily. For dead-end, routine, and low-level jobs, it may also be desirable to state the maximum acceptable standards in order to prevent an overqualified person from taking the job and being dissatisfied.

Many methods are used to gather data for the job specifications, but the most popular ones are observation, the questionnaire, and the interview.

Job specifications provide the foundation for performing the personnel function effectively. They will aid greatly in recruiting, selecting, and placing employees in your firm and in deciding what wages and salaries to pay. They will also be valuable in personnel training and development and in deciding transfers and promotions.

A service station dealer wanted to hire an "experienced attendant." He believed it was unnecessary to specify the attendant's duties because, "He'll know what the job is." But is this true? Ser-

---

[1] Rudolph Ralphelson, *Finding and Hiring the Right Employee* (Washington, D.C.: Small Business Administration, 1972), Small Marketers Aids, No. 106.

vice station attendants have different kinds of duties, including working at the pumps selling gasoline, lubricating cars, changing tires, and doing repair work during slack times at the pumps. If the dealer needed a repair man but did not so indicate, he could waste considerable time interviewing men who were qualified only for driveway work.

If you do not want to go to the extreme of preparing job specifications, you should at least establish *job descriptions* for the most important positions. These are merely statements of duties and responsibilities of the job itself, and do not include personal characteristics and qualifications. (See Figure 18–1 for a sample job description.)

WHERE TO FIND NEW EMPLOYEES

Once you have decided what type(s) of employees you need for a given job, the next step is to decide where to seek them. There are only two basic sources: from *within the firm* through promotion, upgrading, or transfer; and from *outside the company* through recruitment and selection. More specifically, there are four sources usually used by small businessmen:

1. Qualified people from within the organization.
2. Personnel from competing firms in the same industry.
3. Organizations outside the industry.
4. Educational institutions.

Positions can be filled by existing personnel by promoting qualified individuals from lower levels, or transferring them from other parts of the organization where they are not needed as badly. An alternative is to upgrade the abilities of an employee who is not presently qualified, but who can be trained and developed for the new position.

Some outside sources are:

1. Former employees.
2. Friends and relatives of employees by means of "referrals."
3. Personal applications received in person or through the mail.
4. Competing firms.
5. Labor organizations.
6. Employment agencies, either public or private.
7. Educational institutions, including high schools, business schools, vocational-technical schools, junior colleges, colleges, and manufacturers' training schools.
8. Leased manpower.

To utilize the internal source most effectively, you should consider using the currently popular process of "job enlargement," or preferably,

FIGURE 18–1
Sample Job Description

Job title: Office and credit manager

Supervisor: Store manager

Job Summary

Responsible for all office and credit functions of the store. Has control of store's assets and expenditures. Helps manager administer store's policies and methods. Exercises mature judgment and initiative in carrying out duties.

Duties

1. Inspects sales tickets for accuracy and completeness of price, stock classifications, and delivery information. (Daily)
2. Prepares bank deposits, listing checks and cash, and takes deposit to bank. (Daily)
3. Keeps sales and expenses record sheets, posting sales and expenses, and accumulating them for the month. (Daily)
4. Processes credit applications: analyzes financial status and paying record of customers, checks references and credit bureau to determine credit responsibility. (Daily)
5. Sends collection notices to past-due accounts, using mail, telephone calls, and personal visits (if necessary) to collect. (Daily)
6. Sells merchandise during rush hours of the store. (Daily)
7. Checks invoices of outside purchases to verify receipt, quantity, price, etc. Gets store manager's approval. (Weekly)
8. Does all bookkeeping and prepares financial and profit-and-loss statements of store. (Monthly)

Duties	*Approximate Time Spent on Each Duty (percent)*
Bookkeeping	40
Credit and collection	20
Selling on retail floor	20
Inventories and stock control	10
Miscellaneous functions	10

Source: *Personnel Management.* Administrative Management Course Program, Topic 6 (Washington, D.C.: Small Business Administration, 1965), p. 56.

"job enrichment." By means of job enrichment, the duties of a few different jobs may be combined into one job.

One of your machine operators, in addition to handling his regular production runs, might also be assigned to set up his machine, inspect his completed work, service his machine, or perform other duties.

Job interest and satisfaction may be increased for some of your employees by rotating them among a few to several jobs or by rearranging their work places to permit them to enjoy more group interaction.
Advantages of using the internal source for your personnel include knowledge concerning the person's capabilities, strengths, and weak-

nesses. Promotion from within will probably also build the morale of all employees (except, perhaps, the individual who is jealous).

Disadvantages of the internal source may be the lack of anyone capable of filling the vacant job or willing to take it, and the possible inbreeding produced by excessive reliance on this source.

You should first decide what kind of personal qualifications you are seeking and then choose the sources most likely to produce people with such qualifications. Some of these methods are expensive in terms of your time and money, while others are free. Also, the results are not always worth the cost of using the method.

A *balanced program* of using people from each source is superior to using either the internal source or the external source exclusively. You should have a balanced policy of promoting from within and recruiting from outside when the need arises.

HOW TO RECRUIT NEW PEOPLE

There are many methods you can use in recruiting new people. These include:

1. School and college scouting.
2. Advertising, using newspapers, trade journals, radio, billboards, and window displays.
3. Private and public employment agencies.
4. Employee referrals.

The following is an example of using an external source and two methods of recruiting:

A retail store manager put a "help wanted" sign in the window. He found this practice to be time-consuming, because many unqualified applicants inquired about the job. Furthermore, when he disapproved an applicant, he stood the risk of losing the business of the applicant plus his friends and family. The manager also found that newspaper advertising reached large groups of job-seekers. But it also brought in many unqualified people. If the store's telephone number was included in the ad, calls tied up his line and customers could not reach the store.

In order to fill his vacancy, the manager should have considered using the services of either a public or a private employment agency, or he should have obtained leads from his present employees.

HOW TO SELECT PEOPLE FOR GIVEN JOBS

Mistakes in selecting and placing personnel in your firm can be greatly reduced if you use an orderly and systematic procedure for choosing the right people. While no one method is generally acceptable, the following procedure illustrates one effective method which can be used in filling a position.

1. Review the job specifications for this position.
2. Consider your present employees, for one of them may be able to perform the job acceptably, or become qualified if his abilities are upgraded.
3. Look outside the company and recruit applicants if none of your present employees can fill the job.
4. Use an application blank in gathering information from applicants.
5. Prepare for interviews with applicants by listing the points you need to cover.
6. Conduct the interviews.
7. Bring the supervisor of the prospective employee into the act; you may even want him to do the interviewing.
8. Use psychological tests[2] to determine the applicant's knowledge, skills, and attitudes.
9. Check on qualified applicants with their previous employers.
10. Arrange for the applicant to take a physical examination.
11. Decide whether the applicant should be hired on a trial basis.
12. Conduct an orientation program for the new employee.
13. Decide whether the employee should be retained after a pre-arranged probationary period.

Figure 18–2 shows this suggested selection procedure in graphic form.

Application Blank

Application blanks are used at the time a candidate applies for employment, and may be submitted in person or by mail. The candidate lists employers for whom he has worked, titles of jobs he has held, and the length of employment with each company. He describes his background, education, marital status, military status, and other useful data. The blank should be carefully designed to provide information that you need about the candidates, but it should not be a "hodge-podge" of irrelevant data developed from the application blanks of other firms. The completion of the blank by the applicant will provide you a sample of his neatness, thoroughness, and ability to answer questions. Since many states have restrictions concerning the kinds of questions that

---

[2] A word of caution is in order at this point. The Equal Pay Act of 1964, the Civil Rights Act of 1964, the Age Discrimination Act of 1967, and other acts; and Executive Orders 10925, 11246, 11375, 11491, 11616, and others prevent discrimination against prospective employees on grounds of race, creed, color, sex, nation of origin, or age. You should be certain that your selection procedure conforms to national and local laws and customs.

FIGURE 18–2
Flow Chart of Selection Procedure

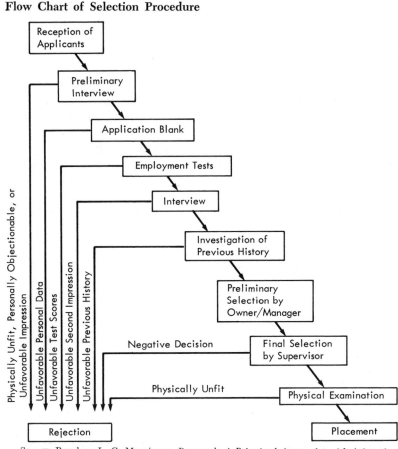

Source: Based on L. C. Megginson, *Personnel: A Behavioral Approach to Administration* rev. ed. (Homewood, Ill.: Richard D. Irwin, Inc., 1972), pp. 267 and 274.

may be included on an application blank, you should check any laws which your state may have governing such practices.[3]

Interviewing

In preparing for the interview, you should use the information in the application blank to learn about the applicant in greater detail. You should know beforehand the questions you need to ask to get the other information you need. Your personal experience with the job may provide some questions. In order not to overlook anything significant

---

[3] W. F. Robe, *Matching the Applicant to the Job* (Washington, D.C.: Small Business Administration, 1972), Management Aids for Small Manufacturers, No. 185.

during the interview, you should list the points that should be covered. You should ask the applicant specific questions, such as:

1. What did you do on your last job?
2. How did you do it?
3. Why did you do it?
4. What job did you like best? Least?

Compare your list of questions with the job specification to see that you are matching the individual's personal qualifications with the job requirements.

If you are observant and perceptive during the interview, you can obtain some impressions about the candidate's abilities, personality, and attitudes toward work, as well as evaluate appearance and speech. You can also provide information about your company and the job. Remember, the applicant needs facts to decide whether to accept or reject the job, just as you need information to decide whether or not to offer it. The interview may be individual or group, and may be structured or nondirective in nature.

The supervisor of the prospective employee should have an important role in this procedure. In fact, you may want the supervisor to conduct the interview as well as evaluate the application blank. If you are the interviewer, however, you should at least have the supervisor meet the applicant and show him the job and the work area. Failure to let the supervisor participate can lead to unfavorable attitudes later.

The interviewing may occur in one or two stages. Some firms have a *preliminary interview* during which the application is completed and general observations of the applicant are made. A later, *more penetrating interview* may then be held to probe his attitudes, belief system, and willingness and desire to work. The method you choose will depend upon the time available and the importance of the position to be filled.

Employment Tests

Through using employment tests, you can determine the candidate's intelligence quotient (I.Q.), skill, aptitude, vocational interest, and personality. *I.Q. tests* are designed to measure one's capacity to learn and solve problems and to comprehend complex relationships, and are particularly useful in selecting employees for managerial positions. *Proficiency and skill tests* are tests of ability to perform a particular trade, craft, or skill, and are useful in selecting operative employees. *Aptitude tests* are used to predict how a person might perform on a given job, and are most applicable to operative jobs.

Vocational interest tests are designed to determine the areas of major interests of the applicant, as far as work is concerned. Interest does not guarantee competence, but it can result in the employee working and trying harder. A limitation of the test is that it can be "faked."

Personality tests are designed to measure whether the applicant is an "introvert" or an "extrovert," the total personality structure, and emotional adjustment and attitudes. These tests, along with inventories of emotional maturity, are often used to evaluate interpersonal relationships and see how the person might fit into your organization. "Faked" answers can also arise in using these tests. In addition to their use in selection, these tests are valuable in evaluating present employees for promotion and as a basis for consulting with employees.

Aptitude tests are, by far, the most reliable indicators of an applicant's skill level. On the other hand, intelligence and personality tests should be interpreted by professionals. You may be able to obtain some testing assistance from your state employment service offices.

If tests are used as a basis for making any personnel decision, they must be valid; that is, there must be a high degree of correlation between the test scores and objective measures of performance on the job.

Checking References

The small business manager is often victimized by employees whose credentials are not checked thoroughly. The importance of your checking applicants' references carefully cannot be overemphasized.

Reference checks provide answers to questions concerning the candidate's performance on previous jobs. They are helpful in verifying information on the application blank and statements made during interviews. They are also useful in checking on possible omissions of information and clarifying specific points. Three sources of reference are:

1. Academic.
2. Personal.
3. Previous employers.

Checks made by telephone or in person with business references are preferred to written responses. The writer of a letter of reference may have little or no idea of your job requirements. Also, past employers are sometimes reluctant to write poor letters of reference. Be sure to ask specific questions about the candidate's performance, as well as determining whether former employers would consider rehiring the person.

Physical Examination

The applicant's health and physical condition should be matched to the physical requirements of the job. You should require that each applicant be examined by a physician before hiring. The examination could reveal physical limitations which would limit job performance. Also, it will help you comply with your state's workmen's compensation laws by providing a record of the employee's health at the time of hiring. Compensation claims for an injury which occurred prior to his employment with you could be prevented. This step is usually last, as it is ordinarily the most expensive one.

Decision to Hire

After completion of the selection procedure, you are in a position to decide whether the applicant should be hired on a trial basis or rejected. The final decision whether the employee matches the job requirements should be made only at the end of a probationary period. Furthermore, by that time, the employee should know your company sufficiently well to decide whether to stay. Probationary periods should be set for the various jobs in your company, with length depending upon the type of work. Some jobs may require six weeks, and others six months—depending on how long it takes to learn to perform the job acceptably.

HOW TO INTRODUCE NEW PEOPLE TO THEIR JOBS

Frequent discussions should be held with a new employee during the orientation program. Several should be held during the first day and during the first week. The purpose of these talks is to determine that the new employee has the necessary facts about you and your firm and about your objectives, policies, and rules. You should also inform the employee of your ideas of what performance is expected.

A formal interview with the employee may be appropriate at some point during the first month. Its purpose would be to correct any mistaken ideas that the employee may still have about the job, and to determine whether the employee feels that you and your people are fulfilling your commitments to him.

During the orientation and follow-up period, you should evaluate the new employee's performance compared to your expectations. You can also start to point out any shortcomings, as well as strong points. Another formal meeting should also be held at the end of the probationary period. You will then state whether you are going to keep the employee or not.

During the probationary period, you can depend upon personal observations of the new employee. You can also check with the supervisor concerning progress and receive volunteer comments from co-workers.

When you make the final decision concerning retention or dismissal, again refer to the job specification. Review it item by item. The new employee's supervisor should do the same. The two evaluations should be compared. If your decision is to keep the new employee, discuss both strong points and weak ones. Encourage the employee to keep trying to improve. State when to expect a merit increase in pay. If you decide the employee is to be rejected, the parting should be as graceful as possible.

SUMMARY

Some ideas on selecting people to help you operate your business are offered in this chapter. It should be strongly emphasized that we know you may not be able to use all these ideas in your firm, especially when it is new and small. And yet, you may be able to use some of the thoughts in an informal way, even if you don't have formal programs.

This chapter has covered (1) manpower planning, (2) source of new employees, (3) recruiting new people, (4) selecting people for given jobs, and (5) introducing new people to the job.

In doing *manpower planning*, you should (1) develop job specifications, (2) forecast the total number of people needed in each category, (3) develop manpower plans, (4) inventory the skills of all your present personnel, (5) compare your plans with your inventory so you can identify shortages, and (6) determine the sources of supply from which you can recruit the extra people needed.

Some specific sources from which you might be able to recruit new personnel were given.

In *recruiting* people, you can use (1) school and college scouting, (2) advertising, (3) private and public employee agencies, and (4) employee referrals.

In *selecting* people, you need to (1) review the job specifications for the position, (2) consider your present employees, (3) recruit applicants from outside the company if none of your employees can fill the job, (4) use an application blank in gathering informaton from applicants, (5) prepare for interviews with applicants by listing the points that you need to cover, (6) conduct the interviews, (7) bring the supervisor of the prospective employee into the act, (8) use psychological tests, (9) check on qualified applicants with their previous employers, (10) arrange for a physical examination, (11) decide whether the applicant should be hired on a trial basis, (12) conduct an orientation program for the new employee, and (13) decide whether the employee should be retained after a definite probationary period.

After the person is hired, it is important that you *introduce him to the job* properly, for this is where most labor turnover begins.

QUESTIONS FOR FURTHER DISCUSSION

1. According to Lawrence Appley, what is the primary duty of every manager?

2. What does manpower planning entail in the small company?

3. Explain the significance of this statement: Job specifications provide the foundation for performing the personnel function effectively.

4. What specific sources for finding new employees are usually used in small businesses?

5. Give some of the advantages and disadvantages of using the internal source of labor supply.

6. What methods can be used by small business managers in recruiting new people?

7. What is needed for you to have a successful selection procedure?

8. How would you prepare for, and conduct, an effective interview with an applicant?

9. What are some sources of reference that the small business manager may use in investigating applicants?

10. Why should a physical examination be required of an applicant?

11. Why is a probationary period needed for new employees?

12. How should new people be introduced to their jobs?

19

Developing and Maintaining Your People

In the last chapter, you learned about planning your manpower requirements, selecting the sources from which you would recruit your employees, determining how to recruit them, and doing the actual selection of people. Now that you have selected and placed your people, you need to be concerned with:

1. Training and developing them into productive workers.
2. Setting their wages and salaries.
3. Evaluating their performance.

This chapter covers these topics in depth.

TRAINING AND DEVELOPING YOUR PEOPLE

The ultimate efficiency of your business will be determined by the interaction of two related factors:

1. The caliber of the people you hire, including their inherent abilities, and their development through training, education, experience, and motivation.
2. The effectiveness of their personal development by you after they are hired.

This is called *personnel development,* and may be defined as an attempt to increase the employee's productive capacity up to the highest level of the job to be performed.

Need for Training

Not only must your new employees be trained, but also the present ones must be retrained and upgraded in order to adjust to rapidly changing job requirements. Some of the more general reasons for you to emphasize growth and development are:

1. Readily available and adequate replacements for present personnel who may leave or move up.
2. Freedom to use advancements in technology because of a more highly trained staff.
3. A more efficient, effective, and highly motivated work team, which increases the company's competitive position.
4. Adequate manpower resources for expansion programs.

More specific results which you will probably receive from training and developing your workers include:

1. Increased productivity.
2. Reduced turnover.
3. Increased financial rewards.
4. Decreased costs of materials and equipment.
5. Less supervision required.
6. Higher morale.

Your employees also have a stake in development, for they acquire a greater sense of worth, dignity, and well-being as they become more valuable to society. They will receive a greater share of the material gains that result from their increased productivity. These two factors will give them a sense of satisfaction in the achievement of personal and company goals.

Methods of Training

You, as the small business manager, will have available various methods of training nonmanagerial employees. These methods include:

1. On-the-job training (OJT).
2. Apprenticeship.
3. Internship.
4. Outside training.

On-the-job training consists of the employees receiving training while they perform their regular jobs. Thus, they are both producers and learners. An effective program consists of these steps:

1. Planning what is to be taught the employee.
2. Establishing a time schedule for the employee to follow.
3. Providing feedback to the trainee concerning his progress.

The purpose of *apprenticeship training* is to develop well-rounded individuals who are capable of performing a variety of jobs. It usually involves learning a group of skills which, when combined, gives one a trade. The program is usually a long-term process, covering from two to seven years, and a union is often involved in administering it.

Internship training is a combination of school and on-the-job training. It is usually used with employees who are prospects for marketing or clerical positions, or who are being prepared for management positions.

Outside training consists of the employees being trained at schools outside the company. Usually, the company reimburses the employees for all or part of their tuition expenses.

Other forms of development which you probably can use on a limited basis are *Programmed instruction* (sometimes called "learning machines"), *educational television, extension courses,* and *correspondence courses.*

Outside Assistance You Can Use in Training

There are many outside programs available to help you train employees. You can probably use some of the following.

All states have *vocational-technical education* programs whereby vocational-technical schools assist firms by conducting regular or special classes where potential employees can become qualified for skilled jobs, such as machinist, lathe operator, power-machine operator, and so forth.

Another training activity for new employees is the *vocational rehabilitation* programs sponsored by the U.S. Department of Health, Education, and Welfare in cooperation with state governments. These programs provide counseling, medical care, and vocational training for physically and mentally handicapped individuals.

The *Manpower Development and Training Act of 1962,* as amended, provides a program of federal assistance in training unemployed and underemployed workers. You would hire these individuals and pay their wages. The government reimburses you for part of those wages, instructor fees, and materials and supplies used and provides advice and consultation on training problems and in developing training programs. You do the actual training yourself.

Title V of the Economic Opportunity (Antipoverty) Act of 1964 authorizes state welfare departments to provide training programs for welfare recipients or members of their families. The individual is hired by you and you do the training, with the government paying the cost of training.

The *Defense Department* has invited many companies to train servicemen who are about to be released from service. This cooperative effort, called "Project Transition," has been fairly successful in bridging the difficult period of transition from military to civilian life.

The *JOBS (Job Opportunities in the Business Sector) Program,* which was launched several years ago by NAB (the National Alliance of Businessmen), encourages you—the employer—to submit proposals for contracts to provide on-the-job training for the disadvantaged, hard-core unemployed. You are paid for any additional costs incurred because of limited qualifications of those hired and trained. The state *public employment offices* are used for recruiting, selecting, and counseling the trainees.

The *National Apprenticeship Act of 1937,* which is administered by the Bureau of Apprenticeship and Training in the Labor Department, sets policy for apprenticeship programs. Write to this Bureau for help in conducting such a program.

Some Guidelines for Developing People

Some specific basic guidelines which can be of great help to you in developing and conducting your training and development programs are:

1. The objectives of the development activities should be established.
2. Trainees should be carefully selected.
3. Qualified instructors and proper instructional techniques should be used. Be aware that good managers are not necessarily effective trainers.
4. Some method of evaluating the results of the training program should be established.
5. Trainees should not be brought along faster than they can absorb the training and demonstrate the skills. On the other hand, they should not be permitted to stagnate in the program.
6. Feedback on performance should flow from both trainers and trainees. The former should periodically report results to trainees and to you, and the latter should also submit written reports periodically to you on their progress.
7. Learning is stimulated by motivation. When trainees finish the program, they should have new and challenging assignments with appropriate compensation or position increases.

Developing employees for your competitors should be avoided! Yet, your firm will probably experience some degree of personnel turnover. People die, become disabled, retire, or quit. Voluntary separations, or quitting, is a key indicator. If these separations occur often, you should determine the reason. Among the reasons may be poor supervision, dead-end jobs, or poorly trained or motivated employees.

SETTING WAGES AND SALARIES

Another important duty you have is setting wages and salaries for your people. Their earnings must be high enough to motivate them to be good producers, yet low enough for you to maintain a satisfactory earnings level.

Rewarding Nonmanagerial Employees

There are two aspects of wage and salary administration which are particularly relevant to small business. People work for monetary and nonmonetary rewards. *Nonmonetary* rewards are a form of psychic income. They often motivate us even when monetary income fails to do so. (See Chapter 10.)

As for monetary rewards, you should understand that both the *absolute* and *relative* amounts of income received are important to employees. They are concerned with their *absolute* level of pay so far as it is adequate to meet their needs. However, they are also concerned about their *relative* level of income when compared with what their fellow workers are making. In fact, an employee could be quite satisfied with the amount of absolute pay, but highly disgruntled because an associate at an equal or lower status is receiving higher pay.

Setting Rates of Pay. Some important factors to consider when setting rates of pay are:

1. Effort: Employees like to believe they are paid in proportion to their physical and mental expenditures.
2. Time: The time spent performing a job should be directly related to the amount of pay.
3. Your ability to pay.
4. The standard and cost of living, including changes in the cost of living in the area.
5. Legislation, including laws establishing minimum wages and hours for which overtime is paid.
6. Unions, including wage patterns established through collective bargaining—whether or not your firm is unionized.
7. Supply and demand for workers, which are reflected in the wages received by employees with similar skills in the area.

One way you can provide more equitable wages and salaries is to use either formal or informal *job evaluation,* whereby the relative worth of each job to your firm is determined. The job evaluation process can be done in a number of ways, but the *ranking system* and the *point system* are the two most commonly used. The small business manager who performs his own job evaluation generally ranks jobs in some ascending or descending order, depending upon their relative values to the company. Professional consultants performing job evaluation programs for small businesses generally use the point system.

In the *ranking system,* you compare the worth of each job as a whole with every other job, and assign a monetary figure to it. The system is simple, relatively inexpensive, and requires little paper work. Its disadvantages are the lack of definite standards on which to determine the ranking and the difficulty in finding raters with sufficient knowledge of the jobs.

In actual practice, prevailing rates and classifications are used extensively by small business managers. In other words, managers pay greater attention to the so-called "going rates" in the community for similar jobs in establishing their companies' wage and salary structure.

Other Aspects of the Wage and Salary Administration Program. Some other aspects you should consider in compensating your employees are:

1. The manner in which the employees will be paid: by wage or by salary.
2. What is the wage and salary structure in your firm.
3. Whether to adopt a wage incentive system.
4. The extent of employee benefits—such as life insurance; hospitalization, sickness, and accident insurance; and pension plans—you will provide your workers.

A *wage incentive system* may be an effective motivational tool, particularly in a small manufacturing plant. Purposes of the plan can include increased production, reduced waste, and better use of machinery. Employees' productivity, skill, effort, and attitudes can then be rewarded on a more equitable basis. The oldest and most frequently used plan is a straight piece-rate system, whereby a given rate is paid for each unit produced.

Another plan is a *cash bonus based on profit.* Often, young employees prefer "cash-in-hand" because of their need for cash and the effects of inflation.

A company reviewing its employee benefit program was considering a pension program. A detailed analysis proved that the existing plan of a monthly cash bonus based on company profits and a year-end cash bonus based on 11 months profits provided the best incentive.

But whatever the plan, it should be simple and easy to administer. Also, it should be clearly understood and accepted by the employees.

Other motivational possibilities are:

1. Using bonuses as morale boosters, particularly during seasonal slacks or other "slow" periods.
2. Controlling absenteeism through incentive compensation.
3. Using profit-sharing plans to stimulate productivity.

You could also consider using one or more of the following employee benefit programs: money-purchase pension plan, pension plan, and bonus awards. Most small businesses can afford these deferred-compensation programs whose purpose is to help attract and hold quality employees. The Internal Revenue Service has approved model plans which contain all the forms and agreements needed to establish a comprehensive, simple, and flexible program. You can choose from a wide variety of plans—from mutual funds, banks, insurance companies, and others—in tailoring a program to your company's needs.

If you desire to give your employees a retirement income based on a fixed dollar contribution by the company, the *money-purchase pension plan* is appropriate. Deposits for all employees in the plan must be the same percentage of pay. You should consider this plan only if your company has relatively stable earnings.

Under a *pension plan,* you can provide your employees with retirement benefits that can be computed at any time. The plan is dependent neither on profits nor on pension-fund investments. It will necessitate an actuarial study.

Requirements for a successful employee benefit plan are:[1]

1. Your company's plan should be the right type for your purpose.
2. Generally, your company's contribution should be at least eight percent of the employee's salary or wages.
3. Your company needs an average annual return of at least six to eight percent from investment of the plan's funds in order to underwrite the benefits.
4. You should remind and inform your employees about the benefits and value of their plan at least annually.
5. Your plan should be reviewed periodically and kept up to date in its benefits.

You may want to consider using the "cafeteria" or "smorgasbord" approach when determining what employee benefits to provide. Under this system, all employees receive a statement of the amount (in dollars)

---

[1] Harold A. Hobson, Jr., *Selecting Employee Benefit Plans* (Washington, D.C.: Small Business Administration, 1972), Management Aids for Small Manufacturers, No. 213.

they are entitled to receive for such benefits. Each person then tells you how to allocate the money between a variety of programs available. Advantages of this system are increased employee awareness of the value of the fringe benefits, freedom of choice, and personalized approach.

You may also want to consider *bonus awards* for outstanding performance. A certain sum of money or gifts are given to outstanding employees.

> The owner-manager of a small company decided to eliminate paid vacations and sick leave. Instead, all employees were given 30 days annual leave to use as they saw fit. At the end of the year, they were paid at regular rates for the leave not used. Employees had previously had to prove they were actually ill when sick leave was taken, and they had to apply for personal leave in advance. The results attained from the new program were reduced unscheduled absences and overtime pay, and happier, more productive employees.[2]

Don't be misled into believing that employee benefits are not expensive. As desirable and necessary as they are in attracting and holding employees, they constitute one of your major costs of production. According to the U.S. Chamber of Commerce, the amount of these benefits paid by the average firm (large, medium, *and* small) in 1969 was 30.8 percent of payroll.[3]

Other Financial Benefits. There are two other financial programs which you should know about. If you use them, by all means call in experts to aid you!

The *Keogh Plan* (HR 10) permits you as a self-employed person or a partner in a partnership to have a tax-deferred retirement program. Up to $7,500, or 10 percent of earned income, whichever is lower, may be withheld from your current income and invested.

Under the *keyman deferred compensation plan,* a contract is drawn between you and your key employee. Your firm agrees to invest annually a specified dollar amount or percent of wages. Your firm holds title to these assets until the retirement, disability, or death of the employee, when the benefit becomes payable to him or his beneficiary.

Rewarding Management Personnel

A well-conceived and effectively-operated management compensation plan can help you motivate your top assistants. It can also help you know your employment costs for these assistants.

---

[2] Jack H. Feller, Jr., *Keep Pointed toward Profit* (Washington, D.C.: Small Business Administration, 1972), Management Aids for Small Manufacturers, No. 206.

[3] *Employee Benefits, 1971* (Washington, D.C.: Economic Analysis and Study Group, Chamber of Commerce of the United States, 1972), p. 6.

Determining Level and Form of Reward. The level of pay for these managers depends on many factors. Some of the more important of these variables are:

1. The kind of industry you are in.
2. The size of your firm.
3. The company's geographic location.
4. The responsibilities of each position.
5. The pay method used (bonus or nonbonus).
6. Growth (rapid or steady) of your company.

You should establish a salary range, adjust present salaries to that range, and periodically review your compensation plan. The salary range for each position should have a minimum for beginners, intermediate figures for advancement, and a maximum. Responsibility should be the determining factor for the required spread in a range. For example, at the vice presidential level, a 60 percent spread may be needed, while for lower management positions, a 40 percent spread might be sufficient. In establishing a salary range, you could establish the competitive salary as the midpoint. Examples of percentage spread are shown below:

	Range of Salaries		
Percentage Spread	*Minimum*	*Midpoint*	*Maximum*
40	$10,000	$12,000	$14,000
50	$15,000	$18,750	$22,500
60	$20,000	$26,000	$32,000

After you have established salary ranges, you should compare the salaries you are currently paying your managers with the ranges. Provided that your assistants' performances merit adjustment, and if your company has the ability to pay, you should adjust current salaries to the appropriate place in the ranges.

A vital question is: What should you do when a substantial difference exists between the manager's current salary and what his salary should be? You should consider these guidelines:

1. Do not take any hasty action, but consider carefully possible effects of your actions.
2. If the current salary is greater than what it should be, try to upgrade the manager's performance. A promotion may be a possible solution. However, a promotion should not be created in order to justify an excessive salary.
3. If the current salary is less than what it should be, determine the

cost of bringing the salary into line and develop a plan for raising it to the desired level.

Since pay levels and practices are constantly changing, you should compare your compensation plan with competitive practices at least annually. Information on competitive salaries may be obtained from local surveys, including those done by chambers of commerce, informal contacts at service clubs or industry conventions, and national surveys conducted by trade associations.

Using Financial Rewards to Motivate. If your business is growing rapidly, your compensation program normally should be designed for the type of manager who is willing to take risks. Even if the salary is less than he could receive elsewhere, if a substantial bonus is paid for results and if good opportunities for promotion exist, he will be motivated to produce for you. On the other hand, if your firm's sales and profits are growing slowly, your compensation plan probably should emphasize salary and perhaps an attractive retirement plan.

One effective bonus plan is to use *profit sharing*. Such plans usually have four features:

1. The bonus payments are directly related to company profits, and a predetermined formula is used to determine the amount of profits that will be provided for bonuses.
2. Participation in the plan is reserved for managers whose performance significantly affects profits.
3. Payments are based on each manager's performance.
4. Bonuses are paid promptly.

The bonus formula usually consists of a percentage of the company's profits before taxes, but after providing a normal return to the owner(s). For top assistants, bonuses for superior performance are commonly 50 to 60 percent of their salaries.

APPRAISING YOUR EMPLOYEES' PERFORMANCE

Your firm should have an effective personnel appraisal or employee evaluation system to enable you to answer the question: How well are my people performing? Under such a system, each employee's performance and progress are evaluated and rewards are given for above-average performance. Often, this method is used in determining merit salary increases.

If a Management by Objectives program (See Chapter 10) or its equivalent is not being used, *merit rating* is based upon the following commonly used factors:

1. Quantity and quality of work performed.
2. Cooperativeness.
3. Initiative.
4. Dependability.
5. Attendance.
6. Job knowledge.
7. Ability to work with others.
8. Safety.
9. Personal habits.

Each of these factors can be evaluated, for example, as *superior, above-average, average, below-average,* or *poor.* The person's wage or salary is then determined from this evaluation.

Relationships should exist also between merit rating and promotions. The appraisal system can also help you identify marginal employees, as well as point up areas of improvement and possible training and development needs for all your people. The system can also be a valuable ingredient in the Management by Objectives program in determining the degree of success with which objectives are achieved. Under such a plan, each individual manager should be held responsible for establishing written performance criteria used by him for promotion.

SUMMARY

In this chapter, we have discussed (1) training and developing your people, (2) setting wages and salaries for them, and (3) appraising their performance.

The need for developing employees, methods of training, sources of outside assistance, and some guidelines to follow in developing people were also discussed.

The most frequently used *training methods* are on-the-job training, apprenticeship, and internship.

Less frequently used methods of training include programmed instruction, educational television, extension courses, and correspondence courses.

Some basic *guidelines* to follow in developing people are:

1. Have clearly defined objectives.
2. Select trainees carefully.
3. Use only qualified instructors and materials.
4. Evaluate results of development activities.
5. Don't rush the trainees too fast.
6. Provide trainees—and trainers—feedback on their progress.
7. Provide motivation for growth, such as wage or salary increase or promotion.

In setting wages and salaries for nonmanagerial personnel, you should consider such factors as effort, the time spent, your ability to pay, the standard and cost of living, legislation, the role of unions, and the supply of—and demand for—workers in your area.

Two other important considerations in the compensation picture are (1) whether to use a wage incentive system, profit-sharing plan, or bonus system to motivate employees; and (2) the type and extent of employee benefits.

In compensating your managerial personnel, you should establish salary scales, decide where a given manager fits on the scale, and use bonuses or profit sharing to motivate them.

An important part of developing and maintaining your work force is appraising your employees' performance. This involves evaluating their performance relative to some standard, telling them how they are doing, and explaining how they can improve their performance.

APPENDIX: GUIDELINES FOR EFFECTIVE EMPLOYEE TRAINING

Goal of Training	*Yes*	*No*
1. Do you want to improve your employees' performance?	——	——
2. Should employees be prepared for newly developed or modified jobs?	——	——
3. Should employees be prepared for promotion through training?	——	——
4. Should accidents be reduced and safety practices improved?	——	——
5. Should employee attitudes about waste and spoilage be improved?	——	——
6. Should materials-handling be improved in order to eliminate production bottlenecks?	——	——
7. Should employees be trained in order that they can teach new workers in an expansion program?	——	——

Subject Matter of Training		
8. Should standards of quality be taught to the trainees?	——	——

	Yes	No

9. Should trainees learn certain skills and techniques? ___ ___

10. Should trainees learn how to operate equipment more effectively? ___ ___

11. Should product information be taught to the employees? ___ ___

Type of Training
12. Should on-the-job training be conducted? ___ ___

13. Should a combination of on-the-job training and classroom instruction be used? ___ ___

Method of Instruction
14. Should a lecture or series of lectures be used? ___ ___

15. Should demonstrations be used? ___ ___

16. Should operating problems be simulated? ___ ___

Use of Audio-Visual Aids
17. Should outside textbooks and other printed materials be used? ___ ___

18. Should motion pictures, filmstrips, or slides be used? ___ ___

19. Should models of machinery and equipment be used? ___ ___

Use of Physical Facilities
20. Should training be conducted in a conference room? ___ ___

21. Should training be conducted off-premises in a school, hotel, or motel? ___ ___

Timing of Program
22. Should training be scheduled during working hours? ___ ___

23. Should instruction cover a predetermined period of time (e.g., 4 weeks)? ___ ___

Selection of Instructors
24. Should you be an instructor? ___ ___

25. Should supervisors or department heads be instructors? ___ ___

	Yes	No

Selection of Trainees

26. Should employees in lower-rated jobs but who have the aptitude to learn be trainees?   ____ ____

27. Should employees be permitted to volunteer for training?   ____ ____

Cost of Program

28. Should the training program be charged for the space, machines, and materials used?   ____ ____

29. Should trainees' wages be included?   ____ ____

30. Should an employee instructor's pay be included?   ____ ____

Use of Controls

31. Should you check the results of the training against the goals of the program?   ____ ____

32. Should trainee performance data be developed before, during, and after training?   ____ ____

33. Should trainees be followed up periodically by supervisors or department heads to determine the long-range effects of the training?   ____ ____

Publicizing of Program

(Publicizing the training program in the community helps attract qualified job applicants. Publicizing inside the company boosts employees' motivation to improve themselves.)   ____ ____

34. Should pictures be taken at the training sessions and used on bulletin boards and in local newspapers?   ____ ____

35. Should certificates be awarded to employees who complete the program?   ____ ____

QUESTIONS FOR FURTHER DISCUSSION

1. Why should personnel development be emphasized in a small business?
2. Discuss briefly some specific results that are usually received from training and developing employees.
3. Describe briefly the methods of training nonmanagerial employees.
4. Give some guidelines that may be used in developing and conducting training and development programs.
5. Explain some of the factors that should be considered in setting rates of pay.

6. What is job evaluation?
7. Briefly describe the ranking system of job evaluation.
8. What are the purposes of a wage-incentive system?
9. Describe three employee benefit programs.
10. Describe the "cafeteria" or "smorgasbord" approach in determining what employee benefits to provide.
11. What is an effective personnel appraisal (or employee evaluation) system? In the absence of MBO, list five factors that are evaluated.

20

Your Relationships with Your Employees

In the last two chapters, you have read considerably about how to handle your manning problems. Suggestions were made for planning your manpower requirements, recruiting applicants, selecting the most capable people from those available, evaluating your selection procedure, training and developing your employees, compensating them appropriately, and evaluating their performance. But you should also be familiar with other important phases of the personnel function, including:

1. Handling employees' grievances.
2. Understanding legislation that affects your business.
3. Dealing with labor unions.

This chapter covers these topics.

HANDLING YOUR EMPLOYEES' GRIEVANCES

Complaints and grievances will inevitably occur. You should encourage your employees to inform you when they think something is wrong and needs correcting. Also, you should instruct your supervisors how to handle the complaints and grievances. An effective grievance procedure should have these characteristics:

1. Assurance to employees that expressing their complaints will not prejudice their relationships with their immediate supervisors.
2. A clear method from the employees' viewpoint of presenting their

grievances, and a description of how those complaints will be processed.
3. A minimum of red tape and time in processing their complaints and determining a solution.
4. An effective method for employees who cannot express themselves well to present grievances.

Unresolved grievances can lead to strikes. You should listen patiently and deal with a grievance promptly even though you believe an employee's grievance is without foundation. You should thank the employee for bringing the grievance to your attention. Before you render judgment on the grievance, you should think about it carefully and gather pertinent facts. You should inform the employee of your decision on the grievance and follow up later to determine whether the cause of the grievance has been corrected.

You should maintain written records of all grievances (and disciplinary actions) in employees' files. These records are beneficial in your defense against any charges of unfair labor practices which may be brought against you.

UNDERSTANDING LEGISLATION THAT AFFECTS YOUR BUSINESS

The whole area of personnel relations in your business is affected by labor legislation. Some of these laws and their effects on you are now explained.

Unions and Collective Bargaining

You are required by the *National Labor Relations Act of 1935,* as amended by the *Labor Management Relations Act of 1947,* to bargain collectively if a majority of your employees desire unionization. You are forbidden to discriminate in any way against your employees for union activity.

The purpose of the Act was to facilitate the process of collective bargaining, not necessarily to prevent or settle disputes. Under the Act, both you and the union are required to bargain in "good faith" in order that difficulties may be resolved and an agreement reached.

The National Labor Relations Board serves as a labor court and its general counsel investigates charges of unfair labor practices, issues complaints, and prosecutes cases. The Board can issue direct orders, but cannot levy fines or penalties. Only the courts can levy fines or penalties. You can appeal a ruling of the Board through a Circuit Court.

Under "right-to-work" laws in some states, the union shop is outlawed. A union shop clause provides that all employees must join the recognized union within 30 days after being hired.

Payroll Taxes

As a small business manager, you are both a taxpayer and a tax collector. To finance old age and survivor's insurance, you must pay a tax on each employee's earnings and deduct a comparable amount from the employee's salary. Since tax laws are subject to change, you should check the rate and base amount applicable. As the proportion of the aged in the total population rises, it may be anticipated that both taxes and benefits will increase. An unemployment insurance tax is also provided under the *Social Security Act of 1936*. The state government receives most of this tax. It may be as high as three percent on your payroll. If you stabilize employment in your firm, you can have lower rates under merit rating provisions. Maintaining the validity of your tax trust funds is important because of the legal liability associated with them.

Workmen's Compensation

Accidents and occupational diseases are covered under state workmen's compensation statutes. You are required to pay insurance premiums either to a state fund or to a private insurance carrier. Funds accumulated in this fashion are used to compensate victims of industrial accidents or occupational illness. Your premiums will be affected by hazards in your company and the effectiveness of your safety program.

Wages and Hours

Minimum wages and overtime compensation are prescribed by the *Fair Labor Standards Act of 1938*, as amended. The Act specifies a standard work week of 40 hours and overtime compensation at the rate of time-and-one-half for hours in excess of standard. Many states also have wage and hour statutes which specify maximum hours for women and children.

Laws Pertaining to Age

The Fair Labor Standards Act and many state statutes prescribe the minimum age for employees. Typically, these laws specify a minimum of 14 to 16 years with a higher minimum often set for hazardous occupations. On the other hand, the *Age Discrimination in Employment Act of 1967* says you cannot discriminate against potential employees aged 40–64.

Equal Employment Opportunities

In 1964, Congress passed the *Civil Rights Act. Title VII* of this Act, as amended by the *Equal Employment Opportunities Act of 1972*, prohibits discrimination because of race, color, religion, sex, or national origin in hiring, upgrading, and all other conditions of employment. It applies to employers of 15 or more persons.

The *Equal Employment Opportunity Commission* was established by Title VII, and it receives and investigates charges of employment discrimination. In order to stop violations, the Commission may take action itself or go to a U.S. District Court. The Commission promotes *affirmative action* programs to put the principle of equal employment opportunity into practice.

In recruiting applicants for employment, companies no longer may be allowed to rely completely on "walk-ins" or "word-of-mouth" advertising of job openings, especially if their own work force is predominantly of one race. Friends or relatives of present employees cannot be recruited if a company has a disproportionate amount of a certain class of employees. A company cannot set hiring standards with respect to test results, high school diplomas, height, arrest records, manner of speech, or appearance, which result in discrimination on the basis of race, color, sex, religion, or national origin.

Seniority systems should not result in "locking" minorities into unskilled and semi-skilled jobs without providing them lines of progression to better jobs. Equal employment opportunity in promotion decisions should be provided. Training and performance appraisals should be conducted on a nondiscriminatory basis. Discrimination should not exist relative to hourly rates and deferred wages including pensions or other deferred payments. Recreational activities—bowling teams, softball teams, Christmas parties, etc.—should be open to all employees on a nondiscriminatory basis. So far as facilities of a "personal nature" are concerned, an employer should make every "reasonable accommodation" for male and female employees.[1]

Sex Discrimination

Generally, all jobs must be open to both men and women unless the employer can prove that sex is a bona fide occupational qualification necessary to the normal operations of that particular business.

Advertisements cannot be run by a company for "male only" or

---

[1] William H. Holley, Jr. and William N. Ledbetter, "Personnel Practices Take on a New Demeanor," *AMS Report* (December 1973), pp. 79–80.

"female only" employees. This practice may be discriminatory unless sex can be shown as a bona fide occupational qualification. Disqualifying female employees from jobs requiring heavy lifting, night shifts, and dirty work is often illegal unless justification exists for these restrictions. Automatic discharge of pregnant women and refusal to reinstate them after childbirth constitute discrimination.

All employees are entitled to equality in all conditions of employment, including:

1. Hiring.
2. Layoff.
3. Recall.
4. Discharge.
5. Recruitment.
6. Compensation.
7. Overtime.
8. Promotional opportunities.
9. Paid sick leave time.
10. Paid vacation time.
11. Insurance coverage.
12. Training and development activities.
13. Retirement privileges and pension benefits.
14. Rest periods, lunch periods, etc.

According to the *Equal Pay Act of 1963*, an amendment to the *Fair Labor Standards Act of 1938*, you must also pay males and females the same rate of pay for performing the same general type of work.

Environmental Protection

In 1970, the Environmental Protection Agency was created under an Act of the same title to help protect and improve the quality of the nation's environment. Areas covered are:

1. Solid waste disposal.
2. Clean air.
3. Water resources.
4. Noise.
5. Pesticides.
6. Atomic radiation.

Industrial pollution can be prevented or controlled either through waste treatment or process changes or both. Much oil pollution is also preventable. Builders, developers, and contractors—many of them small businesses—can help prevent and control water pollution. Soil erosion, wastes from feedlots, improper or excessive use of pesticides and fertilizers, and careless discarding of trash and junk are among the causes of water pollution.

Due to the actions of the Agency in requiring pollution-control equipment to be installed in "marginal" plants, many of these plants are closing and employees are losing their jobs. If you face this situation as a small business manager you should assist your employees as much as possible in obtaining other jobs. You should work together with community agencies—such as chambers of commerce and industrial development corporations—in trying to attract other businesses and industries to absorb your former employees.

Occupational Safety and Health

The *Occupational Safety and Health Act* (OSHA) was passed in 1970. Its purpose is to assure so far as possible safe and healthful working conditions for every employee and to preserve our human resources. An employee—or his representative—has these five important rights:

1. If he believes that a violation of job safety or health standards exists which threatens physical harm, he may request an inspection by sending a signed, written notice to the U.S. Department of Labor. He may not be discharged or discriminated against for filing the complaint.
2. When the Department of Labor inspector arrives, usually unannounced, the employee's representative may accompany the inspector on the visit.
3. If the employer is cited under OSHA and protests either the fine or the abatement period, the employee can participate at the hearing and object to the length of the abatement period.
4. Concerning exposure to toxic materials or other physically harmful agents, the employee may observe the company's monitoring processes. If an OSHA standard covers the substance, the worker is entitled to information about his exposure record.
5. The employee's authorized representative may request that the Secretary of the Department of Health, Education, and Welfare (HEW) determine whether any substance found in the place of employment has potentially toxic effects. If HEW makes this finding, the Secretary of Labor may institute a procedure to set a safe exposure level for that substance.

Supporters of OSHA claim reductions in lost time and in Workmen's Compensation, decreases in lost wages, lowered medical costs, and higher productivity. Critics believe that the Act has been implemented too rapidly and restrictively, and that compliance costs are so high that a company's competitive position is threatened.

Even though many accidents are caused by the employees' own carelessness and lack of safety consciousness, they cannot receive citations. Instead, employers are responsible that their employees wear safety equipment. Furthermore, employers are subject to fines for unsafe practices irrespective of whether any accidents actually occur. You should provide safety training for your supervisors and employees and discipline employees for noncompliance with safety work rules. The Act has produced increased examination and questioning of management's manning decisions and equipment selection. To illustrate, a union could claim that a crew-size is unsafe or that a machine fails to provide a safe work place. The Act makes compulsory training in forklift truck driving and respirator-wearing.

Five industries in which small businesses predominate—roofing and sheet metal; meat and meat products; lumber and wood products; manufacturers of mobile homes, campers, and snowmobiles; and stevedoring—have relatively high injury and illness rates.

"Dry-run" inspections are not permitted by OSHA inspectors because if they do come to your premises, they are obligated by law to inspect fully, to cite, and to fine. You can request a free health hazard evaluation by the National Institute of Occupational Safety and Health in the HEW. Training may be obtained from OSHA and National Safety Council chapters. Your workmen's compensation insurance carrier may be helpful. However, its approval does not guarantee the same from OSHA. You may also obtain useful information from equipment manufacturers, other employers who have had an inspection, trade associations, and your local fire department. You should provide effective coordination among manufacturing, safety, medical, industrial relations, and so forth.

Occasionally, there is some frustration in attempting to comply with OSHA regulations and standards due to a lack of clarity. In addition, while an OSHA inspector may present you with a citation for noncompliance or may reject the procedure or protective measures being used, definitive corrective information may not be forthcoming. OSHA inspectors are not allowed to offer this type assistance. As this book goes to press, efforts are being made by Congress to satisfy various complaints registered against the OSHA program. You should recognize that the newness of the program and its very nature will keep it in a state of transition for some time. Therefore, you are advised to utilize the resources suggested above, as well as your local chamber of commerce, area planning and development commission, and the Office of the Small Business Administration serving your area. Small Business Administration loans could be available to help you meet safety and health standards.[2]

DEALING WITH LABOR UNIONS

Many small business managers have rather strong personal anti-union feelings because they believe: (1) they have "made it on their own," and employees want to take it away from them; and (2) an individual's

---

[2] Fred W. Foulkes, "Learning to Live with OSHA," *Harvard Business Review,* vol. 51, no. 6 (November–December 1973), pp. 57–67.

drive and initiative are more productive than group-set norms. You should recognize, however, that employees join unions because of their needs, as they perceive them, for a union.

If your company is unionized, you have more constraints on what you can and cannot do in your relations with your people. Your employees may view you more as an economic opponent than as a person with whom cooperation can be expected to obtain mutual benefits. Improving personnel performance is more difficult in a unionized company than in a nonunionized company.

If a union does try to organize your firm, there are certain things you can and cannot do. See the appendixes at the end of this chapter for the things you *can* and *cannot* do.

The purpose of labor unions is to bargain on behalf of their members as a counterbalance to the economic power of the employer. Your employees, through their elected representatives, negotiate with your company for wages, fringe benefits, working conditions, and so forth. The union's principal role is collective bargaining.

If your company is unionized, you should be prepared for the possibility that certain difficulties may occur. Many of your actions and statements may be reported to union officials. You may be harassed by the union's filing unfair labor practice notices with the National Labor Relations Board. Your best defense is to know your management rights under the Labor Management Relations Act.

Bargaining with a labor union involves preparation, negotiation, and agreement. The bargaining is then followed by another phase, living with the contract. *Preparation* may well be the most important step. You should have obtained facts about wages, hours, and working conditions when you sit down at the bargaining table. You should have information on other contracts in the industry and in the local area. Disciplinary actions, grievances, and other key matters that arose during the day-to-day administration of the current contract should have been noted. Current business literature concerning general business and the status of union-management relations in the nation and in your industry can be useful. A carefully researched proposal should be developed well in advance of negotiation of the contract.

Having done this, you should be in a much more favorable negotiating position than if you use a negative strategy of permitting the union to develop its own ideas for a new contract and then you attempt to offer defensive counter proposals. All too frequently, fear seems to pervade the owner's willingness to develop in advance a contract proposal with attractive features that will appeal to the rank-and-file employee. The "I don't want to give away any more than I have too" attitude generally fails to contribute to a viable union-management relationship.

You should recognize the *negotiation* step as being critical, particularly if it is not handled properly. You should not only consider the impact of wages on your company, but also the effects of seniority, discharge rules, and sick leave. You should understand that anything given up now probably can never be regained.

The *agreement* usually consists of these ten clauses:

1. Union recognition.
2. Wages.
3. Vacations and holidays.
4. Working conditions.
5. Layoffs and rehiring.
6. Management prerogatives.
7. Hours of work.
8. Seniority.
9. Arbitration.
10. Renewal clause.

Specifics are set forth in each of these areas, and rules are established which should be obeyed by you. The management prerogatives clause defines the areas in which you have the right to act, free from questioning or joint action by the union.

Once the agreement is signed, you should *live with the contract* until time to negotiate a new one. All of your management personnel should be thoroughly briefed on the contents. Meanings and interpretations of each clause should be reviewed, and the wording of the contract should be clear and unambiguous. Your supervisors' questions should be answered in order that they will be better prepared to deal with labor matters.

Your company's labor relations and personnel practices should be consistent, uniform in application and interpretation, and based on a sense of "fair play." We have observed numerous instances where owners have pursued policies that could be labeled as selfish and greedy; the end product has been unionization, bankruptcy, or both.

To enable you to do the proper thing in a specific labor relations situation, you can obtain advice and/or reliable information from numerous private groups and some government agencies. The *private sources* consist of employers' associations, trade associations, labor-relations attorneys, labor-relations consultants, leader companies, and professors. *Government sources* are federal and state mediators, wage-hour investigators, National Labor Relations Board regional offices, and state industrial relations departments. Leader companies set labor contract patterns in key bargaining sessions and small companies tend to follow their lead. Often, their labor relations staffs are willing to help you. The wage-hour investigator is not only a law enforcement officer, but also is interested *in helping an owner-manager* avoid violations.

SUMMARY

Many thoughts have been presented in this and the preceding two chapters for performing the personnel function. Your firm's personnel program might be considered progressive if (1) selection, testing, placement, and training of all personnel are conducted on an organized and efficient basis; (2) salary and wage rates are fair and equitable for each employee; (3) incentive plans exist for all levels of employees based on an effective set of standards and an active personnel appraisal system; (4) you, or another manager possessing adequate authority, formulate sound industrial relations policies and represent the company in labor negotiations and administer the contract impartially; (5) labor turnover is minimized and employee morale and efficiency improved; and (6) individual records for each employee are kept current for use in an inventory of qualifications.

In addition, you should review each position in your company periodically, perhaps quarterly. Does duplication of work exist? Is work structured so that employees are encouraged to become involved? Can tasks be given to another employee(s) and a position eliminated? Can a job be filled by a part-time person?

> A procedure observed in one firm which seemed to reduce activities and minimize the number of employees was asking each employee this question: "What do you do all day long and why?"

Imagine this hypothetical problem—you must terminate one employee. Who would it be? How would you restructure your jobs? A real solution to this imaginary problem may be to your advantage.

APPENDIX: TWENTY-SEVEN THINGS YOU *CAN DO* WHEN A UNION TRIES TO ORGANIZE YOUR COMPANY

1. Keep outside organizers off premises.
2. Inform employees from time to time on the benefits they presently enjoy. (Avoid veiled promises or threats.)
3. Inform employees that signing a union authorization card does not mean they must vote for the union if there is an election.
4. Inform employees of the disadvantages of belonging to the union, such as the possibility of strikes, serving in a picket line, dues, fines, assessments, and one-man or clique rule.
5. Inform employees that you prefer to deal with them rather than have the union or any other outsider settle grievances.
6. Tell employees what you think about unions and about union policies.

7. Inform employees about any prior experience you have had with unions and whatever you know about the union officials trying to organize them.

8. Inform employees that the law permits you to hire a new employee to replace any employee who goes on strike for economic reasons.

9. Inform employees that no union can obtain more than you as an employer are able to give.

10. Inform employees how their wages and benefits compare with unionized or nonunionized concerns, where wages are lower and benefits less desirable.

11. Inform employees that the local union probably will be dominated by the international union, and that they, the members, will have little to say in its operations.

12. Inform employees of any untrue or misleading statements made by the organizer. You may give employees the correct facts.

13. Inform employees of known racketeering, Communist, or other undesirable elements which may be active in the union.

14. Give opinions on unions and union leaders, even in derogatory terms.

15. Distribute information about unions such as disclosures of the McClellan Committee.

16. Reply to union attacks on company policies or practices.

17. Give legal position on labor-management matters.

18. Advise employees of their legal rights, provided you do not engage or finance an employee suit or proceeding.

19. Declare a fixed policy in opposition to compulsory union membership contracts.

20. Campaign against union seeking to represent the employees.

21. Tell employees you do not like to deal with unions.

22. Insist that any solicitation of membership or discussion of union affairs be conducted outside of working time.

23. Administer discipline, layoff, grievance, etc., without regard to union membership or nonmembership of the employees involved.

24. Treat both union and nonunion employees alike in making assignments of preferred work, desired overtime, etc.

25. Enforce plant rules impartially, regardless of the employee's membership activity in a union.

26. Tell employees, if they ask, that they are free to join or not to join any organization, so far as their status with the company is concerned.

27. Tell employees that their *personal* and *job* security will be determined by the economic prosperity of the company. Profits are an important essential in this picture.

APPENDIX: TWENTY-TWO THINGS YOU *CANNOT DO* WHEN THEY TRY TO ORGANIZE

1. Engage in surveillance of employees to determine who is or is not participating in the union program; attend union meetings or engage in any undercover activities for this purpose.
2. Threaten, intimidate or punish employees who engage in union activity.
3. Request information from employees about union matters, meetings, etc. Employees may, of their own volition give such information without prompting. You may listen, but not ask questions.
4. Prevent employee union representatives from soliciting memberships during nonworking time.
5. Grant wage increases, special concessions or promises of any kind to keep the union out.
6. Question a prospective employee about his affiliation with a labor organization.
7. Threaten to close up or move the plant, curtail operations, or reduce employee benefits.
8. Engage in any discriminatory practices, such as work assignments, overtime, lay-offs, promotions, wage increases, or any other practices which could be regarded as preferential treatment for certain employees.
9. Discriminate against union people when disciplining employees for a specific action and permit nonunion employees to go unpunished for the same action.
10. Transfer workers on the basis of teaming up nonunion employees to separate them from union employees.
11. Deviate in any way from known company policies for the primary purpose of eliminating a union employee.
12. Intimate, advise, or indicate, in any way, that unionization will force the company to layoff employees, take away company benefits or privileges enjoyed, or any other changes that could be regarded as a curtailment of privileges.
13. Make statements to the effect that you will not deal with a union.

14. Give any financial support or other assistance to employees who support or oppose the union.

15. Visit the homes of employees to urge them to oppose or reject the union in its campaign.

16. Be a party to petition or circular against the union or encouraging employees to circulate such a petition.

17. Make any promises of promotions, benefits, wage increases, or any other item that would induce employees to oppose the union.

18. Engage in discussions or arguments that may lead to physical encounters with employees over the union question.

19. Use a third party to threaten or coerce a union member, or attempt to influence their vote through this medium.

20. Question employees on whether or not they have or have not affiliated or signed with the union.

21. Use the word "never" in any predictions or attitudes about the union or its promises or demands.

22. Talk about tomorrow. You can talk about yesterday or today, when you give examples or reasons, instead of tomorrow, to avoid making a prediction or conviction which may be interpreted as a threat or promise by the union or the N.L.R.B.

QUESTIONS FOR FURTHER DISCUSSION

1. What are three characteristics of an effective grievance procedure?
2. How should a manager handle grievances effectively?
3. Describe briefly the Labor Management Relations Act and the Labor Relations Act.
4. Describe the preparation for bargaining with a labor union.
5. How is Old Age and Survivor's Insurance (OASI) financed?
6. What does the Fair Labor Standards Act prescribe?
7. What does the Equal Employment Opportunities Act provide?
8. What effects may the Environmental Protection Act have upon a small company?
9. What is the purpose of the Occupational Safety and Health Act (OSHA)?
10. Why are many small business managers "anti-union"?

WHERE TO LOOK FOR FURTHER INFORMATION

Feller, Jack H., Jr. *Keep Pointed toward Profit*. Washington, D.C.: Small Business Administration, 1972. (Management Aids for Small Manufacturers, No. 206.)

Hobson, Harold A., Jr.   *Selecting Employee Benefit Plans.* Washington, D.C.: Small Business Administration, 1972. (Management Aids for Small Manufacturers, No. 213.)

Murdick, Robert G. et al.   *Business Policy: A Framework for Analysis.* Columbus, Ohio: Grid, Inc., 1972. Credit is given to the authors of this text for many of their ideas which are included in this chapter.

Smith, Leonard J.   *Checklist for Developing a Training Program.* Washington, D.C.: Small Business Administration, 1967. (Management Aids for Small Manufacturers, No. 186.)

Summer, Howard E.   *How to Analyze Your Own Business.* Washington, D.C.: Small Business Administration, 1973. (Management Aids for Small Manufacturers, No. 46.)

Cases for Part VI

VI-1. Metal Fabricators (B)[1]

Metal Fabricators, Inc, is a small firm in Capital City in the southeastern part of the country. It was engaged in fabricating metal products. Practically all the firm's income came from small subcontracts from general contractors in the area. However, since its incorporation in early 1970, the two owner-managers had been attempting to develop and market a sandblasting machine with a new type of control mechanism, which they had developed. Only two of the sandblasting machines, or "pots" as they were called, had been sold, although most of the company's efforts had been directed at this part of the business.

The two owner-managers, Jerry Rogers and Joe Benson, had similar education and work experience. Each had completed about three years of college, including several engineering courses. They were both competent welders and both had served as construction superintendents on several medium-sized projects.

---

[1] Prepared by Arthur D. Sharplin, Louisiana State University. See "Metal Fabricators (A)" in Part III for further details.

Jerry's work experience had been much broader and more successful than Joe's and he was still much in demand as a construction superintendent. In fact, he had turned down several job offers during the last year. Jerry came from a low-income, small-town family and Joe from a relatively well-to-do family in Capital City.

Larry Ford, who owned 51 percent of the stock in the firm, was a local businessman who had devoted little of his time to Metal Fabricators.

As a matter of fact, though, it was at Larry Ford's initiative that Metal Fabricators came into existence. Jerry and Joe were temporarily unemployed, as construction superintendents often are, when Larry asked them if they could build a special type of hopper for Ford's construction company. Jerry and Joe rented a building and welding machine and constructed the hopper. This job led to others and the firm was incorporated in March, 1970. Larry Ford, who purchased most of the stock, appointed Joe as president and Jerry as general manager, with the mutual consent of the two men. Their titles notwithstanding, Jerry and Joe worked side by side to complete the small contracts that they obtained.

As the work load increased, Joe and Jerry soon found that they either had to hire some more welders or turn down some contracts. At first, students at a near-by trade school were hired on a part-time basis. Also, for a while, two experienced welders, who had full-time jobs elsewhere, were hired to work evenings and week-ends. It soon became clear that the work load was sufficiently dependable to support at least three full-time employees, and the following conversation ensued between Jerry and Joe in early 1972:

JOE: I'll call Mr. Smith who teaches over at the trade school tomorrow and ask him to recommend three of his new graduates.

JERRY: Joe, this is rather ticklish work and these trade school boys just don't have the savvy to do the job. We have to watch them every second. And we are spending more time training them than we are actually performing the work.

JOE: Jerry, a good welder will cost us $5.00 an hour. We can get these boys from the trade school for $3.50 an hour.

JERRY: Sure, we pay them about 70 percent as much as we would a good welder, but you give me one good, experienced welder and I can put out more work than I can with all three of those kids. Besides, when we get one of these kids halfway trained, we'll have to pay him $4.50 an hour to keep him.

JOE: We'll still save money while we're paying him $3.50. You and I can do the complicated work and, if we plan and schedule the work right, all the other men will have to do is weld.

JERRY: Well I'm still not convinced, but I'll sure try to make it work. Go ahead and call Mr. Smith tomorrow.

Three young men who had been at the top of their class at the vocational-technical school were hired on the recommendation of Mr. Smith. They started at about 70 percent of the going rate for experienced welders. During the weeks that followed one of the welders found a better job elsewhere and failed to show up for work one morning. Another decided he did not really like welding and quit his job to go to work on a pipeline. When the second welder left, Joe and Jerry had to decide how to obtain replacements.

QUESTIONS FOR DISCUSSION

1. What do you think of the selection procedure of the firm? Explain your answer.
2. How would you improve the procedure?
3. What is your reaction to hiring students directly out of the vocational-technical school rather than recruiting experienced employees?
4. What is your analysis of the wage policy of the firm?
5. What would you do now?

VI-2. Jiffy-Burger Restaurant

About a year ago, Bill Northrup came to Mid City and opened a small drive-in restaurant called *Jiffy-Burger*. Bill had previously worked 15 years for International Oil where he had been in charge of training all new salesmen. The challenge and appeal of managing his own business, however, persuaded him to give up a secure position and invest all his savings in this new venture.

On a recent day, Bill was visiting with his neighbor, Ron. It soon became evident to Ron that his visitor was worried about something, so he asked if Bill was having trouble at the restaurant. The following conversation took place.

BILL: Ron, you just can't imagine the problem I've had since opening that damn restaurant! I never thought it would be this much trouble running my own business. This past year has been a nightmare. Let me tell you about it!

Before opening, I placed an ad in the local paper asking for "hired help." Of the 125 applicants answering the ad, about 100 were high-school dropouts. Of course, I didn't expect college graduates for this type of work, but half of them couldn't even read. It was quite a shock to discover that so many of our younger generation are going into life illiterate. What kind of future do these kids have? They don't seem to have any ambition or desire to improve themselves. Most of them are completely undependable. I spend half of my time replacing boys who just quit. The average employee stays about two months. As a result, I'm always operating short-handed. Even when they show up, I can't get any cooperation from them.

You know, I thought I understood people pretty well, but these kids are impossible. I guess it can be attributed partly to their family background. Take Steve for example. He is 17 years old and his parents have separated. Steve dropped out of school last year and is living with his brother, who is on welfare.

RON: (Interrupting) Can't you do anything to help them?

BILL: I've treated Steve as I would my own son, but he didn't appreciate it. He worked for two months and then just stopped coming. He didn't even tell me he was quitting. If you treat them nice they think you're a 'sucker' and take advantage of you. If you try to reason with them, they resent it. The only thing these kids understand is force. I have to watch them every minute to get any work out of them.

RON: I don't know. It seems that if they were given some responsibility they would show more interest.

BILL: I've tried that. But they won't accept responsibility. In the first place, if I put one in charge, the others resent having to take orders from someone their own age. The petty jealousies are ridiculous. When business is good, I sometimes ask one of the boys to help the man at the grill. The 'grill' man then gets 'huffed up' because someone is taking his job away from him. I just can't get them to work as a team.

RON: Don't they ever become friends? I understand one of the basic needs of restaurant workers is a friendly relationship among themselves.

BILL: Yeah, several of them will pal around together for awhile, but within a week they're fighting among themselves. That's the problem that bothers me. If they could become more cohesive in their informal relationships, they would work together more efficiently. But they aren't even loyal to each other. Every time I walk in, one of them meets me at the door to "rat" on another. The friction resulting from all the conflict usually ends with several quitting. Even when I hire a good worker, within two weeks the group pressures bring him into line. It's just one vicious cycle. I'm afraid to leave them alone for fear of what will happen.

RON: I thought you had a night manager to take charge when you left.

BILL: I did until last week. He was an older fellow and he did a fairly good job. However, I caught him stealing from me.

RON: Did you file charges?

BILL: What good would that do? I'd never get the money back and I would have a hard time proving it was him. I estimated the loss at over $200. When I mentioned it, he just disappeared. This isn't the first time that's happened. I've fired three others for the very same reason.

RON: How could he take that much without your knowing it?

BILL: I thought I had controls to prevent that. We work on a ticket system.

Each item is accompanied by a prenumbered ticket. When the cashier fills an order he removes the ticket and puts it in the cash register. Some days we are short-handed and the manager has to assist with two jobs. When this happened he merely reused some of the tickets and extracted an equivalent amount of cash. By the time I caught on the damage was already done. The other three I caught were taking food, all of which I know they couldn't use.

RON: The way you tell the story, its a pretty hopeless case.

BILL: You haven't heard the worst of it. This, I think tops them all. Last month, in one of my futile attempts to improve the situation, I gave them all a bonus. Beforehand, I carefully explained that the money would be distributed on the basis of hours worked. They all agreed readily that this was fair. However, after I handed it out, half of them became disgruntled and started griping. As a result, the room was in a chaotic state for a week and two employees quit.

RON: Why don't you raise the pay rate and get more qualified workers?

BILL: I can't do that! I'm already paying above the standard rates. I'm having enough trouble breaking even as it is.

RON: Yes, but if you improved the working conditions wouldn't business pick up enough to overcome the added cost? The present situation certainly affects the customers.

BILL: I'm not at all sure that raising the wages would improve the service. The jobs are still the same and adding a few cents to the wage rate won't attract much better people. The only solution is to get out. As soon as the lease expires I'm going to sell the business to some other fool and let him try to make a go of it.

QUESTIONS FOR DISCUSSION

1. What does this case show about the hiring practices of a small business?
2. What does it show about wage and salary problems?
3. What does it indicate about the need for definite personnel policies?
4. What suggestions for improvement could you make to Bill if you were Ron?

VI–3. The Powell Company

The Powell Company was organized in 1972 to provide a service to consumers. In order to start operating, it was necessary that some experienced personnel be hired from an established competitor. The owner of Powell approached several of these potential employees and offered them, (in some cases) the same wages they were earning from their current employers. In other cases, the wages offered were slightly less than those that were being paid by the competitor. Since there was little to be gained financially by the job change, the prospective employees were told of the advantages of getting in on the "ground floor" of the newer, though smaller, organization. The interested individuals were told that as the firm grew and sales and profits increased, it would be management's policy to pay a higher basic wage and also larger employee benefits.

The recruiting policy was relatively successful and several employees were indeed enticed away from the competition.

During the Company's first year in business, sales did not come up to management's anticipation. Analyzing the situation, management decided that in order to increase sales, it should move to a more desirable location where more modern equipment and facilities could improve production. The search for a new location was started and the employees, both the experienced ones who had been hired from the competition, and those who were inexperienced and were being trained, were excited at the prospect of being located in a newer building with more expanded facilities using the latest tools and equipment.

During the period while the new facilities were being readied, there was not a single personnel problem and morale was high. Employee performance was superior and management was proud that none of its employees were "clock watchers."

When the facilities were completed and occupied, morale improved even further. During the first few months, more orders were obtained by the sales force than the firm was able to fill. However, production quotas were met and surpassed. To all concerned it appeared that the Company was well on its way to becoming a leader in its field and was quite profitable.

With the new and expanded facilities, though, came new and unexpected problems. For example, there was an expanded overhead; a larger tax burden; and an increase in the costs incurred for insurance, utilities, and personnel. All these factors contributed to a significant increase in operating expenses.

Management felt it could not fulfill its promise to increase wages and add more employee benefits. The owner, John Powell, said that employees "would just have to wait until the financial position improved before receiving what had been promised them." The implication was that the increases would not be provided until the Company's sales grew to a point where they were sufficiently higher than expenses so that there was a profit.

Mr. Benjamin, the production manager, agreed with Mr. Powell that wages could not be raised at that particular time, but he felt that seeds of trouble had been sewn among the employees. He reported that as far as the employees were concerned, they could only see that sales were high, that production was exceeding expectations, and that unless a detailed report of expenses were shown to them, they would continue to believe that the firm was making a substantial profit and had gone back on its word.

Mr. Powell said he realized that this situation existed, but that he also knew the employees had no justification for looking into the company's financial situation. In view of this, he said, he knew of but one alternative—the one he had previously outlined.

QUESTIONS FOR DISCUSSION

1. What does this case show about the role of expectations in wage and salary administration?
2. What does it show about the relationships between income, expenses, and profits?
3. What did the addition of the new facilities do to the firm's breakeven point?
4. Should the owner show the books to the employees? Why or why not?
5. What would you do now if you were the owner?

VI–4. The Delday Chevrolet Agency[1]

While waiting for key members of his management team to arrive for a special meeting, Paul Day sat pondering the approach he would use to get George Cutter, manager of the Parts Department, to discuss frankly his apparent loss of interest in the continued progress and profitability of the business. Another problem bothering Paul Day was how to announce his undisclosed decision to make Charles Bender, currently Used Car Manager, Business Manager in charge of both used and new car sales.

The Delday Chevrolet Agency began operations in 1965. At that time, Paul Day purchased the City Motor Company which was the oldest

---

[1] Prepared by Frederic A. Brett and Paul Huddleston, University of Alabama.

dealership in the state. At the time of purchase, Paul and his brother, John, also owned and operated the Pontiac–GMC Company and the Delta Finance Company. These two organizations had been given to them by their father, who had amassed a fortune during his lifetime by diversifying his business interests into finance companies, automobile agencies, a chain of funeral parlors, and commercial real estate.

To finance the purchase of the Delday Chevrolet Agency, Paul sold his interest in the Pontiac–GMC Company to his brother, John, and borrowed the remainder from the Delta Finance Company. Because of their respective interests in the latter company, Paul owned 60 percent and John 40 percent of the Chevrolet agency.

Other key members of the agency's management team were: George Cutter, Parts Manager; James Worth, Sales Manager for new cars and trucks; Charles Bender, Used Car Sales Manager; and Ben Martin, Service Department Manager.

George Cutter joined the agency soon after it was founded. Prior to that time he had been Parts Manager for a large General Motors dealership in a nearby city. He had the reputation of being "the best parts manager in the state."

Soon after joining the Delday Agency, Cutter began to sound out the Day brothers on the possibility of getting an interest in the firm. Continued expressions of interest in owning part of the business resulted in the two brothers agreeing to grant his request in January, 1972. An agreement was drawn whereby Cutter would be allowed to buy a one percent per year interest in the agency for a period of five years. In addition, the brothers agreed to give him an equal amount over the same period. Thus at the end of five years, Cutter would own 10 percent of the business. The agreement further provided that the purchase price would be based on book value as of January 1, 1972, and that the annual profit-sharing would be based on percentage ownership as of December 31 each year. John Day actually made the deal with Cutter and although Paul agreed, he did not approve of the loose way in which the agreement was drawn.

In March, 1972, John became interested in politics and ceased to be active in the agency. Five months later he sold his interest in the business to Paul. Mr. Cutter had wanted to buy part of John's interest and was disappointed when John refused to sell him any part of his holdings. Paul was completely unaware of Cutter's attempt to buy part of John's interest until after he had acquired John's stock in the company. In September, 1972, Paul bought John's interest in the Delta Finance Company. This transfer of interest resulted in Paul's owning 90 percent and Cutter the potential owner of 10 percent of the Chevrolet agency.

In September, 1973, Paul applied to the Small Business Administration for a loan to secure working capital for the business. Mr. Cutter did not agree with this method of financing and made demands for a 25 percent interest in the agency. He was very adamant in his demand and threatened to inform General Motors that the agency was a corporation and not a sole proprietorship. The Chevrolet Division of General Motors had a stated policy that each dealership would be a sole proprietorship unless permission for a different legal form was secured at the time the dealership was awarded. The Delday Agency was registered by General Motors as "Paul Day, Owner."

The issue was settled in November, 1973, when Paul bought Cutter's interest for $7,000. This amount was approximately twice Cutter's legal investment. Sale of his interests in the agency did not terminate his employment, as Paul believed that the company could not do without him. Cutter continued to be paid on the basis of four percent of the gross sales of the Parts Department and Service Department. During 1973, his remuneration was about $21,000.

Since November, 1973, Cutter had lost much of his drive and was continually finding fault with how the agency was run. Gross sales in both the Parts Department and the Service Department had dropped considerably and some of the mechanics had voiced their opinion that "George got a rough deal." In May, 1974, Cutter earned about $1,100. Sales were off as much as 50 percent in corresponding months from 1973 to 1974. In 1973, the Service Department showed $6,320 profit for the period January 1 through May 31. A $1,050 loss was reflected in the records for the same period in 1974.

While John Day had been associated with the agency, he had concentrated his efforts in selling used cars and trucks. In December, 1962, Charles Bender was employed as Sales Manager for used cars and trucks. Mr. Bender previously had his own unsuccessful dealership with a competitive automobile manufacturer. Apparently, inadequate financing and his inability to hold good salesmen were the causes of his failure. Bender, however, attributed his failure to the product he was selling and had convinced Paul Day that his potential for developing a top-notch sales organization was unlimited.

Charles Bender came from a prominent and wealthy family in the area which gave him much in common with Paul Day. The two family names, Day and Bender, had been associated with social and economic leadership in the state for well over 100 years. The Bender family was heavily involved in banking and owned and managed the local bank.

Since Bender joined the agency, he had taken over the responsibility of appraising all trade-ins involving both new and used cars. James Worth, Sales Manager for new cars and trucks, openly resented what he considered Bender's intrusion into his sphere of influence. However, he had not protested to Paul Day and was becoming reconciled to the fact that Bender had the inside track where Paul Day was concerned.

Most of the animosity Worth felt toward Bender could be traced to their personalities and background. Bender was a college graduate who had had all of the advantages provided by his family in preparing himself for a business career. Mrs. Bender was also from a socially prominent family and was characterized by Worth as being a typical representative of the "country club set."

Worth, 44 and seven years Bender's senior, stood out in marked contrast to Bender. Worth had little formal schooling and had difficulty in writing and conversing without "murdering" the English language. He had joined the company in 1967 as a salesman. His greatest value to the Agency was his ability to "talk" to the customers from the rural areas and his ability to close a deal. He did extremely well in selling a package (insurance, financing, and so forth), and made a good living on his commissions from sales as well as a percentage of the package.

In 1972, Paul Day employed an experienced salesman from an out-of-state Chevrolet agency to take over as Sales Manager for new cars and trucks, to "relieve him of some administrative duties." The new man did not perform as expected and was discharged after eight months. Worth was temporarily appointed Sales Manager until a replacement could be hired.

This appointment brought about a complete change in Worth. As a salesman he had been uncooperative with Paul and was antagonistic toward the other salesmen. As Sales Manager he became a "100 percent company man, working long hours and doing all in his power to knit the sales group into a smooth-running, friendly organization." At first, the salesmen did not understand the change that had taken place in Worth and kept their guard up in their dealings with him. Several quit their jobs rather than accept Worth in his new position. However, after several months, the new attitude displayed by Worth became more accepted and conflicts with his salesmen became less frequent.

Paul continued to interview prospects for the Sales Manager position but was unable to find anyone "who was as good as Worth." In November, 1973, Paul informed Worth that he could have the Sales Manager position on a permanent basis as long as he continued to perform as well as he had in the past. This added security caused Worth to become even more amiable and conflicts with his salesmen ceased almost entirely.

Ben Martin, Service Department Manager, had been close to Worth when Worth had been a salesman. However, this friendly relationship disappeared when Worth became Sales Manager. Martin had always associated with members of the agency who were more or less dissatisfied with their jobs. Martin was a quiet individual who had not entered into any of the intrigue except to express his opinion that Cutter got a "raw deal" when Paul bought out his interest.

Martin was competent in supervising the mechanics and running the shop. However, since Cutter sold his interest in the agency, Martin closed the shop at five on the dot and had even turned business away if it appeared that overtime would be necessary to complete the job.

QUESTIONS FOR DISCUSSION

1. What factors accounted for George Cutter's opposition to Paul Day?
2. How do you evaluate Paul Day's management of the Delday Agency?
3. From a behavioral viewpoint, how do you evaluate the interaction between James Worth and (a) Charles Bender; (b) the salemen?
4. What approach should Paul Day use with Ben Martin to improve his serving customers?
5. What approach should Paul Day use to motivate George Cutter to improve his effectiveness and efficiency?
6. What criteria should Paul Day use in promoting Charles Bender?
7. How should Paul Day announce his decision to promote Charles Bender to Business Manager?

VI–5. *Dependable Motors, Inc.*[1]

When Dan Cole was discharged from the Navy in January 1970, he took a part-time job at Dependable Motors as a "lot boy" while attending classes at Southern State University. Dan got the job through his uncle who was Finance Manager of the dealership. Jim, a long time buddy of Dan's, who was also attending school, had started work at Dependable as a "lot boy" a few months before Dan came on board. It was Jim who filled Dan in on the details of the job. Their duties included:

> Checking in new cars as they came in; shifting the cars around the lot to keep the stock in order; driving cars bought from other dealers by Dependable; washing cars on the lot with a hose and rag; cleaning cars that were "sold," as well as for the showroom floor; maintaining all keys for the new cars; and many other duties and errands "too numerous to mention."

After arriving at work in the same car every day and punching in, Dan and Jim reported to the office to see what needed to be done

---

[1] Prepared by David R. Kenerson, University of South Florida. Based on a student project done by Doyle Cobb in the author's course in Organizational Behavior.

and in what priority. After this, Dan's uncle or Mr. Clay, his boss, would contact them only if there was a problem or a special job. Work hours were approximatly 1:00–5:30 P.M. Pay was $1.75 an hour. Dan and Jim worked on Saturday mornings only if they got behind in their work and had not been able to catch up by working late on Friday.

A partial chart of the organization is indicated in Exhibit V–1.

EXHIBIT V–1

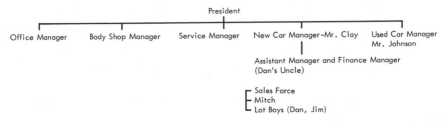

As time went on, both Dan and Jim had to work harder and longer because of the increased work load. There was less time for "coke breaks," for conversation with Mitch, whose job it was to clean up "sold" cars for delivery, and there were fewer trips to other dealers to pick up cars. In fact, Dan and Jim had to spend more and more time checking in new cars in the hot sun, shifting cars around on the lot, and picking up trash and cigarette butts from the plants in front of the dealership.

The boys got little help from Mr. Clay, the New Car Manager. In fact, Mr. Clay seldom took any interest in what they did. Dan's uncle was also very busy doing not only his own work but also much of Mr. Clay's. Dan and Jim thought of Mr. Clay as a playboy who was quite permissive. Mr. Clay never seemed to notice whether the boys' work was done well or not, but Dan's uncle did. If they did a job well, he would say, "Boys, it looks real good, just great." If it wasn't quite up to par, he might give them a hint or just ignore it because he knew they were quite busy.

In August, 1971, Mr. Clay was asked to resign and Mr. Johnson, the Used Car Manager became General Sales Manager.

The organization now appeared as in Exhibit V–2.

EXHIBIT V–2

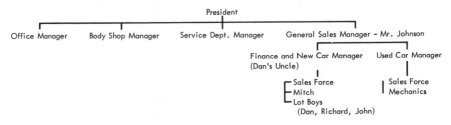

Mr. Johnson wasn't as permissive as Mr. Clay had been. In fact, they were exact opposites. Before the change, most of Dan's jobs were assigned by his uncle. Now, Mr. Johnson and Dan's uncle shared the responsibility of supervising the boys, with Mr. Johnson having the final word if there was disagreement. Under Mr. Johnson, the boys were punching in closer to a specific time, reporting to him more often so that he could keep a close watch on progress, checking with him before punching out to ensure completion of work, working more often on Saturdays than ever before, getting very little time for breaks, receiving less desirable jobs with no additional compensation, getting very few "thank you's" for a job well done, and receiving sharp criticism for work not up to par. Jim soon left Dependable Motors for a part-time job at the Post Office at $4.00 an hour.

After Jim left, Dan had two weeks alone on the job. It soon became obvious that one boy couldn't do the work, so Richard, a 17 year old high school student was hired. Since Dan was older and knew the work, Mr. Johnson left him unofficially in charge of the lot with Richard as his new assistant.

The duties of the job hadn't changed much, but the percentage of bad jobs to good ones increased. Whereas Dan and Jim had been equals, and had received equal treatment, now Richard received most of the undesirable jobs when there was a choice. Trips were a rare event now, but occasionally Dan's uncle called the boys into his office and gave Dan a trip to go on and told Richard the cars on the lot were looking dusty and needed to be washed. Richard resented this, while Dan felt very much like the man in the middle trying to appease management and keep Richard satisfied at the same time.

Early in 1972, a third "lot boy" was hired. John, the new boy, was a hustler. After working two weeks, John caught up. All the cars had been washed and the whole front was free of any paper or cigarette butts. Dan and Richard tried to clue John in on the "facts of life." They told him, "No matter how hard you work, you won't get a raise." John finally became convinced and gradually slowed down, and all three shared the undesirable jobs.

The three boys were now good friends. Dan was accepted as the unofficial boss who got his orders from Mr. Johnson or his uncle and assigned the work equally. However, by now John had become a first-rate slacker. This situation created serious problems for Dan, because with three boys on the lot instead of two, Mr. Johnson expected much more work to be done. In order to get John to work, Richard came up with the idea of drinking beer on their breaks instead of soda pop. It was agreed to do this, only on their breaks in the shed and no more than two cans in an afternoon.

The plan backfired and the results were disastrous. John could not handle two cans of beer, and Richard felt little pain either. They got into water fights and production went down to zero, because Dan had to spend a lot of time breaking up their games.

Dan and Richard agreed that if this conduct continued they would be fired. However, John disagreed and decided to do very little work unless beer drinking was continued. The result was that Dan and Richard had to cover for John when he came to work late or punched out early. In fact, John started sleeping in the cars while they were cleaning them. Threats by Dan and Richard to report John to Mr. Johnson were countered by John's threat to report their beer-drinking activities.

In desperation, Dan went to his uncle and requested that he give John assignments directly and let him work alone. As Dan put it, "Three people are too many working on one car and we just get in each other's way. Richard and I work best as a team, and I think John works best by himself."

Since Mr. Johnson was out-of-town on business for two weeks, Dan's uncle was in charge and handled the change with tact and gave John instructions for the day which were different from those given to Dan and Richard.

John was mad and thought the boys had "ratted on him." Pretty soon he started coming to work late until Dan's uncle started riding him about it. John finally just quit coming to work altogether. One Friday he picked up his final check.

By the time Mr. Johnson got back from his trip, Dan and Richard were just getting caught up in their work. Mr. Johnson was on their back more than ever, and they were getting stuck with all the dirty jobs again. Dan and Richard soon decided to quit, but before they did, they wanted to enjoy things a little and show Mr. Johnson what a real slow-down was like. They "hot rodded" the cars on the lot, "shot the bull" with Mitch and other employees, did very little if any work, got further and further behind, came to work late, punched out early, and cheated on the time clock. Dan decided the next time Mr. Johnson called him about a slow down, he and Richard would quit on the spot. By then they would be so far behind that it would take three weeks to get caught up after training new employees. Mr. Johnson called Dan in the next day.

QUESTIONS FOR DISCUSSION

1. What are the advantages and disadvantages of Mr. Clay's and Dan's uncle's supervisory styles?
2. What are the advantages and disadvantages of Mr. Johnson's supervisory style?

3. How can Dan hope to be successful as an "unofficial boss"?
4. What were the probable causes of the decline in productivity and effectiveness of the "lot boys" under Mr. Johnson's supervision?
5. Who would you prefer to work for, Mr. Clay or Mr. Johnson? Why?

VI–6. Metal Specialties, Inc. [1]

Metal Specialties, Inc., manufactured a series of proprietary metal fabrication items as well as a general line of standard metal products. For several years, annual sales volume had been approximately $1 million per year. The company was closely held by the Jason brothers, John and Bill. During 1968, the company decided to construct a fabricating plant adjacent to its existing plant and operate it as a new activity, to be designated as Fabricators, Inc. It was thought that existing management personnel could be spread over both operations, thereby reducing overhead and increasing profits. The building plan called for the use of existing personnel in the planning and construction process. In exchange for this effort the personnel would receive shares of stock in the new operation. This concept created high morale throughout the parent organization. Each person saw an opportunity for a special reward for his contribution.

Unfortunately, the new plant was not ready for production until almost the middle of 1969. The equipment for the new plant had been designed by personnel of the parent company, and it had been fabricated by the shop people. From the outset, production was impaired by the crudeness and ineffectiveness of the equipment. This hampered output and required modification of the production equipment. During this period, waste and labor costs were excessive.

About the time the new plant was conceived, George Kelley, an "Ivy-leaguer," had been brought in as Director of Corporate Development. John Jason, Corporate President, had felt that if the company were to overcome growth and profit problems, such a person must be brought in from the outside to breathe new life into the company.

For a number of years, Tim Smith had been Sales Manager for the company. Smith was a good salesman and was very conversant with the industry. There was some question, however, as to whether he had

---

[1] Prepared by Curtis E. Tate, Jr., University of Georgia and Dennis M. Crites, University of Oklahoma.

the managerial ability to direct a sales force. In fact, his optimistic sales forecasts usually ran about twice the sales achieved. In late summer, 1969, Smith was relieved of the sales management responsibility and assigned the task of managing the new fabricating plant activity, including production and sales. It had become apparent that the split responsibility of other personnel was interfering with the production and efficiency of both operations. Also, the fabricating plant continued to be plagued with production problems, excessive waste, and an inability to meet delivery schedules. The impact was a sharp reduction of morale in both organizations.

When Smith became General Manager of Fabricators, Kelly was given a special assignment to take over as Sales Manager for Metal Specialties. He was given specific instructions to develop a sales force, including a new person to fill the sales manager's slot. Kelly started with one salesman in addition to himself.

TERMINATION OF THE NEW OPERATION

Failures at Fabricators had imposed such a drain on Specialties' resources that in early 1970 a consolidation of creditors took place. The terms of this arrangement called for equal monthly payments on the outstanding indebtedness for 24 months. If at any time the company were to lose money for three consecutive months, the creditors would take over the operation of Specialties. In addition, the arrangement required the termination of Fabricators and its subsequent liquidation.

An outside group had been appointed as directors to complement the inside group in early 1969. They had foreseen the demise of Fabricators as early as September. They had suggested the activities of Fabricators be terminated, but their entreaties had fallen upon deaf ears.

Upon termination of Fabricators, Smith was put on the payroll of Specialties as Manager of Special Projects. In effect, this left him with little but frustration. John Jason felt a special affinity for Smith because of his long years of loyalty, and was reluctant to terminate his services.

During the last half of 1969, Kelly and his one salesman plowed the territory and brought in sufficient orders to keep the company in the black. However, as time passed Kelly became more unhappy with his personal situation. On more than one occasion Kelly visited with the outside board members and voiced his displeasure. The target date for having a sales organization passed. Kelly still had his one salesman and he was becoming more vocal concerning his unhappiness.

In early December, 1970, the board of directors met for the first time in a year. One of the actions at this meeting was to appoint an *ad hoc* committee to formulate a remuneration plan for Kelly. Professor Joe Sexton of State University was appointed chairman of the committee.

Kelly had earlier presented demands to John Jason that he be given 51 percent of company stock and that his salary be increased from its current annual rate of $20,000. Kelly's rationale for these demands was that the ideas he had suggested—even if not all had yet been implemented—plus the sales he obtained had made a significant contribution to salvaging the company.

It was decided that the three-member committee—Joe Sexton, Ed Snow, and Jack Phillips—would meet weekly until a plan had been formulated for remunerating Kelly. After some discussion it soon became apparent that the committee's assignment had more ramifications than Kelly's problems. The whole company's future was at stake, as was the welfare of both John and Bill Jason. It seemed that to meet Kelly's demands would completely ignore the efforts and contributions that John Jason had made to the company. In addition, Kelly lacked a "track record."

The ad hoc committee held four weekly meetings exploring an ever-widening series of issues. In early January, Snow related an incident to Sexton concerning a bid Kelly had made for a large order. Kelly had bid $0.42 per pound when he knew the competition was bidding $0.39. The material cost to Specialties was $0.30 a pound plus $0.01 for container and $0.02 for transportation. Direct labor costs were negligible, and less than the latter two items. This action of Kelly's distressed the other executives. December sales had been low and the company had suffered a substantial loss.

At the next meeting, the committee agreed to recommend a remuneration plan for Kelly. His salary would be $20,000 per year for the first $100,000 profit. For the next $100,000 profit he would receive another $10,000; and for the next $100,000 profit he would receive an additional $10,000. He would be given an option to purchase stock from John and Bill Jason. The initial payments for his stock would be used to retire personal notes held by the company against John and Bill.

FURTHER INVESTIGATION AND VIEWPOINTS

A formal report was submitted to John Jason including this and other recommendations of the committee. Later Sexton received a call from Kelly requesting a luncheon appointment. As they sat down to lunch, Kelly began to push Sexton for information concerning the committee's recommendations. Sexton replied that the committee had finished its report and it was the responsibility of John Jason to communicate it to him. This left Kelly in not too happy a state, but Sexton tried to convince Kelly that it was John's responsibility to make the interpretation. Sexton indicated that he thought the committee had come up with an equitable solution to Kelly's dilemma.

Later Sexton received a call from Kelly indicating a conversation with John. The proposal John had tendered was in no way in accord with the committee's report. Sexton called John to discuss the discrepancy with him. During the conversation, John proposed that Sexton meet on the next Saturday, in turn, with Smith, Page, and Kelly to determine what each thought his potential was in the company and the contributions that he could make. John also reported that sales and profits during the first two weeks of January were off more than in December. Following this conversation, Sexton did some informal questioning and was told by a reliable source that Smith was an excellent salesman. The source believed that the company was hurting itself by not utilizing his service in a sales capacity.

The Saturday meeting began with an interview with Smith. He was very vocal in expressing his frustration because of the lack of a definitive assignment. At the same time, he expressed his loyalty to the company and his strong belief that he could make a contribution to rebuilding the company. When asked if he would like to return to the road as a salesman, his face broke into a joyous grin with an affirmative answer. Next in order came Page. He initially discussed the opportunity for savings through changed purchasing procedures. He was very vocal in expressing his confidence in Smith's loyalty and capability. Page appeared to lack confidence, however, concerning Kelly and spoke in reserved terms. The matter of the high bid was discussed and Page felt that such actions would destroy the company.

When Kelly came in after lunch, he opened, "Why the hell should we go over this again? We've already been over it." Sexton said, "OK, but there is one thing I want to know. Why did you bid $0.42 on the XCO order?" Kelly almost snapped, "I wanted to put the competition on notice that we are not in the price-cutting business." Sexton, after some further conversation, thanked Kelly for his time and told him that was all for now. Kelly again expressed interest in the terms of the committee proposal but Sexton told him once again that information would have to come from John.

Sexton—mentally reviewing his discussions with Smith, Page, and Kelly—went into John Jason's office to seek his views. He told John that "six more weeks of losses and the creditors will take over and put the company up for sale." Sexton, after briefing John on the three discussions, inquired especially about the role that John had planned for Kelly at the time he had brought Kelly into the company. John reiterated his belief that Kelly had the background that could have helped breathe new life into the company. He mentioned also the value of Kelly's contacts and the influence that Kelly's father had as a member of one of the major investment banking houses. Admittedly disappointed in Kelly's failure to develop the sales force, John did express the view that Kelly's sales had helped keep the company in the black for several months and that Kelly had given him some good ideas. "In fact," said John—pointing to a list of "Managerial Do's" given to him earlier by Kelly—"I think I'd better start using some more of them right away." The first item on the list was that "A manager should delegate." The second item was that "A manager should pull back his delegation in a time of crisis."

"This sounds like that second item applies," Jason stated. "Anything else you learned that I'd better keep in mind as I start changing things?"

Sexton mentioned again his thoughts about Smith's assignment, the need for getting everyone on the road who could sell, and Smith's feelings about being a salesman. He also pointed out that Kelly seemed to believe that "the company will have plenty of orders in April and May." "But," Sexton noted, "it will be too late by then. And if he handles any more bids like he did that XCO order, he won't get the orders even then." Concluding, Sexton told John, "I agree you'd better start changing things—especially on what role, if any, you let Kelly play! And you have to consider why—with such bright promise and good ideas—Kelly seems to be producing so little as things have gotten tighter."

QUESTIONS FOR DISCUSSION

1. Evaluate John Jason's actions as president—including those that appear to be his strengths as well as any that may indicate his weaknesses.
2. Was the idea of bringing in George Kelly a good one? Discuss.
3. Is this an appropriate use of a committee?
4. What are some possible explanations to answer the last point raised by Joe Sexton? Select the two most divergent explanations from among those possible. How do they differ in their consequences and in the action that should be taken?

VI–7. Kellog Motors[1]

Kellog Motors was an automobile agency in a small rural community in the Mississippi delta. Historically, agriculture had been the area's

---

[1] Prepared by Robert A. Rentz, Jr., Scottsdale Memorial Hospital, and Leon C. Megginson, Louisiana State University.

primary economic base with "cotton the king." However, in 1971 growing welfare receipts represented a major portion of the county's income.

Pleasantville, which we shall call the town, had a population of about 6,500 in 1960 and 7,000 in 1970. It was the only town within a county of about 15,000 people, of whom around 40 percent were black. The county experienced over a 10 percent decline in population from 1960 to 1970. It was estimated that most of the loss was from outmigration, especially from the farms in the surrounding countryside.

Like many small towns, Pleasantville had only three automobile agencies—a General Motors dealership; a Ford dealership; and a Chrysler dealership, owned and operated by Mr. J. A. Kellog.

Mr. Kellog was originally from a city near Pleasantville. As a youth he was a good student with natural mechanical inclinations. Upon graduation from high school, Kellog was encouraged by his family, especially an aunt who was a college professor, to enter college and pursue an education in engineering, but he refused. His interest was not in school, he said, but in automobiles.

Starting as a mechanic's helper when 16, he quickly built a reputation as a good mechanic. Three years later he founded his own business. Actually, Pleasantville had no one who knew about automobile repairs until Kellog came there and established his business. After about a year of doing almost all the work himself, he went back to his home town and encouraged two mechanics to come work for him in Pleasantville, as business was good.

Five years later Mr. Kellog became a Chrysler dealer, the same year in which the new car was introduced. Before that time, he had handled Chevrolet, but he dropped the franchise when General Motors tried to force more cars upon him than he wanted immediately before a major model change. He rapidly sold his remaining stock and made room for his new stock of Chryslers while 12 Chevrolets which General Motors said he must take sat refused and in demurrage in railroad cars.

In 1962, the Dodge automobile and truck agency was obtained to increase the firm's market potential. Until that time Kellog had been without a truck line. This addition gave the dealership a full line of products with the Valiant in the compact field, Plymouth and Dodge in both the intermediate and standard-size car class, Chrysler in the medium to luxury car class, and the Dodge in the truck market. Kellog Motors also had a profitable Texaco dealership.

Competing dealerships in Pleasantville have come and gone throughout the lifespan of the firm. The Ford agency has changed hands four times in the past 12 years, and Chevrolet three times. The agencies were more highly organized and formally structured than the Chrysler dealership.

Kellog's only son had a bachelor's degree in business administration and was currently enrolled at State University studying toward a M.B.A.

degree. Respecting his son's education, Kellog often asked him his opinion on various problems of the business. Kervin, the son, who was considering managing the business someday, was interested in its affairs, and attempted to find ways to apply what he had learned in his formal education to the betterment of the business.

One of the problems facing the son was the fact that the dealership was in a small town and was a small sized business, while the young man's education had been directed mostly toward big business. This difference caused conflict between Kervin and his father as the son attempted to apply his knowledge to the affairs of the business. The following exchange is an example:

KERVIN: Dad, I think Brick is mad again about having to grease those cars. He doesn't think a mechanic should have to do that type of work.

MR. KELLOG: I can't help that, Kervin. What should I do when there are several wash and lube jobs to be done and he doesn't have anything to do in the shop? Should I let him sit down back there and pull a laborer off the front to grease cars, or let the wash man both wash and grease them when we are rushed like this?

KERVIN: Well, I don't know. But I've learned that each man should have his own job with distinct duties, and that he should be entirely responsible for them and only them.

MR. KELLOG: Well, that's all right for a big organization, but it will not work for a small business such as this. I don't want anyone to think he has only one job; he is to do anything that needs doing, when it needs doing.

KERVIN: Perhaps you're wrong. I also noticed something else. You don't let the men help make the decisions that affect them. Maybe they would be happier and produce more if you let them have their say in the management of the business; after all, they are a part of it, aren't they?

MR. KELLOG: Now, wouldn't that be fine. What the hell? Do you think those jerks out there know anything about running this place?

KERVIN: Maybe they don't, but if they aren't the right people, then get the right people.

MR. KELLOG: That's easier said than done. That is one of the big problems, and perhaps the biggest problem for a small business today. Where are the right personnel to be found? Today, a good mechanic is almost as hard to find as gold at the end of the rainbow. A good mechanic can make as much as $250 to $300 per week, and yet, no one wants to become a mechanic. Ask boys in high school what they want to be. Practically all of them want to be doctors, business executives, lawyers, engineers, teachers, or perhaps football coaches. I bet you that not a single one answers that he wants to be a mechanic. Who is going to maintain the automobiles of those doctors, lawyers, and engineers? Here is a problem for you, your teachers, and the politicians of the nation. But right now I am looking at the situation from my own point of view.

Mr. Kellog went on to explain that a business man becomes successful by hiring good people and then building an organization around them. A doctor or lawyer is limited to only what he can turn out personally.

However, the business man is different, for his managerial abilities constitute a creative force within himself. He can multiply his productivity many fold. But to do this, he must have the right personnel; he must surround himself with capable men so that he can multiply the amount of production that can be achieved. However, if the right workers are not to be found, he is limited to only what he, individually, can produce.

Kervin knew these facts to be true, for there were very few mechanics available. Also, during the previous 10 years, very few young men had entered the skilled fields. However, it seemed that the problem was even more severe for Kellog Motors than for the larger concerns. Since Mr. Kellog was a skilled mechanic, his customers could depend on him to see to it that their automobiles were repaired when they were supposed to be. If Kervin were in charge, he would not be able to guide the mechanics and ensure that they did the job correctly, as the father had been able to do. Kervin was not accustomed to doing mechanical work.

Another drawback in the small company was that if it were lucky enough to find a good mechanic, he would probably not want to come to a small town and leave a shop where he had established customers. As this question particularly disturbed the young college man, he asked his dad one day:

KERVIN: Dad, what can be done to solve this problem of mechanics? There are many young men who are unemployed, or their folks are on welfare. Why can't they be trained to become craftsmen?

MR. KELLOG: The factories realize the problem and are offering training programs for mechanics. The arrangement is for the dealer to send the mechanic to school for several days at a time to learn to repair specific parts of the auto. The problem is that when you train a mechanic and he becomes good and starts attracting customers, he usually quits and opens a small shop of his own. So you lose the time and money you invested in his training. In Brick's case this would be easy with the emphasis upon "black capitalism," and the government's emphasis upon "civil rights."

KERVIN: If you would put them on a commission basis instead of paying them salary, it would perhaps solve this problem.

MR. KELLOG: Maybe it would. There is one bad thing about the commission method, though. It would perhaps encourage mechanics to be crooked. For instance, he will do jobs on automobiles that don't actually need to be done, or he will make parts replacements when they aren't necessary. Mechanics often make what is called a "double charge," too. That is, if he pulls a wheel off to fix a wheel cyclinder and while he has it off he also replaces the brake shoes, he charges for each of them as a separate job, as if he had to take the wheel off for each job separately.

The son had been studying "democratic leadership" versus "authoritarian management" at school. One of his professors had often said that the manager must create within his subordinates a love for him, which is admittedly hard to do. Otherwise he must create a healthy fear, or respect, among his followers towards him. This problem was acute in the agency, as shown in the following example:

Mr. Kellog: I sent James back to the shop this afternoon with a pair of chains for one of the men to put on a car. He came back and said there wasn't anybody back there. I went back myself and sure enough there wasn't anyone there. So, I walked around the corner and there stood Charley and Brick at the bar on the corner drinking. I said, 'What the hell do you mean coming around here during working hours? I ought to pay you both off right now.' They both left the bar and walked ahead of me all the way back, with me telling them what I thought of them every step of the way.

Kervin: I can't understand why they would do a thing like that. Maybe you have been too hard on them.

Mr.. Kellog: Bull! You have to be hard; you can't be nice to them. Yesterday, during the snow, they had had a hard day putting anti-freeze in cars. Around 10 minutes before quitting time we had everything ready to close up and another car drove in for anti-freeze. I told the driver he would have to wait until the next day, as we were closing. I thought I would be nice to the labor considering how hard they had worked. What I should have done was tell them to open up the shop again and put the anti-freeze in that car. They just don't appreciate what you do for them. You can't be considerate and nice to them—they will take advantage of you every damn time they have an opportunity.

The lack of good mechanics was enough of a problem by itself; however, it had side effects. As a result of the great demand for their services and the relatively few good ones available, they became hard to manage. They knew they were in demand, and did things they would not do otherwise. This may be an example of the problem:

Mr. Kellog: In addition to the shortage of mechanics, the government's ruining the ones who are working. Brick's attitude has certainly changed now that he has so many opportunities to do other things. He's getting hard to live with. In fact, I'm reasonably sure that he has stolen oil from this place to go in his own automobile. The reason I believe this is that he never buys oil for that car of his, yet he buys gasoline and other things for it. I know it doesn't run without oil.

Kervin: He could buy his oil somewhere else.

Mr. Kellog: Why would he do that when he buys other things here? It doesn't make sense. Anyway, he should buy oil here once in a while.

Kervin: I will go along with you on that.

Mr. Kellog: We started keeping a closer check on our oil inventory and James came up five quarts short on Havoline #20, exactly the oil Brick's car requires. I know it went into his automobile.

Kervin: Well, are you going to fire him?

Mr. KELLOG: No, I will just have to watch him closer. He is a good mechanic, and is making me money. What's wrong?

KERVIN: Nothing, I was just thinking.

QUESTIONS FOR DISCUSSION

1. How can a small firm like this find and keep capable employees?
2. Should Mr. Kellog have a more formal organization structure with separate job specifications for each employee? Explain your answers.
3. How would you motivate these employees?
4. With this business, and with these employees, which leadership style would be best? Explain your answer.
5. What would you do about the missing oil? Explain.
6. What does the case show about the problems of manning a small business?

VI–8. Central Plastics, Inc.[1]

Central Plastics, Inc. was a single-plant operation with 25 employees. The company was involved in plastics formulation and compounding, and had been in business for 18 years in the same location.

The physical plant consists of two buildings, an eight-year-old structure used as a warehouse, and an 18-year-old single story structure that housed the production facility, a research and testing laboratory, and administrative offices. Both buildings had been given adequate maintenance and safety emphasis, and the safety record of the firm had been good.

Prior to notification by the OSHA[2] compliance officer, the plant manager, Charles Rainey, had instituted many of the corrections that were needed, based on his own inspection of the facility.

The plant was visited on February 15 by Mr. Steven Smith, Compliance Officer of the U.S. Department of Labor, Occupational Safety and Health Administration. He and Mr. Rainey conducted a walk-around inspection.

---

[1] Prepared by Rudolph L. Kagerer, University of Georgia.

[2] The Occupational Safety and Health Administration set up under the Williams-Steiger, Occupational Safety and Health Act of 1970.

The in-plant memo prepared by Mr. Rainey is shown in one appendix, while the other appendix contains notes on the final conference with Smith.

APPENDIX: REPORT ON O.S.H.A. WALK-AROUND INSPECTION 2/15/74
Distribution: RTH–JPH–DBH–JL–LF–DBP–CAM–James Nolan

Mr. Steven Smith, Compliance Officer, U.S. Department of Labor, Occupational Safety & Health Administration, called on us today, presented his credentials and requested to see certain records and to inspect our facility.

After an initial conference and a check of our medical and accident records, the two of us went around the plant. He made notes, took several photographs, and pointed out situations requiring remedial action. (Please see notes attached). When we had finished the inspection we discussed the results, pinpointing several problem areas.

Mr. Smith said that we will receive a registered letter from his office in about a week if citations are to be issued. The time allowed for correction of violations will be given for each citation listed.

Within 15 days of the receipt of this letter, we may request an extension of time on any of these remedial jobs if this is required. Within this 15 day period also, we may exercise our right to contest the violations cited. Mr. Smith said also that we may call his office informally for a conference over any points in the letter of citation which we do not understand, or which need clarification. All of these provisions will be stated in the letter.

No imminent-danger citation was issued today.

C. A. Rainey
2/15/74

APPENDIX: NOTES ON FINAL CONFERENCE, WITH MR. STEVEN SMITH, O.S.H.A., 2–15–74

1. HIGHLY IMPORTANT: Maintain intact ground wires and plugs on all electrical equipment. Check grounding of 240V, 440V equipment on the floor (tub mixers, etc.)
2. MIX TANK B–4, URETHANE AREA: Need rail on stairway access.
3. VERY IMPORTANT: Identify each switchbox and circuit breaker as

to the outlet or machine which it serves. ALSO: Mr. Smith suggested that we place nonconductive rubber matting under all our high-voltage switchboxes, due to our wet-floor conditions.

4. The CATWALK in the rear of the urethane area should be changed to permit direct up-and-over access instead of the present side-step required. Mr. Smith voiced concern also about the slippery residues on the ladder.

5. Our FORKLIFT TOWER must be provided with an interrupt-switch by which the man on the tower can shut off the engine of the forklift truck, [section 1910.178, m, (12), (ii)]. Mr. Smith also suggested that a third observer be present when the tower is being used, to watch for obstructions and to serve as a safety link between the driver and the man on the tower.

6. 3-ROLL MILLS: Need body-stops and safety controls on in-running rollers. (see copy of section 1919.216,b,1–3) attached.

7. COMPRESSED AIR USED FOR CLEANING: Mr. Smith pointed out the need for reduction of pressure to less than 30 p.s.i. on the hose near the Floflex sifter if it is used for any kind of cleaning. He suggested the use of a chip-guard nozzle and eye protection.

8. SHOP GRINDERS, Plant 1, Plant 2: Need to have spindle-ends covered and work-rests kept adjusted to within 1/8 inch of the wheel. [see copy of section 1910.215,a,(2),(i) and (4)].

9. AISLE MARKING: The major pathways for the forklift truck and for personnel need to be maintained continually by clear markings. Mr. Smith seemed satisfied with the floor markings in Plant 2.

10. We need to locate a FIRE EXTINGUISHER near the paint spray area in Plant 2.

11. We need to maintain the STAIRWAYS in the plant free from the buildup of residues and slippery materials.

In addition to these requirement, Mr. Smith made a number of suggestions during the walk-around:

1. Install grounded plug on Floflex Lab refrigerator.
2. Install cover plate on Floflex lab hood switch.
3. Establish some color-coding or other identifying system for pipes in urethane area.
4. Eliminate slide-bolt locks on urethane area personnel door.
5. Insulate steam pipes near stairway on rear wall of urethane area.
6. Cover solvents kept in open buckets.
7. Post the capacity of 1-ton hoist on either side of the beam. Make periodic checks for wear and stretching of the chain and hook.
8. Provide a chain clip for electrical bonding between drum and pump nozzle in the solvent room.
9. Involve production hourly personnel, as well as management, in a program of regular safety meetings and inspections.

Mr. Smith did feel that housekeeping in the plant was good, considering the type of materials that we process and the amounts used. While commending us on this, he also suggested continual efforts to improve problem areas.

C. A. Rainey
2/15/74

QUESTIONS FOR DISCUSSION

1. If you were the manager what steps would you take immediately?
2. How would you evaluate the seriousness of the inspector's observations, concern, and/or suggestions, as opposed to the "chapter-and-verse" kind of comments?
3. How could a company organize itself so as to feel the minimum impact from an OSHA inspection?

Part **VII**

Maintaining Financial Health

No business is stronger than its financial strength and vitality. Today, among the greatest requirements for success in small business are an appreciation of the importance of financial management, an understanding of financial relationships, and the devotion of time, energy, and initiative to this difficult activity. The rewards are worth effort, though, for this is how your firm will not only survive, but grow and develop.

In this part, you will study the procedures for analyzing and evaluating your financial operations and position in Chapter 21; the "how to" of records keeping in Chapter 22; the need for, and methods to use in, planning your profit in Chapter 23; how to budget and control for financial viability in Chapter 24; and what you can do to safeguard your assets in Chapter 25.

21

Evaluating Your Financial Position and Operation

Your company operates through the decisions made and the activities performed. As the company operates, its financial position changes. Cash received for sales increases your bank balance. But then you spend it for materials, thereby increasing your inventory. At the same time, machines are decreasing in value, goods are being processed by employees, and utilities are being used. The value of your firm is constantly changing.

However, the important question is whether your company is improving its chances of attaining its objectives. One objective is to make a profit, but there are many problems involved. Some companies have made a profit, and still have failed. Profits are not necessarily cash. Profits may be reflected in accounts receivable, and those accounts may not be collectible. Too much money may be tied up in other assets which are not available to pay your bills.

You may have had this trouble in your own finances. Your salary or income may be adequate to pay for your food, clothing, and other operating expenses. However, you may need a new house or car for which you must make a down payment in the form of cash. Your funds are invested in a fixed asset and they are not available for you to use to pay your bills.

We have discussed your accounting records and have mentioned assets, liabilities, owners' equity, income, and expenses. You must make sure that the interrelationships between these accounts are satisfactory.

For example, what amount of cash reduces your income-producing possibilities? An increased investment in building and equipment reduces your ability to pay your operating expenses. Increases in liabilities increase your obligations and monthly payments. Therefore, you need to study your firm's financial structure to assure its being able to do the things that it needs to do. The continued operation of your company depends upon maintaining the proper balance between its investments, expenses, and income. These subjects are discussed in the balance of this chapter, and are divided into two parts:

1. The meaning of each of the accounts and how it affects the company's operations.
2. Methods of evaluating a company's financial condition, and important ratios and their meanings.

We will use The Sample Company as an illustration as we go through the financial analysis.

FINANCIAL ACCOUNTS OF THE FIRM

The financial structure of your firm is reflected in its assets, liabilities, and equity. These accounts are interrelated and interact with each other. See Figure 21–1 for location of the accounts on the balance sheet.

Assets

As has been stated, assets are the physical, financial, or other values which your company has. Assets are divided into *current* and *fixed* assets. Current assets are those that turn over—that is, they change from one form to another—within one year. For example, it is expected that accounts receivable will be paid and converted into cash within one year and that inventory will also be converted into sales within that period.

Current Assets. The first item of current assets is cash. It includes the currency—bills and coins—you have in the cash register, the deposits in your checking account in the bank, and other noninterest-bearing values that you can convert into cash immediately. When cash is available, it means that you can pay today's bills. It is the most liquid of any of the accounts.

A certain level of cash is necessary to operate a business. However, cash does not produce income. Too much cash means that the company has reduced its income-producing capacity. Yet, you cannot pay your bills if you do not have cash. Therefore, a certain level of cash must be maintained, but not at too high a level.

Accounts receivable is a current asset which results from giving credit to customers when they buy your goods. Your company may sell entirely on credit, which should help it maintain a level of sales volume.

FIGURE 21–1

THE SAMPLE CO.
Balance Sheet
December 31, 19–

Assets

Current Assets:
Cash	$ 3,527	
Accounts receivable	30,242	
Inventory	40,021	
Prepaid expenses	523	
Total current assets		$74,313

Fixed Assets
Equipment	$30,250	
Building	20,475	
	$50,725	
Less reserve for depreciation	8,450	
Net fixed assets		42,275
Total Assets		$116,588

Liabilities

Current Liabilities:
Accounts payable	$25,674	
Accrued payables	1,530	
Total current liabilities		$27,204

Long-Term Liabilities
Mortgage payable		10,354
Total Liabilities		$ 37,558

Net Worth (Equity)
Capital stock	$60,000	
Retained earnings	19,030	
Total Net Worth		79,030
Total Liabilities plus Net Worth		$116,588

This is a service which your customers will usually want. While extension of credit implies future payment by the customer, some customers—fortunately, only a few—do not pay their accounts. Care must be exercised to select customers who will pay within a reasonable period of time. Policies should be set on the terms of payment and how much credit will be extended.

Credit is a cost to the company. Cash has not been received and therefore the money can not be used for paying your own expenses or buying other goods. Several means are used to decrease the impact of this, including the following:

1. You may factor your accounts receivable. Under this arrangement, your company sells its accounts receivable and receives cash less a fee.
2. Your company may honor one or more of the many kinds of credit cards.

Note that both types of transactions make it easier for you to pay your company's obligations, but they also result in an expense to the company. This expense may be offset by increased sales (or maybe not a loss in sales) and a reduction in needed assets.

Too large an investment in accounts receivable will place your company in considerable financial strain. Your investments of financial resources in the company must be increased and the chance of your incurring a high expense because of bad debts is increased.

Inventory is an asset which provides a buffer between purchase, production, and sale of the product, as discussed in Chapter 17. A company must maintain some level of inventory to serve the customers when they demand, or request, a product. Some sales are made on the basis of availability. On the other hand, a customer may want a special item and be willing to wait until it is ordered and delivered.

However, there are costs resulting from carrying inventory. Your money is tired up, space is used, products must be maintained and can become obsolete, and so forth. Also, inventory, as such, is not an income-producing asset. The amount of inventory to carry depends upon a judicious balancing of costs. In addition, too high a level of inventory places a financial burden on the firm.

Other current asset accounts might include *short-term investment, prepaid items,* and *accrued income.* Usually, these are only a small percentage of the current assets and need little attention.

Fixed Assets. *Buildings, machinery, store fixtures, trucks,* and *land* are included as fixed assets. The company expects to own them for considerable time and writes off part of their cost each period as a depreciation expense.

Different types of fixed assets have different lengths of useful life. Land is not depreciated; buildings are usually depreciated over a period of 20 years: machinery, over 5–10 years; and store equipment, 2–10 years. The amount of fixed assets should be related to the needs of your company. Idle fixed assets are a financial drain and are usually avoided when possible.

Some companies find it advantageous to rent fixed assets instead of owning them. A retailer rents a store to reduce his need to make a large investment.

Whether you decide to rent or own your fixed assets will depend on the cost of rental, the period cost of owning, the availability of capital, and the freedom to operate.

Liabilities

A company obtains its funds by borrowing, creating an obligation to pay, and by owner investment. The first results in a liability to pay someone; the second results in owner's equity. *The total of the liabilities and the owner's equity always equals the total of the assets.* A company is wise to maintain a proper balance between the higher risk of investment by creditors and the investment by owners. The investment by creditors is divided into current liabilities and long-term liabilities.

Current liabilities are obligations which are to be paid within one year. They include *accounts payable, notes payable,* and *accrued items*—such as payroll—which are services performed for the company, but are not yet paid.

Accounts payable are usually due within 30 or 60 days, depending on the credit terms. The delay in required payment is the service a vendor provides to the buyer. A company maintains current assets to pay these accounts. A check should be made to determine if early payment is beneficial. Some companies offer a cash discount, such as 2 percent if paid in 10 days, for early payment. Maintenance of a high level of accounts payable requires a high level of current assets.

Notes payable, which are written obligations to pay, usually give the company a somewhat longer period before payment is required and usually require payment of interest. An example is a 90-day note.

Bonds and *mortgages* are the usual types of *long term liabilities.* A company contracts these when it purchases fixed assets, and the owners do not have sufficient equity to pay for the assets. Also, *long-term loans* may be used to supply a permanent amount of *working capital,* which is current assets less current liabilities. Small businesses use long-term borrowing as a source of funds much less frequently than do large businesses. This type of borrowing requires current payment of a fixed amount on the principal and a smaller amount for interest. These payments increase the risk to a company during slack times of being unable to meet its obligations.

Owner's Equity

Equity is the owners' share of the company after the liabilities are subtracted from the assets. The owners receive income from the profits of the company in the form of dividends or an increase in their share of the company through an increase in the retained earnings. They also absorb losses, which decrease the equity.

Capital stock is the value the owners invest in the company. A share of stock is issued in the form of a certificate and has a stated value on the books of the company. Additional shares can be sold or issued in place of cash dividends.

Retained earnings are the accumulation of the profits which are not distributed to the owners in cash dividends. *Cash dividends* reduce current assets. Since a company usually does not pay out all its profits in dividends, some earnings are retained as protection for the firm or to provide for its growth. Many small firms have failed because the owners paid out the profits as dividends too quickly. A long-range plan for paying dividends should be established.

The assets, liabilities, and equity accounts form the financial structure of a company at a point in time, but they tend to change from one period to the next. At regular intervals, a *balance sheet* is prepared to show the value of the company and how the funds are distributed.

The financial structure of a company is changed by the profit-making activities of the company. These activities are reflected in the revenue and expense accounts. (Net income = revenue — expenses.) During a given period, the company performs services for which it receives values. The financial values exchanged are shown by the profit and loss statement. (See Figure 21–2).

FIGURE 21–2

THE SAMPLE CO.
Profit and Loss Statement
January 1 through December 31, 19—

Net Sales.		$231,574
Less Cost of Goods Sold		145,631
Gross profit		$ 85,943
Operating Expenses:		
Salaries.	$41,569	
Utilities	3,475	
Depreciation.	5,025	
Rent	1,000	
Building services	2,460	
Insurance	2,000	
Interest	1,323	
Office and supplies	2,775	
Sales promotion	5,500	
Taxes and licenses	3,240	
Maintenance.	805	
Delivery	2,924	
Miscellaneous	875	
Total expenses		72,971
Net Income before Taxes		$ 12,972
Less income taxes		3,242
Net Income after Taxes		$ 9,730

Revenue and Expenses

Revenue is the return from services performed. Revenue is usually called sales income, and is received by the company in the form of cash or credit—an obligation of the customer to pay. Many companies also have other income, such as interest from investments.

Expenses are the costs of performing services. They include material, wages, insurance, utilities, transportation, depreciation, taxes, supplies, and sales promotion. These items become deductions from the revenue as they are used.

Profit

Profit is the difference between revenue and expenses. Profit is often classified as gross, operating, net before, and net after taxes—depending on the type of expenses deducted.

The values of these items are related to each other and to the structure of the company. Earlier, it was stated that a company has fixed assets which are income-producing. Are these assets being used efficiently? To find this, the relationship between the volume of sales income and the value of the fixed assets is determined and evaluated.

METHODS OF EVALUATING THE FIRM'S FINANCIAL CONDITION

Now that we have considered the financial structure and operations of a company, we should consider the methods of evaluating its financial condition. Look at Figures 21–1 and 21–2, which present the financial statements of The Sample Company. Is the company in a good financial position?

In Chapter 23, we will consider a method of analysis called *profit planning,* which can be used to anticipate the position for the coming year. Now, however, we would like to evaluate the company on a broader basis. Out of this evaluation, other changes can be made which may be better than those suggested. Also, the evaluation can lead to a strengthening of the company's financial structure.

The evaluation of the financial condition of a company is based upon establishing relationships between two or more variables. For example, the amount of current assets needed depends on other conditions of a company such as the size of the current liabilities. So, a *current ratio—* current assets divided by current liabilities—shows how easily a company can pay its current obligations. Another comparison can be made by subtracting current liabilities from current assets, with the resulting value called *working capital.* Unfortunately, no standard figures have been determined to be best for you to use, nor have any of them been found which can assure your success. Yet, a reasonable evaluation is necessary. Two sets of values which can be used for evaluation purposes are:

1. A comparison of the current value of ratios with those of the past.
2. A comparison of the ratios of your firm with other similar ones.

Values of Each Ratio in the Past

A change in the value of selected ratios for a firm indicates a change in its financial position. For example, suppose the current ratio for The Sample Company has moved gradually from a value of 1.0 to 3.0. The firm has moved to a more liquid position and, therefore, looks good. However, this improvement may be due to keeping old uncollectible accounts on the books. In that case, the company would not be more liquid. While the trend does indicate a change, only in-depth analyses can determine the causes.

Values of Other Like Companies

Average and range of values for the ratios are published for a large variety of small to large companies. Some of these firms will fail, but the averages are ranges which provide a guide to what other companies are doing. Suppose the current ratio of companies with assets of $250,000 or less is found to be 2.3 to 1, while The Sample Company has a ratio of 3.0 to 1. Again, the company's ratio looks good. However, it may be losing income by maintaining too many nonproductive assets.

In the past, a ratio of 2 to 1 has been used as a rule-of-thumb for the current ratio. However, no one value of a ratio is optimum for all companies.

IMPORTANT RATIOS AND THEIR MEANINGS

The ratios and percentages are valuable in answering a number of questions that you may ask yourself about your company. By obtaining answers to these questions, you can make plans to correct deficiencies in the operations and structure of your company. When a ratio is mentioned, look at Figure 21–3 for the method of computation of the ratios. Spaces are provided for you to compute the ratio for The Sample Company using the data provided in Figures 21–1 and 21–2. Comparable figures for the industry are provided for comparative purposes.

Are you making an adequate or reasonable return on your investment? The *ratio of net profit to net worth* [often called return on investment (ROI)] is used to evaluate this, but several other ratios should be considered to aid in profit planning and to make decisions.

How much return is your company making on its sales dollar? The *ratio of net profit to net sales* provides this information. Suppose The Sample Company makes four cents per dollar of sales. Is the trend up or down? How does it compare with other like companies? If it is dropping, why? Your costs may be increasing without an increase in price. Your competitors may be keeping their prices low and you

FIGURE 21–3
Financial Ratios

Ratio	Formula	The Sample Company	Industry Average (percent)
1. Net profit to net worth	$\dfrac{\text{Net profit before taxes}}{\text{Net worth}}$ = _____		18.4
2. Net profit to net sales	$\dfrac{\text{Net profit before taxes}}{\text{Net sales}}$ = _____		3.1
3. Net sales to fixed assets	$\dfrac{\text{Net sales}}{\text{Fixed assets}}$ = _____		5.8
4. Net sales to net worth	$\dfrac{\text{Net sales}}{\text{Owner's equity}}$ = _____		7.5
5. Current ratio	$\dfrac{\text{Current assets}}{\text{Current liabilities}}$ = _____		1.3
6. Acid test	$\dfrac{\text{Current assets-inventory}}{\text{Current liabilities}}$ = _____		1.0
7. Receivables to working capital	$\dfrac{\text{Accounts receivable}}{\text{Working capital}}$ = _____		1.2
8. Inventory to working capital	$\dfrac{\text{Inventory}}{\text{Working capital}}$ = _____		0.4
9. Collection period	$\dfrac{\text{Accounts receivable}}{\text{Average daily credit sales}}$ = _____ *		43.0 Days
10. Net sales to inventory	$\dfrac{\text{Net sales}}{\text{Inventory}}$ = _____		22.0
11. Net sales to working capital	$\dfrac{\text{Net sales}}{\text{Working capital}}$ = _____		10.0
12. Long term liabilities to working capital	$\dfrac{\text{Long term liabilities}}{\text{Working capital}}$ = _____		0.7
13. Debt to net worth	$\dfrac{\text{Total liabilities}}{\text{Net worth}}$ = _____		1.6
14. Current liabilities to net worth	$\dfrac{\text{Current liabilities}}{\text{Owner's equity}}$ = _____		1.1
15. Fixed assets to net worth	$\dfrac{\text{Fixed assets}}{\text{Owner's equity}}$ = _____		1.2

* If 80% of sales are on credit: average daily credit sales = $\dfrac{\text{annual sales}}{365} \times 0.80 = \dfrac{\quad}{365} \times$ 0.80 = _____.

need to keep yours low in order to compete. You may be trying to obtain a large sales volume at the expense of profit. An increase in sales volume with the same net profit per dollar of sales will increase your ROI, but if you need to reduce the return on a dollar of sales, your ROI may decrease.

Does your company obtain enough sales from its producing assets? This is reflected in the *ratio of net sales to fixed assets*—your fixed assets representing the producing units of the company. This is only a general guide, for so many variables exist—such as leasing instead of owning fixed assets—that the ratio can change with changes in policies. Still, trends and good use of industry data make this a valuable ratio.

Does your company have enough sales for the amount of investment? The *ratio of net sales to net worth* provides a guide to this evaluation. Note that this ratio can be combined with the profit to sales ratio to obtain the ROI.

Can you pay your current obligations? A number of ratios can be valuable to you. The best known is the *current ratio*, that is, the current assets to current liabilities. You may be making a good profit, but not be able to pay your debts, for cash does not necessarily increase when you make a profit.

The *acid test ratio*, that is, the current assets minus inventory to current liabilities, is used to make a further check.

Another check is obtained by using *working capital*, or current assets less current liabilities, as a basis. Working capital is the margin of safety your company has in paying its current liabilities.

The *ratios of accounts receivable and inventory to working capital* provide an insight into the riskiness of the company's ability to make current payments.

How good are your current assets? Cash in hand is the best current asset. Accounts receivable represent what the company will receive in cash from customers some time in the future. However, the older an account is, the greater the expectation of loss. The *collection period ratio*, that is accounts receivable to average daily credit sales, provides a guide as to the "goodness" of your accounts receivable. Suppose The Sample Company has set a 30-day payment period for its customers and its collection period ratio is 50 days. Many accounts are less than 30 days old, so many other accounts must be over two months old. Apparently, Mr. Sample is not adequately checking on those to whom he extends credit, he is carrying bad accounts, or he is not exerting enough effort to reduce the slow payments of accounts. Periodically, each account in accounts receivable should be reviewed for its collectability. A system of control of accounts receivable is discussed in the next chapter.

Inventories can be evaluated in about the same way as accounts receivable. Goods in inventory become obsolete if not sold within a reasonable time. Therefore, inventory should be "turned over" during the year. The turnover rate is expressed by the *ratio of the net sales to inventory*. A turnover of inventory of six times each year for a company is good if turnover for the industry is five. If your company is turning over its inventory too slowly, you may be keeping obsolete goods. Too high a ratio may result from so low an inventory that it is hurting production or not providing necessary customer services.

To obtain an idea of the support that a company is receiving from its current assets, *the ratio of net sales to working capital* may be computed. Accounts receivable and inventory should increase with an increase in sales, but not out of proportion. Payroll and other expense increases require a higher level of cash outflow. On the other hand, too low a ratio indicates surplus working capital is available to service the sales.

How much equity should your company have? Assets are financed by either equity investments or the creation of liabilities. Retained profits are part of equity and can be used to increase your assets or decrease your liabilities. You can maintain a high level of equity with a relatively low level of risk, or a relatively high level of liabilities with a higher expected return on equity.

Most small companies do not like to maintain a large amount of long term debt. The risk is too great. The common ratios used for checking the company's source of funds relationships are:

1. Total liabilities to net worth.
2. Current liabilities to net worth.
3. Long term liabilities to working capital.
4. Fixed assets to net worth.

If any of these are extremely high, the company is in a risky situation. A bad year decreases the income, but the obligation to pay continues.

More questions can be asked and you can develop more relationships to guide you in analyzing your company's financial strengths and weaknesses. Each ratio is an indicator of only part of the company's position. The ratios overlap because a company is a complex system so that a change in the size of one of the accounts, such as cash, will change other values.

The financial ratios for the items on the profit and loss statement are usually expressed in percentages of sales. This information is usually hard to obtain from competing firms, but when it can be, it can point to any out-of-line costs. High cost of goods sold as a percentage of sales income may indicate a poor choice of vendors, inefficient use of material or labor, or too low a price. A high percentage of salaries may indicate an overstaffing of the company.

SUMMARY

This chapter has provided a set of tools for analyzing your company's financial condition and operations. The next chapter presents some methods for maintaining your accounting records. These will help you in your profit planning and control activities discussed in later chapters.

QUESTIONS FOR FURTHER DISCUSSION

1. Compute the ratios listed in Figure 21–3 for The Sample Company.
2. Evaluate the financial condition of The Sample Company.
3. What might be some recommendations you could make to the owner of The Sample Company?
4. Make an evaluation of your personal financial structure and operations. What steps can you take to improve them?

22

Your Accounting Records

Have you ever considered how many records you possess or generate? You probably have in your possession a driver's license, credit cards, student activity card, social security card, and/or checkbook.

Without these records, you would be unable to transact much of your business. When you use one of these, records—or entries in the records—are generated. For example, suppose you use a credit card. This generates a sales slip, an account for you, a bill, and a record of payment. You use the bill to write a check and to deduct the amount from your bank balance. At the same time, you keep some information in your head to save time in filling out forms. While this informal method may be all right for you as a student, it is not sufficient for you as a small business manager. Instead, you need a system of records to aid human memory. A business has a much more extensive set of records than an individual, because it has many more transactions and more people involved.

Earlier in this book, you read about the information needed to make financial, marketing, personnel, and production decisions. Much of the information needed for decision making is carried in employees' heads. However, certain types of information are more valuable if brought together from a variety of sources, related in a systematic way, recorded accurately, kept permanently, and made available to the people who need them. A procedure is needed to provide the needed information in the proper manner.

With the increasing complexity of business, the amount of paperwork has expanded. However, records need to be kept in as simple and inexpensive a manner as possible—while providing the required information. How can this be achieved? By knowing what information is needed, by obtaining and storing information with little copying and recording, and by storing information for easy retrieval, you may achieve this.

The proper design of a record-keeping system is important to a business and need not be too expensive. Yet, any acceptable system will deal effectively with the following factors:

1. What information is needed.
2. Recording the information.
3. The storing of information.

These factors are discussed in detail in this chapter.

WHAT INFORMATION IS NEEDED

In determining what information is needed, you should ask: For what purposes do I want the data? The usual answers are:

1. To plan ahead. Past information can be used for planning the future. Examples might be past sales trends, sales per salesperson, output from a machine, delivery time for a purchase, quality of output of an employee, payment experience from a given customer, and demand for a particular product at a given time.
2. To meet obligations. For example, money is borrowed, material is purchased on credit, delivery is promised for a certain day at a certain price, and taxes are due.
3. To control activities. Many activities are routine, but vital, to the firm and can be checked by a clerk. For example, material ordered has not arrived, inventory has reached zero, losses in supplies are occurring, and too much time is being spent on routine work. By having guidelines and "warning flags," a clerk saves the manager time by performing the control function and obtaining the material.
4. To satisfy the government. For example, the government collects taxes; requires conformance to safety, fair employment, and price control standards; and checks on ethical standards of business practice.
5. To evaluate performance. Evaluation is obtained from review of selected records and reports.

In addition to determining the information needed, you must know how to use it. This involves classifying it into a usable form. The information for accounting purposes has been classified in Chapter 21 as follows:

1. Assets.
2. Liabilities.
3. Owners' equity or net worth.
4. Revenue or sales income.
5. Expenses.

Many other pieces of information are needed, including economic and market conditions, personnel history and capabilities, sources of material, and specifications for products. Systems and procedures need to be established to assure the availability of critical information. This area is beyond the scope of this book.

Service to Customers

These transactions provide both the income and an expense of doing business. When you perform a service—such as the sale of a product, repair of an auto, or rental of an apartment—cash, check, or an IOU is received in exchange for goods and/or labor. Recordings on slips and tapes are used to accumulate the changes in the affected records. For example, the cash sale of a pair of socks increases your cash. Yet, it creates the obligation to pay sales taxes and reduces your inventory of socks. See Figure 22–1 for a flow chart of the transfer of data, cash, and goods. A credit slip is used to reverse the above transaction when goods are returned.

Services Performed for You

These transactions originate your expenses of doing business. Materials, parts, and finished products are purchased to be transformed or sold. Employees are paid for work performed. Electricity is consumed, taxes are paid, advertising promotes the products, and supplies are used. Also, the service performed may increase the assets of the company— such as equipment and machine purchases, building construction, and stock investments. A somewhat different type of service fitting this category is the floating of bonds to obtain cash or credit. All these types of transactions generate obligations and initate transfers of data within an accounting system, as shown in Figure 22–1 and Figure 22–2.

Other Activities

Many matters of a nonaccounting nature initiate other records. Sources for these include inquiry letters, agreements on sales, complaints, and implementation of controls over physical units.

FIGURE 22–1
Accounting for Sales

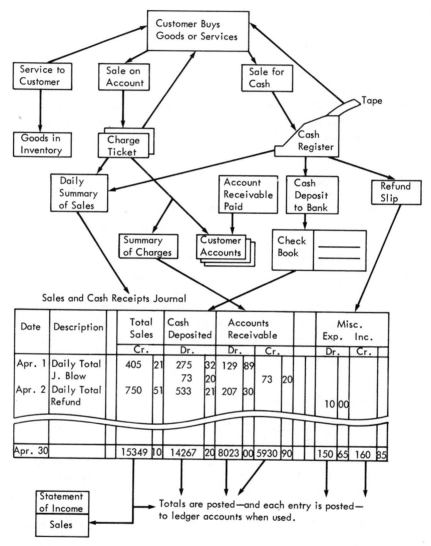

RECORDING THE INFORMATION

All transactions involving accounting information must be recorded so that your accounts will be "in balance." The system used to record the information this way is known as the *double-entry* system of accounting. When a sale is made for cash, income is increased and cash—an asset—is increased by the same amount; conversely, inventory is de-

FIGURE 22–2
Accounting for Purchases

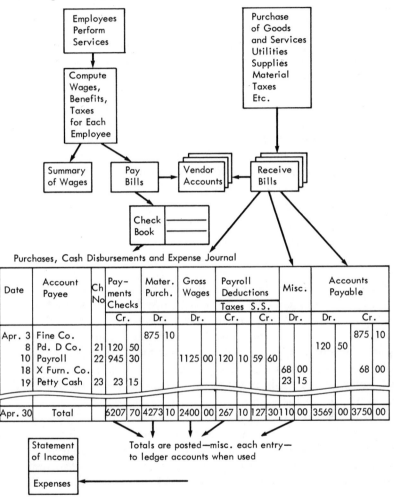

Purchases, Cash Disbursements and Expense Journal

Date	Account Payee	Ch No	Pay-ments Checks Cr.	Mater. Purch. Dr.	Gross Wages Dr.	Payroll Deductions — Taxes Cr.	Payroll Deductions — S.S. Cr.	Misc. Dr.	Accounts Payable Dr.	Accounts Payable Cr.
Apr. 3	Fine Co.			875 10						875 10
8	Pd. D Co.	21	120 50						120 50	
10	Payroll	22	945 30		1125 00	120 10	59 60			
18	X Furn. Co.							68 00		68 00
19	Petty Cash	23	23 15					23 15		
Apr. 30	Total		6207 70	4273 10	2400 00	267 10	127 30	110 00	3569 00	3750 00

Totals are posted—misc. each entry—
to ledger accounts when used

creased. When material is purchased on credit, inventory—an asset—is increased and accounts payable—a liability is increased by a like amount. A machine wears out. So periodically, depreciation is deducted from assets, and expenses are increased by the same amount. Notice in all of these transactions that the changes are made so that the *sum* of assets + expenses = the *sum* of liabilities + equity + income. The amount of the totals may change, but they change by the same amount.

The accounting system starts with the tapes and other items discussed under *sources,* and includes journals and ledger accounts. The journal is the original book of entry, and records the daily transactions in chronological order. To group like items together, the chronological entries are entered individually or as totals in ledger accounts. A ledger account might be set up for each of the accounts listed in Figure 21–1. The amount of detail depends on the needs of your company and its other records. For example, journals and statements may be used to show the income and expenses, whereas only the profit—the difference between income and expenses—is shown in a ledger account. Under all circumstances, the ledger accounts must balance.

Figures 22–1 and 22–2 diagram the flow of data for some of the more common entries in the accounting records of a small business. The following sections discuss some transactions and entries to help you to understand the system of recording information. (The month is used for the time period for adjustments to emphasize the need for frequent review of the results of your operations. Some of the formal accounting illustrated may be performed only once a year, often by an accountant. But, hopefully, the examples explain the concepts.)

Sales

The sale of your products or the service you perform is the source of profit. In every company, a record must be kept of each sale made. The auto repair shop makes a record of the charges to the customer for labor hours and parts used. A *sales slip* is completed when a radio is sold. The number, type, unit price, and total price of the radio should be entered on the slip. On all items sold, the sales tax must be recorded. Cash sales, when cash registers are available, can be recorded on a tape to be used as the sales slip.

Information on the sales forms is used to accumulate the sales income, to reduce inventory, to make analyses for future plans, and—in the case of a credit sale—to enter in the *accounts receivable record* for the customer. To eliminate the totaling of sales slips, cash registers can be used which total the daily sales. When many different items and people are involved, the registers can total by variables, including type of product, sales person, or department. The classification should be aligned with the types of analysis you will make and with the controls to be exercised.

Sales are entered in a *sales journal*. This shows the daily summary or the individual item depending on the detail desired. The sales journal can be multi-columnar paper to provide additional information, such as how much was sold for cash (or credit card and account) in each department, of each type of product, and by each salesman. If you analyze this sheet, it can provide information on sales trends, where the major volume is, or who is selling the most. Figure 22–1 provides an illustration of a sales and cash receipts journal.

The totals of the columns of the sales journal are transferred to the income statement and/or the sales income ledger account.

Cash Income and Outgo

When services are sold, the total of the recordings for cash, credits, and other values must equal the sales income recorded in order to balance the accounts. The accounting for cash is most important, as cash is negotiable anywhere. The person handling cash can mishandle it so that losses will occur. The recording system for cash should be designed and established with care so as to minimize losses.

When sales are made for cash, the goods sold and the cash received should be recorded independently of each other—if possible. Also, in order to maintain control, only certain people are allowed to handle company cash, and only on an individual basis. Each person starts with a standard amount for change, and the cash balance is reconciled each day or more often. The reconciliation checks that the cash on hand equals the beginning cash on hand plus cash sales less cash returns.

The waitress makes out the bill for a customer at a restaurant and a cashier receives the money. The gas pumps record the total gallons pumped, the price, and the total amount of the sale, and the gas station attendant collects the cash. The cash register, placed in view of the customer when he pays his bill, allows the customer to check the cash recording.

Checks are not as negotiable as cash, but are handled with the cash. One extra step is required. To guard against losses from bad checks, a method of identification of the person presenting the check is established. Past experience with payment by check often determines the policy to follow. Some companies accept only cash; some require identification such as driver's license and social security card, the number of which is recorded on the check; and some accept the check without formal identification. A proper balance between safeguarding against losses and making the customer feel he is receiving a personal service should be maintained.

At the end of each day, standard amounts of money are retained to make change the next day and the rest is deposited in the bank. *Deposit slips* are forwarded to the bank with the money and the amount deposited is added to the checkbook stub balance.

Payments are made by check or, if for small items, from petty cash. The *checkbook* can be used as a ledger account by adding bank deposits and deducting each check on the checkbook stubs. Each check is entered in the *cash journal* to show the account to which it is charged.

It often becomes too expensive to pay small bills by check, as for example, payments of $5 and under. A *petty cash fund*—say, $25 or $50 in cash—can be used to pay these bills. Each payment should be recorded on a form to keep track of the account and amount paid. The sum of the amounts on this record, plus the cash in the account, should always total the figure set for the size of the fund. Periodically, the fund is replenished by check to the set figure, and the expenditures recorded transferred to the appropriate accounts in the *cash journal.*

Accounts Receivable

When your customers buy goods using *credit cards* or *open accounts,* each sales slip either is entered on a customer account record or is filed under the customer's name. These records are details of the *accounts receivable account* and are totaled periodically to compare with the account. Any differences should be investigated. At the end of each period—usually a month—all customers' accounts are totaled and bills sent to them. As payments are received, the amounts of the checks are recorded in each customer's account and totaled for entry in the *sales and cash receipts journal.* A discussion of the decisions regarding credit is included in Chapter 24.

Periodically, a review of the individual *accounts receivable records* provides information about the status of the accounts, who is slow in paying, and which accounts need follow-up. The follow-up methods include delinquent notices, personal contact, and use of a collection agency. Some should be written off by charging them to *bad debts* when they cannot be collected. Other information can also be obtained, including identification of your large customers, what kinds of items they buy, and who has stopped buying your services.

Credit card sales are totaled by each credit card company and, after service charges are deducted, are processed through the bank. Gross sales are entered as sales income, as are accounts receivable and cash sales; the service charge is charged to that account; and the accounts receivable or cash account posted, depending on the procedure.

Some transactions—such as installment sales, damaged or lost goods, and income from insurance of damaged equipment—require more complex accounting procedures than are being presented. For these, we recommend consulting with an accountant or studying an accounting text.

Accounts Payable

An operating business incurs many obligations for material and equipment purchases, wages, utilities, taxes, and notes payable. These are reported in a *purchase and cash disbursements journal*. Practically all purchases are paid by check, and the number of individual payments is relatively small.

Bills and *invoices* can be filed by date to be paid, and when paid, filed as a history of *accounts payable*. As each initiating record is received, it is entered in the purchases and cash disbursements journal, as shown in Figure 22–2. Notice the columns used to classify the expenses and the "Miscellaneous" column used for expenses or assets for which there are few bills each month. Columns are used for accounts in which many entries occur during a month. For example, each month many purchases are made of a variety of materials, products, parts, and supplies for which one or more columns are provided. Few purchases of office equipment are made in a year, so they are handled in the miscellaneous column. Utilities might warrant a separate column. As a payment is made, the bill is marked and filed and the amount is entered on the check stub and in the purchases and cash disbursements journal. As with accounts receivable, there are complex transactions about which you should consult an accountant or an accounting book.

Inventory

One of the troublesome records to keep is that for inventory. The problem of inventory was discussed in Chapter 17. A number of methods are used to assist the manager in maintaining records of his stock. All are based on a systematic method of spotting a low inventory item—that is, there are some methods which help "wave a warning flag" when the inventory is below a predetermined standard. These methods include setting aside the standard amount, setting aside an amount of space, making a regular physical count of the items, and for bulky material, flashing a light. A business selling a high volume of many items, like a grocery store, depends on visual inspection of the number of items on the shelf by several people, each assigned to certain items. For slower-moving and fewer items, the paper work is not increased very much by keeping a *perpetual inventory record*. (See Figure 17–4.) All the methods require determining the amount of the minimum or standard amount left in inventory before ordering.

A record is made of the sale and the physical movement of an item when it is sold. The recording of the removal to expense is handled in two ways. First, for high-volume and a multiplicity of items, the purchased items are charged to expense directly and adjusted at the end of the period for the inventory obtained by a physical count of the items. This reduces the volume of transfer recordings out of inventory into expense required of the second method. The second method uses perpetual inventory recordings described above, with added columns in the form for dollar values of units. The total cost of units used is the material expense. This method is usually used by manufacturing companies.

Expenses

Your business will purchase services from other people, and these will become expenses as they are used. Material is transformed and sold, electricity is used, machines decrease in value, and insurance protection is based on time. The bases of payments for these costs of doing business vary from daily to over five years, and an item's use may be delayed for years. In order to determine your true profit, income and expenses must be determined for the same period, say for January, 19—.

Many small businesses compute their profit on a cash basis rather than on the accrual basis. The *accrual basis* makes adjustments to align income and expenses. The *cash basis* charges the items as they are actually paid. The cash basis is used for simplicity and, as will be seen, is not a pure cash procedure. The cash basis assumes that payments and use are in the same period or that payments do not vary from one period to another. The analysis of the method to choose should balance the validity of the result against the cost of getting a more accurate picture.

The procedure for obtaining the expenses by the accrual method is:

1. Obtain the values for all assets, payments, and obligations.
2. Determine how much of each has been used during the period.
3. Transfer the used portion to expense, reduce the asset, or increase the obligation.

A number of examples of this procedure are shown below. (See Figure 22–3 for sample recordings of each.)

1. *Material for sale in a retail store.* The expense of material = beginning inventory + purchases — ending inventory.
2. *Insurance.* Insurance may be paid monthly, quarterly, or annually for the period ahead. Usually, annual payments reduce the cost and, by spreading the payment of different policies over the year, payment can be distributed to different months. Insurance is usually charged to expenses when paid and, for monthly statements, one-twelfth is charged to expenses and the remainder of payments placed in an asset account for prepaid insurance. This adjustment is not necessary when the monthly payment is close to one-twelfth the annual cost (the latter is a cash-basis type of accounting).
3. *Wages and salaries.* These expenses are paid regularly after the employees have performed a service for the business. By paying salaries for a month at the end of the month, salaries are the expense

FIGURE 22–3

Examples of Recordings and Adjustments of Transactions

1. Receive order for material X, $100, entered when received.
   Used $80 of material X, entered at end of period.

Cash		Material Purchase Expense		Material Inventory	
$100 ←		→ $100	$20 ←	→ $20	
(decrease)		(increase)	(decrease)	(increase)	

or

Cash		Material Inventory		Material Expense	
$100 ←		→ $100	$80 ←	→ $80	
(decrease)		(increase)	(decrease)	(increase)	

2. Paid insurance policy, $75, entered when paid.
   Monthly expense of insurance, $50 (1/12 of annual $600), entered
   at end of period.

Cash		Insurance Expense		(cash basis)
$75 ←		→ $75		
(decrease)		(increase)		

or

Cash		Prepaid Insurance		Insurance Expense	
$75 ←		→ $75	$50 ←	→ $50	
(decrease)		(increase)	(decrease)	(increase)	

3. Paid wages, $2,400 (160 hours x $3.00 per hour x 5 workers) (from
   payroll book). Wages paid for last month's work, $480 (32 hours)
   x $3.00 per hour x 5 workers). Work not paid this month, $600 (40
   hours x $3.00 x 5 workers).

Cash		Wages Expense		(cash basis)
$2,400 ←		→ $2,400		
(decrease)		(increase)		

or

Cash		Wages Expense		Accrued Expense	
$2,400 ←		→ $2,400	$480 ←	→ $480	$480 (from last
		$600 ←			→ $600 month)
(decrease)		(increase)	(decrease)	(decrease)	(increase)

4. Have machine which cost $1,300. From machine records, machine
   expense, $20—machine cost, $1,300 less estimated scrap value,
   $100—divided by estimated life, 5 years (60 months).

Reserve for Depreciation		Depreciation Expense	
$20 ←		→ $20	
(increase)		(increase)	

of the month and need no adjustment. When wages are paid, say every two weeks, the payment is for the past two weeks, which often covers work in the previous month. At the end of the month, wages have not been paid for part of the month, so a liability exists for accured wages. Adjustments between labor and accrued wages are made. Subsidiary records are usually kept to compute the wages, salaries, employee benefits, and company payments for social security and so forth.

4. *Machinery, equipment, and buildings.* These are used up over a period of years. On a monthly basis, the expense of a machine

$$= \frac{\text{cost of machine} - \text{sale value at end of expected life}}{\text{expected life}}.$$

This figure remains constant until the assets are sold, added to, or used up.

Maintaining the original cost of machinery and equipment in the records is valuable. The cost of using the machine, which is called *depreciation,* is an estimate and the reduction in value for depreciation is kept in a separate account, called *reserve for depreciation.*

Many other items of expense and income need the same types of adjustment as just discussed. The main points to determine are: How much of the cost is used up during the period? How much is an asset? How much is a liability? Find the easiest way to assign the proper values to expenses, income, assets, and liabilities. These records can now be used for analysis and for making reports.

Financial Statements

During each period—say on a daily or weekly basis—a check should be made of a few critical accounts, such as sales, for trends and other changes which are occurring. This enables you to anticipate changes that may be needed. Shortages or overages of stock may be detected.

Financial statements are prepared from accounting records to aid management in its analyses. They are a profit and loss statement and a *balance sheet* (see Figures 21–1 and 21–2). The accounts are grouped so that a financial analysis can be performed, as discussed in Chapter 21. Profit and loss statements should be prepared monthly, and balance sheets less often,—perhaps semi-annually.

Tax reports are completed for the various government divisions many times during the year. These include reports for income, sales, social security, and excise taxes. As reporting requires an understanding of the regulations which change periodically, you are advised to see the Internal Revenue Service, accountants, or one of the appropriate tax pamphlets on these reports.

THE STORING OF INFORMATION

The records of your company are very important to you and should be treated accordingly. Care should be exercised to see that records are not lost, stolen, burned, or otherwise destroyed. Critical records should be kept in a safe; others may be placed where they are readily available. Systematic arrangements for keeping records can save time and money in processing information and protecting the records.

SUMMARY

How we hate records keeping! Yet, it is now essential for survival as a small business or even as an individual, especially at income tax preparation and auditing time.

Considerable detailed, specific, and practical material was furnished in this chapter which should be of help to you in coping with this problem. Specifically, we made suggestions for dealing effectively with: (1) deciding what information is needed; (2) locating sources where information can be found; (3) recording information in appropriate places; and (4) storing it where it can be retrieved when needed.

We also provided tables, figures, journals, and statements to serve as guidelines for you to use in your business.

QUESTIONS FOR FURTHER DISCUSSION

1. What management decisions do you need to make?
2. What information do you need to make those decisions?
3. For what purposes does a business want information?
4. How can the needed information be classified?
5. What are some sources of information you need?
6. Discuss the recording of information.
7. Discuss the following: sales account, cash income and outgo, accounts receivable, accounts payable, inventory, and expenses.

23

Planning Your Profits

When you "read" the profit and loss statement in Figure 21–2, you may tend to read the statement in the following order: "The Sample Company received $231,574 in sales, expended $145,631 for cost of goods sold, had $72,971 of other expenses, and had $12,972 left over as profit." It seems that profit was a "leftover."

Neither you nor Mr. Sample, owner-manager of The Sample Company, can do anything about the past. However, you can do something about the future. Since one of your goals is to make a profit, you should plan your operations so that you attain the profit you feel you should make from the business. The steps you need to take to achieve this goal during the coming year are:

1. Establish your profit goal.
2. Determine your planned volume of sales.
3. Estimate your expenses for planned volume of sales.
4. Determine your estimated profit based on plans reached in (2) and (3).
5. Compare your estimated profit with your profit goal.

If you are satisfied with your plans, you can stop after completing Step 5. However, you may want to check further to determine whether improvements can be made—particularly if you are not happy with the results of Step 5. The following steps may help you understand better how certain changes in your business activities may affect your profit. They are:

6. List possible alternatives which can be used to improve your profit position.
7. Determine how costs vary with changes in sales volume.
8. Determine how profits vary with changes in sales volume.
9. Analyze your alternatives from a profit standpoint.
10. Select changes in your plans, if any, and implement the changes through the use of budgets.

You should be realistic when going through these steps; otherwise you may not be able to attain your goals. You may feel the future is too uncertain to make such plans, but the greater the uncertainty, the greater the need for planning.

> The president of a company said that his forecast was too inaccurate to use, so he had stopped forecasting. The company was not very successful, and he had to sell out.

> Recently, the owner of a small business complained that she could not forecast next year's revenue within 20 percent of actual sales. However, she continued to forecast and plan, because she needed plans from which to deviate as conditions changed.

This chapter deals with the use of the above steps in a company, using The Sample Company as the example. (The details are shown in Figure 23–1.) The next chapter presents some further analyses of a company's profit potential.

Place yourself in Mr. Sample's shoes as he plans for the coming year. He should start making his plans several months ahead of the time to put them into effect, say starting in October for the coming calendar year. In order to present a systematic analysis, we will assume he is planning for the first time. Actually, he should be planning for each month at least six months or a year ahead. This can be done by dropping the past month, adjusting the rest of the months in his prior plans, and adding the plans for another month. This planning will give him time to anticipate needed changes and do something about them.

STEP 1: ESTABLISHING YOUR PROFIT GOAL

Your desired profit must be a specific value which you set as a target. Since you are managing the business, you are paying yourself a reasonable salary. Also, as the owner, you should receive a return on your investment, including your initial investment plus prior earnings left in the business. In order to determine your desired profit, you can com-

FIGURE 23–1

THE SAMPLE COMPANY
Planning the Profit for the Year, 19__

Step	Description	Analysis	Comments
1.	*Establish your profit goals*		
	Equity invested in company	$ 80,000	
	Retained earnings	20,000	
	Owner's equity	$100,000	
	Return desired	$ 15,000	15% × $100,000
	Estimated tax on profit	5,000	25%
	Profit needed before income taxes	$ 20,000	
2.	*Determine your planned volume of sales*		
	Mr. Sample's estimate of sales income	$250,000	8% increase over last year
3.	*Estimate your expenses for planned volume of sales*		

Item of Expense	Actual Last Year	Estimate 19__
Cost of goods	$145,631	$159,100
Salaries	41,569	44,000
Utilities	3,475	3,600
Depreciation	5,025	5,025
Rent	1,000	1,000
Building services	2,460	2,500
Insurance	2,000	2,000
Interest	1,323	1,500
Office expenses	2,775	2,900
Sales promotion	5,500	6,100
Taxes and licenses	3,240	3,400
Maintenance	805	850
Delivery	2,924	3,200
Miscellaneous	875	900
Total	$218,602	$236,075

Step	Description	Analysis	Comments
4.	*Determine your profit based on (2) and (3) plans*		
	Estimated sales income	$250,000	
	Estimated expenses	236,075	
	Estimated net profit before taxes	$ 13,925	
5.	*Compare your estimated profit with your profit goal*		
	Estimated profit before taxes	$13,925	
	Desired profit before taxes	20,000	
	Difference	−$ 6,075	

pare what you would receive in salary for working for someone else, plus the income you would receive if you invested the same amount of money in a savings and loan association, house loans, bonds, or stocks.

Each of these investments provides a return with a certain degree of risk—and pleasure. Say you could invest at a 7 percent return with little risk, what do you feel the return on your business should be? Peter Drucker states that profits are:

> . . . the "risk premium" covering the costs of staying in business.
> . . . the source of capital to finance the jobs of tomorrow.
> . . . the source of capital for innovation and for growth of the economy.
> Profit planning is necessary. . . . The minimum needed may well turn out to be a good deal higher than the profit goals of many companies, let alone their actual profits.[1]

Originally, Mr. Sample invested $80,000 in his company and has left $20,000 of his previous profits in the business. He made about 10 percent on investment this past year. He could make about 8 percent if he invested his money in a good grade of bond. He judges his return has been too low for the risk he is taking and feels that about a 15 percent return is reasonable.

In Figure 23–1, Step 1, he enters his investment, his desired profit, his estimate of income taxes (from the past and after consultation with his accountant), and determines he must make $20,000 before taxes, or a 20 percent return on his investment. Having set his goal, he next turns to the task of determining what his profit before taxes will be from his forecast of next year's plans.

STEP 2: DETERMINING YOUR PLANNED VOLUME OF SALES

A forecast of your sales for next year is based on your estimate of factors including market conditions, the level of your sales promotion, your estimate of your competitors' activities, and forecasts of business activity made by business managers, by magazines such as *Business Week*, by government specialists, and by people specializing in forecasting. Talks with your banker, customers, vendors, and others provide added information.

Mr. Sample has been gathering this information and has been watching his company's sales trend. From these, he estimates he can increase his sales about 8 percent. Thus, he enters $250,000 (1.08 × $231,574) in the figure as Step 2.

---

[1] Peter F. Drucker, *Management Tasks, Responsibilities, Practices* (New York: Harper & Row, Publishers, 1974), p. 114.

STEP 3: ESTIMATING YOUR EXPENSES FOR PLANNED VOLUME OF SALES

To estimate the expenses for next year, you collect the company's costs for the past years. Mr. Sample has listed these for the past year in Figure 23–1, Step 3. (He also has them for the previous years if he needs to refer to them.) These expenses must be adjusted for the planned sales volume, for changes in economic conditions (including inflation), for changes in sales promotion to attain the planned sales, and for improved methods of production.

Mr. Sample has figured that about 63 percent of his income is expended on purchased material and the labor used directly on the goods he sells. He uses this figure (63 percent), adds a one percent increase in the unit costs for inflation, and enters the result, $159,100, for cost of goods. He estimates the value of each of the other expenses, recognizing that some expenses vary directly with volume changes, others do not change at all, and still others have small changes. Each figure for expenses is entered in the appropriate place.

STEP 4: DETERMINING YOUR PROFIT FROM STEPS (2) AND (3)

In this step, he deducts the figure for his total expenses from the sales income, and adds the total of any other income, such as interest. Mr. Sample calculates this amount, and finds that his estimated profit before taxes is $13,925 ($250,000 — 236,075). This amount is slightly better than the $12,972 made last year. (See Figure 21–2.) However, he had thought that the increased volume of sales would increase his profit more than $953.

STEP 5: COMPARING YOUR ESTIMATED PROFIT WITH YOUR PROFIT GOAL

Mr. Sample then compares his estimated profit with his desired profit. He enters the value for these profits in Figure 23–1, and finds that his plan will result in a profit figure which is $6,075 ($20,000 — 13,925) lower than his goal. After pondering what he should do, he decides to follow the rest of the steps.

STEP 6: LISTING POSSIBLE ALTERNATIVES TO IMPROVE YOUR PROFITS

As shown in Figure 23–2, Step 6, there are many alternatives for improving profits available to Mr. Sample. Some of these are:

1. Change the planned sales income by:

   a. Increasing the planned volume of units sold by increasing sales promotion, improving the quality or product and/or service, making the product more available, or finding new uses for the product.

   b. Increasing or decreasing the planned price of the units. The best price may not be the planned one. How will these changes affect

FIGURE 23–2
(continuation of Figure 23–1)

Step

6. Some alternatives:
   a. Increase planned volume of units sold.
   b. Increase or decrease planned price of units.
   c. Decrease planned expenses.
   d. Add other products or services.
   e. Subcontract work.

7. *Determine how costs vary with changes in sales volume*

Item of Expense	Total Estimated Expenses	Fixed Expenses	Variable Expenses
Goods sold.	$159,100	$	$159,100
Salaries.	44,000	20,000	24,000
Utilities	3,600	2,600	1,000
Depreciation.	5,025	5,025	
Rent	1,000	1,000	
Building services.	2,500	2,000	500
Insurance.	2,000	2,000	
Interest.	1,500		1,500
Office expenses	2,900	1,500	1,400
Sales promotion.	6,100		6,100
Taxes and licenses.	3,400	2,500	900
Maintenance.	850	450	400
Delivery	3,200		3,200
Miscellaneous	900	900	
Total	$236,075	$37,975	$198,100

8. *Determine how profits vary with changes in sales volume*

   Total marginal income = sales income − variable expenses
   $$= \$250,000 - \$198,100 = \$51,900$$

   Marginal income per dollar of sales income = $51,900 ÷ $250,000
   $$= \$0.208/\$ \text{ of sales income}$$

   Estimated costs and profits at various sales volumes:

Sales Volume	Fixed Costs		Variable Costs	Profit
$175,000	$37,975	.792 × 175,000 =	$138,600	−$ 1,575
200,000	37,975	.792 × 200,000 =	158,400	3,625
225,000	37,975	.792 × 225,000 =	178,200	8,825
250,000	37,975	.792 × 250,000 =	198,100	13,925
275,000	37,975	.792 × 275,000 =	217,800	19,225
300,000	37,975	.792 × 300,000 =	237,600	24,425

the profit? Have there been price changes in the past and, if so, what has happened? Have there been changes in the attitudes and economic status of the company's customers? Which products' prices should be changed?

c. Combining (*a*) and (*b*). It has been observed, on occasion, that some small business owners become too concerned with selling on the basis of price alone. Instead, you should price for profit and sell quality, better service, reliability, and integrity. Never be entrapped by the cliche, "I won't be undersold," or "I will meet any price." The economic path of life is strewn with many failed businesses whose key to failure was this form of pricing strategy.

2. Decrease planned expenses by:

a. Establishing a better control system. Money may be lost by too many people operating the cash register, by poor scheduling, and by having too much money tired up in inventory. Expenses may be reduced if these areas are spotted and controls are established.

b. Increasing productivity of people and machines by improving methods, developing proper motivators, and improving the types and use of machinery.

c. Redesign of the product. Research is constantly developing new materials, machines, and methods for improving products and reducing costs.

3. Add other products or services:

Costs per unit can be reduced by adding a summer product to a winter line of products, selling as well as using parts made on machines with idle capacity, and making some parts customarily purchased.

4. Subcontract work.

Having listed the alternatives which might be available, Mr. Sample needs to evaluate each of them. Some alternatives may not be good choices now. Their evaluation can be delayed until after deciding on more favorable alternatives. A better understanding of cost and volume relationships is important in evaluating the alternatives.

STEP 7: DETERMINING HOW CHANGES IN COSTS VARY WITH SALES VOLUME CHANGES

Mr. Sample planned for changes in his expenses with an increase in sales volume, as shown in Step 3 of Figure 23–1. He used a simple breakeven chart, which is shown in Figure 23–3. Notice that as the volume of sales changes, the costs of doing business also change. Straight lines are used, because costs are estimated and a straight line adequately approximates the costs.

FIGURE 23–3
Break-Even Chart, The Sample Company

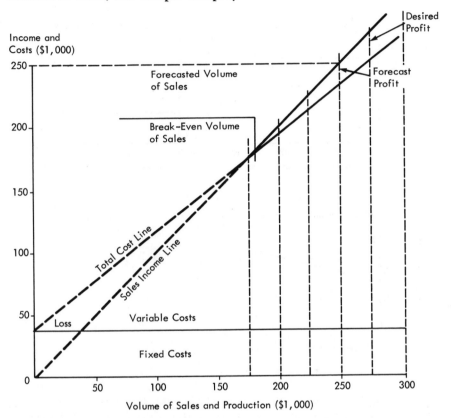

Mr. Sample collected the figures for production volume and costs from his records of the past five years. Production figures and costs for items such as direct materials, depreciation, and office supplies are shown in Table 23–1, and are plotted in Figure 23–4. Note that when the cost of direct materials (A) is plotted in the figure, the cost increases

TABLE 23–1
Data Collected from The Sample Company Records

Year	Production Volume	Direct Materials	Depreci- ation	Office Supplies
1	$110,100	$45,900	$3,100	$2,150
2	139,000	52,900	3,100	2,500
3	165,200	60,700	3,800	1,900
4	205,000	74,800	4,400	2,800
5	231,600	85,100	5,025	2,800
19– (Est.)	250,000	92,000	5,025	2,900

FIGURE 23–4
Costs and Volume of Production

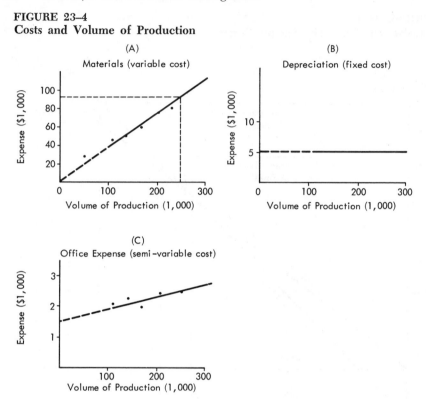

in direct proportion to sales volume, starting at zero cost and zero volume. This is to be expected, as materials used directly in manufacturing the product increase directly as the volume of products increases.

Depreciation (B) is the loss in value of the machinery and equipment as they are used and as they get older. This is similar to the cost of running your car—its value decreases with time. Businesses usually deduct the estimated resale value of an item from its costs and divide the balance by the life of the item—in years—to obtain its annual depreciation cost. Depreciation is called a fixed cost because its cost per year does not change, regardless of the volume of output, until you buy or sell the fixed asset. Other fixed costs, such as rent, are paid each period.

The account, office expenses (C) is shown to illustrate what is called a semi-variable expense. When Mr. Sample plots this cost, the line starts at about $1,500 at zero sales volume, and increases from that amount as the sales volume increases. You can use the graphs to help you in your analysis, but be sure to recognize that:

1. The relationships exist only within limited changes in sales volume. Very high sales volumes may be obtained only by such measures as extra-ordinary sales promotion, added fixed costs for machinery, or increases in overtime. Low sales volumes result in extra costs of idle capacity, lost volume discounts, and so forth.
2. Past relationships may not continue in the future. Inflation or deflation, changing location of customers, new products, and other factors can cause changes in the costs per unit. Mr. Sample recognized a possible increase in the cost of goods sold for the next year, and increased his cost of goods.

Mr. Sample computed fixed and variable costs for each of his items of expense at his planned volume of sales, and entered the figures in Figure 23–2.

STEP 8: DETERMINING HOW PROFITS VARY WITH CHANGES IN SALES VOLUME

How much does profit increase when you increase sales by $1.00? Mr. Sample planned for $250,000 of sales and $236,075 of expenses. Therefore, each dollar of sales will incur a cost of $0.944 ($236,075 ÷ $250,000). However, if he increases his sales $1.00, the extra sales should not cost him $0.944. The fixed costs will stay contant, and only the variable cost should increase. So his cost should increase only by the variable portion. For $1.00 of sales increase, his cost should increase by only $0.792 ($198,100 ÷ $250,000). His increase in profit per dollar of increase in sales volume, often called *marginal income* (MI), is $0.208 ($1.00 — $0.792). What do you think this means to Mr. Sample?

The marginal income (or gross profit) can be determined for each product, and tells you which product is the most profitable.

STEP 9: ANALYZING ALTERNATIVES FROM A PROFIT STANDPOINT

Mr. Sample can compute his cost and profit at several sales volumes in order to give him a picture of the changes in profit. This is shown in Step 8 of Figure 23–2, and is plotted as a graph in Figure 23–3. Note that the sales volume at which the company still makes no profit is close to $175,000, and it can make the desired profit only if sales increase to $275,000.

Mr. Sample can use the marginal analyses to help him in his decision making, as follows:

1. How much can he reduce his price for a sale to bring in more sales volume? He must not reduce it more than 20.8 percent, for if he does he would be paying out more than the extra sales bring in. Any less reduction would contribute to reducing the fixed-cost charges, or increasing the profit.

2. Is it profitable to increase his advertising $2,000 which, Mr. Sample estimates, would increase his sales $15,000? He should obtain additional profits of $3,120 ($0.208 × $15,000) for the $2,000 he paid out. This would give him an added profit of $1,120 ($3,120 — $2,000).

3. Is it profitable to increase the price 2 percent if he can expect a drop of 5 percent in sales? The price increase would result in a marginal income (MI) of about $0.228 ($0.208 + $0.02), and the profit would change to about $16,175 ($0.228 × 0.95 × $250,000 — $37,975), which would be better than the present expected profit of $13,925.

4. What would a reduction of 5 percent in his variable costs do to profit? The MI should increase to $0.2476 [($1.00 — $0.792) × .95], and the profit at $250,000 sales volume would be $23,925 ($250,000 × $0.2476 — $37,975). This looks very good if the means can be found to reduce the variable cost without hurting other operations.

5. Which product is the most profitable?

Other alternatives can be evaluated in much the same manner.

Having made these economic analyses, Mr. Sample is now ready to make his final plan for action.

STEP 10: SELECTING CHANGES IN YOUR PLANS

The selection of the changes, if any, depends on your judgment as to what would be most beneficial to your firm. The results of the analyses you have made in the prior steps provide the economic inputs. These must be evaluated along with your other goals. Cost reduction may result in laying off employees, or a reduction in service to your cus-

FIGURE 23–5

THE SAMPLE CO.
Planned Profit and Loss Statement
For the Year 19_

Sales Income		$250,000
Less		
Cost of goods sold	$155,900	
Other expenses	76,975	232,875
Net profit before taxes.		$ 17,125
Return on investment		17.1%

tomers. But lowering prices may satisfy your goal for a larger volume of sales. Higher prices are risky.

Mr. Sample has just read this book, made the case analyses, and has been studying some other management literature. He feels that he can reduce his cost of goods by 2 percent. Figure 23–5 shows a simplified statement of his planned income and outgo for the next year.

SUMMARY

Profits do not just happen! Planning your operations improves your chances of achieving your profit goals. You can achieve more by knowing your goals, understanding the company's sales income to cost relationships, and determining the best operating plan. You should know where your break-even point is and what the effects of alternative plans would be.

Before making your final plans, you need more information about the financial condition of your company. The next chapter provides you with some more tools for obtaining this information.

QUESTIONS FOR FURTHER DISCUSSION

1. What steps are needed in establishing your future plan?
2. How do you establish your profit goal?
3. How do you determine planned volume of sales?
4. How do you determine planned expenses?
5. What are some alternatives that could improve your planned profit?
6. Explain how you can measure the change in cost because of a given change in sales volume.
7. How can you determine variations in profit because of changes in sales volume?

24

Controlling the Financial Structure and Operation of Your Firm

After your plans have been developed, a system must be designed to help you carry out those plans. Then, the system must be controlled to see that the plans are carried out and objectives are reached. This chapter is designed to help you understand the controls which can be used in your small business.

As shown in Part III, your management functions are planning, organizing, directing, and controlling. Plans are the guides and standards used in performing the activities necessary to achieve your company's goals. A system of controls would help you make actual performance conform to the plans you had made. Any deviation from the plans would point to a need for change—usually in performance, but sometimes in the plans themselves.

Each day, we as individuals exercise controls over our activities and also have controls working on us. We control the speed of the car we are driving. Police officers control our traffic flow. Thermostats in our homes keep the temperature within an acceptable range. Controls are everywhere and are established to assure reasonable accomplishment of some set of objectives.

Regardless of where it occurs, the process of control consists of five steps. They are:

1. Set up standards of performance.
2. Measure actual performance.

3. Compare actual performance with the planned performance standards.
4. Determine if deviations are excessive.
5. Determine the appropriate corrective action required to equalize planned and actual performance.

The steps are performed in all control systems, even though the systems may be quite different. This chapter covers in detail these five steps of control. The following subjects are discussed:

1. Characteristics of control systems.
2. Causes of poor performance.
3. Establishing standards of performance.
4. Obtaining information on actual performance.
5. Comparing actual performance with standards of performance.
6. The design and use of budgets.

CHARACTERISTICS OF CONTROL SYSTEMS

Almost all control systems have the same characteristics. They should be timely, not overly costly, provide the accuracy needed, be quantifiable and measurable, show cause-and-effect relationships, and be the responsibility of one individual.

Controls Should Be Timely

To keep them timely, checks should be made frequently and as soon as practical after they are needed. You cannot wait until the end of the year to find out what your sales are and whether they meet your plans. Some stores check their daily sales for indications that their performance is not meeting expectations. They have many small purchases, and a daily check helps to indicate whether changes are needed. Manufacturers handle fewer transactions on a less regular basis, so that weekly or monthly checks may be sufficient.

The collection of the totals of an activity, such as sales, takes time. Such data collection has been simplified through the use of cash registers with tapes, mini-computers, and other office machines.

A system for fast checks is valuable. The old adage, "It is too late to lock the barn door after the cow has left," applies well to your controls.

Controls Should Not Be Costly

All controls require the time of a person or of some equipment. Often, paperwork is involved. The cost of the control system needs to be balanced against its value to you. It is not economical "to spend a nickel to save a penny."

Also some systems are simple and others are complex and costly. Therefore, you should try to reduce the time of employees, the amount of paper, and your time in collecting information. A systematic, simple inspection of what is on the shelves may give enough information for control without a clerk providing a written or tabulated summary of what has been removed from the shelves. At selected times, extra cost may be justified to provide for more detailed controls.

Controls Should Provide the Accuracy Needed

Inspection for control of quality can take two forms. Either it can test every unit of product or only a sample of the units. Statistical techniques can be applied to many areas of control in order to reduce cost and, in many cases, to improve quality. You can periodically check the output per hour of workers, cleanliness of the stock room, and the cost of paper to obtain a good check of performance.

Performance can vary above as well as below standard. Also, part of the variance from standard cannot be controlled, while part can. But, should you do it if you can? The correction of a variation of a few cents in a $10,000 figure may not be desirable or justified, but may be very significant in a figure of $0.05 per unit.

Controls Should Be Quantifiable and Measurable

The choice of measuring sticks for control is vital. Sales can be measured in dollars, pounds, tons, barrels, gallons, grams, kilograms, meters, or other units of product. Which will give you the information you want for control? Which is the least costly? You should choose the unit that will give you the needed control for the least cost.

Controls Should Show Causes, When Possible

A report that the costs of a manufactured product are higher than past costs may indicate the actual situation, but not explain why. On the other hand, a report that the cost per unit of purchased goods is higher than planned, shows not only the actual situation, but also identifies the source(s) of the higher costs.

Controls Should Be Assigned to One Individual

Because you do not have time to control all activities yourself, you need to delegate the authority for those actions to a subordinate. Give that person authority, provide the necessary resources, and then hold the person responsible for accomplishments.

Selected controls which have these characteristics, and which enable you to meet your plans, will be invaluable to you in managing your business.

CAUSES OF POOR PERFORMANCE

Poor performance can result from many factors in a company. A partial list of some of these activities or nonactivities would probably include the following:

1. Customers not buying the company's product.
2. Poor scheduling of production or purchases.
3. Theft and/or spoilage of products.
4. Too many people for the work to be performed.
5. Opportunities lost.
6. Too many free services or donations.

> A company oriented toward research and development was found to be providing customers with special R and D service without reimbursement for the thousands of dollars spent in this manner. This policy was changed to the company's profit benefit.

ESTABLISHING STANDARDS OF PERFORMANCE

Standards of performance are developed from many sources. Some of these are:

1. Intuition.
2. Past performance.
3. Plans for desired accomplishment.
4. Careful measurement of activities.
5. Comparison with other standards or averages. (See Chapter 16 for a discussion of time standards.)

Once the standards of performance are determined, they may be communicated to the people who are to do the performance by means of policies, rules, procedures, budgets, and statements of standards. (See Part III for a discussion of the first four of these.)

Statements of standards are norms, stated in writing, for employees to follow. They are usually stated in terms of units consumed or of price paid or charged. Illustrations of these are standard hours per unit to produce a good or service, miles per gallon of gasoline used, and price per part for purchased goods. Standards are used to inform the employee of the time to do a job and to measure how well he does it. They are valuable in locating sources of inefficient—as well as efficient—performance.

OBTAINING INFORMATION ON ACTUAL PERFORMANCE

Information on actual performance is obtained through some form of "feedback." It can be obtained by observation, oral reports, written memos or reports, and other methods.

Observation will probably be most satisfying to you, as you are at the scene of action and have direct control over the situation. However, this method is time consuming and you cannot be in all places at one time. Observation time is justified when your knowledge is needed, when your presence may improve the work, or when you are present for other purposes.

Oral reports are less time-consuming, simple, and provide two-way communications. They are the most prevalent type of control used in business.

Written memos or reports are prepared when a record is needed and when many facts must be assembled for decision making. These types of feedback are most costly unless they are the original records. A good record system, as discussed in Chapter 22, is a valuable aid and, when designed, should consider the reports needed.

COMPARING ACTUAL PERFORMANCE WITH STANDARDS

Information about actual performance, obtained by feedback, is compared to standards to determine if any changes are needed. This procedure may be simple or complex. Usually it will be simple, for informal controls exist for most of your decision making. The measures of performance are carried in your head; you make the comparison as you receive feedback; and you make your decisions accordingly. It must be emphasized, however, that this type of control follows the same steps as the more formal types of control. Examples of the use of standards have been discussed in Chapters 15 through 18, and follow the same pattern as control through the use of budgets. The rest of this chapter will cover the design and use of some budgets which are of most value to small business firms.

THE DESIGN AND USE OF BUDGETS

As stated in Chapter 9, a budget can be defined as an itemized summary of probable expenditures and income for a given period of time, which embodies a systematic plan for meeting expenses. The budget system is based on your profit plans for the coming period. As each day, week, or month passes, checks are made to assure progress toward meeting your goals. If actual performances equal the budget, the company is meeting its goals. If they are different, decisions can be made about whether changes are needed. Thus, budgets provide:

1. Guideposts toward your goals.
2. Indications of where trouble exists.
3. Planned actions which need to be taken during the year.
4. At planning time, the feasibility of the plans.

An effective budget system would include close controls in the areas in which poor performance most affects your company. Other areas do not warrant such expense for control, and may be controlled less often. For example, the cost of goods sold by The Sample Company is planned for 63 percent of the sales dollar, and utilities are 1.4 percent. Cost of goods sold may be divided into material and labor, and checked weekly. Utilities might be checked on a monthly basis.

Illustrative budgets presented in this chapter are sales; cash; credit, collections, and accounts receivable; and others.

Sales Budget

The sales budget is the most basic one, for once sales are planned and budgeted, the other budgets can more easily be prepared.

This budget should be the responsibility of a sales manager or you. Let us assume you have a sales manager. You and he should have worked up the sales plan for the coming year. Now, how much does the sales department need to sell each day? The plans for The Sample Company call for sales of $250,000 per year. If the firm plans for 203 sales days per year, it must average $1,230 ($250,000 ÷ 203) per sales day. But some days are good days, and some are poor. You may have noticed seasonal, monthly, and even daily patterns in the past. The daily average can be adjusted upward or downward for each day in the week or for the month.

Another method which can be used to obtain daily, weekly, or monthly sales is to modify the figures for the past year. If you think the pattern of sales for the coming year will be the same as that of the past year, merely change last year's daily sales by a given percentage. Mr. Sample planned to increase his sales by 8 percent, as shown in step 2, Figure 23–1.

How often should you compare actual sales to the budget? A grocery store manager usually makes a daily check, for he finds the daily sales vary considerably from his budget. This is expected, but they should be within range of the budget, and actual sales should range above the expected figure at least as often as below. If they do not, you have a warning signal to do a more complete check or perhaps take some corrective action. Weekly, monthly, and year-to-date summaries provide more stable relationships for control.

Companies may check at longer intervals and may use other types of checks. One owner watches the number and size of contracts at the end of each month. Other managers control by product line, by units of product sold, and by territory. The detail needed for control depends on the nature of the business.

For budgeting purposes, a simple tallying of sales in one column of a control pad, the budget in a second column, and the difference in a third column may be adequate.

Cash Budget

Cash planning is very important if a company is to meet its payments. Cash planning takes two forms: (1) the daily and weekly cash requirements for the normal operation of the business, and (2) the maintenance of the proper balance for all requirements.

The first type of planning tends to be routine. For example, your company may have a fairly constant income and outgo which can be predicted. Policies can thus be established for the level of cash to maintain. Therefore, a procedure should be established to control the level of cash. These operating demands represent a small part of the cash needed and tend to remain fairly constant.

The second type of planning requires a budget for, say, each month of the year. Payments for rent, payroll, purchases, and services require a regular outflow of cash. Insurance and taxes may require large payments a number of times each year. A special purchase, say of a truck, will place a heavy demand on cash. It takes planning to have the *right* amount of cash available at all times.

Figure 24–1 shows one form of a cash budget for three months ahead. Each month is completed before the next month is shown. Lines 1–3 are completed for the cash estimated to be received. The Sample Company expects to receive 20 percent of its monthly sales in cash. A check of its accounts receivable budget (presented in the next section) can provide estimates of the expected cash receipts in January. Other income might come from interest on investments or the sale of surplus equipment.

Expected cash payments, lines 5–12, should include items for which the company pays cash. The Sample Company might list salaries and utilities separately, and combine advertising and selling expenses under sales promotion. Cash is often paid in the month after the service is performed. Examples of this are payments for electricity and for material

FIGURE 24–1

THE SAMPLE COMPANY
Cash Budget Form

	January		February		March	
CASH BUDGET (for three months, ending March 31, 19__)	Budget	Actual	Budget	Actual	Budget	Actual
EXPECTED CASH RECEIPTS:						
1. Cash sales						
2. Collections on accounts receivable						
3. Other income						
4. Total cash receipts						
EXPECTED CASH PAYMENTS:						
5. Raw materials.						
6. Payroll.						
7. Other factory expenses (including maintenance)						
8. Advertising						
9. Selling expense						
10. Administrative expense (including salary of owner-manager)						
11. New plant and equipment.						
12. Other payments (taxes, including estimated income tax; repayment of loans; interest; etc.)						
13. Total cash payments						
14. EXPECTED CASH BALANCE at beginning of the month						
15. Cash increase or decrease (item 4 minus item 13).						
16. Expected cash balance at end of month (item 14 plus item 15).						
17. Desired working cash balance.						
18. Short-term loans needed (item 17 minus item 16, if item 17 is larger)						
19. Cash available for dividends, capital cash expenditures, and/or short-term investments (item 16 minus item 17, if item 16 is larger than item 17).						
CAPITAL CASH:						
20. Cash available (item 19 after deducting dividends, etc.)						
21. Desired capital cash (item 11, new plant equipment)						
22. Long-term loans needed (item 21 less item 20, if item 21 is larger than item 20).						

Source: J. H. Feller, Jr., *Is Your Cash Supply Adequate?* (Washington, D.C.: Small Business Administration, 1973), Management Aids, No. 174.

purchases. Some cash payments can be made at any one of several times. For example, payments on a new insurance policy can be set when your other cash demands are low. The cash budget shows when payment is to be made.

The cash balance on the first of January, plus the month's receipts, less the month's cash payments, provides you with an expected cash balance. A negative balance will require an increase in cash receipts, a decrease in payments, or the "floating" of a loan. In addition, a company should have a certain amount of cash to take care of contingencies. Line 17 is used to show the desired amount needed as a minimum balance. Lines 18–22 show alternative means of maintaining a reasonable cash balance.

A three-month projection is probably the practical minimum estimation for a cash budget. If your company is seasonal or you expect heavy demands on your cash balance, longer periods may be necessary. Also, as you approach the end of January, your performance should be checked and a month added. In Figure 24–1, the budget for February and March is reviewed toward the end of January, and April is budgeted.

The cash budget is a technique for controlling your cash flow so that you can make needed payments and not maintain too high a cash balance.

Credit, Collections, and Accounts Receivable

As previously stated, the extension of credit increases the potential for sales. In Chapter 23, you may have found that the amount in accounts receivable for The Sample Company was large relative to its credit sales. It is potentially dangerous to wait .until the end of the year to find this out. Checks should be made often enough to identify customers who are slow in paying and determine the reason(s) for the slow payments. It is believed that the average retailer loses more from slow accounts than from bad debts.

The best control of losses on accounts receivable starts with their prevention. You will enhance your position if you investigate the customer's ability and willingness to pay and provide clear statements of terms. The level of risk is balanced against the gain from giving credit. Then, establish surveillance of past-due accounts each month so that a slow account will be followed up promptly. As time passes and an account is not paid, the probability of collection decreases. You can expect to collect only about one quarter of the accounts over two years old and none of the accounts over five years old.

A first check should be made of the total amount of your accounts receivable. Chapter 21 discussed the ratios used to evaluate the amount of receivables to sales (collection period). Then a comparison of your planned figures and the actual amounts indicates if the situation is satisfactory overall.

Next, the accounts can be "aged." This is a tabulation of the accounts receivable by their age. Thus, The Sample Company's accounts receivable might be something like the following:

	Age of Accounts					
	30 Days or Less	*60 Days or Less*	*6 Months or Less*	*1 Year or Less*	*Over One Year*	*Total*
Amount	$17,150	$8,102	$2,500	$990	$1,500	$30,242

What should be done? Particular attention should be given to accounts over 60 days past due, and then to the 30–60 day accounts. Remember that most customers are honest, and that you want them to be willing and able to pay.

Mr. Sample's analysis may lead him to write off some accounts as an expense of bad debts and to provide some incentive for earlier payments by slow-paying customers. Bad-debt adjustments should be made at or near the end of the fiscal year. *Uncollectable accounts* receivable create a misstatement of income, and therefore an unjustified increase in your business income tax liability. Unless there exists a reasonable expectation of collecting the account, a good "rule of thumb" is to write off all accounts six months old or older at tax time. Mr. Sample should examine next year's profit plans for the extra cost of bad debts and for a review of his credit policy.

Other Budgets

Many other budgets can be used to control the activities and investments of your company. Each expense can increase gradually without your noticing the change. Have you noticed how fast the cash in your pockets disappears? You know you need to control this, but it is so very hard to do. Some call it being "nickeled and dimed to death." A company has similar problems. Such diverse situations as the following may contribute to this creeping increase in your firm's costs. A clerk is added to take care of the added paperwork, a solicitor comes in for donations, a big customer wants a special delivery, some of the employees use company stamps for personal letters, and inflation increases costs. While it may be unpleasant to do, these costs must be controlled if your firm is to survive.

Detailed control of inventory has been discussed in Chapter 17. An inventory budget can be established for weekly or monthly checks, based on the level of your expected sales. Purchases may be budgeted on the basis of the demand for materials. The budget can then be coordinated with the inventory and cash budgets. Analysis of a similar nature can be performed for other expenses.

Control over current liabilities is tied to expense and cash plans. Fixed assets and long-term liabilities usually change on a fixed basis, except for infrequent changes of equipment and other needs. Capital stock changes are infrequent, and retained earnings change as a result of the operations of the company. Budgets for fixed items can be maintained through a quarterly set of planned financial statements.

SUMMARY

Controls in a small company need to be simple, yet effective. While a small firm cannot spend much money for controls, it cannot afford the risks of any out-of-control activity. Therefore, it must establish at least a basic control system.

Direct control by an owner is possible for a very small business. As the company grows, however, the owner must depend increasingly on subordinates, and must use policies, rules, procedures, and budgets to help control operations. The owner always uses some type of standards of performance, either formally or informally. Also, as the business grows, more information is recorded rather than being remembered. The art is to keep paper work and cost low, and yet maintain effective controls.

QUESTIONS FOR FURTHER DISCUSSION

1. Make a cash budget for your personal use over the next four months.
2. Make recommendations to Mr. Sample for control of his operations.
3. Should a company use a budget for inventory? Explain your reasoning.
4. How should a company with many products, say a drug store, design its sales budget?
5. Who should be made responsible for variances from the budget? Give examples.

25

Safeguarding Your Assets

By now, you have established your business, set up your marketing program, arranged for your physical facilities, hired your people, and started operating. You will face many risks in the management and operations of your company. Insurance provides one of the most important means of safeguarding your business. Examples of the more common, specific business risks you will probably face and which are insurable are:

1. Fire losses.
2. Flood, hurricane, and tornado losses.
3. Business interruptions.
4. Liability.
5. Death, or other loss, of a key executive.
6. Business frauds and thefts.

In deciding what to do about these risks, you should ask: Without adequate insurance, what happens to my company when:

1. I die or become incapacitated?
2. Fire destroys my firm's building and/or inventories?
3. An employee embezzles company funds?
4. A customer is awarded a liability judgment for an accident?

Often when these disasters occur in small companies, the insurance protection is inadequate or nil. Such companies are "forced to the wall," and their future operations severely curbed.

The aspects of insurance covered in this chapter are:

1. Insurance and its limitations.
2. Alternatives to commercial insurance.
3. Guides to buying insurance.
4. Types of coverage.

INSURANCE AND ITS LIMITATIONS

Pure risk always exists when the possibility of a loss is present, but you do not know the possible extent of the loss. To illustrate, the consequences of a fire, the death of a key man, or a liability judgment cannot be determined with any degree of certainty. Yet it is probably impossible to handle the full burden of pure risks through insurance, because the premiums would be so great that it would leave you nothing, or almost nothing, to operate your business.

The principal value of insurance is its reduction of pure risk. In buying insurance, you are trading a potentially large but uncertain loss for a small but certain cost (the expenditure for the premium.) Briefly, you are trading uncertainty for certainty.

You should not attempt to insure situations that should be handled in other ways, such as:

1. Trivial losses. If the potential loss is trivial, even if the peril should occur, you should not insure against it.
2. Unnecessary coverage. If the insurance premium is a substantial proportion of the value of the property, you should not buy the insurance. For example, if the annual premium for a $50 deductible automobile collision insurance policy is $35 greater than the premium for a $100 deductible, the insured would in effect be paying $35 for $50 additional coverage—70 percent of the possible recovery if a single collision occurred during the policy term.

A well-designed insurance program not only provides for losses, but also can provide other values, including reduction of worry, freeing funds for investment, loss prevention, and easing of credit.

ALTERNATIVES TO COMMERCIAL INSURANCE

Methods other than commercial insurance for dealing with risk include: noninsurance, loss-prevention, risk transfer, and self-insurance. Perhaps you can reduce costs related to risks in your company by using one or more of these methods, or by combining them with commercial insurance.

Noninsurance is used by most firms, for they must inevitably assume some risks. You should use this method only when the severity of the potential loss is low and for risks that are more or less predictable, preventable, or largely reducible.

Loss prevention programs involve reducing the probability of loss, such as preventing fire and burglary. These programs usually result in reductions in insurance premiums.

Risk transfer involves transfering the risk of loss to others, as in leasing an automobile under a contract whereby the lessor buys the accident insurance.

For *self-insurance* to be considered, you should have adequate finances and broadly-diversified risks. Often, these requirements cannot be met in small companies. Self-insurance plans should be actuarially maintained with a cash reserve accumulated to provide for losses.

GUIDES TO BUYING INSURANCE

In buying insurance, the two most important factors are:

1. Financial characteristics of the insurer and his flexibility in meeting your requirements.
2. Services rendered by the agent.

Financial Characteristics and Flexibility of Insurer

The major types of insurers are: stock companies, mutual companies, reciprocals, and Lloyd's groups. While mutuals and reciprocals are co-operatively organized and sell insurance "at cost," in practice their costs may be no lower than those of profit-making companies. In comparing different types of insurers, you should use the following criteria:

1. Financial stability.
2. Specialization in types of coverage.
3. Flexibility in the offering of coverage.
4. Cost of protection.

Only after you are satisfied with 1, 2, and 3, should you consider 4.

While you ordinarily rely on your insurance agent to judge the financial stability of insurers, *Best's Insurance Reports* are reliable sources of financial ratings and analyses of insurers if you want to check for yourself.

Some insurers specialize in certain types of coverage and offer you the advantage of greater experience in these lines. For example, Lloyd's groups often underwrite "dangerous" risks which other insurers will not assume.

Some insurers offer you great flexibility by tailoring their policies to meet your needs. Tailoring can be accomplished through the insertion of special provisions in the contracts and/or the provision of certain services to meet particular requirements.

In making cost comparisons, you should not confuse the *initial* premium with the *net* premium. Some insurers have a lower initial rate (deviated rate), while others have a higher initial rate but pay a dividend to the insured.

Valid comparisons of insurance costs are difficult to make, but insurance brokers, independent insurance advisers, or agents may assist you. In general, you should avoid an insurer who offers a low premium.

Services Rendered by Agent

You should decide which qualifications of agents are most important to you, and then inquire about agents among business friends and others who have had experience with them. In comparing agents, some of the things to look for are contacts among insurers, professionalism, degree of individual attention, quality of "extra" services, and help in time of loss.

You should determine whether the agents' contacts among insurers are sufficiently broad to supply all the coverage you need without undue delay and at reasonable cost. Professionalism is indicated by the agent's possession of the *Chartered Life Underwriter* or *Chartered Property and Casualty Underwriter* designations. You want an agent who is willing and able to devote enough time to your individual problems to justify his commission, to survey your exposure to loss, to recommend adequate insurance and loss-prevention programs, and to offer you alternative methods of insurance. He should also be known for serving his clients well in time of loss. The quality of the agent and the companies he represents may be validated by checking with the insurance commissioner of your state or his representative.

TYPES OF COVERAGE

Some of the major types of insurance you should consider are:

1. Fire insurance.
2. Casualty insurance.
3. General liability.
4. Workmen's compensation.
5. Business life insurance.
6. Fidelity and surety bonds.

The standard *fire insurance* policy, excluding endorsements, insures you for only fire, lightning, and losses due to goods temporarily removed from your premises because of fire. In most instances, this basic policy should be supplemented with an extended-coverage endorsement which insures against windstorm, hail, explosion, riot, and aircraft, vehicle, and smoke damage. Business interruption coverage should also be provided through an endorsement, because frequently "indirect" losses are more severe in their eventual cost than are direct losses. To illustrate, while rebuilding after a fire, you must continue to pay salaries of key employees and expenses such as utilities, interest, and taxes.

Casualty insurance consists of automobile insurance, both collision and public liability, plus general liability, burglary, theft, robbery, plate glass, and health and accident insurance. Automobile liability insurance is necessary because firms are often legally liable for the use of trucks and passenger cars, even though they do not own any vehicles. For example, an employee may use his own car on behalf of the employer. In case of accident, the employer is liable. Automobile physical-damage insurance, covering perils such as collision, fire, and theft, is also essential.

General liability insurance is particularly important because, in conducting your business, you are subject to common and statutory laws governing negligence to customers, employees, and anyone with whom you do business. One liability judgment could easily result in the liquidation of your business.

Workmen's compensation and *employer liability* insurance are related to common law requirements that an employer provide his employees a safe place to work, hire competent fellow employees, provide safe tools, and warn his employees of any existing danger. Damage suits may be brought by employees for failure of employers to perform these duties. State statutes govern the kinds of benefits payable under workmen's compensation policies, which typically provide for medical care, lump sums for dismemberment and death, benefits for disablements by occupational disease, and income payments for a disabled worker or his dependents.

Business life insurance can be used in several ways in small firms. A firm can buy, or help buy, group life insurance and health insurance policies for its employees. (See Chapter 19.)

Business owner's insurance is important coverage consisting of:

1. Protection of an owner or his dependents against losses from premature death, disability, or medical expenses.
2. Provision for the continuation of a business following the premature death of an owner.

Business continuation life insurance, which is related to (2), is used in sole proprietorships, partnerships, and closely-held corporations. Advance planning involves the provision of ample cash and its use. Life insurance often provides the cash, and a trust agreement, coupled with a purchase-and-sale plan, provides for its use. The cash can be used to retire the interest of a partner of sole proprietor, or to repurchase the stock of a closely-held corporation. As for life insurance, partners or stockholders may buy sufficient insurance on each other's lives to retire each other's interest in case of death. Or the firm may buy the necessary insurance on the lives of its principal owners.

Fidelity and surety bonds are issued by insurers which guarantee to another firm that your employees and others with whom your company transacts business are honest and will fulfill their contractual obligations. Fidelity bonds are purchased for employees occupying positions which involve the handling of company funds in order to provide protection against their dishonesty. Surety bonds provide protection against the failure of others to fulfill contractual obligations.

SUMMARY

This chapter has described some of the more common business risks your firm will probably face, and has offered some suggestions as to how you can protect yourself against them. They are: fire hazards; flood, hurricane, and tornado losses; business interruptions; liability risks; death or other loss of a key executive; and business frauds and thefts.

The ways of protecting yourself are commercial insurance, noninsurance, loss-prevention, risk transfer, and self insurance. Most small firms use commercial insurance in combination with other methods.

In insuring yourself, remember these important points:

1. You and your agent should evaluate your risks.
2. You should review your present coverage.
3. You should take the necessary action to provide the protection you need.

QUESTIONS FOR FURTHER DISCUSSION

1. Give five examples of the more common, specific business risks which are insurable in small businesses.
2. When does pure risk exist? Give two illustrations of pure risk.
3. Describe two situations in which commerical insurance should not be purchased by small businesses.
4. Besides commercial insurance, describe three methods of dealing with risk in a small business.
5. Cite three criteria that should be used in comparing different types of insurers.
6. Cite four criteria that should be used in comparing agents.
7. Describe business interruption coverage.
8. Cite the common law requirements to which workmen's compensation and employer liability insurance are related.

WHERE TO LOOK FOR FURTHER INFORMATION

Anthony, R. N. *Management Accounting,* 4th ed. Homewood, Illinois: Richard D. Irwin, Inc., 1970.

Anthony, Robert N., and Welsch, Glenn A. *Fundamentals of Management Accounting.* Homewood, Illinois: Richard D. Irwin, Inc., 1974.

Brummet, R. L., and Robertson, J. C. *Cost Accounting for Small Manufacturers,* 2d ed. Washington, D.C.: Small Business Administration, 1974. (Small Business Management Series, No. 9.)

Crowningshield, Gerald R., and Gorman, Kenneth A. *Cost Accounting: Principles and Managerial Applications,* 3d ed. Boston: Houghton Mifflin Co., 1974.

Greene, Mark R. *Insurance Checklist for Small Business.* Washington, D.C.: Small Business Administration, 1971. (Small Marketers Aids, No. 148.)

Gruenwald, A. E., and Nemmers, E. E. *Basic Management Finance.* New York: Holt, Rinehart, and Winston, Inc., 1970.

Hedrick, F. D. *Purchasing Management in the Small Company.* New York: American Management Association, Inc., 1971.

Horngren, Charles T. *Cost Accounting: A Manager's Analysis,* 3d ed. Englewood Cliffs, New Jersey: Prentice-Hall, Inc., 1972.

Katz, B. *Happiness or Misery.* Alexandria, Va.: Overlook Company, 1971.

Kreutzman, H. C. *Managing for Profits.* Washington, D.C.: Small Business Administration, 1968. (Management and Financial Control Series.)

Miller, D. E. *The Meaningful Interpretation of Financial Statements,* rev. ed. New York: American Management Association, Inc., 1972.

Mockler, Robert J. *The Management Control Process.* New York: Appleton-Century-Crofts, 1972.

Moran, Christopher J. *Preventing Embezzlement.* Washington, D.C.: Small Business Administration, 1973. (Small Marketers Aids, No. 151.)

Niswonger, C. Rollins, and Fess, Phillip E. *Accounting Principles,* 11th ed. Cincinnati, Ohio: South-Western Publishing Co., 1973.

Sanzo, Richard. *Ratio Analysis for Small Business,* 3d ed. Washington, D.C.: Small Business Administration, 1970.

Welsch, G. A. *Budgeting: Profit Planning and Control,* 3d ed. Englewood Cliffs, New Jersey: Prentice-Hall, Inc. 1970.

Welsch, Glenn A., and Anthony, Robert N. *Fundamentals of Financial Accounting.* Homewood, Illinois: Richard D. Irwin, Inc., 1974.

Woelfel, B. L. *Financial Audits: A Tool for Better Management.* Washington, D.C.: Small Business Administration, 1972. (Management Aids, No. 176.)

Zwick, Jack. *Handbook of Small Business Finance.* Washington, D.C.: Small Business Administration, 1965. (Small Business Management Series, No. 15.)

Cases for Part VII

VII-1. Tanner's Grocery Store (D)[1]

By March, the profit and loss statement showed a net loss; the liquid capital was almost gone; and Tanner was concerned with money for paying his upcoming tax bill. He sought additional financing, but was unable to obtain it. He wished to re-establish the credit aspect of his business, but could not do so without additional capital. It was suggested that he raise some capital by liquidating some odd lines, including hardware and clothing, of which he had an inventory of $300 to $500. It took four weeks for Tanner to decide to do so, and to place these and other items on special sale. Tanner tried reducing his prices to a 13 percent markup, as the major chain stores in the area did, but raised prices again after a week on the advice of a friend.

Matters grew progressively worse. Tanner no longer held another job, but was absent from the store more than he should have been.

---

[1] Written by Rudolph L. Kagerer and James F. Russell, University of Georgia. See "Tanner's Grocery Store (A), (B), and (C)" in Parts I, II, and III for previous details.

The inventory shrunk as items were sold and were not replaced. Customers complained about the shortage of items on the shelves, and then went elsewhere to purchase their groceries.

Finally in June, Tanner went to the lender and stated his desire to declare bankruptcy. The corporation foreclosed on the store and subsequently sold it back to Greenwaite and his partner for $10,000. The bank undertook to sue Tanner for the remaining $20,000 of the loan, but Tanner proceeded with bankruptcy proceedings. Greenwaite and his partner reported that less than half of the original inventory was found in the store, and they anticipated it would take six months to a year to rebuild the reputation and operation of the store to its former level.

Mr. Bowden, who had served as loan officer for the Corporation and for the bank, stated that the major flaw in Tanner's business abilities was the inability to make decisions, postponing them until it was too late or refusing to change a decision once it was finally made. Tanner had been advised to reconsider the credit issue by the second month of operation, but had done nothing about it. Bowden's final comment was that $1,000 was found in Tanner's checking account, and the final profit and loss statement had shown a profit. He felt that Tanner had just quit, giving up because the work and responsibility were more than he had bargained for.

QUESTIONS FOR DISCUSSION

1. Do you agree with Mr. Bowden's analysis of why Mr. Tanner failed? Explain.
2. Would you have done any differently if you had been the lending institution? Explain.
3. What does the case illustrate about the need for profit planning?
4. What does it show about the importance of cash flow budgets? Other types of budgets?

VII–2. Allied Securities Co.[1]

Mr. John Cain, President of Allied Securities Co. was "the typical salesman type" and had succeeded extremely well in organizing and raising capital for the eight-year-old business which he headed.

---

[1] Prepared by Leon C. Megginson, Louisiana State University.

Very early during the organization of Allied Securities, Cain had hired Steven Brunson, an accountant. Brunson had been made treasurer of Allied and was responsible for all financial planning for the company.

Early in its history, the company had some serious difficulties due to a too-rapid expansion program. During the course of three or four years, all these problems had been resolved and the firm had grown and prospered. During the previous two years, the Company had acquired several new retail outlets which had required a considerable outlay of cash and capital stock. "The acquisitions for cash had brought the company," in Brunson's opinion, "to the point where additional purchases of new retail outlets for a cash consideration might seriously impair the Company's liquidity—that is, the firm's cash position and its ability to borrow more working capital at favorable rates."

Mr. Cain was expansion minded, and took considerable pride in the growth of the organization. By nature, he was primarily interested in most of the technical operational and financial problems of the business, but left these responsibilities to subordinates. Consequently, he did not give too much thought to those problems as they applied to acquisitions. However, he did regard these two problems as possible hindrances to him in promoting growth of the company.

Mr. Cain had a great deal of respect for Mr. Brunson, but regarded him as "a conservative business man overly inclined to want to minimize business risks." For his part, Brunson felt the Company's growth was more than adequate and compared quite favorably with companies having the most progressive management philosophies. Brunson felt the need for a company policy definitely establishing the rate at which expansion should be carried out.

In their discussion of this problem, Mr. Cain liked to point to businesses that had phenomenal growth records and accompanying success. Mr. Brunson pointed out problems of businesses that had grown too rapidly, and how some expansion minded businesses had failed.

QUESTIONS FOR DISCUSSION

1. To what extent should the growth of a firm be determined by the liquidity of assets instead of the available opportunities for acquiring new outlets?

2. Explain some of the problems which could occur from "too rapid expansion."

3. With which of the two men do you agree? Why?

4. What would you recommend to Mr. Cain?

5. If you were Mr. Brunson, what information would you need to support your position?

6. Does a company need a man "inclined to minimize business risks"?

VII-3. Star Electric Shop[1]

Mr. Frank Victor had operated the Star Electric Shop as a sole proprietorship since 1940. In 1970 he was 60 years old. At that time his plans were to retire from the business in January, 1976.

The shop was located in a building in the center of the Shawnee, Oklahoma, business district. Mr. Victor had rented this building from Mr. Jack Walls since 1950.

In December, 1970, according to the terms of the lease agreement which required a one-year's notice of lease termination, Mr. Walls gave Mr. Victor notice that he would have to vacate by December 31, 1971.

In April, 1971, Mr. Victor began looking for a new location for his business. He found two suitable buildings he could rent. One building was located in the downtown area.

Mr. Victor also considered the possibility of constructing a building on some residential rental property he owned. He held this property as an investment and as a possible source of additional income upon his retirement.

He had also thought about getting out of the business and seeking employment in Shawnee. However, he did not consider this a practical alternative, because he felt (1) that he could do no more than recover his investment in inventory, furnishings, and equipment, and (2) his before-tax earnings as an employee could be expected to be no more than $8,000 annually. Furthermore, he had been self-employed for many years and "did not want to forego this freedom."

Because of his age and planned retirement, Mr. Victor was uncertain as to which of the alternatives would be best.

Exhibit III-1 gives actual income and expense data for the shop for 1970 and estimated data for 1971. Because of the growth of the community, Mr. Victor expected the total dollar sales of the shop to increase five percent per year for the period 1971 through 1975. During the period 1961–1970, gross profit averaged 40 percent of sales. Mr. Victor expected this percentage to remain the same. He also expected selling expenses to increase in proportion to sales. He expected other expenses to increase approximately three percent per year. Depreciation of equipment, included in *other* expenses, was $500 per year. Mr. Victor considered three alternatives:

---

[1] Prepared by Milton F. Usry, Oklahoma State University.

Alternative A: Rent Building in Shopping Center. The rent for the building in the shopping center was $125 per month. Mr. Victor estimated he would lose only five percent of his sales volume by moving away from the downtown area. He felt this way because most of his sales were made over the telephone rather than by direct contact with customers.

Alternative B: Rent Building Downtown. The rent for the building located downtown was $200 per month. Mr. Victor did not feel that a move to this location would cause any changes in expected sales or expenses (other than rent).

Alternative C: Construct Building. Mr. Victor owned rental property located on the edge of the downtown business district. A house, duplex, and garage apartment were located on this property. Mr. Victor considered constructing a building on the portion of the property now occupied by the house. He felt this was best, because the area occupied by the garage apartment was not large enough for the type of building he needed, and the rents from the duplex were too high to lose.

Yearly income and expense data for the rental property are given in Exhibit III–2. Mr. Victor expected no changes in these data.

EXHIBIT III–1
Income Statements for Star Electric Shop

	Actual Data (1970)	Estimated Data (1971)
Sales	$50,000	$52,500
Cost of Sales	30,000	31,500
Gross Profit	$20,000	$21,000
Expenses:		
Rent	$ 900	$ 900
Selling	3,000	3,150
Other	4,100	4,223
	$ 8,000	$ 8,273
Net Income	$12,000	$12,727

EXHIBIT III–2
Yearly Income and Expense Data for Rental Property

	Duplex	Garage Apartment	House	Total
Rents	$1,800	$600	$960	$3,360
Cash Expenses	540	180	480	1,200
Net Cash Income	$1,260	$420	$480	$2,160
Depreciation	600	200	400	1,200
Net Income	$ 660	$220	$ 80	$ 960

The cost of constructing the type of building Mr. Victor wanted had been estimated at $20,000. This figure included razing the house, which had been fully depreciated for tax purposes, with all salvaged materials becoming the contractor's property. He could obtain a six percent, 10-year loan from a local savings and loan association, with yearly payments of $2,717 due December 31 of each year. Exhibit III–3 shows a schedule of beginning-of-year balances, cash payments, interest, and yearly reductions in principal.

EXHIBIT III–3
Loan Schedule: $20,000, six percent, 10 years

Year	Beginning Principal	Cash Payments	Interest	Reduction in Principal
1972	$20,000	$2,717	$1,200	$1,517
1973	18,483	2,717	1,109	1,608
1974	16,875	2,717	1,012	1,705
1975	15,170	2,717	910	1,807
1976	13,363	2,717	802	1,915
1977	11,448	2,717	687	2,030
1978	9,418	2,717	565	2,152
1979	7,266	2,717	436	2,281
1980	4,985	2,717	299	2,418
1981	2,567	2,717	150	2,567

Depreciation on the building would be figured on the straight-line method, with a $2,000 salvage value and an estimated life of 20 years. Mr. Victor estimated that maintenance and repairs for the building would cost $250 per year and that gross profit, selling, and other expenses would be the same as for *Alternative B*.

By joint agreement of the city, county, school district, and state, no property taxes are assessed on new business property construction for the first five years. After this time, the estimated annual property tax would be $260.

Mr. Victor believed he could rent the building for $200 per month after his retirement in 1976. In that case, he expected the maintenance and repair costs to remain the same at $250 per year.

QUESTIONS FOR DISCUSSION

1. Prepare projected income statements, by years, for the period 1972–1975, for each of the following alternatives:
   a. Rent building in shopping center.
   b. Rent building downtown.
   c. Construct building.

2. Evaluate the results obtained in Question 1.
3. Compute estimated net *cash* incomes, by years, for the period 1972–1975, for each of the three alternatives identified in Question 1.
4. Evaluate the results obtained in Question 3.
5. Which data are the more useful in selecting the best alternative, those obtained in Question 1, or in Question 3?

VII-4. Ruth's Dashiki (B)[1]

Bill had collected background information about Ruth's Dashiki, but decided he needed more factual information about its finances. He found that although the business had been operating for some time, there was no system of record keeping. Therefore, he found it difficult to make sense of the assortment of paid and unpaid bills, receipts, scraps of paper, and notes Ruth kept. It was apparent that Ruth was unaware of the need for record keeping. She had both a personal and a business checking account, and used them interchangeably. Deposits seldom were recorded. In addition, she frequently used bank checks to make withdrawals without recording them in either account, with the result that the true balance was uncertain. With some guesswork and a great deal of estimating, Bill was able to construct an estimated balance sheet as shown in Exhibit IV–1.

He was able also to rough out a tentative profit and loss statement for October (Exhibit IV–2). October, however, was not a typical month, since renovations were still in process at that time. The figures also were incomplete, for depreciation was not included. The rental of the storefront location was $125 per month. A seamstress was hired at $1.85 per hour, one-half of which would be paid for 15 weeks by the State Department of Labor under an On-The-Job-Training contract. A salary for Ruth was also omitted, although the student learned that she drew out an average of about $150 per week. For subsequent months, the costs of telephone service and insurance would have to be included. He estimated these at $30 and $20 respectively. On the more positive side, sales could be expected to increase. The $609.81 of sales had been

---

[1] Prepared by Donald DeSalvia and Allan Young, Syracuse University. See "Ruth's Dashiki (A)" in Part Two for this background information.

EXHIBIT IV–1

RUTH'S DASHIKI
Balance Sheet
November 1, 19x1

Assets

Current Assets
Cash	$ 53.40	
Accounts Receivable	548.26	
Finished Goods Inventory	245.00	
Materials Inventory	780.82	
Prepaid Expenses	75.00	
Office Supplies	124.16	
		$ 1,826.64

Fixed Assets
Machinery and Equipment.	2,669.00	
Improvement in Property	2,315.65	
		$ 4,984.65
Total Assets.		$ 6,811.29

Liabilities

Accounts Payable.	$1,672.43	
Taxes Payable	60.53	
Notes Payable–SBA	9,000.00	
Notes Payable–Other.	128.10	
Total Liabilities		$10,861.06
Equity.		($ 4,049.77)

EXHIBIT IV–2

RUTH'S DASHIKI
Profit and Loss Statement
October, 19x1

Sales		$609.81
Cost of Goods Sold		
Labor	$184.78	
Materials	121.96	
	$306.74	
Shop Overhead		
Rent	$125.00	
Debt Service.	105.00	
Utilities	10.58	
	$240.58	
Total Costs	$547.32	
Less OJT*.	– 85.87	
Net Cost	$461.45	
Net Profit	$148.36	

* State Department of Labor Reimburse-
ment for On-the-Job-Training.

achieved while renovations were going on and without any promotional activities at all.

As best he could, the student summarized the expenditures from April to November. He knew the firm was seriously short of cash, but Ruth expected to ask the SBA for a third installment. Ruth had obtained a first installment of $2,000, the major portion of which had been used to cover the debts of starting up and running the business up to the time of the loan, and a second installment of $7,000, a good share of which had been absorbed in the relocation and renovation delay costs. He wondered how large a loan would be necessary and how much more the SBA would be willing to advance.

The store consisted of a showroom/salesroom in which items were displayed, and a back room in which they were produced. The equipment used in making the garments is shown in "Ruth's Dashiki (A)." There was sufficient work space and equipment to greatly expand output. The student felt that the average "dashiki" could be made in three or three and one-half hours. Vests took four to five hours, and robes took about five hours. A "dashiki" required one and one-fourth yards of material, as compared with three and six yards for vests and robes respectively. Ruth purchased fabrics from the Fabric Center at prices which varied from $2 to $3 per yard.

The retail price for "dashikis" varied from $17 to $20, depending upon the fabric and the amount of decoration on the garment. Vests sold from $12 to $15, and floor-length women's robes varied from $30 to $35. Ruth also carried some purchased accessories and jewelry. While choir and ministerial robes had also been made originally, there had been no orders for them for several months. Credit sales were frequent and informal. Ruth often allowed people to take garments without a down payment and without specific provisions for payment. As a result, accounts receivable were high. The age distribution of accounts receivable is shown in Exhibit IV–3.

EXHIBIT IV–3

RUTH'S DASHIKI
Age of Accounts Receivable

12 Months and Over	$ 90.20
9–11 Months	65.00
6–8 Months	100.78
3–5 Months	0.00
0–2 Months	292.28
Total Accounts Receivable	$548.26

QUESTIONS FOR DISCUSSION

1. Examine the financial statements that Bill developed. Would you make any changes? If so, explain.

2. What kind of a financial record keeping system do you advise for Ruth?

3. Can a reasonable level of profit be obtained in the future? Show the breakeven point for the company and your estimate of the volume of sales needed for a reasonable profit.

4. How much of a loan would you advise Ruth to ask for? What other sources of funds might be available?

5. How would you advise Ruth to determine her prices? Do present prices appear to be reasonable?

6. What financial analysis tools can be used to determine the condition of the company? What do they show?

7. Evaluate the credit policy of the company.

VII-5. Floyd Bean Bonanza Steak House (B)[1]

During the first two months after Floyd Bean opened Floyd Bean Steak House in December, 1971, he had difficulty finding the right combination of black and white employees to attract a diverse clientele. His initial problem was to get enough customers—both black and white—to maintain enough sales to make a profit, or even to break even. In January, 1972, he hired a white assistant manager who had previous experience in the management of restaurants. Mr. Bean now feels he has a complementary combination of staff and management that will satisfy all his customers.

Another problem Mr. Bean faces is how to increase his sales from Monday through Thursday. During these days he loses a significant percentage of his black customers. He says that the reason for this is that black families in general do not eat out as a family unit until the weekends.

In 1970, 25 Bonanzas topped $400,000 in sales. Average sales of all Bonanzas were $278,000. Mr. Bean expects to do at least $300,000 a year and hopes it will exceed $400,000 with the added help of a party room he plans to add. Bonanza #572 at 3515 Inwood Road in Dallas, without a party room, had net sales of $416,644 in 1971.

---

[1] Prepared by Sydney C. Reagan and Calvin W. Stephens, Southern Methodist University. See "Floyd Bean Bonanza Steak House (A) in Part Two for background material."

At the present, however, Mr. Bean's actual sales are running behind his predictions. For the first six months of 1972, his projected gross sales were $94,309. His actual gross sales for that period, ending June 1972, were $67,045—some $27,264 short of his goal. For the same six-month period, his projected net profit was $743.50. He actually had a net loss for the period of $3,282.66, which is $4,026.16 short of his projection. However, Mr. Bean is still very optimistic that he will eventually increase his sales and meet his earlier projections. See Exhibits V–1 and

EXHIBIT V–1

FLOYD BEAN BONANZA STEAK HOUSE
Statement of Operations
June 1972 and Year to Date

	June 1972		January–June 1972	
	Amount	Percent of Sales	Amount	Percent of Sales
Sales	$15,762.02	100.0	$67,045.49	100.0
Cost of Sales:				
Beginning Inventory	$ 3,677.86		$ 5,036.72	
Purchases	5,825.05		26,105.59	
	$ 9,502.91		$31,142.31	
Less: Ending Inventory	3,478.32		3,478.32	
Cost of Sales	6,024.59	38.2	27,663.99	41.3
Gross Profit.	$ 9,737.43	61.8	$39,381.50	58.7
Expenses:				
Cash, over and short	(5.72)	0.0	(35.61)	0.1
Advertising	551.67	3.5	2,285.39	3.4
Depreciation	413.20	2.6	2,066.00	3.1
Interest	428.73	2.7	2,078.88	3.1
Insurance, general	250.00	1.6	1,250.00	1.9
Insurance, officers life	208.20	1.3	208.20	0.3
Insurance, employees	141.62	0.9	141.62	0.2
Legal and audit	250.00	1.6	1,250.00	1.9
Office			94.17	0.1
Maintenance.	358.87	2.3	1,980.29	3.0
Rent, building.	1,490.60	9.5	7,453.00	11.1
Rent, equipment	283.09	1.8	848.85	1.3
Salaries and wages	3,249.50	20.6	14,894.61	22.2
Supplies	171.47	1.1	977.45	1.5
Security	75.71	0.5	424.53	0.6
Payroll taxes.	169.00		777.08	0.9
Telephone	24.87	0.2	179.11	0.3
Utilities	572.61	3.6	2,487.58	3.7
Franchise royalty.	375.19	2.4	1,605.99	2.4
Rubbish removal			282.00	0.4
Uniforms and laundry	88.67	0.6	1,415.02	2.1
Total Expense	9,097.28	56.7	42,664.16	63.4
Net Profit (Loss).	$ 640.15	5.1	$ (3,282.66)	4.7

EXHIBIT V-2

FLOYD BEAN BONANZA STEAK HOUSE
Balance Sheet
January 1, 1972 and June 30, 1972

Assets

	January 1, 1972	June 30, 1972
Current Assets:		
Cash in Bank	$15,353.80	$ 6,245.19
Cash on Hand	700.00	800.00
Receivables	(55.00)	560.32
Inventory	5,036.72	3,478.32
Prepaid Insurance	1,606.20	2,377.24
Deferred Advertising	446.85	851.29
Total Current Assets	$23,088.57	$14,312.36
Property and Equipment:		
Furniture and Fixtures	$49,585.08	$50,312.08
Less: Accumulated Depreciation	413.20	2,479.20
Total Property and Equipment	$49,171.88	$47,832.88
Other Assets:		
SBA Lease Guarantee	$ 7,267.40	$ 7,064.40
Total Assets	$79,527.85	$69,209.64

Liabilities and Investment

Current Liabilities:		
Accounts Payable	$ 5,167.52	$ 8,369.86
Note Payable—Insurance	990.90	1,418.94
Payroll Taxes Payable	992.14	602.20
Sales Tax Payable	901.67	1,478.14
Accrued Payroll	1,303.71	1,409.41
Total Current Liabilities	$ 9,355.94	$13,278.55
Long Term Debt:		
South Oak Cliff Bank	$44,618.75	$40,837.50
SBA	20,000.00	18,787.22
Motor Enterprises	15,000.00	15,000.00
UCC Venture	5,000.00	5,000.00
Total Long Term Debt	$84,618.75	$79,624.72
Investment:		
Floyd Bean, Investment	($ 7,861.01)	($14,446.84)
Net Profit (Loss) for year to date	($ 4,910.83)	($ 3,282.66)
Less: Withdrawals	1,675.00	5,964.13
Total Investment	($14,446.84)	($23,693.63)
Total Liabilities and Investment	$79,527.85	$69,209.64

V–2 for statements of operations and balance sheets, and Exhibit V–3 for projections by Mr. Bean. The effect of cooperative advertising by all Bonanza Steak Houses in the Dallas area is considered to be highly beneficial to each.

Mr. Bean is considering all his problems and trying to decide how to proceed.

EXHIBIT V–3

FLOYD BEAN BONANZA STEAK HOUSE
1972 Pro-Forma Income and Expense Statement

	January–March	April–June	July–September	October–December	1972 Total
Sales	$43,341.00	$50,968.00	$60,260.00	$63,480.00	$218,049.00
Cost of Sales	16,475.00	20,650.00	24,500.00	25,650.00	87,275.00
Gross Profit	$26,866.00	$30,318.00	$35,760.00	$37,830.00	$130,774.00
Expenses:					
Cash short (Over)	$ 150.00	$ 150.00	$ 150.00	$ 150.00	$ 600.00
Advertising	1,225.00	1,535.00	1,811.00	1,905.00	6,476.00
Depreciation	1,239.00	1,240.00	1,240.00	1,239.00	4,958.00
Interest	1,374.00	1,361.50	1,348.00	1,334.00	5,417.50
Insurance	558.00	558.00	558.00	558.00	2,232.00
Legal and Audit	750.00	750.00	750.00	750.00	3,000.00
Office	60.00	65.00	75.00	85.00	285.00
Maintenance	250.00	150.00	150.00	150.00	700.00
Rent Building	4,350.00	4,350.00	4,350.00	4,350.00	17,400.00
Rent Equipment	531.00	531.00	531.00	531.00	2,124.00
Salaries and Wages	8,517.00	10,320.00	10,350.00	10,500.00	39,687.00
Supplies	1,378.00	1,735.00	2,031.00	2,151.00	7,295.00
Service	1,020.00	1,020.00	1,020.00	1,020.00	4,080.00
Payroll Taxes	619.00	720.00	720.00	729.00	2,788.00
Other Taxes	555.00	555.00	555.00	555.00	2,220.00
Telephone	120.00	120.00	120.00	120.00	480.00
Utilities	1,321.00	1,841.00	1,839.00	1,932.00	6,933.00
Franchise Royalties	1,943.00	2,449.00	2,897.00	3,048.00	10,337.00
Miscellaneous	460.00	570.00	755.00	830.00	2,615.00
Total Expenses	$26,420.00	$30,020.50	$31,250.00	$31,937.00	$119,627.50
Net Profit (Loss)	$ 446.00	$ 297.50	$ 4,510.00	$ 5,893.00	$ 11,146.50
Less Estimated Income Taxes	$ 190.00	165.00	910.00	1,180.00	2,445.00
Net Profit (AT)	$ 256.00	$ 132.50	$ 3,600.00	$ 4,713.00	$ 8,701.50
Less: Withdrawals	2,499.00	2,499.00	2,499.00	2,499.00	9,996.00
Profit for Loan Payment	($ 2,243.00)	($ 2,366.50)	$ 1,101.00	$ 2,214.00	($ 1,294.50)
All Loan Payments	$ 2,871.99	$ 3,184.75	$ 3,198.35	$ 3,212.15	$ 12,467.24

QUESTIONS FOR DISCUSSION

1. Can Floyd Bean afford the assistant manager?

2. What alternatives does Mr. Bean have to increase his weekly sales during the Monday–Thursday lag? Can he afford these alternatives?

3. What steps do you suggest Mr. Bean take to stop the drain on cash reserves?

4. By analyzing the financial statements, what would you say are Mr. Bean's major financial difficulties, other than low sales?

5. Should Mr. Bean reduce his monthly withdrawals of $833 ($10,000 a year)?

6. What do the analyses of the statement of operations, the balance sheet, and the projections of the pro-forma income and expense statement reveal?

7. What adjustments should Mr. Bean make in the pro-forma projections, based on operations from January through June 1972?

VII–6. Solomon Foods[1]

Early in 1970, the management of Solomon Foods was faced with the problem of the financial feasibility of constructing a larger, more competitive retail food store. Management felt it could improve the company's sales and profits by moving from the 3,000 square foot building. Bernard Solomon especially realized that with the limited parking area and poor location it was only a matter of time before annual sales volume of $250,000 would decline below the break-even point of $248,000. And even if sales remained the same, stagnation was as bad as death in the city's competitive retail market. Bernard Solomon believed that an optimum-size store and parking area located in a highly traveled area would afford "economies of scale" plus the psychological advantage of low prices. After management reached an agreement, it was time to sway would-be creditors to its way of thinking.

Solomon Foods was owned and operated as a partnership by Maurice and Bernard Solomon. Maurice T. Solomon had been, for 39 of his 64 years, managing this business. He worked 70–80 hours per week planning, organizing, staffing, directing, and controlling the business.

Bernard M. Solomon, Maurice's son, was a 38 year old businessman who expanded the business to its present size. Through his drive and enthusiastic determination, he had been able to pursuade his father to risk everything in order to achieve progress. But convincing Maurice to risk the business was achieved only by his son's threat to quit, which he made twice.

After many heated discussions with individuals experienced in the retail food industry, and after a determination of the extent of the keen competition in a city of 100,000, it was felt that a 6,000 square foot building was the optimum floor space. A store of that size could be built at a cost not greater than $7.50 a square foot.

Fortunately, an ideal spot not far from the present location could be purchased (on the going-home side of the street) for $11,000. This

[1] Prepared by Robert Crayne, Stephen L. Woehrle and B. D. Perkins, The University of South Dakota.

location was large enough to give a proper ratio of parking area to store floor space (four to one was the suggested ratio, while at their existing location it was only one to four). Also, planned street changes were expected to increase the traffic of homeward-bound workers. With the possible increased traffic in mind, a store plan was drawn so that future expansion to 10,000 square feet would be relatively easy.

After talking with several equipment dealers, management decided that the new store could be completely equipped, exclusive of building costs, for $10.00 a square foot. Existing equipment was close to being fully depreciated, but was still in good condition. Only 50 percent of the required equipment needed had to be purchased. No additional working cash was needed, and only $5,000 more inventory had to be acquired. It was estimated that equal payments over 20 years would require total payment of twice the cost—half to principal and half to interest, taxes, and insurance.

Much thought was given to just how to finance the total cost of the project. It was determined that a loan from the SBA would be most appropriate. But because the SBA had not as yet been approached,

EXHIBIT VI–1

SOLOMON FOODS
Balance Sheet
December 31, 1964 to December 31, 1969

	1964	1965	1966	1967	1968	1969
Assets						
Current Assets:						
Cash	$ 3,954	$ 4,657	$ 3,153	$ 8,377	$ 4,982	$ 7,840
Accounts Receivable	4,238	3,267	1,699	1,316	1,384	1,749
Notes Receivable	12,398	12,398				
Inventory	16,503	15,614	13,794	14,077	15,279	14,783
Total Current Assets	$37,093	$35,936	$18,646	$23,770	$21,645	$24,372
Equipment–Net	22,027	20,010	16,924	13,916	10,766	8,075
Total Assets	$59,120	$55,946	$35,570	$37,686	$32,411	$32,447
Liabilities						
Current Liabilities:						
Accounts Payable*	$ 8,824	$ 8,430	$ 5,101	$10,647	$ 8,121	$ 6,721
Wholesaler Payable	2,725	1,450				1,465
Taxes Payable	1,517	1,499	1,523	1,402	1,350	1,444
Total Current Liabilities	13,066	11,379	6,624	12,049	9,471	9,630
Long-Term Liabilities:						
John Hancock Note	$ 800	$ 800	$ 800	$ 800	$ 910	$ 800
N. Bank Note	1,000	2,620		1,000	1,400	1,000
S. Bank Note	8,322	6,456	4,412			
Total Long-Term Liabilities	$10,122	$ 9,876	$ 5,212	$ 1,800	$ 2,310	$ 1,800
Total Liabilities	$23,188	$21,255	$11,836	$13,849	$11,781	$11,430
Equity						
Total Capital Invested	$35,932	$34,691	$23,734	$23,837	$20,630	$21,017
Total Liabilities and Equity	$59,120	$55,946	$35,570	$37,676	$32,411	$32,447

* Purchases are paid for by the last day of the week on which they were bought.

EXHIBIT VI–2

SOLOMON FOODS
Income Statements
December 31, 1964 to December 31, 1969

	1964	1965	1966	1967	1968	1969
Net Sales.	$260,378	$275,328	$268,132	$265,442	$241,602	$251,747
Cost of Goods Sold	215,542	233,725	228,491	228,093	202,055	211,034
Gross Profit	$ 44,836	$ 41,603	$ 39,641	$ 37,349	$ 39,547	$ 40,713
Expenses						
Outside Labor.	$ 370	$ 184	$ 183	$ 127	$ 92	$ 176
Operating Supplies	1,843	1,825	1,875	2,045	1,932	1,902
Gross Wages*	8,979	8,031	8,098	8,458	8,103	6,943
Repairs and Maintenance . .	556	675	319	534	879	353
Advertising	3,603	3,777	3,193	2,947	3,028	4,163
Bad Debts.	477	409	301	216	67	248
Administrative and Legal . .	626	560	600	600	600	600
Rent	3,420	3,900	3,900	3,900	3,900	4,100
Utilities	3,199	3,116	3,131	3,117	3,415	2,933
Insurance	1,881	1,411	925	520	587	559
Taxes and Licenses	974	996	1,129	1,214	1,215	1,241
Interest	384	1,222	648	449	120	121
Depreciation.	3,167	3,254	3,339	3,338	3,150	2,784
Miscellaneous Expense	1,052	922	906	610	315	300
Total Expenses	$ 30,632	$ 30,282	$ 28,456	$ 28,075	$ 27,403	$ 26,423
Net Profit.	$ 14,204	$ 11,321	$ 11,184	$ 9,274	$ 12,144	$ 14,290

* Owners' salaries are not included in expenses.

EXHIBIT VI–3

SOLOMON FOODS
Pro-Forma Income Statement
December 31, 1969

	Percent of Total Sales
Sales	100.00
Cost of Goods Sold	83.83
Gross Profit	16.17
Expenses:	
Wages and Labor*	6.36
Operating Supplies	1.25
Repairs and Maintenance	0.20
Advertising	1.00
Bad Debts	0.02
Administrative and Legal	0.26
Miscellaneous and Other	0.05
Utilities	1.17
Insurance	0.37
Taxes and Licenses	0.78
Depreciation	1.65
Interest, Taxes, Insurance on Loan	0.91
Total Expenses	14.02
Net Profit.	2.15

* Owners' salaries are not included. In the past Maurice and Bernard Solomon have withdrawn $75 and $125 respectively each week.

management was still faced with the problem of raising long-term capital.

The financial statements for the company are shown in Exhibits VI–1 and VI–2. Competition had been increasing in the retail food business in the past ten years. In moving to the new location, sales (only cash sales would be made) were expected to increase to $9,625 per week. This volume was "extremely conservative in view of the fact that the national sales average for retail food stores was $2.50 a square foot per week." It was anticipated that sales could be increased to the national average by the third or fourth year of operation in the new location. When sales reached the average, the store would be expanded to 10,000 square feet.

A percentage break-down of the projected income statement for the first year appears in Exhibit VI–3. The gross margin was expected to increase to 18 percent when proper departmental controls were established. But in line with the conservative approach throughout the forecast, it was reasonably safe to assume that the margin would not decline below its existing level.

QUESTIONS FOR DISCUSSION

1. Do you feel that management has considered all the factors it should consider before determining whether to relocate?
2. Do you feel the estimates are reasonable? Explain.
3. What are the possible causes for the "total capital invested" to decline? Explain.
4. What sort of profit potential do you feel exists? How do you think break-even points would compare for the present and proposed locations?
5. Do your analyses show the company to be financially sound? Would you loan the company money? How much?
6. How much money should Solomon borrow? Show the cash flow for the next years. Is it adequate?
7. The value of income received today is greater than that received, say, five years from now. A present cost is greater for a company than the same cost in the future. Why are these statements true? Show the present value of estimated future cash income for 10 years.
8. Would you recommend that the company make the proposed move?

VII-7. Ideal Sheen Cleaners, Inc. (B)[1]

Mr. William E. Miller, a respected black businessman of Cleveland, Ohio, had been engaged in various aspects of the laundry and dry cleaning business since 1939. His first business venture as a laundry route operator was financed with an investment of less than $200, of which $50 was obtained from a "loan shark." The assets of the business consisted of a small amount of cash and an automobile which was used to pick-up and deliver laundry between customers and a commercial laundry. He paid the laundry 60 percent of the retail dollar collected from customers for the washing service. Over the years his business grew and expanded until, in 1973, it included: (1) a shirt laundry, (2) a dry cleaning plant, (3) three retail outlets, and (4) several dry cleaning sales and delivery routes. Mr. Miller expected that the business would continue to grow.

Recent financial history of the organization is described in Exhibits VII–1 and VII–2, which contain income statements and balance sheets for

EXHIBIT VII–1

IDEAL SHEEN CLEANERS, INC.
Consolidated Profits and Loss Statements
For Fiscal Years Ending June 30, 1969–1972

	1969	1970	1971	1972
Net Sales	$184,400	$244,400	$262,800	$236,700
Cost of Production	82,300	139,800	128,200	116,900
Gross Profit from Operations	$102,100	$104,600	$134,600	$119,800
Expenses:				
Sales and Delivery	$ 58,000	$ 73,300	$ 78,800	$ 71,700
Administrative	27,700	31,300	30,000	39,100
Total	$ 85,700	$104,600	$108,800	$110,800
Operating Income	$ 16,400	$ 0	$ 25,800	$ 9,000
Other Income	$ 1,400	$ 1,400	$ 1,300	$ 200
Less Other Expenses	$ 3,000	$ 10,000	21,200	$ 18,900
Net Other Income	($ 1,600)	($ 8,600)	($ 19,900)	($ 18,700)
Net Profit before Taxes	$ 14,800	($ 8,600)	$ 5,900	($ 9,700)
Reserve for Income Taxes	$ 2,800	–	–	–
Net Profit after Taxes	$ 12,000	($ 8,600)	$ 5,900	($ 9,700)

---

[1] Prepared by Donald W. Scotton, Jeffrey C. Susbauer, and A. Michael Sibley, The Cleveland State University. See "Ideal Sheen Cleaners, Inc. (A)," Part Three, for previous details.

EXHIBIT VII–2

IDEAL SHEEN CLEANERS, INC.
Consolidated Balance Sheets
For Fiscal Years Ending June 30, 1969–1972

	1969	*1970*	*1971*	*1972*
Assets				
Current Assets:				
Cash on Hand	$ 7,600.00	$ 1,400.00	$ 8,700.00	$ 8,900.00
Notes Receivable	-0-	-0-		
Accounts Receivable	10,200.00	9,000.00	7,800.00	8,200.00
Finished Clothes	14,300.00	21,300.00	19,700.00	32,000.00
Other.	6,100.00	15,000.00	24,600.00	29,500.00
Total.	$ 38,200.00	$ 46,700.00	$ 60,800.00	$ 78,600.00
Fixed Assets:	$117,100.00	$212,800.00	$219,200.00	$227,800.00
Less Reserves for				
Depreciation	18,200.00	33,100.00	48,500.00	61,500.00
Total.	$ 98,900.00	$179,700.00	$170,700.00	$166,300.00
Other Assets	$ 12,300.00	24,500.00	$ 6,100.00	$ 6,100.00
Total Assets	$149,400.00	$250,900.00	$237,600.00	$251,000.00
Liabilities				
Current Liabilities:				
Accounts Payable.	$ 10,500.00	$ 29,900.00	$ 27,200.00	$ 16,600.00
Notes Payable	21,900.00	37,900.00	12,600.00	8,400.00
Miscellaneous Taxes				
Payable	8,600.00	18,100.00	11,100.00	23,800.00
Other.	3,500.00	5,100.00	5,300.00	3,900.00
Total.	$ 44,500.00	$ 91,000.00	$ 56,200.00	$ 52,700.00
Fixed Liabilities:				
Long-Term Notes	$ 62,100.00	$128,100.00	$ 87,800.00	$108,600.00
Mortgage Payable.	-0-	-0-	50,000.00	49,100.00
Reserve for Income Tax . . .	2,800.00	-0-		
Loans from Stockholders . .	-0-	1,000.00	8,900.00	15,700.00
Total.	$ 64,900.00	$129,100.00	$146,700.00	$173,400.00
Net Worth:				
Capital Stock	$ 8,000.00	$ 8,000.00	$ 8,000.00	$ 8,000.00
Earned Surplus	32,000.00	22,800.00	26,700.00	16,900.00
Total.	$ 40,000.00	$ 30,800.00	$ 34,700.00	$ 24,900.00
Total Liabilities and				
Net Worth	$149,400.00	$250,900.00	$237,600.00	$251,000.00

the years 1969–72. An examination of these statements reveals that the business had grown substantially in both sales and total assets.

During 1973, Mr. Miller was considering a number of additional expansion plans designed to increase the firm's long-run profitability and return on investment. These plans included: (1) an increase in the variety of services available at the existing dry cleaning plant and (2) the opening of a retail outlet in Park Center, a large apartment–shopping complex under construction in the downtown area.

Expansion plans at the existing plant called for (1) opening a coin operated laundry, and (2) the addition of drapery and carpet cleaning services. Additional plant and equipment would be needed. Land was available for purchase adjacent to the existing dry cleaning plant. The existing plant had 3,300 square feet of space, and an additional 4,000 square feet of space would be necessary. This would include space for (1) the coin operated laundry, (2) new equipment to clean rugs, drapes, and upholstered furniture, and (3) some replacement equipment to be used for traditional dry cleaning services. This expansion was anticipated to cost approximately $164,900. A breakdown of the costs follows:

Land; Building.	$ 97,000
Drapery and Carpet Cleaning Equipment	13,000
Laundromat Equipment	45,900
Traditional Dry Cleaning Equipment	9,000
Total	$164,900

It was hoped that the addition of the coin-operated laundry and the carpet and drapery cleaning service would draw new customers to the retail store in the existing plant and thus increase sales for traditional garment-cleaning services. The existing dry cleaning plant was operating at only 50 percent of capacity.

The second part of the expansion plan was the opening of a new retail outlet in the Park Center Apartment complex, an urban redevelopment project which would contain 1,000 apartments, a 75-store shopping mall, business offices, and recreational facilities. In addition to Park Center, several other apartment complexes were located within a two-block radius and were thought to be sources of potential customers. Mr. Miller estimated that annual sales through the Park Center Outlet would probably be around $80,000 for the first two years, and might become as high as $200,000 after five or six years.

Mr. Miller had talked with the rental agent for the Park Center, and had tentatively agreed on a 10-year lease with the following terms:

1. For the first 30 months, the base rent would be $1,000 per month, plus 10 percent of all sales volume over $84,000 annually.
2. After 30 months, the base rent would be $1,000 per month, plus 10 percent of all sales volume over $100,000 annually.
3. Other features were estimated to cost about $100 per month, including:
   a. Payment for air-conditioning, heat, and utilities on a metered basis.
   b. Payment of a prorated share of maintenance for the common area of the mall.
   c. Mandatory membership in the Mall Merchants Association, for purposes of joint advertising and promotion of the mall.

The immediate investment required by the Park Center outlet was estimated to be $27,000, mostly for leasehold improvements and equipment. It was estimated that improvements and equipment would have a useful life of approximately 10 years and a negligible salvage value. The outlet would be open 12 hours a day, six days a week. Initially, only one person would be on duty at any time. Salary expense under these circumstances was estimated at approximately $12,000 to $13,000 a year. As business increased, additional staff might be required, and salary expense would then increase.

With a few exceptions, ordinary garment cleaning handled by the Park Center store would be processed at the existing dry cleaning plant. Because excess capacity for this type of cleaning service was available, no new machinery or additional help would be required during the first few years. In the past, the cost of production for garment cleaning averaged about 50 percent of sales. This rate was expected to continue in the future, and was thought to be an appropriate estimate of the cost of processing sales made through the new Park Center store. The annual cost of transporting clothing between Park Center and the plant was estimated at approximately $3,000 per year. Office and administrative expenses would also increase by approximately $5,000 per year.

Mr. Miller made contact with the Shaker Savings Association about financing part of the proposed expansions through the United States Small Business Administration "502 Loan Program." It was his understanding that if the loan was approved, the bank could loan 50 percent (and receive a first mortgage lien or SBA loan guarantee), the Small Business Administration would loan 40 percent, and a local development company would provide the remaining 10 percent. Local Development Companies were specified as an integral part in Section 502 of the Small Business Investment Act of 1958, as amended. The savings association was receptive to such a loan, because it held the mortgage of the existing dry cleaning plant and owned the property Mr. Miller had wanted to buy.

Mr. Miller planned to finance the needed equipment from other sources. He was considering applying for a loan from a commercial bank and a local MESBIC (Minority Enterprise Small Business Investment Corporation.) These investment corporations were made possible under the Small Business Administration Act of 1958 and under the first specialized application of the Small Business Investment Corporation for minority enterprise in 1968. He estimated that the average cost of borrowed funds from all sources would be approximately 7.6 percent per year.

Mr. Miller was optimistic that his plan for revitalizing and expanding his business would work. He was equally optimistic that his past record as a businessman would enable him to receive the financing required.

QUESTIONS FOR DISCUSSION

1. Evaluate the profitability of Ideal Sheen Cleaners for the period 1969 to 1972. For this period, what was the average rate of return after taxes on (1) assets and (2) equity? Is any trend in profitability apparent?

2. Discuss the plan to expand the services offered at the existing dry cleaning plant, considering that current facilities are operated at 50 percent of capacity. What information would be helpful to Mr. Miller in making an expansion decision of this type? How could this information be obtained?

3. Identify the fixed and variable costs associated with the Park Center retail outlet. What level of sales would be necessary to break even (produce zero profit)? What level of sales would be necessary to produce an annual pre-tax profit of $5,000?

4. In light of its present financial condition, does it appear that Ideal Sheen Cleaners will have any difficulty financing the proposed expansions? If you were a banker, under what conditions would you loan the necessary funds to Mr. Miller?

VII–8. *Pictronics, Inc.*[1]

In June of 1963, Mr. Andrews stated: "We have completed more than two years of Pictronics, Inc. operations and feel that we are steadily gaining ground. There have been many problems to overcome but our sales have grown at a satisfactory rate. We have a fine organization of sincere, hardworking people who have faith in the future of our Company."

HISTORY

In 1955, shortly after the end of the Korean War, some graduate engineers organized Technotronics Corporation to rebuild television picture tubes and to develop, manufacture, and distribute other electronic mechanisms and systems having applications in industry. A new plant was constructed in a small town of 2,000 population, located several miles from a metropolitan complex of 1.5 million people.

---

[1] Prepared by Henry Key, Texas Christian University.

Rebuilding of "black-and-white" picture tubes of good quality was eventually achieved, but money spent on research and development for other projects depleted working capital. In 1960, Technotronics Corporation went into bankruptcy.

In June 1960, Andrews, who had recently been placed in charge of sales and collections at Technotronics, became President and General Manager of Technotronics under supervision of a Trustee in Bankruptcy. The trustee reported to the District Court that good profits were earned from June to September, 1960, and the cash position was improved by tightening credits and collections. However, in September creditors and lenders were pressing for liquidation. In order to protect his and his father's sizeable investment, Andrews proposed the creation of Pictronics, Inc., to take over the business, put additional cash in through new stock, and assume the first mortgage loan obligation to the Small Business Administration.

After the trustee's petition to the District Court for permission to liquidate Technotronics was granted, a deal was made with Pictronics Corporation to take over the assets and assume the mortgage note.

THE BUSINESS

Pictronics main business was TV picture tube rebuilding. The average useful life of an early black-and-white picture tube was estimated at three years. Warranty of the tube for the first year of service became standard practice. TV repair shops picked up burned out "dud" tubes for trade–in allowances of $1 to $2 each. A rebuilt picture tube was essentially equivalent to a new "virgin" glass tube, and carried the same one-year warranty. Rebuilding of tubes was carried on by national name-brand manufacturers, regional rebuilders, and local shops in major metropolitan centers. Set owners usually left the choice of a picture tube replacement to the repair shop. Shops preferred rebuilt tubes, because they cost only about half as much as virgin name-brand tubes.

Mr. Andrews believed TV picture tube rebuilding would go from a large number of small local firms to a much smaller number of successful regional rebuilders. A half dozen regional rebuilders like Technotronics, now Pictronics, covered the principal market areas of the U.S.

Some thought had been given to rebuilding color tubes, but the process was much more exacting than for black-and-white tubes. Expensive new equipment would be required, and people would need to be trained to do the work.

Pictronics had found it necessary to make good on warranties of Technotronics tubes in order to maintain good customer relations. Andrews had fought to keep production and deliveries going in order

EXHIBIT VIII–1

PICTRONICS, INC.
Balance Sheets
Years Ended May 31, 1962 and 1963

	1963		*1962*	
Assets				
Current assets:				
Cash		$ 8,430		$ 12,060
Trade receivables	$ 49,190		$ 75,700	
Less: Allowance for doubtful accounts . .	3,740	45,450	4,340	71,360
Federal income tax refund.		13,220		–
Inventories		174,640		107,700
Prepaid expenses		8,580		5,450
Total current assets		$250,320		$196,570
Fixed assets:				
Land		$ 6,500		$ 6,500
Furniture, plant, buildings.	$192,070		$189,090	
Less reserve for depreciation	31,050	161,020	10,770	178,320
Total fixed assets.		$167,520		$184,820
Other assets:				
Escrow accounts	$ 18,250		$ 9,420	
Unamortized organization costs.	6,360	24,610	8,470	17,890
Total Assets		$442,450		$399,280
Liabilities and Equity				
Current liabilities:				
Accounts payable.		$ 53,340		$ 18,280
Notes payable		95,780		55,910
Accrued expenses.		36,140		14,710
Estimated warranty liability from				
predecessor . . . . · . .		5,380		5,380
Estimated federal income tax		–		26,200
Total current liabilities		$190,640		$120,480
Long term mortgage note		153,630		161,900
Total liabilities		$344,270		$282,380
Stockholders' Equity:				
Common stock	$ 94,100		$ 88,470	
Retained earnings.	4,080	98,180	28,430	116,900
Total Liabilities and Equity		$442,450		$399,280

to hold customers and maintain a certain "going concern" value. Sales were on a delivered basis, and for this purpose Pictronics operated a fleet of van trucks on a short-term lease basis.

Accounting and Reporting—Pictronics, Inc. Stock ownership in Pictronics was limited to five individuals who had put up $94,000 in new cash for common stock. The Company was not subject to Securities and Exchange Commission regulations, but creditors, lenders and the Small Business Administration insisted on audited annual financial statements. Frank K. Norton, accountant for Pictronics, explained that the

EXHIBIT VIII–2

PICTRONICS, INC.
Income Statements
Fiscal Years Ending May 31, 1962 and 1963

	1963		*1962*	
Revenue from sales	$1,033,890		$923,080	
Less: Sales returns, discounts, allow-				
ances, federal excise	232,100		146,000	
Net revenue from sales		$801,790		$777,080
Cost of goods sold		685,260		589,000
Gross profit on sales		$116,530		$188,080
Selling expenses:				
Salaries and wages	$ 34,410		$ 32,560	
Freight out	55,210		51,930	
Other selling expenses	12,350	101,970	13,180	97,670
Profit from sales activities.		$ 14,560		$ 90,410
General and administrative expense:				
Salaries and wages	$ 27,150		$ 21,110	
Other expenses	17,520		15,510	
Depreciation—office equipment.	2,460		1,310	
Organization expense amortization. . .	2,110		2,120	
Total general and administrative				
expense		49,240		40,050
Operating profit (loss).		($ 34,680)		$ 50,360
Other expense and income:				
Interest expense	$ 16,040		$ 6,640	
Miscellaneous income	5,560		10,910	
Excess income (expense).		(10,480)		4,270
Net income (loss) before				
federal tax		($ 45,160)		$ 54,630
Provision for federal tax				26,200
Refund due on federal tax . . .		20,810		
Net Profit after Federal Tax				$ 28,430
Net Loss after Federal Tax				
Refund		$ 24,350		

accounting system was modeled on that commonly kept by a trading commercial firm. There was no formal cost accounting system, but statistical cost studies were made from time to time in order to gain information for cost control efforts and for use in inventory valuations.

Comparative condensed financial statements for fiscal years ending May 31, 1962 and 1963 (audited by C.P.A.'s) appear as Exhibits VIII–1 and VIII–2.

QUESTIONS FOR DISCUSSION

1. What "bad effects" left over from the bankruptcy of Technotronics did Pictronics have to overcome?

2. Do you think Andrews was wise in forming Pictronics from Technotronics? What other alternatives did he have? Do they appear to be financially better?

3. Which trends, from 1962 to 1963, look good and which look bad?

4. What accounting and financial controls appear to be necessary? Explain.

5. Prepare some financial ratios to help in analyzing the financial position of the company.

6. Would you have invested your money in the company? Explain.

Part **VIII**

Where Do You Go from Here?

The United States seems to be ahead of other counties in generating effective business enterpreneurs and executive leaders, in conceiving and organizing new business ventures, and in producing and distributing goods efficiently and effectively. It seems to us that the greatest single factor in this country's economic growth and development has been its ability to produce capable industrial and commercial leaders, especially in the more dynamic, innovative, and flexible area of small business.

We have assumed in the past that we were not only leading in this respect, but that we were somehow assured of a continuing supply of such leaders through some process of "natural progression" in both small and large organizations—that the needed managerial talent would naturally work its way to the top. However, it is becoming increasingly clear that this is not necessarily true.

Now there is a great need for more dynamic, aggressive, and personal business leadership with its vitalizing and envigorating force on the lives and fortunes of their organizations. Everything else being equal, this can occur more easily in small enterprises than in large organizations. We believe this is where the real future of American business growth and development lies. It is in the new and growing small firms where the really challenging, stimulating, and rewarding experiences exist—alongside many frustrating disappointments. However, the decision of whether to become a small entrepreneur is yours now that you have explored the unique advantages and disadvantages of small business and know what is required to establish and operate one.

In previous parts of this book, we have looked at the characteristics of small businesses and their owners, the methods of choosing what business to enter, and how to enter an existing business or start a new one; how to manage your firm; and some of the problem areas you will encounter, including marketing, operations, personnel, and financing.

Two problems which are unique to small firms and which you should face are: (1) working in a family business, and (2) providing for your successor. They are discussed in Chapter 26.

Finally, there are several cases which integrate these subjects and provide you with an overview that has not previously been possible.

26

Providing for Management Succession

In most small firms, the development of managerial personnel and the provision for management succession are greatly neglected, often until it is too late to do anything about them. Therefore, now that you have your firm operating successfully, you should answer these questions: If my business is a proprietorship, do I want my wife to manage it when I leave? If my company is a partnership and I leave it, do I want my wife to be a partner? How will my death affect my small corporation? Who will fill my shoes so that I can retire when I choose? Is there someone to operate the firm so I can take vacations or go to training programs or conventions?

You should realize that many children, grandchildren, and other relatives do not have the capabilities—or the interest—to manage your firm. Also, you need to be exceedingly competent to be either a judge of their managerial talent or a teacher to provide management training.

Many of you will start your professional career by working in, or operating, your family's firm or that of your spouse. The following discussion is offered for your benefit.

MANAGING A FAMILY-OWNED BUSINESS

When close relatives work together in a business, emotions often interfere with business decisions. "It's our business," is the motto in a family enterprise. Conflicts sometimes arise because relatives look at the business from different viewpoints. For example, relatives who are furnishing the capital or are the "money-men" may consider only income when judging capital expenditures, growth, and other major matters. Relatives engaged in the daily operations judge money matters from the viewpoint of securing the production, sales, and personnel necessary to make the firm successful. Clearly these two viewpoints may conflict.[1]

The firm's top manager should recognize the extent of the emotions involved and make objective decisions. It is often hard for the manager and other relatives to make rational decisions about the skills and abilities of each other. Also, quarrels and ill feelings of relatives may spread to nonfamily employees. Or, family quarrels may carry over into the firm's operations and interfere with its effectiveness. The manager should not permit the business to be divided into factions. It is necessary to convince nonfamily employees that their interests are best served by a profitable company rather than by allegiance to any particular family member. Another complication that often occurs is that nonfamily employees tend to base their decisions on the family's tensions. They know how their bosses react, and they react accordingly.

Some family-owned companies are handicapped with high turnover among their most capable nonfamily employees. Relatives are sometimes responsible, for they may resent outside talent and make things unpleasant for nonfamily managers. Or, key managers may resign because the lines of promotion are closed to them. A troublesome relative may be discharged (with difficulty), assisted in starting another business in a noncompeting line, exiled to a branch office, or assisted in obtaining a job elsewhere.

Another problem is the family member who has occupied one job after another without being successful in any one of them. But now this person has a job, a title, and a salary—with you. A "ghost," or a lesser manager who knows the job and knows how to perform it, is doing work for which the other person is getting the credit. If the business is incorporated, perhaps the "floater" cannot be discharged because of a major stockholder's complaints. However, the useless manager may be shifted to some newly-created menial position with title and salary, but have no actual job to perform. The "ghost" may be promoted and given proper recognition.

The ceiling on the amount of money a manager can spend without permission from the rest of the family may be too low to permit taking advantage of productive situations—such as a good price on raw materials.

Perhaps the manager is "in a bind" because of emotional involvement.

---

[1] Robert E. Levinson, *Problems in Managing a Family-Owned Business* (Washington, D.C.: Small Business Administration, 1971), Management Aids for Small Manufacturers, No. 208.

For example, it may be necessary to clear routine matters with family members, because they have not let the manager forget past mistakes— particularly if the person is young, an in-law, or a distant relative.

Another difficulty may be that relatives indulge in excessive family talk during working hours, which hampers their performance as well as the performance of others. The manager should set the example and insist that other relatives refrain from family talk while on the job. If the company can afford it, one way to obtain objective control in a family-owned business is to hire an outside professional manager to handle day-to-day operations.

Definite lines of authority and responsibility are an absolute necessity. The responsibilities of family members should be specified and the extent of the authority, duties, and activities should be clearly stated. A non-family employee should be high enough in the organization to be involved in operations and assist in smoothing out any emotional family decisions.

The manager's authority to suspend or discharge flagrant violators of company rules should also be specified. Control is weakened if the manager must make special allowances for "family employees."

A common problem is the hiring of relatives who lack talent. Perhaps such a relative can be assigned to a job that permits contributions without disturbing other employees.

A relative can demoralize an organization through dealings with other employees by loafing, avoiding unpleasant tasks, taking special privileges, or making snide remarks about the manager and other relatives. The manager should assign such a relative to a job involving minimum contact with other employees and requiring no important decisions.

A more devastating aspect of this type of activity is where one of the family members "spies" on other employees.

> In a retail clothing store, the aunt of the owner-president is no-torious for making life miserable for other workers, especially fe-males. She "sneaks" into the ladies room and reports anyone found smoking. The employees always look behind clothing racks before they say anything personal, or derogatory of the family to see if she is listening. They refer to her as "the Gestapo." Needless to say, the morale is constantly low. Turnover is far greater than for compar-able stores.

Often the owner-manager may believe an expenditure should be made in order to improve efficiency; yet, other family members may oppose it because they consider it to be only an expense and money out of their pockets. To overcome this tendency, the manager might base arguments for the expenditure on information which nonfamily employees have derived. Perhaps it is possible to show the relatives that an investment can be recovered in a few years. Outside business advisers—including bankers, accountants, attorneys, or consultants—may assist the manager in convincing the relatives of the merits of the expenditure.

When some relatives in a family-owned business grow older, they frequently develop a desire to maintain the *status quo*. They can block, or at least hamper, company growth. These relatives may be given an opportunity to convert their common stock to preferred stock or to sell some of their stock to younger relatives. Perhaps they can be "gradually retired" through salary reductions over several years and induced to relinquish some of their interest in the firm.

Provisions for paying family members and dividing the profits equitably among them can also be difficult. If the business is a corporation, stock dividends may be appropriate.

The salaries of family members should be competitive with those paid others of comparable rank and ability in the same area. Fringe benefits—such as deferred profit-sharing plans, pension plans, insurance programs, and stock purchase programs—can be useful in dividing profits equitably.

If you are the manager of a family-owned business, you are not alone. Other individuals managing family companies in the same community may provide a source of information and assistance to you. You should exchange ideas with them and learn how they have solved problems similar to yours. Also, if you manage a small corporation, the presence of outsiders on the board of directors can be of benefit to you.

SOME DIFFICULT PROBLEMS WITH MANAGERS

You will have many problems with your managers, whether they are members of the family or not. You should be familiar with three staffing problems, which are particularly difficult in small firms: (1) the managers who thinks only in terms of "the past," (2) the one who "makes work," and (3) the one guilty of work duplication.

The first of these managers retains the old ways and refuses to learn and adopt new methods of management, regardless of how effective they may seem or how needed they are. Either dismissal or transfer to another assignment is appropriate in this case.

The make-work manager may have been hired to perform a specific job—such as doing a market survey—but the need for his services no longer exists. Dismissal or transfer to a more productive position may be appropriate.

The problem of work duplication may exist because two managers are both supervising the same project. Their duties should be reappraised.

If you are faced with similar staffing problems in your company, you should start with one or two changes at a time and see how they work out. You should also try to make changes before they become a dire necessity.

You may be faced with another type of staffing problem when one of your key executives leaves. Some dislocation will inevitably occur, but you usually have some latitude in the kind of replacement you seek. You could consider reorganizing your management, redistributing the present assignments, and using present managers more effectively. The job specifications for a new manager could be written less narrowly, and the range of choice broadened. Your managers should participate in this planning because they will feel that they have contributed to the decision and will accept the newcomer more readily.

Often, your managers will prefer that an individual from within the firm replace a key manager who has left. This attitude usually appears not only in the manager who expects to be promoted, but also in other employees. If you decide upon an outsider, you should discuss the reasons with the manager who expected the promotion and with other managers prior to filling the vacancy.

If you recruit someone from the outside, you should have your people who will be working with the new manager meet and talk with candidates. You should observe their reactions and ask for their evaluations of the prospect. You should seek answers to these important questions: Will the prospect fit into the community? Will the family be able to make the adjustment? You should give the prospective manager ample opportunity to consider your situation carefully before deciding.

You can appraise a prospective manager's ability by considering several kinds of information: records of past performance, personal statements, and evaluations by others. Perhaps a prospective sales manager provides data which show a 60 percent increase in sales volume over the last five years while the sales force rose only 20 percent. The candidate's personal statements may reflect an interest in high-quality, custom-built products with low volume and high margin. You should determine whether there are inconsistencies in the candidate's statements. If you have doubts, you should ask more questions. Concerning others' evaluations, you should not automatically reject the prospect because of a poor reference. The latter may result from a personality conflict, circumstances of resignation, or some other situation which does not affect the prospect's suitability for your company.

In determining compensation, you should review the remuneration of your present managers to see if it is adequate and equitable, if it is properly related to their contributions to the firm, and if it is comparable to that of the new manager. You should probably have a five-year compensation plan in mind for a new manager. Keep in mind that if your offer is too high now you may limit your ability to increase rewards for improved performance in the future. However, you should not drive too hard a bargain. To help make the new manager's interests coincide with yours, you should consider offering a share of ownership in your firm.

When you hire a manager you should discuss with him or her how the relationship can be terminated. There should be some penalty for termination, but it should not be so great that you keep an unsatisfactory manager rather than pay the penalty. You also want to avoid giving the manager a bonus for taking a better job elsewhere. You should not conceal any unpleasant conditions that must be confronted soon after the new manager reports for work.

Some turnover in your middle management group can be beneficial if it does not happen too often. If you have a young manager with ability and ambition, you should be frank about the opportunities you can offer. If such a person should desire to move, you should offer help in finding a better position. This assistance is preferable to his job-hunting without your knowledge.

> One of us was on the Panama Limited train going from Chicago to New Orleans with the owner-manager of a large office in the latter city. He was reading the *New Orleans Times-Picayune* want ads. Suddenly he exclaimed, "That's my telephone number!"
>
> When asked what he meant, he indicated a "position wanted" ad which gave one of his office phones for prospective employers to call. Needless to say, he was very upset with the young man who had placed the ad.

Replacing a manager can sometimes benefit you. For example, suppose a production manager who has excelled in plant layout, tooling, and production methods leaves you. In replacing this person, you might want a manager with a different mix of skills—perhaps including labor relations, employee productivity, and quality of supervision.

PREPARING FOR YOUR SUCCESSOR

What preparations should you make when you are planning to retire, acquire another business, or otherwise turn the business over to someone else? Too often, a small company suffers under these circumstances. Sales may decrease or production may lag. These difficulties can be prevented by preparations which will enable the new manager to pick up where you leave off. The key is to make available to your successor the specialized knowledge which you have accumulated over the years.

You should create a reference source for a new manager by making an inventory of the various kinds of information used to manage and operate your business. The inventory should consist of three kinds of information:

1. Facts about the general administration of the company.
2. Data concerning the firm's finances.
3. Information about operating and technical aspects.

Examples of these inventories are presented in the Appendix with this chapter. This type of inventory should also help you evaluate your firm at any time, so you might want to do it periodically.

You should set down some information about goals and objectives you hope to see the company reach, both before you leave and afterwards. An illustration of this type of objective might be the accumulation of funds to replace an old plant. This program should be supplemented with profit and loss and cash flow projections. These long-range goals should be described in two parts:

1. Steps to be accomplished before you leave.
2. Steps to be accomplished after you leave.

Even though your top assistant should have the same capabilities as you, you should also try to find someone who complements your abilities. Two dynamic and aggressive individuals often clash. "The capable assistant is usually one whose strengths match your weaknesses, rather than one whose strong points match yours."[2]

In order to facilitate a smooth transition, you should bring in the new manager as early as possible. The length of the transition period varies according to your plans, the type of business you are in, the new manager's experience and knowledge, whether the person is a relative or a hired outsider, and the size of your firm. The period may vary from three to five years.

Ultimately, the moment arrives when you must turn over to someone else the business you have created with your own ambition, initiative, and character. If you have built well, it will survive as testimony of your creativity.

SUMMARY

Because of the time, effort, and money you have expended to make your small business a success, it is important that you do everything

---

[2] Med Serif, *Pointers for Developing Your Top Assistant*, (Washington, D.C.: Small Business Administration, 1972), Small Marketers Aids No. 101.

possible to provide for effective management succession. In order to do this, you must make adequate provisions for the selection, development, and motivation of competent professional managers to succeed you and assure your firm's continuation. Some ideas to make this possible have been presented in this part.

APPENDIX: INVENTORY OF INFORMATION USED TO MANAGE AND OPERATE A COMPANY

Inventory of Facts about General Administration

Company History:	Date organized, key founders, and major events.
	Clippings of stories from newspapers and trade journals concerning your company.
	Brochures concerning new products, processses, sales personnel, etc.
Company Organization:	Organization chart.
	Job specifications.
	Description of key employees, including your evaluation of their potential.
	Report of studies made by your employees or an outside consultant on your company.
Policies:	Information on credit and selling terms, vacations, retirement plans, employee loans and advances, etc.
Legal Matters:	Patents, licenses, and royalty agreements.
	Note where each formal document is filed.
	Employment and labor agreements.
	Leases.
	Contracts with suppliers and customers.
	Outcome of past law suits, and pending suits.
Outside Services:	List and brief description of outside professional people who work with your company, including bankers, accountants, insurance agents, advertising agencies, consultants, etc.

Inventory of Financial Data

Profit and loss statements for past ten years.

Copy of most recent balance sheet.

Copy of most recent budget.

Brief description of company's working capital turnover trends, return on investment trends, operating ratios, etc.

List of current bank accounts, including average balances and name of bank employee who handles accounts.

List of prior banking connections, indicating the line of credit and bank officers who arranged it.

List of paid tax bills.

List of insurance policies, including a description of coverages and premiums and name of agent.

Copies of your financial and control reports, with notation about frequency of preparation and distribution.

Copies of procedures or procedure manuals.

Inventory of Operating and Technical Information

Marketing:

List of company's products or services, and notes concerning customer acceptance, profitability, and future potential.

List of geographical areas in which each product is sold, types of customers, and the largest customers.

List of distribution channels.

Brief outline of advertising program, including how it is coordinated with other sales efforts.

Brief descriptions of sales training programs.

Brief description of how prices are set for current and new products.

Brief description of competitors, including a list of their products, location and size of their plants, share of the market, pricing policies, and channels of distribution.

Production:

List of major pieces of equipment. Brief appraisal of efficiency of the plant and equipment.

List of product and manufacturing specifications and process procedures.

List of studies made to improve layout and quality control, replace existing equipment, etc.

Brief description of how production is scheduled and controlled (orders on hand or for stock).

Brief description of standards used for measuring performance and methods for eliminating waste.

Purchasing:

Lists concerning: (1) major materials purchased; (2) names of suppliers; (3) present contracts with suppliers; and (4) procedures for buying, including kind of approval needed for various types of purchases.

Other Areas:

Inventory of knowledge in special areas, including research and development, engineering, quality control, etc.

Source: Frederick E. Halstead, *Preparing for New Management* (Washington, D.C.: Small Business Administration, 1972), Management Aids for Small Manufacturers, No. 183.

QUESTIONS FOR FURTHER DISCUSSION

1. What are some staffing problems an owner-manager should be familiar with?
2. What problem will face an owner-manager when a key manager leaves?
3. Discuss the problems involved in managing a family-owned business.
4. How should a manager prepare to leave and turn the business over to a new manager?

WHERE TO LOOK FOR FURTHER INFORMATION

Halstead, E. Frederick. *Preparing for New Management.* Washington, D.C.: Small Business Administration, 1972. (Management Aids for Small Manufacturers, No. 183.)

Levinsen, Robert E. *Problems in Managing a Family-Owned Business.* Washington, D.C.: Small Business Administration, 1970. (Management Aids for Small Manufacturers, No. 208.)

Robinsen, Joseph A. *How to Find a Likely Successor.* Washington, D.C.: Small Business Administration, 1968. (Management Aids for Small Manufacturers, No. 198.)

Cases for Part VIII

VIII–1. Arthur Adams—Service Station Operator[1]

Art's Universal Station in Morton seemed in a state of chaos as Arthur Adams, the owner, drove up. The gasoline islands were crowded with out-of-state cars, some of which were pulling vacation trailers. Three employees in distinctive Universal Oil Company uniforms were shuttling in and out of the office to write up credit card sales and ring them up on the cash register. Adams pitched in and attempted to clear the jam around the pumps to the point where two employees could keep them under control. Then he turned to the service bays which were also jammed with cars and trucks. An employee was discussing the sale of tires to a customer when Adams intervened and made the sale. The employee was sent to pick up the tires at one of the three buildings in town where Adams stored tires.

With a little direction from Adams, the station quickly was transformed into a more efficient unit. Inside of two hours, two sets of car tires, three sets of truck tires, and a tractor tire were sold. Adams wondered why, on days when he was in the station, sales were two or three times higher than when the station was left with Dale Clinton, his station manager.

---

[1] Prepared by David R. Seymour, Weyerhaeuser Company, and Sydney C. Reagan, Southern Methodist University.

After things settled down at the station, Adams picked up the excess cash and his book work and drove home to work on the books. He dreaded the thought of working on his books, and often procrastinated when he came to do so. "Where does a guy my age learn how to figure how much he is making on each of his operations? I wish I could be sure of an income when I am too old to pump gas. Sometimes I wonder if it wouldn't have been better to have worked at a job where you get a pension in your old age."

The phone rang, and the caller identified himself as Jack Fuller, a representative of Midstates Petroleum Company. Fuller inquired about the possibility of leasing the self-service station and car wash Adams owned about a block from his Universal service station in Morton. Adams replied that "I don't really know what would be a fair rental; Universal leases my Middleville station for $630 a month, and I really don't know if that is a fair price. Let me check with Dunbar at the First National Bank of Morton and see if I can't come up with a fair price. I also want him to tell me how much I can sell it for with the idea of leasing it and operating it myself."

Later that afternoon, as Adams drove back to the Morton station, he wondered how long it would be before an interstate highway would bypass his two Morton stations, which were located on the main regional highway. Even though no interstate was even being proposed, he also was concerned about his other properties along the highway. He had toyed with the idea of putting a restaurant or a motel on land he owned between the old station and the new self-service station and car wash, or perhaps he could use the land he owned across the highway for a KOA campground. These ideas intrigued him, but he reminded himself that he had no experience along these lines and his talents were limited to operating service stations and selling tires. He also remembered he was now 54 years old and had to begin seriously preparing for retirement.

Adams had always been able to sell. After returning from World War II, he drove a soft-drink delivery route. In the early 1950s, he quit the route to try his luck operating a small Universal station in Morton, a town of 1,500 persons. He was so successful, that by 1957 he had exceeded the sales capacity of this one-bay station. But growth prospects were so limited that he told the Universal bulk dealer, Roger Wilkinson, of his intention to try another field when his lease expired.

Wilkinson recognized Adams' potential and decided to build a larger station on the highway if Adams would lease and operate it. Adams agreed to a 10-year lease at $280 per month, and finally moved into this new two-bay station in 1958. By 1965 he had exceeded its capacity.

The population of Morton would not appear to support such a large sales volume, but it was a center for a big ranching area and Art's Universal service was the principal regional supplier of truck and tractor tires. Universal Oil Company had pressured Adams to sell the Universal tire line, but he found it profitable to stock other major brands as well.

In early 1966, Adams tried but was unable to convince Universal and Wilkinson to expand the station. After considerable discussion, Wilkinson offered to sell the station to Adams for $28,000 cash, if Adams continued to pay him rent until the lease expired in 1968. Universal held an option from Wilkinson to buy the station at any time during the lease for $40,000. With Wilkinson's offer in hand, Adams attempted to convince Universal Oil to increase the purchase option to $65,000, so he could expand the station without loss. The Universal representative suggested the company might be willing to renegotiate a lease if Adams would put up a station in Middleville, a city about 200 miles away, located in the middle of rich farmland and oil property. After considerable negotiating, the following "package" arrangement was agreed to in late 1966 by Adams, Wilkinson, and Universal Oil Company:

I. Morton Station:
    A. Ten-year lease agreement with three five-year options:
        1. Universal Oil Company agreed to:
            a. Establish a $510 per month credit. This amount would become a monthly rent payable to Adams should someone else operate the station.
            b. Pay maintenance charges less than $50 per item.
            c. Pay real estate taxes above $600 per year (currently $648).
        2. Adams agreed to:
            a. Transfer his credit of $150 a month to Universal Oil Company in lieu of rent. Universal would have charged a third-party operator a higher rent.
            b. Sell the station to Universal Oil Company at any time during the lease for $65,000.
            c. Expand the station to three service bays.
            d. Pay property insurance, which was currently $375 a year.
            e. Pay maintenance charges of $50 or more.
            f. Pay real estate taxes up to $600 a year.
    B. Financial Data:
        1. Purchase price to Adams of $28,000 plus 24 payments of $280.
        2. Expansion cost to Adams of $25,000, borrowed at 5½ percent for 10 years.

II. The Middleville Station:
    A. Ten-year lease agreement with three five-year options.
        1. Universal Oil Company agreed to:

      a. Pay Adams $630 per month rent.

      b. Pay maintenance charges less than $50 per item.

      c. Pay real estate taxes above $600 per year (currently $550).

  2. Adams agreed to:

      a. Sell the station to Universal Oil Company for $75,000 at any time during the lease period.

      b. Pay the property insurance, which was currently $390 a year.

      c. Pay any maintenance charges of $50 or more.

      d. Pay real estate taxes up to $600 per year.

B. Financial Data:

  1. Land cost to Adams of $22,500;

  2. Building cost to Adams of $48,000 for a three-bay station with 32,000-gallon bulk plant; and

  3. Mortgage terms: $48,000 at 6 percent for 10 years.

By 1971, five years after Adams expanded his Morton station and purchased his Middleville station, a sales capacity problem again confronted Adams. He tried to get Universal to renegotiate the lease so the purchase option price could be increased to cover any added investment necessary to expand the station. By expanding the station without a new lease, Adams would be increasing the probability that Universal Oil would exercise the purchase option. The regional Universal officials agreed to change the lease in early 1971, but the national office refused.

Adams knew that in order to increase tire sales he would have to keep his employees working without interruption in the service bays and keep the one- and two-dollar customers to a minimum. He reasoned that if he opened a self-service station and car wash on the highway about a block from the Morton station on land he had purchased in 1970 for $14,000, he could sell gas for four cents a gallon less and increase the efficiency of his Universal station's tire mounting and service functions. He was able to obtain a loan of $30,000 at eight percent interest payable over a 10-year period. This loan covered the total cost of construction, which was begun in mid-1971.

At that time, Adams' taxable income was in the $36–40,000 range. As his income had increased in recent years, he had used surplus cash to accelerate loan payments on his two Universal stations. He would have paid off both debts in 1974, two years ahead of schedule, but his accountant convinced him to accelerate payments on the carwash and self-service station instead. Adams was looking for another place to invest some surplus cash.

The self-service station and car wash was originally designed to stay open 24 hours and run with a minimum of labor. The gas pumps took one dollar bills and dispensed one dollar's worth of gasoline, while the car wash consisted of pressure wands which customers used to wash their cars, trucks, and tractors. In 1972, the self-service operation began to cut into the gasoline sales at the Universal station. At that time the fire marshall ruled the station could not operate without an attendant, and subsequently the hours of operation were shortened. However, the 1972 volume was high enough to give the self-service station a favorable allotment during the energy crisis.

Adams had considered building some apartments in Morton. He felt there was a demand for apartments, although none had been built in Morton up to that time. He had been looking at other alternatives, including stocks or other securities, but he did not have much faith in this type of investment after investing in mutual funds in the mid-1960s. He was also worried about his Middleville station, because Universal was pressuring him to sell it to the present operator. Adams admitted he needed help in untangling his business arrangements and in planning his financial future, but he did not know where to find it.

QUESTIONS FOR DISCUSSION

1. What is wrong with opeartions of the Morton station? How can operations be made more efficient?
2. What is Adams' marketing strategy (if any)? Develop an improved marketing strategy.
3. Why has Adams had difficulty expanding his business in Morton? Present a plan for expansion.
4. If Adams wished 10 percent per year return on his invested capital in the Middleville station, what price should he have asked in 1971? In 1974?
5. How does the price of the Middleville station, based on return on investment, differ from a price based on the rights to future income and a reversionary (salvage) value of the property? Assume constant values for rent and expenses, a 25-year total economic life for the station, a three percent per year appreciation of land values, and a 10 percent capitalization rate.
6. What would be a fair monthly rental for the car wash?
7. What are the prospects for Adams' other real estate holdings? Determine their potential, and make recommendations for further purchases and dispositions of real estate.
8. In a small town, where can a small businessman get professional assistance for financial and management problems at a price he can afford?
9. What are the problems faced by Adams in investing his surplus capital? Prepare an investment plan for him.
10. How should Adams plan for retirement?

VIII-2. Robertson Rubber Products, Inc.[1]

Many people see the man who owns his own business as "having it made." To them, he is his own boss and can come and go as he pleases. There are no set hours when he must report for duty or stay at work. He can tell people what to do, and they had better do it if they want to keep their jobs. They also believe that he is "making bushels of money."

In reality, small, independent owner-managed businesses are not the panacea commonly thought. This case illustrates the growth and development of one such firm, Robertson Rubber Products, Inc., owned by Mr. Fred Engle. To all who want to be their own bosses, it would be wise to reflect a moment on the pros and cons of owning that "dream venture."

EARLY COMPANY HISTORY

In 1893, Isaiah Robertson founded the company that still carried his name at the time of this case. Mr. Robertson perceived an opportunity to serve industrial customers as a manufacturer's representative with a limited line of rubber products. His son-in-law joined the firm in 1915. The firm began to prosper as he directed its activities to the "after-market" rubber products customers. In 1930, Mr. Robertson hired an experienced rubber products salesman, who convinced him that great opportunities were available in "jobbing" operations.

World War II produced a greatly increased demand for rubber products of all kinds, and the firm expanded operations by adding a manufacturing job shop to produce those small specialty items which large rubber manufacturers were not interested in producing. The company developed a reputation as the place to go with a problem larger firms considered to be of too limited potential volume to warrant the tooling expenses incurred. When the War ended, Robertson Rubber Products had annual sales of nearly $1 million, and had found its niche between the little company that lacked RRPI's skills and the big company that was not interested in the volume of job that Robertson manufactured.

[1] Prepared by Jeffrey C. Susbauer and Donald W. Scotton with research assistance by Christopher French, all of Cleveland State University.

516

RECENT HISTORY

At present, Robertson sales are generated 30 percent from jobbing, and 40 percent from distributing. Of these, the manufacturing operations are the most profitable, while distributing has the least margin. Intense distributor and jobber competition exists in the market area presently served by the company, which is generally confined to the State of Missouri. Manufacturing competition is less intense, since the manufacture of rubber products is a specialized business requiring considerable skill and expertise.

Larger manufacturers cannot compete with Robertson's expertise and overhead rates, and are generally uninterested in attracting the types of jobs Robertson performs. Some competition does exist within the market area served by RRPI from other small rubber products manufacturing concerns, but the impact of over 25 years of experience in this field has contributed to a solid list of satisfied customers. Opportunities generally exist for further manufacturing, jobbing, and distribution expansion of the enterprise without expanding the market territory boundaries.

Shortly after World War II, Mr. Fred Engle came to work for RRP. He later became president of the firm. One factor leading to this position was the fact that "he married the boss's daughter," but it was by no means his only asset. Engle had held a variety of jobs after graduating from Purdue University in 1937 with B.S. and M. S. degrees in Metallurgical Engineering. Among other occupations, he had been a mining engineer and an assistant production manager for a middle-sized corporation prior to serving as a Major in the U.S. Army during the War.

When Engle assumed control of the company in 1949, it had gone through several changes. From its early stages of strictly being a distributor, it had diversified into manufacturing, jobbing, and distribution. Engle's major contribution to continuing this diversification was to change the primary direction of the firm from the "after-market" to the "Original Equipment Manufacturer (OEM)" market. Yet, the firm continued to supply the after-market.

Engle felt that the company could best develop by using its manufacturing facilities. He apparently made the proper decision, because the firm grew from about $250,000 in annual sales when he became president, to nearly $1 million in sales in 1973. In addition, Engle made major modifications to the organization of the firm during his 24-year tenure as owner-manager.

ORGANIZATION STRUCTURE

The Robertson organization was housed in a two-story building in a large city's downtown area of the mid-central region. It employed

18 people, including Mr. Engle. He and his wife owned 90 percent of the stock of the concern. A simplified organization chart is shown in Exhibit II–1.

Engle felt his company was rather unique, and that this was a direct

EXHIBIT II–1
Robertson Rubber Products, Inc. Organization Chart

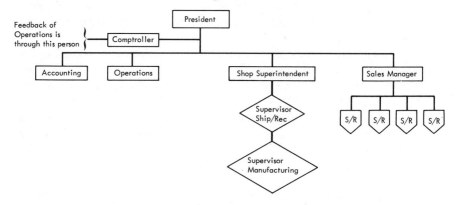

result of his planning and operating philosophy. He noted that most small, closely held, owner-managed firms do not really provide for the succession of the enterprise in the event of the death or retirement of the owner-manager. It is not unusual for such firms to simply dissolve when the principal owner-manager retires or dies.

The Board of Directors of the firm included Mr. Engle and his wife. One long-time employee, who was also a stockholder, was the only other inside director of the firm. Mr. Engle had placed several outside directors on the board to advise him and serve as "devil's advocates" to his whims and plans. He included other business managers, the Dean of the local College of Business Administration, an economist, and a lawyer. Engle believed that, "If the Board does not thwart at least one of my ideas at each session, they are not doing their job." Yet he was free to accept or reject the advice of the Board, because he owned the company.

FINANCIAL AND FISCAL CONTROLS

Though his formal academic background was obtained in engineering, Engle understood that sound financial control systems were essential to the success of his firm. He hired a staff comptroller for the corporation in 1964 to ensure that he was receiving timely information upon which to make decisions and gauge the performance and direction of the firm.

It proved to be a wise decision, in his estimation. As Mr. Engle explained:

> The large firm can make many mistakes, but it is insulated from the shock effect of those errors. In the small firm, a major mistake can have catastrophic effects, because there are few buffers, checks, and balances. At the same time, a properly responsive control system can provide me with the means of finding out about the mistake, and the small size of my operations pays the dividend of my being able to respond more quickly than the large firm can.

Employee Relations: Philosophy

Until 1971, the company did not differ from many small firms. It was run in a paternalistic fashion, with fairly lax work rules, no unionization, and a "happy family" atmosphere. Mr. Engle became concerned that perhaps the family was *too* happy when he noticed his cost of overhead and manufacturing labor rising in relation to previous years' performance.

His corrective action—replacing the manufacturing operations supervisor with a more hard-nosed supervisor—produced the opposite effect from what he had expected. He had hoped the new supervisor would make people more conscious of the need to be productive and improve the manufacturing margin. Instead, the supervisor managed to alienate the hourly employees. They, in turn, sought a union to represent them as their bargaining agent.

Like most owners, Mr. Engle viewed this unionization attempt with uncertainty. He dragged his feet as long as he could, and mounted a counter-campaign. Finally, when he could not legally postpone recognition further, the union became the workers' representative in his shop. After the shock had worn off, he reflected on what was accomplished by unionization:

> Prior to 1971, no strict work rules were really enforced. Everybody in this company had the right to come to my office and complain about their problems. I had to figure out all the wage rates, merit increases, percentages of profit sharing for each employee. We had an in-house grievance system, but it always included my negotiation with the worker and the supervisor. When the union came in, I suddenly found I no longer had to perform most of these functions. The labor contract set the wage rates, fringe benefits package, and laid out procedures for handling disputes. Strangely, the two workers who agitated most for union recognition were not backed by the union when we fired them for infractions of work rules shortly after the union took over. All of a sudden, the union became the enforcer and made the employees 'toe the line.' Also, in exchange for $.15/hour, we negotiated the end

of merit increases and profit sharing for the hourly workers. There are several hourly workers that now wish they did not have to pay the initiation dues to the union and those monthly dues. The union also makes sure production quotas are achieved.

SALARIED AND OFFICER PERSONNEL

Of the 18 people employed by Robertson Rubber Products, nine were included in the categories of officers and salaried personnel. Salaried personnel (6) were distributed among the Accounting, Operations, and Sales functions of the business. All these people shared in any profits the company made each year.

For 30 years, Robertson had had an employee bonus plan, keyed to profitability. In these years, only in 1971 had the company failed to distribute some portion of profit to those employees. In recent years, this distribution had ranged from a high of 24 percent of pre-tax profit to a low (excluding 1971) of 10 percent.

Prior to Mr. Engle's ascendancy to the presidency, profit sharing was the only fringe benefit the company had for employees. Mr. Engle believed that:

> . . . in order to retain good employees and attract competent new ones, there had to be a better fringe package. Therefore, over the years, I have added additional fringes of full hospitalization, a group life insurance policy, and a sickness and accident policy to what the employees could receive from the company. Of course, they have been covered by Social Security for many years.

Under the charter of the company, as amended, Mr. Engle was required to pay a *minimum* of five percent of profits before taxes into the company profit-sharing fund. This was deferred compensation to employees covered. It took three years of continuous employment, full-time, to be eligible for any benefits. Employees' rights to the noncontributory fund became fully-vested after 13 years of continuous employment.

Compensation in the company was perhaps unique when compared to similar practices in government and large private corporations. Mr. Engle commented:

> We have some sales representatives who have not grossed less than $30,000 for years. Their compensation is geared to their productivity, on a commission basis. As a consequence, there are a handful of individuals in this company who earn more than I do. I think this is healthy, and I encourage it. After all, the more they sell, the more worth I have in the company. But you don't find this condition in your normal, run-of-the-mill *Fortune 500* firm.

THE COMFORT STAGE

One of Mr. Engle's problems was the fact that he had been owner-manager of the company for over 20 years. He had guided its growth and development at a rate which compounded more than 10 percent annually. Yet, in 1973, it took about $25,000 in additional working capital to generate growth at the rate previously obtained. He had reached what he described as the "comfort stage"—a position where he obtained sufficient remuneration from the company to support his material needs and desires. Increasingly in the past few years, he had been able to do what he wanted, within limits, and still keep the company on an even keel. In recent months, for example, he had felt sufficiently comfortable about the competency of his subordinates to take off a week at a time to pursue his golfing avocation in various places around the country.

> What do I do now? I've mastered the job. What directions should the company pursue? The corporation is perfectly capable of expanding market territories, if desired. Present accounts can be maintained and new ones can be acquired through normal business expansion without excessive efforts on my part. Should I take more remuneration from the business? Should I sink more into the venture, even at this mature stage? Should I retire, and turn the firm over to someone else with more need to succeed at this point?

> I have no need to expand the company at more than the current inflationary rate. If we are to get ahead of the game we currently play in this economy, it must expand at more than this rate, yet I am very comfortable expanding at the inflation rate and can live very adequately on that kind of expansion. I am no longer driven by the need to achieve success, and this may be incompatible with my employees' needs—particularly the newer ones. At the same time, I am still in charge—the one that makes the ultimate decisions upon which the company sinks or swims. I think the corporation has done right by me. The weight of decision-making will not really pass out of my hands until I relinquish the reins of control. Unfortunately, although the invitation is open, my son-in-law is not interested in joining the firm, and I have some hard decisions to make. I am not independently wealthy, yet my ambition is somewhat less urgent than it was 10, 15, or 20 years ago.

As Mr. Engle told his story, he turned to an article in *The Wall Street Journal*[1] which described a small company in South Dakota, suffering problems similar to his firm's:

---

[1] The article Mr. Engle referred to appeared on Page 1 of the July 26, 1973, Midwest Edition of *The Wall Street Journal*. It was entitled, "The Jacobs Brothers Opt Not to Go Home to Deadwood, S.D.—So Who Will Take Over the Store the Parents Operated?"

Here, this is exactly my dilemma—the locale is different, but the problems are still the same. These people (in the article) have been successful, but they can't interest their children in following in their footsteps. I've still got some years before I would have to retire, but if I wanted to step down tomorrow, the business would have no one to step into my shoes.

Are you interested in being in business for yourself as the owner-manager of a small, closely-held concern? Are you willing to relate to Mr. Engle's situation? He is obviously very capable, self-educated in business, and active. He has tried to provide for continuity and is not willing to let the organization "go to pot." At the same time, he has lost much of the drive to succeed that drove him to expand the firm over the past 24 years.

QUESTIONS FOR DISCUSSION

1. What would you do if you were Mr. Engle?
2. What do you think of his philosophies of management?
3. Is Mr. Engle unique? Or do most other independent owner-managers exhibit the same characteristics?
4. How does Mr. Engle's firm deviate from the typical business school case norm—i.e., the large corporation? How does his attitude toward union-employee management relations deviate? His attitude toward his sales representatives? His attitude toward growth? His attitude toward his market area and customers?
5. What does the case show about the problem of providing management succession in a small business firm?

VIII–3. Hummel Maid, Inc.[1]

Many years ago, Mrs. Lucile Hummel moved into a new house and busied herself making it into a home. It was located in a campus community. There was no dining room rug, but there were several football jerseys of rich gold and brown colors. With characteristic ingenuity, she converted the jerseys into a beautiful braided floor covering.

---

[1] Prepared by M. M. Hargrove, University of Tulsa.

Many people admired the braided rug, and several wanted to know how it was made. Mrs. Hummel—Lu to friends—helped them, and even casual acquaintances, make braided rugs for their own homes. The rugs were handsome and inexpensive. As more and more women tried to acquire the skill, it became evident that most failures were due to the use of poor materials. Soon Lu Hummel was in business selling wool to homemakers. A maid cut the wool into strips by hand in the basement.

Lu's hobby-business was interrupted for several years while she completed her education and became a professional teacher. She was well on her way to receiving her Ph.D., with only her dissertation unfinished, when World War II broke out and her husband was sent to the Southwest. Lu found a teaching position at the University of Tulsa, and soon became the head of the Office Administration Department. She was an enthusiastic, understanding, patient teacher, admired by her students and fellow professors. Her husband returned after the war, and both seemed destined to have separate professional careers—she as a professor and he as an oil company executive.

But her career was again interrupted when the oil company decentralized and transferred her husband to Oklahoma City. In her new home, she reassembled her interests and planned again for her future. She considered an offer to teach at a nearby state university, but decided not to accept. This was her opportunity to revive her rug business.

Wherever she traveled, Lu looked for braided rugs. She found them in the show cases at the Smithsonian Institution, the national shrines of historical Americans, and old homes of colonial origin. She read all available materials written about braided rugs, and she collected hundreds of pictures showing them used with furniture of all periods.

With free time on her hands and her enthusiasm bubbling again, Lu Hummel consulted with her banker and a lawyer recommended by a friend. The banker suggested, "We'll get you some money," and the attorney added, "Let's make a big thing of this." Feeding her high spirits on these bits of professional advice, Lu continued to consider various aspects of her proposed business. Gradually, her thoughts crystalized. She found 20 women willing to buy $20,000 of stock. She incorporated under the name of Hummel Maid, Inc., with common stock totaling $50,000. The women all wanted to help. Fifteen agreed to serve as members of the Board of Directors. They were well known and held responsible positions in the major companies of the city. Lu Hummel retained 52 percent of the stock.

LOCATION

At an early meeting of the Board of Directors, after they had voted themselves a salary of $10 per meeting, the women considered the problem of finding a good location for Hummel Maid, Inc. Lu thought incoming travelers emerging from the Turner Turnpike would want to stop and relax before tackling the traffic of the city by-passes and congested throughways. Or, if traveling toward the East, the drivers would want to stop before entering the turnpike for relaxation, gas and oil, or to get a bite to eat. Near a proposed site, three large service stations cared for the needs of cars. A beautiful new unit of a large chain of motels was across the divided highway. A tourist attraction, Frontier City, was to be located nearby. Here restless children and fatigued adults were invited to watch snatches of life of the old West re-enacted with exciting realism. Tourists were also invited to visit the modern, attractive training school of one of the nation's largest automobile manufacturers.

The directors decided to locate in this vicinity. A contact was made with Mr. A. C. Brown, part-owner and operator of the motel. Mr. Brown owned land along the highway, and offered to sell for $100 a front foot. The lots were 300 feet deep. For the site chosen with 100 front feet, he wanted $10,000 and would hold the deal open for $100 earnest money. After practically no discussion, the directors accepted Mr. Brown's offer and called for $10,000 on unpaid stock to cover the purchase cost.

An attractive building was erected well back on the site so as to allow for parking. The building served as a retail display room, home office, training center for workers, and shipping center. The original cost of the building was $27,500. Furnishings were purchased to enhance the merchandise to be displayed. These appointments eventually cost $10,000. A loan was secured on the real property calling for an annual payment of $2,000 plus interest.

There were many other necessary items. An appropriate sign was acquired. Insurance coverage was provided. Taxes and utilities bills were submitted and seemed high when related to the income of the infant business. Then more help and more inventories were needed, and it appeared obvious that the anticipated increased production must soon get under way.

PROPOSED OPERATIONS

Lu Hummel outlined her proposed operations to her board members. Production would not be done by factory methods. The work would be done in the worker's home. In this way, there would be less capital invested and operating costs would be minimized. Workers would be recruited among housewives and unemployed women of the community who would work during their spare time. Lu Hummel would teach them how to make the rugs. Excellent designs and beautiful woolen materials would be supplied to the workers. Hummel Maid, Inc., would market the rugs for the workers. It would advertise and promote the sales. The Board of Directors approved the program as outlined.

TRAINING

In arranging the teaching room, Lu Hummel used the vestibule school idea, and in this way introduced her workers to the ideals of the good home workshop. At first the lessons were free to all comers, but a $10 charge was made after many women learned the art only to quit after making a single rug. The learners met at 9:30 each Friday morning. These group meetings started with a 20-minute lecture advising the workers what was expected of them, the time they should take to produce a rug, the size and layout of the ideal production room, the size of the work table, what treatment would help if they were affected by wool and dust allergies, transportation procedures, the problems caused by small children being around the work center, and similar items of information. After the lecture, the workers were taught how to make small circular rugs. They developed skill in the proper use of the thumb, which was the key to successful rug making, and proper stitching which made the rugs lie flat. The necessary time was given for each learner to become expert.

WORKERS

For the most part, the workers took unusual pride in their work. They were able to fit their rug work into their family schedules. Generally, farm women were better producers than suburban women. The farm women had fewer distractions. Age of the workers had little to do with the quality and quantity of production. Some young mothers with small children were slow in getting the rugs produced, while others did fast work of acceptable quality. Often, several workers were in one family group. No special physical attributes were needed, but outside interests did interfere. Many women felt a sense of accomplishment from creating a beautiful and useful product, and all agreed that money was only one of their motivators. One woman inherited a substantial estate, but continued to maintain her production schedule. Another worker, almost 90, sold her land to the federal government because it was to be inundated by the waters of a flood control dam. With plenty of money to care for her and being too old to make the big, heavy rugs, she continued to make "mockups" which were sold to dealers.

A distinctive cloth label was signed by each woman and attached to her rugs. The label stated that the rug was an original heirloom rug designed by Lu Hummel, hand braided for the designated customer, the handiwork of the designated worker, specifying the pattern and size, and recorded the register number. The pattern was registered by number so that in years to come the customer could duplicate the order if desired.

PRODUCTION

In production, wool strips were braided first and then sewed by hand with a special concealed stitch. For sewing thread, a heavy grade of waxed linen warp was used. The rugs were heavy, weighing about one pound per square foot. A 9′ × 12′ rug weighed approximately 100 pounds.

More than a hundred color shades were available, and all were vat dyed. If the right color for the customer's decoration scheme was not on hand, a special dye lot was run for a charge of $10 or less.

Standard designs called for circle or oval shapes. Special shapes were available at higher cost, and included rectangular, square, three-circle, multicircle, and half-circle rugs. The customer was asked to provide the color scheme desired. While standard color patterns were ordered by name, custom color patterns were available at no extra charge. Even the standard color patterns could be altered to meet customers' needs and without extra charge.

Five easy specifications to aid the customer in ordering included (1) size; (2) shape; (3) general effect, including light, dark, predominating color, and accent colors (when posible, the customer was asked to send swatches of furniture fabric or wallpaper); (4) pattern; and (5) price. After the order was received, a chart was submitted to the customer with colors attached showing what was to be used in each row. The chart was returned to indicate approval.

The office work connected with each order was no simple task. Acknowledgment of the order was mailed, the shipping date was scheduled, the design of the rug planned and approved, many letters were written to be certain that the customer was satisfied, rug charts were kept, labels recorded, and wool poundages estimated for each color. The colors selected for each rug then had to be dyed in proper quantities. And good records were kept. Lu Hummel once remarked, "Cost accounting is a must. We simply have to know where we stand with our costs."

Lu had learned that she had to be certain about all of her costs of operating, especially before she entered a new market. If her cost records were inaccurate, she made decisions from false information. She knew the close relationship between cost and sales prices. When sales prices were increased, she had to have justification for herself, her dealers, and her customers. She tried never to raise all prices at the same time and to have as few increases as possible. She found that she could raise prices on odd sizes and shapes with little or no objection.

PRODUCTION PROBLEMS

To avoid confusion, workers were asked to notify the office at least three days before they returned a finished rug, so that the next rug could be readied. Workers were scheduled so that not more than two were in the shop at the same time, to keep from wasting time for both the workers and the office staff. The workers were given the following suggestions to help ensure efficiency in the shop when they called:

1. Tie each color of unused wool together to make it easier to put up.
2. Bring sacks of unused wool into the large teaching room for weighing, and be sure your name is on the sack.
3. Take small rugs to back shipping rooms, and large rugs to front.
4. Keep small scraps in a paper sack and short lengths of 1 to 2 feet in another sack so we can put them in our hit-and-miss barrels. Scraps have value!
5. Check in the office to get the materials for the rug inspector to use.
6. While your rug is being inspected, put your colors on the chart for your next rug.
7. The inspector will talk to you privately about the rug and help you with any problems.
8. Take your check sheet and materials from the finished rug to the office and sign your slip.
9. Now get checked out with wool, charts, and supplies for the new rug.
10. Place the due date on your chart. If you feel you can't make it, tell us now! If something comes up later while you are at work on the rug, tell us in time to have someone else take over.

Within two years after moving into the new building, sales poured in and production was increased repeatedly. A group of nearly 100 workers was trained and producing. More workers were needed, and Lu Hummel appealed to trained producers to help find the right type of women. She explained that they could not use a producer who, after she had learned to make small rugs, could not make a 9′ × 12′ size and over. And with so many workers, the money invested in wool increased so substantially that some control was necessary. Lu decreed that only one half the wool needed for a large rug would be issued initially, and the remainder issued only when needed. On rugs up to size 6′ × 9′, all the wool needed was issued with the work order. When it became apparent that special dye problems would delay the production, Lu Hummel gave to the braider a "no-rush" order on which to work if her production should be stopped.

When an order was received for a set of several rugs, all were produced by one person. It was found easier to give the total order to one woman so that all the rugs would be alike. If an order for a set involved unusually large rugs, it was given to two women who lived close together for joint production.

Lu Hummel knew the answers to problems brought to her. She showed the women how to make the firm, even braid necessary for a beautiful rug. A tight braid was difficult to sew and not handsome. She demonstrated how to braid different weights of wool together. She determined that every row put on a rug should add two inches to the size. With this standardization, production control and uniform quality were possible. Through experience, she found that there were several techniques for improving the color beauty. For example, when it was necessary to change shades, it was best done in the corners.

Lu Hummel recalled vividly the crisis precipitated by the regional head of the Wage and Hour Administration. Hummel Maid, Inc., had been reported to the Administration by an unknown informer. A heated discussion ensued about the relationship of the braiders to the company. Lu claimed that the women were independent contractors and that she had no control over their hours of work or their production schedules. She gave the agent the names of 24 braiders with the request that he visit their work centers and learn first hand about this relationship. From his inspection, he determined that the braiders were, in fact independent contractors and could easily make the minimum wage or more per hour. His ruling simplified Lu's relationships with them and with the government.

If an adverse recommendation had been made by the agent, Hummel Maid, Inc., would have had to hire more accounting services, pay more taxes, and incur more office expenses. Actually, the company had operated one year under Social Security. This was discontinued.

The better braiders made substantial supplementary incomes for their families. They averaged $1,200–$1,500 per year. One woman made in excess of $4,000 annually, and another built a $10,000 home from her rug money. Many had added rooms and other improvements to their homes or purchased new appliances.

FINANCES

The original five-year loan had to be refinanced. The loan holder died in April and the loan was due the following September. When the lender's estate was probated, it showed that the principal had been reduced to $19,000. The Southwestern Life Insurance Company was asked for a loan. The company refused to deal with a group of women. However, the company did offer to make a personal loan to Lu Hummel.

Lu owned 52 percent of the stock at the date of organization, and four years later she had increased her share of ownership to 83 percent of the 351 shares outstanding.

Occasionally, differences of opinions occurred among the stockholders. On one such occasion, Lu had to pay almost double per share to get a few directors out of the company. This price was substantially more than the book value of the stock. After a series of attempted negotiations, Lu acquired the land and building on her personal credit, and Hummel Maid paid her rent for their use.

MARKETING THE RUGS

At first, all rugs that could be produced were sold without much effort. One satisfied customer told another, and this word-of-mouth advertising absorbed the limited production. Since the rugs were made of heavy wool, thickly braided, and lasted almost a lifetime with reasonable care, there was little repeat business.

Lu Hummel was astounded at the free publicity her rugs received in *House Beautiful, Better Homes and Gardens, Interior Design, The Wall Street Journal,* and many other publications. She managed a modest advertising program, run in home magazines which she considered helpful in selling the rugs. Chatty, friendly, informative letters sent to current and prospective dealers were effective. Prospective dealers were urged to invest in a sales kit and stock-rugs which, when purchased, entitled them to be listed as official dealers. Kits were sold to dealers at less than half of the actual cost, because experience had shown how much a sales staff needed information and aids in order to present the line. A 30″ × 48″ stock rug made sales efforts even more effective. A few dealers who had sufficient floor space bought sizes ranging up to 9′ × 12′ for display.

The themes repeated frequently in dealer contacts were (1) your profit for each sale is much greater on our rugs; (2) the customer knows the rug was made for her, and when pleased, she becomes an active sales force for your store; and (3) the rugs are "right" for the casual living of today. On special price lists prepared for dealers, prices were stated at retail and the dealer's discount was 40 percent.

The number of dealers increased until there were more than 500 department and furniture stores, carpet shops, and decorators all over the country, including New England, the home of the braided rug. With this expanded sales organization, it was difficult to keep a production-sales balance. Lu recognized these growing pains. Hummel Maid rugs sold too well! What should have been a sweet experience proved to be a major problem of production. Her workers were unable to speed up, so she tried to turn the operation into factory-type production. This didn't work because she could not get workers who took pride in their work. Delivery dates were delayed. Lu philosophized, "You know that the people of Oklahoma talk slowly, and they work the same way; but the beauty of the finished product is well worth the waiting time." After returning strictly to home production, she appealed to her dealers to help her keep high standards of quality and to be understanding if deliveries were slow. Lu explained that if the homemaker had wanted a machine-made braided rug with limited colors, no special design, and a stereotyped look, she would not have ordered a Hummel Maid rug.

MARKETING CHANNELS TRIED

Hummel Maid, Inc., tried many channels of distribution. Word-of-mouth advertising was sufficient during the early years. As production mounted, an attempt was made to combine the retail business with some wholesale activities. This program was gradually replaced by exclusive distributors. It was hoped that these distributors would develop their exclusive territories and would push the rugs more diligently than the wholesalers, who often carried them as a sideline. The dealers provided all customer services and billed their own accounts. Hummel Maid was the supplier and had little customer contact under this arrangement. But sales through these exclusive distributors were disappointing, so the company tried to operate as a wholesale mail-order business. Later, sales representatives replaced the mail-order program. These sales representatives emphasized the wholesale business and did only casual retail business. They tried to get stores with good showrooms as customers. For example, the rugs were displayed in the showroom of Sullivan's on Fifth Avenue, New York, and in the showroom of the Trade Mart in Dallas, Texas. Sales representatives were paid 10 percent commission, which was considered good by the trades people.

ADMINISTRATIVE PERSONNEL

Mrs. Elsie Shidell, Office Manager, started with Hummel Maid two years ago. She learned to design some of the rugs, and worked with independent contractors when needed. She assumed much of the routine work of processing orders, invoicing, preparing materials, keeping records on the workers, and general office work. Her husband worked for an oil-field equipment firm. Mrs. Shidell had worked for 12 years in a retail grocery which she owned jointly with her husband. Prior to the grocery venture, she spent five years as office manager of a tool company and three years as a partner in a small company selling oil field equipment. She had also had a little experience selling in a retail gift shop.

Charles Irvin Springer, Jr., son of Lu Hummel, was 30 years old and married. He had completed three and one-half years of college study in business administration. During his college years, he worked closely with Lu, helping especially with the cutting of wool and the supervising of rug makers. For several years he had created authentic hand-made stage coaches for dude ranchers, movie producers, and other customers. Recently he had been giving his full time to the rug business. He was mechanically inclined and creative.

LU HUMMEL

Lu Hummel drove herself hard in all that she did. Her enthusiasm and optimism were contagious. She liked people, and they responded. About six months ago, she had a severe case of the flu. She had a continuous cold, and knew she was run down. Her hands and feet became swollen and painful. When they turned red and became of major concern, her family physician referred her to Dr. H. C. Johnson, Chief of Staff at a large, new Baptist hospital.

One morning at breakfast, Charles Springer called Elsie Shidell and said, "Dr. Johnson has told mother she has Raynaud's disease and that she will be a convalescent for an indefinite period of time. She doesn't know when, if ever, she can return to the business. Raynaud's disease is not fatal, but she is unable to use her hands, and her feet are also affected. She must be unusually careful because in her exhausted condition she has little resistance to infections and other diseases."

QUESTIONS FOR DISCUSSION

1. How did Lu Hummel combine education and experience to provide a promising and interesting career? Evaluate experience *vs* education.
2. Would men have added to, or detracted from, the operations?
3. The "farming out" system predates the "factory" system. How could it succeed in a contemporary business?
4. What qualities of leadership did Lu Hummel possess? What weaknesses?
5. How strong was the organization? The Board? The Office Manager?
6. What should the company do now that Lu Hummel is ill? What short-range actions should be taken? Long range?
7. Are all managers teachers? Explain.
8. How important is an adequate cost accounting system to a manufacturer? What costs must be controlled?
9. How should braided rugs be marketed?
10. Evaluate the financial strengths and weaknesses of Hummel Maid.
11. Evaluate the attempt at "factory-like" production. Why did it fail?

VIII-4. Bell Associates[1]

Mr. E. N. Bell, founder, owner, and President of Bell Associates, estimates he spends 80 hours per week overseeing the comany's construction jobs, supervising the Tank Lining, Industrial Services, and Construction divisions, preparing bids for upcoming construction projects, making economic feasibility studies, generating new work, inspecting and signing daily work orders, handling personnel problems, and planning the company's expanding activities.

Bell evidenced entrepreneurial characteristics while still in high school and college, and started his own company in 1956. Exhibit IV-1 sum-

EXHIBIT IV-1

History of Mr. Bell and Bell Associates

Early 1950s	Organized grass mowing teams and earned, in summers, $75 to $85 per week. Repaired mowers and cycles, and helped father build houses.
1954	Obtained contract from Warren Company for $15,000 to supply 6″ to 30″ plywood disks to seal tank openings. Netted $7,700 for college payments.
1956	Interviewed for job after graduation, but decided he could make more money by starting his own business. Rented a building, hired a manager and sold and repaired mowers and cycles. Received a B.S. degree in Business Administration.
1958	Bought a 5,000 sq. ft. building, and added golf cart sales and repair.
1960	Sold mower, cycle and cart business. Entered into a partnership arrangement with Mr. Rum to manufacture wood plugs for cores on which paper is rolled. Designed, made and sold cricket boxes.
1962	Dropped the manufacture and sale of cricket boxes. Designed an "indestructible" 5′ × 5′ wooden pallet. Received orders from the Warren Company for these. Took on the management of his father's house construction company. Started making cabinets and related wood items for commercial firms.
1965	Obtained a contract for part of maintenance of building and yard, for waste disposal, and for small construction jobs from Warren Company. Began constructing commercial metal buildings.
1968	Discontinued managing father's business because of heavy workload, and incongruity of managing both union and nonunion work forces.
1969	Moved into a 20,000 sq. ft. building. Sales about $340,000 per year. Incorporated Bell Associates.
1971	Discontinued the company's cabinet and millwork operations. Purchased the tank and pipe lining operations from the Warren Company, and added 10,000 sq. ft. to Bell Associates Building.
1972	Redesigned pallets—steel channels welded to rectangular tubing with wood slats.
1973	In process of dropping waste haulage at Warren Company due to new environmental regulations requiring a $25,000 to $50,000 investment in compacting equipment.

[1] Prepared by Charles R. Scott, Jr., Alonzo J. Strickland III, and Arthur A. Thompson, University of Alabama.

marizes the company's developmental history. At present, Bell Associates has about 90 employees engaged in constructing metal buildings, maintaining building grounds, making pallets, and lining tanks. The company's scope of activities and organizational structure are depicted in Exhibit IV–2 and IV–3.

EXHIBIT IV–2
Organization Chart and Personnel Information

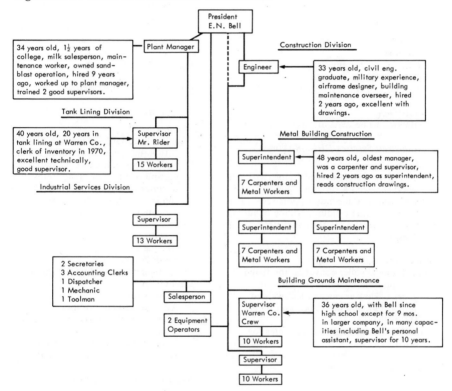

GENERAL CONSTRUCTION

During 1972, Bell Associates completed 12 general construction jobs, the largest of which grossed $200,000. Mr. Bell spends considerable time working up bids and estimates, and he obtains 10 percent of the jobs on which he bids. He prefers jobs in the $150,000 range that can be completed within 90 days, are within a 100-mile radius, and require only one crew. However, Bell is currently involved in bidding on a job which has mushroomed unexpectedly to about $700,000.

Bell maintains that the company's success in bidding on government

EXHIBIT IV–3
Product, Work, and Financial Information
Construction Division

Metal Building Construction (40%)*

Product:
Buildings made of concrete and metal
During 1972, largest four jobs between
$100,000 and $200,000
Subcontracts plumbing, electrical and
masonry work.

Volume:
10 years ago, 15% of the company
revenue
1970, 70% of the revenue
1972, 50% of the revenue
1973, 60% of the revenue (estimated)

Net income:
Estimated to be 2½% of revenue

Industrial Services Division (10%)

Products:
5' × 5' pallets steel welded frame, with
wood slats and 4 vertical pipes.
Stairs, braces, and small support sections requiring welding, drilling bending, etc. usually for the construction
division.

Production facilities:
Bell-designed roller conveyor line fitted
with jig to hold and move parts of
pallet as they are assembled, welded
and bolted. Maximum production is
100 pallets/day.
Job shop arrangement of machines for
other work.

Pallet price: $30 each

Buildings Grounds Maintenance (40%)

Work Description:
Grass cutting
Weed killing
Small building repairing
Storm sewer cleaning
Fence painting
Waste hauling

Income: $150/day/crew

Wages: 70% of income

Net income: $10/day/crew

Tank Lining Division (10%)

Products:
Rubber-lined tanks which can be filled
with liquids, gases, etc., such as acids,
with no corroding effects. Sandblasting and painting of many items such
as concrete mixers, buses, wash pots
and bedsteads is performed to keep
machines busy.

Production facilities:
In the yard:
Sandblaster
Refrigeration building for rubber
In building:
Rubber sprays
Autoclave to cure rubber. One is the
largest in the market area (12 ft.
dia.)
Hand steam units to cure large tanks.
Paint spray for outside of tanks.

Purchase cost from Warren Co.:
$100,000

Sales income:
1971–$96,000 (8 mos. oper.)
1972–154,000 (12% net income)
1973–150,000 (first 3 mos.)

* Bell's estimate of his division of time.

jobs is attributable to his willingness to put up with extra paper work
and to accept close inspection—both of which tend to deter other contractors from bidding on government jobs. Bell ferrets out most of his
leads on new projects from published listings, but he also gets repeat
business from previous customers and inquiries from potential customers.

BUILDING GROUNDS MAINTENANCE

For eight years, Bell Associates has had a crew maintaining part of the Warren Company grounds and buildings, and has recently added a crew to maintain the grounds of two other local companies. This work includes grass cutting, weed killing, making small repairs, and performing miscellaneous maintenance work. For each of these crews Bell Associates receives gross revenue of $150 per day, and from this Bell nets about $10. Also, Bell has used this work as a contact point for learning about and securing other more profitable maintenance related jobs, including cleaning up after major plant changes and performing field engineering services.

INDUSTRIAL SERVICES

Since 1962, Bell Associates has made about 4,000 pallets for the Warren Company and, last year, started manufacturing redesigned pallets to replace the old "indestructable" ones. The local unit of the Warren Company is changing to the new pallet, and Bell expects to raise production from 73 per day to 100 per day as soon as Bell Associates completes the repair of the old pallets. He has trial pallets in several other plants of the Warren Company and also has made contact with several other potential users of the new pallets. Mr. Bell plans to increase the sales of pallets so that he can reduce the price below their current level of $30 per pallet.

TANK LINING

In 1970, Bell bought the machinery and the rights to use the Warren Company's tank lining operation. The Warren Company had been lining tanks since early 1950, but started to phase out the operations in 1965 when its sales were about $300,000 per year. By 1970, Warren had reduced its tank lining output, stopped replacing equipment, and transferred many men to other operations. Bell made the purchase for $100,000 with the provision that the Warren Company allow its tanking lining supervisor, Mr. Rider, to join Bell Associates and furnish necessary technical knowledge. Bell hoped to raise tank lining sales to $250,000 by 1972, though he was aware that demand for tank lining is linked to economic conditions in the textile industry and, further, that improved methods of chemical storage are reducing the number of lined tanks needed.

Bell Associates has been sandblasting storage tanks and many other small items for many years. In addition, it has purchased painting equipment for $7,000 to paint the outsides of tanks and selected small items. Sandblasting and small painting jobs gross $5 to $50 each.

ACCOUNTING

The cost system of Bell Associates is designed to collect costs by job and division. Each day, each construction supervisor records the hours worked on each job by each worker in his crew. Labor rates are applied to the hours to compute the payroll and job and division costs. A computerized payroll system has been considered, but as many as seven wage rates (reflecting regular and overtime hours, union and nonunion, job, and other variations) may be used for a single worker during a given day. The use of computers was deemed impractical. Material and supplies, subcontracting, and job-identified financing costs are assigned to the jobs and divisions. Other costs are collected and prorated over the entire operation, using rates which are determined annually. In working up costs and estimating new jobs, Bell customarily applies a 7½ to 8 percent charge for overhead and profit, and expects a profit of 2½ percent of the bid price. However, Bell states that even with this detailed accounting system he has to "wait until the end of the year to know just where we stand."

In addition, costs must be collected in such a manner that bonuses of 25 percent of division profits can be distributed to five key managers. These bonuses ranged from $1,800 to $3,800 per manager and totaled $10,000 in 1972. However, these managers have questioned the application of the Company's indirect costs in determining their profit bonus.

MR. BELL AND THE COMPANY

Mr. Bell attributes his long work hours to his inability to delegate. For example, he assigned management of building construction to one of his superintendents. But after a trial period, the superintendent asked to be relieved of that responsibility and returned to the supervision of only one crew. Bell has transferred the superintendent's responsibility to the engineer, but by-passes him when Bell feels the decisions go beyond the engineer's fairly limited experience and knowledge. It is Bell's policy, however, to urge each supervisor to train someone to provide a backup for the position.

Bell says he needs to keep in contact with all work, as he is best equipped to deal with the more serious and urgent matters. To facilitate communications, he has located his office in the center of the building in view of the operations and the equipment dispatch board, and has installed radio equipment in company trucks for contact with workers on the jobs.

The company, despite Bell's watchful eye, has experienced several operating incidents which Bell feels should not have occurred. In one recent case, a job had passed final inspection of the architect, but Bell felt it was shoddy and ordered some of the work redone. Although Bell realized this caused some resentment among the work crew, he said, "I cannot have perfection in all things, but I want more than the minimum." In another case, a concrete mixer which had been improperly stored and recorded was stolen and subsequently found not even to be insured. Additionally, several daily work sheets for the Warren Company were found in error, which caused Bell some embarrassment. Now, he inspects and signs each daily work sheet.

Mr. Bell finds himself forced to spend many hours each week resolving personnel problems. Among these are problems of general supervision, lack of job descriptions, interfacing with union and nonunion employees, and the seasonal nature of construction work which interferes with

EXHIBIT IV–4

BELL ASSOCIATES
Income Sheet
For the Year Ending December 31, 1972

Income		
Construction		$1,007,747
Rubber Lining		154,006
Industrial		104,259
Rental		18,784
Total		$1,284,796
Direct Costs		1,090,448
Gross Profit		$ 194,348
Indirect Costs		89,314
Gross Profit after Indirect Costs		$ 105,034
General and Administrative Costs		32,403
Operating Profit		$ 72,630
Other Income	$5,868	
Outgo	9,002	3,134
Net Profit before Taxes		$ 69,496
Provision for Income Taxes		13,097
Net Profit after Taxes		$ 56,399

Indirect Costs			*General and Administrative Costs*	
Auto and truck expense	$ 6,723		Salaries	$21,600
Depreciation	18,513		Payroll taxes	1,169
Employee insurance	8,016		Employee insurance	264
Insurance–other	9,404		Advertising expense	1,595
Maintenance	2,497		Bad debts	1,776
Supplies	2,458		Depreciation	374
Payroll taxes	19,166		Donations	209
Rent	11,950		Dues	984
Utilities	7,823		Legal and accounting	808
Taxes and licenses	2,764		Office supplies	1,545
Total	$89,314		Rent	1,200
			Taxes and licenses	150
			Utilities	400
			Miscellaneous	330
			Total	$32,403

scheduling and manning of work crews. On a recent day, a supervisor waited an hour to talk to Mr. Bell about having to come 15 minutes early each day to thaw out some rubber in order not to delay production. The supervisor hinted about being entitled to extra pay, but Mr. Bell felt it was more a case of frustration than concern with pay. One of Bell's superintendents just left the company to accept an offer of $20,000 per year—$3,000 more than the salary at Bell Associates.

A number of situations involving company equipment also consume much of Bell's time. He finds it hard to turn down small jobs for his idle millwork equipment. He is considering purchasing a van to avoid paying the travel costs for employees on out of town jobs. He feels renting equipment is high-priced financing, and so he owns many pieces of equipment, including air compressors and trucks, which are then rented to others when not in use.

Last year, Bell states, he budgeted too low by 30 percent, and this year it appears that the difference will be even greater. Yet, his net income increased from $15,000 in 1970 to $56,000 in 1972. (See Exhibits

EXHIBIT IV–5

BELL ASSOCIATES
Balance Sheet
December 31, 1972

Assets

Current Assets

Cash	$ 18,074	
Accounts Receivable	195,916	
Inventory	24,794	
Prepaid Expenses	3,146	$241,930

Fixed Assets

Building, Machinery, Equipment	$185,046	
Less reserve for depreciation	41,560	143,476
Total Assets		$385,406

Liabilities and Stockholder's Equity

Current Liabilities

Accounts Payable	$129,343	
Notes Payable	28,625	
Accrued Payables	20,562	$178,530
Long Term Liabilities		92,772

Stockholders Equity

Common Stock	$ 30,000	
Retained Earnings	84,104	114,104
Total Liabilities plus Equity		$385,406

IV–4 and IV–5 for 1972 financial statements.) Even though estimating the future is perplexing, he plans to continue planning and budgeting his operations.

Bell recognizes that his company has expanded and that he has fallen short in defining duties, training new people and keeping up with the company's changing character. As Bell closed up the office, he expressed the thought that "there are so many opportunities for me to improve my business, but I just do not know where to start."

QUESTIONS FOR DISCUSSION

1. How would you evaluate Bell's managerial capacities? What are his strengths and weaknesses?
2. What would you say are the goals of the company? Are they the same as Mr. Bell's?
3. Evaluate the history of the company. Do you believe Mr. Bell made the best choice when he graduated from college? Estimate Bell's salary.
4. Should Bell Associates continue to engage in all its current activities? If not, what should it drop and why?
5. Can Mr. Bell delegate some of his time-consuming activities? If so, what and how? Would it be economical?
6. Evaluate the organizational structure of Bell Associates. Would you recommend a reorganization of the company's divisions? Does Mr. Bell need a general manager to help him oversee the firm's activities? Can he afford to hire such a person?
7. Make a financial analysis of Bell Associates. Is the company in a sound financial position? How profitable is the company?
8. Do you recommend that Bell Associates continue to expand? Should the company bid on the $700,000 job, which will surely increase the company's sales?
9. What will happen to the company if Mr. Bell becomes incapacitated?

VIII–5. Lithograving, Inc.[1]

Thomas Long, Sr., and James Williams faced some crucial issues as they looked over the mass of papers spread across the conference table and stared at each other in silence. Their young and rapidly growing firm had in recent years become the largest and best known in the area for its expertise in the pre-printing activities, supporting much of the local graphic arts industry. Their services included primarily the

[1] Written by Louis P. White and Kenneth R. Van Voorhis, University of South Florida.

production of rubber and metal printing plates for advertising agencies, newspaper and magazine publishers, corrugated box and label manufacturers, and polyethylene and paper packaging concerns.

Although Lithograving's growth in sales was certainly outstripping the gains made by competitors, the two principal owners were beginning to recognize the loss of their earlier opportunities to express technical and artistic creativity as craftsmen. Furthermore, Jim was concerned that Tom's dominating personality and high regard for outside personal friendships and business relationships were hurting their progress.

Each man's thoughts flashed back to their merger in 1966, with Tom becoming President and Jim serving as General Manager of the new firm. Yes, they had correctly appraised the potential for combining Tom's old hot-lead casting business and Jim's production of zinc printing plates. Now, there were new production techniques to explore, including automation and even computerization of certain phases of their processes. Larger size had brought concern for expanding from a local market to regional and perhaps even national influence. The union which had been voted in by the firm's employees more than four years ago was adamant about "getting a decent contract this year." And of course, the financial squeeze being felt by multitudes of small businesses weighed heavily on the minds of these two executives as they pondered the data before them and attempted to decide what to do next.

INDUSTRY BACKGROUND

Traditionally, the graphic arts industry has been localized, with small firms with a few employees striving to meet the needs (particularly, quick deadlines) of a small number of local users. The phase of the industry activities in which Lithograving, Inc., was engaged involved the production of plates to be used by printers, who in turn accomplished the transfer of words and images for the final users—including a wide variety of packaging, publishing, and other message-oriented concerns.

Historically, the industry has been quite specialized and secretive, with individual craftsmen gaining expertise through long years of experience. The recent formation of technical trade associations, coupled with the fact that a number of the larger graphic arts firms now enjoy national reputations, has done much to enhance sharing of technological advances. The application of new lightweight metals, automation using computers, and improved communication and transportation, promise to facilitate increasing geographic dispersion of information and services. Other trends include rising material costs, increased sales revenue per worker, and an increasing number (a majority) of firms employing five to 20 employees.

Lithograving, Inc., with 45 employees, is regarded as an intermediate-size firm, with plants employing 50 or more personnel beginning to account for a sizeable portion of the industry's total business. Many in the industry believe that plants must be at least this large to compete effectively, and the proportion of such plants relative to smaller ones is expected to increase significantly over the next decade. While small independent photo engraving firms will probably continue to hold a niche in the market, it was reported by most managers recently surveyed that these operations will have to offer special services not ordinarily performed by their larger competitors.

The combining of smaller platemaking firms, widening of market areas served, introduction of more automated production processes, and hiring of young, well-educated employees, have led to greater capital requirements. Instead of small firms financed by individuals and partners, the corporate device is becoming more widely used often with very impersonal ownership of equity.

Thus, without examining the technical production processes in any greater detail, it can be inferred that the industry is becoming much more complex. This industry analysis provides the background for an examination of the development of Lithograving, Inc., and the decisions which Tom Long and Jim Williams faced.

DEVELOPMENT OF LITHOGRAVING, INC.

Lithograving, Inc. (LGI) began in 1958 when two entreprenueurs previously conducting separate, but complementary, pre-printing businesses decided to share a common building and other resources. This arrangement preceded by several years the legal merger and formation of a partnership in 1966.

Tom Long had started his "stereo" business (formation of printing matrices on a specially prepared paper substance, using hot lead) in 1953 with only one machine and a total investment of about $5,000. Five years later, Jim Williams (Tom Long's brother-in-law) had begun his "photoplatemaking" operation (production of metal printing plates for subsequent use in preparing stereo or rubber flexoprinting plates) in the same Southeastern city with a similar initial investment of about $5,000.

During the next two years, Tom's firm became the major customer for Jim's products, while Jim served as Tom's primary supplier. When the opportunity arose in 1958 to bring their operations under the same roof, both men found the prospects attractive. From this point, the eventual merger of the two segments seemed to be only natural. Five years later, Tom Long, Jr., who had played an active role in his father's business, was offered one-third ownership (via an additional equity contribution by Tom Long, Sr.), and a corporation was formed.

EXHIBIT V–1

Sales Growth of LGI and Components

	Southeast Stereo and Mat Service (Tom Long)	Southeast Photoplatemaking (Jim Williams)	Lithograving, Inc. (combined business)
1953	$ 12,000	–	–
1958	53,000	$ 17,000	–
1961	102,000	99,000	–
1965	112,000	142,000	–
1969	125,000	196,000	–
1970	150,000	294,000	–
1971	–	–	$463,000
1972	–	–	562,000

The figures in Exhibit V–1 show a rapidly increasing volume of business during the brief existence of LGI and its two former components. The owners were "quite pleased with this record," citing favorable comparisons with industry standards. Tom Long remarked that, "if certain recent changes in newspaper printing operations hadn't been introduced, LGI's sales would be considerably higher yet."

A rapid expansion in the number of employees and the volume of operations occured in 1971–1972. Robert Miller, a young MBA graduate, was hired as Plant Manager in 1971. However, despite a number of indicators of significant improvement in LGIs' operations, a "personality clash" developed between Bob and Tom Long, Sr. Other young graduates of a nearby state university had joined the firm in the last year, but several told Jim confidentially that they were not at all pleased with Tom's "constant interference" with their work. Of particular concern to Jim was the Production Manager's indication that he was actively seeking a better job—not in terms of pay, but in order to be able to make the operating decisions necessary to keep production smooth and efficient.

CURRENT LOCAL SITUATION

LGI had three smaller competitors within a 100 mile radius. With current annual sales of approximately $600,000[2], LGI's volume of business was greater than the total of the other three firms, whose annual sales volumes were approximately $300,000, $100,000 and $100,000.

LGI had half again as many employees as the next largest competitor in the local area, which had slightly fewer than 30 employees. Until 1970, this competitor had more employees than LGI, although its sales

---

[2] Approximately 85 percent, or $510,000 of LGI's sales were derived from the immediate area, with the remainder coming from more distant customers.

had been below the combined figures for Tom's and Jim's former proprietorships since about 1964. The two other area photoengraving firms each had fewer than five employees, having remained quite small since their inceptions.

The volume of local business had leveled off somewhat in the last several years, and LGI had begun to look increasingly beyond its primary market area in order to achieve further sales increases.

LITHOGRAVING STRATEGY

Prior to 1971, Tom Long, Sr., and Jim Williams were quite content to remain a relatively small partnership without striving actively to increase their volume of business. When Tom Long, Jr., was brought into the firm as a third major shareholder and the new young Plant Manager was hired, a new era began at Lithograving. At that time, LGI embarked on a program to attain regional recognition and demand for its services, and eventually to attact a national clientele. In early 1972, a second sales office was opened in an adjoining state, and plans called for the opening of two additional regional sales offices in nearby states during 1973. Tom Long, Jr., was "eager to purchase or construct a second production facility near the first satellite sales office," and the other two major stockholders had begun to consider seriously the idea which they first passed off as "youthful ambition."

Although the two Longs did not typically express their objectives or strategies in writing, a memo (October 1, 1972) written by Jim Williams to company managers and supervisors summarizing the viewpoints of the owners, dealt with a number of broad aims, including: (1) introduction of employee profit sharing and retirement plans, (2) development of a cost accounting system, (3) development of quality control standards, and (4) aggressive sales expansion. These goals were to be completed over the next 12 months.

More immediate priorities were concerned primarily with: (1) increasing the effectiveness of equipment utilization and research and development, and (2) achieving significant sales increases.

MARKETING

As was true of the other smaller and medium-sized firms in the industry, LGI did not actively advertise its services through local or trade media (other than listings in telephone and industry directories), but relied upon previously satisfied clients to "spread favorable comments" regarding LGI's expertise. Jim Williams attended national, regional, and local trade shows and association meetings in order to make the LGI name more widely known on a "professional" basis, as users of photo-plate-making services frequently make new contacts and become prospective clients on such occasions. But the volume of new business generated through such efforts was thought by the owners to be much less significant than that achieved through local "satisfied customer" sources.

Jim Williams' strategy for expanding LGI's position from a small-to-medium-size firm to a prominent national supplier included establishing a number of regional sales offices throughout the country. His plan also involved a shift in emphasis from serving packaging companies to more direct contact with primary national marketing firms selling the products to be packaged. For example, rather than dealing with an intermediate printing or packaging concern, Jim's efforts were directed at serving such firms as Dan River Textile Mills and Winn Dixie Supermarkets.

Tom Long, Sr., on the other hand, devoted "a tremendous effort toward cultivating personal contacts in order to expand business on an informal, friendship basis." It was not uncommon for Tom to "wine and dine" a prospective customer for several evenings, or to send expensive gifts (including color television sets), in order to secure potential contracts. Historically, such practices have been common among smaller proprietors in the industry for years, and the owners felt that "Tom had been quite successful with these efforts in the past."

The third major shareholder, Tom Long, Jr., leaned toward the establishment of a sophisticated network of regional sales offices (and associated production plants), but the company did not have such a network. So, he attempted to emulate his father's style, except he talked about future office openings, (regardless of improbability) rather than using gifts and amenities.

Although the three men discussed their differences and each understood the others' points of view, there had been no overt attempt to formulate a unified strategy or set of marketing policies.

PRODUCTION

The simplified production flow chart in Exhibit V–2 shows that LGI's work involved, in addition to initial scheduling and final quality control and shipping activities, three major production departments: Art, Engraving, and Stereo.

Mike Samuelson, the current Production Manager, was a young college graduate who tried to achieve efficiency through refined production control procedures. Although the plant was relatively small, Mike was quite enthusiastic about a number of the "management science" techniques which he had brought into use at LGI.

Most of the operative employees were "old timers" who had become highly skilled over the years. Despite the fact that "a few had been slow to accept Mike's new efficiency schemes, the majority recognized

EXHIBIT V–2
LGI Work Flow Chart

Process or Department

Explanation

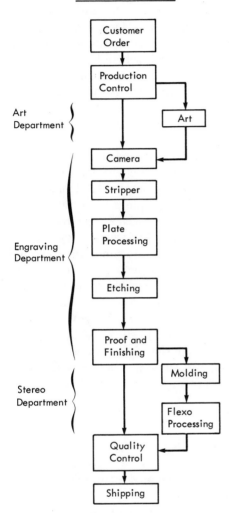

Customer may want metal or rubber printing plates; may supply own design or request art work, etc.

Work order prepared and specifications formulated.

If design is to be created or altered, must be made camera ready (including drawing, typesetting, etc.)

Design shot on "negative" film(s).

Various negatives of complex design combined to produce finished composite.

Stripped negative(s) exposed to metal via carbon arc process. Metal previously chemically treated to make it light sensitive.

Prepared metal plate exposed to acid solution so that some areas eroded away while others (usually the design letters, etc.) remain raised.

Etched plate cleaned and examined for correctness.

Inverse (female) image transferred to "matrix sheets" from engraved metal plate using heat and pressure.

Image again reversed back to original (male) form and transferred from matrix sheets to rubber plates using heat and pressure.

Final checking against specifications, customer order, etc.

Either metal or flexographic plates shipped to customer or intermediate printing firm.

rising productivity and higher pay as a result of technological advances and cooperated fully," according to one of the owners.

In general, Jim Williams was quite pleased with the 60 percent increase in productivity which had occurred in the last year. He monitored the Engraving Department's progress, established goals and policies for this segment of the operation, and could perform any of the steps in the engraving process when special problems arose. Typically though, "he delegated as much as possible and interfered with normal operations as little as possible."

Tom Long, Sr., who secured a fairly large volume of the business via special situations, shifted priorities according to the informal agreements made with clients, not only in the Stereo Department but in the others as well. He had little regard for Mike Samuelson's production control techniques, and frequently interrupted scheduled projects in order to concentrate on rush orders. He was "an extremely hard-working craftsman who was eager to get his hands dirty when the need arose." The regular operators had a great respect for his ability and tended to do as he said, regardless of what orders the Plant Manager or Production Manager might previously have given.

As had been true for the industry generally, the level of productivity per employee at LGI had risen substantially during the last two years. The initial application of automated typesetting in the Art Department promised to produce favorable results. The basic piece of equipment—a "Photon" by trade name—had already been purchased, and the associated type faces (different sizes and styles) for a wide variety of printing needs were being readied for operation. The primary time savings would be achieved through the "shooting" (i.e., taking pictures with the cameras) of individual characters using rapidly accessible type styles and four computer-controlled cameras, rather than having an operator set up a whole rack of type and make the type-face changes manually.

Several new automated installations were planned if the Photon proved successful. Jim Williams indicated that LGI would probably move farther in this direction during the coming year, although Tom Sr. was not convinced that the firm was ready for such investments.

PERSONNEL

One of the major incidents which preceded the "falling out" between Bob Miller, the former Plant Manager, and Tom Sr. was the introduction of a new and radically different set of personnel policies. Bob, who cleared the new ideas with the other Board Members (Jim Williams and Tom Jr., as shown in the LGI organization chart in Exhibit 5–3) despite Tom Sr's. reservations, felt that the operative employees had not been properly motivated in the past. Of paramount importance in the new "Work Policies" was the provision that any employee who completed his standard full day's work would receive normal pay and could then go home, regardless of the time of day. Given the sequential process of work, this really meant that when the group had all processed a standard quota of work (set at a fairly rigorous level), operations for the day virtually came to a standstill with only a small "skeleton crew" remaining in the shop.

EXHIBIT V–3
LGI Organization Chart

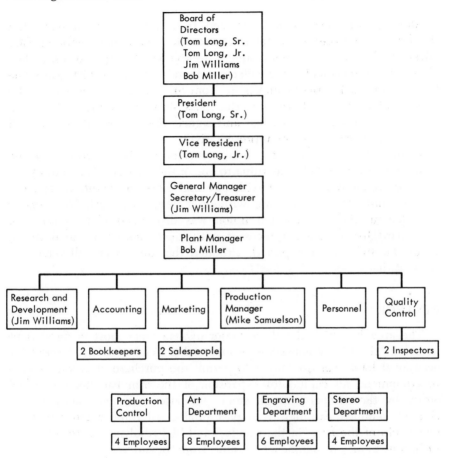

The response of the employees was enthusiastic. Almost immediately, errors went down and productivity rose by over 20 percent. Certain types of work which formerly had created problems along the production line suddenly began to flow smoothly. Jim Williams, Bob Miller, and Mike Samuelson were highly pleased. But Tom Sr. "became increasingly furious as each day passed under the new system." The following comments are typical of his reactions upon walking into the nearly vacant work area toward the end of a shift.

Where the hell is everybody? Bob's just giving the damn plant away these days. You can't make profits by paying the workers more money than anybody else does and then letting them go fishing whenever they please. I work hard to get a new hot contract on a special rush order and there's nobody but me to do the work! I told the Board these ideas were just too far out in left field to work.

Although the owners had assumed from surface appearances that the firm's employees were relatively satisfied with their work at LGI (despite abandoning policies similar to the preceding), in 1967 they elected to be represented for collective bargaining by the Lithographers-Photoengravers International Union. Tom Sr. was against accepting the union, but fearing a strike and other possible union reprisals, he reluctantly consented to its presence and signed the agreements negotiated by LGI's attorney and union representatives.

During 1972, however, the final terms of a labor contract for the year were never settled. According to one of the owners, "The employees, most of whom were content with pay and working conditions at LGI, seemed quite at ease working without a formal contract. Needless to say, though, the international union was displeased and intended to push hard for a signed agreement with much more realistic terms to cover the 1973 contract period, although the union was still relatively weak at that time."

FINANCE

The area in which the three major owners were most in agreement involved "the highly conservative financial policies of LGI." Except for occasional bank loans obtained to permit the purchase of certain pieces of equipment, all capital for expansion of the firm had been supplied either by the owners through stock purchases and personal loans or through retained earnings from past profits. All three wanted to keep ownership of the firm "in the family," and had resolved not to sell stock or borrow money in significant amounts from "outsiders."

All bills incurred by LGI were paid immediately, although the firm did not insist in many cases that its own customers adhere strictly to LGI's "2 percent discount if paid in 10 days, net due in 30 days" policy. Several of Tom Sr's. old friends owed a combined total of over $20,000 in fees for past services at the end of 1971. These "friends" were quick to complain directly to Tom when efforts were made to collect on accounts older than six months. These efforts were backed by firm statements that future services would not be extended until these accounts receivable were considerably lessened.

The purchase of supplies and services had been done on a personal basis by Tom Sr., who felt that "a slightly higher price on a few items is greatly outweighed by new accounts obtained through well-placed outside spokesmen on LGI's behalf."

The other two owners had usually been content to let Tom Sr. "wheel

EXHIBIT V–4

LGI Income Statements*

	1971	1972
Sales	$463,329	$561,580
Cost of Sales		
Sales Discounts	$ 6,252	$ 4,395
Commissions	6,524	4,613
Delivery and Freight	1,440	5,219
Depreciation	24,258	30,997
Materials	74,685	82,128
Repairs and Maintenance	8,782	14,213
Salaries and Wages: Plant	130,430	138,737
Salaries: Sales Representatives	0	10,851
Supplies	10,047	14,484
Utilities	8,205	8,469
Miscellaneous (including royalties outside services, etc.)	4,864	7,017
Total Direct Costs	$275,487	$321,123
Gross Profit on Sales	187,842	240,457
General Operating Expenses		
Advertising	$ 846	$ 1,828
Automobiles (Executives)	5,123	5,881
Bad Debts	827	506
Depreciation	1,064	2,783
Equipment Rental	2,468	3,261
Insurance	5,824	10,863
Interest	936	1,359
Legal and Accounting	5,469	6,570
Rent	12,600	12,600
Repairs and Maintenance	0	4,708
Research and Development	632	1,233
Salaries—Executive	58,500	58,500
Salaries—Office	50,233	72,372
Supplies	5,648	4,867
Taxes—General and Payroll	8,264	19,386
Telephone and Telex	6,023	6,966
Travel and Entertainment	4,097	5,008
Utilities	2,964	3,262
Total General Operating Expenses	$171,519	$221,953
Other Income or (Expense)—Net	14,662	1,926
Income before Income Taxes	30,986	20,430
Income Taxes	9,628	1,024†
Net Income after Taxes	$ 21,358	$ 19,406

* 1971 Combined figures from partnership components used for comparison with 1972 corporation data. Both fiscal years ending June 30.

  † Timing differences in reporting of income after merger resulted in deferring $6,952.00 of currently due $7,976.00 income taxes (as reflected in Balance Sheet).

EXHIBIT V–5

LGI Balance Sheets

October 1, 1971* June 30, 1972†

ASSETS

Current Assets

Cash (Including $35,000 Certificate of Deposit)	$ 68,083	$ 48,701
Accounts Receivable	61,423	58,651
Notes Receivable–Current Portion	1,200	5,867
Inventories–At Cost	7,593	27,876
Prepaid Expenses	1,064	10,157
Total Current Assets	$139,363	$151,252

Other Assets

Notes Receivable–Portion due after 1 year	$ 5,700	$ 19,084
Accounts Receivable–Stockholders	25,923	8,851
Deposits	255	255
Total Other Assets	$ 31,878	$ 28,190

Facilities Used in Business

Plant Equipment	$186,147	$225,830
Office Equipment and Furnishings	35,293	37,906
Leasehold Improvements	18,695	23,893
Motor Vehicles	16,686	21,080
Total Cost	256,821	308,709
Less Accumulated Depreciation	110,379	132,491
Net Facilities	146,442	176,218
Total Assets	$317,683	$355,660

LIABILITIES

Current Liabilities

Accounts Payable–Trade	$ 626	$ 14,633
Accounts Payable–Stockholders	9,506	9,506
Notes Payable–Current Portion.	5,555	24,074
Accrued Expenses	0	2,266
Income Taxes Payable	11,746	7,976
Total Current Liabilities.	$ 27,433	$ 58,455

Noncurrent Liabilities

Notes Payable	$ 3,037	$ 9,164
Deferred Income Taxes	26,190	19,238
Total Noncurrent Liabilities	$ 29,227	$ 28,402

STOCKHOLDERS' EQUITY

Capital Stock

Common, $25 par value; authorized, issued, and outstanding, 1000 shares	$ 25,000	$ 25,000
Capital Surplus	12,000	12,000
Retained Earnings	224,023	231,803
Total Stockholders' Equity	261,023	268,803
Total Liabilities and Equities.	$317,683	$355,660

* Date of Formal Merger and Incorporation.
† End of Fiscal Year.

and deal" in making various financial arrangements. Bob Miller had recommended strongly that the firm could in many instances gain more favorable terms by having several outside suppliers bid competitively on the same items.

Although such concepts as "return on capital employed" and "discounted present value" had not really been considered in LGI's past financial decisions, the owners were quick to point out the success of their operations in terms of growth. The sales figures presented earlier, for example, "compare very favorably with the volumes achieved by both local and national competitors."

Exhibits V–4 and V–5 present financial statements for the time since the firm was incorporated. The owners were pleased with the 20 percent sales gain achieved during this first year of business as a corporation. However, profitability declined slightly in 1972, as expected since expenses were incurred in purchasing and setting up new equipment which promised to increase future profitability.

Despite their expressed satisfaction with these financial achievements, Tom Sr. and Jim Williams had been concerned with cash flow problems. Frequently, checks which had been written in payment of various operating expenses were "held" until sufficient funds were on hand to cover them. Since the owners liked to pay all bills immediately, "this had been a cause of great frustration on a number of occasions."

Both Tom and Jim viewed the cash shortage problem as being one that reflected prices which were too low. Their costs were constantly increasing; wage rates had increased by about 50 percent in 14 years and cost of materials also kept rising. But their prices had stayed about the same for the last 10 years.

Neither Tom nor Jim was willing to "crack down" seriously on customers whose accounts were overdue, although both agreed that if there were some innocuous way to speed up collections, cash flow would be enhanced. Tom's regard for personal friendships usually dominated in questionable situations, for his philosophy was, "You help your customers when they get in a bind, and they'll come through for you."

Since cash on hand at the moment seemed sufficient for current operations, Tom and Jim felt they should probably begin their analysis by concentrating on more general problems. One of Jim's primary concerns was a recent talk with Bob Miller in which the young Plant Manager said he was about to turn in his resignation because of the increasingly frequent clashes with Tom.

QUESTIONS FOR DISCUSSION

1. What are some of the general problems the owners of this firm should consider? Explain.

2. How should they proceed in establishing their overall objection and strategies? What impact would their personal goals and philosophies have upon these decisions?

3. Evaluate the firm's marketing efforts.

4. Evaluate the personnel problems which currently exist or seem likely to arise in the near future.

5. Is LGI currently in financial trouble? In the near future? Explain.

6. Evaluate the firm's production operations.

Index

Index

555

*This book has been set in 10 and 9 point
Caledonia, leaded 2 points. Part titles are 18
point Scotch Roman and chapter titles are 18
point Scotch Roman italic. Part numbers are
24 and 36 point Scotch Roman and chapter
numbers are 72 point Bookman. The size of
the type page is 27 by 45½ picas.*